W9-ARZ-777

VENCEREMOS!

Books by John Gerassi

THE GREAT FEAR

THE BOYS OF BOISE

VENCEREMOS!

VENCEREMOS!

The speeches and writings of
Ernesto Che Guevara

EDITED, ANNOTATED, AND WITH AN INTRODUCTION BY

John Gerassi

THE MACMILLAN COMPANY NEW YORK

Library of Congress Catalog Card Number: 68-22126

FIRST PRINTING

The Macmillan Company, New York
Collier-Macmillan Canada Ltd., Toronto, Ontario
Printed in the United States of America

To my parents, Fernando and Stepha Gerassi, who taught me, not by preaching, but by their example, whatever genuine values I may have about the worth of man

And to my daughter Nina, to whom, I hope, such values will be transmitted

JOHN GERASSI

Contents

Contents by Subject Matter

The articles and speeches of Ernesto Che Guevara in this volume have been arranged chronologically. The specialist, however, may want to read them according to subject matter, and thus I have listed below the entries in five separate categories: On Guerrilla Warfare; On Capitalism and Imperialism; On Human Values and Socialist Man; On Economic Theory; and On Economic Policy. Naturally, since Che often tackled many themes in a single article, this classification cannot be rigid. What I have done, therefore, is either chosen the dominant theme, or else, if various themes are given equal weight, repeated the chapter numbers under the various categories.

Acknowledgments

THIS BOOK was the genuine product of a collective—imbued with a collective spirit. It was produced in one month, mainly because everyone concerned—and two hundred odd of my students at San Francisco State College, as well as scores of student and youth leaders across the country, with whom I keep in close contact—egged me on to get it out fast. Many volunteered to type, proofread, even to cook for me, so I could keep at it as much as possible. One of my SFSC students, Terry Oudes, spent innumerable hours at Stanford University's Hoover Library tracking down Che's speeches and articles, then went through five years of daily *Revolución,* to make sure he did not miss anything. Terry and I were given invaluable help in this task by the Hoover Library's acting curator of the Latin American section, Joseph Bingaman, and the Library staffers.

Many of the translators did not even want to be paid, since they felt so strongly about the book, and gave in only when I assured them that The Macmillan Company had allocated funds for translation. Nancy McKendree Peters, who has translated things for me before, proofread the galleys, an arduous task, since it meant coordinating the terminology of no less than twenty-one different American translators, plus the official Cuban translators. Finding all the material was very difficult and at times almost discouraging, but again, the encouragement of the youth kept me going. Some of those who helped most were in Cuba, friends of mine who went on manuscript hunting expeditions, and by phone, finally made sure I had the things they found. One was Ricardo Valdés; another, who worked with Che for years as his economic assistant and who told me many marvelous stories about him, is Carlos Romeo, a Chilean revolutionary, a beautiful human being, and a great friend; others included Oscar Lugones, who gave me his collection of *Cuba Socialista,* and various staffers of the

Cuban mission to the United Nations, who scrounged through their personal files to come up with Che material.

Here in the States, the list of selfless, idealistic people who translated their enthusiasm into direct action of some kind or other is too long to enumerate. Let me, however, single out Suzanne Pollard, my secretary, who kept being my secretary for a full month without pay (my money had run out) and then spent her off-hours translating two Che works; Helena Bradley, who convinced her husband Chuck (that was easy; he was all for it anyway, and besides, volunteered his own time to proofread part of the manuscripts) and her two children that her typing of the Che material, days, nights, and weekends, was more important than whatever they had planned to do together; Harriet Sheppard, of the SFSC's International Relations Department, where I teach, who volunteered much of her free time to type, proofread, and generally stand by for any emergency as we strove hectically to make our deadline; Cindy Young, a student at SFSC, who typed in the clinch; Jane Pollard (Suzanne's sister) and Helen Garvy, who proofread; James O'Connor, an economist and Cuban expert from San Jose State College, who checked the manuscript and made valuable suggestions; and of course, all the translators, whose names appear in this book, whose dedication was prodigious.

But with all this help, this book would still not have been produced in time had it not been for the care, enthusiasm, and direct participation in the venture by the office of my literary agent, Carl Brandt. When I ran out of money, Carl loaned me some. When I needed permissions, his office got them. And most important, when I needed translators in New York, Carl's personal secretary, Charity Randall, made sure I got them. Working on her own time, as well as on Carl's, with his approval, she tracked down material, got it to the right place at the right time, hounded the luckless translators (most of whom worked days and nights without prodding), to keep them to their schedule, and delivered as promised. Finally, of course, there was my editor at Macmillan, Peter V. Ritner, the editor-in-chief, who rarely agrees with my political views, but always fights to make sure I can express them. He did this, long before he became editor-in-chief, for my first book, *The Great Fear*. And he has done so again now for Che.

In general, however, this book was made possible for a reason few people over forty will understand: That is that America's conscientious youth —those who are upset at the dehumanizing process of our system; those who oppose the war in Vietnam, who are conscious of the terrible price that the whole world, and we as human beings, are paying for our greed, our paternalism, our "superiority," our imperialism; those who are dissenters in America today—admire Che Guevara like no other man of the modern era. Cynics like Walt Rostow may be jubilant that such "romantics" as Che are getting killed (and Rostow does think that the world will be better off when pragmatists replace romantics). But not young America.

Young conscientious America *is* romantic. Our youth care less and less about Rostow and Company's efficiency, profit, stability. They would rather drop out of society than become board chairmen. Rostow will never understand that. Neither will President Johnson, our senators, our policemen, our school administrators, and most of our teachers. That is why they cannot communicate with our youth. But Che can. He did and will continue to do so. He was a romantic. He lived and died for others—for a better world, a world where people can really love, instead of just "coming to terms"; just compromising. That is why Che is so popular among young America. That is why he is not dead.

Wherever death may surprise us, it will be welcome, provided that this, our battle cry, reaches some receptive ear, that another hand stretch out to take up weapons, and that other men come forward to intone our funeral dirge with the staccato of machine guns and new cries of battle and victory.

Let the flag under which we fight represent the sacred cause of redeeming humanity, so that to die under the flag of Vietnam, of Venezuela, of Guatemala, of Laos, of Guinea, of Colombia, of Bolivia, of Brazil—to name only the scenes of today's armed struggle—be equally glorious and desirable for an American, an Asian, an African, or even a European.

Each drop of blood spilled in a country under whose flag one has not been born constitutes experience for those who survive to apply later in the liberation struggle of their own countries. And each nation liberated is a step toward victory in the battle for the liberation of one's own country.

Each and every one of us will pay on demand his part of sacrifice . . . knowing that all together we are getting ever closer to the new man, whose figure is beginning to appear.

Venceremos!

CHE

Introduction

ON OCTOBER 9, 1967, the first news of Ernesto Che Guevara's alleged death reached the United States. The next day, as I was about to enter my classroom at San Francisco State College to teach my course on Nationalism and Revolution in the Third World, I was approached by a nineteen-year-old coed. She had tears in her eyes and a "Make Love Not War" button on her breast. "You don't really believe it, do you?" she asked. "I mean, he couldn't really be dead, could he?"

Naturally, we spent the class period talking about Che, his guerrilla warfare concepts, and his personal commitment. No one really believed at that time—neither the sixty students in the class, nor I—that he was dead. What was amazing, however, was that no one wanted to believe it.

To my knowledge there were no conservatives in the class. But there were many liberals and many pacifists, in addition to the radicals. And yet to all, even if they disagreed with his tactics, the news of Che's possible death was very upsetting and very personal. Che had obviously caught their imagination. They respected and admired him. They knew very little about his life—we had not yet discussed him in class. But they knew enough to realize he was an idealist, a man who lived—and if the present news were correct, a man who died—for other people, for people he had never met, for the poor, for the exploited, for the alienated, for those who feel, perhaps only instinctively, that they are merely tools in their society, tools of greedy and powerful men who do not really care about human beings. Thus, it became apparent to me, as we talked that day, that these liberal and pacifist students felt, incredibly, as if Che had died for them. They wanted to understand why. They wanted to make his experiences relevant to theirs. And since Che had come from a background very similar to theirs, that relevance was much more obvious than American "objective" commentators would ever admit. Indeed, Che had very much the same kind of upbringing as most American students.

Ernesto Guevara was born June 14, 1928, in Rosario, Argentina's most important city after Buenos Aires. His father, also named Ernesto, was an adventurous, swashbuckling, hell-bender, who made and squandered minor fortunes in shipbuilding, maté growing,[1] ranching and real estate, before becoming an architect-builder without an architectural degree. He was very broadminded, very liberal, and never tried to force any of his five children into adopting a rigid pattern of life or belief. He was very proud of his lineage, one branch of which dated back to Viceroy Liniers, an early Argentine grandee.

Another of Guevara's ancestors was Juan Antonio Guevara, who rebelled and fought against the dictatorship of Juan Manuel Rosas, failed, and fled into exile around 1850, winding up in California, where he became the much-feared leader of a Latino band of gold-seekers and rustlers. It was in California that he met and married a Mexican belle, Concepción Castro, and their son, born an American citizen, married a girl named Elizabeth Victoria Lynch, from San Lorenzo, California. The young American couple eventually went to Argentina, and it was there that their son, Ernesto Guevara (Che's father), was born.

Che's mother, Celia de la Serna, was also of aristocratic ancestry, and though she became a wiry Marxist in her old age, she remained proud of the "de" in her name until she died in 1965. Strong-willed, impetuous, ready to pitch into any political argument to defend "underdogs oppressed by domestic capital and Yankee exploitation," Celia also wanted her children to grow up much as their inclinations led them, though, as in the best of American liberal tradition, she tried to guide her children toward "respectable" careers.

Similar in background and temperament, the elder Ernesto and his wife Celia were constantly arguing with one another, and they did not try to hide their disagreements from their children. Although their marriage ultimately failed (they did not live together as man and wife during the last years of their lives) their children grew up with admiration for them both. Partly, this was due to the fact that the parents never argued about such petty subjects as money or status, but about the value of man and his endeavors.

The elder Guevaras were fairly footloose throughout most of their lives. They were in Rosario by chance when their first son was born. Explains the father: "I was in the maté growing business in Misiones Province. My

[1] Maté is a kind of bitter green tea which Argentines, Uruguayans, and Paraguayans drink hot or cold from an oval silver or wooden gourd through an ever-present straw of the same material. Che liked maté and continued to drink it even after he became accustomed to Cuban coffee.

wife and I came to Rosario on business. We did not expect the child for at least another month, but suddenly my wife had pains, and we got her to the hospital. 'Ernestito' was born prematurely, and he was a sick and puny baby."

Eventually four other children followed: Celia, two years younger than Che; Roberto, three years younger than Che, now a prominent lawyer; Anna Maria, four years younger; and finally, Juan Martín, thirteen years younger.

The first eighteen months of Ernesto's life were spent in Misiones. Then the Guevaras abandoned the maté and went to Buenos Aires, where the elder Guevara became a shipbuilder. But he took on another major task—that of turning his sickly baby into a husky youth. He would take him, dressed only in diapers, out onto the cold balcony and sit with him under the sun, and he would give him cold baths. Though Che toughened up, he was always coughing, and it soon became apparent that he had a serious case of asthma. Doctors told the Guevaras that the humid climate of Buenos Aires was not good for asthma, so father Guevara sold out his share of the shipbuilding business to his partner (whose shipyard is now the biggest in Argentina), and the family moved to Córdoba, settling in the hilly, healthy resort town of Alta Gracia when Che was four. "We went there because we wanted to get Ernesto well," says the father, "but there was nothing for me to do, so I built up a library. We lived a good life. I spent all my time with the boy. I took him shooting, taught him to swim, and got him to play soccer and rugby. I saw to it that he spent about three hours each day in the pool in the summer, to relax his chest muscles and get him breathing well."

A childhood friend of Ernesto's remembers that "Alta Gracia had two distinct sections, the upper and the lower. The upper section was the residential area with rows of identical houses built by an English railway company for its executives. The Guevaras lived in a house called Villa Nidia in the main avenue of that section where all the houses looked alike." The Guevara house backed onto what is now the Alta Gracia Golf Club, and the game was already played there at that time; Ernestito became quite good at golf, shooting in the 80's.

Alta Gracia also had its social life. "We had open house for kids," remembers the father. "I taught Ernesto never to care about who his friends' parents were. Butcher and baker, they all came to our house, rich and poor, they were all welcome."

Those years in Alta Gracia changed Ernesto significantly. Still today the father likes to show two photographs: one when Che was four, with arms and legs like matchsticks; the other when Che was fourteen, showing him as a tough, muscular, and confident youth. "Look at the physique," the father says. "Good Córdoba air did that, and the time I spent with the boy.

When I went out pigeon shooting, he came along with his slingshot. He was a good shot with it, too."

Meanwhile, as he grew, Che made up for his poor health with sharpness and willpower. He roamed the town with a gang of urchins who clearly acknowledged his leadership, despite his physical frailty. His father encouraged him to take on small jobs, such as helping in the grape harvest, not for the sake of making money, but in order to mix with peasants and learn how the poorer classes in the Argentine backlands lived.

Occasionally this got him into trouble. Once, when he was invited to a children's birthday party at the swank Sierra Hotel, he showed up looking unkempt. A little girl reacted by saying "Why did they let in the shoeshine boy?" and Ernesto started swinging. His father was called in to put an end to the commotion, but instead, joined his son, charging the "rich bastards," who had ganged up on Ernestito, with his walking stick, until both father and son were thrown out by the hotel staff.

When he was not shinnying up a tree or working at an odd job, Che roamed the fields with his father. When he had an attack of asthma and had to be in bed, he spent the time reading or talking about political and social problems with his old man. There were three thousand books in the Guevara home, and Che was interested in everything from sociology and philosophy to mathematics and engineering—but not books on church or military affairs. Like his father, Che had been born a Catholic and had been baptized, but he never took communion and never took any interest in Catholicism. His father felt pretty strongly about the Church and its "exploitative character." He used to like to say: "Christ was the greatest man on earth, but the Church ruined his preaching. The Church is the biggest business ever invented by Jews and managed by Italians."

One of Che's close friends, José Aguilar, recalls, "We did a great deal of reading in those days. My favorite authors were Jules Verne and Alexander Dumas. My father, who was a doctor, was shocked to find Che reading Freud when he was only twelve. He liked French, which he learned from his mother, who spoke it. I don't remember whether he had a French teacher, but he learned to read poetry in French, and he could spend a whole day reciting it." Che continued to like poetry all his life, and at one point he rather seriously thought of becoming a poet. However, one attempt, the "Song to Fidel," written in March, 1956, is not particularly brilliant. Aguilar also remembers that Che was particularly fond of Pablo Neruda, and used to recite one particular Neruda poem about the Spanish Civil War so often that "some of the lines have been engraved into my memory." The lines were, in Aguilar's rough translation: "It was a lie, a lie made sad reality, whose footfalls were heard in the Madrid that no longer stands."

Che did not start primary school in Alta Gracia until he was seven, because of his asthma. Celia Guevara was once chastised by the local office of the Ministry of Education for not sending her elder son to school. "I was happy that they were concerned, but he could not attend school because of his asthma. He only attended classes regularly during the second and third grades; the fifth and sixth grades he attended sporadically. I taught him his ABC's and later his brothers and sisters would copy the lessons, and he would do them at home." And Che finished each year at the top of his class.

In addition to being an unusual student, he was becoming an activist, getting into his first scrape when he was only eleven. The light and power workers had gone on strike throughout the province, and the company was hiring strikebreakers. Che organized his slingshot gang, and in one night smashed every single street light in the town.

Another facet of Che's personality was his tendency toward sentimentality. When the family dog died of old age, for example, he wept like any middle-class American kid. Then he called his gang together and organized a funeral procession, carrying a handmade coffin through the streets of the town to an empty lot, and with a voice broken by sobs, delivered a heartrending eulogy before giving his friends the signal to lower the casket into the earth.

Che's love for animals did not decrease as he grew. In his last year of medical school, for example, despite protests from neighbors, he risked his life shinnying up a perilous pipe to rescue a sparrow who had caught his wing between two tiles on the roof.

In 1941 the Guevaras moved from Alta Gracia to Córdoba, the capital of the province of the same name, and there Ernestito or "pelado," meaning "the shaved one" because he kept his hair close-cropped, or "el chancho," meaning "piggy" because he never bothered about his dress, entered the state high school. In the summer before school began, however, he went to his father and announced, "I want to see things. I am going on a tour of Argentina, but I will be back in three months, in time for school." His father remembers that although his son was only thirteen, he made no objection, saying "I had to let him go probing, exploring, finding things out for himself, so he could become a man." So off went Che on the first of many tours. He put a small motor on his bike, donned his old leather windbreaker, put his maté gourd and kettle in his knapsack, and went off "probing" with seventy-five pesos (about $5 at that time) in his pocket. Whenever a fit of asthma hit him, he stopped along the road and rested. He slept under trees and worked as a crop-picker whenever he ran short of money. He often went without food for a day at a time, but he toured all northern Argentina and returned in time to enter class in the fall.

His teachers still remember him. One, Diaz Vidal, says that he was a student "who took every opportunity to oppose the Catholic Church, had Marxist ideas, was never distinguished, and was a leftist ring-leader among his classmates."

Another teacher, Alfredo Pueyrredon, says: "He was an outstanding student. He looked and acted much older than he was, and was clearly already grown up with a definite personality, moody and undisciplined, but extremely mature."

At about this time the fortunes of the elder Guevaras took a turn for the worse, and the family could no longer afford the good life. They lived in a smaller home, and Che had no spending money. Thus, he had to work throughout high school for his personal expenses. In one job he succeeded brilliantly for the wrong reason. His friend José Aguilar remembers that "he was compiling a philosophical dictionary for his own personal use. He did it in the office where he was working—on company time. One day the boss arrived when everyone should have been working, but the only one who was working was Che. The boss congratulated him on his conscientiousness and promoted him. The truth is that he was working not at his job but on his dictionary."

Despite having to work at the same time he studied, Che finished school quickly and well. During this period, Guevara Senior organized Spanish refugees from the Spanish Civil War and became very active in politics. His son, too, became politically active, joining the Comando Cívico Revolucionario Monteagudo, a nationalist youth group which eventually fought dictator Juan Perón in street action rather than in political debates. In addition Che also managed to take hiking trips whenever he could and developed a new passion for sports, which he pursued as a way to demonstrate that he could rise above his physical frailty.

In 1947, at the age of nineteen, he entered the University of Buenos Aires as a premedical student. His father thought he would become an engineer; in fact, he looked forward to Che joining him in his new Buenos Aires construction business. But Che decided to become an allergist, in part because he wanted to understand and cure his own allergy. His real reason for wanting to become a doctor, however, was because he had been moved by the death of his grandmother from cancer, for which he hoped to find a cure. He studied, and continued to hold odd jobs, including that of night watchman, reporter for the ultra-nationalist weekly *Acción Argentina*, and clerk at a construction company (not his father's).

It was during this period, also, that his father and mother separated, and Che stayed with his mother. Through her he came to know many Argentine intellectual Marxists. Still, Che remained a nationalist, taking active part in several anti-Perón street brawls and working in the Centro Reformista, the university students' organization. He also played with the San Ysidro rugby team, and he became a familiar sight as he would periodically run to the side where a lineman, keeping pace with him, would hand him his atomizer. Forceful, hard tackling, with a strong frame, he became the pride of his father, who says "He never got depressed, never let himself be gotten down by his attacks."

Che went through six of the seven-year course in three years, passed sixteen major exams in six months, during which time he had no less than forty-five serious asthma attacks. His aunt remembers that when she visited her sister, Che's mother, "We would listen to him gasping, studying lying on the floor to ease his breathing, but he never complained. For him it was a challenge."

During the summers of those years at the University, Che took jobs as a male nurse aboard a freighter and visited nearly every Argentine port. In 1950 he tried to go into business on his own, having invented a concoction based on Gammexane for use as a general insecticide. He patented it, calling it Vendaval, and started manufacturing it in an abandoned garage on almost no funds because he would not accept financial help from his father's friends. "I am not looking to make money for your wealthy pig capitalists," he would say. Thus, he went bankrupt.

After his business failure, Che decided to learn more about the continent. He interrupted his medical studies and with another medical student, Alberto Granados, now a distinguished leperologist and biochemist, set out on a motorcycle. Granados, now living in Cuba, remembers that he first met Che in 1941 in high school: "We Córdoban students, together with students from other schools, had gone on strike against the abuses committed on the campuses. I was arrested and taken to the Central Police Commissariat. Rather than arrested, it would be more correct to say kidnapped, as we were not tried. I asked my brother, Tomás, to bring me food. In jail they did not give us anything to eat. One day Tomás was accompanied by his friend, Ernesto Guevara. I explained to them that if the secondary students all took to the streets, the people would know we were being held, kidnapped without trial. I was amazed at the reply of young Guevara who said 'Nothing doing, Alberto. Take to the streets so that the police can go after us with clubs? Nothing doing. I will go out only if you give me a gun.' "

Granados continues: "Later, after 1945, I was a biochemist in a leprosy hospital 180 kilometers from Córdoba, almost 1,000 kilometers from Buenos Aires. Ernesto visited me on several occasions. After the December examinations, instead of staying in the capital reviewing the subjects for the March exams [the final exams in Argentina], he would put together his knapsack, get on his motorcycle, or sometimes he just used his legs, and travel to different parts of the country. He almost always included in his travels a brief stay at the hospital where I was working. He would say to his fellow students, 'While you stay here preparing for three examinations, I plan to cover the provinces of Santa Fé, northern Córdoba and eastern Mendoza, and along the way study, and pass the courses along with you.' And of course, he did just that, and maybe more."

In 1952, the two friends got on a motorcycle and began their trip through Latin America. They crossed the Andes, but there broke down and junked their motorcycle. From there they continued by hitchhiking, earning money by working in copper mines, as truck drivers, porters, seamen, doctors, and dishwashers. "Traveling without a cent in our pockets, one day we arrived at the gates of the Braden Company mine at Chuquicamata," Granados remembers. "Braden and their cohorts never did learn that in the early part of 1952 the guard who was then sleeping in the sentry box with his feet resting on a pair of military boots was none other than Ernesto Che Guevara. For, in our various odd jobs, we even worked as cops."

From Chile they went on to Machu Picchu, the old Inca capital, and saw how the Indians, downtrodden and exploited by the big landlords and companies and their police, were "brutalized by the constant use of coca, which is given to them instead of food." "One day," says Granados, "I started talking about creating a workers' community in the Andes and then winning over the government to make a revolution for these poor people. I remember that Ernesto smiled and said, 'Make a revolution without firing a shot? Are you crazy?' "

The two Argentines went on to Iquitos, and finally, hungry and penniless, wound up in a leper colony on the shores of the Amazon River. They worked as male nurses for three months, and when the lepers presented them with a balsa wood raft, they followed the river down to Leticia, where the great river arrives at the intersection of three countries, Brazil, Peru, and Colombia. There, they smashed up the raft, earned some money by playing soccer for a local team, bought two airplane tickets to Bogotá, arrived safely but were jailed for illegal entry, escaped and managed to cross the border into Venezuela, heading on to Caracas.

In Caracas, Che met a family friend who was transporting racehorses. While Granados stayed on to become a doctor in a leprosarium, Che flew to Miami with the horses, but was not allowed to stay by American immigration authorities. Having lost a year from his studies, he then decided to fly back with the horses to Buenos Aires, buried himself in his books, and rivaling all medical school records, passed twelve subjects in a few months and received his M.D. degree in March, 1953. "Then," says his father, "he threw it away." Indeed, in July of 1953, Che once again took to the road.

Che began this trip by train and got as far as Bolivia, where in July a young Argentine lawyer, Ricardo Rojo, also arrived, almost penniless. Remembers Rojo: "I was one of many young Argentines roaming South America looking for the excitement unavailable in the drab semipopulist Argentina of Perón. One day I was invited to a cocktail party at the home of a wealthy Argentine resident of La Paz. I used my last clean shirt to go, and I was stunned to see a short, about 5-foot-6-inch, sallow-faced young man standing in a corner wearing a filthy brown jacket, rumpled shirt, spotted shoes, which had no trace of leather left. I was introduced to this young beardless man, and I remember that first impression distinctly, for his fierce brown eyes showed such intensity. This was Che Guevara. He waved his hands as he spoke and jutted out his chin and had a habit of pushing back his long black hair with his bony fingers. He suffered from asthma, and when he spoke, he often went into fits of wheezing and gasping. He told me he was a medical doctor and was on his way to work in a leprosarium in Venezuela [where Granados was still working]. He had little knowledge or interest in politics, but he had a lot to say about injustices throughout Latin America, and eagerly discussed this with anyone who would listen."

Rojo, Guevara, and four other Argentines became chummy and spent many of the following days sitting around cafe tables talking about conditions in Latin America and what to do about them. But the talk after a while got boring, and the six decided to hitchhike to Peru, finally arriving in Guayaquil, Ecuador, in August, 1953. Rojo remembers: "As we saw case after case of exploitation and misery, Guevara began to talk more and more about breaking the system, rather than changing it." Rojo complained that "You just talk of revolution and that is all."

Guevara answered: "Maybe, we will see."

Living in a boarding house on the docks of Guayaquil, the six Argentines tried to find work. Instead, one day they obtained six tickets aboard a United Fruit Company cargo ship on condition that they travel only in pairs. Rojo and the others gratefully set out and waited in Panama for Guevara. After three months they gave up and went on to Guatemala. From Guatemala, Rojo, with Walter Beveraggi Allende, an economist who was returning home from a teaching stint in the United States, and his brother Domingo, decided to drive back down to Argentina. Allende recalls that they "were motoring along the Pan-American Highway from Guatemala to Costa Rica when we got to Piedras Blancas, a small border town, where we had to stop because the road was impassable. Suddenly two bums appeared. They were wearing torn alpargatas, bombachas so very dirty you could not tell what color they were, windjammers, and carrying small haversacks on their backs. One was Che; the other a student from La Plata named Eduardo García. They had walked all the way from Panama. It was some reunion for us five Argentines, most of us victims of the Perón regime, meeting accidentally in the middle of nowhere. Che impressed me as unusual. He was quiet, yet made his presence felt. He had a beautiful face, and was moved by the poverty he had seen in Central America. He looked poor yet full of fight and devotion to some inner ideal. He seemed to feel responsible for all the world's injustices. I felt sorry for him, and I gave him some of my clothes. He had almost nothing, and the clothes on his back were in tatters. We took the boys back to Managua in the car with us. The trip took two days, during which time Che had several asthma attacks. In Managua, Ricardo [Rojo], and I stayed on to sell the car, while Che, my brother Domingo, and García, went on to Guatemala on foot. I had other occasions to see Che during my trips in Central America. Once we came across a group of undernourished, belly-bloated kids. We were on United Fruit land. Che went into one of his rages. He cursed everybody from God to North American exploiters, and wound up with a frightening asthma attack lasting two hours."

Meanwhile Rojo had told Che about what was going on in Guatemala, where the regime of Jacobo Arbenz was nationalizing United Fruit land and launching a social revolution. Che became enthusiastic and decided to go there. He arrived in Guatemala City on Christmas Eve, 1953, and showed up at the house of Juan Angel Muñoz Aguilar, a Honduran married to an Argentine girl and a good friend of Guatemala's ex-President, Juan José Arevalo. Che got a job peddling encyclopedias and moved into a flea-ridden boarding house on Third Avenue, where he paid 50¢ a day for room and board. In order to fight his asthma, he was convinced that he had to eat a good deal of fruit, such as apples, grapes, and pears, but these particular fruits were rare in Guatemala, and thus he grew miserably thin. A Guatemalan friend, Julia de Cobos, remembers that he would spend days on end lying on his back, reading, with his atomizer always within reach.

In the early part of 1954, through Muñoz Aguilar, Che met a Peruvian girl named Hilda Gadea, a member of Peru's Aprista Youth Movement, which was then revolutionary in intent, but is now conservative. Through her, he met Cuban exiles, members of a strange group called the 26th of July Movement, which had launched an attack in 1953 on the Moncada Barracks in Cuba, and whose members were either in jail or in exile. Hilda remembers that "I used to talk to him a lot about Fidel and the things he had done, and Che became a great admirer of Fidel."

This was not the first time Che had met Cuban exiles from the 26th of July Movement. According to Juan Bosch, the former President of the Dominican Republic, who met Che in San José, Costa Rica, "It was there that Guevara first met a group who had participated in the Moncada assault." At that time, says Bosch, "Guevara spoke very little. He would answer questions, but not volunteer information. He would sit to one side and listen. He was in a very bad economic situation, but when I tried to help him, he would never accept anything. He was intensely preoccupied with what he saw. He seemed dissatisfied with all solutions proposed up to that time, and when he was asked specific questions, he criticized all parties, but never defined his own position. However, I am convinced by the way he answered questions that he was not a Communist then."

In Guatemala, Che did not work for the government, though he went to the Ministry of Health and asked to become a staff member in a hospital in Totonicapán and was told that permission would be granted only if he became a member of the Communist party. He angrily told the official to go to hell and stalked out.

So, instead, Che spent a lot of time just talking, mostly to Apristas and other left-wing exiles from Latin America. One of them, a doctor, was Luís Manuel Peñaluer, who went on to become a deputy in Venezuela after the 1958 Revolution. He remembers Che living in really precarious conditions in Guatemala: "For one thing, he had no money, and the asthma bothered him very much. I went several times to take him medicine and to give him shots (including Vitamin C) and once we had to hospitalize him for a week."

When the Arbenz regime was attacked by the CIA-trained and financed troops of Castillo Armas, Che immediately went to its defense. Hilda remembers that "Che encouraged the Guatemalans as much as he could. He kept saying, 'You must fight.' One night when some of the boys escaped from the enemy, Che got them to safety in an embassy. He also transported weapons from one place to another until it was impossible for him to continue, and then he took refuge, as I did, in the Argentine Embassy."

Che himself has said, "I was and still am an ardent admirer of the Arbenz government, though I never occupied a position in that government. When the United States intervention occurred, I made attempts to organize a group of young men like myself to confront the United Fruit interests. In Guatemala it was necessary to fight, and yet almost no one fought. It was necessary to resist and almost no one wanted to do it."

As a political refugee in his embassy, Che was treated as an undesirable. He was confined to the kitchen with orders not to show himself around and he had to work as a busboy. Nevertheless he lived there for almost two months and must have had plenty of time to study the whys of the Guatemalan failure. One of his conclusions was that the revolutionary government of Arbenz did not have enough faith in the people, did not trust them by either arming them or integrating them into the political structure.

Eventually Che was ordered to leave the embassy. Hilda had already left. She had then been jailed, had gone on a hunger strike in jail, had been released, and had managed to get to Mexico by swimming across a small river. Che then did the same thing, and he arrived in Mexico in August of 1954.

On his way to Mexico Che had met Roberto Caceres, a young Guatemalan revolutionary, later known to all Cubans as "El Patojo," whom Che talks about in his account of the revolutionary war. In Mexico they shared a small apartment and earned their living as tourist photographers, using a dilapidated Brownie. Once when Che was told to go away by an American tourist, he turned fiercely toward him and shouted, "You may laugh now, but our day will come." He also worked in a cardiologist lab. Dr. Cornelio Moyano remembers that Che was often at the University working on an experiment with cats and dogs, and "was always busy going and coming, always looking at his watch for the time to do this or that."

Through El Patojo, Che renewed his acquaintance with the Cuban exiles, and as he himself has said, "became friends with Raúl Castro, Fidel's younger brother, the leader of the movement at the time they were planning the revolution in Cuba. I talked with Fidel all night, and by dawn I had become the doctor of the future expedition. In reality, after my experiences all over Latin America, and the *coup de grâce* in Guatemala, it didn't take much to arouse my interest in joining any revolution against tyranny. But my over-all impression of Fidel was that he was an extraordinary man. He confronted and solved the most impossible problems. He had an unshakable faith that once he left Mexico and arrived in Cuba he would fight, and that fighting, he was going to win. I shared his optimism. It was imperative to do something, to struggle, to achieve. It was imperative to stop crying and fight."

Che and Fidel hit it off well from the very first time they met in that summer of 1955. Castro had already set up his table of organization for the expeditionary force, and invited Che as a fighting doctor. They began to train together, growing in number, collecting arms. Under the guidance of the Spanish Loyalist General Alberto Bayo, they began to mold their men into a genuine guerrilla platoon.

Meanwhile, in May of 1955, Che and Hilda had married. Raúl Castro had served as their best man. But Hilda recalls that Che and Fidel did nothing but "plot and talk revolution. I lost my husband to the Cuban Revolution."

It was then that Guevara got his nickname "Che." The Cubans were struck by the fact that he always called his friends "Che" which in Argentine, means "Mac" or "buddy."

Finally, in 1956, after some of the band had been arrested (for general conspiracy) and shortly thereafter had been released, eighty-two of them boarded an old yacht named *Granma* and headed for Cuba. Hilda, now pregnant, stayed behind. Che's first child, a girl named Hilda Beatrice, was born in Mexico while Che was fighting in the hills of the Sierra Maestra.

The eighty-two spent six days aboard the old 62-foot yacht. They weathered a bad storm, during which Che was the only one who was not seasick because he was too busy caring for the others. Hitting the beach on the night of December 2, 1956, they were spotted by the enemy, and were attacked by the Batista air force. The survivors made their way inland, trying to reach the Sierra Maestra. They were again attacked, having been betrayed by their guide. Only seven men reached the safety of the Sierra Maestra after that first encounter. Later it was learned that twelve had survived, and historians are thus talking of "the original twelve." In fact, however, twenty men survived and eventually reached the Sierra Maestra.

From the very start Che was a favorite with the ranks. He objected to being called "Doctor" saying, "We are all warriors." He demonstrated a natural ability to command and was able to inspire confidence in his men.

He was also braver than the others, and his men admired him for it, though as Fidel pointed out in his speech of October 18, 1967, such bravery could be a liability. Said Fidel: "This was one of his principal characteristics: his willingness to instantly volunteer for the most dangerous mission. And naturally this aroused the highest admiration, and twice the usual admiration for a fellow combatant, fighting alongside us, who had not been born here, a man of profound ideals, a man in whose mind stirred the dream of struggle in other parts of the continent and who was, nonetheless, so altruistic, so disinterested, so willing to always do the most difficult things, to constantly risk his life. . . . Che was an incomparable soldier. Che was an incomparable leader. Che was, from a military point of view, an extraordinarily capable man, extraordinarily courageous, extraordinarily aggressive. If, as a guerrilla, he had his Achilles' heel, it was this excessively aggressive quality, his resolute contempt for danger."

Under air attacks Che never showed alarm. He rarely took cover. Usually he would stare at the passing plane and puff calmly on his cigar until the raid ceased. Often he would ignore air attacks entirely and continue doing whatever he was doing. He quickly earned the rank of platoon commander, *i.e.*, lieutenant, taught his men tactics, trained them constantly, and enforced discipline mostly by his own example. Once he shot a guard who had fallen asleep on duty. But at the same time he spent nonfighting evenings reading to his men from Cervantes, Robert Louis Stevenson, Alfonse Daudet, Rómulo Gallegos, and the poems of Pablo Neruda.

When his asthma bothered him and made it difficult for him to hike in the Sierra, Che rode a mule called Martín Fierro (a character in a classic Argentine poem). He was often wounded, from the first day of the landing when he was shot in the neck, right up to December 9, 1957, when in the Battle of Alto de Conrado, as he explained in a letter to Fidel, "I got an M-1 bullet in the foot, which lodged itself there, and at the moment I cannot walk. Ramiro took charge of the column and is going on with a majority of the men to a place of which the guide will tell you. We need a rapid assist with 30.06 and 45 automatics. I am here in safety with an ambush prepared. I am very sorry I ignored your advice, but morale had fallen so low, as a result of the excessive fatigue everyone was feeling, that I considered my presence necessary in the front line. All in all, I took sufficient care of myself, and the wound was an accident." Che limped badly for a long time afterward, bandaging himself as his own doctor.

In the summer of 1958, Che, now comandante (major, the highest rank in the Cuban revolutionary army), led a formidable breakthrough from the Sierra Maestra to the Escambray Hills of central Cuba with the intention of cutting Cuba in two. That march and its ultimate success is eloquently described in this volume. It was during this march and in the battles of Las Villas that Che became close to a Cuban girl who first served the 26th of July Movement as a courier, but now joined Che as a combatant. Her name was Aleida March. Che eventually divorced Hilda, his Peruvian wife, and married Aleida on June 3, 1959—though he remained friends with Hilda, and invited her to Cuba after the Revolution. She still lives there, working for INRA, the Agrarian Reform Institute, and Hilda Beatrice, their daughter, now nearing her teens, has been brought up as a Cuban.

Aleida has often been referred to as Che's secretary, even during the revolutionary period. She points out, however, that "when it was made practically impossible to continue living in Santa Clara because of my revolutionary activity, I decided to join those fighting the dictatorship with arms. I arrived at the camp of Che Guevara and was admitted. I learned quickly how to handle arms, and decided to be one of the soldiers, despite the fact that women were mostly used as nurses. I confess that at the beginning it was very difficult for me, but later I grew accustomed to it, above all after the first encounter with the enemy. Together with Che I made the Las Villas campaign, and took part in all the battles that took place there."

Shortly after the Las Villas campaign, where Batista threw in all his reserves and staked his regime, the barbudos walked into Havana. On January 2, 1959, Che assumed the command of Havana's La Cabana fortress, and two days later issued this victorious salute to the Cuban people: "The peasant is a man of good faith, of high morals, and of an unshakable love of liberty. Men and women of the Sierra Maestra and all the peasants of Cuba were the principal fighters in this battle. Now that the struggle is over, one of the fundamental steps will be giving the Cuban peasant the treatment he justly deserves."

On January 9, 1959, the Cuban Council of Ministers made Che Guevara a Cuban citizen, and at that time, he legalized "Che" (without an accent over the "e") as part of his name.

His main concern, at first, was foreign policy. In June, 1959, he went on extensive trips through Africa, Asia (including Hiroshima), and Europe. He returned on September 8, 1959, and got to work on the agrarian reform. On October 7, at a meeting of the National Institute of Agrarian Reform (INRA) presided over by Fidel, Che was named chief of the Industrial Department, and much of the credit for its success is due to him.

On November 26 of that year Che took over the national bank and made Cuba's new banknotes famous by signing them simply "Che." The first question he asked of his subordinates when he took over the bank was "Where has Cuba deposited its gold reserves and dollars?" When he was told, "In Fort Knox," he immediately decided to sell, converting the gold reserves into currencies which were exported to Canadian or Swiss banks. Thanks to this foresightedness, Cuba was not caught in a bind—indeed, it would have been bankrupt—when the United States seized all Cuba's assets in the United States.

Both at INRA and at the bank, Che's routine was very taxing, especially for foreign bankers. He often worked as much as thirty-six successive hours, lunching and dining at his desk. His business appointments usually began after 2 A.M., and never did he accept the idea of the business lunch. He used to say, "Business lunches waste too much time, and you can't talk with food in your mouth."

Whenever he did have a moment off at home with Aleida who worked (and still does) for the Cuban Federation of Women, Che learned to enjoy classical music, especially Beethoven, and of course he read avidly, as always. He ate simply: steak, if possible, lettuce and tomato salad, Spanish cognac, and inevitably, maté. He dressed equally simply: a faded fatigue uniform with shirt hanging over the pants, black paratroop boots, and a beret, which he took off rarely. Always erect, usually puffing on a Monte Cristo No. 4 cigar, Che tried to keep out of the limelight as much as possible, and only because Fidel insisted did he make public speeches. He never tried to imitate Fidel; instead he spoke calmly, almost as if delivering a lecture, using an index finger to point through the air for emphasis. His early speeches have been lost, but from 1960 on they have been recorded, transcribed, and are represented in this book.

At cabinet meetings Che never hesitated to argue or disagree with Fidel, and he, more than anyone, set the tone for the dialogue that began right from the beginning among revolutionary leaders. That dialogue has continued to this day.

From the very outset Che's main concern was establishing Socialist Man in Cuba. In this he was willing to sacrifice efficiency—though he was very efficient—and thus clashed almost at once with the Communist party's traditional thinkers. These Communists always insisted—and still do, everywhere—that one ought to build a socialist economy before one tries to change man. Che, on the other hand, felt that a socialist economy in itself is not worth the effort, sacrifice, and risks of war and destruction if it ends up encouraging greed and individual ambition at the expense of the collective spirit. Still, as the dialogue raged, Che was good at his job.

In the early days, when the United States and Cuba were still trying to find ways of interaction, Walter Sauer, executive vice president of the Export-Import Bank, an official arm of the United States Treasury Department, had occasion to talk with Che about finances. He commented later: "Guevara knows and understands foreign exchange, balance of payments, etc., and in fact he understands finance and economics, and he knows exactly where the hell he is going. . . . It was just like talking to another banker, except that the son of a bitch is an orthodox Marxist."

As director of the bank Che was in charge of import permits, and from the beginning he tried to cut down on imports as much as possible in order to build up Cuba's reserves and get Cubans to become more self-sufficient, even at the risk of great shortages. One day, it seems, a group of girls employed at Havana's famous department store, El Encanto, went to see Che to ask him to increase the import quota, "or else we will be without jobs in a few days." One of the girls explained that "Lots of us are married and have children to support, and if the store collapses, we will be in the street." Che asked them to come back the next day and "I will have a solution." The next day the girls returned to Che's office and he received them with a big smile. "Your problem is solved," he started to tell them, but the girls drowned out his words as they broke into applause. Finally he explained: "Cuba is producing a big crop of tomatoes this season. All of you can go to the fields and pick tomatoes, and you will make a better living from that than at the store." He issued no import permit to El Encanto.

In 1960 Che traveled again a great deal, going to Czechoslovakia, Russia, China, and Korea. From each he brought home sound commercial agreements for the development of Cuba. Then in 1961 he moved on to become the Minister of Industry and spent a great deal of time and effort convincing workers that both their duty and their personal satisfaction were to be found in working for the collective, for the community, not for individual material rewards.

In April of that year he reassumed his military duties in the armed forces and participated in the counterattack against the Bay of Pigs invaders. Then, in August, he headed the Cuban delegation to the Punta del Este conference where the Alliance for Progress was enacted. It was there that I met him for the first time.

On August 10, 1961, I was at Montevideo's Carrasco International Airport covering the event for *The New York Times*. There were about two thousand Fidelistas waiting patiently but loudly, waving flags and posters. Secretary of the Treasury Douglas Dillon arrived first that warm pleasant afternoon. He was immediately surrounded by a batch of us reporters, photographers, protocol men, and every other type of credential holder—but no people. The long black limousines were waiting, but Dillon decided to make a little arrival speech and pulled out his prepared text.

Just as he began to read, however, a whining buzz muffled out his words, and the crowd let out a tremendous roar. A Cuban Airline Britannia had started banking down. Dillon tried to continue to read, but no one was listening. The youngsters behind the police lines were shrieking and Dillon's words could not carry very far anyway. As Che's plane taxied to a stop, Dillon found himself alone with his aides, embassy staff members, and protocol men. Even the United States correspondents abandoned him to rush over and see Che. Dillon folded up his speech and disappeared in his black limousine. The new arrival, Che Guevara, in olive green fatigues and beret, was applauded, cheered, hugged, even kissed, as he tried to push his way to a small pink Chevy waiting for him. Days before the conference the Cuban Embassy tried to rent the usual diplomatic cars, but were told by all rent-a-car dealers that all their cars had been rented. Later, we of *The New York Times* staff covering the conference had no difficulty renting a car. However, as the car news was made public, scores of Uruguayans volunteered to lend their private cars, and thus Che, after waving to his fans, shaking hands, and patting me on the back as I tried to ask him a couple of quick questions, which he could not answer due to the crush of people, got into a loaned pink Chevy and drove up the west coast of Uruguay to the resort town of Punta del Este. I did the same. My assignment, until I had to return to Montevideo six days later to cover a mammoth pro-Castro demonstration, was "Cover Che Guevara."

The Cuban delegates stayed at the most modest of the major hotels at Punta del Este, the one called Playa (beach), and occupied two full floors. Off-duty bodyguards, delegates' wives, Che's elder sister, who had come over from Argentina, and friends, all ate at two huge round tables at one end of the dining room.

Che was not especially warm to those he did not know, but he was pleasant and greeted everyone who greeted him. The Playa was only a short walk across a treeless park from the casino, which had been renamed Building of the Americas. It was there, at the gaming tables, that Latin America's sovereignty was gambled away for Alliance goodies. Each time a session ended, Che and his entourage ambled leisurely back through the park. Once an unshaven, burly, local fisherman headed his bicycle straight for Che. One of the bodyguards, who was edgy because known anti-Castro Cubans were all over the place (with credentials from the continent's reactionary press), began to reach for his pistol. But the fisherman shouted "Comandante!" and grabbed both of Che's arms, saying "I want you to know that our government may be against you, the governments of this hemisphere may be against you, but we the people, the poor, are with you. Don't let us down." Then he rushed off before Che, visibly moved, could even utter a *Thank You.* It was Che's only moment of hesitation.

In the off-hours of the conference, Che could be quite a talker. One night, three Argentine correspondents and I sat up until 4 A.M. while he discussed his adventures in the Sierra Maestra. I wrote shortly thereafter (in 1962), "Through his 'army experiences' talk, we discovered a keen observer, extremely intense and in a great hurry. He gave us the impression that he was convinced he would soon die and that he must accomplish everything he can as fast as possible." I asked him that night about the executions in Cuba and about his relationship with Russia and the break with the United States. He answered, as I reported then:

> Without Russian aid we'd starve. . . . Every social revolution has to have its Stalinist phase. Let's hope ours lasts only a short time. . . . We had to nationalize United States industry, and when we did the United States cut us off. I'm sure that if we really were Commies, we'd get along fine, just like Russia and the United States get along, with tourism, plenty

of trade, exchange students and the rest. It's too bad, though; it will mean many shortages for us. We will run out of food. Our busses will stop. Everything will go down until we can raise the food we need and manufacture our own busses. If we can last until then, the United States is lost, because as soon as Latin America sees our economy going up, more revolutions will explode. That's why the United States must destroy us—before we recover completely, before we have rebuilt our economy.[2]

My over-all impression of Che as I remember it was that he was extremely dedicated, extremely honest, and extremely human, though he had a distance, perhaps even a shyness, which made those other qualities difficult to perceive. Apparently he had difficulty showing personal affection, even to his parents, as the letter to them in this volume makes clear. In any event I was convinced that he was not a Communist in most of the traditional senses of the word. He believed in a socialist economy. He believed in Socialist Man. He was convinced that these two goals can be achieved by man and was dedicated to working for their realization without taking orders from any foreign power. He only felt scorn for those who took such orders. Indeed, one night at the Punta del Este conference, two Argentine Communist hacks arrived at the Playa Hotel and passed through the lobby where we were talking. Che quipped to them, "Hey, why are you here, to start the counterrevolution?" I put that quote into my book on Latin America and I remember at the time (in 1963 when the first edition came out) being ridiculed by many of the critics who looked upon Che as a traditional Communist. Of course, now that his feud with the party hacks is well known, no one would disbelieve that quote.

Between Punta del Este in 1961 and the summer of 1964, when I saw Che again, he continued to devote all of his energies to creating the Cuban Socialist Man, the Cuban Socialist economy—to getting the best possible deals from socialist countries. He traveled to Russia in 1962, to Switzerland in 1963 and 1964 for the United Nations Conference on Trade and Development, to Algiers in early 1964, and again to Algiers later that year. During all this time he waged an untiring battle against bureaucratism, against Party coldness, against castes and prejudices.

In July 1964 I went to Cuba as a correspondent for *Newsweek,* and there renewed my acquaintance with Che. I met him one night at the Algerian Embassy, which was celebrating the day of its revolution, and we began to chat about some of the basic problems involved in all revolutions, specifically in the Cuban. Suddenly he stopped, and said, "But wait, you are here representing what?"

I told him, *"Newsweek."*

"Ah," he said, "I won't speak to you in that capacity," and feigned moving away from me. Then he stopped, turned, and said, "But of course

[2] *The Great Fear in Latin America,* (New York, The Macmillan Company, 1963), Collier, 2d edition (1966), pp. 257-58.

if you want to speak 'como hombre' we will continue." By this he meant more than that our talk was to be off the record. He meant that it would have to be a give and take, an honest relationship, not one in which I might be pumping him for facts, and he telling me things to impress me. Naturally I agreed, and during the next three weeks I had a few opportunities to talk to him at length. I never took notes; therefore I am reconstructing from memory three years later. But I recall very clearly my impression—and his main concerns.

It was quite clear to me that he had reached the conclusion that the United States will never stop or even modify its imperialism so as to allow any country of the underdeveloped world in which it has interests to develop for its own good. No underdeveloped country will ever be allowed to develop its own industry if that industry would compete with American industry. No underdeveloped country would ever be able to enjoy the benefits derived from a structure that is absolutely corruption free, that is dedicated to building up the lowest members of society to the level of the highest. Che gave me the impression then he was totally convinced that from then on no individual revolution could succeed unless it was tied to a revolutionary process implanted in the whole underdeveloped world; that the traditional Washington-Moscow "peaceful coexistence" line was a sell-out, a compromise. He was convinced that each compromise of the revolutionary ideals corrodes the Revolution itself. Over and over again in this book, this theme is repeated, even in such an early article as "The Sin of the Revolution," written in 1961.

In our discussion of Lenin, Che made me feel that he looked upon that great revolutionary as almost tragic, as a man who knew that a society built on material incentives was doomed to fail morally, and yet the man who instituted the New Economic Policy. That policy, as successful as it was, brought back material incentives at the expense of moral incentives, and with it the goal of creating a new man was abandoned for the sake of creating a powerful state. Che never criticized Lenin, but he lamented the result of the NEP. Che himself, it seemed to me, was not interested in setting up a powerful state. He was interested only in building a society in which all men shared the collective spirit through the fullness of their individual aspiration. He was a genuine individualist in that to him the greatest expression of the individual was total commitment to the collective. One of the great classics in that kind of argumentation by a Marxist-Leninist thinker is his speech on Revolutionary Medicine, delivered as early as August 1960.

By 1964 Che had understood that all institutions must work toward such social goals; that not even the National Bank can afford to be a mere instrument for financing development. As a revolutionary institution, it must work for the social needs of a new society. His debate with orthodox Marxist economists on this theme has passed almost unnoticed in the non-socialist world, but in Cuba it has become the most important of all theoretical discussions—and Fidel has clearly agreed with Che (see Castro's "Criterios de Nuestra Revolución," *Cuba Socialista*, Año V, No. 49, Sept., 1965).

To Che the debate was crucial, for it affected the whole orientation and structure of Cuba's socialist economy. If all our efforts are to be directed at creating Socialist Man, Che would argue, then the Theory of Value (as dependent on supply and demand) is wrong; Value becomes defined according to the moral and social worth of a product, not its market worth. Likewise, if Socialist Man is more important than socialist efficiency, then, Che would say (and he says it in this book quite explicitly), the worth of an enterprise is its social function, not its financial success. Thus the bank should budget enterprises according to their social value, as Che did when he ran the bank, and not give loans at interest to state enterprises, which tends to force their managers to become obsessed with the results (as is the case in Russia). Che's whole attitude toward prices, sacrifices, import restrictions, new factories, electrification, communications, etc., was governed by his one fundamental principle that no matter how much you change a society, no matter how much you restructure it, unless you create a new man, unless you change attitudes, it all ends up in greed, lust, and ambition.

Thus, for Che, the Revolution, and its work beyond the armed struggle, is basically directed at and justified by the setting up of a genuine "love generation," to use a New Left term.

But Che understood more than any man I have ever met that love cannot exist between master and slave. He knew that such relationships have to be destroyed, first. And he knew that once destroyed, the new relationship—love—does not spring forth automatically. Love does not come out of an establishment from above. It comes from the roots, from people, working at it from below. Love, Che would say, is not a flash of lightning, an instantaneous mystical happening. It is an effort. It is something that one builds up gradually by working at it.

Before people can work at their love, however, and gain pleasure from the other's pleasure, gain satisfaction from satisfying the other, they must first be able to communicate. In order to communicate they have to be equals. A rich man who "loves" a poor man is offering charity, not love. Thus, he who wants to belong to the Love Generation must first be committed to destroying the Hate Generation, sponsored by the greedy, by the know-it-alls, by the masters. Thus it was to me quite understandable when I heard that Che had left Cuba and gone elsewhere to help destroy the masters. For in Cuba, by 1965, the New Man was being created by the New Men. The commitment of the new generation was total.

Unquestionably many Cubans over thirty have had, and continue to have, a hard time adapting to the Cuban Revolution. But the new generation does not adapt. It leads. It throws itself into it so completely that Che could look upon Cuba as having definitely and irrevocably launched itself on the road to the creation of the Socialist Man. Thus, with a deep heart, but with a sense of satisfaction, he could leave Cuba to begin anew.

He left sometime in 1965, went to Vietnam, to the Congo, and to various places in Latin America. He was at one point in Guatemala, at another in Venezuela. He certainly went through Peru, also perhaps Colombia. On February 15, 1966, the day of his daughter's tenth birthday, he sent her a note from "somewhere in Latin America," saying: "You must know that I am far and will stay away from you for a long time, doing what I can to fight our enemies. It's not much what I do, but I hope you will always be proud of your father, as I am proud of you. Remember that many years of struggle are still ahead, and even when you will be a woman you will have to take part in it. In the meantime, you must prepare yourself, be very revolutionary, which, at your age, means to learn a lot, the most possible, and to always be ready to support just causes. . . ."

In August 1967 Che was in Argentina, where some of his old friends, people I have known since 1960, saw him. Then he went to Bolivia, or perhaps returned to Bolivia, and began the struggle from scratch.

It is fairly clear from his diary, assuming it is authentic, and from his friends with whom I have communicated, that Che was somewhat disappointed at the slow process of revolution in Bolivia. But that is because Che was a man in a hurry, a man who knew in 1961 that he would soon die.

It is true, as Fidel has pointed out, that Che tended to be careless with his own safety. But he was plagued with many personal obstacles—not only his asthma but also a fantastic allergy to mosquito bites, each of which would swell into a bubble the size of a walnut. It is also true, as Fidel pointed out, that Che was absolutely convinced that he was not indispensable, that he could die and that the cause would continue. There is no reason to doubt this. But neither can one doubt that as Fidel said, "men of his experience, men of his caliber, of his unique capacities, are not common," and such an individual should not die in small, relatively unimportant encounters. But Che believed to the end that history is made by men, in the plural, not by any individual man.

Apparently Che was caught in a small skirmish in Bolivia, was wounded and captured alive, and then was murdered by a shot in the heart the next day. Information on the way he died is contradictory, and perhaps we will never know the truth. It is quite clear, however, that he is more alive today than when he lived, for he is the only example in the history of social revolutions of a man having reached the top and then voluntarily started from the bottom again. He is, thus, the Garibaldi of social revolutions. Above all else he has shown the world that failure is never final, and when it is for the people that a man fights, there will always be another to carry on after he is gone.

When he was killed, *The New York Times* reported that the Bolivian guerrilla operation was over; only the mop-up of six stragglers remained. In the month that has ensued since then, no less than thirty skirmishes with Bolivian guerrillas have been reported in the press, mostly by Reuters. More than any theoretical work on how examples create progress and generate their own momentum, Che has proved it by his actions. He is a hero in Hanoi, in the Congo, in Algeria, in Tanzania, in every country of Latin America, in the ghettos of the United States. As Julius Lester of the Student Non-Violent Coordinating Committee (SNCC) wrote: "It is not important that Comrade Che is dead. It is only important that he lived, and that is all that is important for each of us. . . . To destroy Comrade Che they will have to destroy all of us—the dispossessed; and this they cannot do."

In the history books he will, in due course, be recorded as one of the great contributors to Marxist-Leninism. I say "in due course" because contemporary critics, those who look at the writings and speeches in this book, for example, will inevitably find clichés, misstatements, and factual errors, not to mention sheer bad writing. There is no doubt that some of what Che wrote and said was written and said badly. There is no doubt that many of the articles included herein will have historical value only. They are sometimes dull and repetitious. Their style varies from brilliant to vulgar; their insights range from profound to common. Still, in any history of Marxist-Leninist thinkers twenty years from now, Che will rank as a great theoretician. I hope this book gives the fairest possible representation of his work—except of course, for his book, *Guerrilla Warfare*, which has already been published. And I hope the book will help the historian, the political scientist, the humanist, and the activist to face squarely the problems of today—as Che faced them, honestly and totally.

Che was first and foremost an activist himself. He thought hard and well, reading everything he could find, going into every problem as deeply as he could. He was, as Fidel has said, ". . . a communist revolutionary, a true Communist, he had a boundless faith in moral values, he had a boundless faith in the conscience of man. And we should say that he saw, with absolute clarity, moral resources as the fundamental lever in the construction of communism in human society." But he was primarily a doer, a revolutionary activist.

That was what led him to Guatemala, to Cuba, to Bolivia. It is that faith and activism that lead the new Ches today, men who still believe in men, who are still convinced that we can build a decent society in which all men respect one another, and in which all men can communicate with each other as full-bodied human beings who are still persuaded that "we can make it," that *venceremos!*

CHAPTER I

Canto a Fidel[1]

Vámonos,
ardiente profeta de la aurora,
por recónditos senderos inalámbricos
a librear el verde caimán que tanto amas.

Vámonos,
derrotando afrentas con la frente
plena de martianas estrellas insurrectas,
juremos lograr el triunfo o encontrar la muerte.

Cuando suene el primer disparo y se despierte
en virginal asombro la manigua entera,
allí, a tu lado, serenos combatientes,
nos tendrás.

Cuando tu voz derrame hacia los cuatro vientos
reforma agraria, justicia, pan, libertad,
allí, a tu lado, con idénticos acentos,
nos tendrás.

Y cuando llegue al final de la jornada
la sanitaria operación contra el tirano,
allí, a tu lado, aguardando la postrer batalla,
nos tendrás.

El día que la fiera se lama el flanco herido
donde el dardo nacionalizador le dé,
allí, a tu lado, con el corazón altivo,
nos tendrás.

No pienses que puedan menguar nuestra entereza
las decoradas pulgas armadas de regalos;
pedimos su fusil, sus balas y una peña.
Nada más.

[1] Written in Mexico, 1956 and printed in *Unión* (Havana), Año 6, No. 2, April–June 1967.

Y si en nuestro camino se interpone el hierro,
pedimos un sudario de cubanas lágrimas
para que se cubran los guerrilleros huesos
en el tránsito a la historia americana.
Nada más.

Song to Fidel[2]

Let us go,
Fiery prophet of the dawn,
On silent spatial roads,
To free the verdant isle you love.

Let us go,
Brow studded with Martí's rebellious stars.
As we set out to vanquish infamy
Let us vow to overcome or die.

When the jungle awakens in virginal surprise
At the sound of your initial shots,
There, repeating the barrage,
You'll find us at your side.

When your voice clamors to the wind:
Land! Justice! Liberty! Bread!
There, a choir in counterpoint,
You'll find us at your side.

And at the end of the quest,
When tyranny's sore must be excised,
There, ready with swath,
You'll find us at your side.

The day the dragon licks its flank
Where liberating darts have struck,
There, dreams inhabiting the heart,
You'll find us at your side.

Never think our carat could diminish
At sight of alien-armed bemedalled fleas.
We'll seize their rifles, bullets, and . . . a rock.
Nothing more.

[2] Translated by Tana de Gámez.

Then, should battle iron freeze our stance,
Give us a shroud of Cuban tears
To drape over the warrior bones
As America's history bears them on.
Nothing more.

MEXICO, 1956

CHAPTER 2

The Revolutionary War[1]

FOREWORD

FOR *some time I had contemplated writing an account of the Cuban Revolution that would include all its aspects and phases. Many of our Revolution's leaders have expressed this intention—either privately or publicly—but our tasks are many, the years pass, and the memory of the insurrectional struggle grows dim, making it difficult to pinpoint events that already are part of America's history.*

I present here a series of personal memories of attacks, skirmishes, and battles in which I participated. It is not my intention that this fragmentary story, based on recollection and a few hastily written notes, should be considered a full account of the Revolution. On the contrary, I hope the subject may be elaborated by many of the men who played a role in the struggle.

My participation in the war was limited to specific areas of Cuba. Therefore I could not possibly describe events and battles that occurred elsewhere. To help our comrades to add their accounts in chronological order, I begin with our first battle; the only one with Fidel taking part in which our forces were not victorious: the surprise attack at "Alegría del Pío."

There are many survivors of these actions and each is invited to contribute his personal recollections of these events to the written records of our history. We ask only that the narrator be truthful, and that, in an attempt to clarify his position, he not unjustifiably enlarge on his true role or pretend to have been where he was not. We would ask that after writing a few pages to the best of his ability, he make a critical examination of his

[1] Originally published as *Pasajes de la Guerra Revolucionaria*, (La Habana: Ediciones Unión, 1963). Official Cuban Government translation by Eduardo Bernat. (Havana, Book Institute, 1967.) Guevara's allusions to himself appeared as "we" in the Cuban translation (ed.).

efforts and eliminate every doubtful fact that does not contribute to the authenticity of his account. In this spirit I begin my memoirs.

ALEGRÍA DEL PÍO

Alegría del Pío is a place in Oriente Province, municipality of Niquero, near Cabo Cruz. At this very spot, on December 5, 1956, Batista's forces discovered our hiding place.

We were exhausted from a long, painful trek; more painful than long, to tell the truth. We had landed on December 2, at a place known as the Playa de las Coloradas. We had lost all our equipment, and had trudged for endless hours through marshlands and swamps. We were all wearing new boots and by now everyone was suffering from blisters and footsores, but new footwear and fungus were by no means our only enemies. We had reached Cuba following a seven-day voyage across the Gulf of Mexico and the Caribbean Sea, without food, plagued by seasickness and aboard a far-from-seaworthy vessel. We had left the port of Tuxpán November 25, at a time when a stiff "northerly" was blowing and all small craft had been warned to stay in port. All this had left an indelible mark upon our troop, made up of rookies who did not know what the word "combat" meant.

All that was left of our war equipment was our rifles, cartridge belts, and a few wet rounds of ammunition. Our medical supplies had disappeared, and most of our knapsacks had been left behind in the swamps. We had spent the previous night in one of the canefields of the Niquero Sugar Mill, owned by Julio Lobo at the time. We had managed to mitigate our hunger and thirst by eating sugar cane, but due to our lack of experience we had left a trail of cane peelings and bagasse all over the place. Not that the guards looking for us needed any trail to follow our steps, for it had been our guide—as we found out later—who had betrayed us. We had let him go the night before—an error we were to repeat several times during our long struggle, until we learned that civilians whose personal records were unknown to us were not to be trusted while in dangerous areas. It was a serious blunder to release that man.

By daybreak of the fifth we could barely walk. On the verge of collapse, we would walk a short distance and then beg for a long rest period. Orders were given to halt at the edge of a canefield, in a thicket close to the dense woods. Most of us slept throughout the morning hours.

At noon we began to notice unusual signs of activity. Air Force "Piper" planes, as well as other type small planes together with small private aircraft, began to circle our hiding place. Most of our men went on cutting and eating sugar cane without realizing that they were perfectly visible to those flying the planes, which were now circling at slow speed and low altitude. I was the troop physician, and it was my duty to treat the blistered feet. I recall my last patient that morning: His name was Humberto Lamotte, and that was to be his last day on earth. I still remember how tired and worn out he looked as he walked from my improvised first aid station to his post, still carrying his shoes in one hand.

Comrade Montané and I were leaning against a tree, eating our meager rations—half a sausage and two crackers—when a rifle shot broke the stillness. Immediately, a hail of bullets—at least this is the way it looked to us, this being our baptism of fire—descended upon our eighty-two-man troop. My rifle was not one of the best; I had deliberately asked for it because I was in very poor physical condition due to an attack of asthma that had bothered me throughout our ocean voyage, and I did not want to be held responsible for the loss of a good weapon. I can hardly remember what followed the initial burst of gunfire. Almeida approached us requesting orders, but there was nobody there to issue orders. Later, I was told that Fidel had tried vainly to get everybody together into the adjoining canefield, which could be reached by simply crossing a path. The surprise attack plus the heavy gunfire had been too much for us. Almeida ran back to take charge of his group. A comrade dropped a box of ammunition at my feet, and when I reprimanded him for his action he looked at me with an expression of anguish and muttered something like "this is no time to bother with ammunition boxes." He continued on his way toward the canefield and disappeared from view. He was murdered by Batista's henchmen some time later. Perhaps this was the first time I was faced with the dilemma of choosing between my devotion to medicine and my duty as a revolutionary soldier. There, at my feet, were a knapsack full of medicine and a box of ammunition. I couldn't possibly carry both of them; they were too heavy. I picked up the box of ammunition, leaving the medicine, and started to cross the clearing, heading for the canefield. I remember Faustino Pérez, kneeling and firing his machinegun-pistol. Near me, a comrade named Arbentosa was walking toward the canefield. A burst of gunfire hit us both. I felt a sharp blow on my chest and a wound on my neck, and I thought for certain I was dead. Arbentosa, vomiting blood, and bleeding profusely from a deep hole made by a 45 caliber bullet, yelled: "they have killed me!" and began to fire his rifle at no one in particular. Flat on the ground, I turned to Faustino, saying: "I've been hit!"—what I really said is unprintable—and Faustino, still firing away, looked at me and said: "Oh, it's nothing," but I could see by the look in his eyes that he considered me as good as dead.

Still on the ground, I fired a shot in the direction of the woods, following an impulse similar to that of the other wounded man. Immediately, I began to figure out the best way to die. I recalled a Jack London story where the hero, aware that he is bound to freeze to death in the wastes of Alaska, leans calmly against a tree and prepares to die in a dignified manner. That was the only thing that came to my mind at that moment. Someone on his knees said that we had better surrender, and I heard a voice—later I found out it was Camilo's—shouting: "No, nobody surrenders here!," followed by a four-letter word. Ponce came at a run, breathing hard, and showed me a bullet wound (I was sure the bullet must have pierced his lungs), and said "I'm wounded," and I replied coolly "me, too." Then Ponce, and other comrades who were still unhurt, crawled toward the canefield. For a moment I was left alone, just lying there waiting to die. Almedia approached, urging me to go on, and despite the intense pain I dragged myself into the canefield. There I met comrade Raúl Suárez, whose thumb had been blown away by a rifle bullet, being attended by Faustino Pérez who was bandaging his hand. Then everything became a blur of airplanes flying low and strafing the field, adding to the confusion, amid Danteesque as well as grotesque scenes such as the sight of a comrade of considerable *avoirdupois* who was desperately trying to hide behind a single stalk of sugar cane, while in the middle of this turmoil another man kept on yelling: "Silence!" for no apparent reason.

We organized a group headed by Almeida. This group included Lieutenant Ramiro Valdés, now a major, and comrades Chao and Benítez. With Almeida leading, we crossed the last path among the rows of cane and reached the safety of the woods. The first shouts of "fire!" were heard in the canefield, and tongues of flame and columns of smoke began to rise. I cannot remember exactly what happened; I felt the bitterness of defeat, and I was sure I was going to die. We walked until the darkness made it impossible to go on, then decided to lie down and go to sleep all huddled together in a heap. We were starving and thirsty and the mosquitoes added to our misery. This was our baptism of fire on December 5, 1956, in the outskirts of Niquero. It was the beginning of what would later become the rebel army.

BATTLE OF LA PLATA

Our first victory was the result of an attack upon a small army garrison at the mouth of La Plata River. The effect of our victory was electrifying. It was like a clarion call, proving that the Rebel Army really existed and was ready to fight. For us it was the reaffirmation of our chances for total victory.

On January 14, 1957, shortly after the surprise attack at Alegría del Pío, we came to a halt by the Magdalena River. A piece of firm land, originating at the Sierra, juts out between the Magdalena and La Plata. Fidel gave orders for target practice as an initial attempt at some sort of training for our troops. Some of the men were using a weapon for the first time in their lives. We had not washed for many days, and we seized upon the opportunity to go swimming. Those who were able to do so changed into clean clothes. At that time we had 21 weapons in operating condition: nine rifles, equipped with telescopic sights, five semiautomatic rifles, four bolt rifles, two Thompson submachine guns, and a 16-gauge shotgun. That afternoon we climbed the last hill before reaching the outskirts of La Plata. We were following a trail marked specially for us by a peasant named Melquíades Elías. This man had been recommended by our guide Eutimio. Our guide was essential to us, and he seemed to be the prototype of the rebel farmer, but later he was apprehended by Casillas, who, instead of killing him, bribed him with an offer of $10,000 and the rank of lieutenant if he managed to kill Fidel. Eutimio came close to fulfilling his bargain, but he lacked the courage to do so. However, he was very useful to the enemy because he informed on the location of several of our camps.

At the time, Eutimio was serving us loyally. He was one of the many peasants fighting for their lands in the struggle against the landowners, and anyone fighting them was also fighting against the guards at the landowners' service.

That day we captured two peasants who turned out to be our guide's cousins. One of them was released, but we kept the other one as a precautionary measure. The next day, January 15, we saw the La Plata army barracks, under construction, with a zinc roof. A group of half-naked men were moving about, but we could tell they were soldiers. Just before sundown, about 6 P.M., a boat came in, some guards landed, and others got aboard. We did not quite make out the maneuver, so we postponed the attack to the following day.

At dawn of the sixteenth we began watching the army post. The boat had disappeared during the night, and no soldiers could be seen anywhere. At 3 P.M. we decided to approach the road leading to the barracks and take a look; by nightfall we crossed the shallow La Plata River and took our positions on the road. Five minutes later we took two farmers into custody. One of them had a record as an informer. When we told them who we were and reassured them that no harm would befall them, they gave us some valuable information: the barracks held about fifteen soldiers. Also, that Chicho Osorio, one of the region's most notorious foremen, was to go by at any moment. These foremen worked for the Laviti family latifundium. The Lavitis had established an enormous feud, holding on to it by means of a regime of terror with the help of characters such as Chicho Osorio. Shortly afterwards, Chicho showed up, astride a mule, with a little Negro boy riding "double." Chicho was drunk. Universo Sánchez gave him the order to halt in the name of the Rural Guards and immediately Chicho replied: "Mosquito." It was the password.

We must have looked like a bunch of pirates, but Chicho was so drunk we were able to fool him. Fidel stepped forward and, looking very indignant, said he was an army colonel who had come to find out why the rebels had not yet been liquidated. He bragged about going into the woods, which accounted for his beard. He added that the army was "botching things up," etc. In one word, he cut the army efficiency to pieces. Sheepishly, Osorio admitted that the guards spent all their time inside the barracks, eating and doing nothing but occasional useless rounds. He emphasized that the rebels must be wiped out. We interrogated him discreetly about friendly and unfriendly people living in the area, and we kept tab on his replies, backwards: when Osorio called somebody a bad man we knew he was one of our friends, and so on. We had about twenty-four names by now, and Osorio was still jabbering away. He told us how two men had been killed, adding: "but my General Batista, set me free at once." He spoke of having slapped two peasants who "had gotten a little out of hand," adding that the guards would not do such a thing; on the contrary, they let the peasants talk without punishing them. Fidel asked Osorio what he would do if he ever caught Fidel Castro, and Osorio, with a very expressive gesture, replied: "We'll have to cut his —— off." He said the same thing about Crescencio. "Look," he said, showing us his shoes (they were the kind of Mexican-made shoes our men wore), "these shoes belonged to one of those sons of bitches we killed." Without realizing it, Osorio had signed his own sentence. At Fidel's suggestion, he agreed to accompany us to the barracks in order to come upon the soldiers unexpectedly and prove to them they were badly prepared and not fit for their duties.

As we neared the barracks, with Osorio in the lead, I still did not feel so sure that he had not become wise to our tricks. However, he kept going on, in complete ignorance, for he was so drunk he could not think straight. When he crossed the river to get near the barracks, Fidel told Osorio that military rules called for the prisoner to be tied up. The man did not resist and he went on, this time as a prisoner, although he ignored this fact. He explained to us that the only guards were set up at the entrance of the barracks under construction and at the house of a foreman named Honorio. Osorio guided us to a place near the barracks, near the road to Macío. Luis Crespo, now a major, went on to scout around and returned saying that the foreman's report was correct. Crespo had seen the barracks and the pinpoints of light made by the guards' cigarettes.

We were just about ready to approach the barracks when we had to pull back into the woods to let three guards on horseback go by. The men were urging a man whom they had taken prisoner to walk faster as they followed him on horseback, hurling all sorts of insults at him. They passed very close to me, and I remember the peasant saying: "I'm just like one of you fellows" and the answer by one of the men whom we later identified as Corporal Basol: "Shut up and keep going or I'll use the whip on you!" We all thought the peasant was out of danger by remaining out of the barracks at the moment of our attack. However, the following day, when the guards heard of the attack, they murdered him at El Macío.

We had twenty-two weapons ready for the attack. It was a crucial moment because we were short of ammunition. The army post had to be taken, for a failure would have meant spending all our ammunition, leaving us practically defenseless. Lieutenant Julio Díaz—later killed at the battle of El Uvero—Camilo Cienfuegos, Benítez, and Calixto Morales, armed with semiautomatic rifles, were to surround the palm-thatched house on the right side. Fidel, Universo Sánchez, Luis Crespo, Calixto García, Fajardo—brother of our physician, Piti Fajardo, killed at the Escambray—and I, would attack the center. Raúl and his squad and Almeida with his would attack the barracks on the right side.

We approached to within forty meters of the barracks. By the light of a full moon Fidel opened the hostilities with two bursts of machinegun fire and all available rifles joined. Immediately, we demanded the enemy's surrender, but we got no results. Murderer-informer Osorio was executed as soon as the battle broke out.

The attack had begun at 2:40 A.M., and the guards put up a much stiffer resistance than we had expected. A sergeant armed with an M-1 opened up with a burst every time we asked them to surrender. We were given orders to use our old, Brazilian-type hand grenades. Luis Crespo and I threw ours but they did not go off; Raúl Castro threw a stick of dynamite with the same negative result. It became necessary to get close to the houses and set them on fire even at the risk of our own lives. Universo Sánchez made a futile attempt, and Cienfuegos also failed. Finally, Luis Crespo and I got close to one of the ranches and set it on fire. The glare gave us an opportunity to see that it was a place for storing coconuts, but the over-all effect intimidated the soldiers and they gave up the fight. One of them, trying to escape, ran smack into Luis Crespo's rifle; Crespo shot him in the chest, took the man's rifle, and continued firing toward the house. Camilo Cienfuegos, entrenched behind a tree, fired upon the fleeing sergeant and ran out of ammunition.

The soldiers, almost defenseless, were being wiped out by our bullets. Camilo Cienfuegos was first into the house, where shouts of surrender were being heard. Quickly, we took stock of our booty: eight Springfields, one Thompson machine gun, and about one thousand rounds; we had fired approximately five hundred rounds. In addition, we now had cartridge belts, fuel, knives, clothing, and some food. Casualties: two soldiers dead, five wounded. We took three prisoners.

Our men had not suffered a single scratch. We set fire to the soldiers' quarters, and after taking care of the wounded—three of them were seriously wounded and we were told later that they had died—we withdrew. One of the soldiers later joined the forces under Major Raúl Castro's command, was promoted to lieutenant, and died in an airplane accident following the war.

Our attitude toward the wounded was in open contrast to that of the tyranny's army. Not only did they kill our wounded men; they abandoned their own. This difference made a great impact upon the enemy and it was instrumental in our victory. Fidel gave orders that the prisoners be given all the medicines to take care of the wounded. I was appalled at this decision because, as a physician, I felt the need of saving all available medicine and drugs for our own men. We freed all civilians and at 4:30 of the seventeenth we started for Palma Mocha, arriving there at dawn and continuing on to the most inaccessible zones of the Sierra Maestra.

A most depressing scene awaited us: The day before, an army corporal and one of the foremen had warned all the families living in the area that the Air Force was to bomb the entire zone, and the exodus toward the coast had begun. No one knew of our presence in the area, so it was evidently a maneuver on the part of the foreman and the rural guards to take the land away from the peasants. Unfortunately, their stories had coincided with our attack, making the lie appear as the truth. Terror was rampant among the peasants and it was impossible for us to stop their flight.

This was the first victorious battle of the rebel armies. It was only in this battle and the one following that we had more weapons than men. Peasants were not yet ready to join in the struggle, and communication with the city bases was practically nonexistent.

BATTLE OF ARROYO DEL INFIERNO

Arroyo del Infierno is a little stream running into the Palma Mocha river. Walking alongside the stream, skirting the surrounding hills, in a direction away from the river, we came upon a small gorge where two small palm-thatched huts were located. We set up camp, but as usual, we kept away from the huts.

Fidel expected the army to come looking for us and be more or less successful in finding us, so he decided to set up an ambush to capture a few soldiers. To this aim men were conveniently set up at various points. Fidel kept a constant check-up on our lines and defenses. On January 19 we were reviewing the troops, and an accident occurred that could have had grave consequences. I used to wear a corporal's helmet, a trophy of the La Plata battle. I wore the helmet with great pride as I reviewed the troops, but since the review was held in the middle of the woods, the advance guard heard us coming, and all they could distinguish was a group led by a man wearing a helmet. Fortunately, it was weapon-cleaning time, and Camilo's rifle was the only one in condition to fire. Camilo opened fire on us and immediately realized his mistake; the first shot missed the mark, and then his automatic rifle jammed. This proves how tense we all were, waiting for the fight as a sort of relief from this tension. These are the times when even the coolest men feel a slight tremor in their legs, and everyone is anxiously awaiting that great moment of war: combat. However, we were far from yearning for a fight. We fought because we had to fight.

At dawn of the twenty-second we heard a few shots near the Palma Mocha area. This made us renew our efforts to strengthen our lines and take good care of ourselves while waiting for the enemy troops.

Expecting the soldiers to be nearby, we skipped breakfast and lunch. Crespo and a few other men had discovered a hen's nest and we used to steal the eggs, always leaving one so as not to discourage the hen in her task. That morning Crespo decided that as long as we had heard shots nearby, we might as well eat the last egg. At noon we saw someone in one of the huts, and at first we thought it was one of our comrades who had disobeyed the orders to stay away. It turned out that the man exploring the hut was a soldier. Later on the number of soldiers increased to six. Finally, some of them left, and three men remained. We could see the man on guard taking a good look all around. Then he picked up a few leaves, placed them behind his ears in a sorry attempt at camouflage, and sat in the shade with a placid look on his face, which was clearly distinguishable through the telescopic sight. Fidel opened fire, hitting the man, who fell crying out something that sounded like "Oh, mother!" and lay still. Shooting became general, and two other soldiers fell. Then I saw another soldier trying to hide near the other hut. From an elevated point, all I could see was his legs, because the overhanging roof covered the rest of him. My first shot missed, but the second one hit him. As he fell, his rifle hit the ground bayonet-first and remained stuck there. Covered by Crespo, I reached the house, and I could see the man was dead. I took his ammunition, rifle, and other belongings. He must have died instantly because rigor mortis was setting in quickly, probably due to his exhaustion following his last journey through the woods.

It was a fast and furious battle, and soon we were on our way into hiding, having fulfilled our plans.

When we took inventory it turned out that we had spent about 900 rounds and taken in 70 from a cartridge belt and one rifle. This rifle was a Garand that went to Efigenio Ameijeiras, now a major, who used it for the major part of the war. We counted four enemy dead, but months later we found out through an informer that there had been five. It was not a complete victory, but neither was it a Pyrrhic one. We had exchanged blows with the enemy under difficult circumstances, and we had passed the test.

This raised our spirits and allowed us to keep on climbing toward the most inaccessible places in order to escape larger groups of enemy soldiers. We crossed the mountains, and now we were traveling parallel to the Batista soldiers who had also run away crossing the same mountain tops to get to the other side. For two days our troops and theirs marched almost side by side without being aware of it. Once they spent the night in a hut, separated from the hut we were in by only a narrow river and a couple of road bends. The soldiers were led by a lieutenant by the name of Mosquera. His name and his fierce reputation were well known all over the

Sierra. It is worth mentioning that the shots we had heard prior to the battle had killed a man of Haitian descent who had refused to guide the soldiers to our hiding place. If the soldiers had not murdered this man, they would have found us less prepared for the battle.

Once again we were overloaded; most of us were carrying two rifles each. This did not make our traveling easy, but our morale was quite different from that following the Alegría del Pío disaster. Only a few days before, we had defeated a smaller number of men entrenched in an army post; now we had defeated a column on the march, of greater strength than ours, and we were able to verify how important it is, in this type of war, to eliminate the advance guard, because an army cannot move without an advance guard.

AIR ATTACK

Following our victorious battle against Sánchez Mosquera's men, we traveled along the banks of the La Plata river. Then we crossed the Magdalena and returned to a zone familiar to us: Caracas. But conditions there were much different from those existing when we had first hid in that very same hill. At that time everyone in the area supported our struggle; now Casillas' troops had passed by, leaving a trail of terror. The peasants had disappeared, and all that remained was their huts and a few animals which we had to kill in order to get some food. Experience had shown us that it was not safe to stay in the houses, so after we spent one night in one of these lonely huts, we returned to the woods and set up camp near a waterfall, almost at the top of Caracas hill.

There I received a note from Manuel Fajardo, asking me if it was possible that we might lose the war. Our reply, independent of the state of euphoria following some victory, was always the same: The war would be won. Fajardo explained that he asked the question because "Gallego" Morán had told him it was impossible to win the war; that our cause was lost. Morán had ended by inviting Fajardo to give up the struggle. I reported to Fidel, but I found out that Morán had taken care of telling Fidel that he was going to lay out a few "feelers" to test the troops' morale. Fidel and I agreed that this was not the most adequate system, and Fidel addressed the troops, urging a more strict discipline and explaining the perils involved if discipline was not observed. He also announced that the crimes of insubordination, desertion, and defeatism were to be punished by death.

The situation was not a happy one. Our column lacked cohesion. It had neither any ideological awareness nor the esprit de corps that can only be attained through hard, bitter struggle. Day after day more comrades would ask to be released and to be assigned to missions in the cities—although this involved even greater dangers—but it was evident that they simply could not stand the rough going. Nevertheless, we maintained our day by day routine. Morán went here and there, trying to locate some food and making contacts with neighboring peasants.

This was the general state of affairs on the morning of January 30. Eutimio Guerra, the traitor, had asked Fidel's permission to go visit his sick mother; Fidel had agreed and had even given him some money for the trip, which Eutimio had said would take several weeks. We were still unaware of many strange things, which later became quite clear due to Eutimio's behavior following his return. He said he had been near Palma Mocha when he found out that the army was hard on our trail, and had tried to warn us but all he found was the bodies of dead soldiers in the house of Delfín, a peasant who lived near Arroyo del Infierno, where the battle had taken place; he had followed our vague trail until he found our camp. What actually happened was that Eutimio had been captured by the army and now he was working as an enemy agent. He had been promised a large sum of money and a military rank as a reward for murdering Fidel.

As part of his plan, Eutimio had left the camp on the night of the twenty-ninth. In the early hours of January 30 we heard the sound of airplane engines. Our field kitchen was set up two hundred yards downhill, near a brook. Suddenly we heard a plane diving and the rattle of machine-guns, followed by the bombs falling. We still lacked experience and it seemed to us that the gunfire came from every side. Fifty caliber shells explode on contact with the ground, and we received the impression that they came from the woods, in addition to the air strafing. We thought we were surrounded by the enemy.

I was assigned the mission of waiting for the members of the advance guard and picking up a few utensils we had abandoned following the attack. The meeting point was La Cueva del Humo. Accompanied by Chao, a Spanish War veteran, I waited for our men, but they did not show up there. Carrying a heavy load, we followed a trail and finally sat down to rest. Then we heard sounds and saw Guillermo García—now a major—and Sergio Acuña coming from the same trail we had followed. They were members of the advance guard. After a brief consultation, García and I returned to the camp to be met by a scene of desolation. Everything was silent now, and the planes were gone. In a unique display of marksmanship, never again repeated throughout the entire war, the Air Force had hit our field kitchen smack on the nose. The stove was cut in half. A bomb had hit our advance post, but luckily, the men had already abandoned it. Morán, who had gone scouting with another man, returned alone, saying that he had seen the planes—five of them—and that there were no soldiers in the vicinity. All five of us started out, carrying our heavy loads. Suddenly we came upon a scene of horror: our peasant friend's house had burned to the ground. All that was left was a cat, meowing sadly, and a pig that took off into the woods as soon as he saw us. We had heard about Cueva del Humo, but were not sure about its location. We spent a sleepless night, waiting for our comrades and fearing an encounter with the enemy.

On January 31 we camped atop a hill overlooking some orchards. We explored an area we believed to be Cueva del Humo, but found nothing. Sergio thought he had seen some men wearing baseball caps, but he was late reporting to us, and we could not see anyone. We went with Guillermo to explore the bottom of the valley near the Ají. A friend of Guillermo's gave us some food, but everybody in the area was scared to death. This man said that Ciro Frías' merchandise had been seized and burned by the guards, his mules had been impounded, and the muleteer had been killed. The soldiers, who had arrived that morning, were under the command of Major Casillas, who had spent the night near the house.

On February 1 we were still in our camp, in the open air. At 11 A.M. we heard shots, followed by the sound of someone calling for help. This was too much for Sergio Acuña, who silently dropped his rifle and cartridge belt and disappeared into the woods, deserting his post. Taking our campaign diary, we entered a list of items he had taken with him: a can of condensed milk and three sausages. We were very sorry about the milk and sausages. A few hours later we heard noises, and not knowing whether Sergio had betrayed us, we prepared to defend ourselves. It turned out to be Crescencio, leading a large group, including some of our men plus a group from Manzanillo led by Roberto Pesant. Missing from our group were: Acuña, the deserter, Calixto Morales; Calixto García; Manuel Acuña; and a new recruit, who apparently got lost during the shooting.

Once again we started toward the valley, and on the way down we distributed the items the men from Manzanillo had brought. This included a surgery kit for me and a change of clothes for every man. We were moved by the sight of initials that the girls from Manzanillo had embroidered on our uniforms.

The following day, February 2, two months after the "Granma" landing, we were a homogeneous group: We had ten more men from Manzanillo and we felt stronger and more confident than ever before. We held long discussions on the subject of the surprise air attack and we all agreed that the smoke from the open field-kitchen had served as a beacon for the planes. For many months—perhaps for the duration of the war—the memory of that surprise attack remained with us, and no open-air cooking was ever again done, for fear of unpleasant consequences.

At that time we would have found it impossible to believe that Eutimio Guerra, the traitor, had been a passenger in the observation plane carrying Casillas and had pointed out our hiding place. His story about his mother's illness had been a pretext to go out and locate Casillas and tell him about our location.

For a long time Eutimio Guerra played an important negative role in the development of our war of liberation.

SURPRISE ATTACK AT ALTOS DE ESPINOSA

Following the surprise attack, mentioned in the prior chapter, we left Caracas hill, in search of more familiar areas where we could establish direct contact with Manzanillo, receive additional aid, and get some information on the situation in the rest of the country.

Therefore, we returned to the Ají, traveling through familiar territory, until we reached old Mendoza's house. On the hillsides we had to cut our way through the brush, using our machetes, and we made little progress. We spent the night on one of the hills, with practically nothing to eat. I still remember what I consider one of the greatest banquets I ever attended: Crespo showed up holding a can containing 4 sausages, the results of his "savings," for his friends. Crespo, Fidel, and I, together with some other man, ate the meager ration with great joy. Our journey continued until we reached the house "to the right of Caracas hill," where old Mendoza was to give us some food. In spite of his fright, this loyal peasant would welcome us every time we passed by, urged by Crescencio or some other friendly peasants who were now part of our troop.

It was a painful journey for me. I was suffering from an attack of malaria and both Crespo and the unforgettable Julio Zenón Acosta nursed me throughout the entire trip. It was not our habit to spend the night indoors, but my condition and that of Morán, who was always finding an excuse to get sick, made it necessary for us to sleep in one of the houses, while the rest of the men kept watch outside. The only time they used the house was when they had to eat.

It was necessary to "clean up" our group. We had a few men of very low morale and others who were seriously hurt, among them Ramiro Valdés, now Minister of the Interior, and Ignacio Pérez, one of Crescencio's sons, later killed in action bearing the rank of captain. Ramiro had received a blow on one knee, already weakened by wounds received in the "Moncada" attack, so we had to leave him. Several other men left, but we considered their defection very advantageous to our troop. I remember one of them who was overcome by an attack of nerves and suddenly, in the stillness of the woods, began to shout that he had been sent to a camp where there was plenty of food and water and an antiaircraft defense, and now he was being chased by planes, and there was no place to hide, no food, and no water. This was the impression most men received during the first few days of war. Later on, those who stayed and passed the first tests would become accustomed to the filth, the lack of water and food, and the lack of safety, placing all their trust in their rifles as well as in the cohesion and resistance of the small guerrilla group.

Ciro Frías, accompanied by a few new men, arrived. He told us a series of stories which caused quite a lot of confusion. Today we smile when we think of it, but at that time it was no joke: He had been told that Díaz Tamayo was about to make an about-face and was "dealing" with the revolutionary forces; that Faustino had been able to collect thousands of dollars; in one word, that sabotage was rampant, and the end of the government was drawing near. There was also a sad note, but one that served as a warning: Sergio Acuña, the deserter, had gone to some relative's house; there he began to brag about his heroic deeds in the Sierra and was heard by a man named Pedro Herrera, who informed the police. The notorious Corporal Roselló—later executed by the people—arrested Acuña, tortured him, fired four shots into him, and hung him. It was a great lesson for our troop: It showed the value of cohesion and the futility of trying to escape from a danger that threatened every one of us. It also made it imperative for us to move to another location; presumably, the boy might have talked before he was murdered, and he knew Florentino's house, where we were at the moment. A curious incident occurred which we did not quite understand until some time later: Eutimio Guerra had said that he had dreamed about Acuña's death. He even added that Corporal Roselló had been the killer. This led to a long philosophical discussion on whether or not it was possible to predict any event by means of dreams. Part of my daily routine was to lecture the men on some cultural or political subject, and I explained that such a thing was not possible; that it was due to an extraordinary coincidence; that we all expected Acuña to end that way, and that we all knew that Roselló was running wild all over that zone, etc. Universo Sánchez settled the whole affair by saying that Eutimio had the habit of telling tall stories and that someone had probably told him the whole story; we must remember that Eutimio had left the day before and had returned with fifty cans of milk and a flashlight. One of the most staunch supporters of the theory of "illumination" was the forty-five-year-old peasant Julio Zenón Acosta. He was my first pupil in the Sierra. I was doing my best to teach him to read and write, and wherever we stopped, we'd take up the lessons. We had reached the stage of distinguishing A from O, E from I, and so on. Julio Zenón, not thinking of the years gone by, but rather of the years to come, had put his heart into the task of learning how to read and write. Perhaps he could be a very good example to other peasants who were his comrades at that time, or to others who have heard about him. Julio Zenón Acosta gave us great aid in those difficult times. He never tired, he knew the zone well, and he was the first to run to the aid of a comrade in trouble, or help a city man who was still unfamiliar with his surroundings. He would bring water from a distant stream, start the fire, and find the right kind of kindling to get the fire going on a rainy day. He was our all-around man.

One night, only a short time before we discovered he was a traitor, Eutimio complained that he had no blanket and asked Fidel to lend him one. It was a cold February night, up in the hills. Fidel replied that if he gave Eutimio his blanket they would both be cold; that it was better to share the blanket, topped by two of Fidel's coats. That night, Eutimio Guerra, armed with a 45 caliber pistol that Casillas had given him to use against Fidel, and two hand grenades that were to be used to cover his getaway once the crime was committed, slept side by side with our leader. Universo Sánchez and I had made it a point to stay close to Fidel and that night Eutimio had said to us: "I am very interested in this business of the watch. We must be on guard all the time." We explained that three men were on guard nearby. We, the Granma veterans, and a few of Fidel's trusted men always took turns protecting him. Thus, Eutimio spent an entire night lying side by side with the Leader of the Revolution, waiting for his chance to murder him, but he never gathered enough courage to do it. Throughout the night, a great part of the Revolution depended on the thoughts of courage, fear, scruples, ambition, power, and money, running through the mind of a traitor. Fortunately for us, the sum total of inhibitory factors emerged triumphant, and the night passed without any incident.

We had left Florentino's house and were now settled in a ravine. Ciro Frías had gone home and returned with a few hens and some other food. Hot soup and other viands were our reward for a long, rainy night in the open. Somebody said Eutimio had been around there too. Eutimio used to go in and out at will; we trusted him and we had accepted his explanation of his trip to see his sick mother, the story about the Caracas hill battle, etc. He said his mother had recovered from her illness. The man was extremely audacious. We were in a place called Altos de Espinosa, near a chain of hills, such as El Lomón, Loma del Burro, Caracas, and others, that were under constant aerial attack. Eutimio would say: "I told you they'd strafe Loma del Burro today." The planes would come and strafe the hill, and Eutimio would jump to his feet, bragging about his accurate forecasting.

On February 9, 1957, Ciro Frías and Luis Crespo went foraging for food as usual. Everything was quiet, and about 10 A.M. a young peasant named Labrada, who had recently joined our group, captured a man nearby. It turned out to be one of Crescencio's relatives, a salesclerk in Celestino's grocery store, where Casilla's soldiers were stationed. The boy reported that there were close to 145 soldiers in the house. We checked, and we saw a few of them, far away on a barren spot. Our prisoner told us that he had spoken to Eutimio, who had told him that the zone was to be bombed the next day. Casilla's men moved about but we could not determine which way. Fidel became suspicious; Eutimio's strange behavior was beginning to dawn upon us and we began to comment on it. At 1:30 P.M. Fidel gave orders to leave, and we went to the top of the hill to wait for the comrades who had gone scouting. Ciro Frías and Luis Crespo returned, saying that everything was normal. Suddenly Frías requested silence, saying that he had seen someone moving around. He cocked his rifle and at that moment we heard a shot, followed by a volley. There was the sound of volleys and explosions coming from the place we had previously occupied and which was now being torn apart by the concentrated fire. We left our position at full speed, and some time later we found out that Julio Zenón Acosta had been killed atop the hill. The uneducated peasant, who had been able to comprehend the enormous tasks that the Revolution was to face following its triumph; the man who was getting ready to lend a hand in these tasks, was dead. Our group had become dispersed. My knapsack—my pride and joy—full of medicines, reserve food, a few books, and blankets, was left behind. I managed to pull out a blanket that had belonged to Batista's army, a trophy of the La Plata battle, and started to run.

Soon I met a small group of men: Almeida, Julito Díaz, Universo Sánchez, Camilo Cienfuegos, Guillermo García, Ciro Frías, Motolá, Pesant, Emilio Labrada, and Yayo. We took off in an oblique direction, trying to avoid the shots. We did not know where our other comrades were, or what had happened to them. We could hear shots at our rear, and we knew our trail was an easy one to follow because we were moving fast and did not have time to erase our tracks. At 5:15 P.M. we reached a craggy spot, where the woods ended. We made up our minds to wait there until darkness set in because if we tried to cross the open space by daylight, the enemy would see us. If they followed us to our present location, we could still defend ourselves, protected by the rugged terrain. However, the enemy did not show up, and we went on, guided by Ciro Frías, who was slightly familiar with the area. It had been suggested that the group be broken into two patrols, allowing for faster moving and a less conspicuous trail, but Almeida and I voted againt the idea. We wanted to keep the group intact. We reconnoitered the area, called Limones, and held a meeting, because some of the men wanted to get away from there. Almeida, head of the group, based on his rank of captain, gave orders to continue to El Lomón, where Fidel had called for a meeting. Some of the men argued that the place was familiar to Eutimio, and we would find the soldiers there. We had no doubts about Eutimio being a traitor, but it was Almeida's decision to obey Fidel's orders.

We met Fidel on February 12, near El Lomón, in a place called "Derecha de la Caridad." Then we heard the whole story about Eutimio. It began with his arrest by Casillas following the La Plata encounter. Instead of killing Eutimio, Casillas had bribed him to kill Fidel. Eutimio had given away our position in Caracas; he had given the order to bomb Loma del Burro because it was in our itinerary—we had changed it at the last moment—and had organized the concentrated attack on the spot of Cañón del Arroyo, where we withdrew with only one casualty, thanks to Fidel's quick thinking. We verified the death of Julio Acosta, and it was said that some guards had been killed and others wounded. I must confess that neither the dead nor the wounded was any of my own doing; at the time, I had executed a "strategic retreat" at full speed. Now we were all together, excepting one comrade lost the day before. Raúl, Ameijeiras, Ciro Redondo, Manuel Fajardo, Echeverría, Morán, and Fidel; in all, eighteen of us. This was the "Reunified Revolutionary Army" on February 12, 1957. A few comrades had already given up, and a few rookies gave up their guerrilla war right then and there. A Granma veteran was also missing. His name was Armando Rodríguez, and he carried a Thompson machine gun. For the last few days he had looked so alarmed and frightened every time we heard shots around us, particularly if the shots came from all sides, that we began to describe his expression as a "surrounding maneuver look." Every time a man's face showed the look of a trapped animal, we expected something unpleasant to happen. That type of look was incompatible with guerrilla warfare. Our friend with the "surrounding maneuver look" got into high gear, as we used to say in guerrilla jargon, and took off. Some time later we found his machine gun abandoned in a peasant's hut, a great distance away. Undoubtedly, the man was gifted with a good pair of legs!

END OF A TRAITOR

Once our little army was organized, we decided to abandon the El Lomón region. On the way, we made contacts with peasants and established bases necessary for our survival. We kept going away from the Sierra Maestra, toward the plains where we could get in touch with the comrades operating in the cities.

We passed by a hamlet called "La Montería" and camped in a thicket of woods near a stream, in a plantation owned by Epifanio Díaz, whose sons had joined the Revolution.

We wanted closer contact with the 26th of July Movement. Our nomad existence made it practically impossible to contact its members.

Actually, we were two distinct groups, of different tactics and strategy. The great split that months later was to place the Movement's unity in danger had not yet materialized, but one could feel that the concepts were different.

It was on this farm that we met the outstanding figures of the Movement in the city, among them three women, well known to all of Cuba today: Vilma Espín, now President of the Federation of Cuban Women and Raúl Castro's wife; Haydée Santamaría, now President of the Casa de las Americas and Armando Hart's wife; and Celia Sánchez, our beloved comrade in every movement of the struggle, who was soon to join our group for the duration of the war. There was also Faustino Pérez, an old friend and Granma comrade, who had come to report to us on his mission to the city and rush back once again. Shortly afterward he was taken prisoner.

We met Armando Hart, and I then had my only opportunity to spend some time with the great leader from Santiago, Frank País.

Frank was one of those men who make a lasting impact at first sight. His present photos are quite accurate, but it was his eyes that impressed me most. It is very difficult to write about a comrade now dead, whom I saw only once, and whose life is well known to everyone. All I could see in his eyes was the fire of a man possessed by a cause, with faith in it. It was evident that he was an extraordinary person. Today he is called "the unforgettable Frank País," and that is the way I feel about it, although I saw him only once. Frank is another comrade whose life would now be devoted to the common task of the Socialist Revolution; he is part of the enormous price that our people had to pay for their freedom.

He gave us a silent lesson in order and discipline, cleaning our dirty rifles, taking stock of the ammunition, and keeping every round in place. Since that first day I made a pledge to take care of my weapon. I kept my pledge, too, although I must say I was never too meticulous.

The little thicket of woods was the scene of other interesting events. For the first time we were to be interviewd by a reporter, and a foreign reporter at that. This man was Matthews, who brought with him a small box-type camera, with which he took the pictures that were so widely disseminated and later disputed in the stupid statements of one of Batista's ministers. The interpreter was Javier Pazos, who later joined the guerrillas where he remained for a long time.

I was not present at the interview. Fidel told me later that Matthews had asked concrete questions. He had asked no "loaded" questions and seemed to sympathize with the Revolution. I remember Fidel's comments about how he had given an affirmative reply to Matthews' question as to whether Fidel was an antiimperialist. Fidel had objected against the delivery of armaments to Batista and had told Matthews that the arms were not for intercontinental defense but rather to be used against the people.

Matthews' visit was a short one. Once he left, we got ready to leave. We were warned to keep our eyes open because Eutimio was somewhere nearby. Almeida was ordered to go and capture him. Accompanying him were Julito Díaz, Ciro Frías, Camilo Cienfuegos, and Efigenio Ameijeiras. Ciro Frías overpowered Eutimio—not a difficult task—and brought him to us. He was carrying a 45 caliber pistol, 3 hand grenades, and a pass signed by Casillas. By then Eutimio was convinced that he was to be executed. He fell to his knees at Fidel's feet and simply asked to be shot, saying that he deserved to die. He seemed to have aged all of a sudden; his temples were gray, something I had never noticed before. There was a tense moment. Fidel began to berate Eutimio, and Eutimio kept asking to be shot. We will never forget the moment when Ciro Frías, who was a close friend of Eutimio's, began to talk to him. He spoke of all the favors he had done for him, of how he and his brother had always helped Eutimio's family. Then he confronted him with his crime: First, Eutimio had informed on Ciro's brother, and the boy had been murdered; next, Eutimio had tried to have our entire group exterminated. It was a long, pathetic statement that Eutimio heard without uttering a word. He was asked if he had something to say, and he said he wanted the Revolution, that is, us, to take care of his children.

The Revolution kept its promise. Eutimio Guerra is simply a name that comes to mind when writing these notes, but otherwise it has been forgotten, perhaps even by his own children. Under a different name, they are now attending school, receiving the same treatment as all other sons of the people, preparing themselves for a better life, but some day they will have to be told that the peasant who let himself be tempted by power and money, in addition to recognizing his crime, never asked for clemency—which he knew he did not deserve—but instead asked our leader to be kind and benevolent to his children.

At that moment, a tremendous storm broke out, and it got very dark: Amidst a veritable deluge, interrupted by lightning bolts and thunder, the life of Eutimio Guerra was snuffed out, and no one heard the shot that killed him.

We buried him the following day. A little incident occurred when Manuel Fajardo tried to place a cross over the grave. I objected, saying that it would involve great danger for the owner of the farm. Then Fajardo carved a cross on a nearby tree. That is the only sign showing the resting place of a traitor.

Morán quit at that time. He knew we did not care for him, and that we all thought of him as a potential deserter. He had previously disappeared for some days with the excuse that he had been trailing Eutimio and had become lost in the woods.

Just when we were ready to depart, we heard a shot and found Morán with a bullet in his leg. Comrades who happened to be near him held long arguments among themselves. Some of them said the shot was an accident, while others claimed that Morán had done it on purpose so as not to stay with our group.

Morán's later behavior, his act of treason, and his death at the hands of the Guantánamo revolutionaries, make it quite evident that he shot himself intentionally.

We finally left the farm. Frank País had promised to send us a group of men around the beginning of March: The rendezvous was to be at Epifanio Díaz's house, near El Jíbaro.

BITTER DAYS

The days following our departure from Epifanio's farm were, at least for me, the most painful of the war. These notes are an attempt to describe the effect upon our men of the initial stage of the revolutionary struggle. If this passage, more than the others, contains more references to myself, it is only because it is related to the other episodes, and to leave them out would mean a loss of continuity.

Our revolutionary group was made up of seventeen men of the original group and three new recruits: Gil, Sotolongo, and Raúl Díaz. These men had arrived in the Granma, had hidden away somewhere near Manzanillo, and when they heard of our whereabouts, they made up their minds to join us and share our fate. It was very difficult for us, at the time, to increase our army. Some men came, but others would leave. The struggle demanded a tough physical condition and a high standard of morale, and we lived under the threat of continuous attack.

We traveled without any fixed destination, hiding in small wooded areas in a zone where cattle had cleared most of the vegetation. One night we heard, on Fidel's little radio, that one of the men who had left with Cresencio had been captured. Eutimio had already told us that the man had been arrested, but we had never found out officially. Now at least we knew he was alive. It was not always that a man survived one of the Batista army's "interrogations." Frequently we heard rifle and machine gun fire directed toward the wooded areas. The soldiers spent a lot of ammunition but never dared to enter the woods.

On February 22 I wrote in my diary that I was beginning to feel the symptoms of an attack of asthma. I did not have any antiasthmatic medicine left. The date for the new rendezvous was set for March 5, so we still had to wait several days.

During that period we just moved about aimlessly, killing time and waiting for Frank País's men, who were to bring additional weapons. It had been decided that our group was to be strengthened in firepower rather than in number, and that every available weapon in Santiago was to be brought to the Sierra Maestra.

Once we spent a very uneasy day by a stream near La Majagua, where there was practically no vegetation. This was in a valley named Las Mercedes. It is very hard to remember exact names now. At dusk, we reached the house of a peasant called Emiliano. He was another one of those peasants who became frightened every time they met us, and yet they risked their lives for us and contributed to the development of our Revolution. It was the rainy season in the Sierra, and night after night we would get soaked to the bone, so we now headed for the peasants' huts despite the danger of meeting the soldiers who were everywhere.

My asthma was so bad I could hardly walk, and we spent another night near a house, among a thicket of coffee trees. It was February 27 or 28. Censorship had been discontinued, and the radio was pouring out news about everything that had occurred during the last few months.

There was talk about terrorist attacks and Matthews' interview with Fidel. That was the moment when the Minister of Defense made his famous statement that Matthews' interview was a lie and demanded that the photographs be published. Hermes was the son of old Emiliano, and at the time he was the one who would look for food and show us the way. On the morning of the twenty-eighth he did not make his usual rounds, and Fidel issued immediate orders to move to another place overlooking the roads. About 4 P.M., Universo Sánchez and Luis Crespo were watching the road and saw a large troop coming from the direction of Las Vegas. We had to move fast to reach the hillside and cross to the other side before the troops cut us off, but it was not difficult because we had seen them in time. Mortar and machine gun fire broke out, headed in our direction, which proved that Batista's men knew that we were somewhere in the vicinity. Everybody made it to the top, but for me it was a terrible experience. I was practically choking by the time I reached the top of the hill. I remember Crespo's efforts to make me walk. Every time I said I could not go on and asked to be left behind, Crespo would revert to our jargon and snap at me: "You, son-of-a-bitch from Argentina, either you walk or I'll hit you with my rifle butt!" Then he would pick up his load, and practically carry me and my heavy knapsack to the top; all this under a heavy downpour.

We reached a small hut at a place called Purgatorio. Fidel put on a great performance, impersonating a "Major González" of Batista's army, in search of rebels. The host was both courteous and cool, but another man, a neighbor, was a real toady. I was too ill to enjoy fully the dialogues between Fidel, in his role as Major González, and the man, who insisted on giving advice to Fidel and kept saying that he could not understand why this boy Castro was out there in the woods, fighting.

Something had to be done about me; I simply could not go on any longer. When the chatty neighbor left, Fidel told the host who he really was and the man threw his arms around him, saying that he belonged to the Orthodox party, that he was a follower of Chibás, and that he was ready to help out in every way. It was necessary for the peasant to go to Manzanillo and establish some contact, or at least buy some medicine. Even the man's wife was not supposed to know that I would be near the house. Our latest recruit, a man of doubtful reputation, was assigned as my guard. In a generous gesture, Fidel gave me a Johnson rifle, a real jewel. Then we all made a big show of leaving together, and a few yards away my companion —whom we called "the teacher"—and I went into the woods to hide and wait. The latest news was that Matthews had made a telephone call, saying that the photographs were to be published while Díaz Tamayo insisted that the whole thing was a lie; that nobody could get past the troops surrounding the rebels. Armando Hart was in prison, charged with being the second leader of the Movement. The date was February 28.

Our man had fulfilled his mission, and I got my adrenalin. The next ten days were the most bitter days of the struggle in the Sierra: I was dragging myself from tree to tree, using my rifle as a crutch, accompanied by a thoroughly frightened man who went practically out of his mind every time I coughed—he was so afraid someone would hear me—but we finally made it back to Epifanio's house. It had taken us ten days to cover a distance easily covered in one day's march. We did not make it in time for the rendezvous scheduled for March 5. Our slow movements and the circle of soldiers surrounding the zone kept us from reaching the house until March 11.

Several things had happened, already known to the members of the household: in a place called Altos de Meriño, Fidel's group had become separated under the mistaken impression that they were soon to be attacked. Twelve men had followed Fidel and six had gone with Ciro Frías. Ciro's group fell into an ambush but, luckily, they all escaped. Now they were all back, and only one of them, Yayo, who came back minus his rifle, had stopped by Epifanio's house on his way to Manzanillo, and told the whole story. Frank País' troop was ready, although Frank had been arrested. We spoke with the leader of the troop, a man called Jorge Sotús, bearing the rank of captain. He told us it was impossible to make the rendezvous by March 5 because the news about their coming had leaked out and the roads were infested with soldiers. We took every measure to insure the arrival of the troop, estimated to be close to fifty men.

REINFORCEMENTS

On March 13, while we waited for the reinforcements, we heard the news of the attempt to kill Batista. We heard the names of some of the dead. First, José Antonio Echeverría, student leader, then the others, among them Menelao Mora. Innocent persons were killed, too: The following day we heard that Pelayo Cuervo, an Orthodox party leader, who had always maintained a firm position against Batista, had been murdered. His body appeared in some desolate spot of the aristocratic residential section of the country club known as "the little lake." A strange paradox: Pelayo Cuervo's sons and their father's murderers participated in the thwarted invasion of Playa Girón. They had come to "liberate Cuba from communist oppression."

A few details escaped through the curtain of censorship surrounding the frustrated attack on the Presidential Palace. I had never met the student leader, Echeverría, but I had met a few of the others in Mexico during a 26th of July Movement-Students' Directorate meeting aimed at taking steps toward common action. These men were: Faure Chomón, who became Cuban Ambassador to the U.S.S.R.; Fructuoso Rodríguez; and Joe Westbrook. All three of them had participated in the attack.

As everyone remembers, the attack was thwarted before the men could reach the third floor of the Palace, where Batista was. What could have been a victorious *coup* had turned into a massacre. Only a handful of the attackers had managed to escape from the Presidential Palace.

Our reinforcements were scheduled to arrive on the fifteenth. We waited for hours, but no one came. They arrived the following day, exhausted, saying that unexpected events had delayed their departure. They came in trucks owned by a rice planter, who later became so frightened about being implicated in the affair that he took refuge in an embassy, then departed for Costa Rica, and returned to Cuba as a hero, aboard a plane carrying some arms. His name: Hubert Matos.

Only thirty of the fifty-man troop were armed: They had two machine gun rifles, a Madzen, and a Johnson. The few months spent in the Sierra had turned us into full-fledged veterans, and the new troop looked, to us, as full of defects as our original *Granma* troop: no discipline, lack of decision, and inability to adapt to the new surroundings. The group, led by Sotús, captain, was divided into five squads, each composed of ten men led by a lieutenant. This rank had been conferred by the organization in the city, pending ratification. The squad leaders were: a comrade named Domínguez, later killed at Pino del Agua; René Latour, guerrilla organizer in the plains, killed close to the end of the war; "Pedrín" Soto, our old *Granma* comrade who had joined us at last, was later to be killed in combat and awarded the rank of Major, posthumously, at the Frank País Second Front; Pena, a student from Santiago, who reached the rank of major—he committed suicide some time after the triumph of the Revolution—and Lieutenant Hermo, the only group leader who survived the two-year war.

Our greatest problem was our inability to walk. Jorge Sotús, the chief, was the worst offender: he was always at the rear, setting a horrible example. I had been ordered to take command, but when I told Sotús he said that he had orders to turn the troop over to Fidel and no one else; that he was still my commander, etc., etc. I still had a little complex about being a foreigner and did not wish to resort to extreme measures, although it was easy to see that the men were not at ease. Following a few short marches, which seemed terribly long due to the men's lack of training, we came to the place where we were to have our rendezvous with Fidel Castro. There we met the men who had become separated from Fidel: Manuel Fajardo, Guillermo García, Juventino, Pesant, the three Sotomayor brothers, and Ciro Frías.

The contrast between the two groups was tremendous. Ours was well disciplined, compact, and hardened. Theirs was suffering from the usual ills. They were not accustomed to eating only one meal a day; if they found the meal unpalatable, they refused to eat. Their knapsacks were loaded with useless items, and in order to make them lighter, they would rather get rid of a can of condensed milk than a towel—this is practically high treason in guerrilla warfare!—so we made it a point to follow their trail and pick up any food they discarded. Once we settled in our camp, there was a tense period brought about by constant friction between Sotús—who was quite an authoritarian but lacked the gift of getting along with others—and the troops. We were forced to take special measures, and René Ramos, whose *nom de guerre* was Daniel, took charge of the machine gun squad at the exit of our hideout, in order to avoid any trouble.

Sometime later Sotús was sent to Miami on a special mission. There he betrayed the Revolution when he met Felipe Pazos, whose boundless ambition for power made him forfeit his commitments and appoint himself interim president, in a shoddy maneuver in which the United States State Department played a major role.

As time went by Captain Sotús showed signs of rehabilitation, and Raúl Castro offered him his chance; the Revolution has always given everyone a chance. However, he began to plot against the Revolutionary Government. He was sentenced to twenty years' imprisonment, and aided by one of the prison guards, he escaped to the counterrevolutionaries' lair: the United States of America.

But let us get back to our story. We tried to help Sotús, easing the tension between him and the men, and explaining the need for discipline. Guillermo García went to Caracas zone, looking for Fidel, and I made a little tour to pick up Ramiro Valdés, whose leg had partially healed. Fidel arrived on the night of March 24. He and his twelve stalwart comrades were an impressive sight. What a contrast between these men, with their long beards and their makeshift packs, and the new arrivals wearing clean uniforms, carrying well-made packs, and all clean shaven! I made a full report of our problems and we held council to decide on future action. Members of the council were: Fidel, Raúl, Almeida, Jorge Sotús, Ciro Frías, Guillermo García, Camilo Cienfuegos, Manuel Fajardo, and I. Fidel criticized my behavior for not exerting my authority, leaving it in the hands of Sotús, a newcomer—although there was no feeling of animosity toward him—whose attitude, in Fidel's judgment, should never have been condoned. New platoons were organized, comprising the entire troop, to form three groups commanded by Captains Raúl Castro, Juan Almeida, and Jorge Sotús. Camilo Cienfuegos led the vanguard, and Efigenio Ameijeiras, the rear guard. My position: staff physician. Universo Sánchez was appointed staff squad leader.

The new arrivals added to our troops' efficiency. In addition, we had two machine gun rifles, even though they were old and badly worn. Nevertheless we now constituted a considerable force. We studied our next step and my opinion was to attack the nearest post we could find. That would be a good test for the new men. Fidel and the other members of the council were of the opinion that the men should march for long periods, to become accustomed to the rigors of jungle and mountain life as well as the long treks over rugged hills. We held a short, elementary, guerrilla training practice, and departed due east. Our plan was to cover long distances, looking for some group of soldiers upon whom to pounce.

Full of enthusiasm, we marched on to carry out our plan. The climax was to come at the battle of El Uvero.

FORGING THE TEMPER

The months of March and April 1957 were devoted to the reorganization and training of the rebel troops. Our army was made up of eighty men, distributed in the following manner:

The four-man vanguard was led by Camilo; Raúl Castro led one platoon of three lieutenants who in turn led one squad, respectively. These were Julio Díaz, Ramiro Valdés, and Nano Díaz. The two comrades named Díaz were not related. They were both killed in the battle of El Uvero. Nano was from Santiago, and today the Díaz brothers' refinery in Santiago bears his name and the name of his brother who was murdered in Santiago de Cuba. Julito was from Artemisa, a veteran of the Granma and the Moncada. Jorge Sotús' lieutenants were: Ciro Frías, killed at the Frank País Front; Guillermo García, now chief of the army of the Western sector; and René Ramos Latour, killed while bearing the rank of major. Then came the staff, or General Command, led by Fidel, Commander-in-Chief; Ciro Redondo; Manuel Fajardo, now a major; Crespo, major; Universo Sánchez, now a commander; and me as physician.

The platoon that usually followed the column was led by Almeida, captain, and Lieutenants Hermo, Guillermo Domínguez, killed at Pino del Agua, and Pena. The rear guard was led by Efigenio Ameijeiras, lieutenant, and three other men.

We learned to cook by squads. Our group was so large that the squad system allowed for a better distribution of food, medicine, and ammunition. There was a veteran in most squads, teaching the new men the art of cooking and how to get the best nourishment out of our foodstuffs. They also trained the men in packing their knapsacks and the correct way of walking through the Sierras.

It would take an automobile only a few hours to cover the distance between the right hill of El Lomón and Uvero. To us it meant weeks of slow walking taking every precaution, carrying out our program of training the men for the coming battles as well as for a new life. We came to Altos de Espinosa, and we, the veterans, kept a guard of honor by the grave of Julio Zenón. I found a piece of the blanket I had left behind during my "strategic retreat" and shoved it into my pack, swearing that I would never again lose any equipment that way.

Paulino was my new assistant. He helped me in the transportation of medicines, and this way I could devote a few minutes every day to the attention of the men. We passed by Caracas hill, recalling our encounter with the enemy air force, thanks to Eutimio's treachery, and found a rifle, which one of our men must have left there the day of the attack. We no longer had a surplus of rifles; on the contrary, we needed more. We had entered a new stage. A qualitative change had taken place. Throughout a wide zone, the enemy was careful not to come face to face with us; of course, we were not too crazy about meeting them, either. The political situation showed evident signs of opportunism. Pardo Llada, Conte Agüero, and other characters of similar type, made long-winded speeches, reeking with demagoguery, calling for harmony and peace, and timidly criticizing the government. The peace government had spoken; the new Prime Minister, Rivero Agüero, had made a pledge to go to the Sierra if necessary, in order to bring peace to the country. However, a few days later, Batista declared that there was no need to speak with Fidel or the rebels; that Fidel was not in the Sierra, and therefore there was no point in talking with "a bunch of bandits."

Thus, Batista showed his determination to carry on the fight—the only point on which we wholeheartedly agreed—at any cost. Colonel Barreras was then named chief of operations. Barreras was famous for embezzling the funds for the soldiers' rations. Later on he was appointed military attaché to Venezuela, and when the Batista regime came to an end, he was still sitting comfortably in his office in Caracas.

Among us there were at the time three pleasant characters, who served to furnish our movement with a little advertising service; especially in the United States. Two of them gave us a little trouble, too. They were three Yankee boys who lived in the Guantánamo Naval Base and had left their homes to join our struggle. Two of them never heard a shot in the Sierra; worn out by the climate and the privations, they asked newspaperman Bob Taber to take them back. The other one fought in the battle of El Uvero and later retired, quite ill, but at least he did participate in a battle. The boys were not ideologically prepared for a revolution; all they did was give vent to their spirit of adventure while in our company. We felt a sort of affection for them, but we were glad to see them go. I was especially glad, because as a physician I was constantly busy with their various maladies. They simply could not stand the rigors of our campaign.

It was during those days that the government took a group of newspapermen for an airplane ride over the Sierra Maestra, to prove that there was nobody down there. It was a bizarre operation, and it convinced no one. This was another demonstration of the methods used by Batista's government to deceive the public, together with the use of all the Conte Agüeros disguised as revolutionaries, who made daily speeches in a vain effort to fool the people. I must mention here that, at last, I was going to get a canvas hammock. This was a royal gift, which I had not yet been awarded, in keeping with the guerrilla law: A canvas hammock went to those who had already made their own out of burlap sacks. Anyone could make himself a burlap hammock; this made him a candidate for the next canvas hammock; but the lint made my asthma worse, and I was forced to sleep on the ground. Not having a burlap hammock I was not entitled to a canvas hammock. It was a really vicious circle: one of the daily events that are part of each man's individual tragedy.

Fidel realized my plight and broke all the rules, awarding me the precious hammock. I will always remember this happened by the banks of the La Plata river, the day we ate horse meat for the first time.

The horse meat was not only a luxurious *pièce de résistance*; it was the acid test of the capacity of adaptation. Peasant members of our guerrilla force became quite indignant and refused to eat their portion of horse meat. Some of them looked upon Manuel Fajardo as a murderer. He had worked in a slaughterhouse, and a great event, such as the slaughtering of a horse, called for the hand of a professional.

The horse belonged to a peasant named Popa, who lived across the river. I feel confident that following the anti-illiteracy campaign, Popa must be able to read and write by now. If he ever lays his hands on the magazine *Verde Olivo*—where these notes were originally published—he will undoubtedly recall the night when three murderous-looking guerrilla fighters knocked at his door, mistook him for an informer, and added insult to injury by taking his old, moth-eaten horse, which a few hours later was to become a meal of exquisite taste for some of us and a test for the prejudiced bellies of the peasants, who felt that they were committing an act of cannibalism by chewing on their old friend.

A FAMOUS INTERVIEW

By the middle of April 1957 we returned to the area of Palma Mocha, near Turquino Peak. Our most valuable men for that type of mountain warfare were those of peasant extraction.

Guillermo García and Ciro Frías, leading groups of peasants, went back and forth, scouting, foraging for food, and catching up on the latest news; they were the real mobile vanguard. When we reached Arroyo del Infierno, all the peasants came out to welcome us and tell us about the attack: who had guided the soldiers to our hideout, the number of casualties, etc. They were experts at relaying information.

Fidel did not have a radio then, and he asked a peasant to lend him his. This way we could hear the news direct from Havana. The so-called guarantees had been reestablished, and the newscasts were a little more informative.

Guillermo García, wearing the uniform of a corporal of the Batista forces, and accompanied by two peasants, went out to look for the informer. They got their man and told him that the colonel wanted to see him. When he saw us, he realized that everything was lost. Cynically, he told us about his liaison with the army, and how he had told "that s.o.b. Casillas" that he would guide the soldiers, because he knew where we were hiding, but that no one had paid any attention to him.

A few days later the informer was executed. We received a message from Celia telling us that two United States reporters were on their way to interview Fidel under the pretext of the young "gringos" who had been with us. She also sent some money given by sympathizers of the Movement.

We decided that Sardiñas, who knew the Estrada Palma zone well, would be the guide of the newspapermen. We had been devoting all our time to making contacts with peasants, thus creating contact centers and permanent camps, and increasing our zone of operations. We already had several spots where we could store our provisions; they were also used as relay points for messenger work all over the Sierra.

People of the Sierra have an extraordinary capacity for covering long distances in the shortest possible time. We were always fooled by their version of "a half hour's walk," or "just over the hill." This type of information is always exact—for a peasant—although their concept of time, and the meaning of an hour, are completely different from that of the city folks.

Three days later we received the news that six people were climbing toward the zone of Santo Domingo: two women, two "gringos," and two others. However, there were some contradictory stories: It was said that the guards had been informed, and they were surrounding the house where the new arrivals were. News travels fast in the Sierras, but it also becomes distorted. Camilo went out, leading a platoon, ready to liberate the two United States newspapermen as well as Celia, whom we knew to be part of the group. They brought them to us safely. The false information had been caused by the movement of soldiers following a tip given by some backward peasants.

On April 23, Bob Taber and a cameraman arrived. They were accompanied by Celia Sánchez and Haydée Santamaría. There were also representatives of the Movement in the plains: "Marcos" (or "Nicaragua"); Major Iglesias, now governor of Las Villas, who was then in charge of activities in Santiago; and Marcelo Fernández, coordinator of the Movement, later vice president of the National Bank. The latter spoke English and was appointed interpreter.

We spent a few days engaged in diplomatic sparring, showing the United States men our strong force and evading any indiscreet questions. The interviews went on pleasantly. They, in turn, answered our questions with a full understanding of our primitive way of life, although they never became accustomed to it. Neither did they have anything in common with us.

Our group was increased by the arrival of "El Vaquerito"—the cowboy

—one of the most beloved figures of our revolutionary war. He told us that he had been looking for us for over a month. He said he was a native of Camagüey, and we proceeded to interrogate him. A rudimentary course of political orientation came next; this was frequently my task. Vaquerito did not have any political ideas. He seemed to be a wholesome, happy boy, who looked upon the whole thing as a great adventure. He was barefoot, and Celia gave him a pair of Mexican-style shoes, with lots of engravings. With the new shoes and a big straw hat he looked like a Mexican cowboy, so he was stuck with the nickname.

Vaquerito never saw the end of the revolutionary struggle. He was killed the day before we took Santa Clara. He was the leader of the suicide platoon of Column 8. We all remember his extraordinary good humor, and his bizarre, devil-may-care attitude in the face of danger. He was an inveterate liar; his stories were always an intricate network of truth and fiction, and at the end the listener was completely unable to discern where truth ended and fiction began. But when it came to his activities in the war, he was truly amazing: starting as a messenger, he graduated first to soldier, then to leader of the suicide platoon. The same fantastic, incredible deeds he was so fond of talking about, he repeated in the battlefield. By the time he met his death, his bravery had become legendary.

Once I asked Vaquerito to tell us about his life. He began his story, and secretly, we kept track of the dates. When he finished his long, amusing story, we asked him how old he was. He must have been about twenty, but once we tallied up on the various dates and countless adventures, it turned out that Vaquerito must have been hard at work five years before he was born.

Comrade "Nicaragua" brought the news that there were still several weapons in Santiago; these were leftovers from the frustrated attack on the Palace. They included ten machine guns, eleven Johnson rifles, and six "muskets," as he called them. There was more armament, but the Movement was contemplating the establishment of another front in the zone of Miranda sugar mill. Fidel opposed the plan, giving them permission to take only a few of these weapons, ordering that as many as possible be sent to us in order to reinforce our equipment. We were ready to leave, to avoid coming face to face with some soldiers in the vicinity, when we decided to go climb Turquino Peak. This was a symbolic gesture; to climb our highest mountain. We were now on the crest of the Sierra, very close to Turquino.

Taber's interview ended at Turquino. Moving pictures were taken which were later shown on TV in the United States, at a time when no one took us too seriously. For example: a peasant joined us and told us that Casillas had offered him $300, a cow, and a calf as reward for killing Fidel; the United States was not the only one who made mistakes on the price of our maximum leader.

Our altimeter showed that Turquino was located 1,850 meters above sea level. We had never tested the device, but it seemed to work well at sea level. Curiously, this height was quite different from the one appearing on official records.

An army company was following our steps, and Guillermo and a group of men went out to harass them. I was still fighting my asthma and was bringing up the rear, as usual in that case. As long as I could not go into battle, I had to surrender my Thompson submachine gun. It took me three days to get it back, and it was very unpleasant for me to go about unarmed, expecting an attack at any time.

Bob Taber and two newspapermen left our column and arrived safely at Guantánamo. We went on along the Sierra and the foothills, exploring new areas, making contacts, fanning the flame of the Revolution, and increasing the legend of "the bearded ones." A new spirit permeated the Sierra. Peasants would come and greet us, no longer fearful. We, in turn, had more confidence in them. Our relative strength had increased, and we felt safe against any surprise attack; we also felt that a closer bond existed between us and the peasants.

ON THE MARCH

Throughout the first two weeks of April we marched toward our objective. Beginning near Turquino, we crossed zones that later became the scene of many battles: Santa Ana, El Hombrito, Pico Verde. We found Escuedro's house and went on to Loma del Burro. Our trip toward the east was intended to pick up some weapons sent from Santiago and hide them in the Loma del Burro zone, close to Oro de Guisa. One night I got lost in the woods and remained lost for three days, until I met some people in a place called El Hombrito.

It dawned upon me at that moment that we were equipped with everything necessary for survival: oil, salt, canned food and milk, a kit for starting a fire, and a compass. Up to that time I had placed great trust in that device.

Realizing I was lost, I had used my compass without any results. I had finally come to a peasant's house, where they gave me the right directions. We all found out later that in rugged places like the Sierra Maestra a compass will indicate only a general direction, but never a definite course. The only way to set a course is by being throughly familiar with the area or by the use of experienced guides. This was to be my personal experience, one I began to operate precisely at the zone of El Hombrito.

My return to the column was an exciting affair. I was received with great demonstrations of affection and was told that I had just missed attending the trial of three informers, one of whom, named Nápoles, had been sentenced to death. Camilo had presided over the tribunal.

I was carrying on my duties as a physician, and everytime we arrived at some village or hamlet, the people would come to me, looking for relief.

My task was a monotonous one: I did not have too many medicines to choose from, and most cases were quite similar, typical of life in the Sierra: toothless women, who had aged prematurely, children with tremendously swollen bellies, parasitism, rickets, and avitaminosis. Of course, some cases still remain, but the sons of poor women are now studying at the Camilo Cienfuegos School City; they have grown; they are healthy. Quite a contrast with the first undernourished, puny-looking contingent that arrived at our original school city.

I remember a small girl who kept watching me as I listened to the women who came to me, with an almost religious attitude, in an effort to find out the reason for their various illnesses. As the girl's mother approached my "office"—a corner of an old palm-thatched hut—the little girl said to her: "Mamma, this doctor tells every one of them the same story."

The little girl was right. My experience as a doctor was limited; moreover, every one of them had told me, unwittingly, the same horrible story. What would have happened if the doctor had come to the conclusion that a young mother of several children complained of fatigue following her daily task of carrying a bucket of water from the stream to her house, simply because she did not have enough to eat? It is useless to try to explain the reason for that fatigue to a woman of the Sierra. She will argue that she has done that kind of work "all her life" and it is only now that she gets this sudden feeling of tiredness. There is the whole sad story: People in the Sierra grow like wild flowers, unattended. Then they fade away, constantly busy at a thankless task. It is due to our daily contact with these people and their problems that we become firmly convinced of the need for a definite change in the life of our people. The idea of an agrarian reform became crystal-clear, and communion with the people ceased to be a mere theory and became an integral part of ourselves.

Guerrillas and peasants began to merge into a solid mass. No one can say exactly when, in this long process, the ideas became reality and we became a part of the peasantry. As far as I am concerned, the contact with my patients in the Sierra turned a spontaneous and somewhat lyrical decision into a more serene force, one of an entirely different value. Those poor, suffering, loyal inhabitants of the Sierra cannot even imagine what a great contribution they made to the forging of our revolutionary ideology.

Guillermo García was promoted to captain, taking command of all new peasants joining the columns. Perhaps comrade Guillermo has forgotten the date of his promotion, but it is right here in my notebook: May 6, 1957.

Haydée Santamaría left the following day. Fidel had given her instructions to establish all the necessary contacts. Then we received the news that Major Iglesias ("Nicaragua") had been arrested. He was supposed to bring the weapons, and now we were at a complete loss, not knowing what to do. Still, we continued on our way.

We came to a little depression near Pino del Agua, at the very edge of the Sierra, where there were two abandoned huts. One of our patrols captured an army corporal. He was known for his many crimes, dating back to Machado's regime, and a few of us suggested that he be executed, but Fidel refused. We simply left him in the custody of the new recruits, who did not even have rifles, warning him that any attempt to escape would mean death.

Most of us went ahead to see if the weapons had arrived. It was a long walk, even though we did not carry packs; we had left them at the camp. We did not find the weapons, and of course we put the blame on Nicaragua's arrest. We were able to purchase some food and return with our load: not the load the men had been expecting, but a welcome load just the same.

We returned slowly, bordering the crests and being very careful on the open spaces. We heard shots ahead of us and became alarmed because one of our men had gone ahead in order to reach the camp as soon as possible. He was Guillermo Domínguez, a lieutenant, recently arrived with the men from Santiago. We prepared for a fight and sent out a scouting group. The group came back with Fiallo, a comrade from Crescencio's group. He came from our base camp and said that he had seen a dead man on the road; he added that there had been an encounter with some guards who had withdrawn toward Pino del Agua where there was a large detachment of troops. We moved forward and came upon the body of a dead man.

It was Guillermo Domínguez. His body was naked from the waist up, showing a bullet wound in the left elbow and a bayonet wound in the chest. A shotgun blast had literally blown his head apart. Apparently, he had been killed with his own gun. Several buckshot pellets were clearly visible around his head.

It seems that the guards were looking for their comrade, our prisoner, and heard Domínguez coming. He must have been quite confident, because he had made the same tour the day before. He was captured by the soldiers at the time that Crescencio's men were on their way to us. Crescencio's group came upon the soldiers from the rear, and began firing. Then the soldiers killed Domínguez, and escaped.

Pino del Agua is a sawmill camp up in the Sierra, and the road taken by the soldiers was an old lumber trail that we had to follow for one hundred yards and then take up our narrow trail. Our comrade had not taken the necessary precautions, and it was his luck to meet the soldiers at the lumber trail. This served as a lesson to all of us.

THE ARMS ARRIVE

Near Pino del Agua sawmill we killed the horse that had belonged to our prisoner, the corporal. It was a magnificent animal, but certainly of no use to us in the jungle, and we were short on food. There is a touch of irony in this story: The corporal had insistently repeated that the horse belonged to a friend of his. Now, sitting on the ground and drinking horse soup, he still kept repeating his friend's name and address, in case we ever had an opportunity to return the horse.

We heard over the radio that our Granma comrades had been sentenced; also that one of the judges had voted against the verdict. The man was Urrutia, whose honest gesture was rewarded by his appointment to interim president of the republic. The gesture, per se, had no other significance than that of being a gesture of dignity. Undoubtedly, it was, at the moment. But the aftermath was the establishment of a bad president, incapable of understanding the political process that was to follow, incapable of understanding the depth of a revolution not made to fit his reactionary mentality. His character, and his reluctance to take a determined stand, caused plenty of trouble. The climax came when—faced by the people's unanimous hostility—he presented his resignation as president of the republic. It happened at the time when the people of Cuba were getting ready to hold their first 26th of July celebration.

One day, a contact man from Santiago, named Andrés, arrived with the welcome news that the arms would be delivered within a few days. A sawmill on the coast was set for the rendezvous. The Babún brothers, who owned the sawmill, were handling the operation. They expected a great profit from their participation in the Revolution. Further events made them drift apart, and three of the sons of one of the members of the Babún firm attained the dubious privilege of being part of the counter-revolutionary element captured at Playa Girón.

It is a curious thing to observe how at that time many people had the idea of profiting by the Revolution. They did little favors here and there, everyone of them expecting great rewards from the new state. In the Babún case, the reward was to be concessions for commercial exploitation of forests, which would include the eviction of peasants, thus increasing the latifundia of the Babún household. We now had a new addition to our group: a United States' newspaperman, Hungarian by birth, named Andrew Saint George. He belonged in the same class with the Babúns.

He was careful to show his less dangerous side, appearing as a mere newspaperman, but he was an agent for the FBI. I was appointed to take care of him because I was the only one who spoke French, and none of us spoke English. In all sincerity I must say that he did not look like a dangerous character, but after our second interview he had no qualms about being taken for an agent. We went on, skirting Pino del Agua, to the source of the Peladero river, marching through rugged areas and always carrying a heavy load. We continued to a stream named Del Indio, where we spent two days. Passing through small villages, we established a sort of nonlegalized revolutionary state. Sympathizers were told to report everything that went on including, of course, any move made by the enemy.

Always, we stuck to the woods. On some rare occasions we would sleep in some hut close to the woods. Daytime was spent under the protection of the tall trees, under a canopy of leaves, and always on guard.

Our worst enemy at that time of the year was the "macagüera," a species of gadfly so called because it lays its eggs on the Macagüa tree. The macagüeras would bite every unprotected part of our bodies, our skin was far from clean, and the constant scratching caused abscesses. Our legs, wrists, and necks always bore the marks of the macagüera.

On May 18 we heard about the arms and of what they consisted. Everyone got very excited, because we all wanted to improve our individual armament. We all hoped to get something; either a new weapon or a used one that might have belonged to one of the veterans who would be issued a new weapon. We also heard that the moving pictures that Bob Taber had shot at the Sierra Maestra had been very successful in the United States. Everyone was happy, with the exception of Andrew Saint George. After all, in addition to being an FBI agent he was also a newspaperman, and he felt that he had been "scooped." The following day he left the Babún zone, aboard a yacht bound for Santiago de Cuba.

A man had escaped, and we became very alarmed because everybody knew about the new weapons. We sent patrols after him, and they returned after several days with the news that the man had taken a boat for Santiago. We suspected he had gone to inform the authorities but we found out later that his desertion was due to lack of physical and moral capacity to face the hardships of our life. In any event we had to take extreme precautions. Our fight against the lack of physical, ideological, and moral preparation of the combatants went on relentlessly, but the results were not always successful. Men would find the flimsiest excuses to justify their demand to be released and if the answer was in the negative, desertion would follow. We must remember that desertion meant death; the execution was to be carried out at the spot where the deserter was apprehended.

That night the arms came, and it was the most beautiful sight in the world. There they were, the instruments of death, on exhibit before the hungry eyes of every fighter: three machine guns, with their tripods, three Madzen machine gun rifles, nine M-1 carbines, ten Johnson automatic rifles, and six thousand rounds of ammunition. Although the M-1's were allotted forty-five rounds apiece, they were distributed according to each man's merits and time spent in the Sierra. One of them went to Ramiro Valdés, now a major, and two others were given to Camilo's advance guard. The other four were to cover the tripod machine guns. One machine gun rifle went to Captain Jorge Sotús' platoon, one to Almeida's, and another to the Staff; that was my weapon. The tripod machine guns were distributed as follows: one for Raúl, one for Guillermo García, one for Crescencio Peréz. Such was my initiation as a direct combatant. I had participated in combat, but my steady position was that of physician. For me, it was the beginning of a new stage.

I will always remember the moment when the old rifle, one of inferior workmanship, was given to me. At that moment it was a precious gift. Four men had been appointed to operate the weapon. These men were to follow opposite paths: the Beatón brothers, Pupo and Manolo, were executed by the Revolution for the murder of Major Cristino Naranjo, and their subsequent escape to the Sierras de Oriente, where they were captured by a peasant; the other one was a fifteen-year-old child who always carried the enormous weight of the gun's magazines. The boy, named Joel Iglesias, is now president of Rebel Youth, and a major in the rebel army. The fourth man, now a lieutenant, was named Oñate, but we nicknamed him "Cantinflas." Our struggle to increase the ideological and combative strength of our troop did not end with the arrival of the arms. On May 23 Fidel ordered the release of more men, among them a complete squad. This reduced our forces to 127 men, most of them armed, including 80 equipped with very good weapons.

Of the entire squad released, including its leader, only one man remained. He was Crucito, who later became one of our most beloved combatants. He was a natural poet, or balladeer, and he would hold long contests with the city poet Calixto Morales, one of the Granma men, who called himself "the country nightingale." Crucito would always end his songs with a scornful refrain that went something like "you old Sierra buzzard."

Crucito had written songs about the Revolution, beginning with the departure of the Granma from Mexico. He would sit, smoking his pipe, and compose lyrics. There was a shortage of paper in the Sierra, so Crucito learned the words by heart. Not a single line of verse remained when he was killed in the battle of Pino del Agua.

In the sawmill zone we had the invaluable aid of Enrique López, an old childhood friend of the Castros. He worked for the Babúns and was our contact man for supplies and safe travel throughout the zone. The area was crisscrossed by narrow roads, which were used by the army trucks, and we had set up several ambushes, but never succeeded in capturing a truck. Perhaps this contributed to the success of the coming operation, one that had the greatest psychological impact in the entire history of the war: the battle of El Uvero.

On May 25 we heard that an expeditionary group, led by Calixto Sánchez, had arrived aboard the launch *Corintia* and landed near Mayarí. A few days later we heard about the disastrous outcome of that expedition. Prío Socarrás had the habit of sending his men to die, but he never bothered to accompany them. The news of the landing and its aftermath made us realize that it was imperative that we begin diverting maneuvers against the enemy to give the survivors a chance to reach some place where they could reorganize themselves and go into action. We did this out of sheer solidarity with the men, although we did not know their social makeup nor the real purpose of the landing.

On the occasion, we held an interesting debate, with Fidel and I the leading characters. I argued that we should not waste the opportunity to seize one of the army trucks; that we should devote ourselves specifically, to catch one of them as it went carelessly by us. On the other hand, Fidel had the operation of El Uvero in mind, and he maintained that the decision was a just one; it would be much more important and a very great success to capture the army post at El Uvero. The psychological impact would be tremendous and the event would be known throughout the country, something that would never happen if we seized a truck. Such an incident could easily be reported as a simple accident, with a few casualties. In that case, even though some people might suspect the truth, nobody would know about our effective existence as a fighting force in the Sierra. This did not mean discarding the idea of seizing a truck, but it was not to be the focal point of our activities.

Now, several years after that debate where Fidel had the last word but did not convince me, I must recognize that the decision was a just one; it would have been of very little advantage to us to carry out some action against a patrol traveling by truck. Of course, our desire to fight made us adopt drastic positions, lacking the patience, and perhaps even the vision, to see faraway objectives. Anyway, we had come to the final preparations for the El Uvero action.

BATTLE OF EL UVERO

Once we had settled on our objective, the next step was to plan the attack. We had to find out about the number of soldiers, sentry posts, type of communications, access roads, civilian population and its distribution, etc. Comrade Caldero, now a major in the rebel army, did a wonderful job in this department. Caldero, I seem to remember, was the sawmill manager's son-in-law.

We presumed that the army had more or less precise information about our presence in the zone, because we had captured two informers who confessed that Casillas had sent them to find out about the rebel army's whereabouts and its meeting points. The sight of the two informers, pleading for their life, was disgusting as well as moving, but the laws of war could not be disregarded in those difficult moments, and both men were executed.

That same day the staff and all the officers held a meeting, and Fidel announced that we would go into action within the next forty-eight hours. He told us to remain fully dressed and equipped, ready to leave. No instructions were given at the time.

Caldero was to be the guide. He knew the post at El Uvero, every way in and out, and every access road. We started on our way at night. It was a long march—about sixteen kilometers—but luckily, all downhill, along the roads built by the Babúns. Yet, it took us about eight hours to cover the distance because of the extreme precautions taken as we neared the danger zone. Finally, the orders came, and they were very simple: Take the sentry posts and riddle the wooden structure holding the garrison.

We knew that the post had no major defenses except a few logs distributed around the building; the strong points were the sentry posts, of four soldiers each, placed strategically outside the building. Our staff was to be established atop a hill overlooking the post, a good vantage point from which to direct the action. It was easy to approach within close range of the post by crawling through the dense woods. We had strict orders not to shoot toward the civilian area where women and children lived. The manager's wife, who knew of our plan, also lived there, but she had refused to leave in order not to arouse suspicion. The civilians were uppermost in our minds as we took our positions to begin the attack.

El Uvero post was located at the very edge of the water so we had to attack only three sides.

Platoons led by Jorge Sotús and Guillermo García were sent to the spot overlooking the road running alongside the coast. It was Almeida's job to liquidate the sentry post facing the mountain more or less to the north; Fidel was to be at the hill overlooking the post, and Raúl was to make a frontal attack. I was assigned an intermediate post with my machine gun rifle and my aides. Camilo and Ameijeiras were to attack from the front, between my position and Raúl's, but they lost their way in the dark and began the attack at my left. Crescencio Pérez's platoon was to advance along the road leading to Chivirico and stop any reinforcements coming that way.

We expected the attack to be of short duration, due to the element of surprise, but minutes went by, and we still could not place our men in the ideal positions. Our guides, Caldero and one of the zone's guides, named Eligio Mendoza, went back and forth with reports. Soon it would be daybreak, and the planned surprise attack was doomed to fail. Jorge Sotús sent word that he was having trouble pinpointing his target, but it was too late to figure out new maneuvers. When Fidel opened fire with his rifle we were able to locate the post by the flashes of the soldiers' fire. I was up on an elevated area and was able to see the post, but the distance was too great, and we moved in, looking for a better position.

Everybody was advancing: Almeida was headed for the sentry post covering the entrance, and on my left I could see Camilo's cap, with a piece of cloth sticking from the back, Foreign-Legion style, but bearing the insignia of the Movement. We went on advancing, amidst heavy gunfire, taking all the necessary precautions.

We began to receive reinforcements: men who had become separated from their units. A comrade nicknamed "Bomba," Mario Leal, and Acuña joined our small group. The soldiers were putting up a stiff resistance, and now we had reached the flat, open spaces where we had to be very careful of the soldiers' accurate fire. I was about fifty or sixty meters from the enemy's advance guard and saw two soldiers come out of a trench. I fired, but they took refuge in one of the houses. Firing toward the houses was out of the question, so we kept pressing forward across open ground, and the bullets kept whizzing by. I heard someone moaning, and I thought perhaps he had a wound in his head. I made a quick inspection of the wound: the bullet had hit him on the temple. Leal was fainting, and his side was paralyzed; I can't recall whether it was his left or right side. The only bandage I could lay my hands on was a piece of paper, so I placed it on the wound. Joel Iglesias came to help Leal, while we continued the attack. A few seconds later Acuña fell. We could no longer advance, and we kept firing toward a trench and getting plenty of return fire. We were gathering our courage to go for a final attack, as the only means to finish the enemy's resistance, and at that very moment, the post surrendered.

It takes only a few minutes to describe the battle, but the actual time was two hours and forty-five minutes, counting from the opening shot to the time we entered the post. On my right, I believe it was Víctor Mora, and other comrades had captured several soldiers who had put up a last struggle; a soldier came out of the trench in front of us, holding out his weapon in a gesture of surrender; we could hear cries of surrender coming from all sides. We ran toward the building, and there was a burst of machine gun fire. It was that last burst that killed Lieutenant Nano Díaz.

Reaching the civilian area, we captured the two soldiers who had escaped my fire, and also the post physician and his assistant. A curious incident occurred, involving the physician, a calm, gray-haired man whom I never saw again. I do not know if he is now part of our Revolution. I was never too much of a physician, and the number of wounded men being carried in was on the increase. Moreover, I was not too inclined to Medicine at the moment. When I went to turn the wounded over to the army physician he asked me how old I was and the date of my graduation. I told him I had several years experience and he said: "Look, you take care of this; I have just graduated, and I have very little experience." His lack of experience and his fear at finding himself a prisoner had made him forget whatever he knew about his profession. From that moment on I had to exchange my soldier's uniform for a physician's robe; actually, all I did was wash my hands.

Following the combat, one of the bloodiest we ever had, we began to gather data, and now I am able to present a more general picture; up to now the story was based on my personal experience. What happened was more or less as follows. When Fidel opened fire, giving the signal to begin, everybody began to attack the predetermined objectives, and the army returned the fire, especially toward the hill where Fidel was. Julito Díaz was killed while standing next to Fidel. The soldiers' resistance was increasing, and it was practically impossible to press on toward our goal. The most important task had been given to Almeida, at the center. He was to liquidate the sentry post to open way for his men and Raúl's. We were told how Eligio Mendoza, the guide, had grabbed a rifle and joined the attack. He was a very superstitious man, and when he was warned to take care of himself, he scornfully replied that his "saint" would take care of that. A few seconds later he was practically cut in two by a burst of machine gun fire. The enemy's fire was heavy, and we lost a few men. We were finding it very difficult to gain any distance through the center. Jorge Sotús, on the road to Peladero, tried a flank maneuver, accompanied by his assistant, nicknamed "The Policeman," but the latter was killed almost immediately, and Sotús had to dive into the sea to escape. Others in his platoon made an effort to advance, but were repelled. A peasant named Vega was killed, Manals was hit in the lungs, Quike Escalona was hit in the arm, hand, and buttocks. Hiding behind the log barricade, the soldiers were cutting our small troop to pieces. Almeida called for a final attack to take the enemy position. Cilleros, Maceo, Hermes, Leyva, and Pena were wounded, and Almeida himself was hit in the left leg and shoulder. Moll was killed. However, this last rush overtook the sentry post and opened our way to the fort. On the other side, Guillermo García's accurate machine gun fire had killed three soldiers; another one tried to escape and was also killed. Raúl, his platoon divided into two groups, began a rapid advance toward the post. It was the attack carried out by Guillermo García and Almeida that turned the tide; they had liquidated their respective enemy posts, allowing for the final attack. A praiseworthy performance was that of Luis Crespo, who left the staff to join the fight.

As we reached the building, where somebody was waving a white handkerchief, someone in our troop must have fired, and the enemy replied with a burst that killed Nano Díaz, who had been using his machine gun very effectively against the soldiers. Crescencio's platoon was practically out of action due to a jammed machine gun, so they had continued covering the road from Chivirico, and had captured two soldiers who had tried to escape along that road. The battle had lasted two hours and forty-five minutes, and no civilians were hurt, despite the intense fire.

Our casualties were: Moll, Nano Díaz, Vega "The Policeman," Julito Díaz, and Eligio Mendoza, dead; Leal and Cilleros, badly wounded. Others, more or less seriously wounded, were Maceo, hit on the shoulder; Hermes Leyva, surface wound in the chest; Quike Escalona, right arm and hand; Pena, shot in the knee; Manuel Acuña, right arm; and Manals shot in the lungs, no other symptoms: a total of fifteen comrades out of action. The enemy had nineteen wounded, fourteen dead; fourteen had been captured, and six had escaped. A total of fifty-three men, they were commanded by a second lieutenant who had raised the white flag after he was wounded.

We had 80 men, and the enemy 53; a total of 133, with 38—over one-fourth—out of action in less than two and a half hours fighting. It had been a reckless, wide-open attack upon an enemy that was badly protected, and we must admit that both sides showed tremendous courage. For us, it was a victory that meant that our guerrillas had reached full maturity. From that moment on, our morale increased enormously, our determination and hope for victory also increased, and although the months that followed were a hard test, we now had the key to the secret of how to beat the enemy. This battle sealed the fate of every garrison located far from larger concentrations of troops, and every small army post was soon dismantled.

One of the very first shots fired in the combat had cut off telephone communication with Santiago, and the enemy recognizance planes arrived hours later, when we had already reached the mountain. The following will give an idea of the concentrated fire we had poured into the army post: in addition to the fourteen dead soldiers, there were three dead parakeets—the guards had five of these as pets—and it must have taken a veritable deluge of bullets to hit such small animals.

My return to the medical profession had its sad moments. My first patient was Cilleros. A bullet had broken his right arm, had gone through his lungs and imbedded itself in his spine, paralyzing his legs. His condition was very serious, and all I could do was give him some drugs and bandage his chest tightly, so that he could breathe a little more comfortably. We tried to save his life by doing the only thing we could do at the time: take the fourteen prisoners with us and leave our two wounded men, Leal and Cilleros, with the enemy, under the guarantee of the doctor's word of honor. When I told Cilleros about our decision, adding a few words of comfort, he looked at me with a sad smile on his lips which was more eloquent than any word. He knew this was the end. We knew it too, and I was tempted to kiss him on the forehead, but I realized that it would mean signing his death sentence. It was my duty not to make his last moments any worse by doing something that would only confirm what he already suspected. I said a fond goodbye to my two comrades. They insisted on staying with us, even if it meant death for them, but it was our duty to fight for their lives to the last minute. We left them there, fraternizing with the wounded soldiers, who had also been taken care of to the best of our ability.

Our comrades were treated very decently by the enemy soldiers but one of them, Cilleros, never reached Santiago. The other one survived and was sent to the Isle of Pines prison. He still bears the marks of that important episode of our revolutionary war.

We loaded one of the Babúns' trucks with every sort of item, principally medicines, and went on to our hideout in the mountain, where we arrived in time to attend the wounded and pay our last respects to the dead. We expected that the army would be in hot pursuit, and we decided that every man who was able to walk was to go as far as possible from the place. The wounded were to remain with me, and Enrique López was to find transportation, a hideout, a few helpers to carry the wounded, and contact men to bring medicines.

Throughout the night we kept discussing the battle. No one slept, and they all had something to say about what they had seen or done. Out of curiosity I kept a record of the enemy dead and wounded—according to the storytellers—and they seemed to surpass the actual number of enemy soldiers. Each man's story reached the realm of fantasy. This and other similar experiences taught us that all data should be checked and rechecked by several persons. In our exaggeration we went so far as to demand physical proof, such as items taken from enemy soldiers, before we accepted it as an enemy loss. Our main concern was to broadcast the truth. This was the central theme of any information given by the rebel army, and we made every effort to make our comrades realize how important it was to have respect for truth, and to realize that truth was to be placed above transitory victory.

At dawn we bid farewell to the victorious troop. I remained with Joel Iglesias and Oñate, a guide named Sinecio Torres, and Vilo Acuña—now a major in the rebel army—who remained to take care of his uncle.

NURSING THE WOUNDED

The day following the Uvero battle we could see enemy planes circling. They had been at it since dawn. Once we said good-bye to the comrades, we began to erase every sign of our entrance into the woods. We were only one hundred yards away from a road and were waiting for Enrique López to begin the transfer of our wounded men.

Almeida, Pena, Escalona, and Manais were unable to walk. Manuel Acuña, Hermes Leyva, and Maceo could move about with difficulty. Vilo Acuña, Sinecio Torres, the guide, Joel Iglesias, Alejandro Oñate, and I were to protect them, transport them, and nurse them. Hours later a man came to tell us that Enrique López could not help us; his daughter was ill, and he had to leave for Santiago. He was to send us some volunteers, but they never came.

It was a serious situation; Escalona's wound was infected, and we could not tell how badly Manals was hurt. We scouted the nearby roads and found no soldiers, so we decided to take them to an abandoned hut located three or four kilometers away, where there were plenty of chickens.

Two of the sawmill's workers helped us to carry the wounded, who had been placed on hammocks. The following day, after a good chicken dinner, we left the spot. We had remained practically in the same place, too near to the roads that could be used by enemy soldiers. We started our journey—a short one, but a very difficult one—toward a ravine called Del Indio; we crossed it and then climbed to a hut owned by a peasant named Israel, who lived with his wife and a brother-in-law. It was a rough trip but we finally made it. Those wonderful people even offered us the couple's bed so that our wounded men could get some sleep.

We had left some weapons at our former camp, most of them in bad condition. There were other implements, too: things that we had to abandon as the weight of the wounded men made our traveling increasingly difficult. It seemed that we always left something behind us in some hut or camp, and we wanted to get back this time and erase all signs that might lead to us. Our lives depended on it. At the same time, Sinecio, the guide, went to get some friends of his who lived in the zone of Peladero.

Acuña and Joel said that they had heard strange voices on the other side of the mountain. We thought the time had come to put up a fight, since our duty was to defend our precious load of wounded comrades: we kept going ahead, wanting the encounter to take place as far as possible from the hut. We found prints of bare feet on the same trail we had used before. Then we heard the voices of men apparently engaged in careless conversation. I had my machine gun ready, and flanked by Vilo and Joel, I came upon the group of men. They were the prisoners that Fidel had set free at El Uvero, and they were looking for a way out of the woods. Most of them were barefoot, and an old corporal, practically exhausted, expressed his admiration for us and for our experience in moving about the woods. They had no guide; all they had was a pass, signed by Fidel. Taking advantage of the great impression we had made upon them, we warned them not to enter the woods again.

We spent the night in the hut. At dawn we returned to the woods and sent the peasant to go catch some chickens for the wounded men. We spent the entire day waiting for him and his wife, but they never returned. Some time later, we heard that they had been arrested, and the soldiers had forced them to guide them to our former camp. Fortunately, we had moved out one day before.

We kept a strict vigilance and would never have been taken by surprise, but we could not predict the outcome of a battle under such unfavorable conditions. Sinecio returned that night with three volunteers: an old man named Feliciano and two others, who later became members of the rebel army. They were Banderas, who was killed in the battle of Jigüe, bearing the rank of lieutenant, and Israel Pardo, the oldest member of a large family of fighters; he is now a captain. These men helped us transfer the wounded to another hut while Sinecio awaited the peasants who were to bring our food. Of course, we did not know that they had been arrested. We suspected a trap, and made up our minds to leave our new hideout. We ate a frugal meal, consisting of some vegetables dug from around the hut. The following day, six months after the Granma landing, we were on our way. Each stage of our march was short, and incredibly tiring for anyone unaccustomed to mountain traveling. We could only carry one hammock, which had to be tied to a strong branch which could be carried on the shoulders of two or four men. The branch would literally tear the bearer's shoulders to pieces, so every ten minutes or so we had to change bearers. Six or eight men are needed to carry a wounded person in this manner. Almeida half-walked, half-dragged himself along from tree to tree until Israel made a short cut through the woods, and we met the bearers.

We arrived at the Pardo's at dusk, following a tremendous rainstorm. It had taken us twelve hours to cover a distance of four kilometers.

Sinecio was our salvation. He knew every road and every person in the zone. It was he who managed to get Manals out and send him to Santiago, and we were getting ready to send Escalona too, as his wounds were still badly infected. We heard all sorts of contradictory news: Celia Sánchez had been arrested; Celia Sánchez had been killed, etc. It was said that an army patrol had captured Hermes Caldero. We did not know what to believe, and some of the reports were really frightening, since Celia, for example, was our only safe, confidential contact. Her arrest would mean isolation for all of us. Fortunately, the news about Celia turned out to be false. Hermes, however, was arrested and managed to survive a long jail sentence.

A man named David, a foreman for one of the landowners, was very helpful. He had slaughtered a cow for us, near the coast, and we had to go and bring in the pieces. This had to be done at night and I sent a group of men led by Israel Pardo, and a second group led by Banderas. Banderas was quite undisciplined, and he made the men carry the entire load. It took them all night to bring the meat. A small troop was being organized, which I was to lead since Almeida was hurt. Aware of my responsibility, I told Banderas he was no longer a combatant; that unless he improved his behavior, he was to remain as a sympathizer. He did improve. Although he was no model of discipline, he was an alert man of great ingenuity, and he had come face to face with reality through the medium of the Revolution. He had been working a small parcel of land wrested from the woods, and lived in a small hut with two small pigs and a dog. One day he showed me his sons' photograph; they lived with his ex-wife in Santiago. Banderas said he hoped that once the Revolution had succeeded, he could go somewhere to work a piece of good land, not this inhospitable scrap of land practically hanging from the Sierra. The man had a passion for agriculture.

I told him about the cooperative, but he was unable to understand. He wanted to work the land by himself and for himself. Gradually, he began to understand the advantage of collective work, the use of farm machinery, etc. Banderas would have been a vanguard fighter in agricultural production. At the Sierra, he improved his reading and writing, and he was really preparing for the future. He was a wide-awake peasant, who knew the value of self-sacrifice when it comes to writing a new page in history.

I held a long interview with David, the foreman. He was on his way to Santiago, and he wanted a list of the things we were in need of, so that he could get them for us. He was the typical foreman, faithful to his boss, with a great scorn for peasants, and a racist to boot. However, after the army arrested him and tortured him, his main concern, when he saw us again, was to explain that he had refused to talk. I do not know if David is still in Cuba; perhaps he followed his bosses, whose possessions have already been confiscated by the Revolution. I must say he was a man who, at that moment, felt the need of a change; he felt that a change was forthcoming, although he never imagined the change might reach him and his world. The structure of the Revolution is based upon many sincere efforts made by humble men; our mission is to bring out the best in everyone and turn everyone into a revolutionary. The Revolution is made up of Davids who did not understand too well, of Banderas who did not live to see the dawn, of blind sacrifices, of unrewarded sacrifices.

We who are able to witness the Revolution's accomplishments must remember those who fell by the roadside and do our utmost to decrease the number of laggards.

THE RETURN

We spent the entire month of June 1957 nursing the wounded of the Uvero battle and organizing the small group that was to join Fidel's column.

David was our contact man with the outside. His timely advice, in addition to the food he always managed to find, made our situation quite bearable. We did not know Pancho Tamayo then. Old Pancho, a peasant, was another contact man, and his cooperation will always be remembered. Pancho was killed by the Beatons, after the triumph of the Revolution.

Sinecio began to show a lack of revolutionary morals. He used the Movement's funds to get drunk, he would not obey orders, and once, following one of his escapades, he brought back eleven unarmed men. We tried to avoid any enlistment of unarmed men, but the peasants kept bringing more and more young men who were anxious to join us. Our column was visited by more than forty people, but on the other hand, desertions continued, with or without our permission, so our effective troops never amounted to more than thirty men.

My asthma became worse, and I was reduced to an immobility similar to that of the wounded men. I used to relieve my condition by smoking the dry leaf of the "clarín"—that is the Sierra's remedy—until we received the medicines and I was able to recuperate, but our departure was still postponed. We organized a group to recover all the weapons rendered useless following the Uvero attack; we could still repair them and use them once again.

In our position, all those old rifles, more or less serviceable, including a 30 caliber machine gun, became a potential treasure, and we spent a whole night looking for them. Finally our departure was set for June 24. This was our group: five men, still recovering from their wounds, five assistants, ten new men from Bayamo, two who had recently joined us just because they "felt like it," and four other from that zone; total, twenty-six. We started out with Vilo Acuña in the advance guard, followed by the commanding staff which I led because Almeida could hardly walk, and two other squads lead by Maceo and Pena. Pena was a lieutenant. Maceo and Vilo were soldiers, and the highest rank was held by Almeida, who was a captain. We did not leave on the twenty-fourth because of several incidents. A guide was coming with another man, or perhaps it was a new shipment of medicine and food. Old Tamayo went back and forth bringing news, canned food, and clothing. We had to find a cave to store some food. Our contacts in Santiago had materialized, and David had brought back such a load that nobody could carry it; at least not our troop, made up of convalescents and raw recruits.

On June 26 I made my debut as dentist, although at the Sierra I was known by the modest title of "tooth-puller." My first victim was Israel Pardo, now a captain in the army, who did not fare too badly. The second one was Joel Iglesias, and I thought that if I ever wanted to extract his ailing canine tooth, I would have to use a stick of dynamite. I must confess that I failed, and Joel finished the war with his tooth still in his mouth. My lack of experience and lack of anesthetic forced me to resort to "psychological" anesthesia, which in plain language means insulting the patients whenever they complained about the pain.

Whenever we announced our departure, someone would leave, only to be replaced by newcomers. Tamayo brought four men, among them Félix Mendoza, who carried a rifle. He told us that the army had caught them off guard, and his comrade had escaped, while he, in turn, had jumped off a cliff. Later we found out that the "army" was a patrol led by Lalo Sardiñas. They had found our man's friend, and he was now a member of Fidel's troop. Evelio Saborit, now a major in the Rebel Army, also joined us.

With the addition of Félix Mendoza and his group, we increased our number to thirty-six, but the next day three men left us, to be replaced by others, and we went back to thirty-five. However, as soon as we started out, the number of men decreased. We were now on the foothills of Peladero, climbing a very short distance at each stage.

The news over the radio described a picture of violence all over the island. On July 1 we heard about the death of Josué País, Frank País' brother, and others, in Santiago. The city was the scene of continuous struggle. Despite our short journeys some of the new recruits began to feel depressed and asked to be sent to the city "where they could be more useful." On the way down we passed Benito Mora, at the hill known as The Bottle. He played the gracious host in his little hut perched at the edge of the Sierra. Shortly before our arrival at Benito's, I had spoken to the men telling them that we were about to face difficult, dangerous days, that the enemy was nearby, and that we might have to go on for several days, always on the move, with very little food. Some of them were decent enough to express their fear and leave immediately, but a man named Chicho spoke on behalf of his group, saying that they were ready to "go on to their death" if necessary. Soon after our visit to Benito we camped near a stream and received a great surprise when the same group approached us and told us that they would like to leave the guerrillas. We agreed to their demands and jokingly nicknamed the stream "Death's Stream." After all, this was where Chicho and his confrères had ended their activities as guerrillas.

Now we were only twenty-eight, but the following day two new men, ex-army men, came to the Sierra to the fight for freedom. They were Gilberto Capote and Nicolás. They were guided by Arístides Guerra, another contact man who became of inestimable value to our column. We used to call him "The Food King." The "King" helped us at all times, carrying on missions much more dangerous than just fighting. Several times he drove caravans of mules from Bayamo to our zone of operations.

As we continued our short journeys, we tried to have our men familiarize themselves with the use of firearms. We appointed the two army men as instructors in dismantling and putting together the weapons, dry-run firing, etc. Unfortunately, no sooner had the lessons begun when an instructor's gun went off, accidentally. The man was demoted, and we began to look upon him with a certain degree of suspicion, although his look of genuine consternation made it very difficult for us not to believe he was truly sorry about the whole thing. Neither he nor the other man could stand the constant moving, and they left with Arístides. Alberto Capote did return some time later. He died a hero's death at Pino del Agua, bearing the rank of lieutenant.

We left the house of Polo Torres at La Mesa, which later became one of our centers of operations, and went on, guided by a peasant named Tuto Almeida. We had to reach La Nevada and join Fidel, crossing the north slope of the Turquino. On our way we saw two persons who ran away when they saw us, and we had to chase them for quite a distance before we caught them. They were two Negro girls, Adventists, and absolutely against any sort of violence. However, they gave us their full support at that moment and continued doing so for the duration of the war.

We ate a hearty meal and rested. Then, as we neared Malverde, which we had to cross in order to get to La Nevada, we were told that there were soldiers all over the zone. Following a short meeting between our so-called staff and the guides, we turned back and headed for the Turquino; a much rougher road, but less dangerous under the circumstances.

Our little transistor radio kept us well informed, although the news was quite alarming: heavy fighting in the Estrada Palma zone, Raúl badly wounded, etc. Now I cannot remember whether the news came through our radio or by the Sierra grapevine. We did not dare believe information that had been proven false on other occasions, but we did our best to rush toward Fidel's location. Marching through the Sierra at night, we came to the house of a peasant known as El Vizcaíno—the Basque—who lived in the foothills of Turquino. He lived alone in his little hut, and his only friends were some books on Marxism, which he kept carefully hidden away under a rock, far from the hut. He was proud of his Marxist militancy, which no one in that zone suspected. He showed us the way, and we continued our slow march. Sinecio was now getting further away from his base of operations and for a peasant like him, who was now practically an outlaw, the situation was alarming. One day, carrying a rifle, he joined another man named Cuervo, who was doing sentry duty with a Remington rifle. A half hour later I went to see what was going on; I did not trust Sinecio any longer, and the rifles were a treasure to be well guarded. When I got to the sentry post, they were both gone. Banderas and Israel Pardo went after them, despite the fact that they were carrying revolvers and the two escapees had rifles. The men had disappeared.

It is hard to maintain a high morale among a troop with practically no armament, without direct contact with the head of the revolution, stumbling through the darkness, lacking experience, surrounded by enemies, who appeared as giants if one were to listen to the peasants' tales. Men from the plains, not used to the rough going over mountains, added to the crisis. There was an attempt at escape, led by a man called The Mexican, who once reached the rank of captain, but is now living in Miami; another traitor to the Revolution.

I heard about the escape through Hermes Leyva, Joel's cousin, and called for a confrontation in order to solve the problem. The Mexican swore by all his ancestors that he had no intention of leaving us; that all he wanted was to have his own guerrilla group to kill informers, because there was no action in our group. Actually, his plan was to kill informers and rob them. A typical bandit's behavior. Later, at the battle of El Hombrito, we lost only one man: Hermes Leyva. All suspicion fell upon the Mexican, but we could never prove that he had murdered Leyva.

The Mexican remained, swearing on his honor as a revolutionary, etc., that he would never try to escape or encourage anyone to do so. Following a few short, tiring marches we reached the zone of Palma Mocha, in the western slope of Turquino, where we received a great welcome from the peasants and established direct contact, due to my new profession as "tooth puller," which I practiced with great enthusiasm.

Once again we had a good meal and rested up for a fast move toward our old friendly zones of Palma Mocha and El Infierno, where we arrived June 15. Emilio Cabrera, a peasant living in the area, reported that Lalo Sardiñas had set up an ambush nearby, involving great peril to his house in the event a fight began.

On June 16 our column met the platoon belonging to Fidel's column, led by Lalo Sardiñas. Sardiñas told us he had been forced to join the Revolution. He was a store owner who used to bring us food when we were in the plains. One day he was taken by surprise, and he had to kill a man. Then he took the way to the Sierra. Now he had instructions to lie in wait for Sánchez Mosquera's columns. Once again Sánchez Mosquera, an obstinate man, had come to Palma Mocha and had found himself practically surrounded by Fidel's column. He evaded the trap and went full speed to the other side of Turquino.

We had heard about the presence of troops nearby and had seen the trenches. What we did not know was that what we considered a sign of a sustained offensive against us was really a sign of an enemy retreat, signifying a complete qualitative change in the character of the operations in the Sierra. We were now strong enough to encircle the enemy and force them to flee under the threat of complete annihilation.

The enemy learned their lesson well. The soldiers made only sporadic raids on the Sierra, but one of the most tenacious, aggressive, and bloody officers of the enemy army was Sánchez Mosquera. In 1957 he was only a lieutenant; following the last battles of the general offensive on the part of the army, which ended in defeat, he was promoted to colonel. He had a meteoric career as regards promotions. He was also extremely successful in robbing the peasants of everything they owned every time he set foot on the labyrinths of the Sierra Maestra.

TREASON IN THE MAKING

It was a pleasure to look at our troop. Close to two hundred men, well disciplined, with increased morale, and armed with good weapons, some of them new. The qualitative change I mentioned before was now quite evident in the Sierra. There was a true free territory, safety measures not so necessary, and there was a little freedom to carry on conversations at night while resting in our hammocks. We were allowed to visit the nearby villages and establish closer ties with the peasants. We were moved by the hearty welcome given by our comrades.

Felipe Pazos and Raúl Chibás were the "prima donnas" of the moment, although they were complete opposites. Raúl Chibás lived under the shadow of his brother's reputation—for Eddie Chibás was the symbol of an era—but he had none of his brother's virtues. He was neither expressive nor intelligent. Only his absolute mediocrity allowed him to be the principal figure of the Orthodox party. He spoke very little, and he wanted to leave the Sierra at once.

Felipe Pazos had a certain personality. He was rated as a great economist and had a reputation for being an honest person. His reputation for honesty was due to the fact that he did not steal from the public funds during his period as president of the National Bank, under Prío Socarrás' regime, a regime marked by extreme larceny and embezzlement. Many people would think this was a great achievement—to remain pure throughout a regime of debauchery and thievery. He deserved credit, yes, but only as an official who followed his administrative career, turning a deaf ear to the country's great problems. However, can anyone imagine a revolutionary who will not speak up against the inconceivable excess and abuse rampant at the time? Felipe Pazos managed to keep his mouth shut, and left the post of president of the National Bank—following Bastista's *coup*—surrounded by an aura of virtue: honesty, intelligence, and a great experience as an economist. Petulantly, he expected to come to the Sierra and take over. This pint-sized Machiavelli thought he was destined to control the country's future.

It is very possible he was already planning to betray the Revolution; perhaps this came later. Yet, his position was never clearly defined.

Protected by the joint declaration which we will analyze later on, he appointed himself delegate of the July 26th Movement in Miami, and he was on the verge of being appointed interim president of the republic. Through this maneuver, Prío made sure that he had a faithful man within the provisional government.

We did not have much time to talk, but Fidel told me about his efforts to turn out a really militant document which would set the basis for a declaration of principles. This was a difficult task when faced by these two "stone age" brains, inmune to the call of the people's struggle.

Fundamentally, the manifesto reiterated "the establishment of a great civic revolutionary front comprising all opposition parties, all civic institutions, and all revolutionary forces."

Several proposals were submitted: "the establishment of a civic revolutionary front in a common front of struggle"; the appointment of "a figure designated to preside over the provisional government." The document stated that the front did neither request nor accept intervention by any other country in the internal affairs of Cuba; it "did not accept any military junta as a provisional government of the republic"; the determination to separate the army from politics and insure the safety of the armed forces against political intrigue and influence; elections to be held within one year's time.

The program to be observed by the provisional government included the freedom of all political prisoners, civilian and military; absolute guarantee of freedom of the press and radio, and all rights, individual or political, to be guaranteed by the constitution; appointment of interim mayors in all municipalities, following consultation with the district's civic institutions; suppression of embezzlement in all forms, and establishment of measures aimed at increasing efficiency of all state organizations; establishment of the administrative career; democratization of trade union politics, promoting free elections in all trade unions and industrial workers' federations; beginning of an intense anti-illiteracy campaign and public education on civic affairs, pointing out the citizens' rights and duties to society and the country—"to establish the bases for an agrarian reform aimed at distribution of untilled lands, giving ownership to all sharecroppers, tenants and squatters having small lots of land, either private or state-owned, provided the former owners are compensated"; establishment of a foreign policy safeguarding our currency's stability and aimed at investing the country's credit in productive works; expedition of the process of industrialization and creation of additional employment opportunities.

In addition, there were two points of special emphasis: "First: The need to appoint, from this moment, the person who will preside over the Provisional Government of the Republic, to prove to the entire world that Cubans can become united under a slogan of freedom; to support the person who, for his impartiality, capabilities, and honesty, can personify such a slogan. "There are many able men in Cuba who can preside over the Republic." Felipe Pazos, one of the cosigners, felt quite confident that there was only one man for the presidency: himself.

"Second: that this person be appointed by an ensemble of civic nonpolitical institutions, whose support would safeguard the president from any political commitments, thus insuring clean, impartial elections.

The document also stated "it is not necessary to come to the Sierra for any discussions. We can have representatives in Havana, Mexico or wherever it becomes necessary."

Fidel had pressed for more explicit statements regarding the agrarian reform, but it was very difficult to crash through the wall of the two "stone age" characters; "to establish the bases for an Agrarian Reform aimed at the distribution of untilled lands," was the kind of policy with which the newspaper *Diario de la Marina* might agree. To make it worse, there was the part reading: "provided the former owners are compensated."

The Revolution did not comply with some of the commitments, as originally stated. We must emphasize that the enemy broke the pact expressed in the manifesto when they refused to acknowledge the authority of the Sierra and made an attempt to shackle the future revolutionary government.

We were not satisfied with the commitment, but it was necessary; at the time, it was progressive. It could never last beyond any moment that would represent an obstacle for the development of the revolutionary movement. In this matter, the enemy helped us to break the uncomfortable bonds and gave us the opportunity to show the people what their real intentions were.

We were aware that this was a minimal program, limiting our own efforts, but we had to recognize that it was impossible to impose our will from the Sierra Maestra; for a long period of time, we would have to depend upon a whole series of "friends" who were trying to use our military strength and the people's great trust in Fidel for the Machiavellian maneuvers, and above all, to maintain imperialist domination of Cuba, through the importing bourgeoisie, closely linked with the United States owners.

The manifesto had its positive sides: it mentioned the Sierra Maestra and it clearly stated: "Let no one be deceived by Government propaganda about the situation in the Sierra Maestra. The Sierra Maestra is an indestructible bulwark of freedom. It is part of the hearts of our people and it is here that we will know how to do justice to the faith and the confidence of our people." The words "we will know how" meant that Fidel and only Fidel knew how. The other two were incapable of following the development of the struggle in the Sierra; not even as spectators. They left the Sierra immediately. Chibás was arrested and beaten by the police. Both men managed to get to the United States.

It was the well planned *coup:* A group of representatives of the most distinguished Cuban oligarchy arrived at the Sierra "in defense of freedom," signed a joint declaration with the guerrilla chief isolated in the wilds of the Sierra, and returned with full freedom to play their trump card in Miami. But they overlooked one most important point. Political *coups* always depend on the opponents' strength, in this case, the weapons in the hands of the people. Quick action by our chief, who had full confidence in the guerrilla army, averted the development of the treacherous move. Months later, when the outcome of the Miami pact became known, Fidel's fiery reply paralyzed the enemy. We were accused of being "divisionists" trying to impose our will from the remote regions of the Sierra, but the enemy had to change its strategy and look for a new trap: the Caracas pact.

Our manifesto, dated July 12, 1957, was published in the newspapers. To us, the declaration was simply a short rest period on our march forward. Our main task—to defeat the enemy army in the battle field—must go on. A new column was being organized, with me as captain, and there were other promotions. Ramiro Valdés was promoted to captain, and his platoon joined my column. Ciro Redondo, too, was promoted to captain and was to lead a platoon. The column included three platoons; the first platoon, the advance guard, was led by Lalo Sardiñas, who was also the detachment's second-in-command. Ramiro Valdés and Ciro led the other two, the column was made up of close to seventy-five men, heterogeneously dressed and heterogeneously armed; however, I was very proud of them. A few nights later I was to feel prouder, closer to the Revolution, anxious to prove that my officers' insigna were well deserved.

We wrote a letter of greetings and appreciation to "Carlos"—Frank País' underground name—which was signed by all the officers of the guerrilla army who were able to write. Many of the Sierra peasants did not know how to read or write, but they were an important part of our column. The signatures appeared on one column and next to it there was another column showing the signer's rank. When my turn came, Fidel simply said: "make it major." Thus, in a most informal manner, I was promoted to major of the second column of the guerrilla army, later known as column number four.

The letter, written while resting in a peasant's house, was the guerrilla fighters' warm message to their brother in the city, thanking him for his endless struggle to obtain supplies for us and lessen the enemy's pressure upon us.

There is a tinge of vanity hiding somewhere within every one of us, and I was no exception. I was the proudest man in the world when I was promoted to major. My insignia, a small star, was given to me by Celia. The award was accompanied by a gift: a wristwatch purchased in Santiago. My first mission was to set a trap for Sánchez Mosquera, but he was the smartest of all the Batista henchmen and had left the zone.

Something had to be done to justify the semi-independent life we were to lead in what was to be our new zone, so we began to plan a series of great deeds.

It was imperative that we celebrate the glorious date of July 26, and Fidel gave me free rein to do whatever I could, provided I took the necessary precautions. We had a new doctor with us: Sergio del Valle, now a major in our revolutionary army. He, too, practiced his profession within the limitations of the Sierra.

We had to prove that we were alive because we had received a few setbacks on the plains. Weapons that were to be used to open another front at Miranda sugar mill had been seized by the police, and several valuable leaders, among them Faustino Pérez, had been arrested. Fidel had opposed the division of forces but had given in to the insistence of the plains. The results were clear evidence of the correctness of his thinking, and from then on we devoted ourselves to strengthening the Sierra Maestra as the first step toward the extension of the guerrilla army.

ATTACK ON BUEYCITO

Several problems arose due to our independent life. Now it was necessary to establish a rigid discipline, organize the command, and set up some sort of staff in order to insure the success of future combats. It was not an easy task, due to the lack of discipline among the new men.

No sooner was the detachment organized when a dear comrade, Lieutenant Maceo, left on a mission to Santiago. We never saw him again. He was killed in the city.

William Rodríguez and Raúl Castro Mercader were promoted to lieutenant, in an effort to consolidate a small guerrilla force. One morning we heard the unpleasant news that a man called Wong "the Chinaman," had deserted, carrying with him his 22 caliber rifle, a most valuable weapon under the circumstances. It was presumed he had returned to his neighborhood in the foothills of the Sierra. Two men were sent to chase him, but we lost all hope when Israel Pardo and Banderas returned following a fruitless search for other deserters. Taking into account Israel's strong physical condition and experience with the surrounding area, he was ordered to join my group, for special missions.

We began to work out a very ambitious plan: to attack Estrada Palma first, at night, then continue on to the nearby towns of Yara and Veguitas, seize the small army posts, and return to the mountains. This would mean taking three enemy positions in one single attack, depending on the factor of surprise. We did some target practice, using ammunition sparingly, and found every weapon in good shape, with the exception of the Madzen machine gun rifle which was old and dirty. We wrote to Fidel asking whether or not he approved our plan. We received no answer from Fidel, but on July 27 we heard the news on the radio: Raúl Castro, leading two hundred men, had attacked Estrada Palma.

The magazine *Bohemia,* in the only uncensored issue of that time, published a special article showing the damage our troops had inflicted on Estrada Palma, where the army headquarters had been destroyed. The article mentioned Fidel Castro, Celia Sánchez, and a myriad of revolutionaries who had come from the mountains. It was a mixture of truth and myth, as usual, and the reporters could never figure out what had happened. The attack had been carried out by a small group of men led by captain Guillermo García. Actually, there was no battle because Barreras had expected the twenty-sixth of July to be the date for strong attacks and had withdrawn his forces, not trusting his position. What came to Estrada Palma was something like an expedition. The next day the army began the pursuit of our guerrillas, and one of our men was caught asleep near San Lorenzo.

When we heard the news we made up our minds to move on and attack some other post on a date as close as possible to July 26 in order to maintain a state of affairs favorable to the insurrection.

On our way to La Maestra, near a place called La Jeringa, we were met by one of the men who had gone in search of the deserter. He said his comrade had told him that he was a close friend of Wong's and could not betray him. Then he invited him to desert, saying that he was not returning to the guerrillas. Our comrade had warned him to stop, and when the man kept going away, he shot him. I gathered my troop on a hill nearby and told them that they were going to witness the outcome of an attempt at desertion. I explained why the crime of desertion was punishable by death, the only sentence that could be applied to anyone betraying the Revolution. We marched by the body of the dead man, single file. Many of our new comrades were shaken by the sight of death, by the sight of a man who had attempted to leave his post. Perhaps many of them were moved more by a certain affection toward the man, together with a political weakness—understandable at that time—than by a feeling of disloyalty to the Revolution. These were hard times, and the shooting of the man was considered as exemplary. It would be meaningless to mention the names of the protagonists in this drama. Let us simply say that the deserter was a young man, a humble peasant of that very same zone.

We were now traveling through familiar zones. On July 30 Lalo Sardiñas contacted an old friend, one of the zone's merchants named Armando Oliver. We set a rendezvous in a house on California zone, and there we met the merchant and Jorge Abich. We told Abich of our intention to attack Minas and Bueycito. We were risking a great deal by confiding in these people, but Lalo had full confidence in them.

Armando reported that Casillas visited these zones on Sundays. Following the inveterate habits of all army officers, he had a girl friend there. However, we were more inclined to carry out a quick attack, based on surprise, rather than trust to luck and try to capture this notorious officer. The night of July 31 was set for the attack. Armando Oliver was to get trucks, guides, and a sapper, whose job was to blow up three bridges between the Bueycito road and that of Manzanillo-Bayamo. The following day at 2 P.M. we started our march toward the Maestra. It took us two hours, and once there, we hid our knapsacks and went on our way. It was a long walk, and on the way we passed a few houses. There was a party going on in one of the houses, and we stopped and gave the people a lecture, holding them responsible for any leaks about our whereabouts. Then we continued on at full speed. Of course, in this case there was no great danger involved; there were no telephones or any other means of communication in the Sierra. An informer would have to run fast to get ahead of us.

A comrade named Santiesteban had a truck ready for us, together with two others which Oliver had sent. Sardiñas climbed aboard the first truck; Ramiro and I got on the second one; Ciro and his group boarded the third; and we began the three-hour trip to the town of Las Minas. Practically all the army vigilance was focused upon Las Minas, so it was our job to keep anyone from going to Bueycito. We left a rear guard, headed by Vilo Acuña, and went on to the outskirts of Bueycito.

At the entrance to town we stopped a coal truck and sent it ahead with one of our men to check up on the sentries. We knew that sometimes the army would set up a post and everybody going in or out would be searched. This time there was no sentry. Every soldier was peacefully asleep.

Our plan was simple, although a little pretentious: Lalo Sardiñas was to attack the west side of the post, Ramiro would encircle it, and Ciro was to attack the front, using the staff's machine gun. Oliver was to arrive in an automobile and turn his headlights on the guards, then Ramiro was to break in and capture everybody. Guards sleeping at home would be taken by surprise. Lieutenant Noda's squad kept their eyes open for any road traffic prior to the attack, and William was sent to blow up the bridge connecting Bueycito with the Central highway.

The plan never materialized. It was too much for a group of men unfamiliar with their surroundings and lacking experience. Ramiro lost some of his men in the dark, arrived late, and the automobile never came. There was a tense moment when we were placing our men and the dogs began to bark furiously.

I was walking along the town's main street when a man came out of a house. I gave him the order to halt and the man, taking me for a comrade, replied: "Rural Guard." When I pointed my gun at him, he jumped into the house and I could hear furniture and glass flying around inside. He escaped through the back of the house. I suppose it was something of a silent agreement between us: I did not want to raise an alarm by firing, and in turn, he did not warn his friends.

We were still looking for favorable positions when the sentry came out, puzzled by the dogs' barking and perhaps by the noise made by my unexpected meeting with the soldier. I came face to face with the sentry. I was ready with my Thompson, and he was carrying a Garand rifle. Israel Pardo was standing next to me. I gave the man the order to stop, and he made a slight move. For me, that was more than enough: I pressed the trigger and nothing happened. Israel tried to fire his 22 caliber rifle and it jammed. I cannot imagine how Israel escaped unhurt. All I remember is running like a madman under the rain of bullets from the soldier's Garand. I turned a corner and stopped to get my gun back into firing condition. The soldier had inadvertently given the signal to start the attack, since his shots were the first heard that night. When the fire became generalized, the soldier hid behind a column, and that is where we found him when the attack ended. It had taken only a few minutes.

While Israel went on to make contact, the shooting ended, and we received the surrender. Ramiro's men had attacked the building as soon as they heard the first shots. They had riddled a door leading to the back of the building.

We found twelve soldiers, six of whom were wounded. We had lost one man, Pedro Rivero, a newcomer to our ranks, who was shot in the chest.

Three others were slightly wounded. Once we had removed everything that was useful to us, we set the building on fire and boarded the trucks. We had captured the sergeant and an informer named Orán.

It was already daylight, and everybody in town was offering us beer and cold drinks. The bridge to the highway had been blown up, and we blew up another small bridge over a stream. The sapper came back with Oliver, and he remained with us as a full-fledged member. He was a priceless acquisition. His name was Cristino Naranjo. He became a major and was murdered by counterrevolutionaries after the triumph of the Revolution.

Our group came to Las Minas where we stopped and held a little meeting. Playing his role to the hilt, one of the Abich, a storekeeper, asked us in the name of the people, to release the sergeant and the informer. We replied that we kept them as prisoners to safeguard the lives of the inhabitants, but as long as the people insisted, we would agree. Thus, we settled two things: the prisoners were released and the townspeople were safe. On the way to the Sierra we buried our comrade in the town's cemetery. Very few recognizance planes were flying over us at the time, so we stopped at a grocery store to take care of the wounded. One man had been shot in the shoulder, a surface wound, but it had torn the flesh away, making the treatment a little difficult; the other one was hit in the hand by a small caliber bullet. The third man had a tremendous bump on his head. It seems that the army mules became frightened during the battle and began to kick right and left. One of the kicks landed on the wall and a piece of plaster had landed on our comrade's head.

At Altos de California, we left the trucks and distributed the arms. Although my participation in the battle had been insignificant and none-too-heroic, since I had presented my posterior to the few shots fired in my direction, I took a Browning machine gun rifle, the best one in the post. I threw away the Thompson and its unpredictable ammunition. The best fighters were given the best arms, and those who performed worst were given leaves of absence; these included the "wets," a group of men who had fallen into the river when they had tried to escape at the beginning of the battle. Among the best fighters we can mention Captain Ramiro Valdés, who led the attack, and Raúl Castro Mercader, who played a decisive role in the short battle.

Back in the hills we heard about the state of siege and the censorship. We also heard the terrible news of Frank País' death. Frank had been murdered in the streets of Santiago, and this represented an enormous loss to the Revolution. It was the end of one of the purest, most brilliant figures of the Cuban Revolution. The people of Santiago and Havana, in fact the entire population of Cuba, went into the spontaneous August strike, the government's partial censorship became complete, and we entered a new stage, one of absolute silence on the part of the pseudo-oppositionists, on one hand, and of savage murders committed by Batista's henchmen all over the island, on the other. This time, the people of Cuba were ready for war.

When Frank País was murdered, we lost one of our most valuable fighters, but the people's reaction to the crime showed that additional forces were joining the struggle and the people's fighting spirit had increased.

BATTLE OF EL HOMBRITO

The column had been organized less than a month before, and already we had begun our sedentary life in the Sierra. We had camped in a valley called El Hombrito—The Little Man—because two superimposed rocks, on the summit of the Sierra, resembled the figure of a small person.

Ours was a troop of new recruits, and the men had to be trained before they undertook difficult tasks, and yet we had to be ready for battle at any moment. It was our duty to attack any enemy units that dared invade what was already "free territory of Cuba," that is, a certain section of the Sierra Maestra.

On the eve of August 29 a peasant reported a large number of soldiers headed for the Sierra through El Hombrito road leading to the valley. We were very skeptical about false reports, so I told the man that he would be subjected to all sorts of punishment if he happened to be lying, but he kept swearing that it was all true, that the soldiers were now at the farm of Julio Zapatero, two kilometers from the Sierra.

That night we got into position. Lalo Sardiñas' platoon was hidden among some ferns, and their duty was to hit the enemy as soon as they were stopped. Ramiro Valdés and his men, with less firepower, were to begin an "acoustic" attack to start the alarm. Although not powerfully armed, they were in a less dangerous position as the enemy had to cross a deep ravine to get close to them.

The trail the enemy had to enter was on the edge of the hill, where Lalo was ambushed. Ciro was to carry on an oblique attack, and I, with the best-armed men, was to open the hostilities. The best squad was Mercader's, so they were positioned as shock troops to reap the fruits of victory. Our plan was a simple one: When the enemy reached a curve on the trail, making an almost 90° turn around a rock, I was to let ten or twelve men go by, then shoot the last one in order to separate those men from the rest. My sharpshooters would quickly annihilate the others, Raúl Mercader's squad would take the dead soldiers' weapons, and we would all withdraw, covered by the rear guard under Lieutenant Vilo Acuña.

At dawn, from Ramiro Valdés' position, we noticed some activity around Zapatero's house. A few men were walking in and out, putting on their helmets. We knew that the peasant had been telling the truth. We were all ready for action.

I took my position as we kept our eyes on the enemy soldiers who were beginning their slow climb. I waited for what seemed an interminable period of time, my finger on the trigger of the Browning rifle, ready for the battle. We could hear their voices and shouts as they went on, not suspecting an ambush. The first man went by, then the second. They were so far apart from each other I began to think there would not be any time to wait for twelve of them to pass. As I counted six, I heard a shout and one of the soldiers raised his head in a gesture of surprise. I opened fire, hitting the sixth man. The fire became generalized, and at the second burst of automatic rifle fire the six men disappeared from the trail. I told Mercader's squad to attack, while a few volunteers joined the attack on the same spot; now we had opened fire from both sides. Lieutenant Orestes and Mercader were on their way in, and other men, protected by a rock, concentrated their fire on the enemy column that was part of a company commanded by Major Merob Sosa. Rodolfo Vázquez took the weapon away from the man I had wounded. Unfortunately, the man was only a medical corps man whose entire equipment consisted of a 45 caliber revolver and a few shells. The other five men had thrown themselves down a ravine, escaping along the bottom of a dry stream. Soon we heard the first bazookas fired by the enemy, now recovered from the unexpected attack.

A Maxim machine gun and my rifle were our only heavy-caliber weapons, but the Maxim would not work and Julio Pérez could not do anything with it.

On Ramiro's side, Israel and Joel Iglesias, armed with their puny weapons, had advanced toward the enemy. Shotguns went off everywhere, adding to the soldiers' confusion. I ordered the two lateral platoons to retreat, then followed them leaving the rear guard to cover up until Lalo Sardiñas' platoon withdrew. We had already planned a second line of resistance.

Vilo Acuña caught up with us and told us of Hermes Leyva's death. We came face to face with a platoon sent by Fidel, whom I had warned about the imminent battle with superior forces. Ignacio Pérez was at the head of this platoon. Retreating to about one thousand yards away, we set up our new ambush. The soldiers came to the plateau where the attack had taken place, and we watched as they burned the body of Hermes Leyva, in a savage act of revenge. In our impotent fury, all we could do was to fire our rifles while they returned our fire with their bazookas.

I found out that the shout that provoked my hurried shot was a remark made by one of the soldiers. He had shouted something like "this is like a picnic!" probably indicating that he was getting close to the summit. The attack proved our lack of combat training, since we had been unable to fire accurately at an enemy no further than twenty yards away. Even so, it was a big victory for us: we had managed to stop Merob Sosa's column, and they had now withdrawn. We had also obtained one small weapon, but at a very high price: the life of one of our comrades. We had accomplished all this armed with inefficient arms, against a complete company of at least 140 men, well equipped for modern war, who had launched a large amount of bazooka fire—perhaps even mortars—against us, although their attack had been just as haphazard as ours.

Following the battle, a few men were promoted, among them Alfonso Zayas, who was made a lieutenant. Next day, we talked with Fidel, and he was very happy with the results of an attack he had launched against the soldiers in Las Cuevas. Some of our comrades had been killed: Juventino Alarcón, of Manzanillo, one of the first to join our guerrilas; Pastor; Yayo; Castillo; and Oliva, a great fighter and a fine boy, whose father was a lieutenant in Batista's army.

Fidel's attack had been quite important, since it was not an ambush but an actual attack on a camp which was fairly well defended. The enemy had suffered many losses and had abandoned their position the following day. One of the heroes had been "Pilón, the Negro," a great fighter. They told us Pilón had come to a hut where he saw a series of strange-looking lengths of pipe next to a number of small boxes. They were bazookas, but neither Pilón nor any of us had ever seen one at close range. Pilón was wounded in a leg and had to abandon the hut, and we lost a great opportunity to get our hands on these weapons, so valuable against small fortifications.

Our battle had new repercussions. A few days later, an army dispatch announced five or six dead. In addition to burning our comrade's body, the soldiers had murdered five or six peasants whom Merob Sosa suspected of having reported to us about the army's whereabouts. Those poor peasants were murdered and their houses were set afire. I remember the names of Abigail, Calixto, Pablito Lebón—of Haitian descent—and Gonzalo González, all far removed, or at least partly removed from our struggle. They knew about our cause, they suspected we were in the zone, but they were completely innocent of our ambush. We knew very well the methods used by Batista's officers to obtain information, and we kept our moves secret. In case a peasant happened to go by an ambush we kept him with us until the attack was over.

The battle proved that it was easy, under certain circumstances, to attack enemy columns on the march. We realized the advantage of firing upon the head of the column and of trying to kill the leading men, immobilizing the rest of them. We continued this practice until it became an established system, so efficient that the soldiers stopped coming to the Sierra Maestra and even refused to be part of the advance guard. Of course, it took more than one battle for our system to materialize. At the time, we were satisfied to analyze our small victories together with Fidel. They were indeed victories, these battles between a well-equipped army and our poorly prepared soldiers.

This was more or less the moment when the soldiers abandoned the Sierra. The only man who ever came back, in a show of audacity, was Sánchez Mosquera, the bravest as well as the most notorious murderer and thief among Batista's military officers.

"EL PATOJO"

A few days ago, the news from Guatemala included the deaths of several patriots, among them Julio Roberto Cáceres Valle.

In our profession as revolutionaries, amidst the class struggle shaking the entire continent, we find that death is a frequent accident. But the death of a friend, who was our comrade during difficult moments as well as during many moments of hopeful dreaming, is always painful. Julio Roberto was a great friend. He was small and rather weak, physically, so we nicknamed him "El Patojo" which in Guatemalan slang means "little one" or "child."

While in Mexico, El Patojo had witnessed the birth of the idea of a Revolution. He had offered his services as a volunteer, but Fidel did not want to involve any foreigners in this project of national liberation in which I had the honor to participate.

Shortly after the triumph of the Revolution, El Patojo sold his few belongings and came to me. He occupied several positions in public administration and became chief of personnel of the Industry Department of INRA—National Institute of Agrarian Reform—but he was never too happy with his jobs. He was looking for something different: his country's liberation. Like all of us, he had undergone a deep transformation. He had changed from a bewildered boy who had left his country without fully understanding the reason for defeat, into the fully conscious revolutionary that he now was.

The first time I saw El Patojo, he was aboard a train. We were running away from Guatemala, following Arbenz' overthrow. Our destination was Tapachula; then Mexico City. He was much younger than I, but we soon became close friends. Together we made the trip from Chiapas to Mexico City, facing the same problems. We were poor and beaten, and we had to make a living amidst indifferent, if not hostile, surroundings.

El Patojo was completely broke, and I had only a few pesos. I purchased a camera, and we became clandestine photographers, taking pictures of people visiting parks, etc. Our partner was a Mexican who owned the laboratory where we developed and printed our photographs. We became thoroughly familiar with Mexico City, walking from one end to the other, delivering our miserable photos, and struggling with our customers in an effort to convince them that the little child in the print really looked beautiful and that the price of one Mexican peso for such a work of art was a tremendous bargain. We practiced our profession for several months and managed to eat quite regularly. Gradually we fared a little better, until the adventures of a revolutionary life separated us. I have already explained why Fidel did not want our small army to be a mosiac of nationalities.

El Patojo continued his life as a newspaperman, studying Physics at the University of Mexico, cutting short his studies, going back to the University, without getting ahead. He made his living working at various occupations, never asking for anything. To this day I cannot say whether that sensitive boy was too timid or too proud to recognize his weaknesses and personal problems, to approach some friend and ask for help. El Patojo was an introvert, a man of great intelligence, well educated, and endowed with tremendous sensitivity, which, toward the end, he had devoted to serving his people. Already a party man, he belonged to the Guatemalan Workers' party, he had acquired great discipline, and he was a good prospect as a revolutionary cadre. There was very little left of his former touchiness and proud demeanor. The Revolution cleanses men, improving and developing them, as the farmer corrects the defects on a plant and brings out its best qualities.

In Cuba, El Patojo and I shared the same house, as becomes old friends, but the old mutual confidence no longer existed. On a few occasions I suspected what El Patojo was after: I had seen him hard at work, studying one of his country's native languages. One day he came to me and said he was leaving, that the time had come for him to do his duty.

El Patojo had no knowlege of military training. He simply felt that it was his duty to return to his country and fight, weapon in hand, in an attempt to imitate our guerrilla warfare. We held a long conversation, a rare thing at the time. I limited my recommendations to three points: constant mobility, constant mistrust, and constant vigilance. Mobility: Never stay in the same place, never stay more than two nights in the same spot, never stop moving from one place to another. Mistrust: At the beginning, do not trust your own shadow, never trust friendly peasants, informers, guides, or contact men. Do not trust anything or anybody until a zone is completely liberated. Vigilance: keeping constant guard and scouting, setting up camp in a safe spot, and above all never sleeping with a roof over your head, never sleeping in a house that can be surrounded. It was a synthesis of our guerrilla experience, the only thing I could give my friend. Could I tell him not to do it? By what right? We had tried something when it was considered impossible, and now he was convinced that it was possible.

El Patojo departed, and a short time later we heard about his death. As always in these cases, we hoped that there had been some mistake, perhaps a mix-up of names. Unfortunately it was true: his own mother had identified the body. Others, too, had been killed: a group of his comrades, perhaps as intelligent and as self-sacrificing as El Patojo, but unknown to us.

Once again there is the bitter taste of defeat. The question left unanswered: Why not profit by the experience of others? Why weren't these simple instructions obeyed? Every effort was made to find out exactly how El Patojo had died. The exact facts are still unknown, but one could say that the zone was badly chosen, the men's physical condition was below par, they were too trusting, and above all, there was not enough vigilance. The repressive army came upon them by surprise, killing a few; the men were dispersed, and the soldiers caught up with them once again. Some were captured, and others, like El Patojo, were killed in the battle. Once the guerrillas lost cohesion, the rest was probably an open manhunt, similar to what happened to us at Alegría del Pío.

Once again, young blood has been spilled on American soil in the struggle for liberty. Another battle has been lost. Let us take time off to cry over the fallen comrades, while we continue to sharpen our machetes. Based on the unfortunate as well as valuable experience of our beloved dead, let us adopt the firm resolution not to repeat mistakes, and to avenge the death of every one of them by winning battles and attaining liberation.

At the time of his departure, El Patojo made no recommendations. He mentioned no one. He had no personal belongings with which to be concerned. However, common friends in Mexico brought me some verses he had written in a plain notebook. They are a revolutionary's last verses. They are also a song of love to the Revolution, to the motherland, and to a woman.

The final recommendation in these verses must have the characteristics of a command directed to the woman whom El Patojo met and loved, here in Cuba.

Take it, it is only a heart
hold it in your hand
and at daybreak,
open your hand
and let the sun's rays warm it. . . .

El Patojo's heart has remained with us, waiting for the lover's hand, and the loving hands of an entire people, to allow the sun to warm it on the dawn of a new day that will shine for Guatemala and all America. Today, there is a small school of statistics named "Julio Roberto Cáceres Valle" at the Ministry of Industry, where El Patojo left numerous friends. Later, when Freedom comes to Guatemala, his beloved name must appear on a school, a factory, or a hospital, anywhere where people struggle and work in the construction of the new society.

CHAPTER 3

On Underdevelopment[1]

As you know, if you have ever listened to any of my speeches on television, I have almost only one theme, at least one central theme, which is the industrialization of the country.

After that first period, during which we were all guerrilla soldiers with gun in hand fighting against tanks and infantry, or taking charge of provisions or sewing up a wound, there followed a period in which out of logical necessity each person in the revolutionary government had to devote himself to some more specific task. He had to begin to specialize in this task because the tasks of government demand such specialization.

Fidel remembered how in the Sierra we had once set up a small shoe factory, and from that time we became industrialists . . . and now we are already well on the way, and we shall continue; we shall continue with devotion and pride, observing how a country through ingenuity, by developing all its strength, unearthing its hidden strengths, transforms itself from an economic colony into a power which makes itself felt throughout the world.

Naturally, to begin with, Cuba's great impact has been as a political force—as the embodiment of all underdeveloped countries struggling for their freedom. The two elements of revolution are interrelated—the goal of those countries fighting for their freedom is to become industrialized in order to gain that freedom. Industrialization is a long and painful task which requires the contributions of a large number of technicians. We shall have to break down many prejudices, leap over many barriers and work untiringly.

Comrade Fernandez complained—or at least pointed out—that this is

[1] Speech delivered May 20, 1960, reproduced in *Obra Revolucionaria*, Año 1960, No. 6. Translated by Paul Bundy.

but a small sample of industry, and he is right. It is small in the size of the industries, the numbers of workers they employ, and in relation to the tremendous technical apparatus necessary to operate them. This Cuban industry should serve as a preview of things to come. It should be the zero mark on the thermometer. From this point, year by year, we shall mark the growth of our industries and demonstrate how the Cuban people, supported by the strength of the agrarian reform and by the even greater strength of our united will to prosper, progressively create the foundations which will free Cuba from "underdevelopment."

You know that this undertaking has been begun in steel production, food production, the chemical industry, mining, chemical products derived from the sugar cane industry, which is particularly important in the case of Cuba, and above all most quickly, most visibly in the progress achieved by the Agrarian Reform.

If you had seen the exhibition at the beginning of its tour of the country, as well as today at its close, you would have the opportunity to note the enormous number of new industries, especially those pertaining to agriculture. You would see how in these last six months, in the short lapse of time between the initial departure and the present arrival of this exhibition, a great number of special industries concerned with the transformation of agricultural products had been established throughout the country. You would see the variety of industries under INRA, some of which have only begun production again after long periods during which they couldn't compete with foreign products, and some of which have been established in the last six months. You would also notice another kind of change. For example, you would see that a certain notice or advertisement for an industry now has a small sign which reads, "Now Operated by the Revolutionary Government." This change shows the other side of industrialization, the decision to carry out the economic policy of the country along the lines that have been prescribed, along lines to be adhered to and not to be violated. If they are violated, government action will be taken. Besides this, you will see a large number of small industries functioning again thanks to the intervention of the Ministry of Labor, which will turn them over to the Industrial Department of INRA. In short, you would see a decidedly different panorama from the one you will see today. And, if instead of today this exhibition were to appear a year from now, the change would be incredible. The number of industries which the revolutionary government is going to install in line with industrialization plans elaborated entirely in Cuba, with the help of many countries of the world and exchanges already in progress, is indeed astounding.

Already the initial plans for the steel industry are being elaborated. It will probably be located in Oriente Province, and in five years it will provide the total steel needs of Cuba. Generally speaking, the basic plans for all the industries I have mentioned are already being implemented.

However, the most important factor does not lie here, but rather in the large quantity of manufactured goods derived from the small factories which will be built in Cuba. And I stress its immediate importance because the main task of the revolutionary government is not to industrialize for the mere sake of industrialization, but rather because industrialization means a better standard of living. And our primary aim is to give a better standard of living to everyone. One has to begin with those who have the lowest standard—the unemployed. Thus the importance of small industry and agriculture, which with a small investment provides work for a great number of people who are now unemployed. Thus, given our understanding of the situation and the willingness of the Cuban people, we can appeal to everyone to participate in what will be our major undertaking in the next two years, perhaps for the next two and a half years: that by 1962 there will be an end of unemployment in Cuba. We must work incessantly for the success of this goal of the people in order to show all countries—those that believe in us, those that do not believe in us, and those that hate us—that a government based on the faith of the people and concerned only with their welfare can, in but a few years, guarantee the well-being of all its inhabitants. This is the great undertaking, the great task of our leaders, the great undertaking of each person who lives in Cuba and believes that the revolutionary government will interpret his wishes correctly, that is to say the wishes of the majority of the Cuban people.

We are now embarked on that effort that will mark our liberation from the onerous label of "underdevelopment": the great leap to achieve full employment in record time.

This great attempt to see that every person is able to work is a task which depends upon you and us. Each one of you should do what each of us does in the government. Each day you should think of how we can give work to more Cubans. You should be constantly alert to new sources, new opportunities that present themselves, which the people within their districts and throughout the republic can discover. You should meet with laborers, peasants, office workers, or students and discuss the best way to enable the country, given its needs and possibilities, to increase the number of people who work, at the same time seeing to it that the work is more productive.

Now you see the little we have in the way of industries. But try to see them not as they are today, but rather with eyes for the future. Look at them as they will be tomorrow or the day after—see their significance for the present, at this zero point on the thermometer of 1960—and carry yourselves into the industrialized country of the future, to that great industrialized nation of the Caribbean which will be the Cuba of tomorrow.

CHAPTER 4

On Sacrifice and Dedication[1]

A REVOLUTION like ours, a people's revolution, made by the will of the people, for the people, cannot advance unless each conquest, each step forward, is taken by the full mass of the public, by the entire mass of the people. And to take those steps, and take them enthusiastically, you must know the revolutionary process, you must know that those steps must be taken, and that they must be taken gladly. And you also have to know, whenever you make a sacrifice, why you are making it, because the road to industrialization, which is the road to collective well-being in this age of economic empires, isn't an easy one. On the contrary, it is an exceedingly difficult road.

And I would like to say still more. As all the rebellions and popular movements in all the underdeveloped regions of the world challenge the most aggressive exponent of economic imperialism, the United States of America, that power is going to turn with even more force on its nearest and most rigidly dominated territory, which is, obviously, America; and within America, that *mare nostrum* of theirs, which is the Caribbean.

That is, this great thrust, this great awakening of the peoples that is being seen in Korea, in Turkey, in Japan—to mention only the most dramatic examples outside the Continent—involves a danger for Cuba. Of course, we must realize, without false modesty, that to a considerable extent we have inspired for these developments.

There is an obvious awakening of the underdeveloped peoples, and to some extent the Cuban example, particularly in the Americas, has contributed to it. Obviously, this is true more in the Americas than in a country like Japan, with a population of ninety million or a little less and

[1] Speech to a Havana assembly of workers, delivered June 18, 1960, reproduced in *Obra Revolucionaria,* Año 1960, No. 11. Translated by Lewis H. Rubman.

with a very powerful industry. But, in any case, it has been shown that the strength of the colonial powers is not so great when they are faced with a people determined to destroy it.

That is the positive part of our mission, which will appeal to international solidarity if any aggression arises. And when I speak of aggression, I mean real aggression, not petty aggression: I do not mean economic aggression like the one the House of Representatives of the United States is about to unleash against Cuban sugar.

That is, our road is difficult, and our strength is the unity of the workers, the peasants, and all the underprivileged classes that must march forward into the future.

Now, this talk was aimed directly at the working class—not at the peasants, but at the workers—for two reasons. First, because the peasants have completed their first historical stage. They have fought bravely to win their right to the land and are beginning to receive the fruits of that victory—they are completely with the Revolution. The working class still has not received the fruits of industrialization, the fruits of the revolutionary movement's determination. And it has not received them because the first thing that had to be done was to establish the base for industrialization, and that base was established, precisely, by changing the pattern of landholding. That is to say, the base was established by the agrarian reform.

We have already covered that part of the road, and we are starting, with hopes for a great effort, on the road to industrialization. At this moment the role of the working class defines itself. Either the working class completely comprehends all its duties and all the importance of this moment and we triumph, or it does not realize them, and industrialization becomes one more of the lukewarm attempts America has made to save itself from the colonial yoke.

I want to tell you this bluntly and analyze the facts exactly, because among revolutionaries it is good to know all the faults that each of us has and to try to correct them. It is no secret that the strength of the revolutionary movement centered around the peasants at first, and then around the workers. And there was a reason for it. The first reason was that the strongest insurrectionary movement operated in the countryside, and that the most prestigious of the insurrection's leaders, Fidel Castro, was in the countryside. But there also are very important socioeconomic reasons, and it is a fact that Cuba, like all underdeveloped countries, does not have a forceful proletariat.

In many industries, especially in the new industries—closely associated, furthermore, with monopoly capital—the worker sometimes turned out to be a privileged individual. While a sugar worker had to sweat as long as the sun was out for three months of the year—and go hungry for the other nine months—in industry some types of workers could work all year and earn five or six, or more, times as much as the sugar worker. This marks a great difference and therefore establishes a principle of division, which is what colonial powers constantly try to create and maintain: the principle of the division of the working class whereby the privileged try to reap their privileges and the underprivileged try to rise, not in a mass, but by individual initiative, thus destroying the solidarity of the working class.

That is why, after our triumph, we have even had arduous struggles against the representatives of Mujalism, representatives of the old CTC[2] gang, and this too has braked the advance of the workers' movement. Today we can not say that these old representatives of another age have been completely annihilated, but they *are* in the process of being destroyed. Those who have made mistakes are in the process of correcting those mistakes. And those who knowingly harmed the people are being eliminated, bit by bit. Nonetheless, the working class still retains much of the spirit that made it see only one difference: between the worker and the boss—a simplistic spirit that led all analysis to precisely this great division: workers and bosses.

And today, in the process of industrialization, which gives such great importance to the state, the workers consider the state as just one more boss, and they treat it as a boss. And since this is a state completely opposed to the State as Boss, we must establish long, fatiguing dialogues between the state and the workers, who although they certainly will be convinced in the end, during this period, during this dialogue have braked progress.

I could give various current examples, but it is not worth the effort to discuss individual cases and point the finger at anybody because I am convinced that most of those examples are the product of exactly that point of view that must be rooted out, and not of bad faith or of a desire to interfere with the Revolution. What should be clear in all of these instances is what Fidel said the other day: The best labor leader is not the one who fights for his comrades' daily bread. The best labor leader is the one who fights for everybody's daily bread, the one who understands the revolutionary process completely, and who, analyzing it and understanding it in depth, will support the government and convince his comrades by explaining the reasons for the revolutionary measures. And this does not mean that the labor leader should become a parrot, simply repeating what the government says through the Ministry of Labor, or through any other ministry.

Of course the government will make mistakes too, and the labor leader will have to call attention to its mistakes, and he will have to call attention to them forcefully if those mistakes are repeated and if they are not corrected. It is nothing but a procedural problem. The fact is that today there is a whole series of people's representatives in the government, and they are there to serve the people and are ready and willing to correct all the

[2] Confederación de Trabajadores Cubanos, the Cuban Labor Federation (ed.).

mistakes we make. I say "we" because no one is exempt. A group of young men who, without any previous experience, has to take command of an accelerated process of development in the face of the military and economic power of the Continent, of the so-called "Western World," naturally is going to make mistakes. And that is the job of the labor leader: go to him and show him the mistake and, if necessary, convince him of it, and keep on going upward to the highest levels of the revolutionary government until the mistake is corrected. And show your comrades what the mistake is and how to combat it, how things have to be changed, but always do this by discussion.

It is inadmissible, and it would be the start of our failure, for the workers to have to go on strike, for example, because the employer-state—and I am talking about the process of industrialization, that is, of the majority participation in the state—adopted so intransigent and totally absurd a position as to force the workers to strike. This would be the beginning of the end of the people's government, because it would be the negation of all we have been upholding. But the government *will,* on occasion, have to ask sacrifices of certain types of workers. It has asked them, and twice the sugar workers have responded, have shown themselves to be—I say this sincerely—the most combative and class-conscious working group, the workers most aware of their revolutionary duties. But, at some time or another, we will all have to face up to those duties and temporarily renounce some of our privileges or rights at a given moment, for the common good. That's the job of the labor leader: to recognize that moment, to analyze and make sure that the workers' sacrifice, if it is necessary, be the smallest possible one, but at the same time, to show the worker comrades that the sacrifice is necessary and to explain why, and to make sure that everyone's convinced. A revolutionary government cannot demand sacrifices from above; they must be the result of everyone's will—of everyone's conviction.

Industrialization is built of sacrifices. A process of accelerated industrialization is no lark, and we will see this in the future. The monopolist companies already have struck a blow, or rather have shown their claws, because they have not struck yet, in the case of petroleum. The petroleum affair is something that would have marked the weakening of the revolutionary government, or its total downfall, only a few years ago. Fortunately, today there are powers who have petroleum and have absolute independence in selling that petroleum, and furthermore, have the power to deliver that petroleum wherever they sell it, no matter what power they offend.

That is, the present division of world power is what has let Cuba cross the dividing line between colonies and free nations, to gain control of her natural resources and of her basic industries.

The subsoil was not worth anything to us if we still did not know if there was any oil there, and you have got to prospect for oil, and that is very expensive. And we had to find enough power to run all our industries.

You all know that practically 90 per cent or more than 90 percent of a country's power in this day and age depends on electricity; and 90 per cent or more of electricity, in a country like Cuba, depends on petroleum. That is, petroleum was the strategic point from which a great battle had to be launched. We knew that sooner or later this battle would be launched, but we approached the foreign companies through legal channels, and they then showed us their monopolistic sovereignty, trying at that time to create a problem, just as they will try to create other, more serious problems, later.

Now I tell you that there is a power that has petroleum, which has the ships to deliver petroleum, which has the desire to deliver petroleum, and which has the power to bring it here.

If we had not had that source of petroleum, we would be facing a difficult dilemma right now. The dilemma would be either to muddle through or to return to the age of our aborigine ancestors, with a slight advance—no more—because we would have horses and mules, which they did not have, but practically all of Cuba's industries would be paralyzed. Obviously, that is an intolerable situation. I can not make myself even think of that choice. Fortunately we have another one, and we must advance.

That does not mean, not by any means, that the danger is over, that our triumph is assured, and that all we have got to do is analyze the problems of industrialization. It is not for nothing that most of you here today are in militia uniforms. Perhaps vigilance and training are more necessary now than ever, and perhaps many of us will have to die defending the Revolution. But the important thing is—and this is what it means to be a good revolutionary—that we have got to work, knowing that that moment could come and foreseeing it, but developing our work force as if that moment never would come, always thinking of the peaceful construction of the country, because we have the right to think of it, and because it is the ideal solution. If they attack, we will have to defend ourselves. If enemy bombs destroy what is rightfully ours, tough luck. After we win, we will rebuild. But today we have got to think of nothing but construction.

This leads us to analysis, to a balance sheet of what we have today, of what we have economically and politically. And we have, we can say, a revolutionary government. I do not think there is much doubt about this, that ours is a revolutionary government, that it is a government of the people and that it is fundamentally pledged to raise the level of its people's life and to create the conditions necessary for the people to achieve happiness. We also have something very important, something that has not always been emphasized: We scared off the last invasion. The first and most important thing was that the people's representatives be in the government, *then* there was a people's government. But a government needs to support itself with something, and that something is, unfortunately, an army, which you must have, a body which is parasitical—although ours, largely, is an exception,—but a body that you have got to have. If this body had been the old army, we would be in La Cabaña, if we were lucky, now. That is why it is so important that the people and the army be one and that the revolutionary government be able to count on the rebel army and on the rebel militia, fused into one.

Furthermore, we have a geographic location and an exuberant nature, which allow us an extraordinarily great development. We have unexplored mineral riches. We are, for example, the world's second largest nickel producer—or at least the second largest in the western world—and nickel travels in the head of every missile and every rocket and in the armor of every tank, and was, until recently, found in the most delicate weldings of combat aircraft. That is, it is a strategic mineral, a mineral of the future. Perhaps we have oil, and we certainly have iron—difficult to process, but we have it—and we have various other minerals. We need some, like coal, but we are looking for a way to get it.

We also have that extra ordinary source of wealth, sugar cane, and the capacity to convert all our sugar cane into a chemical sugar industry, which would be a source of inexhaustible wealth.

That is the picture of our assets. Now there are also our liabilities. In the first place, we have the same imbalance as any other underdeveloped country. We are a monoproducing country, sugar-producing, which has let its entire life revolve around one product, a country where only sugar mills and the group of importers of manufactured goods purchased with the money from those mills have flourished. But because we have governments that did not fight hard enough to sell our product but sold out to the economic system dominated by the colonial powers—by the United States in this particular case—we never looked for new markets for our sugar. Although a large part of the world eats less sugar than it might; although a large part of the world is greatly increasing its buying power and is ready to buy sugar, we were blind to reality.

We had the quota system. That system gave the latifundistas more land than was necessary. That kept agricultural technique from advancing at all, because the *latifundista* did not have to do anything but leave his fields alone, cut them once a year, give them a little attention, and on the average, renew them every seven years.

For this reason a country with Cuba's wealth, a country with Cuba's exuberance, particularly suited for sugar cane, has a completely second-class yield. That is, agricultural techniques are at a minimal level.

We also have—we all know this—to put it in the nicest way possible, an air base ninety miles from our shores, a base for all kinds of war criminals, a potential base for all kinds of aggression. It does not matter what type, from their diplomatic aggressions in this country to all kinds of paid assassins in other countries. And the level of aggression against Cuba is becoming exceedingly high. We are in the strategic heart of the Caribbean, we have a base—we could call it an enemy base—on our territory, which is constantly causing friction, which threatens to become the Maine of this age. And above all we have the dangerous honor of being the "bad example" for Latin America, because when Eisenhower takes a tour, he requires the protection of tear gas. In short, the poor president's situation is most critical.

And then our president comes, often getting a cool official reception from some nervous government functionaries, but receiving an extraordinary popular acclaim. He is our pride and our strength, but he is also, in some ways, our danger: He is the "bad example." And the colonial powers try to isolate us from other governments. It is impossible to isolate us from the people. Isolate us gradually. I think Fidel once spoke of the strategy of substituting Cuba for the Dominican Republic: Break relations gradually with the dictator; then, lo! there is a new dictator in America. Go besiege Cuba so that, at the right moment, when the fruit is ripe, you can gobble it.

That is the danger we face, our external danger, of which I was speaking. Now, we have got to move forward, no matter what political dangers we face. We have simply got to measure our economic possibilities and handicaps, and after we have measured them, after we have realized our possibilities, we must take firm steps to achieve our industrialization. Now, the first thing we have got to do is fix some sort of goal, some sort of limit to our ambitions. What are our primary goals? Our greatest goals? The great lines we must follow? From the political point of view, the first thing we want is to be masters of our own destiny, to be an independent country, a country free from foreign interference, a country that seeks out its own system of development without interference and that can trade freely anywhere in the world. And then, or perhaps earlier, much earlier, we want to improve the people's living standard, improve it as much as possible, ambitiously, but calculating the strength of our problems, and that is where we have to make distinctions.

Let us not worry about the political problem. We have made our decision, and the people support us enough so no one will bring us to our knees because of a political problem. But we have to make sure that our development does not cost the people any more than necessary. We know that people are discontented about a shortage of many everyday articles—all consumer items. Stop to realize that the colonialists taught us to use them. For instance, chewing gum or dolls—they come ready-made from the United States. We have become accustomed to having these things, and then, when they are scarce, we complain. People begin to wonder if this government is really going to raise the standard of living, or if it is going to take away such important things as chewing gum.

Naturally, there can be mistakes in all of this, because it is difficult to hit the nail exactly on the head. But what you have got to remember is that there are many luxury items and you can do without them without suffering. But now, at this moment, there are 300,000 men and women in Cuba without work. And being without work usually means going hungry. And going hungry means getting weak, being the prey of disease—to live, in a word, in misery.

We can not, and we have got to say this with absolute frankness, we can not have all the chewing gum we want, all the peaches we want, all the pear juice, newly imported in its little cans, we want and at the same time create sources of work for 300,000 unemployed and secondary sources of work for another 300,000 underemployed.

It is an enormous task. If you think of the work force, you will find that it is 2,330,000. That is, it is calculated that the work force is a third of the population. There are 300,000 unemployed, 13 percent. This would not be so bad, but there are another 300,000 underemployed. And a tragic example of this is the sugar workers, almost 300,000, who work a few months, the field workers especially, for low wages, and then they do not work for the rest of the year.

Now, the duty of our revolutionary government is, above all, in economic terms, to take care of the unemployed, in the first place; to take care of the underemployed in the second place. That is why we have fought hard against wage increases, because wage increases also mean one less man working. The nation's capital is a hard fact. We can not create it with a little printing press. The more money we create, the less that money is worth. So that capital is a single entity, and with that capital we have got to develop our country. We have to plan carefully so that each industry, each field worked, is the one that gives the most employment, because our duty is, I repeat, first of all, before anything else, to see to it that no one goes without food in Cuba; then, to see that everyone eats daily; after that, in addition to that, to see to it that everyone in Cuba dresses and lives decently; later, to see to it that everyone has the right to free medical attention and a free education.

But the first step is unemployment. That is what we have to think about, and we have to remember that saving foreign exchange is not a sport, but an overriding necessity, and that every penny saved is a penny that is going to be invested in a company that will give work. All right, I am getting a bit ahead of myself, because another question we have to ask ourselves, and of course we have already done it since you have to be systematic, is how to develop our economy, by what means?

Basically, there are two ways, which have their own variants, but there are two ways. One of them is called the free enterprise way. It used to be expressed by a French phrase, which in Spanish means "let be." All economic forces, supposedly on an equal footing, would freely compete with each other and bring about the country's development. That is what we had in Cuba, and what did it get us? I have often cited examples, because they are monstrous and show how deeply a people can enslave itself by economic means, without realizing it in the slightest.

Of course, there also was a dictatorship, but all this could have been done without any dictatorship. For example, there is a company—now in government hands—called Cubanitro. It is a company that will cost at least twenty million pesos. We will have to expand it, and it will cost much more. It is a useful company. That twenty-million-peso company was the property of a group of shareholders who had supposedly invested 400,000 pesos. However, those 400,000 pesos were lent by a bank. Thus, a man with only an idea and initiative can become the owner of a twenty-million-peso factory, can become one of Cuba's greatest millionaires overnight.

Besides that, this is a well-made factory. There were other cases where the investment was not in the factory itself, in the industrial business of producing. After all, if you give a man twenty million pesos, and he gives jobs to some workers and develops the country's industry, it is not so bad. But there were cases where the twenty million pesos were given, but the motive was not industry; the business was buying machinery. They invested eight or ten million pesos in something or other, and the rest stayed in businessmen's pockets. They did not worry about the plant. The plant was destined to go bankrupt.

The revolutionary government has had to reorganize. For example, Técnica Cubana, a paper factory which is a classic example of this, designed to do nothing but steal money out of loans. Those are two examples, on the level of the state—because it was the state's money that was loaned—on the level of free enterprise. This is, if not the picture of all industrial enterprises, the picture of all enterprises, which as they got stronger and stronger, began to make deals with the soldiers of the moment, with the politicians in power, and to gain more advantages.

Another example of free enterprise is the letter that Fidel once read from Radio Cremata, in which he told of his services to the Cuban Electric Company while he was a representative of the Cuban people. That is another example of free enterprise.

And in addition to all that, in addition to this manifest harm and this will to rob, there is the other example of free enterprise: the quantity of idle factories. Why? For two reasons: because, in the first place, those factories belong to small businessmen, petty Cuban capitalists who have to compete with the great monopolistic firms, which, when they have a competitor, simply lower their prices. In worldwide terms, which is how these firms function, it costs them very little. But a small firm goes completely broke in six months. And the other reason for those closed factories is the anarchy that we had here. In any free enterprise system, when one man starts a screw factory and business is good, his neighbor thinks that screw factories are a great business, and starts one of his own. But, at the same time, there are two more who were thinking of it and open *their* factories. The result is that all of a sudden you have four screw factories in a market that can accommodate one screw factory, and you see the result in closed factories.

Another result of free enterprise is that with that system of unemployment and that system of allowing economic forces to fight among themselves, the worker has to sell himself as a thing that works, competing against the worker next door who is also hungry, and who also sells himself. And the capitalist simply buys the cheapest merchandise: One of them is hungrier than the others, or weaker than the others, or betrays his class interests, and sells himself cheaper. That is the one who gets the job: He is the privileged one, and the one who clears the path so that the rest will have to follow him and accept those conditions. That is the other result.

Sometimes the opposite is the case. Free enterprise shows—as opposed to the state, or to the national capitalistic firms—the effectiveness and the price of a foreign monopolist firm. They pay higher salaries. They turn the worker into a privileged individual. That worker is the one who can enter a foreign company, who can receive a high salary, and who must only be loyal to that "good" company that takes a profit, like the petroleum companies for example, of thirty-odd million pesos, year after year.

I was just complaining about a Cuban who pockets twenty million pesos, but it turns out that the petroleum companies pocket thirty-four million every year, not twenty million to last a lifetime. And the electric company, yes, and the telephone company, and all those great international leeches—they have a system: slightly higher salaries.

That is the way they divide the working class. Then, right away they start to say that the people who work for those companies are special, that they have their own club, an exclusive club, and that no Negroes work *there,* because that is a white man's privilege—they have a whole series of dividing instruments. That is another of the results, and of course it is visible, because they are all palpable examples of the system that used to reign in Cuba and which they want to sell us now as the only possible and democratic system for developing the country.

But there is another system. It is the system in which we face up to ourselves and tell ourselves, "we are revolutionaries, the revolutionary government, the people's representatives." And who do we have to make these industries for, who has got to benefit, if not the people? And if the people must benefit, and we are the people's representatives, we, the government, should carry the weight and the direction of industrialization, so that there will not be any anarchy. When we need one screw factory, there will be one screw factory. When we need a machete factory, there will be *one* machete factory, not three. Let us save the nation's capital.

Besides this, when we need a basic industry, although it does not make money, although it is not the best business, we will build that great basic industry, because that is going to be the base for the entire road to industrialization.

Besides all this, we will never have to break a strike, or break up a workers' demonstration with a trick or base maneuvering, with any divisionary process. We should never reward the worker *or* the professional with a higher salary than the prevailing one, than the just one, in order to gain a social advantage or to destroy someone, because that is a nonrevolutionary procedure. But we will always try to keep the workers' salaries as high as the industry will allow, always considering full employment our first duty, and after jobs for the unemployed, more work for the underemployed.

Besides this, there is a great difference between the two types of development, free enterprise development and revolutionary development. In one of them, wealth is concentrated in the hands of a fortunate few, the friends of the government, the best wheeler-dealers. In the other, wealth is the people's patrimony. It can be developed much more quickly and can, at the same time, be unified within the total industrial panorama and place each business venture at the service of the nation's total development. There will not be any delivery of our wealth to foreign monopolies. Besides that, we will go about rescuing our stolen riches from the foreign monopolies.

Those are the basic differences between the two roads with which we are faced: the road of free enterprise, on the one hand, and the revolutionary road, on the other. We, the Cuban people, have chosen the revolutionary road. Our firms are the ones Fidel once called "People Company, Inc."

If you analyze what we have done so far, you will see that we have been faithful to this road of development. We began it the way we had to begin it, with the most timid of laws that still contributed to the people's wellbeing. We lowered electric rates, lowered rents, and cleaned up public administration. Beginning at that moment, came the law that marked the turning point in our road, because until that moment when we lowered the electric rates, the telephone rates, the rents, and cleaned up the public administration, this was what the partisans of laissez-faire, of free enterprise, asked of us. They were happy. All right, there were some that had apartment houses, and they were not happy. The Electric Company was not happy. The Telephone Company was not too happy either. But the great foreign monopolies, even they were happy. This was what they wanted, an honorable government, a popular government that would simply raise living standards a bit and have a good reputation. That would be the perfect government. You could have a government more representative of great western democracy like Figueres's, for example, because Figueres[3]

[3] José "Pepe" Figueres led a successful nationalist revolution in Costa Rica in 1948, then became President and, according to Latin American leftists, sold out to U.S. interests (ed.).

is a *latifundista,* as well as other things, but that was the ideal. Now it turns out that after this came the Agrarian Reform, and then things got complicated. In the first place there is the United Fruit Company, which you all know is directly related to the State Department of the United States. It was unhappy, to say the least.

You can see the government's decision to resolve the people's problems, not merely to talk, to be demagogic. Step by step our wealth, the public patrimony, is increasing, and with it our ability to act, now that we have the land and distribute it among the peasants and farm workers, now that the sugar cooperatives are developing our factory system on the level of the agrarian reform and on other levels and as, at the same time, we are creating the conditions necessary to incorporate all the Cuban people into the revolutionary process so they can advance united into the future. As small things, the confiscations of the property of war criminals and of fraudulent speculators, began to give the people more strength.

That is when the aggression started. Airplane attacks, bombardments of Havana. The aggression provoked new revolutionary laws: the Petroleum Law, the Mining Law. We went on advancing along this road. They threatened to suspend the quota, we signed a covenant with the Soviet Union. They cut off our credit with the banks, we signed profitable covenants with some communist countries and with others, like Japan. That is, we diversified our foreign commerce, waiting for them to strike, because anyone who knows anything about the way these people operate, ought to know that when they strike, which they will do sooner or later, it will be drastic, because the monopolies never play fair. When they see that all their chances of milking a country's resources have ended, they attack it, sometimes directly, as in the age of the Big Stick, or economically. That is why we could see, in the case of the sugar quota, that something like what happened was inevitable, because Cuba always faced the same dilemma: Either we did what we had to do and faced aggression, or we became the most representative "Figuereses" of our continent. And we always tried to keep from being "Figuereses," because that is the negation of the people's aspirations, the most bloody joke there is, to disguise yourself as a democrat. It is even better to be a Somoza, since everyone knows what he is, than to disguise yourself as a patriot, as a revolutionary, as a leftist "but moderate," as they say, to betray all the people's interests. We could never do that. We could not talk the language of revolution and chat, in the rear doorway, with the great monopolies. We have chosen a very difficult road, we believe that it is very just, and all the people have accompanied us along it.

Now, in the middle of the battle—the double battle, the battle that can come, the physical defense of our coasts, or the battle for the country's industrialization—after analyzing the problems this country has had, we discover what are the basic duties of the working class.

Of course there are many duties, but in economic terms there are three great obligations, three obligations that sometimes even conflict with the common denominator the working class has made of its aspirations and its struggles against the ruling class, because one of the great obligations of today's working class is to produce well. When I say "produce," the workers can say "that is just what the bosses said, and the more we produced, the more money we gave them, and the less they needed some comrade, and we caused the unemployment and increased concentration of wealth." That is true. That is why there is an apparent contradiction. But production right now has got to be, precisely, the production of wealth so that the state can invest more in the creation of sources of work, and it has got to be the type of production that does not cost anyone his job. We have got to invent constantly, develop popular initiative, in order to create new sources of work, sources that will demand the greatest possible development.

You know that there are several systems for evaluating an investment. There are investments, for example, of a high concentration of capital, of more than ten thousand pesos for each worker employed. In general, they yield much higher earnings. Then there are investments of a small capital concentration, which come to one or two thousand pesos per worker. That yields less profit, but it is what suits our present needs—to develop all our industries that can employ many people for a small cost. We need this first, and I emphasize it, because it is the necessary foundation for eliminating unemployment and for creating, in addition, the technical base necessary for taking our second step, which is complete industrialization.

I wanted to save this document. The comrades at CMQ gave it to me, and it is an outstanding example of what the working class should do. It is nothing more than the idea of saving the spools of all the country's typewriter ribbons, not the ribbons but their spools, to avoid having to import these items. This is another of the great duties of the working class, which is tied to the duty to produce, to save, always to develop its initiative so that not one centavo is spent unnecessarily. The wasted centavo does not help anybody, and if it is not put to work it will never help the workers. And each centavo saved is put into our foreign trade, or into the National Treasury. That is, it makes possible the development of another source of work.

Production and thrift are the basis of economic development—production and thrift, I repeat, for the benefit of the workers. You can not ask anyone to make sacrifices, to be more careful, to work harder every minute for someone else's benefit. It would be unjust to demand that. We *are* asking this wherever the state takes direct control of a factory's operation. More and more, the major factories—the ones we will build, of course—will be state-owned. The State's role will increase and the duty of the working class will increase too. But in all our privately owned industries, we must also avoid waste, take care of the machinery, because we have not been careful with the machinery.

We are, in many respects, beginning to learn. But we have learned somewhat irresponsibly, on every level. You all know very well, for example, that the drivers from La Cabaña are "dangerous." They have now learned, in the cars we took over from the hierarchy of the old regime, but they learned to drive irresponsibly. The result has been that you see some two-year-old Cadillacs that look antediluvian, all dented, all broken, all scratched. The same thing has happened with our tractors, and this is much more important, because, after all, what does it matter if we destroy a Cadillac? No new one is going to come. More money is not going to be spent. At least a Cadillac is less important. But to break down a tractor is important, because a tractor means production, and when a machine is broken through a worker's carelessness, you must repair that machine. If it is not repaired, it does not produce. You must, every one of you, pay attention and learn as much as possible.

Moreover, the third great obligation of the workers, besides producing and saving, is organizing. Organizing, not in the old sense of organizing as a class against another class, but to organize in order to give more to the Revolution, which is to give more to the people, which is to give more to the working class. Because, for example, the difference between the working class and the peasants is going to decrease until it becomes zero. There is already a group of 300,000 agricultural workers which is going to work the land with more and more mechanized methods. They are being transformed more and more into technical workers, and this is how everyone is being transformed into a worker, everyone who is directly concerned with production, and we have got to go on developing thus and thinking of the nation as a whole.

That is, we have got to do exactly the opposite of what we have been used to doing. They had us used to a circle. We could cite the union, if there was a union, and then the neighborhood, the family, and then the individual, one person, who was the most important. Sometimes you could consider your child the most important; generally you considered yourself the most important. We have got to try to do the opposite. We have got to try to consider ourselves, the individuals, the least important, the least important cogs in the machinery, but with the requirement that each cog function well. Most important is the nation. It is the entire people of Cuba, and you have got to be ready to sacrifice any individual benefit for the common good.

And thus successively, each human grouping is more important than the individual; the whole group of a sector of the working class is more important than a work center's union, and all the workers are more important than one. That is something we have got to understand. We have got to organize ourselves anew to change the old mentality.

Change the mentality of the union leader, whose job is not to shout against the boss or to set up absurd rules within the order of production, rules that sometimes lead to featherbedding. The worker who today collects his salary without earning it, without doing anything, is really conspiring against the nation and against himself.

Now, these are the three basic elements, as I see them, the three duties of the working class. For this you must have, before anything else, understanding, understanding of the problems, understanding of revolutionary development, and then specific knowledge, knowledge of the factory where you work, even more knowledge of the machine you use, and knowledge of the entire system of production. And that should be a duty and right claimed by all workers, a duty to learn, to know your machine perfectly, to repair it and to improve it if possible: your machine, your section, and the entire process of production. But in addition to being a duty, this is a right that should be demanded of your administrators.

The relationship between the workers and the administrators of the state-owned or jointly controlled factories should become ever closer, so they can exchange their experiences. It is not the same thing to direct a great, complex industrial complex, or to direct an industry, as it is to work in an industry. You see the problems in a different perspective, just as I am looking at you from here in one way, and you are looking at me in another. It is exactly the same. Workers and administrators, even today in the revolutionary government, see the problems from different perspectives. What we have to do is see to it that the administrator gets to the work bench, or that the worker rises to the administrator's desk, and the two exchange experiences and see the whole process in the same way, because then they will have seen it from all sides, and they will resolve it.

And you will see how many of the demands on labor that are still being made today will be withdrawn. There are factories that already are completely government-owned, where a worker, for example, has discovered a way to produce more with his machine, and his foreman has forbidden him to produce more. I will not say that this is a reason, but it *is* a false interpretation of the situation; it is a false interpretation of the revolutionary movement; and the first thing we have to think is that all the old modes of thought have been swept out by history, that we have to begin to think all over again and to know that we have a head on our shoulders and that we have to use it, and that we have to analyze each and every one of our problems with a clear mind.

The labor leader and the rank and file worker will then participate in the productive process and will be responsible within it. We have not been able to advance further because there are even factories where you can not discuss things, because there is a hostile syndicate, or because the workers still have not discovered the real meaning of the problem. And if the syndicate speaks with the administration, they think that the syndicate is a sellout leadership. All these things should disappear, because our job, the job of industrializing the country, the most important job of present-day Cuba, can not be done, by any means, with the will of only a few or with the genius of a few, or of one man. Our job is to see the best road and to explain it, but the people's job is to help us see that road, to cooperate with all its strength to make the march along that road a rapid one and always to correct mistakes with a constructive method.

Up until now we have only given ourselves a few goals, some of them timid enough, in order to reach them, because we are still not sure of how well the working mass will understand the importance of each problem. We have proposed, for example, to double the yearly income of each Cuban in ten years. Today each Cuban, dividing all the income in Cuba by the number of inhabitants, has an annual income of four hundred-and-some-odd pesos. If you divide 415 pesos, by the twelve months of the year, you will see what each Cuban really earns during the year, and it is very little. Of course, there are lots of women and children who do not work, but it is still little.

In ten years we intend to raise the per capita income somewhat more than nine hundred pesos. That amount, twice today's per capita, is one of the major efforts we can make, and in spite of the fact we are saying it modestly, it is something that has never been done in America. In America that would mean an annual increase in the buying power of the people, in the people's income, of some 7 percent, and in some countries of America it is increasing at 1 or 2 percent and in others it is decreasing. That is, it will be an enormously accelerated development, and it would be even more accelerated if everyone understood exactly what his duty was. I am not complaining. Certainly to achieve this would be a fabulous triumph. That is, we are going to achieve it and it will be a fabulous triumph.

Another goal we have set for ourselves demands more attention and it is that by the end of 1962, that is within exactly two and a half years, we want to eradicate unemployment in Cuba. You can not applaud that; that is nothing but a goal, and we can all applaud it if we reach it, or hiss at ourselves if we fail. But it is everybody's job, the job of the government and of the people united, and the great obligation of solidarity of everyone who has enough to eat with those who have nothing or almost nothing.

Naturally, one of so many collective jobs we have got to do is the joint administration, by workers and the government, of each business. For example, the ability of the working class and its democratically elected leaders is being tested by the hotel problem.

(Someone yells that in four days of government intervention the number of hotel guests has increased by four thousand.) Of course this initial victory is not the definitive victory. The hotels are a difficult problem, because they were built and operated in Cuba with a colonial mentality, for the tourist who came here to leave his dollars at the gambling table or in some other pleasant place. That is, for the great master who came to his Caribbean possessions to drop off a little of what those possessions gave him during the year. We should not forget that.

Now we have got to change the system, and the mentality, and the structure of the tourist trade completely. Tourists will come if they come, from the United States. The ones with enough sense and enough guts to oppose all their threats will come. In addition, [Latin] American tourists who want to see the revolutionary process close at hand will come, and moreover, those hotels should be filled with our citizens—with Cubans from all over the island, who travel across her, learning about her. That is, we must overturn the tourist system entirely, and it is not an easy job. Now, I am sure that those who will do that job best are precisely the leaders the workers have elected, in collaboration with the revolutionary government.

Some time ago, in an earlier speech, I promised, as chief of the Department of Industrialization, a mixed government system of factories. Of course we have not forgotten this. That system is still being studied. It is going a bit slowly because it is not so simple, because there are a lot of problems to be considered, but it is still being studied and within a short while it will be put in practice in all factories.

To sum up: At this moment the duties of the working class are: to produce, and remember that is to produce without unemployment, produce more, create more wealth, more wealth that will be transformed into more sources of work; to economize as much as possible, not only on the level of the state, but on whatever level a real national saving is possible; to sharpen its revolutionary vigilance to discover new resources and new ways of working which will be beneficial for the nation; to organize, organize in order to bring the greatest force to the collective task of industrialization. To do all these things requires study in order to comprehend the revolutionary process which will lead us to absolute unity and to the greatest firmness—study of the processes of production, of the level to which each worker can rise, in order, precisely, to discover the innovations that will enable us to produce more and save more.

That is my message for today.

CHAPTER 5

On Saying No! to Yankees[1]

ONCE again we are gathered together in this tribunal, which of all the revolutionary tribunals of Cuba is the one which best represents the dignity of her people, the dignity and the fighting spirit of Cuba.

At the dawn of this Revolution, when the people, having just won the battle for their liberty, were exercising revolutionary justice, their enemies, encouraged by the foreign press, attempted to diminish that justice and shorten its reach. Then, for the first time, the people gathered here said *no* to foreign intervention, and revolutionary justice took its inexorable course. At the same time it followed the course of the deepening revolution, until Cuba was converted into the vanguard of America.

It was at that moment that imperialism loosed its pack of hounds, themselves sons of this people. From Florida they pounced on a defenseless Havana, and in one single day of darkness, killed and wounded her helpless children. And once more the people came together in this tribunal to pit their militant faith against foreign intervention of any kind. The Revolution continued to grow more profound. Although they tried to halt it with increasingly severe economic measures, it continued forward despite everything. Then, once and for all, they removed their mask, revealing hidden beneath it the garrote, used so often in America. Nor did they disguise it with pretty words. They no longer even talk about freedom; now they talk about their lost prey. And they threaten more and more violently, with the impotent rage of the wild beast, who, although she has watched the gradual escape of the prey from her claws on every continent of this planet, yet she wishes to maintain in the backyards of all her colonial possessions, each and every sinecure upon which the American way of life was erected.

[1] Speech delivered before the Presidential Palace in Havana on July 10, 1960, reproduced in *Obra Revolucionaria*, Año 1960, No. 13. Translated by Beth Kurti.

North American diplomacy, crippled physically and mentally, is staggering.

Today Cuba is no longer becoming, as she was until recently, the vanguard of America. Today we hold a position of still greater danger and greater glory. Today we are practically, because of the compelling circumstances, the arbiters of world peace. The immense responsibility of the position which Cuba occupies is of tremendous importance, for the world is going too fast for the limited capacity of North American diplomacy.

We planned to gather here to proclaim once again that we could not be bowed, that to attack Cuba would mean sending a torrent of blond invaders to certain death in every house and every field on this privileged island. We have discovered, however, that the warning of the Prime Minister of the Union of Soviet Socialist Republics has changed the character of our threat. The invasion of Cuba now would signify more than the destruction of all her buildings by enemy bombs, more even than the massacre of our children, our women, and all our people by the enormous superiority of the enemy and its air power. It would also mean something else, something that must make the Northern hierarchs stop to think; it would mean that atomic rockets could erase, once and forever, the country that today incarnates colonial avariciousness.

Let them take heed, those sons of the Pentagon and of North American monopolies who until now have paraded their arrogance up and down the lands of America; let them think it over carefully. Cuba is no longer a solitary island in the middle of the ocean, defended only by the vulnerable breasts of her sons and the generous breasts of all the helpless of the world. Cuba is now, in addition, a proud Caribbean island defended by the missiles of the greatest military power in history.

But they have responded to the Soviet warning with renewed boasting. The former President of the United States was questioned at the retreat where he has spent the last trying years of what could have been a glorious life, what could have been the incarnation of democracy fighting against European fascism. He answered that, despite Soviet warnings, the United States will fulfill its duty with respect to Cuba. And we all know the nature of that duty. It is the same duty that took to account a sovereign nation, as is Mexico, for its expression of indignation at the violent and bestial economic aggression unleashed against Cuba. This duty of the United States is the same duty that compelled it to assassinate the patriot Sandino and put into power in Nicaragua the justly hated Somoza. The duty of the United States was to give arms and planes, first to Batista and then to those who continue his work. But the greatest and most brilliant of American duties has been to place and maintain in power for thirty years our "good friend" Trujillo.

Thus do the rulers of the most powerful nation of this hemisphere understand their duties. These are our "good neighbors," those who would defend us, who place a military base on our soil and pay us two thousand pesos a year for it; the sower of atomic bases on all the world's continents, the barons of oil, tin, copper, and sugar—the heirs of monopoly.

The greatest aspiration of our people is to win all our victories with the strength of our own children. We cannot rest on the laurels of others, for we do not know the lengths to which our powerful neighbors will be carried by their madness.

And if, disdaining all our admonitions, they still want to come to trample this Cuban territory, they are caught in an extraordinary new world situation. The balance of power has shifted definitively, and the forces of peace and peaceful coexistence have triumphed. The strength of these forces is increasing daily, as every day their retaliatory power becomes more and more terrible.

Yet we cannot be tranquil by any means; first, because this people won its own liberty, and each conquest of its freedom was accomplished with the sweat and work and blood of its sons. We see the risk of the whole world becoming a huge atomic bonfire, and we must be prepared for that day. If others, more powerful than we, take it upon themselves to destroy great concentrations of troops, we must be ready to destroy, in our turn, all types of physical aggression against our country. Our militias must be more vigilant than ever, our army more cautious, our entire people must be ready at all times to repel aggression, even if it does not occur. And if the shadowy danger of war passes away definitely and forever, we must remain united and vigilant in order to continue the economic battle for the right to call ourselves a free nation. We must keep working, we must keep striving to produce more and more, to be self-supporting, to achieve technical advances, to make culture more accessible to all, and to unite our people in a single column to march toward the future.

But if anyone has doubts; if anyone in this country believes all this is mere boasting in the face of the powerful ones who intend to attack us; and if even our friends think that our people are not able to withstand the approaching pressures; we must demonstrate rapidly that we are.

And today, as proof of this, as a message to all of them and also as a message to our highest leader, who is not with us today, as the total expression of the will of a people, let us raise our voices and make Fidel's radio vibrate. From every Cuban mouth a single shout: "Cuba sí, Yankees no! Cuba sí, Yankees no!"

CHAPTER 6

On Revolutionary Medicine[1]

THIS simple celebration, another among the hundreds of public functions with which the Cuban people daily celebrate their liberty, the progress of all their revolutionary laws, and their advances along the road to complete independence, is of special interest to me.

Almost everyone knows that years ago I began my career as a doctor. And when I began as a doctor, when I began to study medicine, the majority of the concepts I have today, as a revolutionary, were absent from my store of ideals.

Like everyone, I wanted to succeed. I dreamed of becoming a famous medical research scientist; I dreamed of working indefatigably to discover something which would be used to help humanity, but which signified a personal triumph for me. I was, as we all are, a child of my environment.

After graduation, due to special circumstances and perhaps also to my character, I began to travel throughout America, and I became acquainted with all of it. Except for Haiti and Santo Domingo, I have visited, to some extent, all the other Latin American countries. Because of the circumstances in which I traveled, first as a student and later as a doctor, I came into close contact with poverty, hunger, and disease; with the inability to treat a child because of lack of money; with the stupefaction provoked by continual hunger and punishment, to the point that a father can accept the loss of a son as an unimportant accident, as occurs often in the downtrodden classes of our American homeland. And I began to realize at that time that there were things that were almost as important to me as becoming a famous scientist or making a significant contribution to medical science: I wanted to help those people.

[1] Speech delivered to militiamen on August 19, 1960, reproduced in *Obra Revolucionaria,* Año 1960, No. 24. Translated by Beth Kurti.

But I continued to be, as we all continue to be always, a child of my environment, and I wanted to help those people with my own personal efforts. I had already traveled a great deal—I was in Guatemala at the time, the Guatemala of Arbenz—and I had begun to make some notes to guide the conduct of the revolutionary doctor. I began to investigate what was needed to be a revolutionary doctor.

However, aggression broke out, the aggression unleashed by the United Fruit Company, the Department of State, Foster Dulles—in reality the same thing—and their puppet, called Castillo Armas. The aggression was successful, since the people had not achieved the level of maturity of the Cuban people of today. One fine day, a day like any other, I took the road of exile, or at least, I took the road of flight from Guatemala, since that was not my country.

Then I realized a fundamental thing: For one to be a revolutionary doctor or to be a revolutionary at all, there must first be a revolution. Isolated individual endeavor, for all its purity of ideals, is of no use, and the desire to sacrifice an entire lifetime to the noblest of ideals serves no purpose if one works alone, solitarily, in some corner of America, fighting against adverse governments and social conditions which prevent progress. To create a revolution, one must have what there is in Cuba—the mobilization of a whole people, who learn by the use of arms and the exercise of militant unity to understand the value of arms and the value of this unity.

And now we have come to the nucleus of the problem we have before us at this time. Today one finally has the right and even the duty to be, above all things, a revolutionary doctor, that is to say a man who utilizes the technical knowledge of his profession in the service of the revolution and the people. But now old questions reappear: How does one actually carry out a work of social welfare? How does one unite individual endeavor with the needs of society?

We must review again each of our lives, what we did and thought as doctors, or in any function of public health, before the revolution. We must do this with profound critical zeal and arrive finally at the conclusion that almost everything we thought and felt in that past period ought to be deposited in an archive, and a new type of human being created. If each one of us expends his maximum effort toward the perfection of that new human type, it will be much easier for the people to create him and let him be the example of the new Cuba.

It is good that I emphasize for you, the inhabitants of Havana who are present here, this idea: In Cuba a new type of man is being created, whom we cannot fully appreciate here in the capital, but who is found in every corner of the country. Those of you who went to the Sierra Maestra on the twenty-sixth of July must have seen two completely unknown things. First, an army with hoes and pickaxes, an army whose greatest pride is to parade in the patriotic festivals of Oriente with hoes and axes raised, while their military comrades march with rifles. But you must have seen something even more important. You must have seen children whose physical constitutions appeared to be those of eight- or nine-year-olds, yet almost all of whom are thirteen or fourteen. They are the most authentic children of the Sierra Maestra, the most authentic offspring of hunger and misery. They are the creatures of malnutrition.

In this tiny Cuba, with its four or five television channels and hundreds of radio stations, with all the advances of modern science, when those children arrived at school for the first time at night and saw the electric light bulbs, they exclaimed that the stars were very low that night. And those children, some of whom you must have seen, are learning in collective schools skills ranging from reading to trades, and even the very difficult science of becoming revolutionaries.

Those are the new humans being born in Cuba. They are being born in isolated areas, in different parts of the Sierra Maestra, and also in the cooperatives and work centers. All this has a lot to do with the theme of our talk today, the integration of the physician or any other medical worker, into the revolutionary movement. The task of educating and feeding youngsters, the task of educating the army, the task of distributing the lands of the former absentee landlords to those who labored every day upon that same land without receiving its benefits, are accomplishments of social medicine which have been performed in Cuba.

The principle upon which the fight against disease should be based is the creation of a robust body; but not the creation of a robust body by the artistic work of a doctor upon a weak organism; rather, the creation of a robust body with the work of the whole collectivity, upon the entire social collectivity.

Some day, therefore, medicine will have to convert itself into a science that serves to prevent disease and orients the public toward carrying out its medical duties. Medicine should only intervene in cases of extreme urgency, to perform surgery or something else which lies outside the skills of the people of the new society we are creating.

The work that today is entrusted to the Ministry of Health and similar organizations is to provide public health services for the greatest possible number of persons, institute a program of preventive medicine, and orient the public to the performance of hygienic practices.

But for this task of organization, as for all the revolutionary tasks, fundamentally it is the individual who is needed. The revolution does not, as some claim, standardize the collective will and the collective initiative. On the contrary, it liberates man's individual talent. What the revolution does is orient that talent. And our task now is to orient the creative abilities of all medical professionals toward the tasks of social medicine.

We are at the end of an era, and not only here in Cuba. No matter what is hoped or said to the contrary, the form of capitalism we have known, in which we were raised, and under which we have suffered, is being defeated all over the world. The monopolies are being overthrown; collective science is scoring new and important triumphs daily. In the Americas we have had the proud and devoted duty to be the vanguard of a movement of liberation which began a long time ago on the other subjugated continents, Africa and Asia. Such a profound social change demands equally profound changes in the mental structure of the people.

Individualism, in the form of the individual action of a person alone in a social milieu, must disappear in Cuba. In the future individualism ought to be the efficient utilization of the whole individual for the absolute benefit of a collectivity. It is not enough that this idea is understood today, that you all comprehend the things I am saying and are ready to think a little about the present and the past and what the future ought to be. In order to change a way of thinking, it is necessary to undergo profound internal changes and to witness profound external changes, especially in the performance of our duties and obligations to society.

Those external changes are happening in Cuba every day. One way of getting to know the Revolution and becoming aware of the energies held in reserve, so long asleep within the people, is to visit all Cuba and see the cooperatives and the work centers which are now being created. And one way of getting to the heart of the medical question is not only to visit and become acquainted with the people who make up these cooperatives and work centers, but to find out what diseases they have, what their sufferings are, what have been their chronic miseries for years, and what has been the inheritance of centuries of repression and total submission. The doctor, the medical worker, must go to the core of his new work, which is the man within the mass, the man within the collectivity.

Always, no matter what happens in the world, the doctor is extremely close to his patient and knows the innermost depths of his psyche. Because he is the one who attacks pain and mitigates it, he performs an invaluable labor of much responsibility in society.

A few months ago, here in Havana, it happened that a group of newly graduated doctors did not want to go into the country's rural areas, and demanded remuneration before they would agree to go. From the point of view of the past it is the most logical thing in the world for this to occur; at least, so it seems to me, for I can understand it perfectly. The situation brings back to me the memory of what I was and what I thought a few years ago. [My case is the] story all over again of the gladiator who rebels, the solitary fighter who wants to assure a better future, better conditions, and to make valid the need people have of him.

But what would have happened if instead of these boys, whose families generally were able to pay for their years of study, others of less fortunate means had just finished their schooling and were beginning the exercise of their profession? What would have occurred if two or three hundred peasants had emerged, let us say by magic, from the university halls?

What would have happened, simply, is that the peasants would have run, immediately and with unreserved enthusiasm, to help their brothers. They would have requested the most difficult and responsible jobs in order to demonstrate that the years of study they had received had not been given in vain. What would have happened is what will happen in six or seven years, when the new students, children of workers and peasants, receive professional degrees of all kinds.

But we must not view the future with fatalism and separate all men into either children of the working and peasant classes or counterrevolutionaries, because it is simplistic, because it is not true, and because there is nothing which educates an honorable man more than living in a revolution. None of us, none of the first group which arrived in the Granma, who settled in the Sierra Maestra, and learned to respect the peasant and the worker living with him, had a peasant or working-class background. Naturally, there were those who had had to work, who had known certain privations in childhood; but hunger, what is called real hunger, was something none of us had experienced. But we began to know it in the two long years in the Sierra Maestra. And then many things became very clear.

We, who at first punished severely anyone who touched the property of even a rich peasant or a landowner, brought ten thousand head of cattle to the Sierra one day and said to the peasants, simply, "Eat." And the peasants, for the first time in years and years, some for the first time in their lives, ate beef.

The respect which we had had for the sacrosanct property right to those ten thousand head of cattle was lost in the course of armed battle, and we understood perfectly that the life of a single human being is worth a million times more than all the property of the richest man on earth. And we learned it; we, who were not of the working class nor of the peasant class. And are we now going to tell the four winds, we who were the privileged ones, that the rest of the people in Cuba cannot learn it also? Yes, they can learn it, and besides, the Revolution today demands that they learn it, demands that it be well understood that far more important than a good remuneration is the pride of serving one's neighbor; that much more definitive and much more lasting than all the gold that one can accumulate is the gratitude of a people. And each doctor, within the circle of his activities, can and must accumulate that vaulable treasure, the gratitude of the people.

We must, then, begin to erase our old concepts and begin to draw closer and closer to the people and to be increasingly aware. We must approach them not as before. You are all going to say, "No. I like the people. I love talking to workers and peasants, and I go here or there on Sundays to see such and such." Everybody has done it. But we have done it practicing charity, and what we have to practice today is solidarity. We should not go to the people and say, "Here we are. We come to give you the charity of our presence, to teach you our science, to show you your errors, your lack of culture, your ignorance of elementary things." We should go instead with an inquiring mind and a humble spirit to learn at that great source of wisdom that is the people.

Later we will realize many times how mistaken we were in concepts that were so familiar they became part of us and were an automatic part of our thinking. Often we need to change our concepts, not only the general concepts, the social or philosophical ones, but also sometimes, our medical concepts.

We shall see that diseases need not always be treated as they are in big-city hospitals. We shall see that the doctor has to be a farmer also and plant new foods and sow, by example, the desire to consume new foods, to diversify the Cuban nutritional structure, which is so limited, so poor, in one of the richest countries in the world, agriculturally and potentially. We shall see, then, how we shall have to be, in these circumstances, a bit pedagogical—at times very pedagogical. It will be necessary to be politicians, too, and the first thing we will have to do is not to go to the people to offer them our wisdom. We must go, rather, to demonstrate that we are going to learn with the people, that together we are going to carry out that great and beautiful common experiment: the construction of a new Cuba.

Many steps have already been taken. There is a distance that cannot be measured by conventional means between that first day of January in 1959 and today. The majority of the people understood a long time ago that not only a dictator had fallen here, but also a system. Now comes the part the people must learn, that upon the ruins of a decayed system we must build the new system which will bring about the absolute happiness of the people.

I remember that sometime in the early months of last year comrade Guillén arrived from Argentina. He was the same great poet he is today, although perhaps his books had been translated into a language or two less, for he is gaining new readers every day in all the languages of the world. But he was the same man he is today. However, it was difficult for Guillén to read his poems here, which were popular poetry, poetry of the people, because that was during the first epoch, the epoch of prejudices. And nobody ever stopped to think that for years and years, with unswerving dedication, the poet Guillén had placed all his extraordinary poetic gift at the service of the people and at the service of the cause in which he believed. People saw him, not as the glory of Cuba, but as the representative of a political party which was taboo.

Now all that has been forgotten. We have learned that there can be no divisions due to the different points of view of certain internal structures of our country if we have a common enemy and a common goal. What we have to agree upon is whether or not we have a common enemy and whether or not we are attempting to reach a common goal.

By now we have become convinced that there definitely is a common enemy. No one looks over his shoulder to see if there is anyone who might overhear—perhaps some agent from the embassy who would transmit the information—before giving an opinion against monopolies, before saying clearly, "Our enemy, and the enemy of all America, is the monopolistic government of the United States of America." If now everyone knows that is the enemy, and it is coming to be known also that anyone who fights against that enemy has something in common with us, then we come to the second part. Here and now, for Cuba, what are our goals? What do we want? Do we or do we not want the happiness of the people? Are we, or are we not fighting for the total economic liberation of Cuba?

Are we or are we not struggling to be a free nation among free nations, without belonging to any military bloc, without having to consult the embassy of any great power on earth about any internal or external measure that is going to be taken here? If we plan to redistribute the wealth of those who have too much in order to give it to those who have nothing; if we intend to make creative work a daily, dynamic source of all our happiness, then we have goals toward which to work. And anyone who has the same goals is our friend. If he has other concepts besides, if he belongs to some organization or other, those are minor matters.

In moments of great danger, in moments of great tensions and great creations, what count are great enemies and great goals. If we are already agreed, if we all know now where we are going—and let him grieve to whom it will cause grief—then we have to begin our work.

I was telling you that to be a revolutionary you have first to have a revolution. We already have it. Next, you have to know the people with whom you are going to work. I think that we are not yet well acquainted, that we still have to travel a while on that road. You ask me what are the vehicles for getting to know the people besides the vehicle of going into the interior, of observing the cooperatives, of living in the cooperatives and working in them. Not everyone can do this, and there are many places where the presence of a medical worker is very important. I would say that the revolutionary militias are one of the great manifestations of the solidarity of the Cuban people. Militias now give a new function to the doctor and prepare him for what was, until a short time ago, a sad and almost fatal reality for Cuba, namely, that we were going to be the victim of an armed attack of great breadth.

I ought to warn you that the doctor, in that function of soldier and revolutionary, should always be a doctor. You should not commit the same error which we committed in the Sierra. Or maybe it was not an error, but all the medical comrades of that period know about it. It seemed dishonorable to us to remain at the side of a wounded man or a sick one, and we looked for any way possible of grabbing a rifle and going to prove on the battlefront what we could do.

Now the conditions are different, and the new armies which are being formed to defend the country must be armies with different tactics. The doctor will have an enormous importance within the plan of the new army. He must continue being a doctor, which is one of the most beautiful tasks there is and one of the most important in war. And not only the doctor, but also the nurses, laboratory technicians, all those who dedicate themselves to this very human profession, are of the utmost importance.

Although we know of latent danger and are preparing ourselves to repel the aggression which still exists in the atmosphere, we must stop thinking about it. If we make war preparations the center of our concern, we will not be able to devote ourselves to creative work. All the work and all the capital invested in preparing for a military action is wasted work and wasted money. Unfortunately, we have to do it, because there are others who are preparing themselves. But it is—and I say this in all honesty, on my honor as a soldier—the truth is that the outgoing money which most saddens me as I watch it leave the vault of the National Bank is the money that is going to pay for some weapon.

Nevertheless, the militias have a function in peacetime; the militias should be, in populous centers, the tool which unifies the people. An extreme solidarity should be practiced, as I have been told it is practiced in the militias of the doctors. In time of danger they should go immediately to solve the problems of the poor people of Cuba. But the militias offer also an opportunity to live together, joined and made equal by a uniform, with men of all the social classes of Cuba.

If we medical workers—and permit me to use once again a title which I had forgotten some time ago—are successful, if we use this new weapon of solidarity, if we know the goals, know the enemy, and know the direction we have to take, then all that is left for us to know is the part of the way to be covered each day. And that part no one can show us; that part is the private journey of each individual. It is what he will do every day, what he will gather from his individual experience, and what he will give of himself in the exercise of his profession, dedicated to the well-being of the people.

Now that we have all the elements for our march toward the future, let us remember the advice of Martí. Although at this moment I am ignoring it, one should follow it constantly. "The best way of telling is doing." Let us march, then, toward Cuba's future.

CHAPTER 7

"We Are Practical Revolutionaries"[1]

CUBA'S is a unique Revolution, which some people maintain contradicts one of the most orthodox premises of the revolutionary movement, expressed by Lenin: "Without a revolutionary theory there is no revolutionary movement." It would be suitable to say that revolutionary theory, as the expression of a social truth, surpasses any declaration of it; that is to say, even if the theory is not known, the revolution can succeed if historical reality is interpreted correctly, and if the forces involved are utilized correctly. Every revolution always incorporates elements of very different tendencies, which nevertheless coincide in action and in the revolution's most immediate objectives.

It is clear that if the leaders have an adequate theoretical knowledge prior to the action, they can avoid trial and error whenever the adopted theory corresponds to the reality.

The principal actors of this revolution had no coherent theoretical criteria; but it cannot be said that they were ignorant of the various concepts of history, society, economics, and revolution which are being discussed in the world today.

Profound knowledge of reality, a close relationship with the people, the firmness of the liberator's objective, and the practical revolutionary experience gave to those leaders the chance to form a more complete theoretical concept.

The foregoing should be considered as introduction to the explication of this curious phenomenon which has intrigued the entire world: the Cuban Revolution. It is a deed worthy of study in contemporary world history: the how and the why of a group of men who, shattered by an army

[1] *Verde Olivo*, October 8, 1960. Translated by Saul Landau and John Gerassi. Excerpts from this translation were published in *Studies on the Left*, Vol. 1, No. 3, 1960, and permission to reprint is herewith gratefully acknowledged to James Weinstein.

enormously superior in technique and equipment, first managed to survive, soon became strong, later became stronger than the enemy in the battle zones, still later moved into new zones of combat, and finally defeated that enemy on the battlefield, even though their troops were still very inferior in number.

Naturally, we who often do not show the requisite concern for theory will not run the risk of expounding the truth of the Cuban Revolution as though we were its masters. We will simply try to give the bases from which one can interpret this truth. In fact, the Cuban Revolution must be separated into two absolutely distinct stages: that of the armed action up to January 1, 1959, and the political, economic, and social transformations since then.

Even these two stages deserve further subdivisions; however, we will not take them from the viewpoint of historical exposition, but from the viewpoint of the evolution of the revolutionary thought of its leaders through their contact with the people. Incidentally, here one must introduce a general attitude toward one of the most controversial terms of the modern world: Marxism. When asked whether or not we are Marxists, our position is the same as that of a physicist or a biologist when asked if he is a "Newtonian," or if he is a "Pasteurian."

There are truths so evident, so much a part of people's knowledge, that it is now useless to discuss them. One ought to be "Marxist" with the same naturalness with which one is "Newtonian" in physics, or "Pasteurian" in biology, considering that if facts determine new concepts, these new concepts will never divest themselves of that portion of truth possessed by the older concepts they have outdated. Such is the case, for example, of Einsteinian relativity or of Planck's "quantum" theory with respect to the discoveries of Newton. They take nothing at all away from the greatness of the learned Englishman. Thanks to Newton, physics was able to advance until it had achieved new concepts of space. The learned Englishman provided the necessary stepping-stones for them.

The advances in social and political science, as in other fields, belong to a long historical process whose links are connecting, adding up, molding, and constantly perfecting themselves. In the origin of peoples, there exist a Chinese, Arab, or Hindu mathematics. Today mathematics has no frontiers. In the course of history there was a Greek Pythagoras, an Italian Galileo, an English Newton, a German Gauss, a Russian Lobatchevsky, an Einstein, etc. Thus in the field of social and political sciences, from Democritus to Marx, a long series of thinkers added their original investigations and accumulated a body of experience and of doctrines.

The merit of Marx is in suddenly producing a qualitative change in the history of social thought. He interprets history, understands its dynamics, predicts the future, but in addition to predicting it (which would satisfy his scientific obligation), he expresses a revolutionary concept: The world must not only be interpreted, it must be transformed. Man ceases to be the slave and tool of his environment and converts himself into the architect of his own destiny. At that moment Marx puts himself in a position where he becomes the necessary target of all who have a special interest in maintaining the old—similar to Democritus before him, whose work was burned by Plato and his disciples, the ideologues of Athenian slave aristocracy. Beginning with the revolutionary Marx, a political group with concrete ideas establishes itself. Basing itself on the giants, Marx and Engels, and developing through successive steps with personalities like Lenin, Stalin, Mao Tse-tung, and the new Soviet and Chinese rulers, it establishes a body of doctrine and, let us say, examples to follow.

The Cuban Revolution takes up Marx at the point where he himself left science to shoulder his revolutionary rifle. And it takes him up at that point, not in a revisionist spirit, of struggling against that which follows Marx, of reviving "pure" Marx, but simply because up to that point Marx, the scientist, placed himself outside of the history he studied and predicted. From then on Marx the revolutionary could fight within history. We, practical revolutionaries, initiating our own struggle, simply fulfill laws foreseen by Marx, the scientist. We are simply adjusting ourselves to the predictions of the scientific Marx as we travel this road of rebellion, struggling against the old structure of power, supporting ourselves in the people for the destruction of this structure, and having the happiness of this people as the basis of our struggle. That is to say—and it is well to emphasize this once again—the laws of Marxism are present in the events of the Cuban Revolution, independently of what its leaders profess or fully know of those laws from a theoretical point of view. Those events began before the landing of the "Granma," and continued long after, and included the landing itself, the setting up of the second guerrilla column, the third and the fourth, the invasion of the Sierra de Cristal, the establishment of the second front, the general strike of April and its failure, the setback of the great offensive, and the invasion of Las Villas.

Each of those brief historical moments in the guerrilla warfare framed distinct social concepts and distinct appreciations of the Cuban reality; they outlined the thought of the military leaders of the Revolution—those who in time would also take their position as political leaders.

Before the landing of the "Granma," a mentality predominated that to some degree might be called "subjectivist": blind confidence in a rapid popular explosion; enthusiasm and faith in the power to liquidate the Batista regime by a swift, armed uprising combined with spontaneous revolutionary strikes and the subsequent fall of the dictator. The movement was the direct heir of the Orthodox party, and its main slogan was "Shame Against Money," that is to say, administrative honesty as the principal concern of the new Cuban Government.

And yet, in *History Will Absolve Me,* Fidel Castro had noted the bases which the Revolution has now almost totally established, but which have also been surpassed by it, as the Revolution has affected the economy more and more profoundly, and this in turn has brought about a similar deepening of the revolutionary process in the political field, with obvious national and international consequences.

After the landing came the defeat, the almost total destruction of the forces, and their regrouping and integration as guerrillas. Characteristic of those few survivors, imbued with the spirit of struggle, was the understanding that to count upon spontaneous outbursts throughout the island was a deception, an illusion. They understood also that the fight would have to be a long one, and that it would need vast *campesino* participation. At this point, the *campesinos* entered the guerrilla war for the first time. Two forces—hardly important in terms of the number of combatants, but of great psychological value—were unveiled. First, the antagonism that the city people, who comprised the central guerrilla group, felt toward the *campesinos* was erased. The *campesinos* had distrusted the group and, above all, feared the barbarous reprisals of the government. Two facts revealed themselves at this stage, both very important for the interrelated factors: to the *campesinos,* the bestialities of the army and all the persecution would not be sufficient to put an end to the guerrilla war, even though the army was certainly capable of liquidating the *campesinos*' homes, crops, and families. To take refuge with those in hiding was a good solution. In turn, the guerrilla fighters learned the necessity, each time more pointed, of winning over the *campesino* masses, which required, obviously, that they be offered something they desired very much. And there was nothing that a *campesino* sought more than land.

After that came a nomadic stage in which the rebel army kept gaining zones of influence. It could not remain in these areas for any length of time, but then, neither could the enemy. As a result of a series of combats a rather fluid front was mapped. Then, on May 28, 1957, at Ubero, an attack was launched against a well-armed, well-situated garrison, which had ready access to reinforcements, due to its position by the sea and its airport. The rebel victory was very costly: some 30 per cent of the rebel forces were killed or wounded. But it showed that the forces could sweep down from the mountains and wage successful battles in the fields, that they could come after the enemy rather than wait for it to pursue them.

Shortly thereafter, the first segregation took place, and a second rebel column was organized. It went into combat immediately. The two columns attacked Estrada Palma the twenty-sixth of July, and five days later, Bueycito, which is thirty kilometers away. From then on the battles were more important. We were beginning to stand firm against enemy counterattacks. We resisted all its attempts to penetrate into the Sierra. And we maintained our vast front areas.

In the process the guerrillas were now gaining strength from local *campesinos,* and some recruits from the cities. This led us to develop new columns still, and from February 1958 on, these columns began to take the over-all offensive. Column number three, led by Almeida, reached close to Santiago, while number six, named in honor of Frank País, who had died a few months earlier, and led by Raúl Castro, managed to cross the main highway in the first few days of March and established itself in the hills around Mayarí, there creating the Second Oriental Front, "Frank País."

Our successes became known, as they filtered through government censorship, and the people of Cuba began to look forward, for the first time, to a rebel victory. It is then that from Havana the idea of a nationwide struggle was discussed, specifically developing the idea of a general revolutionary strike.

The function of the rebel army would then be mainly one of an "irritating thorn," or catalyst, for the over-all struggle. In those days, our guerrillas became increasingly more daring and successful, and it is then that the heroic legend of Camilo Cienfuegos was born, as his column went into combat, successfully, in the lowlands of Oriente for the first time—under strict central orders.

Nevertheless, the general strike was badly organized and planned, for it did not take into account the workers' own struggle, their unity, or their concept of revolutionary activity. The general call for the strike was launched over a clandestine radio, but the specific date, to be kept secret until the last minute, was to be announced by word-of-mouth, and this manner of communication was not capable of reaching all the people. The strike not only failed, but many valiant and dedicated revolutionary leaders were gunned down in the process.

As an example of what went wrong—and someone should one day investigate this curious fact—Jules Dubois, the spokesman for North American monopolies, knew ahead of time the day when the strike was to start.

In any case, the failure of the strike made it clear that only through armed struggle could the government be toppled. It became imperative, therefore, that such a struggle be accelerated and intensified and that it lead to the final confrontation and defeat of the government forces on the field of battle.

By then, of course, we had established close bonds with the *campesinos.* In the liberated areas we had established a rebel administration, with civil and penal codes. We set up a judicial system, distributed foodstuffs, and levied taxes. Neighboring zones also felt our influence, and in the next two months we waged three major offensives, which caused a thousand deaths among the enemy, completely demoralizing it, which increased our strength from new volunteers by six hundred actual fighters.

It was then clear that we could not be defeated; every path in Oriente became a sieve for enemy casualties. All counteroffensives by the enemy failed. And then, Camilo Cienfuegos, leading column number two, and I, in charge of column number eight, named for another hero of our revolution, Antonio Maceo, were ordered to cross the province of Camaguey in order to establish ourselves in Las Villas and thus cut the enemy's communication lines.

This task changed the correlation of forces, as our two small columns, which included 80 and 140 men, crossed during a month and a half, the lowlands of Camaguey, while constantly surrounded or combatting an army numbering thousands of men. We made it, and went on to cut the island in half.

It may seem strange, incomprehensible, and even incredible that two columns of such small size—without communications, without mobility, without the most elemental arms of modern warfare—could fight against well-trained, and above all, well-armed troops. Basic was the characteristic of each group: The more uncomfortable the guerrilla fighter is, and the more he is initiated into the rigors of nature, the more he feels himself at home; his morale is higher; his sense of security, greater. At the same time he has learned to risk his life in every circumstance that might arise, to trust it to luck like a tossed coin. In general, as a result of this kind of combat, it matters little to the individual guerrilla whether or not he survives.

The enemy soldier in the Cuban example which at present concerns us, is the junior partner of the dictator; he is the man who gets the last crumbs left by a long line of profiteers that begins in Wall Street and ends with him. He is disposed to defend his privileges, but he is disposed to defend them only to the degree that they are important to him. His salary and his pension are worth some suffering and some dangers, but they are never worth his life: If the price of maintaining them will cost it, he is better off giving them up; that is to say, withdrawing from the face of guerrilla danger. From these two concepts and these two moralities springs the difference which would cause the crisis of December 31, 1958, Batista's downfall.

Meanwhile, the superiority of the rebel army became clearly evident, as did, with our arrival in Las Villas, the popularity of the 26th of July Movement with everyone: the revolutionary directorate, the second front of Las Villas, the Popular Socialist party, and even some small guerrilla bands of the Authentic Organization. This was due in great part to the magnetic personality of our leader, Fidel Castro, but also to the just cause of our revolutionary line.

Here ended the insurrection. But the men who arrived in Havana after two years of arduous struggle in the mountains and plains of Oriente, in the lowlands of Camaguey, and in the mountains, plains, and cities of Las Villas, were not the same men, ideologically, who landed on the beaches of Las Coloradoas, or who took part in the first phase of the struggle. Their distrust of the *campesino* had been converted into affection and respect for his virtues; their total ignorance of life in the country has been converted into a knowledge of the needs of our *guajiros;* their flirtations with statistics and with theory have been solidified by the cement which is practice.

With the banner of agrarian reform, the execution of which began in the Sierra Maestra, these men confronted imperialism. They knew that the agrarian reform was the basis upon which the new Cuba must build itself. They also knew that the agrarian reform would give land to all the dispossessed, and that it would dispossess its unjust possessors; and they knew that the greatest of the unjust possessors were also influential men in the State Department or in the government of the United States of America. But they had learned to conquer difficulties with bravery, with audacity, and above all, with the support of the people; and they had now seen the future of liberation which awaited us on the other side of our sufferings.

To reach these conclusions, we traveled far and we changed a lot. As our armed struggle changed qualitatively in the course of actual battle, so too did the social composition of the guerrillas and the ideological understanding of our leaders. This happened inevitably, because each battle, each confrontation, broadens, widens and therefore changes its participants. And this is the revolutionary process, to mature from each event. The *compesino* learns to believe in his own vigor. He gives the revolutionary army his capacity to suffer, his knowledge of the terrain, his love of the land, his hunger for the agrarian reform. The intellectual, of whatever type, throws in his mite, beginning to mold the theoretical framework on this knowledge. The worker contributes his sense of organization, of unity. Above all these, there is the rebel army, which proves to be much more than just an "irritating thorn," but on the contrary contributes the most important lesson, leading the masses to experience it, that all men can get rid of their fear of torment.

Never before was the concept of interaction so clear to us. We could feel with our bones how this concept deepened and matured in us, teaching us the value of armed insurrection, the strength that any man has when, with a weapon in his hand and the will to win in his heart, he confronts other men who are out to destroy him. And we learned from the *campesinos* that there is no limit to the efforts, to the sacrifices that we can all make when we are fighting for the destiny of the people.

Thus, when bathed in *campesino* sweat, with a horizon of mountains and clouds, beneath the radiant sun of the island, the rebel chief and his men entered Havana, a new "history climbed from the winter's garden with the feet of the people."

CHAPTER 8

The Sin of the Revolution[1]

REVOLUTIONS, accelerated radical social changes, are made of circumstances; not always, almost never, or perhaps never can science predict their mature form in all its detail. They are made of passions, of man's fight for social vindication, and are never perfect. Neither was ours. It committed errors and some of these were paid for dearly. Today we know of another error, which did not have repercussions, but which demonstrates how true are the popular sayings, "water seeks its own level," and "birds of a feather flock together."

When the invasion troops, in pain, their feet bloodied and festering due to sharp grasses, with only their faith still intact, reached the tributaries of the Escambray after forty-five days of marching, an unusual letter caught up with them. It was signed by Comandante Carrera and it informed the column of the revolutionary army under my command that it was not allowed to go to the Escambray without making its purpose very clear. Before going on, I was to stop in order to explain my actions to him. Threatened with encirclement every day, we were supposed to halt in open ground—in our condition!—from which we were able to escape only by the rapidity of our movement! This was the essence of a long and insolent letter. We continued forward, surprised and saddened because we had not expected this from those who were supposed to be our comrades in arms. But we were determined to resolve any problem by complying with the orders of Fidel Castro, commander in chief, who had clearly ordered that we work toward the unity of all combatants.

We arrived at the Escambray and camped near Del Obispo peak, which can be seen from the city of Sancti Spíritus, and which has a cross on its summit. There we were able to establish our first base, and immediately we

[1] *Verde Olivo*, February 12, 1961, Año 2, No. 6. Translated by Morton Marks and Robert Novick.

went to look for a house where one of the most precious articles to a guerrilla was supposed to be waiting for us: shoes. There were no shoes. They had been taken by the forces of the second Escambray front, in spite of the fact that they had been obtained by the 26th of July Organization. Everything boded ill. Nevertheless, we managed to stay calm and spoke with a captain, of whom we later learned that he had killed four soldiers of the people who had wished to go to take their place in the revolutionary ranks of the 26th of July Movement and abandon the second front of Escambray. We also had an interview, unfriendly but not stormy, with Comandante Carrera. He had already drunk half a bottle of liquor, which was approximately half his daily quota. Personally, he was not as gross and aggressive as in his letter of a few days earlier, but we sensed that he was an enemy.

Later we met Comandante Peña, famous in the region for his raids on the peasants' cows. He emphatically refused to permit us to attack Güinía de Miranda because the town was in his zone. We argued with him that the zone belonged to all, that it was necessary to fight, and that we had more and better arms and more experience. He simply told us that our bazooka was balanced by his two hundred shotguns, that two hundred shotguns had the same fire power as one bazooka. Finally, he said, Güinía de Miranda was scheduled to be taken by the second front, and we could not attack. Naturally we did not pay any attention, but we knew that we were facing dangerous "allies."

After many offenses, too many to enumerate, by which our patience was put to the test infinite times, and because of which we endured more than was fitting, in accordance with the correct line of comrade Fidel, we arrived at a "modus vivendi" by which we were permitted to institute the agrarian reform in the zone belonging to the second front, but they would continue to collect tribute. Collect tribute—the order of the day!

This story is long. We occupied the major cities of the country after a long and bloody struggle. We counted on the Revolutionary Directorate as good allies. Those men, smaller in numbers and less experienced, did all they could to contribute to our common success. On the first of January there appeared a revolutionary order which required that all fighting forces come under my command at Santa Clara. The second national front of Escambray, by command of their leader, Gutiérrez Menoyo, was placed under my orders. There were no problems. We then gave the order that they wait for us because we had to settle the civilian affairs of the first large liberated city.

In those days it was difficult to control things, and before we knew what had happened, the second front, behind Camilo Cienfuegos, had "heroically" entered Havana. We thought that this could be a maneuver [by the guerrillas of the second front] to try to strengthen themselves, to take a position, to speed things. We already knew what they were like, but each day we got to know them even better. They effectively took the most strategic positions, according to their way of thinking. In a few days the first bill arrived from the Hotel Capri for $15,000 for food and drink for a small number of hangers-on. It was signed by Fleitas.

When the time came for giving out commissions, almost a hundred captains and a good number of comandantes aspired to state sinecures. This was in addition to a large and "select" nucleus of men presented by the inseparable pair of Menoyo and Fleitas, who wanted a whole series of posts in the state apparatus. They were not extremely remunerative jobs, but they all had one characteristic: They were the positions in which, in the prerevolutionary regime, one could steal. Assessors, tax collectors, all the places where money would pass through their avid fingers were the goal of their desires. This was a part of the rebel army with which we had to live.

From the first days serious differences arose which at times culminated in an exchange of violent words; but always our proper revolutionary wisdom prevailed, and we gave way for the sake of unity. We maintained the principle. We did not allow any stealing, nor did we give key posts to those who we knew had treachery on their minds. However, we did not eliminate them; we temporized—all for the benefit of a unity which was not properly understood. This was a *sin of the Revolution*.

This was the same sin that paid off very well for the Barquíns, Felipe Pazos, Teté Casuso, and so many more sinecure holders whom the Revolution kept on to avoid confrontation, trying to buy their cooperation with a tacit understanding between those who were paid off and a government which they were waiting for the right moment to betray. But the enemy had more money and more methods of subverting the people. After all, what could we offer to people like Fleitas and Menoyo, except a job demanding work and sacrifice?

Those men, who lived off the legend of a struggle, in which they did not participate, deceiving the people, looking out for jobs, trying always to be where money was, pushing into all the ministerial cabinets, deprecated by all true revolutionaries, these men were an insult to our revolutionary consciences. Constantly, by their presence, they showed us our sin—the sin of compromise in the face of the lack of revolutionary spirit, in the face of the actual or potential traitor, in the face of those weak in spirit, in the face of the coward, in the face of the bully.

Our conscience has been cleansed now because they have gone in boats to Miami. Thank you, "bully boys" of the second front. Many thanks for relieving us of the execrable presence of makeshift comandantes; of captains of jest; of heroes ignorant of the rigors of campaigns but not of the easy shelter of peasants' houses. Thanks for giving us this lesson, for showing us that one cannot buy consciences with favors from the revolution. This lesson is strict and exacting for all. Thanks for showing us that we must be inflexible in the face of error, weakness, deceit, bad faith; that we must stand up to denounce and punish wherever we find any vice which sullies the high principles of the Revolution.

Let the example of the second front; let the example of our beloved and good friend, the thief Prío, remind us of reality. It is no shame to call a thief a thief, because we ourselves, in honor of that which we conveniently christened "revolutionary tactics," called the thief "ex-president," when the "ex-president" was not calling us despicable communists, as he does now, but rather saviors of Cuba.

The thief is a thief, and he shall die a thief; at least, a cunning thief, not one who in some countries, in desperation, must snatch a crumb in order to feed his children. The other—he who robs to obtain drugs, women, or liquor, in order to satisfy his base animal instincts—shall be a thief all his *life*.

There they are together, those who bruise our conscience: the Felipe Pazoses, who sell their honor to the highest bidder in order to be placed in charge of "serious" institutions; the Rufo Lópezes or Justo Carilloses who danced in order to "accommodate" themselves to the situation and find a fast way to the top; the Miró Cardonases, eternal optimists, incorrigible thieves involved in killing the people, the "tough guys" whose "exploits" were enacted among the peasants they killed in Escambray, spreading a terror even greater than that of the rural police. They are our conscience. They point out to us our sin, a sin of the Revolution, which must not be repeated. This is the lesson we must learn.

Revolutionary conduct is the mirror of revolutionary faith, and when someone calls himself a revolutionary and does not act as one, he can be nothing more than heretical. Let them hang together, Venturas and Tony Varonas, who squabbled among each other, the Príos and the Batistas, Guitiérrez Menoyos and Sánchez Mosqueras—assassins who killed in order to satisfy their greed, and who did so in the name of freedom. Thieves and sellers of honor, opportunists of every kind, candidates for the presidency—what a bunch!

How much they have taught us! Thanks a lot.

CHAPTER 9

Cuba—Exception or Vanguard?[1]

The working class is the creative class; the working class produces what material wealth exists in a country. And while power is not in their hands, while the working class allows power to remain in the hands of the landlords who exploit them, in the hands of the speculators, in the hands of the monopolies, in the hands of foreign and national interest groups, while armaments are in the hands of those in the service of these interest groups and not in their own hands, the working class will be forced to lead a miserable existence no matter how many crumbs those interest groups should let fall from their banquet table.

—FIDEL CASTRO

NEVER in America had an event taken place of such extraordinary character, such deep roots, and such transcendental consequences for the destiny of the continent's progressive movements as our revolutionary war. This is true to such an extent that it has been appraised by some as the decisive event to occur in America, on a scale of importance second only to the great trilogy of the Russian Revolution, the victory over Nazi Germany and the subsequent social transformations, and the victory of the Chinese Revolution.

Our Revolution, which has been heterodox in its forms and manifestations, has nevertheless followed the general lines of all the great historical events of this century characterized by anticolonial struggles and the transition toward socialism.

Nevertheless, some groups, whether out of self-interest or in good faith, have claimed to see in our revolutionary war a series of exceptional qualities whose relative importance in the general social and historical context they tend to overstress to the point of making them determining factors. People point out the distinctiveness of the Cuban Revolution when they

[1] *Verde Olivo*, April 9, 1961, Año 2, No. 14. Translated by Fernando Alegría.

compare it with the lines of other progressive parties of America, and they affirm, as a consequence, that the forms and the paths of the Cuban Revolution are unique, and that in other American countries the historical transitions will be different.

Admittedly there were exceptions which give the Cuban Revolution its particular characteristics. It seems to be a clearly established fact that in every revolution there are specific factors, but it is no less true that all revolutions will follow certain general laws whose violation is not within the reach of a particular society's possibilities. Let us analyze, then, the factors which constitute the supposed distinctiveness of the Cuban Revolution.

The first and possibly the most important and original factor is Fidel Castro Ruz, whose name in but a few years has reached historical proportions. The future will provide the definitive appraisal of our Prime Minister's merits, but to us, his contemporaries, he is comparable to Latin America's greatest historical figures. What are the exceptional circumstances which surround Fidel Castro? There are various qualities in his life and in his character which make him stand out dramatically from his comrades and followers. Fidel is a man of such great personal qualities that in whatever movement he participates he takes command. In effect this is what he had done throughout his career, from his student days to the premiership of our country and to the position of spokesman for the oppressed peoples of America. He has the qualities of a great leader, which when added to his audacity, strength, courage, and untiring perseverance in discovering the will of the people, have taken him to the place of honor and personal sacrifice which he occupies today. He has other important qualities, such as a capacity to assimilate knowledge and experiences quickly, to understand the totality of a given situation without losing sight of details, an unbounded faith in the future, and a breadth of vision which allows him to see further and more accurately into the future than his comrades. With these qualities, with his capacity to unite, to oppose debilitating divisions, to lead all the actions of the people, with his love of the people, his faith in the future, and his capacity to predict it, Fidel Castro did more than anyone else in Cuba to create out of nothingness the formidable apparatus which today is the Cuban Revolution.

Nevertheless, no one would affirm that in Cuba there were special political or social conditions which differed totally from those in other Latin American countries, or that these differences accounted for the triumph of the Revolution. Neither would one affirm that in spite of these differences Fidel Castro made the Revolution. Fidel, a great and able leader, directed the Revolution in Cuba. He chose the form and the moment by interpreting the profound political undercurrents which predisposed and prepared the people for the great leap toward revolutionary paths. There were also certain conditions which were not unique to Cuba, but of which it will be difficult for other people to take advantage, because imperialism, unlike some progressive groups, learns from its mistakes.

The condition we might label exceptional is that North American imperialism was disoriented and failed to fathom the genuinely far-reaching aspects of the Cuban Revolution. This partly explains many of the apparent contradictions of the so-called North American "fourth power." The monopolies, as is common in these cases, began to think of a successor to Batista precisely because they knew that the people were opposed to him and were looking for a leader of revolutionary mind. What more intelligent stroke than to depose the unserviceable dictator and replace him with the new "boys" who would, in good time, serve the interests of imperialism? Imperialism repeatedly played this card from its continental deck, and lost pitifully. Before our triumph they suspected us, but they did not fear us. Emissaries of the State Department went several times, disguised as reporters, to penetrate into the depths of the mountain Revolution, but they failed to diagnose any symptoms of imminent danger. When imperialism was ready to react, when it realized that the group of inexperienced young men who marched in triumph through the streets of Havana had a clear view of their political duty and an unrelenting will to fulfill that duty, it was already too late. And thus, in January of 1959, the first social Revolution of the Caribbean and the most profound of all the American revolutions was born.

We do not believe one can consider exceptional the fact that the bourgeoisie, or at least a good part of the bourgeoisie, favored the revolutionary war against the tyranny at the same time that it supported and promoted movements to find negotiated solutions which would permit them to replace the Batista government with elements disposed to put a brake on the Revolution.

Taking into account the conditions in which the revolutionary war broke out and the complexity of the political tendencies which opposed the tyranny, neither is it exceptional that some big landowning elements adopted a neutral attitude, or at least a nonbelligerent attitude, toward the forces of the insurrection.

It is understandable that the national bourgeoisie, oppressed by imperialism and by a tyranny whose troops pillaged their holdings, should look with sympathy when the young rebels of the mountains punished the armed servants of imperialism who composed the mercenary army.

Thus nonrevolutionary forces aided the coming of revolutionary power.

Analyzing further, we can add another distinctive factor, which is that in the majority of districts of Cuba the peasant had been progressively proletarianized by the demands of large-scale, semimechanized, capitalist farming and had entered upon a new level of organization which gave him a greater class consciousness. We should mention this. But we should also point out that in the primary territorial area of the rebel army, made up of the survivors of the destroyed column which made the "Granma" voyage, the peasantry had different social and cultural roots from those found in the areas of large-scale, semimechanized Cuban farming. The Sierra Maestra, which was the scene of the first revolutionary settlement, is a place where the peasants who had fought against the large landholders took refuge. They went there to find a new parcel of land which they snatched from the state or from some voracious landholder in the hope of making a little money. They struggled perpetually against the demands of the soldiers allied to the large landholding power, and their horizon was limited to the hope of securing a property title. The soldier who integrated our first peasant guerrilla army came from the section of this social class which is more aggressive in its love and posession of the land, that is, which is most strongly imbued with *petit bourgeois* spirit. The peasant struggles because he wants land for himself, for his children; he wants to till it, to profit from it, and enrich himself through his labor.

Despite his *petit bourgeois* spirit, the peasant quickly learns that he cannot satisfy his desire to possess land without first destroying the large landholding system. Radical agrarian reform, the only type which can give land to the peasant, collides directly with the interests of the imperialists, large landholders, and sugar and ranching magnates. The bourgeoisie is afraid of colliding with those interests. The proletariat is not. Thus the process of the revolution unites the workers and the peasants. The workers support the demands made against the large landholders. The poor peasant, given control of the land, loyally supports revolutionary power and defends it against imperialist and counterrevolutionary enemies.

There do not seem to be any other exceptional factors. We have been generous to extend them this far. Now let us look at the permanent roots of all the social phenomena of America, the contradictions which are maturing in the heart of present societies and may provoke changes which can attain the magnitude of a revolution like the Cuban Revolution.

In chronological order, although it is of less importance at the moment, there is the large landholding system; it was the basis of the economic power of the ruling class during the period which followed the great anti-colonial revolutions of the last century. But the large landholding class which exists in all Latin American countries is, as a general rule, far behind the social events that stir the world. In some places, however, the more alert and clairvoyant members of this class perceive the danger and change the nature of their investments, advancing at times to the point of mechanizing agriculture, tranferring a part of their interests to industries, or becoming commercial agents for the monopolies. In any case, the first wars of liberation never managed to destroy the large reactionary landholding powers, which bind the peasant to the soil. This is the phenomenon that is prevalent in all the countries of America and has been the foundation of all the injustices committed since the King of Spain ceded the great land grants to those very noble Spanish conquistadors, leaving, in the case of Cuba, the natives, creoles, and mestizos only the unappropriated royal lands, that is the land left in the center where the boundaries of three circular landholdings meet.

The large landholder realized, in the majority of the countries, that he could not survive alone, so he rapidly joined in an alliance with the monopolies; that is with the strongest and most ruthless oppressors of the American people. North American capital arrived to exploit the virgin lands, to withdraw investment from the "benefited" country.

America was the field of interimperialist struggles. The "wars" between Costa Rica and Nicaragua; the separation of Panama from Colombia; the infamy committed against Ecuador in her dispute against Peru; the struggle between Paraguay and Bolivia; are but expressions of this gigantic battle between the great monopolistic powers of the world, a battle decided almost completely in favor of the North American monopolies after the Second World War. From then on the Empire has dedicated itself to perfecting its colonial possessions and to erecting barriers to prevent the penetration of old and new competitors from other imperialist countries. All this results in a monstrously distorted economy, which has been described by the economists of imperialism with an innocuous vocabulary indicative of the profound pity they feel for us. They call our miserably exploited indians who are reduced to ignominy, "little indians"; they use the term "colored" for negro or mulatto people who are discriminated against, converted into instruments both as a people and as a class; they invent terms to divide the laboring masses in their struggle for better economic conditions; they call us, the people of America, "underdeveloped."

What is underdevelopment?

A dwarf with an enormous head and a swollen chest is "underdeveloped," insofar as his weak legs or his short arms do not coordinate with the rest of his body; he is the product of a teratological phenomenon which has distorted his development. That is what we are in reality, we the modestly called "underdeveloped." In truth we are colonies, semicolonies, or dependent countries. We are countries with economies distorted by the actions of imperialism, which has abnormally developed the industrial or agricultural resources necessary to complement its complex economy. "Underdevelopment," or distorted development, carries with it a dangerous specialization in raw materials, containing a threat of hunger for all our people. We, "the underdeveloped," are those of the single crop, the single product, and the single market. A single product whose uncertain sale depends upon a single market, which imposes and sets conditions: This is the great formula of imperial economic domination which is combined with the old and always useful Roman formula, "divide and conquer."

The system of large landholding, then, through its connections with imperialism, shapes completely the so-called "underdevelopment," which results in low salaries and unemployment. This phenomenon of low salaries and unemployment, sharpened by the cyclical variations of the economy of the system, is the vicious common denominator of all the countries of America from the Rio Bravo to the South Pole. This common denominator, which we are stressing and which should serve as the basis of analysis for all who concern themselves with social phenomena, is called *hunger of the people*; that is, exhaustion from being oppressed, abused, exploited to the maximum; exhaustion from selling miserably one's labor for fear of joining the enormous mass of unemployed, so that the maximum of profit is squeezed from each human body only to be squandered in the orgies of the owners of capital.

Thus we see that there are great and inescapable common denominators in Latin America, and that we cannot say that we have been exempted from any of the related evils which result in the most terrible and permanent of them all: hunger of the people. Large landholding, as a form of primitive exploitation or as the expression of capitalist monopoly of the land, conforms to the new conditions and becomes allied with imperialism, the form of exploitation and monopolistic capital that goes beyond national boundaries, to create economic colonialism, euphemistically called "underdevelopment," which results in low salaries, underemployment, unemployment, and hunger of the people. All this existed in Cuba. Here, too, there was hunger, and one of the highest percentages of unemployment in Latin America; here imperialism was more ruthless than in other places in America, and here large landholding existed as much as in any other American country.

What did we do to free ourselves from the great specter of imperialism, with its entourage of puppet government leaders in each country and its mercenary armies ready to defend the puppet and the whole social system of exploitation of man by man? We applied a few formulas, which we have already mentioned as discoveries of our empirical medicine for the great ills of our beloved Latin America, an empirical medicine that rapidly became part of scientific truth.

The objective conditions for the struggle are created by the hunger of the people, the reaction to that hunger, the fear induced to suffocate the popular reaction, and the wave of hatred which repression originates. Absent from America were the subjective conditions of which the most important is the consciousness of the possibility of victory by violent means in the face of the imperialist powers and their internal allies. Those conditions are created in the process of the armed struggle which progressively clarifies the necessity of the change (and permits one to predict it) and the defeat of the army and its final annihilation by the popular forces (as the necessary condition of any genuine revolution).

Having pointed out that the conditions are fulfilled through the exercise of armed struggle, we have to explain once again that the scene of that struggle should be the countryside, and that from the countryside, with a peasant army pursuing the great objectives for which the peasantry should fight (the first of which is the equitable distribution of land), we will then move to take the cities. Based on the ideological force of the working class, whose great leaders discovered the social laws that govern us, the peasantry of Latin America will provide the great liberation army of the future, as it has already done in Cuba. That army created in the countryside, in which the subjective conditions for the taking of power mature, will proceed to conquer the cities from the outside, uniting itself with the working class, thus increasing its ideological wealth. It will defeat the oppressor army in skirmishes and surprise attacks at the beginning and in major battles at the end, when it has grown to the point where it can abandon its guerrilla form in order to become a large popular army of liberation. The stage for the consolidation of revolutionary power will be the liquidation of the old army, as we have already said.

If all these conditions present in Cuba existed in the rest of the Latin American countries, in other struggles to win power for the dispossessed classes, what would happen? Would it be feasible or not? If it is feasible, would it be easier or more difficult than in Cuba? Let us mention the difficulties which in our view will make the new revolutionary struggles of America harder. There are general difficulties for all the countries and more specific difficulties for some whose level of development or national peculiarities are different. We mentioned at the beginning of this paper that we could consider as exceptional factors the attitude of imperialism, disoriented in the face of the Cuban Revolution, and to a certain extent, the attitude of the national bourgeoisie, also disoriented, even looking sympathetically upon the action of the rebels due to the pressure of imperialism on their interests (a situation which is, indeed, common to all our countries). Cuba has drawn the line in the sand again, and again we see Pizarro's dilemma: on the one hand, there are those who love the people, and on the other, those who hate the people. Between them, each time a bit more definitely, the line divides the two great social forces, the bourgeoisie and the working class, which are defining with increasing clarity their respective positions, as the process of the Cuban Revolution advances.

This is to say that imperialism has learned well the lesson of Cuba, and that it will not allow itself to be caught by surprise in any of our twenty republics, in any of the colonies that still exist in America. This means that vast popular struggles against powerful invading armies await those who now attempt to violate the peace of the sepulchers, the Roman peace. This is important, because if the Cuban liberation war was difficult, with its two years of continuous struggle, anguish, and instability, infinitely more difficult will be the new battles which await the people in other places in Latin America.

The United States speeds up the delivery of armaments to the puppet governments that appear threatened; it makes them sign pacts of dependency to make it legally easier to send instruments of repression and murder and troops charged with these duties. Moreover, they increase the military training of the soldiers in the repressive armies, so that they will serve as an efficient spearhead against the people.

And the bourgeoisie? In many countries of America there are objective conflicts between the national bourgeoisies struggling to develop and the imperialism which inundates the markets with its products in order to destroy in unequal competition the national industrialist, as well as other manifestations of struggle for value and wealth. In spite of these conflicts the national bourgeoisies are not capable, in general, of sustaining a consequential struggle against imperialism. They fear the popular revolution more than the sufferings under the oppressive and despotic domination of imperialism, which destroys nationality, affronts patriotic sentiments, and colonizes the economy. The great bourgeoisie openly opposes the revolution and does not hesitate in allying itself with imperialism and landowners to fight against the people and to cut off their access to revolution.

A desperate and hysterical imperialism, willing to go into all sorts of manipulations while giving armaments and even troops to its puppets to annihilate any people who should rise up; a ferocious *latifundismo* showing no scruples, experimenting with the most brutal forms of repression; and a higher bourgeoisie, ready to cut off, by whatever means, the paths toward popular revolution. These are the great allied forces which directly oppose the new popular revolutions of Latin America.

These are the difficulties, which one must add to the usual ones in this type of struggle, under the new conditions of Latin America since the consolidation of the Cuban Revolution.

There are other difficulties even more specific. Countries that, although still unable to accomplish an effective industrialization, have developed their light and middle industry or have undergone a process of population concentration in large urban centers, find it more difficult to prepare guerrillas. Moreover, the ideological influence of dense population centers inhibits guerrilla warfare and encourages peacefully organized masses. All this gives rise to a certain "institutionalization," which in more or less "normal" periods makes conditions less harsh than the usual ones inflicted upon the people.

It might even be conceived that a possible quantitative change in the number of revolutionary elements in Congress could one day bring about a qualitative change. Given present conditions, this hope, in our view, is groundless in Latin America. While the possibility is not excluded that change in any country may be initiated through electoral means, the prevalent conditions in Latin America make that possibility remote.

Revolutionaries cannot predict all the tactical variants that may present themselves in the course of the struggle for their liberation. The real capacity of a revolutionary is measured by his being able to find adequate revolutionary tactics to meet each change in the situation—to keep all tactics at hand and to exploit them to the maximum.

CHAPTER IO

On Economic Planning in Cuba[1]

WE are initiating a new series of popular university lectures on economics. This is not the most appropriate time for such a task. The blood of the patriots and martyrs who defended our independence is still fresh on Cuban soil, as is the blood of the invaders who tried to tread our land under the protection of a foreign power.

Moreover, this is the eve of the day on which the people will proclaim their revolution, the first socialist revolution of Latin America. Nevertheless, we must return to our economic task. It is not so glamorous as political tasks of the defense of the nation, but it is of great importance.

The Ministry of Industry has had a relatively short life, but it had some antecedents. The economy of free Cuba began with INRA. When the peasants were given land, it became necessary to develop industries to utilize the raw materials they produced and to make consumer goods for the masses. This led to the creation of the Department of Industrialization in INRA. The department slowly began to acquire such importance that it became a separate ministry early this year.

The Cuban Ministry of Industry is designed to suit the newness of our economy and the changes taking place. It may be changed again in a few months because we adapt ourselves to the necessities imposed by our difficult task. This task is all the more difficult because we, the chiefs of the ministry, are learning by doing. Naturally there will be errors, and they must be corrected. But the total number of errors is small compared with those of the past.

The Ministry of Industry does not direct all the industries of the country, nor is it in charge of all industrialization. There are two very important agencies that lie outside this ministry. The industrialization of livestock

[1] Television speech delivered April 30, 1961, inaugurating the countrywide popular university program. Monitored by the Fair Play for Cuba Committee, San Francisco, California.

and agricultural products is administered by a special department of INRA. In addition, the Public Works Ministry is in charge of industries connected with construction and is in charge of all building.

The Ministry is, of course, headed by a minister. He is assisted—and this is an innovation in Cuba taken from the experience of the socialist countries—by a council of directors composed of the heads of the various departments of the ministry and by four undersecretaries. This council meets weekly.

The ministry has two functions. One is the direct administration of the nation's industries, and the other is related to economic planning. The Undersecretariat of Economy plans for future investments and the Secretariat for Construction plans for new industries. The Undersecretariat of Basic Industry takes care of Cuba's most important industries. These industries are divided into industrial groups, each of which is called a Consolidated Enterprise. The Undersecretariat of Light Industry acts more like such secretariats do in other countries.

The path of industrialization has two aspects. One is that the government is heading toward established goals with the aid of laws and decrees, and to this end, has nationalized the principal industries. The other aspect results from the fears of a defeated class and political upheavals like those that have been taking place in Cuba for the past two years.

The goods of those who engaged in activities against the security of the state were the first to be confiscated. The petit bourgeoisie placed itself on the side of the revolution and began to work. The other part of the bourgeoisie began conspiring, and some members of this group have fled. They left a number of small industries, which we had to take over in order to provide work.

This is a continuing process. We tried to put an end to it by giving assurance. However, they continue to leave—some because they wish to return as conquerors, and some from fear. Some engage in subversive activities until they are discovered by our immense intelligence service—all the people of Cuba.

In this way we are presented with a small business employing, say seven workers. There are no machinery, no sanitary facilities, and no organization. But there are seven men who must work for their families. Naturally we take care of them in any way we can.

We have a serious problem trying to deal with such small enterprises. The unemployment problem was very great here, and all the small industries were staffed by employees who worked with primitive tools in primitive ways. If we were to mechanize all these industries so that a few men could do the work of many, the rest might remain unemployed. We cannot permit this.

A case in point is the tobacco industry, where machinery which could replace hundreds of workers already exists. And to compete on the world market, we must mechanize. In the sugar industry we are now producing six million tons and have hopes of exceeding nine million tons in coming years, but we must mechanize. At the moment we are having trouble getting enough people to cut cane. They prefer other jobs because cane-cutting is hard work, so we must mechanize.

We must also mechanize our ports. The Soviet Union has developed detergents to clean out their tankers and prepare them for other cargoes. For example, the Russians provide us with four million tons of oil annually, and this year they are buying 2.7 million tons of sugar from us. Their ships can come with oil and return with sugar. But this necessitates the elimination of many workers who are earning their living from a job that is the work of past eras.

This is one of the vital problems facing us, and we will face it by guaranteeing the livelihood of all those whose work may be affected. That is the task of the executive sector of this ministry.

The Consolidated Enterprise has its own characteristics, but it is really much the same as a Combine in the socialist countries. For example, the Consolidated Enterprise for sugar administers the 160 mills that are operating in the country. The central office is in Havana and is answerable directly to the minister for the functioning of this industry. Each enterprise is responsible to the undersecretariat that controls it and plans for it. Each enterprise has a plan, a budget, and quotas. It must surrender its production to the Ministry of Internal Commerce or to the other industries of the state apparatus. These enterprises make no profit for themselves. All profits they produce belong to the Cuban State.

Another function of the ministry is planning. We speak of an economic plan for the country, a socialist plan. The fundamental condition for this is control of the means of production. We already control the means of production, but is this enough? No! We must also know all the statistics, all the economic factors. As we know, the capitalist system left no statistics, so the government is working on them now.

Once we have this knowledge, we must have goals. But we must be realists. We cannot do everything in five years, but we must plan for the development of whatever is most necessary. When all these things are done, we still cannot plan. There are two more factors: unity of action and popular support. The people must support and understand our plans, and we must know of what they approve and disapprove. Then we can plan.

A few days ago the sugar workers issued the slogan, "Six million tons on the first of May." When I heard this, I was surprised because I knew of the slow progress of the harvest. So I called in the administrator of mills. He said that it was the workers' initiative; that he had not been consulted. Today is April 30. That means that 400,000 tons would have to be produced today, and that is clearly impossible. Why did this happen? Because there was no plan. This is purely constructive criticism. We must be realistic, and we must plan.

The industrialization of our country poses some special problems. Cuba had been a country without a fleet, but with a fabulous amount of foreign trade. Because of its sugar production Cuba had a foreign trade more than half as great as Brazil's. But it was also because of its sugar production that Cuba was an underdeveloped country.

One of the first reforms we instituted was the substitution of Cuban products for imports wherever possible. This was the first phase of industrialization. For industrialization we need technicians in all phases of industry. Another important factor is raw material. Cuba is a country of enormous wealth, and there is no tropical product which it cannot produce. It has everything necessary for industrialization.

We have supplied the need for capital through aid from the socialist countries. In a few years we will have developed from an agricultural into an industrial state. But we do not intend to abandon our sugar production. We think we can not only develop it, but can find more markets. We cannot say now how much sugar we will produce in 1965. However, sugar must continue to be an important factor in our development.

Another of our great resources is mining. We have three basic minerals: iron, nickel, and copper. In addition, we have chromium, manganese, and other minerals of lesser importance.

How have we developed our mining industry? Our two main problems were a complete lack of knowledge of our national territory and total lack of experts. We are overcoming these problems with the aid of socialist countries. Fundamentally, the Soviet Union is the nation that has given us aid within the framework of the planning Cuba has outlined. The Soviet Union has been mainly concerned with long-range mineral prospecting.

To give you an idea of how work is being done in the Soviet Union, which is a technically developed nation, and how work is being done in Cuba, I can say the following: The chief Soviet geologists belong to a southern Soviet Republic which has nine million inhabitants. They have fifteen thousand geologists. We have six million inhabitants, and taking into account all the geologists which we have imported—Soviet, Chilean, Peruvian, Mexican, and others—we have two hundred. And if we were to count only the Cuban geologists, I think that we could count them on the fingers of our two hands. In other words, we are completely lacking in technology.

And I wish to explain why we are now being visited by so many foreign guests. It is simply because the empire was not interested in our technological development; or better yet, because it was interested in keeping the knowledge of geology from Cuba. The North Americans were interested in keeping us in the state in which we found ourselves. For example, the Moa Bay Mining Company, which is now called the Pedro Soto Company in memory of a martyr of our Revolution, was a very modern United States company engaged in the extraction of nickel. This company had several Cuban engineers working for it, but there was not a single Cuban at the head of any of the various departments. All the department heads were

North American; the Cubans took orders. Occasionally they could do things, but they did not have access to secrets. Today the heads of all the departments are Cubans, and they are aided by Soviet technology.

Mining is the basis of the development of a nation. A nation which does not have iron has serious problems. Without iron a nation cannot develop an adequate steel industry.

First I wish to tell you that we have signed contracts with the Soviet Union to make a geological study of a quarter of our national territory. They are now starting a study of six thousand kilometers, which represents approximately 5 per cent of our territory.

The laterite deposits in the Nicaro zone of northern Oriente are among the richest sources of potential wealth. They contain low-grade iron ore, as well as lead, sulphur, and nickel. Nickel extraction is now under way.

These mines have resources estimated at about three billion tons, and this is very important to Cuba. There is a technological problem resulting from the difficulty of separating chromium and iron, but tests are being made, and I am sure the problem will be solved, eventually. Here are Cuba's great reserves of iron. But iron can also be found in laterites in Pinar del Rio and in the south of Oriente, and in other mines—old ones, developed by United States owners, and new ones, which we are opening. In all, we have enough iron for sixty years.

We have two nickel plants: Nicaro, the old United States plant, and Mao, the new United States plant, which probably will go into operation in June. This will be an achievement of the revolutionary government. The Moa plant was completed by the imperialists just as the nation was being liberated, and it was never put into operation.

In Pinar del Rio there is potential wealth in the form of copper. The task is now to develop the old deposits and to search for new ones. We also have large quantities of manganese in the Santiago area. We have chrome in the north of Oriente, in Camaguey, and in Pinar del Rio. We are also studying the use of peat for the generation of electric power.

A very important thing is missing. It is petroleum. You know that many United States companies in Cuba confined themselves to the refining of petroleum. Cuba is an important factory in the Caribbean. It had good ports and communications and offered low production costs. So three colossi installed refineries here: Shell, Esso, and Texaco. They received petroleum from Venezuela, refined it here, and sold it to the United States and to Caribbean countries.

When the revolutionary government took to the path of development, petroleum production in Cuba was small and supplied less than 1 per cent of the country's needs. There was little interest in developing petroleum production; perhaps there was even interest in concealing the fact that there was petroleum here.

We have begun an interesting investigation with the few Cuban experts we possess and with Soviet experts. The Soviet experts pointed out two probable locations of large petroleum deposits and will develop special technology for use in these places. There are clear indications that we do have petroleum in Cuba and our experts and those of our foreign friends will try to find as much as possible.

We have contracted with the Soviet Union for the development of a steel plant with a capacity of 1.3 million tons, to be carried out in several stages. In this connection, the Santiago de Cuba area has been decided upon as suitable for the establishment of our first steel plant.

Here are our steel plans: The Soviet Union has agreed to set up a plant that will produce 250,000 tons by 1964. In addition we will develop a plant we found in Cuba. It was a product of anarchic capitalist development called Antillana de Acero. It was badly designed and poorly utilized. In two years this plant will produce 250,000 tons.

To carry out the development of steel production, mining and industry, we need electric power. At present we have installations with a capacity of 620,000 kilowatts in Cuba. In addition, there are sugar mill installations with a capacity of about 300,000 kilowatts, which are functioning badly. We hope to obtain about 6,000 additional kilowatts in the next five years—most to be developed by the socialist nations and some by nations of the dollar area. In other words, in the next five years we will double our electric power production.

The production of construction materials is of prime importance in the development of our industry. The three principal materials are ceramics, bricks, and cement. We have had problems in this regard. Two brick kilns are not operating at the moment because of the imperialist blockade. But the capacity will be increased in any event. The present production of 900,000 to 1,000,000 tons of cement is insufficient for national consumption. We are contemplating doubling this production within the next five years.

For some time to come, agriculture will be the basis of our development. We have large-scale cattle production which utilizes much land. We must have irrigation projects and we must produce fertilizers. By 1965 approximately one million tons of fertilizer will be used in Cuba. We must have our own factories to produce this amount.

We will now turn to consumer goods. But first I must speak about food, for the industrial picture of the nation cannot be clear without plans for food for the next five years. We must consider the self-sufficiency of our agricultural production. Some crops, such as wheat, olive oil, and wine grapes will have to be omitted. In producing other crops, the proper utilization of foodstuffs for canned goods and the development of light industry will have to be taken into account.

We must also contemplate the development of the textile industry. There was practically no cotton when the revolutionary government assumed power. In a few years we will have all the cotton we need, and we will double our textile production capacity. Because of the serious problems created by the imperialist blockade, we have had to change the type of cotton, and some factories have been closed. During the Five Year Plan, with the aid which we are now receiving, we expect to be able to increase production. In a few days a new factory with 15,000 spindles is to be opened. We are receiving 200,000 more spindles in the next four years: 50,000 from the Chinese People's Republic and 150,000 from the German Democratic Republic. In addition we are to receive 3,500 new looms. At the end of the five years we will have just about achieved self-sufficiency in textiles.

The situation is different with regard to leather. We are a nation of cattle producers, but we have been troubled by bad techniques, bad cattle, and bad cattle fodder. We plan to develop our cattle industry and become exporters of meat, leather, and leather products. This is a long-range task, and we plan to begin to develop it during the Five Year Plan.

Another important factor in industrial development is the mechanical arts. In this field we have contracted with Czechoslovakia for a complete factory for the manufacture of two thousand tractors, five thousand trucks, one hundred stationary motors, three thousand motorcycle motors, and so forth, in one phase of one year. This will give us a basis for the manufacture of our vehicles. In 1965 we will begin to manufacture automobiles. We have decided to devote the first stage of our development to the manufacture of vehicles for industry.

In the field of aviation we are without technological resources, so we will continue to purchase planes. But we will leave our traditional markets for the markets of those nations that now lead in technology.

As for maritime transportation, we will begin the task of becoming a seafaring nation by contracting, within the next few days, with the Polish Republic for a dockyard with all the factories related to this industry. We plan to produce fishing boats of small tonnage in the first phase of our program, and ships of ten thousand tons for trans-Atlantic trade in the second phase.

I have received several letters from Cienfuegos about the placing of this industry there. There are many factors to be considered in placing industries. One must consider the population as a working force and determine whether the population is in need of work and if there are heroic actions to be rewarded.

For example, something must be given to the people of Playa Girón who resisted the weight of the enemy aggression so well. They have suffered losses of life and property; their wives and children have been murdered. It is necessary to go to this zone and take care of them.

There are also important economic factors which regulate the placing of industries: the availability of electricity, water, communications, and raw material. This will give you an idea of how industry will be distributed throughout Cuba.

But first I must issue a notice. Not all these factories have been decided upon yet. If it is necessary, we will have to adjust the locations and make changes. I am giving you this notice in order to be sure that the people will not become angry if a factory is planned for one place and we then have to change its location for some reason.

So now we can begin. In the Zavalo area of Pinar del Rio there will be a plant for the processing of silicone. This zone is rich in silicone. A plant for the processing of kaolin will be located on the Isle of Pines. In the Artemisa area of Pinar del Rio ceramics will be produced. In Camaguey there will be an aluminum plant and a glass combine.

We have not tried to establish too many industries in Havana Province because we want to balance the map of the nation insofar as possible. Until now all the branches of the foreign companies have been established near Havana. We have placed in Havana the industries that are most important from the strategic and technical points of view, but we have tried to place heavy industry in areas where the necessary raw materials are available.

In Havana there will be an electro-technical combine composed of factories for the production of television and radio receivers, a factory for light rubber products, a battery factory, a typewriter assembly plant, a centralized industrial laboratory, a seamless copper factory, and a textile factory.

In Batabano factories for the production of office equipment—pencils, fountain pens, and so forth—will be established. The location of these factories in Batabano is an example of how political factors determine the location of a factory. These factories are of little importance and can be placed anywhere. They have been put in Batabano to give work to port workers and to fulfill an old promise made by the revolutionary government to compensate dock workers who had lost the tourist trade. Now they will be employed in easier work and will be better paid.

A fertilizer combine has been placed in Matanzas. This will be an enlargement of the Cuban-Nitro company. We are negotiating in regard to this factory, not with a socialist nation, but with a private, capitalist firm, which has worked very well with us. As there is a problem of dollars, we are negotiating payments and other details. Also planned for Matanzas are a sodium chloride plant and a textile factory. In Cardenas there will be a lock factory, a nonferrous metal foundry, and production of gas pumps and steam valves.

In Cienfuegos there will be a lumber combine, a mechanical combine, a diesel motor and compressor factory, a sewing machine factory, an electro-technical combine, an electric motor factory, a water pump factory, and others.

In Santa Clara there will be a combine for the production of household articles. There will also be a mechanized electric-arc steel foundry, purchased in the Soviet Union. The electric arc is from Poland, but it is to be operated in the mechanized combine. There will also be a small tool factory, a plastic articles factory, and a small plant for the assembly of cameras.

In Holguín there will be an electro-technical combine with a factory for the production of all types of transformers. In Sagua de Tanamo, for the time being, there will be a light wire factory for the production of needles and pins. This is the city which was so savagely bombarded by the dictatorship, and so far we have not been able to repay them for their sacrifices. In Bahia de Nipe there will be two nickel plants.

In Guantánamo there will be an agricultural tool factory and a file factory. Santiago will be transformed into one of the largest industrial centers of the country. One of the steel plants is being planned for Santiago, as well as a factory for the production of automobiles, tractors, and trucks.

A new petroleum refinery, which has been purchased in the Soviet Union, with a capacity of approximately one million tons a year also will be established in Santiago. There will also be a wire factory and a factory to produce galvanized iron for electrical installations.

This is the program of what the nation is going to do. This panorama has been planned optimistically, with the idea that the progress of the forces of peace make an aggression increasingly improbable. This is our dearest wish.

However, we must take into account the facts of reality. One of the first problems we must consider is the imperialist aggression. What point can this aggression reach? I cannot say. The words of Mr. Kennedy, so full of a profound conviction of a special destiny, full of a fascist conceit, full of arrogance and a concentrated anger because for the first time he was not able to fulfill his designs in America easily, makes it impossible for us to know what the future attitude of the United States will be. And this is very important also from the point of view of industrial construction, because we will have to add to construction the task of reconstruction.

What is assured is that victory will be ours. But we do not know what degree of destruction the imperialist attack may bring us. This time the destruction fell on undefended families, and our militiamen and our soldiers died in the fight in the Playa Girón zone, as did some of our pilots. The loss was entirely of a military nature, if one wants to call it that. However, among the new prospects is the destruction of industries and sabotage. We can even expect that enemy planes will come to bomb us, because they have already done so. And in this eventuality, we cannot estimate what we will have to rebuild.

We have been witness to what happened in Korea, for example. There, North American aerial superiority destroyed every sign of life on the surface of the earth. They did not leave a single house standing. They wiped out the cattle. But today, after only a few years, Korea is preparing to produce 2.5 million tons of steel—much more than we will produce at the end of this Five Year Plan. The resurgence has been extraordinary. All the sufferings instill in the people the inspiration to work hard; they fortify the people, who find new energy when they are imbued with an ideal and see justice is a possible goal.

In addition that was a different epoch. At that time the Soviet Union was just emerging from a great war, the fiercest war that humanity has ever experienced. It did not have, or had not yet perfected, the atomic bomb. Its planes were inferior to the United States planes. The desire for peace, of a nation which had lost twenty million inhabitants, was very strong.

Korea had to maintain itself under conditions very different from the present conditions. I believe that it will not be the same if another aggression is carried out, and an attempt is made to create another Korea in Cuba.

But all this is guesswork. The sad impression today is that world peace depends on the rage, the hysteria, of a fascist ruler in a nation that is directly involved in fascism. That is why we have to consider this as a factor of our industrialization. Among the problems is that of knowing what amount of our industrial wealth we will have to rebuild and to estimate it in terms of time, money, employment of workers, and materials.

Of course this is not the only problem. We also have internal problems —serious problems. We presented one of these problems when we spoke about our Five Year Plan. It is the lack of basic knowledge in a nation in which technology has never been developed, in a nation which did not even know its own wealth and which was absolutely dependent on the North American giant, on the great technical capability of the United States, on North American infallibility, and whose technical knowledge was limited to catalogues for ordering parts that had broken.

This has had an important influence on us—not only in the technical field, by limiting the capability of our personnel in the practical sense, but also by limiting us ideologically, and this is an important point. United States technical personnel have entirely different characteristics from those we are trying to give the technical personnel in Cuba. In the United States the technician is in a separate category, between the large mass of exploited people and the small group of exploiters. He receives more crumbs from the banquet than the workers. This view of the technician, completely removed from real life, has been imposed in Cuba. One can frequently hear, even from those technicians who support the revolutionary government, the statement, "I am a technician." This is said in justification of the fact that he had work under Batista, under the Cuban Socialist government, under Prio, or under anyone else, because he belongs to this special category, completely removed from society. This attitude is a creation of imperialism.

We have had to fight against this, to try to change this view. A nation cannot be built in a laboratory. It must be built with the strength of the people; it must be built by uniting the people. That is why we want each of our technicians to be part of the people. That is why we have difficulties at present.

Some of our technicians are adapting themselves to these changes and are improving, but there are still some who are left over from the previous era. That is why we are determined to create a new man, the man who comes from the working class, from the peasant class, the man who is a product of the Revolution.

Despite the fact that the type of technician we now have is not the ideal type, we have preferred him to having no technicians at all, and in many cases we had to be left with none at all. Many of them left, and they are leaving every day. It is no secret from anyone that every day some man who has been bought, or who simply cannot withstand the new climate of Cuba (I must say that in order not to be unjust), goes into exile.

Construction has been and continues to be difficult. We have had to accelerate the instruction of those who could be instructed. But this is the great task of construction, and this is the miracle that a people can achieve when filled with the holy idea of production and the realization of their aspirations.

Now for the secondary problems we have to face. For example, there is the changeover to different technology. The United States still uses inches, yards, and pounds, while almost all the other nations in the world use the metric and decimal systems, which are much more logical. This seems a small thing, but it brings complications when one must use machinery and equipment designed for the metric system. Our workers have to make the adjustment.

You know there is a fundamental difference between the socialist nations which now supply our raw material and the United States. The United States has an extraordinarily developed consumer-goods industry. The socialist nations are primarily engaged in developing their heavy industry. In the socialist nations everything is planned. If there is a need for one million glasses, then one million glasses are produced. The glasses are all the same, and there is no competition. In the capitalist nations the finish of a product is of great importance and creates competition in the market. Thus our machinery, which was adapted to the production of a fine finish for a product, sometimes had to be changed to satisfy the great demand of the population.

In addition we have had the problem of the imperialist blockade of raw material. This blockade is uneven for many reasons. It is uneven because it is sometimes in their interests to sell. It is uneven because the interimperialist conflict is so great that they cannot prevent the sale of some products. The harm lies in not selling. They lost profits. Then they select certain strategic articles and work on them.

Because of the shortage of strategic raw materials, we have had to close some plants. For example, they did not sell us ammonia. Cuba-Nitro has not yet completed the ammonia plant, and as we cannot at the moment import ammonia from the Soviet Union (you know that ammonia is an industrial product in great demand), the Cuba-Nitro plant is at a standstill. The same thing has happened with other plants. Some are working at half their capacity. In general this means that our ambitious plans could not be fulfilled.

We made our production plans on the assumption that we would have all the raw material needed and all the spare parts we would require. We started to work enthusiastically on our plan, which had not been announced because it was a preparatory plan. The real development plan will begin in 1962.

We made an error similar to the one made by our comrades in the sugar industry. We did not go to the masses. We made a laboratory plan. We estimated the capacity of the plants already installed, we estimated the production, and this was our working plan. Today we can see clearly that the masses did not participate in the plan, and a plan that lacks the participation of the masses is a plan that is always threatened with defeat.

Under these conditions we were unable to fulfill our plan. Fundamentally, we have achieved only 25 per cent of our plan in the steel industry. But even so, we increased production by 75 per cent in one year. This shows us the large number of installations in Cuba that were idle. Our task was to put our full capacity to work. But we failed because we lacked raw material and because we had not discussed our plans with the masses. Another of our problems is coordination with agriculture. We must perfect this coordination.

Now I wish to talk about relations with the workers. The working classes still are unaware of their potential, their duties, their rights. There has been much propaganda about voluntary work—the cutting of sugar cane by people who do not participate directly in production. You know that sugar cane is processed the day it is cut. When the worker takes off on Sunday, even though there is still unfinished work, just because he has made enough to cover his most pressing needs, it shows there is no spirit of improvement in his life, that there is a lack of understanding of the needs of the Revolution. The Sunday sugar cane cutters of Havana help a great deal, and the weekly production of sugar cane in Havana Province is steadily increasing. But what I wanted to stress is that the working class is not putting forth its full effort.

We are living in a time of revolution, a Revolution that has proclaimed itself a socialist revolution. And socialism is not just a word, it is the result of economic factors and factors of conscience. That is why we still have much to do in this connection.

The masses must be interested in knowing what an economic plan is, what their duty is, how they can protect the interests of the workers in each factory. These are problems which must interest the masses. They must be constantly aware of what happens in their factories and relate this to the entire life of the nation.

We are trying to get the workers to be thoroughly aware of their Revolution. We have two important plans to that end. One will be made public soon. They are the emulation plan, and the plan for educating the workers.

Part of the emulation plan is for synchronizing productivity and rewards, and involves work standards. The first stage in the emulation plan is that of organization. The worker must help keep the factory clean, think of caring for his machine, realize the problem of raw materials, protect his factory against sabotage, and contribute by his work and his study to national production.

The education plan begins with the lowest technical capacity required for working with the machines in the factory. Schools and universities will make it possible for the worker to keep advancing as far as engineer or even president of the republic. So work and study together will make the worker into a qualified technician. That is the big task.

All this work could not be done without two things: One is the country's determination, and the other is aid from the socialist countries. Both these things are united and complement each other. We receive aid from the socialist countries because they see the nation's determination, and the nation is more determined because it receives aid.

Our first measures annoyed the North Americans somewhat, but our real struggle began with the agrarian reform. Agrarian reform is the first point of the inclined plane that leads to socialism. The reform affected thousands of caballerias of land belonging to United States monopolistic enterprises.

That brought reaction at once from the empire, which did not seek to compromise. Rather, it at once sought to make this government knuckle under. So the dilemma arose immediately. Either we would go ahead on this path, or we would kneel. Continuing on this road brought more imperialist pressure, and then there were in quick succession the mining law, the oil law, the oil siege, and confiscation of the oil companies. They took away the sugar quota, and we nationalized the sugar mills. We nationalized the electric company. It was a fast and spectacular exchange of blows, and at the beginning of this year our Premier was able to announce that we had entered a socialist era.

This is not the time to define socialism. For our work in industry, we should know that socialism is characterized by the people's ownership of the means of production, which serve the people. Besides that purely economic basis, there is an aspect of consciousness that is of great importance.

I hope that soon the Premier, who I believe will close this series of lectures, or somebody else, will give a clear explanation of these problems.

It is important to stress that without such a clear awareness of the rights and duties of the people in the new phase, it is impossible to really enter into and work in a socialist society such as we want. A socialist society is absolutely democratic; it is based on the needs and aspirations of the people, and the people have a major role in all decisive points.

CHAPTER II

On Growth and Imperialism[1]

LIKE all other delegations, we must begin by thanking the government and the people of Uruguay for the warm welcome we have received on this visit.

I should also like to express my personal thanks to the chairman of the meeting for his gift of the complete works of Rodó, and to explain to him that I am not beginning these remarks with a quotation from that great American for two reasons. The first is that I went back after many years to *Ariel,* looking for a passage that would represent at the present time the ideas of a man who is more than Uruguayan, a man who is our American, an American from south of the Rio Grande; but throughout his *Ariel* Rodó speaks of the violent struggle and opposition of the Latin American countries against the nation that fifty years ago was also interfering in our economy and in our political freedom, and it is not proper to mention this, since the host is involved.

And the second reason, Mr. Chairman, is that the chairman of one of the delegations here present gave us a quotation from Martí to begin his statement. We shall, then, reply to Martí with Martí. To Martí with Martí but with the anti-imperialistic and anti-feudal Martí who died facing Spanish bullets, fighting for the freedom of his country and by Cuba's freedom, trying to prevent the United States from spreading over Latin America, as he wrote in one of his last letters.

At that international monetary conference recalled by the President of the Inter-American Bank when he spoke of the seventy years of waiting, Martí said:

[1] Speech at the Special Meeting of the Inter-American Economic and Social Council of the Organization of American States in Punta del Este, Uruguay, August 8, 1961. Guevara was chairman of the Cuban delegation at the conference, which ratified the United States proposal (the Alliance for Progress), and he abstained at the final ratification. Official OAS translation.

> He who speaks of economic union speaks of political union. The nation that buys commands, and the nation that sells serves; it is necessary to balance trade in order to ensure freedom; the country that wants to die sells only to one country, and the country that wants to survive sells to more than one. The excessive influence of one country on the trade of another becomes political influence. Politics is the work of men, who surrender their feelings to interests, or who sacrifice part of their feelings to interests. When a strong nation gives food to another, it makes use of the latter. When a strong nation wants to wage war against another, it forces those who need it to ally themselves with it and to serve it. The nation that wants to be free must be free in commerce. Let it distribute its trade among other equally strong countries. If it is to show preference for any, let it be for the one that needs it least. Neither unions of American countries against Europe, nor with Europe against a country of the Americas. The geographic fact of living together in the Americas does not compel political union except in the mind of some candidate or some babbler. Commerce flows along the slopes of the land and over the water and toward the one who has something to trade, be it a monarchy or a republic. Union with the world, and not with a part of it; not with one part of it against another. If the family of republics of the Americas has any function, it is not to be herded behind any one of them against the future republics.

That, Mr. Chairman, was Martí seventy years ago.

Now, having performed the basic duty of recalling the past and reciprocating the delegate's courtesy to us, I shall pass on to the fundamental part of my statement, an analysis of why we are here and the characteristics of this conference. And I must say, Mr. Chairman, that in the name of Cuba I disagree with almost all of the statements that have been made, although I do not know if I disagree with the speakers' innermost thoughts.

I must say that Cuba interprets this as a political conference; Cuba does not acknowledge a separation of economic matters from political ones; it understands that they always go hand in hand. That is why there can be no experts speaking of technical matters when the fate of the peoples is at stake. I shall explain why this is a political conference. It is political because all economic conferences are political, but it is also political because it was conceived against Cuba and against the example represented by Cuba in the entire Western Hemisphere.

Let us see if this is not true. On the tenth, in Fort Amador, Canal Zone, General Decker, instructing a group of Latin American military personnel in the art of repressing peoples, spoke of the Montevideo Technical Conference and said that it is necessary to help it. But that is nothing. In his message of August 5, 1961, read at the inaugural session, President Kennedy said the following:

"Those of you at this conference are present at an historic moment in the life of this Hemisphere. For this is far more than an economic discussion or a technical conference on development. In a very real sense it is a demonstration of the capacity of free nations to meet the human and material problems of the modern world."

I could continue with a quotation from the Prime Minister of Peru, when he was referring to political subjects; but in order not to tire the delegates, since I foresee that my statement will be somewhat lengthy, I shall refer to some of the statements made by the "experts," and here I use quotation marks, taken from Topic V of the Agenda.

On page 11, at the end, and as a definitive conclusion, it says: "Establishing, both at the hemisphere and the national levels, regular procedures for consultation among labor union advisory committees, in order that they may play an influential role in the policy development of the programs that may be agreed upon at the Special Meeting."

And to reinforce my statement, so that there may be no doubt about my right to talk politics, which is what I plan to do in the name of the Government of Cuba, here is a quotation from page 7 of that same report concerning the same Topic V:

"Any delay on the part of democratic information media in assuming their duty to defend, unflaggingly and without material compromise, the essential values of our civilization, would be of irreparable damage to democratic society and would put those same media in imminent danger of losing the freedoms they now enjoy, as has been the case in Cuba"—Cuba, spelled out in full—"where today the press, radio, television, and motion pictures are all under the absolute control of the Government."

That is to say, fellow delegates, that in the report under discussion Cuba is judged from the political standpoint. Very well. Cuba will speak the truth from the political standpoint, and from the economic standpoint, too.

We are in agreement with only one thing in the report on Topic V prepared by the experts, with one single sentence which describes the present situation:

"Relationships among the peoples of the Americas are entering upon a new phase," it says, and that is true. It is just that this new phase is beginning under the sign of Cuba, Free Territory of the Americas, and this conference and the special treatment given to all of the delegations, and the credits that are approved, all bear the name of Cuba, whether the beneficiaries like it or not, because there has been a qualitative change in the Americas, a change that has enabled a country to rise up in arms, destroy an oppressive army, form a new people's army, stand up to an invincible monster, await the monster's attack, and defeat it also.

And that is something new in the Americas, gentlemen; that is what has led to this new language and to the fact that relations are easier among all, except, naturally, between the two great rivals of this conference.

At this moment Cuba cannot even speak of the Americas alone. Cuba is part of a world that is under anguishing tension, because it does not know if one of the parties—weaker but the more aggressive—will commit the clumsy blunder of unleashing a conflict which necessarily will be atomic. And Cuba is watchful, fellow delegates, because it knows that imperialism will succumb, wrapped in flames, but it knows that Cuba would also pay with its blood the price of the defeat of imperialism, and it hopes that this defeat may be achieved by other means. Cuba hopes that its sons may see a better future, and that they will not have to pay the price of victory with the lives of millions of human beings destroyed by atomic fallout.

The world situation is tense. Our meeting here is not only because of Cuba, not in the least. Imperialism has to make sure of its rear guard, because the battle is being waged on all sides, at a time of deep anguish.

The Soviet Union has reaffirmed its decision to sign a German peace treaty, and President Kennedy has announcd that he would even go to war over Berlin. But it is not Berlin alone, it is not Cuba alone; there is Laos, and the Congo, where Lumumba was murdered by imperialism; there is divided Vietnam and divided Korea; Formosa in the hands of Chiang Kai-shek's gang; there is Argentina, prostrate, and now they want to divide it, too; and Tunisia, whose people the other day were machine-gunned for committing the "crime" of wanting to recover their territory.

That is the way it is in the world today, fellow delegates, and that is how we have to see it in order to interpret this conference and be able to arrive at the conclusions that will permit our countries to move toward a happy future and orderly development, for otherwise they may become appendages of imperialism in the preparation of a new and terrible war; or they may also be bled by civil strife when their peoples—as almost all of you have said—tired of waiting, tired of being deceived again, start on the path that Cuba once started on: to take up arms, to fight on their own soil, to take away the weapons of the foreign army that represents reaction, and to destroy to its very foundations an entire social order that was made to exploit the people.

The history of the Cuban Revolution is short in years, Mr. Chairman, but rich in deeds, rich in positive facts, and rich, also, in the bitterness of the aggressions it has suffered.

We shall spell out some of them, so that it may be clearly understood that it was a long chain of events that led us here.

In October 1959, only the agrarian reform had been carried out as a basic economic measure by the revolutionary government. Pirate airplanes, coming from the United States, flew over Havana and, as a result of the very bombs they dropped, plus the fire from our anti-aircraft batteries, two persons were killed and half a hundred wounded. Later, there was the burning of the cane fields, which is economic aggression, aggression against our wealth, and which was denied by the United States until an airplane—pilot and all—exploded, and the evidence proved beyond the shadow of a doubt the source of the pirate aircraft. This time the American Government was kind enough to apologize. The España sugar mill was also bombed by one of these aircraft in February 1960.

In March of that year, the steamship *Le Couvre,* which was bringing arms and ammunition from Belgium, exploded at the docks of Havana, causing a hundred dead, in an accident which the experts classified as intentional.

In May 1960, the conflict with imperialism became open and acute. The oil companies operating in Cuba, invoking the right of might and ignoring the laws of the republic that clearly specified their obligations, refused to refine the petroleum we had purchased from the Soviet Union, in the exercise of our free right to trade with the whole world and not with one part thereof, as Martí put it.

Everybody knows how the Soviet Union responded, sending us, with real effort, hundreds of ships to carry 3,600,000 tons per year—our total imports of crude petroleum—to keep in operation all of the industrial machinery which works on the basis of petroleum today.

In July 1960 there was the economic aggression against Cuban sugar, which some governments have not yet perceived. The differences became more acute, and the OAS meeting took place in Costa Rica in August of 1960. There—in August 1960, as I said—the Meeting [of Consultation of Ministers of Foreign Affairs] declared that it "Condemns energetically the intervention or threat of intervention, even when conditional, by an extracontinental power in the affairs of the American republics" and declared that "the acceptance of a threat of extracontinental intervention by any American state endangers American solidarity and security, and that this obliges the Organization of American States to disapprove it and reject it with equal vigor."

That is to say, the American republics, meeting in Costa Rica, denied us the right to defend ourselves. This is one of the strangest denials ever made in the history of international law. Naturally, our people are a little refractory with respect to the voice of technical meetings and they met in the Assembly of Havana and approved unanimously—more than a million hands raised to the skies, one-sixth of the country's total population—the Declaration of Havana, which states in part as follows:

> The People's National General Assembly reaffirms—and is sure that in doing so it is expressing the common criterion of the peoples of Latin America—that democracy is incompatible with financial oligarchy, with the existence of discrimination against the Negro and the excesses of the Ku Klux Klan, and with the persecution that deprived scientists such as Oppenheimer of their jobs, that for years prevented the world from hearing the wonderful voice of Paul Robeson, a prisoner in his own country, and that led the Rosenbergs to their death, in the face of the protests and the

horror of the whole world and despite the appeals of the leaders of various countries and of Pope Pius XII.

"The People's National General Assembly of Cuba expresses the Cuban conviction that democracy cannot consist merely in the exercise of an electoral vote which is nearly always fictitious and is directed by large landowners and professional politicians, but rather in the right of the citizens to decide their own destinies, as this People's Assembly is now doing. Furthermore, democracy will exist in Latin America only when its peoples are really free to choose, when the humble are no longer reduced—by hunger, by social inequality, by illiteracy, and by the judicial systems—to the most hopeless impotence.

And further, the People's National General Assembly of Cuba condemned "the exploitation of man by man, and the exploitation of the underdeveloped countries by imperialist financial capital."

That was a declaration of our people, made before the world, to show our determination to defend with arms, with blood, with our lives, our freedom and our right to control the destinies of the country, in the way that our people deem most advisable.

Later came many skirmishes and battles, sometimes verbal, sometimes otherwise, until in December 1960 the Cuban sugar quota in the United States market was definitively cut. The Soviet Union responded in a way which you already know, other Socialist countries did likewise, and contracts were signed to sell four million tons throughout the socialist area at a preferential price of four cents, which naturally saved the situation for Cuba, which unfortunately is still a single-crop country, like the majority of the American nations, and which was as dependent on one market and one product—at that time—as the other republics are today.

It seemed that President Kennedy had inaugurated the new era which had been spoken of so much. In spite of the fact that there had also been a rough verbal exchange between President Kennedy and the Prime Minister of our government, we hoped that things would improve. President Kennedy gave a speech in which he gave clear warning of a series of positions to be taken in the Americas, but he seemed to be announcing to the world that Cuba's case should be considered as something that had already taken shape, as a "fait accompli."

We were then mobilized. The day after Kennedy's speech, we ordered demobilization. Unfortunately, on March 13, 1961, President Kennedy spoke of the "Alliance for Progress." On that same day, there was a pirate attack against our refinery in Santiago, Cuba, which endangered the installations and took the life of one of the defenders. So once again we were faced with a *de facto* situation.

In that speech, which I have no doubt will be memorable, Kennedy also said that he hoped that the people of Cuba and the Dominican Republic, for whom he expressed great friendship, might rejoin the society of free nations. One month later the events at Playa Girón took place, and a few days later [former] President Trujillo was mysteriously assassinated. We were always the enemies of President Trujillo, and we are just establishing the bare facts of the case, which to this date has not been clarified in any way.

Later, there came a true masterpiece of belligerency and political ingeniousness, which wound up under the name of the White Paper. According to the magazines, which say so much in the United States, even provoking President Kennedy's anger, its author was one of the distinguished advisers of the United States Delegation with us today. It is an accusation full of misrepresentations of Cuba's real situation, conceived in preparation of what was forthcoming.

"The revolutionary regime betrayed their own revolution," so said the White Paper, as if it were the judge of revolutions and how to make revolutions, and the great evaluator of the revolutions of the Americas.

"The Castro regime [in Cuba] offers a clear and present danger to the authentic . . . revolution of the Americas . . ." because the word "revolution," as one of the members of the presidential staff said, also needs to clean up once in a while.

"The Castro regime refuses to negotiate on a friendly basis . . ." despite the fact that many times we have said that we would sit down on an equal footing to discuss our problems with the United States, and I wish to take advantage of this opportunity, Mr. Chairman, to affirm once more on behalf of my government that Cuba is willing to sit down to discuss on equal footing anything that the delegation of the United States may wish to discuss, on a strict basis of nothing more than no previous conditions at all. That is to say, our position in this matter is very clear.

The White Paper called upon the people of Cuba to engage in subversion and revolution "against the Castro regime"; however, on April 13, President Kennedy once more spoke and categorically affirmed that he would not invade Cuba and that the armed forces of the United States would never intervene in Cuba's internal affairs. Two days later, unidentified aircraft bombed our airports and made ashes out of most of our air force, an ancient remnant that the Batista people had left behind in their flight.

In the Security Council, Mr. Stevenson gave emphatic assurances that it was Cuban pilots, of our air force, "unhappy with the Castro regime," who had done this thing and he stated that he had talked with them.

On April 19 there was the unsuccessful invasion, when our entire people united and on a war footing, showed once again that there are forces stronger than generalized propaganda, forces stronger than the brute force of arms, and values more important than the values of money. They crowded down the narrow ways that led to the battlefield and many of them were massacred en route by the enemy's superior aircraft. Nine Cuban pilots with their old planes, were the heroes of the day. Two of them gave their lives; seven are outstanding examples of the triumph of the arms of freedom.

Playa Girón was over, and to say nothing more about this, since "confession takes the place of evidence," fellow delegates, President Kennedy took upon himself the total responsibility for the aggression. Perhaps at that time he did not recall the words he had uttered a few days before.

We might have thought that the history of aggressions had ended; however, as the newspapermen say, "I've got news for you." On July 26 of this year, groups of armed counterrevolutionaries at the Guantánamo Naval Base lay in wait for Major Raúl Castro in two strategic places, in order to assassinate him. The plan was intelligent and macabre. They would shoot at Major Raúl Castro as he traveled down the highway from his house to the rally with which we were celebrating the anniversary of our revolution. If they failed, they would dynamite the base, or rather, they would detonate the already dynamited bases of the box from which our companion Raúl Castro was to preside over that patriotic rally. And a few hours later, fellow delegates, American mortars, located on Cuban soil, would open fire on the Guantánamo Naval Base. The world would then clearly explain the case to itself: the Cubans, exasperated because in one of their private quarrels one of those "Communists they have there" was assassinated, launched an attack on the Guantánamo Naval Base, and the poor United States had no choice but to defend itself.

That was the plan that our security forces, considerably more efficient than they were thought to be, discovered a few days ago.

So, because of all these things I have related I believe that the Cuban Revolution cannot come to this assembly of distinguished experts to speak of technical matters. I know that you are thinking, "and furthermore, because they don't know," and perhaps you are right. But the basic thing is that politics and facts, so stubborn that they are constantly appearing in our midst, prevent us from coming to speak of figures or to analyze the perfect accomplishments of the I–A ECOSOC experts.

There are a number of political problems floating around. One of them is political and economic: the question of the tractors. Five hundred tractors is not an item of exchange. Five hundred tractors is what our government considers as possible reparations for the material damages caused by 1,200 mercenaries. They would not pay for a single life, because we are not in the habit of measuring the lives of our citizens in terms of dollars or equipment of any kind. And much less the lives of the children and the women who died there in Playa Girón.

But we would like to add that if this seems to be an odious transaction stemming from the days of the pirates, that is, to exchange human beings—whom we call worms—for tractors, we could exchange human beings for human beings. We address ourselves to the gentlemen from the United States. We wish to remind them of the great patriot, Pedro Albizu Campos, dying now after years and years spent in the dungeons of the empire, and we offer them anything they want for the freedom of Albizu Campos; and we wish to remind the countries of the Americas who have political prisoners in their jails that we could make a trade. No one responded.

Naturally, we cannot force this trade. It is simply in the hands of those who believe that the freedom of the "brave" Cuban counterrevolutionaries —the only army in the world that ever surrendered completely, almost without casualties—who believe that these people should go free, then let them free their political prisoners, and all the Americas will have shining jails, or at least the political jails will cause no worries.

There is another problem, also of a political and economic nature. It is, Mr. Chairman, that our air transport fleet, plane by plane, is being kept in the United States. The procedure is simple: some ladies get on board with weapons hidden in their clothing; they hand these to their accomplices; the accomplices shoot the guard, put a pistol to the pilot's head, the pilot makes a beeline for Miami, a company—legally of course, because everything is done legally in the United States—files a claim for debts against the Cuban State, and then the plane is confiscated.

But it so happens that one of many patriotic Cubans—and there was also a patriotic American, but he is not one of ours—a patriotic Cuban who was traveling around there, and without anybody's telling him anything, he decided to amend the record of twin-engine plane thieves, and he brought a beautiful four-engine plane to Cuban shores. Naturally, we are not going to use that four-engine plane, for it is not ours. We respect private property, but we also demand the right to be respected ourselves, gentlemen; we demand the right of having no more farces; the right of having American agencies that can speak up and tell the United States: "Gentlemen, you are committing a vulgar abuse; you cannot take planes away from a State, even though it is against you; those airplanes are not yours; return them or you will be punished." Naturally, we know that unfortunately there are no inter-American agencies having that much strength.

We appeal, however, to this august gathering, to the sentiments of fairness and justice of the delegation of the United States, to normalize the situation of the respective airplane robberies.

It is necessary to explain what the Cuban Revolution is, what this special affair is that has made the blood of the empires of the world boil, and has also made the blood of the dispossessed of the world—or at least of this part of the world—boil, but with hope.

It is an agrarian, antifeudal, and anti-imperialist revolution, transformed by its internal evolution and by external aggressions into a socialist revolution, and it so proclaims itself before the Americas; it is a socialist revolution.

It is a socialist revolution that took land from those who had much and gave it to those who worked on that land as hired hands, or distributed it in the form of cooperatives among other groups of persons who had no land to work, not even as hired hands.

It is a revolution that came to power with its own army and on the ruins of the army of oppression; that took possession of this power, looked round about, and undertook systematically to destroy all of the previous forms of the structure maintained by the dictatorship of an exploiting class over the exploited class.

It completely destroyed the army as a caste, as an institution, but not as men, except for the war criminals, who were shot, also in the face of public opinion of the hemisphere, and with a very clear conscience.

It is a revolution that reaffirmed national sovereignty, and for the first time raised the issue, for itself and for all countries of the Americas and for all peoples of the world, of the recovery of territories unjustly occupied by other powers.

It is a revolution with an independent foreign policy; Cuba comes here to this meeting of the American States as one among many Latin American countries; it goes to the meeting of the nonaligned countries as one of their important members; and it sits in on the deliberations of the Socialist countries and these look upon it as a brother.

It is a revolution with humanistic characteristics. It feels solidarity with the oppressed peoples of the world; solidarity, Mr. Chairman, because, as Martí also said, "A true man should feel on his cheek the blow against the cheek of any man." And every time an imperial power enslaves any territory, it is striking a blow at all of the inhabitants of that territory.

That is why we fight, indiscriminately, without asking questions about the political system or the aspirations of countries that are fighting for their independence; we fight for the independence of those countries; we fight for the recovery of occupied territory. We support Panama, that has a strip of its territory occupied by the United States. We say Malvinas Islands, not Falkland Islands, speaking of those that lie south of Argentina, and we say Isla del Cisne [Swan Island] when speaking of the island that the United States snatched away from Honduras and from which vantage point it is committing aggression against us by telegraph and radio.

We fight constantly here in the Americas for the independence of the Guianas and the British West Indies; where we accept the fact of an independente Belize, because Guatemala has already renounced its sovereignty over that part of its territory; and we fight also in Africa, in Asia, anywhere in the world where the powerful oppress the weak, so that the weak may gain their independence, their self-determination, and their right to govern themselves as sovereign states.

Our country—and excuse my mentioning this—on the occasion of the earthquake that devastated Chile, assisted that nation as far as it was able with its only product, sugar. Small assistance, but nonetheless it was help given that demanded nothing in return; it was simply a gift to a friendly people, of something to eat to carry them through those difficult hours. That country does not have to thank us, and much less does it owe us anything. Our duty led us to give what we gave.

Our revolution nationalized the national economy; it nationalized the basic industries, including mining; it nationalized all our foreign trade, which is now in the hands of the State and we began to diversify, trading with all the world; it nationalized the banking system in order to have in its hands an effective instrument for the technical control of credit according to the needs of the country.

Our workers now participate in the direction of our planned national economy, and a few months ago, the revolution carried out its urban reform, which gave each inhabitant of our country the house in which he lived, to be his property, the one condition being that he would continue paying the same amount he had been paying, in accordance with a table, for a certain number of years.

It took many steps to affirm human dignity, one of the first having been the abolition of racial discrimination—because racial discrimination did exist in our country, fellow delegates, in a more subtle form, but it did exist. The beaches in our island formerly could not be used by the Negro or the poor, because they belonged to private clubs and because the tourists who came from other places did not like to go swimming with Negroes.

Our hotels, the large hotels of Havana, built by foreign companies, did not permit Negroes to sleep in them, because the tourists from other countries did not like Negroes.

That is what our country was like. Women had no equal rights; they were paid less for the same work, they were discriminated against, as is the case in most of our American countries.

The cities and the rural areas were two zones in permanent struggle against each other, and the imperialists obtained from this struggle sufficient manpower to be able to pay the laboring man poorly and sporadically.

All of these things were subject to our revolution, and we also accomplished a true revolution in education, culture, and health.

This year illiteracy will be ended in Cuba. One hundred and four thousand instructors of all ages are traveling through rural Cuba teaching 1,250,000 illiterates to read—because there were illiterates in Cuba; there were 1,250,000 of them, many more than the official statistics of previous times had indicated.

This year we have extended compulsory primary education to nine years, and free and compulsory secondary education for all of the school population. We have carried out university reform, giving all the people free access to higher culture, to modern science and technology. We have greatly emphasized our national values as opposed to the cultural deformation produced by imperialism, and the expressions of our art are applauded by people all over the world—not by all, since in some places our art is not admitted; we are emphasizing the cultural heritage of our Latin America, giving annual prizes to writers from all parts of the Americas, the prize for poetry, Mr. Chairman, having been won by the distinguished poet, Roberto Ibáñez, in the last contest; the social function of medicine is being extended for the benefit of humble farm and city workers; there are sports for all the people, as reflected in the 75,000 who paraded on July 25 in a sports festival held in honor of Major Yuri Gagarin, the world's first cosmonaut; the beaches have been opened to all without distinction as to color or ideology, and also free of charge; and there are the Workers' Social Centers, converted out of all the exclusive clubs in the country—and there were many.

So then, fellow delegates, the time has come to speak of the economic part of the agenda. Topic I, very broad, also prepared by very brainy experts, deals with planning for the economic and social development of Latin America.

I shall refer to some of the statements made by the experts, with the idea of refuting them from the technical standpoint, and I shall then express the points of view of the Cuban delegation as to what development planning is.

The first inconsistency that we see in the paper is contained in the following sentence: "The view is often expressed that an increase in the level and diversity of economic activity brings in its wake improvements in health conditions; it is the conviction of the group that such improvements are desirable in themselves, that they are an essential prerequisite for economic growth, and that, therefore, they must be an integral element in any meaningful development program for the region."

This is also reflected in the structure of the loans of the Inter-American Development Bank, since in the analysis we made of the first 120 million loaned, we found that 40 million, that is, one-third, was directly for loans of this kind: for dwellings, water systems, sewers.

This is a little . . . I don't know, but I would almost call it a colonial condition. I get the impression that what is intended is to make the outhouse a fundamental thing. This improves the social conditions of the poor Indian, the poor Negro, the poor man who leads a subhuman existence. "Let's build him an outhouse and then, after we build him an outhouse, and after he is educated to keep it clean, then he can enjoy the benefits of production." It should be noted, fellow delegates, that the subject of industrialization does not appear in the analysis made by the experts. To the experts, to plan means to plan outhouses. As for the rest, who knows how it will be done?

If the Chairman will permit, I want to express deep regrets, in behalf of the Cuban delegation, at having lost the services of an expert as efficient as the one who headed this First Group, Dr. Felipe Pazos. With his intelligence and his capacity for work, and with our revolutionary activity, in two years Cuba would be the paradise of the outhouse, even though we would not have even one of the 250 factories we have begun to build, even though we would not have agrarian reform.

I ask myself, fellow delegates, are they trying to pull somebody's leg? Not Cuba's—Cuba is not in this, since the Alliance for Progress is not made for Cuba but against it and there is no provision for giving it a cent—but the legs of the other delegates. Don't you get a slight feeling that your leg is being pulled? Dollars are given to build highways, dollars are given to build sewers. Gentlemen, what are highways and roads built with, what are sewers built with, what are houses built with? You don't have to be a genius to answer that. Why don't they give dollars for equipment, dollars for machinery, dollars so that all of our underdeveloped countries, all of them, may become industrial-agricultural countries at one and the same time? It really is sad.

On page 10, speaking of the elements of the development planning, in Point 6, it shows who is the real author of this plan.

Point 6 states: "It can furnish a sounder basis for the provision and utilization of external financial assistance, particularly inasmuch as it provides more efficient criteria for judging individual projects."

We are not going to furnish sounder bases for the provision and utilization because we are not the ones who provide; you are the ones who receive, not those who provide; we—Cuba—are the ones who look on, and the United States is the one that provides. This Point 6, then, was drafted directly by the United States; it is a recommendation of the United States; and this is the spirit of this whole bungling thing called Topic 1.

Now I wish to state one thing for the record: We have spoken a great deal about politics; we have charged that this is a political confabulation and in our conversations with other delegates we have emphasized Cuba's right to express these opinions, because Cuba is attacked directly in Topic 5.

However, Cuba has not come here to sabotage the meeting, as has been asserted by some newspapers or by many spokesmen of foreign news agencies. Cuba has come to condemn what is subject to condemnation from the standpoint of principles, but it has come here to work harmoniously, if that is possible, to try to straighten this out, this thing that was born misshapen, and it is willing to cooperate with all the delegates to straighten it out and make it a nice project.

The Honorable Douglas Dillon mentioned financing in his speech; that is important. In gathering together to speak of development we have to speak of financing, and all of us have gathered together here to speak with the only country that has capital for financing.

Mr. Dillon has said [in substance]: "Looking toward the coming years and toward all sources of external financing—international institutions,

Europe, and Japan, as well as the United States, new private investments, and investments of public funds—if Latin America takes the necessary internal measures"—a prior condition—"it can logically expect that its efforts"—it isn't even that if it takes the measures, the funds will be granted, but rather that "it can logically expect"—"that its efforts will be met by an inflow of capital of at least twenty billion dollars in the next ten years. And most of these funds will come from public resources."

Is this what there is? No, there are 500 million dollars approved, that is what is being spoken of. This must be clearly emphasized, because it is the heart of the question. What does it mean?—and I assure you that I am not asking this for ourselves, but rather for the good of everybody—what is meant by "if Latin America takes the necessary internal measures," and what is meant by "it can logically expect"?

I believe that after the work of the committees or whenever the United States representative deems it appropriate, it will be necessary to pinpoint this part a little, because twenty billion is an interesting figure. It is nothing more than two-thirds of the figure that our Prime Minister announced as being necessary for the development of America; a little push more and we get to the thirty billion mark. But we have to get those thirty billion cash on the barrelhead, one by one, in the national treasuries of each of the countries of America, except for this poor Cinderella, who will probably get nothing.

This is where we can help, not by blackmail, as is being looked for, because it has been said: "No, Cuba is the goose that lays the golden eggs; Cuba is there, and as long as Cuba is there, the United States will give." No, we have not come here like that; we have come here to work, to try to fight on the level of principles and ideas, so that our countries may develop, because all or almost all of the delegates have said that if the Alliance for Progress fails, nothing can halt the wave of popular movements—I use my own terms, but this is what was meant—nothing can halt the waves of popular movements, if the Alliance for Progress fails, and we are interested in not having it fail, insofar as it may mean for the Americas a genuine improvement in the standard of living of their 200 million inhabitants. I can make this statement here in honesty and all sincerity.

We have diagnosed and foreseen the social revolution in the Americas, the real revolution, because events are shaping up otherwise, because an attempt is being made to halt the people with bayonets, and when the people realize that they can take the bayonets and turn them against those who hold them, those who hold them are lost. But if it is wished to lead the people along the path of logical and harmonious development, by long-term loans up to fifty years at a low interest rate, as Mr. Dillon announced, we are also in agreement.

The only thing, fellow delegates, is that we must all work together so that this figure may be made firm here and to make sure that the Congress of the United States will approve it, because you must not forget that we are faced with a presidential and legislative system, not a "dictatorship" like Cuba, where a representative of Cuba stands up and speaks in the name of the government, and is responsible for his actions. But things have to be ratified there, and the experience of many of the delegates has been that often the promises made have not been ratified there.

Well, I have a lot to say on each of the topics, so I shall hasten along here and then discuss them in a fraternal spirit in the committees. Just a few general figures, some general comments.

The rate of growth that is advanced as a very fine thing for all the Americas is 2.5 per cent net. Bolivia announced 5 per cent for ten years, and we congratulate the representative of Bolivia and tell him that with a little effort and mobilization of popular forces, he could say 10 per cent. We speak of 10 per cent development with no fear whatsoever; 10 per cent is the rate of development foreseen by Cuba for the coming years.

What does this mean, fellow delegates? It means that if all countries continue on the road they are now following, when all the Americas, which at present have a per capita income of around $330, obtain an annual growth of 2.5 per cent in their net product, somewhere around 1980 they wjll have $500 per capita. Of course, for many countries this will be really phenomenal.

What does Cuba expect to have in 1980? A per capita net income of $3,000—more than the United States has now. And if you don't believe us, that's all right too; we're here to compete, gentlemen. Leave us alone, let us develop, and then we can meet again twenty years from now, to see if the siren song came from revolutionary Cuba or from some other source. But we hereby announce, with full responsibility, that rate of annual growth.

The experts suggest the replacement of inefficient latifundia and dwarf holdings with well-equipped farms. We say: Do you want to have agrarian reform? Then take the land from those who have a lot and give it to those who have none. That is the way to conduct agrarian reform, the rest is a siren song. The way to do it, whether you give land divided into parcels in accordance with all the rules of private property; whether you give it as collective property, or whether you have a mixed system—as we do—depends on the individual characteristics of each country. But agrarian reform is carried out by liquidating the latifundia, not by settling some far off place.

And I could talk like this about redistribution of income, which in Cuba was effectively achieved, because you take from those who have more and permit those who have less or have nothing to have more, because we have carried out our agrarian reform, we have carried out our urban reform, we have reduced electricity and telephone rates—which, parenthetically, was our first skirmish with the foreign monopolistic companies—we have made workers' social centers and child centers where the workers' children go to get food and live while their parents work, we have made popular beaches, and we have nationalized education, which is absolutely free. In addition, we are working on a comprehensive health plan.

I shall speak of industrialization later, because it is the fundamental basis of development, and that is how we interpret it. But there is a very interesting point—that is, the filter, the purifier, the experts, seven of them, I believe. Once again, gentlemen, there is the danger of "outhouse-ocracy," stuck in the middle of the plans by which the countries want to improve their standard of living; another case of politicians dressed up as experts and saying yes here and no there; yes, this and that—but in reality because you're an easy tool of the one who furnishes the means; and you, no, because you've done this wrong—but in reality because you're not a tool of the one furnishing the means, because you say, for example, that you cannot accept aggression against Cuba as the price of a loan.

This is the danger, without counting the fact that the small countries, as is the case everywhere, receive little or nothing. Fellow delegates, there is only one place where the small ones have a right to "kick," and that is here, where each vote is a vote. This matter has to be voted, and the small countries—if they are ready to do so—can count on Cuba's militant vote against the idea of the "seven," meant to "sterilize," to "purify," and to channel the credit, with technical disguises, along different lines.

What is the position that will really lead to genuine planning, fully coordinated but not subordinated to any supranational agency?

We believe—and that is how we did it in our country, fellow delegates—that the prior condition for true economic planning is that the political power be in the hands of the working class. This is the *sine qua non* of true planning for us. Furthermore, it is necessary that the imperialistic monopolies be completely eliminated and that the basic activities of production be controlled by the state. With these three ends well tied together, one can begin planning for economic development; if not, everything is lost in words, speeches, and meetings.

In addition, there are two requisites which will make it possible or not for this development to take advantage of the latent potentialities lying within the people, who are waiting for them to be awakened. These are, on the one hand, rational central direction of the economy by a single power with authority to make decisions—I am not speaking of dictatorial powers, but decision-making powers—and, on the other, the active participation of all the people in the job of planning.

Naturally, in order to have all the people participate in planning, the people must own the means of production; otherwise, it will be difficult for them to participate. The people will not want to, and the owners of the companies where they work won't either, it seems to me.

We can speak for a few minutes about what Cuba has obtained by following its path, trading with the world, "flowing along the slopes of commerce," as Martí put it.

Up to this time we have contracted for loans amounting to 357 million dollars with the socialist countries, and we are engaged in conversations—which really are conversations—for a hundred and some million dollars more, with which we shall have reached 500 million dollars in loans during these five years. These loans, which give us possession and control over our economic development, amount to 500 million dollars, as we just said—the amount that the United States is giving to all the Americas—just for our small republic alone. This, divided by the population of Cuba and transferred to the Americas, would mean that to furnish equivalent amounts, the United States would have to give 15 billion pesos in five years, or 30 billion dollars—I speak of pesos or dollars, because in my country they are both worth the same—30 billion dollars in ten years, the amount requested by our Prime Minister; and with this, if there is wise direction of the economic process, Latin America would be something altogether different in only five years.

Let us go on now to Topic II of the Agenda. And, naturally, before analyzing it, we shall state a political question.

Our friends in these meetings—and there are many of them, even though it may not seem so—ask us if we are willing to come back in the family of Latin American nations. We have never left the Latin American nations, and we are fighting against our expulsion, against being forced to leave the family of Latin American republics. What we do not want is to be herded, as Martí said. Just that.

We denounce the dangers of economic integration of Latin America, because we know the examples of Europe, and furthermore, Latin America has already learned to the depths of its being what European economic integration cost it. We denounce the danger of having the processes of trade within free trade associations completely vested in the hands of international monopolies. But we also wish to announce here in this conference, and we hope our announcement will be accepted, that we are willing to join the Latin American Free Trade Association, as just another member, criticizing what ought to be criticized but complying with all the requisites, just as long as respect is given to Cuba, to its particular economic and social organization, and provided that its socialist government is accepted as an already consummated and irreversible fact.

And in addition, Cuba must be given equality of treatment and a fair share in the advantages of the international division of labor. Cuba must participate actively and it can contribute a great deal to improve many of the great "bottlenecks" that exist in the economies of our countries, with the help of planned economy, centrally directed and with a clear and well-defined goal.

However, Cuba also wished to propose the following measures: it proposes the initiation of immediate bilateral negotiations for the evacuation of bases or territories in member states occupied by other member states, so that there may be no more cases like the one denounced by the elegation of Panama, where Panama's wage policies cannot be applied in a part of its territory. The same thing happens with us, and we should like this anomaly to cease, speaking from the economic viewpoint.

We propose the study of rational plans for the development and coordination of technical and financial assistance from all of the industrialized countries, without ideological or geographical distinctions of any kind; we also propose that guarantees be requested to safeguard the interests of the weaker countries; we propose the prohibition of acts of economic aggression by some member states against other member states; guarantees to protect Latin American businessmen against the competition of foreign monopolies; the reduction of United States tariffs on industrial products of the integrated Latin American states; and we state that as we see it, external financing would be good only if it took the form of indirect investments that met the following conditions: The investments should not be subject to political requirements and should not discriminate against state enterprises; they should be applied in accordance with the interests of the receiving country; the interest rates should not exceed 3 per cent and the amortization period should not be less than ten years and subject to extension in case of balance of payments difficulties; the seizure of or confiscation of ships and aircraft of a member country by another should be prohibited; and tax reforms should be initiated, removing the tax burden from the working masses and providing protection against the action of foreign monopolies.

Topic III had been dealt with just as delicately as the others by the experts; they have approached this matter with a gentle pair of tweezers, lifted the veil slightly, and let it drop immediately, because this is a tough subject.

"It might have been desirable—and it was tempting—" they said, "for the Group to formulate broad and spectacular recommendations. But it was impossible to do so because of the numerous and intricate technical problems which would have had to be resolved first. Therefore, the recommendations actually set forth were confined to those considered technically feasible."

I don't know if I am overly perspicacious, but I think that I can read between the lines. Since there have been no verdicts, the delegation of Cuba specifically presents what should be achieved by this meeting: a guarantee of stable prices, without any "could" or "might," without any "we would examine" or "we shall examine," but just guarantees of stable prices; expanding or at least stable markets; guarantees against economic aggression, against the unilateral suspension of purchases in traditional markets, against the dumping of subsidized agricultural surpluses, and against protectionism for the production of basic commodities; creation of conditions in the industrialized countries for the purchase of primary products that have been subject to a higher degree of processing.

Cuba declares that it would be desirable for the delegation of the United States to state in the committees whether it will continue to subsidize its production of copper, lead, zinc, sugar, cotton, wheat, or wool. Cuba asks whether the United States will continue pressuring to stop member countries from selling their primary product surpluses to Socialist countries, thus increasing its own market.

And now we come to Topic V of the Agenda. Topic IV is nothing more than a report, but this Topic V is the other side of the coin.

On the occasion of the Costa Rica Conference Fidel Castro said that the United States had attended "with a bag of gold in one hand and a club in the other." Here today the United States comes with a bag of gold—fortunately a larger bag—in one hand, and the barrier to isolate Cuba in the other. It is, in any case, a victory of historic circumstances.

But in Topic V of the Agenda a program of measures is established for Latin America for the regimentation of thought, the subordination of the labor movement, and, if it can be done, the preparation of military aggression against Cuba.

Three steps are foreseen in reading it: mobilization, as of now, of Latin America media of information and publicity against the Cuban revolution and against the struggles of our countries for their freedom; the formation, at a later conference, of an Inter-American Press, Radio, Television, and Motion Picture Federation that will enable the United States to direct the public opinion organs of Latin America, all of them—right now there are not many that are outside its sphere of influence but it seeks them all—to exercise monopolistic control over new information agencies, and to absorb as many of the old ones as possible.

All of this is something extraordinary, which was announced here in all calmness and which in my country gave rise to deep discussion when something similar was done in a single instance. This is an attempt, fellow delegates, to establish a common market for culture, organized, directed, paid, mastered; the culture of all the Americas at the service of imperialistic propaganda plans, to show that the hunger of our peoples is not hunger but laziness. Magnificent!

To this we answer: The organs of public opinion of Latin America must be exhorted to support the ideals of national liberation of each Latin American country. An exhortation must be made for the exchange of information, cultural media, press organs, and for direct visits between peoples without discrimination, gentlemen, because a United States citizen who goes to Cuba nowadays faces five years of prison upon returning to his country. The Latin American governments must be exhorted to guarantee the labor movement freedom to organize independently, to defend the interests of the workers, and to struggle for the true independence of their countries. We call for a total and absolute condemnation of Topic V as an imperialistic attempt to domesticate the only thing that our countries have been saving from disaster: national culture.

I shall take the liberty, fellow delegates, of presenting an outline of the objectives of Cuba's first plan for economic development during the next four years. The general growth rate will be 12 per cent, that is, more than 9.5 per cent per capita, net. In the industrial field, the plan calls for the transformation of Cuba into the most highly industrialized country of Latin America in relation to its population, as may be seen from the following figures:

First place in Latin America in the per capita production of steel, electric power, and, except for Venezuela, in petroleum refining; first place in Latin America in tractors, rayon, shoes, textiles, etc.; second place in the world in the production of metallic nickel (up to now Cuba has produced only concentrates); nickel production in 1965 will amount to 70,000 metric tons, which is about 30 per cent of world production; and, in addition, it will produce 2,600 metric tons of metallic cobalt; sugar production of 8.5 to 9 million tons; and the commencement of the transformation of the sugar industry into a sugar-chemical industry.

In order to do this, which is easy to say, but which will require an enormous amount of work and the effort of an entire people and a very large amount of external financing, furnished from the standpoint of aid, not spoliation, the following measures have been adopted: more than one bilion pesos are going to be invested in industry—the Cuban peso is equivalent to the dollar—in the installation of 800 megawatts of electric power. In 1960, the installed capacity—except for the sugar industry, which operates seasonally—amounted to 621 megawatts. The installation of 205 industries, of which the twenty-two more important ones are the following: a new plant for refining nickel ore, which will raise the total to 70,000 tons; a petroleum refinery for two million tons of crude petroleum; the first steel mill, with a capacity of 700,000 tons of steel, which in this four-year period will reach 500,000 tons; the expansion of our plants to produce seamed steel tubes, amounting to 25,000 metric tons; tractors, 5,000 units per year; motorcycles, 10,000 units per year; three cement plants and expansion of the existing ones for a total of 1.5 million metric tons, which will raise our production to 2.5 million per year; metal containers, 291 million units; expansion of our glass plants by 23,700 metric tons per year; one million square meters of flat glass; a new plant for making bagasse fiberboard, 10,000 cubic meters; a bagasse cellulose plant, 60,000 cubic meters, in addition to a wood cellulose plant for 40,000 metric tons per year; an ammonium nitrate plant, 60,000 metric tons; a plant for simple superphosphate, for 70,000 tons, and 81,000 metric tons of triple superphosphate; 132,000 metric tons of nitric acid; 85,000 metric tons of ammonia; eight new textile plants and expansion of existing ones with 451,000 spindles; a kenaf bag plant for sixteen million bags; and so on to others of lesser importance, going as high as 205 at the present time.

These credits have been contracted for thus far as follows: 200 million dollars with the Soviet Union; 60 million dollars with the Chinese People's Republic; 40 million with the Socialist Republic of Czechoslovakia; 15 million with the Romanian People's Republic; 15 million with the Hungarian People's Republic; 12 million with the Polish People's Republic; 10 million with the German Democratic Republic; and 5 million with the Democratic Republic of Bulgaria. The total amount contracted for to the present time is 357 million. The new negotiations that we hope to conclude soon are basically with the Soviet Union which, as the most highly industrialized country of the socialist area, is the one that has given us the most support.

As for agriculture, Cuba intends to achieve self-sufficiency in the production of foodstuffs, including fats and rice, but not in wheat; self-sufficiency in cotton and hard fibers; production of exportable surpluses in tropical fruits and other agricultural products which will triple the present levels of exports.

With respect to foreign trade, the value of exports will be increased by 75 per cent over the 1960 figure. There will be a diversification of the economy; with sugar and sugar by-products amounting to around 60 per cent of exports and not 80 per cent as at the present time.

With respect to construction; the plan calls for elimination of 40 per cent of the present housing deficit, including *bohíos,* which are our rural shacks, and a rational combination of building materials so that use of local materials may be increased without sacrificing quality.

There is a point that I should like to dwell on for a moment, and that is education. We have laughed at the group of experts who placed education and health as *sine qua non* conditions to starting on the road to development. To us this is an aberration, but it is no less true that once the road to development is started, education should progress parallel to it. Without adequate technological education, development is slowed down. Therefore, Cuba has carried out a complete reform of education; it has expanded and improved educational services and has prepared over-all education plans.

At the present time it ranks first in Latin America in the allocation of funds to education; we devote 5.3 per cent of our national income to it. The developed countries allocate between 3 per cent and 4 per cent, and the Latin American countries between 1 per cent and 2 per cent of their national income. In Cuba, 28.3 per cent of the state's current expenditures are for the Ministry of Education, and including other agencies that spend money for education, this figure increases to 30 per cent. The Latin American country that ranks second in this respect allocates 21 per cent of its budget to this purpose.

The increase in our budget for education from 75 million in 1958 to 128 million in 1961 represents an increase of 7 per cent. And total expenditures for education, including the campaign against illiteracy and school construction amount to 170 million, or twenty-five pesos per capita. In Denmark, for example, twenty-five pesos per capita per year are spent on education; in France, fifteen; in Latin America, five.

In two years, ten thousand schoolrooms have been provided and ten thousand new teachers appointed. Ours is the first country in Latin America fully to satisfy all primary instruction needs of the school-age population, an aspiration of the UNESCO Principal Project for Latin America by 1968, which has already been fulfilled in Cuba.

These measures and these really marvelous and absolutely accurate figures we present here, fellow delegates, have been made possible by the following action: nationalization of teaching, making it secular and free, and making possible the total utilization of its services; establishment of a system of scholarships to guarantee the satisfaction of all the needs of the students, in accordance with the following plan: 20,000 scholarships for basic secondary schools, grades seven to nine; 3,000 scholarships for preuniversity institutes; 3,000 for art instructors; 6,000 for the universities; 1,500 for courses in artificial insemination; 1,200 for courses on agricultural machinery; 14,000 for courses in sewing and dressmaking and basic domestic science training for farm women; 1,200 for training of teachers for the hill areas; 750 for beginners' courses for primary school teachers; 10,000 including both scholarships and study grants, for students preparing for technological teaching; and in addition, hundreds of scholarships for the study of technology in the socialist countries; establishment of one hundred centers of secondary education, so that each municipality will have at least one.

This year in Cuba, as I already stated, illiteracy is being wiped out. It is a wonderful sight. Up to the present time, 104,500 brigade members, almost all of them students between the ages of ten and eighteen, have flooded the country from one end to the other, going directly to the cabins of the farm people and the homes of workers, to convince the old people who no longer want to study and thus to eliminate illiteracy.

Whenever a factory eradicates illiteracy among its workers, it raises a flag announcing this fact to the people of Cuba; whenever a farm cooperative becomes free of illiteracy among its members, it hoists a similar pennant; and there are 104,500 young students, who have as their insignia a book and a lamp, to carry the light of education into the backward areas, and who belong to the "Conrado Benítez" Brigades, named in honor of the first martyr of education of the Cuban Revolution, who was hanged by a group of counterrevolutionaries for the serious crime of being in the mountains of our country teaching the people how to read.

This is the difference, fellow delegates, between our country and those that are fighting against it.

One hundred and fifty-six thousand volunteer fighters against illiteracy, workers and professionals, work part time in this teaching field; 32,000 teachers head this army, and only with the active cooperation of all the people of Cuba could figures of such magnitude have been achieved.

This has all been done in one year, or rather, in two years: seven regimental headquarters have become school campuses; twenty-seven barracks have become schools; and all of this while there was danger of imperialistic aggression. The Camilo Cienfuegos school campus at the present time has five thousand pupils from the Sierra Maestra and is building units for twenty thousand pupils; we intend to build a similar campus in every province; each school campus will be self-sufficient in food, thus initiating the farm children in agricultural practices.

In addition, new teaching methods have been instituted. Primary school enrollment increased from 602,000 in 1958 to 1,231,700 in 1959; secondary school enrollment from 21,900 to 83,800; business schools, from 8,900 to 21,300; technological schools, from 5,600 to 11,500.

Forty-eight million pesos have been invested in school construction in just two years.

The National Printing Office guarantees textbooks and other printed material for all school children free of charge.

Two television networks, covering the whole country, make possible the use of this powerful medium for mass education. Likewise, the entire national radio system is at the disposal of the Ministry of Education.

The Cuban Institute of Motion Picture Art and Industry, the National Library, and the National Theater, with representatives throughout the whole country, complete this great system for the dissemination of culture.

The National Institute of Sports, Physical Education, and Recreation, whose initials are INDER, promotes physical development on a massive scale.

This, fellow delegates, is the cultural picture in Cuba at this time.

Now we come to the final part of our statement, the part containing definitions, because we want to establish our position very clearly.

We have denounced the Alliance for Progress as an instrument designed to separate Cuba from the other countries of Latin America, to sterilize the example of the Cuban Revolution, and then to bend the other countries to the wishes of the imperialists.

Permit me to offer full proof of this.

There are many interesting documents in the world. We shall distribute to the delegates some documents which came into our hands and which show, for example, the opinion held by the imperialists of the government of Venezuela, whose foreign minister attacked us harshly a few days ago, perhaps because he understood that we were violating laws of friendship with his people or his government.

However, it is interesting to point out that friendly hands sent us an interesting document. It is a report on a secret document addressed to

Ambassador Moscoso in Venezuela by his advisers, John M. Cates, Jr., Irvin Tragen, and Robert Cox.

This document, in one of its paragraphs, states, speaking of the measures Venezuela must take in order to have a real Alliance for Progress, directed by the United States:

> Reform of the Bureaucracy. All plans that are made [speaking of Venezuela] all programs initiated for the economic development of Venezuela, either by the Venezuelan Government or by United States technicians, will have to be implemented through Venezuela's bureaucracy. But, as long as the civil service of that country is characterized by ineptitude, indifference, inefficiency, formalism, party favoritism in the granting of jobs, corruption, duplication of functions, and the building of private empires, it will be practically impossible to have dynamic and effective projects go through the government machinery. Therefore, a reform of the administrative structure is possibly the most basic need, since not only would it be directed toward correcting a basic economic and social imbalance, but would also imply a reconditioning of the very instrument which should shape all of the other basic reforms and development projects.

There are many interesting things in this document which we shall place at the disposal of the delegates; for example, where it speaks of the natives. After the natives are taught, the natives can be permitted to work. We are natives, and nothing more. But there is something interesting, fellow delegates, and that is the recommendation made by Mr. Cates to Mr. Moscoso as to what has to be done. It reads as follows:

> The United States will be forced, probably sooner than is expected, to point out to the right-wings, the oligarchy, the nouveaux riches, the national and foreign economic circles in general, the military, and the clergy that in the long run they will have to make a choice between two things: either contribute to the establishment in Venezuela of a society based on the masses, maintaining at the same time their status quo and their wealth, or face the loss of both (and perhaps death itself before the firing squad) [this is a report by Americans to their Ambassador] if the forces of moderation and progress are displaced in Venezuela.

Then this is completed, giving the picture and all the machinations by which this conference began to develop, with other reports of secret instructions sent to Latin America by the United States Department of State concerning the "Cuban case."

This is very important, because it shows where the lamb's mother was. It says—and I shall take the liberty of quoting a few extracts from it, though we shall distribute it later, in deference to the brevity that I have already violated somewhat:

From the beginning, it was generally understood in Latin America that the United States backed the invasion, and that it would therefore be successful. The majority of the governments and the responsible sectors of the people were prepared to accept a *fait accompli,* although there were misgivings about violation of the principle of non-intervention. The Communists and other strongly pro-Castro elements immediately took the offensive with demonstrations and acts of violence directed against United States agencies especially in Argentina, Bolivia, and Mexico. However, these anti-American and pro-Castro activities received limited backing and produced less results than might have been expected.

The failure of the invasion discouraged the anti-Castro sectors, who considered that the United States should do something dramatic to restore its damaged prestige, but it was received with glee by the Communists and other pro-Castro elements.

It continues:

In most cases, the reactions of the Latin American governments were not surprising. With the exception of Haiti and the Dominican Republic, the republics that had already broken or suspended relations with Cuba expressed their understanding of the United States position. Honduras joined the anti-Castro camp, suspending relations in April and proposing the formation of an alliance of Central American and Caribbean nations to have it out with Cuba by force. The proposal—which was also suggested independently by Nicaragua—was quietly dropped when Venezuela refused to back it up. Venezuela, Colombia, and Panama expressed serious concern over the penetrations of the Soviets and of international Communism in Cuba, but favored some sort of collective action by the OAS—"collective action by the OAS" brings us into familiar ground—to deal with the Cuban problem. A similar opinion was expressed by Argentina, Uruguay, and Costa Rica. Chile, Ecuador, Bolivia, Brazil, and Mexico refused to support any position that would imply intervention in Cuba's internal affairs. This attitude was probably very strong in Chile, where the Government found strong opposition in all circles to open military intervention by any State against the Castro regime. In Brazil and in Ecuador the matter provoked serious splits in the Cabinet, in Congress, and in the political parties. In the case of Ecuador, the intransigent pro-Cuban position adopted by President Velasco was shaken but not altered by the discovery of the fact that Ecuadorean Communists were being trained in that country in guerrilla tactics by pro-Castro revolutionaries. [Parenthetically, and this is my comment, that is a lie.]

Likewise, there are few doubts that some of the previously uncommitted elements in Latin America have been favorably impressed by Castro's capacity to survive a military attack, supported by the United States, against his regime. Many of those who had previously hesitated to commit themselves, assuming that the United States would in time eliminate the Castro regime, may now have changed their minds. Castro's victory has shown them the permanent and workable nature of the Cuban revolution [this is a report by the United States.] In addition, his victory has no doubt aroused the latent anti-United States attitude that prevails in a large part of Latin America.

In every respect, the member states of the OAS are now less hostile toward United States intervention in Cuba than before the invasion, but a majority of them—including Brazil and Mexico, which accounted for more than half the population of Latin America—are not willing to intervene actively or even to join a quarantine against Cuba. Nor can it be expected that the Organization would give its prior approval to direct intervention by the United States, except in the event that Castro were to be involved beyond a doubt in an attack against a Latin American government.

Even if the United States were successful—which seems improbable—in persuading a majority of the Latin American states to join in a quarantine against Cuba, the attempt would not be completely successful. It is certain that Mexico and Brazil would refuse to cooperate and would serve as a channel for travel and other communications between Latin America and Cuba.

Mexico's long-standing opposition to intervention of any kind would not be an unsurmountable obstacle to collective action by the OAS against Cuba. The attitude of Brazil, however, which exercises strong influence over its South American neighbors, is decisive for hemisphere cooperation. As long as Brazil refuses to act against Castro, it is probable that a number of other nations, including Argentina and Chile, will not wish to risk adverse internal repercussions to please the United States.

The magnitude of the threat represented by Castro and the Communists in other parts of Latin America will probably continue to depend basically on the following factors: (a) The ability of the regime to maintain its position; (b) its effectiveness in showing the success of its way to dealing with the problems of reform and development; and (c) the ability of non-Communist elements in other Latin American countries to furnish feasible and popularly accepted alternatives. If, by means of propaganda, etc., Castro can convince the disaffected elements existing in Latin America that basic social reforms are really being made [that is to say, if the delegates become convinced that what we are saying is true] that will benefit the poorer classes, the attractiveness of the Cuban example will increase and it will continue to inspire leftist imitators in this entire area. The danger is not so much that a subversive apparatus, based in Havana, may export the revolution, but that increasing poverty and unrest among the masses of the Latin American people will give the pro-Castro elements an opportunity to act.

After considering whether we intervene or not, they reason as follows:

It is probable that the Cubans will act cautiously in this regard for some time. They probably are not desirous of risking the interception or discovery of any acts of piracy or military supplies coming from Cuba.

> Such an eventuality would result in a greater stiffening of Latin American official opinion against Cuba, perhaps to the point of giving tacit backing to United States intervention, or at least of providing possible reasons for sanctions by the OAS. For these reasons, and because of Castro's concern over the defense of his own territory at this time, the use of Cuban military forces to support insurrection in other areas is extremely improbable."

And so, for any of you delegates who have any doubts, the government of the United States announces that it would be very difficult for our troops to intervene in the national affairs of other countries.

> As time goes by, and in view of the absence of direct Cuban intervention in the internal affairs of neighboring states, present fears of Castroism, of Soviet intervention in the regime, of its "socialist nature"—the quotation marks are theirs—and the repugnance against Castro's police-state repression will tend to diminish and the traditional policy of non-intervention will be reaffirmed.

It goes on to say:

> Aside from its direct effect on the prestige of the United States in that area—which undoubtedly has dropped as a result of the failure of the invasion—the survival of the Castro regime might have a profound effect on American political life in the coming years. It is preparing the scene for a political struggle on the terms promoted by Communist propaganda for a long time in this Hemisphere, with the "popular" [in quotation marks] anti-American forces on the one hand and the dominant groups allied with the United States on the other hand. The governments that promise evolutionary reforms for a period of years, even at an accelerated pace, will be faced with political leaders who will promise an immediate remedy for social ills through the confiscation of property and the overturning of society. The most immediate danger of Castro's example for Latin America might well be the danger to the stability of those governments that are at present attempting evolutionary social and economic changes, rather than for those that have tried to prevent such changes, in part because of the tensions and awakened hopes accompanying such social changes and economic development. The unemployed city-dwellers and landless peasants in Venezuela and Peru, for example, who have been waiting for Acción Democrática and APRA to make reforms, are an easy source of political strength for the politician who convinces them that the change can be made more quickly than has been promised by the Social Democratic movements. The popular support at present enjoyed by groups seeking evolutionary changes, or the potential support they might normally obtain as the Latin American masses become more politically active, would be lost to the extent to which extremist political leaders, using Castro's example, might arouse support for revolutionary change.

And in the last paragraph, gentlemen, our friend present here says:

> The Alliance for Progress might well furnish the stimulus to carry out more intensive reform programs, but unless these programs are started quickly and soon begin to show positive results, it is probable that they will not be enough of a counterweight to increasing pressure from the extreme left. The years ahead of us will almost certainly witness a race between those forces that are attempting to initiate evolutionary reform programs and those that are trying to generate support by the masses for fundamental economic and social revolution. If the moderates lag behind in this race, they might in time be deprived of the support of the masses and caught in an untenable position between the extremes of the right and the left.

These, fellow delegates, are the documents that the delegation of Cuba wanted to present to you, to make an unvarnished analysis of the "Alliance for Progress."

We all know the innermost feelings of the Department of State of the United States: "We have to get the Latin American countries to grow because otherwise we shall get a phenomenon called 'Castroism,' which is awful for the United States."

Well, then, gentlemen, let us have the Alliance for Progress on these terms: Let there be a genuine growth in the economies of all of the member countries of the Organization of American States; let them grow, so that they may consume their products, not to become a source of wealth for United States monopolies; let them grow to ensure social peace, not to create new reserves for a future war of conquest; let them grow for us, not for outsiders. And to all of you, fellow delegates, the delegation of Cuba wishes to say with all frankness: We, with our own conditions, want to be a part of the Latin American family; we want to live together with Latin America; we want to see it grow, if possible, at the same pace we are growing, but we are not opposed to its growing at a different pace. What we do demand is a guarantee of nonaggression against our borders.

We cannot stop exporting an example, as the United States wishes, because an example is something intangible that transcends borders. What we do give is a guarantee that we will not export revolutions, we guarantee that not a single rifle will leave Cuba, that not a single weapon will leave Cuba for battle in any other country of America.

What we cannot assure is that Cuba's ideas will not be applied in any other country of America, and what we do assure you in this conference is that if urgent measures of social improvement are not adopted, the example of Cuba will take fire in various countries, and then that comment which gave so much food for thought, uttered by Fidel on a certain twenty-sixth of July, and which was interpreted as aggression, will again be true.

Fidel said that if social conditions remained as they were, "the cordillera of the Andes would be the Sierra Maestra of the Americas."

We, gentlemen, call the Alliance for Progress the alliance for our progress, the peaceful alliance for the progress of all. We are not opposed to being left out in the distribution of credits, but we are opposed to being left out of participation in the cultural and spiritual life of our Latin American peoples, of which we are a part.

What we shall never accept is a curtailment of our freedom to trade and to have relations with all countries of the world, and what we shall defend ourselves against with all our strength is any attempt of foreign aggression, whether it comes from an imperial power or from any Latin American organization that incorporates the desires of some to see us wiped out.

To conclude, Mr. Chairman, fellow delegates, I want to tell you that some time ago we held a meeting of the Staff of the Revolutionary Forces of my country, a staff to which I belong. The matter concerned aggression against Cuba, which we knew was coming, although we did not know when or where. We thought it would be large, indeed it would be very large. This took place before the famous warning by the Premier of the Soviet Union, Nikita Khrushchev, that his rockets could reach beyond Soviet borders. We had not requested that aid, and were not aware of that willingness to aid us. That is why we held our meeting, knowing that an invasion was coming, to face our final fate as revolutionaries. We knew that if the United States invaded Cuba, there would be a blood bath, but in the end we would be defeated and expelled from all inhabited areas of the country.

Then we, the members of the staff, proposed that Fidel Castro withdraw to a mountain redoubt, and that one of us take charge of the defense of Havana. Our Prime Minister and chief, speaking in words that ennoble him—as do all of his acts—then answered that if the United States invaded Cuba, and if Havana were defended as it should be, hundreds of thousands of men, women, and children would die under the thrust of Yankee weapons, and that the leader of a people in revolution could not be asked to hide in the mountains, that his place was there with the beloved fallen, and that there, with them, he would fulfill his historic mission.

The invasion did not materialize, but fellow delegates, we maintain that spirit. That is why I can predict that the Cuban Revolution is invincible, because it has a people and because it has a leader like the one who is ruling Cuba.

That is all, fellow delegates.

CHAPTER 12

On the Alliance for Progress[1]

CUBA finds itself obliged to abstain from the general voting on the document, and will go on to explain, with a few details, the reasons for this abstention.

In the speech which it delivered in a plenary session, this delegation warned about the dangers facing the meeting of the Alliance for Progress and expressed its belief that in the Alliance it could see the beginning of a maneuver directed toward isolating the Cuban Revolution.

Nevertheless, the Cuban delegation explained that it came disposed to work in harmony, to discuss the guiding principles of our Revolution, and to attempt to coordinate, with all the other countries, a joint action aimed at drawing up documents which would express not only real present situations, but also the common goals of all nations.

Unfortunately, the Cuban delegation sees that its aspiration cannot be fully realized. Mr. President, Cuba drew up twenty-nine proposals for the Resolution, in which we dealt with many of the fundamental problems that—in our view—are afflicting Latin America, disturbing its development, and providing the conditions that permit the action of foreign monopolies.

Cuba pointed out the contradiction between the insignificance of the objectives and the grandiosity of the proclamation. People spoke here about a challenge to destiny; they spoke of an alliance which was going to guarantee the well-being of all the inhabitants of Latin America, and they used many grandiloquent words.

Nevertheless, when we finally determine what the decade of democratic progress is going to be, we encounter the fact that, with a net annual income increase rate of 2.5 per cent per inhabitant, it would require ap-

[1] Speech delivered at the Punta del Este Conference of the OAS—Inter-American Economic and Social Council, August 16, 1961. Official OAS transcript translated by Suzanne Pollard.

proximately a century to reach the present level of the United States. This is obviously a high standard of living, but it is not an unreachable goal, nor can it be considered absurd for the countries of the world and of Latin America.

Furthermore, calculating (naturally, a calculation that has no scientific basis and serves only as a means of expression of ideas) that the process of development of the presently underdeveloped countries and that of the industrial nations remain in proportion, the underdeveloped countries would have to wait five hundred years before reaching the same revenue per inhabitant as the developed ones.

We understand that when the situation in Latin America is as it is—and we have come together at this economic conference for some purpose—we cannot speak about such large goals and present such small objectives.

Regarding health and education, the goals have also been very modest; in some cases, more modest than those that have been proposed by international organizations, such as UNESCO, for several years now; goals our country has exceeded in some cases, but which it hopes to exceed completely within five years.

Regarding housing, there is no definition of goals, and we cannot even find a qualitative definition of what the industrial development is going to be.

Furthermore, we notice a certain imprecision of objectives regarding agriculture, in that it is considered on the same level on large landed estates and on small ones, and at no point is there a discussion of the action of foreign owners, disturbers of the economy of many Latin American countries.

Cuba felt that if many of these already-stated goals were maintained more or less in an equal form, as in the original documents placed before us for consideration, and if the system of private investments directed from abroad were maintained, it would be impossible to arrive at the necessary bases for truly establishing that right to get underway to which the peoples of Latin America are entitled, the right to establish the bases for a healthy economy which would permit increased rhythms of growth.

Furthermore, during the course of the conference, the Cuban delegation asked on repeated occasions what was the mechanism for the distribution of resources of the so-called Alliance for Progress, and whether Cuba could have recourse to these resources. These two questions have not been answered.

With respect to the economic integration of Latin America, Cuba pointed out that integration is not a panacea, nor can it serve as an alternative to basic socioeconomic reforms. Nevertheless, it stated that if countries with different forms of economic and social organization were part of this integration, then Cuba would show itself willing to join the economic integration of Latin America, as long as its socioeconomic individuality was respected.

Furthermore, Cuba indicated as a prerequisite to solid integration the full sovereignty of the countries in all their territories, and it referred specifically to the Guantánamo Base, which exists within the territory of Cuba, and to the Panama Canal.

In addition, another series of requests was made. Some of these, in one form or another and sometimes quite cut-down from their original intention, have been incorporated into the permanent documents of this meeting. But there are others, such as the necessity for security for the ships and airplanes of all the member nations, which were not even discussed.

With respect to raw materials, we pointed out the incalculable prices of the markets; we denounced economic aggression and demanded that it be condemned and proscribed; we indicated the necessity for diversifying the exportations from Latin American countries, augmenting the variation of raw materials, incorporating new products into the exportations, opening new markets; and we explicitly pointed out the markets of the socialist world, which now have a global increase rate of 10 percent.

Cuba criticized subsidies and the "dumping" of raw materials on the part of the industrialized nations, and pointed out the risks that accumulation of agricultural surpluses or reserves of strategic minerals can represent to the markets of raw materials. The proposals and warnings made by Cuba were echoed by several countries, and we might say that Cuba echoed their proposals and advice as well, since naturally, many of these problems are common to our underdeveloped countries.

Nevertheless, the final document, in practice, totally limited the real intention of the promoters of these ideas, so that they ended up practically innocuous. For example, while the Cuban delegation proposed the abolition of restrictions on importation and subsidies to the internal production of raw materials from the industrialized countries, the final document speaks only about reducing, and abolishing if possible, these restrictions.

The same thing occurred in many other instances. Concrete propositions which had a definite purpose were converted into vague declarations, in that they include the points or phrases: "if it is possible," "within the regulations," "when conditions permit," "if they require it," "if they permit it," etc., so that escape clauses are immediately established.

As a fact—to give an idea of the maintenance of prices in agriculture in the year 1955—according to the FAO, and using the facts we have on hand, we can say that the United States gave the sum of 2,525 million dollars, a much greater sum than any that has been given in one year up to now.

The present document offers no effective guarantee whatsoever that the production subsidized by the United States will not continue to expand.

It would take a great deal of time to continue with the list of all the proposals in which Cuba participated with a constructive spirit, attempting to form effective resolutions aimed at bringing about an understanding which would give a complete guarantee to the smaller countries and to the underdeveloped countries in general. From this point—without injuring the sovereignty of any member nation, nor even the sovereignty of any powerful nation, which for reasons of its industrial development has special conditions in comparisons to the others—we could go on to begin this new era, which has been so widely discussed.

Later the declaration was made which was presented yesterday and on which we worked. Cuba abstained with respect to this declaration, because we found many points that had been changed, some completely in meaning and some in form, as has been occurring in the course of this meeting.

The fundamental point is that, once again, the United States did not answer the Cuban question. This silence must be interpreted as a negative response, and therefore Cuba will not participate in the Alliance for Progress. It is difficult to support an alliance in which the ally is not going to participate at all. Furthermore, the fundamental root of our troubles has not been attacked; namely, the existence of foreign monopolies which interfere with our economies and also tie our international policies to outside dictates.

There has not been a condemnation of economic aggression, for which Cuba has always strongly hoped, since it has felt profoundly the harshness of this aggression.

There has been an insistence on solving Latin America's problems through a monetary policy, in the sense of considering that monetary changes, changes in currency, are going to change the economic structure of the countries, while we have insisted that only a change in the total structure, in the relations of production, can ensure the real creation of conditions for the progress of nations.

There has also been an insistence on free enterprise, which, as it is in the public domain, is philosophically condemned in Cuba as exploitation of man by man. In practice, it hardly exists in our territory, and will play no part in our new programs of development.

For all these reasons Cuba can not sign this document, honored delegates.

Nevertheless, I wish to state that it has been a constructive piece of work; I wish to state that Cuba did not feel itself to be alone during the course of the conference. There were many meetings to which it was not invited—and naturally it can make no judgments on the content of the conversations that took place in these meetings—but we know that the principal theme in many of these was Cuba, and we also know that Cuba had good friends, people of absolute conviction in their ideals and statements, who maintained a favorable attitude toward Cuba.

So we have been able to arrive harmoniously at the end of the conference, and we believe we have been able to demonstrate that our intention was always that of collaborating in the aggrandizement of the inter-American system, based on a real independence and friendship of nations, and not on the dependency of all under the direction of one.

We feel that Cuba has obtained some satisfactions, and basically we feel that a new perspective is opening up for Latin America. In spite of this our delegation cannot sign the document.

We note that in one paragraph there is an explicit admission of the existence of régimes different from those that have the philosophy of free enterprise. Also, for the most part, there is an admission of the existence of a country within the conclave of Latin American nations which presents a series of specific characteristics differentiating it from the rest, but nevertheless permitting it a place in the total, since it is named explicitly in one place.

For this reason we believe that the first real bond of peaceful coexistence in Latin America has been established. We also believe that a first step has been taken toward a recognition, on the part of those governments decidedly against ours and against our system, at least of the irreversible nature of the Cuban Revolution and of its right to be considered as an independent state, with all its peculiarities, even if they do not like its system of government.

The government of the United States has voted affirmatively on all the parts of this document, and in this respect we believe that it has also taken a positive step, establishing the fact that there can exist régimes whose philosophy affects that of free enterprise in this part of Latin America. We believe this to be a very positive step.

We have always been willing to discuss our difficulties with the government of the United States, which have been the subject of many talks and some conferences in these years and in this part of the world, and we have systematically stated that we could do this at any place, the only condition being that no preconditions be set to such a meeting.

Once more our government deliberately states this readiness. It is not begging for any kind of rapprochement, nor is it soliciting any type of truce; it is simply pointing out its position and establishing clearly, before all friendly nations, the fact that Cuba's desire is to live in peace with all the nations of the continent who desire this as well.

Nevertheless, we feel that danger is still floating in the atmosphere. To be crudely explicit, we would be false to the characteristics of the Cuban Revolution if we did not state that we are aware, as is everyone, that this meeting is in some way tied to a foreign ministers' meeting at which the case of Cuba is to be discussed. We understand that many steps have been taken in this direction, to search for affirmative votes for the meeting.

However, we note a new constructive fact. Years ago the foreign ministers met to condemn Guatemala, and an economic conference was planned.

More or less the same thing happened in Costa Rica. Now an economic conference is meeting, and the foreign ministers will meet afterward.

We feel this to be a great step forward, and furthermore we hope that this foreign ministers' meeting will not take place. This would be an even greater step forward. But now we must state the fundamental dilemma of this era, which is really a crucial time for the nations of the world—a dilemma that is also of importance to Latin America.

Many delegates, perhaps all of them, have asked themselves: If the Alliance for Progress fails, what will happen? And this is an extremely important question. The United States has felt the pressure of the nations of the world. It has seen that the situation in Latin America, as in the rest of the world, is extremely tense, and that it tends to attack the basis of the imperialist regime so deeply that it is necessary to look for a solution.

This Alliance for Progress means to look for a solution within the guidelines of economic imperialism. We feel that, under these circumstances, the Alliance for Progress is going to fail. In the first place (without wanting to be offensive in any way) I tend to doubt that it is possible to dispose of twenty-one billion dollars in the next few years. The administrative obstructions of the Great Country to the North have characteristics such that at times—such as now, I believe—there is the threat of charging interest on foreign loans of up to five million dollars. If there are such threats for such small quantities, one can imagine what there will be for quantities as large as the one I have mentioned.

Furthermore, it has been explicitly established that these loans will basically go to foment free enterprise. And since there has been no form of condemnation of the imperialist monopolies which are established in each of the Latin American countries, or in almost all of them, it is logical to suppose also that the debts that would accrue would serve to develop these monopolies. This, undoubtedly, will provoke a certain boom in industry and business and thereby bring in gains for the business enterprises. Within the system of free exchange, in which almost all the countries of Latin America live, this will mean a greater exportation of capital to the United States. So the Alliance for Progress, in the long run, would turn into a source of financing of foreign monopolistic enterprises on the part of the countries of Latin America.

But, in addition, since in no part of the document has there been a deliberate decision regarding fundamental points, such as the fixing of prices of raw materials; since there is no limit to how low these prices may be set; since there is absolutely no obligation to establish limits to them, it is very likely that in the coming year the present tendency will continue, and that the prices of raw materials of Latin America will fall lower and lower.

In that case it is presumable that there will be a continuous deterioration of balance of payments of each of the Latin American countries, and to this there will also be added the operation of monopolies that export capital. All of this will result in lack of development—just the opposite of what the Alliance for Progress intends to achieve.

This lack of development will bring about more unemployment. Unemployment means a lowering of salaries; in order to make up for the state budgets, which cannot be filled because of lack of profits, there will begin the inflationary process which we all know so well. And, at that point, in almost all the countries of Latin America, a document from the International Monetary Fund will enter the scene.

This is how the real plan for the countries of Latin America will be carried out. There are only two possible solutions: to meet popular discontent head on, with all the consequences this implies; or to begin moving toward a liberation of foreign trade, which is fundamental for our economies, to develop an independent economic policy and to stimulate the development of all the internal potential of each country. And all these things, naturally, are within the framework of independent foreign policies, which will bring about the necessary conditions for this entire task of development of trade with countries in other parts of the world.

Naturally, not all the countries will be able to do this, because special conditions are necessary. In the first place, great courage will be needed. Within the system in which most of us live, the statesmen will have to make an about-face in their economic and foreign policy, thereby immediately coming into conflict with foreign monopolies. The masses will support the governments that enter into conflict in order to defend the standard of living of their citizens. But the masses, when they defend a position, also make demands. Then the governments will be faced with a double threat, which they will not always be able to resolve: on the one hand, the pressure from the imperialist monopolies; on the other, the pressure from the masses which are demanding more. In order to really find a solution, a government will have to break down all the structures, take its place at the side of the masses, and begin a complete revolution. But we can not talk about revolutions without talking about the path governments can follow, without arriving in turn at the outbreak of revolutionary processes.

Confronted with this dilemma, the statesmen must realize that if they have the necessary courage to confront the problem, to satisfy a large part of the hopes of the masses, and not to give in to foreign monopolies, they will be able to make some progress.

However, we sadly note that historical example demonstrates that in this dilemma, governments are afraid of pressure from the masses, and tend to ally themselves with monopolies and the importing segment of national bourgeoisies, taking the first step toward repression.

For a policy of this type to succeed, it must be able to count not only on a national bourgeoisie that is strong, aggressive, anxious to overcome, and conscious of its ideals, but also on an army capable of understanding the current situation of Latin America and the world. Whether this is possible or not is a question we cannot answer.

The other choice is that of popular discontent. Popular discontent will augment, under these conditions, to the point where once again two historical conditions will be created, and it will be necessary to resolve them: Either the governments will be substituted, through popular elections, by new ones—this time with the direct participation of the masses in power—or a state of civil war will be established. If you progress to governments with mass participation, once again there will be created the great contradictions between the people, who attempt more and more to advance along the road to gaining their rights, and the national armies, which in general defend different social systems and which still have weapons in their hands. There you have the seeds of another civil war.

If the governments succeed in liquidating the movement of the masses and maintaining an iron control of the state apparatus, there will constantly hang over them the danger of internal wars, for which Cuba declares from this time on that it will not be responsible. And these wars, developing first under very difficult conditions in the most mountainous regions, will little by little come to dominate the countryside, then besiege the cities and one day they will move on to take over political power for the popular masses.

This, Mr. President and Honorable Delegates, is the message Cuba has felt obligated to express before you all; what it sees as really underlying the Alliance for Progress, the dangers it sees in it, and what it predicts for the future of the people if all international meetings simply become tournaments of oratory, as they have been up to now.

Therefore, although Cuba declares its support for many of the aspirations of this Punta del Este Charter, it regrets that it is not able to sign it at this point; it repeats its desire for friendship among all the peoples of the Continent; it clearly establishes its position of willingness to discuss any bilateral problem with any American country; and it appreciates the spirit of cooperation in which all the honorable delegates have listened to the comments of the Cuban delegation: its statements, its advice, and its continued, perhaps a bit repetitious and tiresome, explanations.

Thank you very much.

CHAPTER 13

Our Industrial Tasks[1]

THE Cuban Revolution enters a new stage of its institutional life in 1962. A stage termed *planning* will be governed during the first year by the organizational process. *Planning* and *organization* are more or less twin terms, but we differentiate between them. Planning is the organization of both the economy and the general life of the nation in accordance with broad, compatible, balanced lines, aimed at deriving the maximum values from society's dormant reserves. Organization is the preparation of all of the administrative agencies—down to the last detail—in order to carry out effective planning.

The planning period is necessary because certain phenomena have already taken place, and others are imminent, which are of great importance in developing an effective global approach to economic problems.

Cuba was, and is, a monoculture, and it was, in absolute terms, a country with only one market. In addition Cuba was a semicolonial country with the characteristic traits of semicolonial countries: much unemployment; unemployment disguised as public employment; import of foodstuffs and other consumer goods that could be produced within the country; a proliferation of a mercantile bourgeoisie allied to imperialist exporters.

The panorama offered by the country when the Revolution took charge was that of a so-called representative democracy structured in the economic sector according to established norms. There was the usual profusion of inept agencies utilized by the state bureaucracy, all the important posts being taken by homegrown capitalists or foreign agents. And there was an absolute incongruity between the immediate needs of the nation and the institutions that had been conceived for the purpose of serving the interests of the native oligarchies, and in the end, existed to serve their masters in the north. The economic structure, thus, was geared to our dependence on

[1] *Cuba Socialista*, Año II, No. 7, March 1962. Translated by Melvi Tallers.

the United States. This was not at all surprising, since economic relations condition a country's institutional life. The spectrum was reduced to a single product, sugar. There were large reserves of sugar as well as the means to increase stock if it were necessary. Imperialism dominated the entire apparatus of the product's international distribution. There was a large army of unemployed, at times numbering 600 thousand persons, ready to serve as a counter force against any pretensions organized labor (as well as other victims of the stagnant situation of the country) might have. There were a series of industries manufacturing their products with imported raw materials, with imported machinery, using imported replacement parts. There was an agriculture lacking development, suffocated by the competition from the imperialist market and from the latifundia. The latifundia (absentee landlords) devoted the lands to sugar cane or to extensive cattle raising, preferring to import foodstuffs from the United States. In brief, there was a distortion in the country's economy and an almost total stagnation.

When we first entered into the field of international commerce, we found that the economic policy of the dictatorship had greatly diminished our currency reserves. This situation made it very difficult to maintain the continuous flow of necessary raw materials for our industries, and the flow of consumer goods for our population.

The situation was critical and our inexperience was great. Because we did not know how to find quick solutions, we remained quite inactive. However, during the first year of the revolution we never lost sight of the central question facing our economy: What line should we adopt, and with what intensity would we pursue it?

We can say that the Agrarian Reform Law and the seizure of the National Bank were the most significant acts taken during the first year. The former created the basis for the struggle and established the first link in the chain of clash and counterclash with imperialism. This was to lead us in a direction that, though not outlined in advance, was foreseeable. It was to lead us to new and more just and suitable forms of organization. Toward the end of that year the seizure of the National Bank gave the state control of the currency, although the rest of banking remained in private hands.

This work of the Cuban Revolution was the beginning of what was to be the great struggle of the following year. The great problems that would definitively change the structure of the country in 1960 were not as yet blueprinted. The recovery of ill-gotten properties, many of which were industrial installations, and the purchase of certain industries by the Revolution (in addition to the embryonic plans) made it necessary to create the Department of Industrialization within the National Institute of Agrarian Reform. This Department, conceived to carry out major tasks, could not produce full results at the beginning since the direction that would give perspective to developmental goals was lacking. The first endeavor was to achieve a determination, even if only a preliminary determination, of the industries that it was necessary for the country to have.

The first simple and tentative lines were drawn for the development of an industry based upon the replacement of imported goods of uncomplicated manufacture. Lists were made of those imported products that ranked highest in our import history. Based upon this date, we searched for fiscal backing while leaning upon long-term foreign aid in order to develop our basic industry.

Throughout 1960, starting with the visit of the Vice Prime Minister of the Soviet Union, Anastas Mikoyan, the socialist countries sent their representatives to Cuba, and credit agreements were signed to build a good number of basic industries.

The Soviet Union granted us credit of 100 million pesos for the iron and steel industry, some electric plants, a refinery and a geologic survey of one-fourth of the national territory. Czechoslovakia granted us credit for an automotive plant; China credited us with sixty million pesos for the construction of twenty-four different plants; Romania, fifteen million; Bulgaria, five million; Poland, twelve million; and the Democratic Republic of Germany has offered us ten million pesos for 1963. The most important plants receiving backing, in addition to those mentioned above, are a shipyard to be constructed with Polish aid; a nickel installation backed by additional Soviet aid; a textile operation financed by the People's Republic of China and the German Democratic Republic; and cement plants.

The technical advisory missions from the socialist countries offered primary recommendations as they completed their work. Simultaneously, the Department of Industrialization was beginning to grow with the income from many new state industries. Some of the state industries had been acquired (intervened) through a labor ministry law against owner-abandonment of work centers, some were purchased, some were acquired as the result of laws against the traitors, and some as the result of the major nationalization law, which in addition to liquidating the banks and all North American property in Cuba, acquired a good number of properties held by local capitalists. They all became public property.

It was too much for our existing Department of Industrialization. Thus, we had to come face to face with the task of restructuring the Ministry of Industries. Carrying out this job has taken us all of 1961. Meanwhile offers of credit materialized, and contracts, which made it possible for us to set a general base for development, have been signed. There were, however, huge gaps and disproportions, due to the total lack of any previous planning, and due to the existing plan which was dictated by life itself and was surrounded by all sorts of mistakes, which although we can see them clearly today, we were not capable of foreseeing.

This entire process of gaining experience in planning has been characterized by a series of mistakes and approximations until a global concept of development was reached. The basis of a global concept of development is an emphasis upon agriculture, which constitutes the central link of the plan. The plan is the basis for industrialization and leads the way to important directions of industrial specialization. We shall discuss this after we have analyzed, in some detail, the process of our search.

During 1961 we studied the plan, albeit less than perfect, which will be carried out during this year, 1962. It cannot be a perfect plan because, among other things, annual plans must be elements of a long-range plan. Circumstances have made it imperative that we tailor our general plan of investments (the most important in the long run) to commitments established by early contracts already signed with friendly countries. Production plans must suit the objective possibilities inherent in our own raw material production as well as our true capacity for import. The capacity is determined by our own exportable surplus and the possibility of supplies from foreign countries.

Our present plan, with its imperfections, will be far superior to the outline that served as our guide during 1961. The present plan, with balance, includes production, costs, wages, supplies, investments, and finances. It is, in addition, related to life itself. The first plan was merely a written expression of our good intentions, anticipating maximum supplies and assistance from technical personnel to draw the maximum yield in accordance with the capacity of operating facilities. It was a bureaucratic plan isolated from the masses and not linked to reality.

The industrial realizations of the Revolution are limited to small factories producing consumer goods and the cessation of production that was started by the dictatorship for other goals. This can be utilized by the people.

The sulphometallic plant, "Patrice Lumumba," in Pinar del Río, is an example of the absurd form of investment. This factory, a technical jewel, produces sulphuric acid (three hundred metric tons daily at full capacity). This is an enormously important product in industrial countries with well-developed chemical industries. However, our chemical industry is small. We will not be able to take advantage of the factory's production capacity until another, soon to be built, factory is constructed. It will utilize, at the same location, the sulphuric acid being produced. There is also the problem of supplying the Patrice Lumumba plant with such raw materials as pyrite, which must be extracted from a nearby mine. All the preliminary information necessary for obtaining raw materials required for the operation of the factory was not carefully investigated.

We have demonstrated typical traits of capitalist anarchy carried to extremes in countries that, like Cuba, suffered the development of a bureaucratic bourgeoisie more concerned with its commissions than with industrial benefits. It would be well to stress that the first actions of the Revolution could not escape this legacy of improvisation, which together with both the lack of statistical data and development concepts, was inherited from the immediate past. We did not place proper emphasis on taking the fullest advantage of our own resources. We aimed at substitutions for imported finished goods, without seeing clearly that to do so one must first have the raw materials necessary for manufacture.

Let us look at some examples. Within the coming months a brush factory will start production. This factory will operate with imported raw materials. A screw factory will operate with imported raw material until we have our iron and steel foundry. A factory for picks and shovels will produce with imported raw materials. Factories for welding electrodes will operate with imported raw materials. Barbed wire factories will produce with imported raw materials, and there are others in the same situation.

Everything indicates that we have lacked the basis for raw material production. Steel is one of the fundamental pillars of a country with our characteristics. We are already developing a steel works with Soviet aid, and we must proceed with the highest possible speed in line with our strength and the actual conditions. Until we have it, we shall not be able to take the first steps toward walking alone.

Today we can see the result of our initial policy of replacing imports without worrying about the raw materials required by the factories assigned to production. We continue, in large measure, to depend upon foreign commerce to solve our problem. However, in the industrial sector, the possibilities of supply by foreign commerce are limited by the development of other sectors of the economy and by the life of the country, which demands materials from abroad. Agricultural development requires new investments; the population needs more consumer goods because employment facilitated by the Revolution has enormously increased consumption; public health requires more materials of all types in order to do its work fully; education needs a range of materials of all types, including books and publications, in order to fulfill its obligations; the transportation industry, to function effectively, requires a great deal of equipment. Although investments in electrical power are materializing nearly as fast as the need develops, there is a need for additional large investments to provide for the planned expansion of our economic life, which will insure the growth of the economy's entire production base.

Although this is a country with an abundance of raw materials for cement, there was only one location—Nuevitas—where the production capacity had been more or less studied. This is where the factory, financed by the Democratic Republic of Germany, will be located. We shall try to meet the short-term demands by enlarging the cement factory in Santiago, and we will eventually add two more factories.

Cement, however, is not the only thing. For example, electrical material is needed, and there is none. We must develop an entire industrial branch in order to supply the largest quantity of this material. We have possibilities but we are constantly blocked by a lack of foresight in not already having factories that can process our own wealth and convert it into raw materials for new factories.

The machinery industry is underdeveloped. We lack a technical base for proper development and for adaptation to our own potential and to the economy's industrial and agricultural specialization. Fertilizers are backward; we lack the chemical basis to establish an adequate supply of agricultural fertilizers. The chemical industry is barely developed. The paper industry, with its broad potential, is very poor. The same is true of the plywood industry. We can see that there is a large disproportion between what is developed and what should be developed. We lack the economic strength to quickly create new industries as their need logically develops as a result of complementary investments.

Our efforts in the immediate future will be directed at finding the optimum harmony between the various industrial branches. This harmony must be based upon both the objective reality of our distorted development and the new distortions that have arisen during these initial years of industrialization. At the same time we are dedicating ourselves to specialized areas, which in addition to fulfilling our own needs, allow us to offer a surplus to the socialist world in relation to the international division of labor within the socialist world.

As we gain technical excellence we must, within the harmonious framework of the basic developmental plan, give impetus to the creation of specific lines which will permit us to enter into the export market. This production should be based upon the ability to obtain the majority of raw materials from within the country. It must also be based upon the possibility of attaining adequate technical proficiency and stable markets for our surplus production.

We must initially direct ourselves toward four areas of development: metallurgy, naval construction, electronics, and sucrochemistry.

The agricultural sectors, like the food industry, deserve a separate study, since our surplus exports will be based upon this area. In concert with agriculture we must develop a sophisticated specialization in mechanics and chemistry. This will, in turn, produce the technologies and means suited to a rapid development. The National Institute for Agrarian Reform (INRA) will be in charge of this task.

Rapid advancement in the above-mentioned areas is possible because of our wealth in ferrous minerals. In addition to quantities of iron ores such as hematites and magnetites, we have laterites, our treasure, which offer us nickel, cobalt, chromite, and iron. An institute in Leningrad is studying the technological problems of separating chromite and iron. It is conceivable that these problems will be solved. In addition to chromite, manganese, and silicon, we have the necessary materials for common alloys with which a good specialization within the field of metallurgy can be developed. This does not take into account that nickel, as a result of its importance in inoxidizable steel, also has highly significant uses in the development of chemistry. It is also important in rocketry as an essential element of the alloys utilized in the production of space flight components.

To complete the picture a country must have complementary materials such as chromite, magnesite, dolomites, limestone, etc. We have an abundance of these. We lack only coal for coke and for inexpensive electricity. These lacks are important, but we can import coal, and as we are able to utilize our own petroleum and such other combustibles as peat and coal-bearing rocks, and as modern units are incorporated, adding to the efficiency of the system, the capacity to generate power will double, and electricity will become cheaper.

We also have copper. It is basic to the electrical industry, and due to its excellent price within the world market, is important to a number of light industries.

The shipping industry's potential is of great importance to Cuba. Rather than being a separate entity, the shipping industry is made up of an industrial complex: metallurgy, various types of engines, cables, electrical and electronic equipment, carpentry, etc. In 1965, when the industry is in its infancy, Cuba will need to transport over eight million tons of cargo. It is estimated that a minimum of 160 ships will be needed if each carries a full ten-thousand-ton capacity and can make five round trips to Europe within a year. Since the trading nations will be carrying some cargo in their own ships, Cuba's minimum requirement will be eighty vessels. We must also consider other important branches of naval construction, like ships for coastal traffic (the most inexpensive domestic transport), and the creation of a fishing fleet geared to our potential.

Opposing this idea, since motors and a number of components will not initially be manufactured in Cuba, is the huge investment that we must make in foreign products for many years.

We believe that there are several excellent reasons in favor of developing this industry. The lack of major industry in socialist countries will tend toward an increasing demand for ships. The countries of Latin America lack a shipping industry. There is a possibility of developing industries complementary to shipping that fit into the plan of industrial development. Finally, in terms of foreign exchange, a ship earns 500,000 pesos per round trip to Europe (2,500,000 pesos for five round trips). This represents an excellent return for a country such as ours—a maritime exporter par excellence.

Sucrochemistry is another extremely important area. Our present, and easily expandable, production capacity of 7,500,000 tons per year provides us with an excellent economic base. Work currently underway promises to be successful. Fermentation processes, taking advantage of known techniques, are being used, and new processes are being studied. Paper pulp made with bagazo is already a reality. This, and the possibility of producing synthetic fibers and plywood with that pulp, should be developed further. We are also experimenting with bagazo in the production of plastics. If this proves to be industrially feasible, it will create an industrial branch that will solve our problem of plastic supply. This will then allow us to direct our energies toward the difficult and more costly peat and petroleum technology.

Sugar cane's industrial uses (and the experiments being conducted with Cuban machinery, concerning cultivation and the mechanization of cutting and harvest) will make it possible to produce the consumer product much more cheaply. This will make it possible for us to compete in the price war being maintained against us by the capitalist distributors. The prime industrial task at this moment is to reduce the cost of sugar production.

The fourth undertaking will be audacious. Any country beginning to build socialism must, in order to achieve success, struggle for the initial economic base. The production capacity must be utilized to create the surplus that is possible. At first this productivity can be achieved by means of rationalization of production, and to some degree, through the conscious effort of the workers. Ultimately, due to a shortage of workers, it will be necessary to gradually automate all of the production processes by entering the world of electronics. It can be argued that the electronic industry's newness and complexities can be completely mastered only by a limited number of countries. We believe that this is one more reason for us to speed its study and development. The world is advancing toward the electronic era. The marvelous Soviet cosmic research achievements are based as much upon extraordinary developments in electronics as upon the development of space combustibles. There is every indication that electronics will become the gauge of a country's development. The country that masters this science will lead. We shall make this effort with revolutionary daring. We will join those countries that most rapidly adapt themselves to the technological events of the times.

It must be pointed out that before we can arrive at automation we must concern ourselves with the rationalization of work and give impetus to more and more technical methods of production. This will bring forth increasing socialization until total socialization is achieved throughout the country. The process will take place gradually. We will be immediately compensating those who were expropriated. As has been happening in recent months, we will give owners who wish to continue in the particular industry an opportunity for satisfactory work.

To take the first strong steps along the road we have described, we must make every effort to take advantage of our natural resources. We must create the technical base required for the detection, development, and industrialization of our mines and oil fields. We must zealously develop every cubic meter of the national territory within the shortest possible time.

We must also expend full energy on machinery development—a prerequisite for the development and maintenance of industry. In every sense of the word, 1961 has been a year of patches. This was true of the machinery we had to struggle with in order to make replacement parts as well as possible to avoid paralyzing stoppages. This year, 1962, will be the year of transition. While we continue the struggle to maintain our machinery equipment in good condition, we must make a qualitative leap. We must give the maximum impetus to the campaign to produce our own machinery. This is indispensable for the development of an industry with certain attributes of independence. The production of new machinery will, by duplicating the machinery in existence, give both the Cuban laborer and the Cuban technician more means of production. It will, basically, have the special quality of promoting revolutionary daring on the technical level. It will also enlist a considerable number of laborers for the highest forms of technical work, such as the production of complex tools for their own use. There are two important reasons for pushing this campaign. First, the above-mentioned production of machinery will stimulate and promote revolutionary boldness and imagination. Second, the relative specialization toward branches such as agricultural machinery will, by not being dependent upon imported machinery, allow us greater flexibility in our own plans. The general outlook and needs will change as we add an iron and steel works and develop, with blast furnaces and rotatory ovens and machinery constructed in Cuba, a special steel suited to our possibilities and characteristics. We will then be able to take our own steps.

We still lack, however, an indispensable complement. Without scientific, technical, and technological training of all the cadres at all levels, and without special attention given to finding and developing future leadership, the entire plan will remain a mere dream. Massive mobilization is necessary to accomplish this.

We must do much to achieve our objective. We must give follow-up courses to the laborers who have recently become literate; provide radio and television courses which will bring all laborers up to the sixth grade level; give a minimum of technical training to all laborers; train workers with some basic education to be specialized workers; train specialized workers to be technicians; organize and develop courses for the production units; raise the technical and cultural level of administrators; define the university courses of greatest importance to industry and the number of professionals required and make proposals to the authorities. As a final step our own scientists, after investigating and studying how to take the utmost advantage of our riches, must develop our own technology.

To give cohesion to this enormous and variegated work we must create a socialist conscience by enlisting the workers in all of the practical tasks of the building of socialism; in participation in the management of the factories and enterprises and in the centers of technical study; in the planning of the economy. In brief, there must be conscious participation at every moment throughout the industrial development.

We must add that the entire task of education is intimately linked to production. Thus it will be part of the responsibility of the Ministry of Industries.

This work outline is made up of ideas. If we wish it to become a reality we have to perform concrete tasks. Our initial and most urgent task is to organize production units. This will take all, or at least a great part, of 1962. One of the most important organizational tasks is to establish and improve the specific regulation of production units. A smooth working relationship between the production enterprises and the ministry must be systematized. Heavy emphasis must be placed upon bookkeeping procedures within the enterprises. This is the only way to bring the mystification, murkiness, and anarchy we are leaving behind to an end. We shall work earnestly on statistics so that we may offer the definitive knowledge necessary for future plans. Without adequate statistics we will lack a valid departure point and confidence in the development of future plans. Statistics must relate to the bookkeeping of the enterprises. We must work toward a mechanization of the bookkeeping and toward the effective centralization of statistical and accounting information. The final stage of this process will be mechanical data processing and the use of electronic computers.

Urgent measures will be taken to perfect the plan's control mechanisms. Adequate inventory control and effective controls of the production units and administrative personnel, aimed at clearly defining both the form and the lines of communication, will allow us to establish good control of the plan. The methods will be gradually improved as we gain valuable experience.

We had proposed, as a national goal, to eliminate unemployment by the end of this year. This project has not been forgotten. We are not certain that the goal will be completely attained. However, we know that unemployment is no longer a fundamental problem. Toward the end of the year there will be a strong demand from many sectors for labor. Another major feature of our former semicolonial system is disappearing. There is no longer any unemployment in the countryside. There will instead be a shortage of workers for the upcoming sugar harvest. Thus we can start to work on increasing our agricultural productivity. Increasing productivity in our industrial enterprises may appear to be more difficult, but it shall be attempted during the coming year. Since an extra individual in an organization constitutes a social unemployed, we will be able to rationalize functions. We will remove surplus workers from production units and pay them a fair salary for studying technical courses through which they can develop proficiency.

In a regime of social justice the contradictions between technical advances and full employment must be resolved through unproductive expenditures. The expenditures should be evaluated, and emphasis will be given to preparing technical cadres. We must also make note of activities such as construction. There, a man can replace a machine. This serves as a method to easily regulate unemployment, and when there is a demand for more labor, mechanization can make it available. Thus the process is effectively flexible and controllable.

We must establish precise work standards after the general organization lines are determined. One of the cardinal tasks of the year now beginning will be to formulate and carry out these work standards. With them we shall control production and move toward a steady increase in worker productivity throughout the economy.

We are still greatly dependent upon imported raw materials. Increasing direct work productivity will not be important if we are unable to bring in sufficient quantities of raw materials, for if our factories are unable to operate at full capacity we will have to subsidize laid-off workers until sufficient production materials are on hand. There are, however, other indirect methods of increasing production ability. All industries facing supply shortages must stock carefully to maintain raw materials and reduce costs.

To discover our own raw materials and develop new export products we must appeal to the inventiveness of our workers. Success in this area might help us to acquire the overseas materials and machinery required for our factories to operate. The appeal must be made in the spirit of fraternal competition rather than in a cold bureaucratic manner. The contest (emulation) is shared by all. It contains the elements of a sporting event, but it acquires meaningfulness by the participation of the human conglomerate, when this conglomerate joins the struggle, forms cadres, and draws the maximum effort and intelligence from all. This creates the obligation to aim at perfecting the rational utilization of industrial development and the time to achieve victory. The degree of success of this socialist contest will give much of the rhythm to industrial development.

It will be the ministry's responsibility to select the best workers, those who have earned monthly prizes, and send them to schools where the qualities they have demonstrated in production can be developed. Thus the working class, through its best sons, can produce the technicians and administrators of the future.

Volunteer work to increase production by improving the yield of less advanced sectors is one aspect of a socialist education which finds expression in emulation. Last year this type of work was initiated with marked success. It focused itself within the people's sugar harvest. However, it did not maintain the same rhythm after the harvest. We must perfect volunteer work so that it is not merely a factor of increased production. It should also become a source of education for the masses and a means of fraternal contact with the peasants. Thus it will foster maximum teamwork between the city and the country.

The struggle against absenteeism is an educational process. Absenteeism is a defect of national importance which becomes worse among the higher paid jobs. Cuba will derive great benefits if the masses understand the immorality represented by a man living without working the average number of hours per month considered necessary. These benefits will be particularly true if those who preach the message are excellent examples.

We must insist totally upon the duty of our workers and administrators to offer the finest quality of goods possible to the people. All revolutionary workers have the duty to raise the quality of the products they manufacture. This is especially true of the goods for popular consumption. By establishing the suitable standards and by working on the proletariat's sense of responsibility, we hope to greatly improve the quality as well as the presentation of industrial products.

Salary differences provoke one of the Revolution's most serious problems. In the socialist regime, and even during the earlier period of struggle, the masses' great hope was to achieve, in addition to a proper salary, an equalization of payments for similar types of work. This did not happen, and in fact, it is not presently happening. Women have been made the equal of men, and salaries in equivalent jobs within a given establishment tend to be equal. The salaries among different establishments for jobs requiring similar qualifications and demanding similar efforts, however, are not coordinated.

A single scale of salaries, with all qualifications considered with complete fairness, would be the correct thing. This is not practical, for it would have a deleterious effect upon the budgets of a great many workers who through strenuous efforts snatched a few crumbs from capitalist enterprises and succeeded in rising above the average remuneration. Another solution would be to raise the salaries of all other workers to the level of the first. This, by throwing enormous quantities of money into circulation, would create great economic problems. No one would benefit for the true salary increases only when there is an increase in the social product (more goods to distribute).

An intermediate method, however, does exist. This would consist of creating a single salary scale, studying it, discussing, and finally approving it, throughout all levels, with the workers participating. It would be applied to new incomes or to promotions within a given category and respecting previous salaries of the workers.

It could be objected that this violates the principle of "equal work, equal salary." Today, in all truth, this is respected only within the same establishments. Our socialist country must aim at socialization of the nation's patrimony. Therefore all jobs should be established as a whole, independent of the factory or enterprise to which they may belong.

For example: Although the jobs are similarly classified, a laborer in a mine earns several times less than a laborer in a brewery. The salary difference is based upon the fact that a mine yields less income than a brewery. Because of this, brewery workers were able to squeeze more from their bosses. This was fair in those times. It is not just today. It would be incorrect for a miner and a brewery worker to earn different salaries simply because the brewery produces more income. This would ignore the fact that both are now socialized properties.

If the single salary system were established, a worker presently earning $250 a month while working at a job classified at $200 per month should continue to receive the larger figure. If this compañero were promoted to a new job classified at $230 per month, he would not receive an increase, since he would still earn the larger figure. However, if he were to receive another promotion and qualify for $260 per month, he would be in a position to receive an increase, since his existing salary would be below the salary corresponding to the new post.

With this method Cuba could establish complete salary justice within a few years.

As can be seen, we have tasks ahead of us. This imperative and heavy work should be the result of the determination of all the people. The fundamental importance of collective discussion and massive participation in working out production plans is considered the most significant lesson of the work in preparation for the plan. All of the basic agencies of the factories and enterprises must orient the work of the working class and unite it to the work of their administrators. This will solidify it into one united decision. All should participate in production assemblies where work progress is controlled. All should be concerned daily through the Union (the body representing the working class) with the work of the factories. All, through representation by their best technical cadres, will be present in the Technical Advisory Committees. Thus the quality and quantity of work will improve as greater confidence and awareness is acquired by the working class. A nucleus of active revolutionaries comprise the vanguard of the proletariat and of these mass units. Their task is revolutionary orientation and vigilance, and through example and teaching, to give impetus to all of the great goals of the Revolution.

Although the administrator or director must work collectively with all mass agencies and be advised by the technical personnel available to him, he is ultimately responsible to the ministry for the final decisions he makes. He must, therefore, be ruled at all times by the disciplines of the ministry and apply common sense each time he makes a decision. Our school for administrators is responsible for improving their knowledge and shaping industry's new administrators. It is always kept in mind that the administrator is the main link in the interlocking chain of production. He must have political understanding in addition to administrative ability. He must have an awareness of the justice of our revolution as well as education, organizational ability, executive ability, and disciplinary ability. This is fundamental.

With the prospective National Plan outlines; with our plan for 1962 underway; with our plan to raise the cultural, ideological, and technical standards of the workers being realized; with our plan for new machinery construction beginning to materialize; with the rapid liquidation of unemployment, which will permit us to restructure our industry; with the increase in production as we manage to have adequate supplies; with the creation of new export items; with technological work; with the aid of friendly countries aimed at raising the qualifications of specialists in the new branches—we shall, *based upon our own experiences,* establish a sound foundation for independent development.

As can be appreciated, this is an enormously important task, which requires lengthy preparation. If we spend this entire year on it, and we come out ready to undertake the long-range works with our production units completely organized, with the possibility of pouring the entire resources of the ministry into the development of new investments, which will complete and liberate the economy—we shall then have succeeded fully. Our success will be lessened to the degree that we are unable to fulfill these aspirations. If many of these aspirations fall by the wayside, the pace of the Revolution will be held back. I do not mean by this that we confront a difficult situation. These are the same growing pains suffered by other countries who in a similar situation have chosen rapid industrial development as the initial direction for their transformation into agricultural-industrial countries.

We work under conditions infinitely superior to those that faced the first socialist country, the Soviet Union. They achieved it alone, without friends, without credits, encircled by ferocious adversaries, in the midst of a bitter struggle within their own territory. We are working under conditions far superior to those of the People's Republic of China and those faced by the people's popular republics of Europe. They emerged from a disastrous war at a time when the Soviet Union could not lend its entire support, since it was deeply involved itself in the task of tremendous reconstruction.

We undertake our work in this second half of the twentieth century, an epoch that includes among its traits the transition toward socialism assisted by the superior technology and the great spirit of the Soviet Union, the People's Republic of China, and other friendly countries. We do it from a relatively comfortable point of departure; with an educational, technical, cultural, and economic mass level less backward than that which confronted our sister countries.

We are beginning the real planning tasks with many advantages. We hope to make the best of them in order to arrive, within the shortest possible time, at socialism.

CHAPTER 14

The Cadre, Backbone of the Revolution[1]

It is unnecessary to insist on the characteristics of our Revolution; on its original, partly spontaneous form, which produced the transition from a liberating national revolution to a socialist one. The same applies to the many stages rapidly experienced in the course of this development, which was led by the same protagonists who appeared in the first act at Moncada, passed through Granma, and ended in the declaration of the socialist nature of the Cuban Revolution. New sympathizers, cadres, and organizations were all added to the weak organic structure of the initial movement, until it formed the popular base that characterizes our Revolution.

When it became clear that a new social class had taken power in Cuba, it also became evident that it would place great limitations on the exercise of state power. This was due to the condition in which we found the state, with no cadres to deal with the enormous number of tasks that had to be carried out in the state apparatus, in political organization, and on the whole economic front.

Right after the taking of power, bureaucratic offices were given out haphazardly; there were no major problems, because the old structure had still not broken down. The apparatus moved with the slow, worn-out gait of an old and almost lifeless beast. But it did have an organization, and in it, enough coordination to maintain itself through the power of inertia, while disdaining the political changes that were being produced as a prelude to the changes in the economic structure.

The 26th of July Movement, deeply wounded by the internal struggles between its left and right wings, could not get down to constructive efforts. The Popular Socialist Party [Cuban name of the traditional Communist party] having suffered from fierce attacks, and from the fact that it was

[1] *Cuba Socialista*, No. 13, September 1962. Translated by Morton Marks and Robert Novick.

illegal for years, had not been able to come up with interim cadres to meet the new responsibilities that were now facing it.

When the first state interventions in the economy took place, the task of looking for cadres was not very complicated. They could be chosen from the ranks of many people who had the minimal qualification for exercising leadership. But with the acceleration of the process—beginning with the nationalization of the North American enterprises, and afterward, of the large Cuban enterprises—there appeared a real need for administrative experts. In addition, a desperate need was also felt for production experts, owing to the exodus of many of them, who had been attracted by better jobs offered by the imperialist companies in other parts of America or in the United States itself. The political apparatus also had to make an intense effort, in the middle of the work of building a structure, to give ideological attention to the masses who were coming into contact with the Revolution, and who were very anxious to learn.

We did the best we could, but there were difficulties. There were many errors in the administrative part of the executive body. Enormous mistakes were made by the new administrators of enterprises, whose responsibilities were too great. We also made large and costly errors in the political apparatus, which little by little was becoming a peaceful and cozy bureaucracy. It was virtually seen as a springboard for promotions and for bureaucratic positions of varying importance, and was totally cut off from the masses.

The central cause of our errors lay in our lack of feeling for reality at a given moment. The lack of middle-level cadres—the tools we needed—was weakening our perception and changing the party into a bureaucratic agency, placing administration and production in danger. The cadre policy was clearly set up as a synonym of mass policy. The watchword was to establish contact with the masses once again; a contact which had been closely maintained by the Revolution during its first stages. We needed to establish this contact through the most suitable apparatus. It would have to be suitable as much in response to the needs of the masses as in the development of its political orientation. In many cases political ideas had been transmitted only by the appearances of Prime Minister Fidel Castro or some other leaders of the Revolution.

At this point we may ask ourselves, what is a cadre? We should say a cadre is an individual who has reached a sufficient level of political development to be able to interpret the general directives issued by the central power, to assimilate them, and to transmit them as ideas to the masses. Besides this, he must perceive the people's wishes and deepest motivations. He is an individual of ideological and administrative discipline, who knows and practices democratic centralism and knows how to evaluate the methodological contradictions in the method so as to take maximum advantage of their multiple facets. In production, he knows how to practice the principles of collective discussion, personal decision, and responsibility. His faithfulness is proven, and his physical and moral courage is equal to his ideological development, so he is always ready to face any struggle and to give his life to the Revolution. Furthermore, he is capable of self-analysis, which allows him to make necessary decisions and practice creative initiative, while maintaining discipline.

The cadre, then, is a creator, a leader of high stature, a high-level political expert who can, through dialectical reasoning, head his production sector and educate the masses from his vanguard political position.

This exemplary man, characterized by hard-won virtues, is present among the Cuban people; we meet him every day. The essential thing is to take advantage of all the existing opportunities to develop him to the utmost, to educate him, to draw from his personality the greatest benefit, and to make it into the most useful value for the nation.

A cadre develops through daily tasks. But the tasks should be undertaken in a systematic way, in special schools, where competent teachers, who are at the same time examples for the student body, encourage the most rapid ideological advances. In a regime which is starting to build socialism, we cannot have cadres who lack a high degree of political awareness. But this means more then the learning of Marxist theory. It must also be required that an individual take responsibility for his acts and possess discipline which lessens any passing weakness without excluding a high level of initiative. He must be constantly preoccupied with all the problems of the Revolution. To develop cadres, one must first establish the selective principle among the masses. It is among the masses that we must seek nascent personalities, tested by sacrifice, or people who are now beginning to show their growth, and bring them to special schools, or lacking that, we must at least give them more responsible duties which will heighten their skills in practical work.

We have been finding a multitude of new cadres these last years. But their development has been uneven, since our young comrades have found themselves facing the reality of revolutionary creation without an adequate party orientation. Some have been triumphant, but there are many who have not been able to do it completely and have stayed in the middle of the road, or have simply got lost in the bureaucratic labyrinth or in the temptations of power.

To assure the triumph and the total consolidation of the Revolution, we need to develop different kinds of cadres. First, the political cadres that will serve as the basis for organizing the masses and will teach them through the activity of the United Party of the Socialist Revolution are already beginning to be prepared by courses at national and provincial schools of revolutionary education and with studies and study aids at every level. Military cadres are also needed. To achieve this we must make use of the selective process that the war carried out among our young combatants, since a good many were left alive; they have no great theoretical knowledge, but have been tested under fire. They have been tested under the harshest battle conditions and have complete faithfulness to the revolutionary regime. Their development has been closely linked to the revolutionary regime, since the first guerrilla skirmishes in the Sierra.

We must also promote economic cadres who are dedicated specifically to the difficult tasks of planning and organizing the nascent socialist state. It is necessary to work with the professionals, encouraging youth to take up the more important technical careers to try to give to science the tone of ideological enthusiasm which will guarantee quicker development. It is imperative to create an administrative apparatus that will know how to take advantage of the specific technical knowledge of the others, and to direct the enterprises and other state organizations according to the strong rhythm of the Revolution.

For all of them, the common denominator is political awareness. This does not mean unconditional support of the principles of the Revolution, but rather reasoned support, great capacity for sacrifice and dialectical capacity for analysis. This capacity will permit people to make steady contributions at every level to the rich theory and practice of the Revolution. These comrades must be selected from the masses, applying the sole principle that the best will stand out, and to the best will be given the greatest opportunities for development.

In all these areas, the function of the cadre—in spite of occupying different positions—is the same. The cadre is the driving force of the ideological engine which is the United Party of the Revolution. We could call it a dynamic propeller of this engine, in the sense that it is the part which assures its correct functioning. It is dynamic in the sense that it is not a simple transmitter of slogans or demands, but rather a creator that will aid the development of the masses and the instruction of the leaders, serving as a point of contact between them. Its mission is one of vigilance, making sure that the great spirit of the Revolution does not disappear or doze or slacken its rhythm. It is a sensitive responsibility; it transmits what emanates from the masses, and instills in them what the party teaches.

The development of the cadres is, then, the primary task of the movement. The development of the cadres has been taken up with great initiative by the revolutionary government, through its scholarship programs following selective principles, through workers' study programs offering different opportunities for technical training, through the development of special technical schools, secondary schools, and universities; and finally, through the promotion of study, work, and revolutionary vigilance as the bywords of our whole country. This is development based fundamentally on the Young Communist League, from which cadres of every type must emerge, including the cadres who will lead the Revolution in the future.

Closely tied to the concept of "cadre" is that of the capacity for sacrifice, for demonstrating by one's own example the truths and watchwords of the

Revolution. The cadre, as political leader, must win the respect of the workers by his actions. It is indispensable that he count on the respect and affection of the comrades whom he must guide along the paths of the vanguard.

For all this there is no better cadre than the one who will influence the masses in the assemblies where outstanding workers are chosen, workers who will be integrated into the PURS[2] together with the old members of the ORI who pass all the necessary selective tests. At first they will be a small group, but will have an immense influence among the workers. And their number will increase as the advance of socialist consciousness makes work and total commitment to the people's cause a necessity. With immediate level leaders of this caliber, the difficult tasks that face us can be completed with few mishaps. After a period of disorder and faulty method, a correct policy has been achieved and will never be abandoned. With the ever-renewed impulse of the working class—an inexhaustible fount filling the ranks of the future PURS—and with the guidance of our party, we begin in earnest the task of forming cadres which will guarantee the forceful development of our Revolution. We cannot fail in this undertaking.

[2] Partido Unido de la Revolución Socialista, the old (to 1965) name for Cuba's new Communist party (ed.).

CHAPTER 15

On Being a Communist Youth[1]

ONE of the most satisfying tasks of a revolutionary is to observe, as the years pass, the gradual formation, exaltation, and fortification of the institutions that were born at the dawn of the Revolution. It is rewarding to see the conversion into true institutions which have vigor and authority among the masses, of those organizations which began on a small scale and were gradually transformed through daily work and contact with the masses into powerful manifestations of the revolutionary movement of today.

The Union of Young Communists is almost the same age as our Revolution, although this organization has had different names and different forms. Originally, it grew out of the rebel army, and perhaps it was from the army that it derived its name. It was an organization allied to the army; its purpose was to initiate Cuban youth into the massive tasks of national defense, which was the most urgent problem and the one most in need of a rapid solution.

In the former Department of Education of the rebel army, both the Association of Young Rebels and the National Revolutionary Militias were born. Later they acquired lives of their own. The latter became a powerful aggregate of armed citizens, representative of the entire armed people, who worked with the army for our defense. The former became an organization for the political participation of Cuban youth.

As the Revolution consolidated itself and we were able to delineate on the horizon new tasks to be accomplished, our comrade Fidel suggested changing the name of the youth organization. The change expresses its principles. The Union of Young Communists is directly oriented toward the future. Its backbone is the vision of the luminous future of socialist society. This society lies ahead, on the other side of the difficult pass at

[1] Speech delivered to an assembly of Communist Youth on October 20, 1962, reproduced in *Obra Revolucionaria,* Año 1962, No. 30. Translated by Beth Kurti.

which we now stand on our road to the construction of a new society. The road leads from total reliance upon the dictatorship of class, through socialist society, toward our final destination: a society without classes, the perfect society, the society you will be in charge of constructing, orienting, and directing in the future.

Toward this end the Union of Young Communists raises its symbols, which are those of the entire Cuban people: study, work, and the rifle. And on their banners the members display their tribute to two of the most exemplary of Cuban youths, both of whom died tragically, before they were able to see the results of this battle in which we are all engaged: Julio Antonio Mella and Camilo Cienfuegos.

On our second anniversary, in this period of feverish construction, of constant preparations for the defense of the country, and of greatly accelerated technical and technological work and education, we must continue always to ask ourselves: What is the Union of Young Communists and what should it be?

The Union of Young Communists may be defined in a single word: *vanguard*. You, my friends, must be the vanguard of all movements: the first to make the sacrifices the Revolution demands, no matter what these sacrifices entail; the first in study; the first in the defense of the nation.

And you must set these goals for yourselves, not only as an expression of the will of Cuban youth, not merely as a job for great masses molded into an institution, but rather as the daily, personal tasks of each one of the members of the Union of Young Communists. Your organization is the key that makes it possible to carry out the initiatives of the leaders of the Revolution, the initiatives executed on many occasions by our Prime Minister, and the initiatives that spring from within the working class. All of these initiatives must be transformed into precise directives and clear ideas in order to facilitate subsequent action.

If there is no organization, after the initial impulse, ideas lose their efficacy, fall into routine and conformism, and end up as no more than a memory.

I am warning you because many times in this short yet very rich period of our Revolution, many great initiatives have failed and have fallen into oblivion due to the lack of the necessary organizational apparatus to sustain them and put them into effect.

At the same time, each and every one of you must keep in mind that to be a Young Communist, to belong to the Union of Young Communists, is not a favor conceded by someone to you, nor a favor conceded by you to the state or to the Revolution. To belong to the Union of Young Communists ought to be the highest honor of a youth in the new society. It ought to be an honor which he would fight to defend every minute of his existence. It is in addition, an honor to persevere and to hold up for recognition one's own individual name within the great name of the Union of Young Communists.

Thus we shall advance even more rapidly—by accustoming ourselves to think as an entity, to act upon the initiatives that we are offered by the workers and by our highest leaders, and at the same time, by acting always as individuals, permanently concerned with our own actions, permanently concerned with protecting our own names and the name of the organization to which we belong.

Years from now we will be able to look back and survey the results of our labors. There have been great achievements in the life of the Union of Young Communists. One of the most important and spectacular of these has been its contribution to the defense of our country.

The youths who first—some of them—climbed the five summits of the Turquino, those who enrolled in military organizations, all those who shouldered the rifle in time of danger, were ready to defend the Revolution wherever enemy invasion or action was expected.

The youths of Playa Girón[2] had the honor of being able to defend our Revolution, to protect the institutions we have created with our sacrifices, the gains achieved by a whole people through years of battle. On Playa Girón, in seventy-two hours of fighting, our entire Revolution was preserved.

The intention of the enemy was to create a beachhead, with an inner airport, sufficiently strong to allow aggression on our entire territory; to bombard it mercilessly; to convert our factories into ashes; to reduce our means of communication to dust; to ruin our agriculture; in a word, to sow chaos in our country. The determined action of the people wiped out the imperialist attempt in only seventy-two hours.

Young people who were still children covered themselves with glory. Some are here today as representatives of that heroic youth; others have left at least their names as a memory and as an inspiration to new battles and new acts of heroism.

At the time when the defense of our country was our primary task, our youth was present. Today the defense of the country continues to occupy first place in our duties. Yet we must not forget the unity of aims expressed by the maxim that guides the Union of Young Communists: There can be no defense of the country by the exercise of arms alone. We must defend our country, rather, by constructing with our labor and by forming new technical cadres to accelerate her growth in future years. At the present time this task is acquiring enormous importance, equal to that of the direct exercise of arms.

When problems of defense arose, youth responded. Young soldiers answered the call of the Revolution and invaded every corner of the country. As a result, after a few months of hard battle—in which there were martyrs of the Revolution and martyrs of education—we were able to announce a situation new to America: Cuba was free of illiteracy.

Study at all levels is one of the tasks of youth even now. Study mixed

[2] The beach at the Bay of Pigs (ed.).

with work, as in the case of those young students who are harvesting coffee in Oriente, who utilize their vacations to pick a crop which is important not only to our country's foreign trade, but also to us, who consume great quantities of coffee every day. This work is similar to that of eradicating illiteracy. It is a labor of sacrifice which one performs cheerfully, joining with fellow students in the mountains of our country to spread our revolutionary message.

These works are very important because the young communists within the Union of Young Communists are receivers as well as givers. In some cases they receive more than they give—they acquire new experiences. They learn from the experience of new human contacts. From the peasants in the field they find out about life and work in remote areas and about all that must be done to elevate those regions to the level of our more habitable rural areas and our cities.

The Young Communist gains revolutionary experience and revolutionary maturity. Those who perform these tasks of teaching or picking coffee, in direct contact with the people, whom they have traveled far to help, receive—I can swear it[3]—more than they give, and what they give is a great deal.

This is the education best suited to a youth preparing for communism: a form of education in which work ceases to be the obsession it is in the capitalist world and becomes a pleasant social duty. It is engaged in happily, to the accompaniment of revolutionary songs, amidst fraternal camaraderie and human relationships which are mutually invigorating and uplifting.

Furthermore, the Union of Young Communists has made great strides in its organization. There is a great difference between that weak embryo that began as an appendage of the rebel army and the organization as it is now. Everywhere, in every work center, in every administrative body, everywhere they can be of service, there are Young Communists working for the Revolution. This organizational progress must be considered as another important achievement of the Union of Young Communists.

Nevertheless, friends, on this difficult road there have been many problems, many great difficulties, many bad mistakes, and we have not always been able to overcome them. It is obvious that the Union of Young Communists, as a younger social organization and a little brother of the Integrated Revolutionary Organizations, should always listen—with respect—to the voice of experience and learn from colleagues who have done more work in all areas of revolutionary activity.

But youth has to create. A youth who does not create is an anomaly, in reality. The Union of Young Communists has lacked a bit of creative spirit. It has been too docile, too respectful, and not sufficiently determined to deal with its own problems.

[3] Guevara often went to the fields as an ordinary volunteer to work on agricultural production (ed.).

Today all this is changing. Our comrade Joel talked to us of the beginnings of jobs in Granjas. These are examples of how you are beginning to break away from total dependence—which gets absurd—on the older organization and to think with your own heads.

But the fact is that we, and our youth along with the rest of us, are convalescing from a disease, which fortunately did not last long, but which influenced greatly our retardation in the ideological development of our Revolution. We are all convalescents of that disease called sectarianism.

To what did sectarianism lead us? It led to mechanical imitation, to formal analyses, to the separation between leaders and masses. This was the case even in our Dirección Nacional, and it was directly reflected here in the Union of Young Communists.

If we—disoriented by the phenomenon of sectarianism—were unable to interpret the voice of the people, which is the wisest and most orienting voice of all; if we did not succeed in receiving the vibrations of the people and transforming them into concrete ideas, exact directives, then we were ill-equipped to issue those directives to the Union of Young Communists. And since the dependence was absolute and the docility very great, the Union of Young Communists floated like a small boat cut adrift from its great ship—our revolutionary organizations, which were themselves adrift.

All that the Union of Young Communists was capable of producing were small initiatives, which were transformed into hackneyed slogans, at demonstrations that lacked ideological profundity.

Comrade Fidel severely criticized the extremism and the slogans. All those things Fidel criticized, which you know well, were a reflection of the sickness that oppressed our Revolution.

We have emerged from that stage. We have completely obliterated it. Nevertheless, our organizations always advance a little more slowly than we do. It is like a disease which causes a person to lose consciousness. When the disease leaves, the brain regains its mental clarity, but the parts of the body are not yet able to coordinate their movements. The first days after leaving the bed one's gait is unsteady, until little by little a new sureness is attained. We are on that path.

Therefore, we must define and analyze objectively all our organizations in order to continue to progress toward health. We must know—so that we do not fall, so that we do not stumble and end up on the ground, that we still walk with an uncertain step. We must know our weaknesses so that we can correct them and gain more strength.

That lack of self-initiative is due to our ignorance, for a long time, of the dialectic which moves mass organizations. We forgot that organizations like the Union of Young Communists cannot be simply an executive board or something that constantly sends directives to its base without receiving anything from it in return.

It was thought that the Union of Young Communists and all Cuban organizations were organized on a single line: a single line which extended from the head to the foundations, but which did not have a return cable to bring up communications from the bottom. A double and constant exchange of the experiences, ideas, and directives that seemed most important, the ones that could orient the work of our youth, was what was needed. At the same time the interchange would have allowed the weakest points of the work to be spotted.

We see how even today our young people, almost like romantic heroes, would give their lives a hundred times for the Revolution, and how they march en masse to any concrete or immediate task to which they are called. At times, nevertheless, they miss work because of a Young Communists meeting or because they went to bed late after discussing some new initiative of the Young Communists, or they simply do not go to work, just because, without a real reason.

When one sees a voluntary work brigade, one assumes it contains Young Communists; in many cases there are none; not even one. The leader had to go to a meeting, someone else was sick, and another had not been informed. The result is that the fundamental attitude, the vanguard attitude of the people, the attitude of the living example that moves and inspires everyone—as did the young people of Playa Girón—this attitude is not carried through in practice. The seriousness of purpose that today's youth must have in order to fulfill its great commitments—and the greatest of these is the construction of a socialist society—is not reflected in concrete work.

Huge weaknesses exist, and it is necessary to work on them—to work on organization; to work on pinpointing the sore spot, the place where there are debilities to correct; to work on each one of yourselves so that you are able to understand clearly in your consciences that no one can be a good Communist who thinks about the Revolution only at times for sacrifice or combat or heroic action, times that permit him to rise above the common and the ordinary. No one can be a good Communist who remains mediocre in his work, or less than mediocre.

How can this be possible, when you already bear the name of Young Communists, the name we, as a guiding organization and a guiding party, still do not have? You are to construct a future in which work will be man's greatest dignity, in which work will be a social duty as well as a true human pleasure and the maximum act of creation. Everyone must be interested in his own work and in that of others, in the advancement of society day by day.

How can it be possible that you, who already have that name, disdain work? There is some deficiency: a lack of organization, of inspiration, of work; a failing which is certainly human. Every one of us—everyone, I think—likes best that which breaks the monotony of life, that which, every once in a while, suddenly makes one aware of his own value and the value he has within society.

I can imagine the pride of those of our comrades who, for example, were defending their homeland against Yankee planes, when suddenly someone had the luck to see his bullets reach their target. This is the happiest moment in a man's life. He never forgets it. Nor will those comrades who lived through this experience ever forget it.

But we too must also defend our Revolution, the one which we are carrying on every day. In order to defend it, we must build and fortify it with that work that youth today does not like or that, at least, it considers the last of its responsibilities. Youth maintains toward work the old mentality, the mentality of the capitalist world—that is, the attitude that work is, yes, a duty and a necessity, but a sad duty, an unfortunate necessity.

Why does this happen? Because we have not yet given to work its true meaning. We have not been capable of uniting the worker with the object of his work. And, at the same time, we have not imparted to the worker a consciousness of the importance of the creative act he is performing every day.

The worker and the machine are still two different and antagonistic things. We must concern ourselves with this situation in order to mold new generations of men who will take the greatest interest in their work. They will know how to find in their work a permanent and constantly changing source of new emotions—how to make of work something creative, something brand new.

Because this is perhaps the weakest aspect of our Union of Young Communists, I have emphasized the point. Into the gaiety of this anniversary celebration I have inserted a small drop of bitterness to hit the sensitive spot and cause youth to react.

We spent today in an assembly in which we discussed competition in the ministry. Many of you probably have already discussed competition in your work centers and have read a lengthy paper which is circulating. But what is the problem of competition, comrades? The problem is that competition cannot be directed by papers that attempt to regulate it, order it, and give it a framework. The rules and the model are necessary only later, for the comparison of the work of the enthusiastic people who are already competing.

When two comrades begin to compete, each one at a machine, after a while they begin to feel the necessity of a set of standards to determine which of the two produces more on his machine, what quantity of the product, how many hours of work, the condition of the machine afterwards, its general upkeep—many things. But if, instead of two comrades in genuine competition, to whom we would give the norms they request, we are dealing with two others who merely count the minutes until they can go home, then of what use are regulations, and what function do they fulfill?

In many ways we are working with standards and making a structure for something that does not exist. A framework must have content, and the purpose of a set of regulations, in these cases, is to define and limit an already created situation. The regulations ought to grow out of socialist competition with overflowing enthusiasm in all the work centers in Cuba. And yet, when I asked, at the assemblies at those centers, why the secretary of the Young Communists was not there and how many times he had attended, I found out he had attended a few times, but the Young Communists had not attended.

In the course of the production assembly, discussing these and other problems, the Young Communists, the nucleus, the Federation of Women, and the Committees of Defense and the Syndicate, naturally became filled with enthusiasm. At least they became filled with an internal heat, with a bitterness and a desire to improve, a desire to demonstrate that they were capable of doing what has not yet been done—motivating the people. Then, quickly, everyone committed himself to work toward competition at all levels of the entire ministry, to discuss regulating the competition once it has been established, and to come back in two weeks to present the accomplished fact, with all the ministry in competition.

That is mobilization. People have already understood and felt internally—for each of these comrades is a great one—that there was something weak in their work. They have become filled with wounded dignity and have determined to resolve the problem. That is how it should be done. To remember that work is the most important thing. Pardon me if I insist again and again on this point, but the fact is that without work there is nothing. All the riches of the world and all humanity's values are nothing more than accumulated work. Nothing can exist without that. Without the extra work that is carried out to create more surpluses for new factories and for new social installations the country cannot advance. No matter how strong our armies are, we will always have a slow rhythm of growth. We have to break away from that, break away from old mistakes, and display them in the public light, analyze them everywhere, and then correct them.

I want to present to you now, comrades, my opinion, the vision of a national director of the ORI, of what a Young Communist should be. We shall see whether we are all in agreement.

I believe that the first thing that should characterize a Young Communist is the honor he feels because he is a Young Communist: that pride that leads him to show the world he is a Young Communist. He does not keep his honor secret or reduce it to formulas, but expresses it at all times; it comes from his spirit, and he is inspired to demonstrate it because it is the symbol of his pride.

Beside this, there should be a great sense of duty toward the society we are building, as human beings, with our neighbors, and with all the men of the world.

That is something that must characterize the Young Communist. In addition to this, there should be a great sensitivity to all problems, a great sensitivity to injustice; an independent spirit, whenever something arises that is not right, no matter what anyone says about it; to concern himself with all that he does not understand; to discuss and ask for clarification of what is not clear; to declare war on formalism, on all types of formalism; to be always open to new experiences, to conform to the great experience of humanity, which for many years has been advancing on the path of socialism; to be aware of the concrete conditions of our country, to the realities that exist in Cuba; and to think—each and every one of us—about how to go about changing reality, how to improve it.

The Young Communist ought to decide to be first in everything, to fight to be first, and to feel frustrated when he is forced to occupy any other place; to fight to be better, to be first. Of course not everyone can be first, but one can be among the first, in the vanguard. He should decide to be a living example, a mirror for those comrades who do not belong to communist youth organizations; to be an example also to older men and women. Those who have lost faith in life and a certain youthful enthusiasm always respond to inspiration and good example. That is still another task for the Young Communists.

Together with all this, a great spirit of sacrifice, there ought to be a spirit of sacrifice not reserved for heroic days only, but for every moment. One ought to sacrifice oneself to help a companion with his little jobs so that he can finish his work, his studies, so that he can improve in any way possible. One ought always to be attentive to the human mass that surrounds one.

This means that every Young Communist must be essentially human, so human that he responds to the best in human beings, brings out the best a man has to offer by means of work, study, and the exercise of continued solidarity with his people and with all the peoples of the world. He must develop his sensibility to the maximum, to the point that he feels anguish when a man is assassinated in any corner of the world, and he feels elation when in some corner of the world a new banner of liberty is raised.

The Young Communist cannot be limited by the frontiers of a territory; he must practice proletarian internationalism and feel it as something of his own. He must remember, as we all must remember—all those who aspire to be Communists here in Cuba—that he is a real and inspiring example for our whole America. Even more than for America, he is an example for other countries of the world who fight on other continents for liberty against colonialism, against neocolonialism, against imperialism, against all the forms of oppression by unjust systems. He ought to remember always that we are a lighted torch, that we are the same mirror that each of us is individually for the people of Cuba. We are that mirror in order that all the peoples of America may see themselves, all the people of the oppressed world who are fighting for their liberty. And we must be worthy of setting that example. Every hour, every minute, we must be worthy.

This is what we believe a Young Communist ought to be. And if we are told that we are romantics, that we are inveterate idealists, that we are thinking about impossibilities, that one cannot find an almost archetypal human being among the masses of a people, we have to answer a thousand times that we can. Yes, we can. We know for a fact that a people can continue advancing, doing away with human pettiness, as we have been doing in Cuba during these four years of Revolution. A people can perfect itself as we have all been perfecting ourselves, day by day, settling accounts intransigently with all those who lag behind and are not capable of marching to the rhythm of the Cuban Revolution. It should be this way, it has to be this way, and it will be this way, comrades. It will be this way because you are Young Communists, creators of the perfect society, human beings destined to live in a world from which everything old and decadent, everything that represents a society whose foundations have just been destroyed, will have disappeared forever.

In order to achieve this, we all must work every day, work in the direction of inner improvement, of augmenting our knowledge and increasing our comprehension of the world around us. We need to inquire and learn and become well acquainted with the why of things; to feel as one's own the great problems of humanity.

Then, at a given moment on an ordinary day sometime years from now—after making many sacrifices, yes, after perhaps having found ourselves often at the edge of destruction—having seen, perhaps, the demolition of our factories and having reconstructed them anew; after having witnessed the assassination, the murder of many of us, and having rebuilt what may have been destroyed; after all of this—some fine day, almost without realizing it, we shall have created, together with the other peoples of the world, the communist society, our ideal.

Comrades, to speak to youth is a very great task. One feels the desire to transmit many things youth already comprehends. There are many things that I would like to say about all our endeavors and desires; about how, unfortunately, many of them are shattered when confronted with everyday reality and how we have to begin all over again; about the moments of weakness and about how contact with the people—with the ideals and the purity of the people—infuses in us renewed revolutionary fervor.

There are many things we could talk about. But we must also fulfill our duties. And I avail myself of this opportunity to explain, with completely malicious intention if you like, why I am leaving you. I am leaving you because I am going to carry out my duty as a voluntary worker in a textile factory. We are competing with groups in two other textile factories.

I want to tell you, honestly, that the Ministry of Industry is last in competition, that we have to make a greater effort, constantly, to be able to progress, to be able to keep our promise to ourselves to be the best. We aspire to be first because it is painful to be last in socialist competition.

The situation, simply, is that the same thing has happened here as has happened to many of you. The competition has been cold, a little bit artificial, and we have not known how to enter into direct relations with the mass of industrial workers. Tomorrow we shall have an assembly to discuss these problems and to try to resolve them all, to look for union, to establish the common language of an absolute identity among the workers of that industry and us, the workers of the ministry. After having achieved what we propose, I am certain that we will increase production greatly and be able, at least, to fight honorably for the top places.

In any case I will tell you the results at the assembly next year. Until then.

CHAPTER 16

Against Bureaucratism[1]

OUR Revolution was, in essence, the product of a guerrilla movement that initiated its armed struggle against tyranny and crystalized with the taking of power. The first steps as a revolutionary state, as well as the early period of our formation as a government were strongly colored by the fundamentals of guerrilla tactics as a type of state administration. *"Guerrillerismo"* transferred the experience of armed struggle from the mountains and fields of Cuba into the various administrative and mass organizations, which meant in practice that only the important revolutionary slogans were followed (and often interpreted in different ways by and large) by all the administrative and social organizations. The way to solve specific problems was left to the free will of each of the leaders.

Spreading across the whole complex structure of society, the fields of action of these "administrative guerrillas" often came into open conflict, resulting in continuous friction, orders and counterorders, different interpretations of the law, which led some of these organizations, in a few cases, to retaliate by issuing their own policies in the form of decrees, totally disregarding the policies of the central body. After a year of painful experiences, we came to the conclusion that it was most essential to change our whole style of operating and to reorganize the state apparatus in the most rational way, following the planning methods known in our sister socialist countries.

As a countermeasure, strong bureaucratic structures, which characterized this first stage of our socialist state, began to be set up, but the backlash was too strong, and a whole series of structures, the Ministry of Industries among them, began a policy of functional centralization which overly curtailed the initiative of the administrators. This policy of centralization is understandable due to the lack of middle structures and to the

[1] *Cuba Socialista*, No. 18, Feb., 1963. Translated by Bernardo García-Pandavenes.

former anarchic spirit, but it demanded an overzealousness in the compliance with directives. At the same time, the lack of adequate means of control made it quite difficult to locate administrative mistakes at the time they occurred, a practice that was shielded by the use of the "libreta."[2] As a result, both the most conscientious and the most timid cadres would restrain their momentum so as to keep in line with the slow motion of the administrative machinery, while others continued to carry on without the slightest regard for any authority. All this led to the creation of new control measures to put a stop to such activities. And this is how our Revolution began to suffer from the practice we have dubbed "bureaucratism."

Obviously, "bureaucratism" does not stem from the inception of socialist society, nor is it its expected component. The state bureaucracy had existed since the time of the bourgeois regimes with their atmosphere of patronage and servility, for behind the budget a large number of opportunists used to hang around making up the "court" of the politician of the moment. In a capitalist society, where the whole state apparatus is at the service of the bourgeoisie, its importance as an administrative organ is very small; its importance lies in being penetrable enough to allow the passage of opportunists and closed enough to catch the citizenry in its mesh.

Given the weight of the "original sins" latent in the former administrative structures and the situations later developed with the advent of the Revolution, the evil of "bureaucratism" began to spread with great force. If we were to search out its roots at the present moment, we would find new reasons to add to the aforementioned; namely, three fundamental reasons.

One of these reasons is the lack of inner motivation. By this we mean, the lack of interest of an individual in serving the state when handling and mastering a given situation. It is rooted in a lack of revolutionary consciousness, or in any case, in a kind of conformism when confronted with a problem.

A direct and obvious relationship may be found between the lack of motivation and the lack of interest in solving problems. In this case, whether this failure in ideological inner motivation is the result of an absolute lack of conviction or of a sense of exasperation resulting from facing the same insoluble problems time and again, the individual or group of individuals takes refuge in "bureaucratism," fills out forms, salvages his sense of responsibility, and establishes a written defense either for the purpose of continuing to vegetate or to defend himself against the irresponsibility of others.

Another reason is the lack of organization. In attempting to destroy the "guerrilla style" of working without sufficient administrative experience, dislocations and bottlenecks ensue which unnecessarily slow down the flow of information from below and of instructions or orders emanating from the central structures. Sometimes the latter or the former take a wrong turn

[2] *Libreta*, literally *notebook*, is the ration card (ed.).

and get misplaced. On other occasions they are expressed in badly put together directives—pure gibberish—contributing to further distortions.

The absence of organization has as its basic characteristic a failure in the methods used to face a given situation. We can see plenty of examples of this in the ministries, whenever problems are handled by means other than the suitable ones, or whenever they are dealt with through the wrong channels and get lost in the labyrinth of red tape. "Bureaucratism" is the shackle that chains the type of functionary who tries to solve his problems any which way, bucking the established order again and again, without finding any solution. It is quite common to see how a goodly number of civil servants put in requests for more personnel as their only means of carrying out a task otherwise quite easily solved by using a little brain-power—thus creating new sources of totally unnecessary red tape.

For the sake of honest self-criticism, we ought never to forget that the economic direction of the Revolution is responsible for most of the bureaucratic evils: State structures were not set up according to a master plan of which the inner workings had been thoroughly studied, leaving a wide enough margin to speculate on administrative techniques. The central economic structure, the Central Planning Board (*Junta Central de Planificación*),[3] did not fulfill its task of direction, and could not fulfill this task simply because it lacked sufficient authority over the other bodies. It was not set up to give correct orders on the foundations of a given system; neither did it have adequate controls or the help of an over-all plan. Excessive centralization without ideal organization put the brakes on any spontaneous actions without being replaced in turn by correct and timely directives. A series of minor decisions obstructed our view of the large problems, thus bringing their solution to a stand still, without any rhyme or reason. Last minute decisions carried out suddenly, without any previous study, were characteristic of our work.

A very important third cause is the absence of a body of technical knowledge sufficiently developed to enable making the right decisions within a short time. The inability to do just this leads to the necessity of accumulating many experiences of little value so as to attempt to extract a conclusion from them. Discussions are usually endless, with none of the participants having sufficient authority to impose his criteria. After one, two, or more meetings, the problem continues until it either works itself out, or else it becomes necessary to pick any solution, no matter how unsuitable.

The almost total lack of knowledge supplied, as we have said, by a long series of meetings, brings about "meetingism," which boils down to an absence of guidelines for solving any problem. In these cases, bureaucratism, in other words the dead weight of red tape and of indecision having to do with the development of the whole society, is the fate of every one of the affected bodies.

[3] Often referred to in the chapters that follow as *Juceplan* (ed.).

These three fundamental reasons affect the institutional life of the whole country, either one institution after the other or in different combinations; and the time has come to break loose from their negative influence. It is necessary that new concrete measures be taken to make every state bureaucracy more flexible, in such a way as to establish a fixed center of control, which would hand over to the directors the control of key sectors of the economy, and would give free reign to initiative, thus bringing into play the development of the forces of production based on rational foundations.

If we know the causes and effects of bureaucratism, we are then able to study exactly the possibilities of correcting this evil. Among our main problems we consider that of organization to be the most serious and the one we should attack with all the strength that is required. To do this we must change our style of working. We must set the problems up according to priorities, assign specific tasks to each decision-making body, and establish concrete relations between and among all of them, moving horizontally outward from the center of the economic decision-making structure to the last administrative unit, forming a network of economic relationships among its various components. At present this is the immediate task within our reach, and has the added advantage of transferring to other fronts a large number of those who are uselessly employed, those who do not work at all, and those whose jobs are of minimal importance or duplicate the work of others without any apparent results.

Simultaneously, we must develop with great effort, a political program to eliminate the lack of inner motivation; *i.e.,* the lack of political clarity, which shows itself in a lack of productivity. The paths to follow are: continuous education by means of concrete explanations of every task; the arousing of interest in specific jobs among the administrative employees; the setting of example by vanguard workers on the one hand, and the instituting of drastic measures to eliminate the parasites, either those who hold an attitude of deep hatred toward socialist society or those who totally dislike working.

Finally, we must correct the inferiority brought about by our lack of knowledge. We have initiated the gargantuan task of transforming this society from one end to the other in the midst of imperialist aggression, of an ever harsher blockade, of a complete change in technology, of severe shortages of raw materials and food, and of a mass flight of the very few qualified technicians we have. Under these conditions we must seriously commit ourselves to the most persevering work with the masses, to be able to fill all the openings whether caused by traitors leaving or by the ever-increasing demands on skilled labor due to the rapid rhythm imposed on our development. This is why training holds a top priority in all the plans of the revolutionary government.

The training of the active labor force starts in the labor centers themselves at the most elemental level: the elimination of the last vestiges of illiteracy still found in the most remote areas; follow-up courses, then followed by courses in workers' betterment, for those beyond a third-grade education; courses of Minimum Technical Skills for workers at a higher level, extension courses to turn skilled workers into assistant engineers; university courses for every kind of professional and administrative personnel. The aim of the revolutionary government is to turn our country into a huge school, where study and the successful completion of these studies will be one of the basic factors in the improvement of the conditions of the individual, not only economically, but also by helping him to find his proper moral place in society in accordance with his qualifications.

If we succeed in unraveling the web of red tape, the intricate connections among all the structures and their internal departments, in diminishing the duplication of functions and the frequent "man holes" into which our institutions stumble; if we find the roots of every problem and work out organizational norms—at first elementary, more complex at a later date—then we are on the front lines battling against the indifferent, the confused, and the lazy; we will reeducate and educate the masses, we will incorporate them into the Revolution and eliminate the rejects, and at the same time, without respite, we will continue unflinchingly, in the face of whatever obstacles, the major task of education at every level; then we shall be in a position to do away with bureaucratism in a very short time.

The experience gained through our last mobilization[4] has led to our holding discussion sessions in the Ministry of Industries to study the phenomenon that, when we were in the thick of things, when the whole country mustered all its energies to resist the enemy, industrial production did not fall, absenteeism disappeared, problems were solved at an unexpected rate. After analyzing this event, we came to the conclusion that several factors converged which were instrumental in destroying the basic causes of bureaucratism. There was a great patriotic and national upsurge in the majority of the Cuban people to resist imperialism, and every worker, on every level, became a soldier for the economy, ready to solve any problem.

The ideological inner motivation was the result of foreign aggression. All structural norms were reduced to indicating only what should *not* be done, and the main problem to be tackled: to keep up production above all else, to keep up production of certain items with an even greater degree of emphasis, and to free the enterprises, factories, and bodies from all secondary functions, even those that might be necessary under normal social conditions.

The special degree of responsibility assumed by each individual forced him to make quick decisions; we were faced with a national emergency and we had to make decisions even if they were wrong; we had to make them right on the spot; this was done in many instances.

We have not yet made the final evaluation of the mobilization, and

[4] During the October 1962 "Missile Crisis" (ed.).

obviously, the balance in purely economic terms cannot be positive, but it was definitely favorable in terms of ideological mobilization, in the deepening of the consciousness of the masses. What is the lesson to be drawn? That we must make our workers, laborers, farmers, and clerks understand in their bones that the danger of imperialist aggression still hangs over our heads, that there is no peace, and that our main duty is to strengthen the Revolution day by day, for this is our only insurance against an invasion ever taking place. The higher the cost to the imperialists in taking this island, the stronger our defenses, and the deeper the consciousness of our sons and daughters, the more the imperialists will ponder the risk. But at the same time, the economic development of our country brings us closer to a greater social welfare. Let the grand example of our mobilization against imperialism become a permanent accomplishment—this is our ideological task.

We must weigh carefully the responsibilities of each functionary, establish them as nearly rigidly as possible within fixed boundaries, from which he should not depart, and within these limitations, we must give the broadest possible latitudes. At the same time, we must make a study of whatever is of fundamental importance as against whatever is secondary in the work of the different units in each state structure and place limits on the secondary, stressing the fundamental, allowing for greater expediency. And we must demand that our functionaries take action, establish deadlines to carry out instructions laid down by the core structures, and exercise proper control. And we must pressure them into making decisions within a reasonable period of time.

If we carry out this whole task, bureaucratism will disappear. It is not only a task for a single organization; neither is it limited to all the economic structures of the country; rather, it is the job of the whole nation, *i.e.,* of the leadership organizations, mainly of the United party of the Revolution (PURS) and the mass organizations. Every one of us must work toward fulfilling this urgent goal of the moment: *War against bureaucratism; streamlining of the state apparatus; production without any restraints and responsibility for production.*

CHAPTER 17

On Socialist Competition and Sugar Production[1]

THIS has been a long meeting. Many interesting ideas have been presented. It has been left for me to sum things up, and I will try to make it just that, a summary no longer than what has already been said.

I am just going to take up three matters: the subject of competition, some thoughts on sugar cane production, and the subject of mechanization.

I want to tell you something about competition, because competition is very important. It is very much a weapon of the socialist state. But it is also a double-edged sword, and you must know how to use it.

Competition cannot be like a ball game where the loser throws oranges at the referee. Competition should be fraternal. Why? So that everyone increases production. It is a weapon to increase production. Not only that, but it is also an instrument to deepen the consciousness of the masses, and the two must always go together.

We shall always insist on this double aspect of the progress of socialist construction. The construction of socialism is not work alone. The construction of socialism is not consciousness alone. It is work and consciousness, development of production, development of material goods through work and development of consciousness. Competition must fulfill these two goals, these two functions.

Therefore, what should be the greatest aspirations of a winner? For another to come and surpass him, surpass his record at the next opportunity, and help him, moreover, to surpass his record.

What is the purpose of this kind of competition? To increase the national level of production. To win there is not important, except in a local sense, where the winner can be deservedly proud. But we must not let competition become rivalry. We must remember always that we are not in

[1] Speech delivered at a Camaguey meeting of sugar cutters on February 9, 1963, reproduced in *Obra Revolucionaria,* Año 1963, No. 5. Translated by Robert MacLaren.

a ball game, but in a stage of the construction of socialism. That is why it is so important.

In other words, fencing competition helps to develop the arm, to develop the body of the person who fences with it. But this body should be developed harmoniously and serve an additional function. Not merely, in the case of the fencer, to look at himself in the mirror and see how well he parries, or to practice positions in front of the mirror. Its function should also be to develop; and in our case, to develop the consciousness of the masses and develop production.

Therefore, what must we try to do? Break all records and set new goals for another to reach the following day, if possible, and then surpass them again and again. In these matters competition should always be considered in this same way.

Goals can be surpassed. Not just one, but all can be surpassed. Do not look so much at the favorable conditions that help one or another province to be ahead, but rather look more closely at the unfavorable factors that cause a poor working performance in a province.

We have, for example, three provinces that have promised to be first in the next confrontation. Naturally, there will only be one first place, unless there is a three-way tie, which is not very likely. It is natural to strive for first place, but you should at the same time help your comrades. The province of Camagüey needs ample help. It has accomplished a great deal, especially in the political area, with discussions among the masses. There has been a greater awareness of the importance of sugar cane in our economy, and much has been accomplished in the first month of this harvest.

Now one thing must not be overlooked. There has been plenty of work repairing the sugar mills, and all the provinces have faced basically the same problems, the only difference being in how well the work was organized. And in this area Oriente province has been the leader. Oriente has shown organization and training at all levels, and again, as last year, Oriente is a front runner in all phases of this competition.

Not only in the task of transporting the cane to the mill, but in the logical savings that can be made in the repair work and in the tackling of other problems that come up constantly at the sugar mills—in all these areas Oriente has performed magnificently.

In other words, we must recognize that the province that can be a model for all the rest in the production of sugar is Oriente. We must all learn from their work experience. They have one very interesting feature. I don't know if they exist in Camagüey, but at least not to the same extent as in Oriente. These are the Red Battalions.

I had the opportunity to be with some cane cutters a few weeks back. Truly it is in the extraordinary spirit of the cane cutters that comprise the Red Battalions that the force of the Revolution, the core of the Revolution, can be seen. They are avant-garde battalions, very close-knit groups. They average hundreds of arrobas[2] daily. I have attended discussions, sometimes discussions between brigades, occasionally violent ones, where the head of a brigade was complaining because he had two inexperienced cutters. They have a name for them in Oriente . . . What do they call greenhorn cutters? They have a special name for them, I can't think of it right now . . . well, it doesn't matter.

The problem was that the head of the brigade had two new men and two old men. They also have a special nickname. [Someone from the audience shouts out "cortazo"] Right. Codazo. Something like that. Cortazo. That's it.

The head of the brigade said, "I can take on anyone, but my brigade can't compete. Nevertheless, I want to be with my brigade. This is a unit and we have to fight, and next year we will be better."

In other words, there was a very strong spirit of unity, of comradeship among the cutters. Every brigade captain, naturally, works more and better than the rest of the cutters. They don't worry about difficulties, about food, about this or that thing. The main thing is to cut cane. They have a dream of finishing up there in Oriente, and, like Maceo,[3] pushing on all the way to Pinar del Río, if necessary.

This is the spirit of our field laborers, and what a moving spirit it is. It is the spirit of the avant-garde workers who preach by their example, clearing the way in front of the Revolution. It is an experiment to be studied and put quickly into practice in every province.

Oriente, before the beginning of the harvest, was busy organizing its Red Battalions. In Oriente the Secretary of the ORI is a seasoned cane cutter, so it is easy for him to be at the head of his battalions. I think that if we put comrade Felipe at this position, it will be hard for him, but he can use a cutting machine and work some days. This will give him renewed spirit. And we can give Benito a machine too.

Now, comrades, I have a little criticism. You know I have a mania for criticism every time I find myself in front of a microphone. I am going to make a criticism of Camagüey province. You have done a fantastic job in a wide number of areas. Nevertheless, every problem is blamed on not enough workers, not enough workers, and not enough workers. And there hasn't been enough enthusiasm for the machines. There hasn't been enthusiastic, tenacious work with machines. And machines cut and pick up the cane. They have passed the test.

Camagüey's problems can only be half solved this year.

I have seen assemblies in many places, but at the first sign of a difficulty, the operators start protesting. Another bad thing: They begin to figure out how much they were told they were going to earn, and how much they are

[2] An *arroba* is a twenty-five-pound unit (ed.).
[3] A hero of the liberation struggle (ed.).

actually earning, or what they earned before, and what they earn now. And then they begin to say, "No. It isn't enough." In some places the same thing happened with the cane-gathering machine operators, although this attitude has practically disappeared because the machine has proven itself. It is an efficient machine. It gives a greater yield to the cutters. The other day we were looking at a cane field that was burned in the area of the Ciro Redondo sugar mill. There was a brigade of only three persons: a comrade over sixty years old and his two sons, who cut eight tons in their winning effort. Nevertheless, the average yield there of the winning brigade was nine and a quarter tons. But everybody can cut over six tons with ease when it is done with machinery.

In other words, there are solutions within the provinces themselves. I told you that this year Camagüey's problem can be resolved, can be resolved half way. If you win the competition, I will bet Oriente will not be able to restrain themselves, and they will complain about the cutters they sent over. Las Villas, although they sent very few, will also gripe about it, and so will Havana, without counting the fact that sometimes the cutters they send are very bad cutters, even though good workers.

I have already come across two cases where people vital for production were cutting cane. This is not progressive. It is all right for a few days, but it is not good as a system. We had established that only those workers who would not seriously interrupt production in an industry could be taken out, because otherwise it really would not solve the problem. Now, if instead of being used for cutting cane with machetes, these comrades were used as cutting machine operators, they could produce a lot more, because the work is less specialized, requires less skill and less physical endurance, and can be done by anybody. In other words, there are solutions.

And another point: There is no other way for Cuba in general to advance, and especially for Camagüey, but through mechanization. So we must take what there is and develop it and be inventive with it.

This year a thousand cutting machines will be manufactured. In a few days the first five hundred will be ready, and almost all of them will come here. Then there will be thousands more. Some should arrive before the end of the harvest. If for each of these machines there are workers who think about what they are doing and cherish their machines, there will be one or two thousand heads thinking about these machines. It is a machine that is still in the experimental stage, and will probably undergo many changes, but herein is the potential for a thousand inventors interested in it. And everyone that works a little with it will soon find something wrong, something to correct, something to add, some way to perfect the machine. In just a few days of operation many things have been changed, and a lot of experience acquired. Some additions are really important. The blade has been greatly simplified, and the machine is now doing a very good job with a much smaller one.

This is where the emphasis must be put, in all of Cuba, and primarily in Camagüey. And not sometime in the future, and I say this because on the way here I was listening to Comrade Alfredo Menéndez and others, who were saying, "No. Not this year for the cane cutters." I say "yes" to the cane cutters; this year! This year, yes!

This is a problem that must be quickly solved. Comrades at the sugar mills have put forth a great effort. At the "Ecuador" mill they are making eighty or ninety machines; at the "First of January" mill they are also making some; and at the "Ciro Redondo" too; in other places they are turning out cutters and here in Camagüey too. These machines should be put into use immediately.

Learning to use them is easy for the average tractor operator. It is true that the machines break down, and I can give you statistics, but the majority of the breakdowns are caused by the lack of experience of the operators. With a little practice the machine does not break down, and it gives a high yield.

That is what I wanted to tell you about competition; in other words, the sense in which it should be taken. One must realize that it is not just a simple game; that it is a weapon of the Revolution, and a weapon that has an objective: the development of the consciousness of the entire nation concerning the necessity of productive work that will create greater riches. It also helps to find out where good work is being done and to study the reasons for the good results.

This year I was asking if the "Chile" sugar mill was in first place. It is among the leaders. Last year it was the winner. It is not just luck that has put it at the top two years running. What is the reason? The reason is that they are doing a good job there. In what ways? That is what we need to find out: if it is only a technical achievement, if it is a political achievement, or if it is due to the organization of all the factors pertaining to the production of sugar.

And this leads to the second subject, which is the production of sugar. Comrade Menéndez explained to you that a mill is a sugar factory, and what must be analyzed is the final product and the efficiency in producing the sugar. Now well and good. The final product is sugar, but practically, the economy of the entire country, to a greater or lesser degree, is dedicated to the production of sugar. A large area of the country directs itself toward the mill, where the sugar is processed. And thus it is logical for the mill to be a crucial part of the production of sugar.

Sugar production is made up of many factors. They begin in the laboratory with the search for new varieties. There is patient study, over many years, of the varieties, deciding to what uses each type can be put.

When we know that we are going to mechanize, we have to think about the varieties that are suitable to mechanization; in the growing of the cane, how to make the terrain suitable; even in the arrangement of the furrows so the cane can be cut by machine; in the constant checking on the progress of this work, the actual organization of the cutting, the loading, the transporting to the mill at the time of the harvest. It is all a very complex task.

When the Sugar Commission meets, not only must the Department of Industries and INRA meet; the party must get together to mobilize; and the unions, to mobilize and work according to the needs. The Department of Transportation must meet to see what it can contribute, and a whole series of industries that must provide means for production. The Interior Commerce Department must proportion the necessary supply for the population in these times when there is no surplus. And even the Exterior Commerce Department must foresee the basic necessities of the harvest. The entire economic apparatus of the government must act on these tasks.

Now, everything centers on the mill. So we insist on the importance that it has, not so that it can dictate to agriculture, but so that it exercises sufficient weight in the entire process of production, which does not begin when the cane comes to the mill, but when the scientists are developing new varieties in accordance with ideas already established and accepted by the Economic Planning Office.

In other words, we must have a single road, a single opinion, a single voice. And everyone should see it clearly and work in that direction.

I think that the sowing of the cane fell behind this year. Not all the goals were met last year. Certainly the entire weight of agriculture that falls on INRA is very great, and INRA has a superhuman task to correct past mistakes, but the importance of sugar cane should never be forgotten. This would be a childish extreme. To think that we are being more revolutionary by attacking sugar cane as representative of imperialist exploitation is doing just that. The Garands that we had in the mountains were the same Garands that the oppressive army had. They just changed hands. Nobody thought of kicking a Garand, or locking it up, or burning it because it had belonged to the army. It was a weapon and now was used with a different purpose.

The organization of the sugar industry was very complex. It had fifty years of experience behind it in Cuba. The sugar mill had become, however, the absolute dictator of the entire economy. Yet the apparatus set up cannot be disregarded, nor can the experience and experiments of the sugar companies be disregarded. All of this must be converted into a solid body that functions under a single command, not the Consolidated Sugar Company, but rather the Revolutionary Government Directorate, yet reserving for the mill its deserved importance.

It is at the mill that many problems are going to be solved, problems which cannot yet be solved in the fields. In the areas outside the provincial capitals the mill can be a big brother to the small local industries, because it is at the mill that there are experienced workers and an organization that has gone on unbroken for many years.

In other words, we should not make the same error that agriculture made by destroying the old, the outdated, simply because it was the outdated, without having the new. Much of the old, a very great part, must be changed, but it must be replaced. Every time something is destroyed, something must be put in its place.

This is very important and must be stressed constantly so that everyone understands it very well. It is not just a desire to give orders, but simply a logical reason for the mill to provide basic guidance in the harvesting, while allowing as much freedom and autonomy as possible.

For example, now they are checking the competition. The efficiency of the mill is being studied, and there have emerged all the problems that you are aware of from the long debate between Camagüey and Oriente over the changes in the point evaluation of the competition.

Why is this happening? Well, because we now have a more technical concept of what a sugar mill should be, which is just what we are investigating by checking the creaky points of the mills in order to evaluate their real efficiency.

This is very important because we are condemned, or simply forced—and it is the same thing—to produce sugar for many years yet in order to maintain our export balance and thus acquire the many products we need from abroad.

In today's newspapers they tell about the long-term credit that the Soviet Union has extended us. What is this credit for? It is not for building industries, which is the usual reason for extending credit. It is to pay the existing deficit with the Soviet Union. In other words, to pay off all that we owe the Soviet Union for having purchased more than we delivered. How did this happen? Because of small harvests there was not enough sugar, which is our money until other crops, little by little, supplant the sugar industry.

And if the sugar industry, that is, sugar, the final product, is so important, then every aspect of sugar production has this same importance. And in agriculture we cannot forget sugar cane, and we must think about the sugar cane not only as agriculture but in terms of the final product, sugar, and adapt everything to the optimum conditions, so sugar will be produced in the most efficient manner possible.

For us the most efficient way is the third point we are going to consider. It is mechanization. And for this, I have already said, agriculture must be organized. Now there is the very important work of the organization of the cutting, collecting, and transporting of the sugar to the mill, and the very important factor of changing the consciousness of the workers in respect to the machines.

Just as it was easy at a given moment to rid the countryside of bosses, so it seemed a simple thing to liquidate the inspectors without anyone protesting. It was a change in the mentality of the people, and everybody accepted it.

Now, a problem as important, as basic, as changing the attitude of the worker toward the machine is accepted only very slowly. It means many discussions, many meetings, many demonstrations to each worker, with pencil and paper, that he is going to earn more.

And I ask myself why so many demonstrations must be made, when the Red Battalions did not ask how much they were going to earn before going out to the fields.

The workers are going to earn more when things are well organized with the machinery. But this is not the basic thing, which is that mechanization is indispensable to the Revolution and to the economic development of the country. This is what counts first. This is the primary reason. Then come the others. Then can come the demonstration, more or less incidental, that more will be earned. But the important thing is that mechanization is necessary and indispensable. How is it that the same militiamen who are ready to die any time they are asked and defend the Revolution with the highest spirit, the first thing they do is take out pencil and paper to figure out the wages, if the Revolution is what counts first?

Now, why does this happen? Because it has not been well enough established that what counts is the Revolution, and machinery is fundamental. Why? Because many comrades seated here did not have the least bit of confidence in the machine, and many still have their doubts. I did not point at anybody in particular. I just swept my hand across the audience in general.

But, for example, I am going to use a name. Comrade Mongo Castro has no confidence in the machine, but we have agreed that he is going to make a test with all the efficiency and the enthusiasm he has in order to see what the machines can really do. And in the next competition we shall see if the machine really is or is not efficient. There are many comrades who did not have faith. Actually, it was a rather daring step.

There is not a country in the world that has a thousand machines, and of course, there is not a country in the world that has decided to produce a thousand machines without any prototype. Until now it has only occurred to us. There is no good record to emulate, but I think that we know how to play the flute, and now we must learn to play the concerto that comes after having played the flute.

Now I am going to make my personal boast. Monday I began cutting by machine. At first the expected happens; the joints break, this breaks, that breaks. We even had an accident. Some comrades were not cautious. The machine is dangerous. Guards must be made for it. The teeth that cut the cane are very dangerous. They almost cut off the leg of one of the comrades. After that they began to produce.

That machine is cutting fifty tons where they are trying it out, and everybody is complaining. Naturally, all the conditions are not the best. Nevertheless, I have cut 45,000 *arrobas* this week. This isn't anything to applaud;[4] I am giving an example and showing the record for someone else to break tomorrow. Forty-five thousand *arrobas,* a novice operator who did not go through school.

Yesterday I cut 10,500 *arrobas* in an eleven to twelve hour working day. This morning, with a faster machine, a Soviet tractor which is more powerful, I cut 7,600 *arrobas* in six and a half hours of work. The machines can cut at least 800 *arrobas* per hour in typical fields. That is the yield if you really push. I would say that it is work for two operators.

You cannot expect people to be on tractors for twelve hours straight. Besides, time is needed for maintenance, and naturally, experiments are being conducted with teams of mechanics who are maintaining them.

Yesterday, in ten hours work, one blade tooth came loose, and that was the only thing that went wrong. In the six and a half hours today, there was not a single interruption to interfere with the cutting. A machine will mean some interruptions, because it is far from perfect.

Here in Camagüey I have cut well over 100,000 *arrobas* in two weeks. This means that a machine, given the same conditions, can cut 200,000 in a month. And if the thousand tractors start operating, it would mean 200,000,000. This is a considerable amount. It is a meaningful amount. And something else: A tractor makes people work—makes them run.

Some workers follow after the tractor and cut the cane that it leaves. The tractor is not perfect. It does not cut every stalk. Some are missed. These workers cut them so the tractor can continue on to the next row. These men really have to run. They put in a hard day's work.

Now then, this will mean that four machete cutters will have a fairly easy job to do. Laborers with less skill can gather the cut cane that is on the ground.

There are different methods. In some places the separating is done first, but I think this is a waste of time and can be done after the cutting. If a worker takes out his frustration on the tractor, he will not be able to do anything with it. He is the one who will say that it is no good if the tractor happens to stop in the first row. The tractor is going to be used. When it breaks down, find out why. Study the problems involved. Study the defects. This way you can become expert operators in very little time.

As for the harvesting machine, there is nothing about which to argue. It easily picks up an average of ten thousand *arrobas*. And now a very important matter. The harvesting and cutting machines are attachments to the tractor. The tractor is the soul of the machine and yet it is so badly maintained. Often it needs oil, or pulleys break. There are a lot of problems with the tractor because there are not adequate maintenance crews.

[4] All of Guevara's speeches were always interrupted by applause, such as here. I have eliminated such mention throughout (ed.).

This no longer has anything to do with the machine itself. We need to have special maintenance crews on every farm where they are running tests. The cutting machine is a rather complicated machine with many bolts and many chains. It is still in the experimental stage.

In a short space of time there have been many innovations. One has been made with only four blades, and longer ones at that. These were made for test purposes. The result? Fantastic, much better than the sixteen-tooth blade. It cuts the stalk a lot cleaner. The cutting machine, as it now is, cuts cleaner on the average than the workers using machetes do. Some men cut very clean but they are exceptional. The average professional machete cutter does not cut as clean as the machine does. This is a very important point in favor of the machine. All this about the machine destroying the stalk or uprooting it is a thing of the past.

There is a new problem: the separating. A lot of experiments have been made to find out the best way to do it. And there is always the possibility of developing new varieties of cane that will separate more easily. Genetics may well provide the answer. But already on the mechanical side there are many experiments underway, any one of which may give results.

But we must consider the tractor with a critical attitude and a desire to find answers to its problems. This is what we must accomplish. This, basically, is the task that is before Camagüey today. The first five hundred cutting machines will be ready about February fifteenth, and they are coming to Camagüey. Thus Camagüey has its work cut out for it.

We need five hundred or one thousand inventors, depending on whether there are one or two men operating each machine, looking into the problems, changing anything that they think will improve its efficiency, as long as it is not something basic that would wreck it. In this way a great body of knowledge will be built.

Next year we will not turn out a thousand cutting machines as we are doing this year. We will be more cautious and manfacture more harvesting machines because they present fewer problems. Also, the harvesting machine works all over Cuba, and the machete cutters obtain a higher yield cutting for the harvesting machine. They just cut low down, cut the shoots, and throw it in a pile at the side. The stacking machines, after a little practice operating them, will stack as well as by hand. Now, not every type of equipment will be able to be used. The ox and the high wagon cannot be used. Here problems will arise that will take some thinking to solve: how to use the existing equipment, the existing organization, in order to have the stacking machines working at full capacity.

Over by the Ciro Redondo mill the other day a team of stackers was working in perfect conjunction with trucks as an emergency measure because stalks were burning. The results were extraordinary.

[*Someone from the audience:* What? Is cane burned? Ah! It turns out that a machine cuts the cane, collects it, and separates the chaff. I drew up a plan of it and showed it to Paquito Herrera, who I think is here. He saw it. But what I wanted to ask you was if you intend to make this machine or not, because I wrote and said that the comrades in our department—the lathe operator, the welder, everybody—are ready to experiment and begin to make this machine right here if the government says to do it. Five or six days ago, in the Department of Industries, I spoke with the engineers Guerra and López Vigueiras. The latter sent for me to show me the motor that I told you would work. So the government needs only to give the go-ahead sign to get things started. I brought a letter to give to you, because it turns out that the machine can prune. I explained this to you with a wealth of details, and I specify in the letter how this machine separates the chaff, how it harvests, and how it adapts itself to the various differences in terrain. This machine existed in 1930, and when I was small, I saw it operating. I sketched for you the transmission, the shafts, the chains, how the fans work, and many details. Comrade Paquito Herrera sent me to the laboratory where I am working out the blueprint.]

[*Guevara:*] I want to do some consulting with people who know, because I do not know that much about machinery. But there is a problem. It seems that, at the present time, these combination machines cannot solve the problem in Cuba because the combination machine which cuts, separates, collects, and loads the wagon, averaging 40,000 *arrobas,* would have to make six trips with the wagon behind. So it would be a very costly operation.

Now innovations like this are appearing every day. We have a Technical Department studying the innovations. All the ideas are good, but those for making a new, entirely different machine cannot have the same consideration as ideas for improving the existing machines. Why? Because the apparatus is already set up for making a specific type of machine, one on which many things can and ought to be changed.

Make a new machine? For one thing, the combination machine is a permanent machine. And the tractor should fit it. It would probably need a heavier tractor than the forty-five or fifty horse power tractor we are now using. That is one of the many problems.

On the other hand, when the harvesting is finished, the cutter can be taken off and the tractor is ready to be used for other tasks. Any repair shop can take the cutter off the tractor in an hour or an hour and a half. In other words, it has its many uses during the harvest, and then immediately afterward, the tractor can be used for any other job. For this reason we decided on a model based on all these needs.

We may develop new ideas for loaders, harvesters, for more complex machinery, and sometime we may convert over to them. In the United States there are many machines of this type, but they are in places that harvest five or six times the average here. On such a larger scale it would indeed be worthwhile. The machine can work slowly and can be gathering it up at a high speed because it picks up a large quantity of cane over a small area.

Under our agricultural conditions, with 40,000 *arrobas* of cane to the *caballería,* six rows are needed to fill a cart. And a heavy cart that keeps getting heavier cannot be dragged along. A motor would be needed to move it.

The loading machine is very simple. It is an inverted tractor with an arm like a crane and with teeth. The cutting machine has an apparatus that is added to it and taken off after the harvest. In other words they are very simple machines that can be used with a tractor. We must remember that we are not rich and do not have all the equipment we need. If we can put them to alternative uses, so much the better; better for the farms, especially.

Now then, all these ideas are wonderful. Everything that contributes to solving the problem of the mechanization of the cane operations is important, and we must continue to listen to every comrade who has ideas for this. We must continue to work in every direction. We have not adopted a definitive type of machine. We have simply chosen a type to develop for the time being. These thousand machines will be giving us new perspectives as we put them into use.

For the present what we have got to try to do during this harvest is average at least 200,000 *arrobas* a month with these machines. This is a hard and difficult task. Some mills will not be able to accomplish this. This machine will not work on every type of terrain. Rocks, tree trunks, and steep slopes can be too much for it. But in any case, there is an enormous number of fields in Cuba where this machine can operate. Especially in Camagüey, a flat province with numerous conditions compatible to mechanized harvesting, and moreover, a province where the manpower shortage is a serious problem.

This is the task that lies ahead of us here. Bringing about full mechanization in this province, this pioneering province, and in all the others as well, is an undertaking as important as the grinding of the cane, the work of purifying the sugar, or producing a better sugar at the mill. Every province has cutting and harvesting machines, so they can try them out and see what they can do.

Not a while from now, but tomorrow, the record of 1,500 *arrobas* cut in a day should be broken. Tomorrow someone should cut 11,000, 12,000, or 15,000. And keep on setting new records with the machine, and finding out its defects and correcting them.

This, I think, is the task for Camagüey. And next year this will be the task for all of Cuba. We shall have to make the same careful preparations for mechanization that we made for this year's harvest. Last year much was improvised. This year we have worked especially hard and have set up committees even at the local level to tackle the problems that have arisen.

Remember that our machinery is not anything like it is for the capitalist countries, where it competes with man or enslaves him. Every worker should see how the machine frees him. The machine truly serves man when the exploitation of one man by another is abolished. This is what we are trying to do: to make the machine an instrument for freeing the peasant, giving him more free time, giving him more free time to become educated, to develop himself in every way, to his fullest capacity. It is this for which we are all striving. This man of the future will have to be a man with as simple and pure a heart as the man of today, and moreover, will have the mental capacity to make new discoveries that will gradually put nature to work for mankind, for the benefit of humanity.

Those of us here, in our little Cuba, at the same time that we are taking on the gigantic task of struggling against imperialism, of setting an example for all of Latin America, of carrying on a deadly struggle without a letup, we must also make technical advances to provide a base, a foundation, so that we can progress completely on our own, without having to bring in technicians from other countries to teach us each and every thing; so that we can walk on our own feet; so that we can create our own society with our own technical ability, our own character, our own way of life, and be a strong and prosperous country.

This is a task that will take years to accomplish. But as with any task long or short, to finish it, it must first be started. And now, this moment, the indispensable step has been taken to begin. Now you can go forward with your own inventiveness and drive. In a few years machines will be commonplace, and if someone hears about cutting and loading by hand, he will regard it as bestial, inhuman work, a thing of the past to which one can no longer return.

Remember that there are no machete cutters in Cuba. And not because they have left. Those who used to cut cane are still here, but they chose to do anything except cut cane. Why? Because cutting cane is hard. Cutting cane is exhausting. It is the furthest thing from fun. And besides, the cane field never ends.

For all these reasons, comrades, we have to emphasize mechanization. And what I am saying here to Camagüey should be heard by comrades everywhere in the country. Wherever machines are used, we urge people to think about improvements and come up with new ideas.

And now, comrades, the next competition will be within a month, with three provinces saying that they will win. Conrado kept the other comrades from speaking, so they couldn't say the same. Probably one or two more would have done so. I think that Matanzas would be more modest because conditions there are poor.

In any case the competitive effort should continue, but always remember what was said at the beginning of this resume, which is getting a bit lengthy. Competition is a weapon which will help us increase the output of sugar, which will mean more money to buy the materials we need from abroad, and at the same time helps create in our country a spirit of constructive work.

And so the winner of the next competition should have as its foremost aspiration another province passing its mark in the following competition.

And now to work, to work with this attitude.

And so, comrades, I do not think we will be present at the next competition, but I do plan to attend the following one in Santa Clara and will see you there. See you then.

CHAPTER 18

On Party Militancy[1]

WE decided, with the comrades who are the organizers of this province and of our party, to attend your meeting in view of the importance that the Textilera de Ariguanabo has for the country. At the present time it is the unit with more workers than any other in the country, which means it is the largest industrial center our country possesses. Besides, it is a key factor in one of the most important industries devoted to contributing to the welfare of our people. It provides clothing, one of the most basic things our revolution must give the people, whatever the conditions and whatever the difficulties we face.

We have also come in order to analyze this new process, by which a series of concepts in the party organization has changed, and because there is, here, a return to the masses.

As you have deemed fitting—still more, as you have sanctioned—the members of the Partido Unido de la Revolución Socialista who leave this work center are men who can count on the unanimous support of their fellow workers. The nuclei being formed at this time—the party organizations—can henceforth count on all necessary backing, and they can abandon the almost underground and conspiratorial quality that for some time was the keynote of the work of our ruling party.

All that murkiness in which the men lived in those clandestine cells, which were chosen mechanically and without evaluating the comrades' qualities with sufficient analysis, is changing into a new structural form in which it is the masses who decide, at the lowest rung of the ladder, which model-workers should be proposed as party members.

Hence the enormous difference. Hence also the enormous strength the ruling party can acquire. Consistent with a whole series of changes in the

[1] Speech delivered to textile workers on March 24, 1963. Published in *Ediciones de la Comisión de Orientación Revolucionaria del P.U.R.S.* April, 1963. Translated by Leonard Mades.

structure and in the whole conceptual scheme of the party, the latter is placing itself firmly at the head of the proletarian state. With its example, with its sacrifice, with the thoroughness of its thinking, and with the boldness of its actions, the party is guiding each one of the stages of our Revolution. Nevertheless, not everything is perfect yet—far from it. Many things must be adjusted.

We need go no further than the few statistics we were just establishing. One hundred and ninety-seven comrades have been recognized as having all necessary qualities for membership in the Partido Unido de la Revolución Socialista at this work center, where there are three thousand workers. "What is the exact figure?" asks the public. All right, four thousand; it is all the same, for statistical purposes. One hundred and ninety-seven comrades have been chosen from among them, but there are only five women among the 197. Yet the percentage of women who work here in Ariguanabo is much greater than this 2½ shown by our statistics. This indicates that there is a failure to integrate women, on the basis of equal rights and conditions, into the activity relating to the creation of a socialist society. It would be well for us all to begin analyzing the reason why in each place.

There are two causes that, it would seem, appear clearer and more determinative. One of them is that women have not really freed themselves from a series of ties binding them to a tradition of the dead past. For this reason they do not join the active life of revolutionary workers. Another may be that the mass of workers—the so-called strong sex—think that women are still not sufficiently developed, and these men take advantage of the majority they constitute. In places like this men are more in evidence, and their work attracts more attention. Thus it is a little forgotten that the role of women is discussed subjectively.

A few months ago—just a few—we had to transfer a capable female official at the Ministry of Industry. Why? Because she had a position that often required her to go out into the provinces with inspectors or with the head, the director-general. This comrade, who was married (I believe to a member of the Rebel Army), could not go out alone; her husband would not consent to it. She had to make all her trips subject to her husband's being able to leave his job and accompany her to whatever place she had to go.

This is a boorish example of discrimination against women. Does a woman perchance have to accompany her husband each time he has to go into the interior or any other place so that she can watch him, lest he succumb to temptation or something of that sort?

What does this indicate? Well, simply that the past continues to weigh upon us and that the liberation of women should consist of the achievement of their total freedom—their *inner* freedom. It is not a matter of a physical restriction which is placed on them to hold them back from certain activities. It is also the weight of a previous tradition.

We are living in a new era, an era in which a socialist society is being created. All forms of discrimination are being swept away, and the only remaining dictatorship that counts is the dictatorship of the working class —the class organized on top of the classes that have been defeated. There is still a long way ahead of us that will be full of struggle and unpleasantness until we achieve the perfect society, which is the classless society—the society in which all differences will disappear. At our present stage no other dictatorship but the dictatorship of the proletariat as a class is acceptable.

The proletariat has no sex: It is all men and women taken together, who at all places of work in the nation, struggle consistently to reach a common goal.

This is an example of all there is to do. But naturally, it is only one example among many. Many things remain to be done. Without our going back to the time before the triumph of the Revolution, there are still many traditions belonging to the later past, that is, the past that pertains to our prerevolutionary history.

Whoever aspires to be a leader has to be able to face or, rather, expose himself to the verdict of the masses. He must be confident that he has been chosen or proposed as a leader because he is the best of the good—on account of his work, his spirit of sacrifice, and his constant sense of belonging to the vanguard in all the struggles the proletariat must carry on daily in order to create a socialist society.

This still weighs us down. Our organizations are not totally free of this sin that has become part of our very young revolutionary traditions and has begun to do harm. We must banish totally everything that means thinking that being elected a member of some organization of the masses or of the ruling party of the Revolution—being chosen a leader in one of the Revolution's different activities—permits a comrade to enjoy the slightest opportunity to get something more than the rest of the people. We refer, in other words, to the policy of rewarding excellence with material things, to rewarding with material things the one who has shown greater conscientiousness and spirit of sacrifice.

There are two things that are constantly conflicting and dialectically becoming part of the process of creating a socialist society. On the one hand, material incentives are made necessary by our having emerged from a society that thought of only material incentives, and we are creating a new society on the foundation of that old society through a series of transformations in the minds of the people of that old society. On the other hand we still do not have enough to give each individual what he needs. For these reasons, interest in material things will be with us for a time during the process of creating a socialist society.

But precisely for this reason the function of the vanguard party is to raise the opposite banner as high as possible—the banner of interest in nonmaterial things, the banner of nonmaterial incentives, the banner of men who sacrifice and hope for nothing but recognition by their comrades. Such is the approval you have shown today to the comrades you have chosen to become part of the Partido Unido de la Revolución.

Material incentives are something left over from the past. They are something that we must accept but whose hold on the minds of the people we must gradually break as the revolutionary process goes forward. One type of incentive is definitely on the rise; the other must definitely be on the way to extinction. Material incentives will not play a part in the new society being created; they will die out as we advance. We must establish the conditions under which this type of motivation that is operative today will increasingly lose its importance and be replaced by nonmaterial incentives such as the sense of duty and the new revolutionary way of thinking.

Comrades, we have now taken the first steps. We can say that the Partido Unido de la Revolución officially exists at this work center. It is composed—to start with, at least—of 197 comrades. Which qualities have been looked for in them? You know which they are because you yourselves have chosen the comrades. You know the spirit of sacrifice, the camaraderie, the love of country, the vanguard spirit in each phase of the struggle, the spirit of the leader by example, who leads with modesty that a party member must possess. But the new party member must also be a man who feels the new truths in his bones and feels naturally that what is a sacrifice for ordinary people is, for him, simply a daily occurrence—something that must be done and is the natural thing to do. In other words, he must be a man who completely changes his definition of certain duties in his daily life and toward the duties of a revolutionary in a process of development like ours, which is going on under an imperialist siege.

A few days ago, in one of the unfortunately frequent meetings we have still not been able to rule out, one of our comrades told the latest joke (the latest joke, at least, which has reached my ears), which referred to the party's constitution. It was about a man who was going to join the party and was told by the section members that he had to work overtime, set an example, utilize the hours of the day to further his education, do volunteer work Sundays, volunteer for work every day, forget all vanities, devote all his time to working, and participate in all existing organizations of the masses. He was told, finally: "And, besides, you must at all times be ready to give your life for the Revolution. Are you ready?"

The man replied: "All right; if I am going to lead the life you say, what do I want it for? I'll be glad to give it."

Why? It is the old concept that is expressed in this joke. Whether it is counterrevolutionary or revolutionary, I do not know, but certainly it is profoundly counterrevolutionary in spirit. Why? Because it is precisely a vanguard worker and member of the ruling party of the Revolution who experiences all these hardships (that are called sacrifices) with a new interest and as part, not of a duty that is imposed upon him, but of one that, coming from within him, he performs with enthusiasm.

The most trivial and boring things are transformed, through the power of his interest, from the inner effort of the individual—from the deepening of his awareness in important and substantial matters—into something he cannot fail to do without feeling bad, into what is called sacrifice. Not sacrificing then becomes the real sacrifice for a revolutionary. In other words, categories and concepts now change.

The perfect revolutionary, the member of the ruling party, must work every hour and every minute of his life, during these years of very hard struggle that lie ahead of us. He must work with constantly renewed and growing interest. This is fundamental.

This is what is meant by the Revolution. It means that a man is a revolutionary within himself and feels like a revolutionary. When he experiences this, the concept of sacrifice develops new modalities.

The militant in the Partido Unido de la Revolución is a Marxist. He must know his Marxism and consistently apply dialectical materialism in his analysis, in order to be able to interpret the world correctly.

But the world is big and wide, and it has many structures. It has passed through many different civilizations and in some parts of the world, at the present time, there are still social strata, or peoples who live in the most primitive of societies known to man: primitive communism. Slavery, too, exists, unfortunately; and there is much feudalism, in Latin America for example. Capitalism in its last phase, imperialism, also exists. So do the peoples who are starting to create a socialist society, and those who, like the Soviet Union, are beginning to create a communist one.

But even when the different peoples belong to the same social system—be it capitalism, socialism in its formative stage, or any other system—they have arrived at this historical period by different routes and under conditions peculiar to each nation.

Because of this, Marxism is only a guide to action. The great fundamental truths have been revealed. With them as a starting point, and using dialectical materialism as a weapon, the situation in each part of the world can be interpreted. That is why no construct can be the same as another; all have special characteristics that are peculiar to their formation.

The characteristics of our revolution are also special. They cannot be disassociated from the great truths or be interpreted without a knowledge of the absolute truths revealed by Marxism; these were not invented or established as dogma but discovered through analysis of the development of society. But there will be special conditions, and the members of the Partido Unido de la Revolución will have to be creative. They will have to deal with theory and create practice in accordance with theory and with the special conditions of this country in which it is our lot to live and struggle.

In other words, the task of creating a socialist society in Cuba must be faced by fleeing mechanical thinking like the plague; mechanical thinking leads only to stereotyped methods. It leads only to clandestine cells, favoritism, and a whole series of evils within the revolutionary organization. We must proceed dialectically, relying upon the masses and always being in contact with them. We must lead them by their example, utilize Marxist ideology, utilize dialectical materialism, and be creative at all times.

In view of this, how could we define the most important tasks of a member of the Partido Unido de la Revolución? There are two fundamental ones, two which are repeated constantly and are the foundation on which the entire development of our society rests: production for the people's use, and the intensification of awareness.

It is superfluous to explain to you why production is so important, because production must be something that is always one of a party member's major preoccupations.

If socialism is not a beneficent society, it is not a Utopian system based upon man's goodness as a man. Socialism is a system that is reached by a historical process, and it has as its basis the socialization of the fundamental means of production and the equitable distribution, within a framework in which there is production of a social nature, of all the wealth in that society. It is the same means of production capitalism created: the great factories, the great capitalist plantations, the great capitalist farms, the places where man's work has been done communally, in association. But in that era the fruits of his labor were enjoyed individually by the capitalists, the exploitative class, which was the legal owner of the means of production.

Things have changed now. But the basis is still the same: a social class, a social structure which comes along and necessarily depends upon the preceding one. In the formative stage of socialism this is the basis of development of all our production.

Why is the intensification of awareness the other one of the two most important tasks of a party member? Well, awareness is even more important than production, if one can imagine such a thing. It is so important because of the new characteristics shown by the developmental processes of the societies of this century.

When Marx made his analysis of the various societies, the known ones were the primitive societies, feudal society, and before that, slave society. Capitalist society was also known. What Marx did was analyze the reason for each one and demonstrate that everything was related to production. He showed that man's thinking is generated by the environment in which he lives, and that this environment is determined by production relationships. However, on delving more deeply in his analysis, Marx did something even more important: He demonstrated that, historically, capitalism had to disappear and make way for a new society—socialist society.

But as time went by, Lenin carried the analysis further and came to the conclusion that the transition from one society to another was not a mechanical transition. Conditions could be speeded up to the maximum by what we might call catalysts. (The term is not Lenin's but mine, but it contains the central idea.) In other words, if there were a vanguard of the proletariat capable of enunciating the fundamental demands of the proletariat, of having a clear idea of what direction to take, and of trying to seize power so as to establish the new society, headway could be made and intermediate stages could be skipped. Moreover, a socialist society could develop in a single isolated country, even under the most terrible imperialist siege, such as the one the Soviet Union had to face. And that, then, is the basic reason why awareness is so important.

We have discovered that the process of the historical development of societies can, in certain cases, be shortened, and that the vanguard party is one of the fundamental weapons for shortening it. Consequently, having learned the lesson taught by the Soviet Union forty-five years ago, we applied it. We were able to speed things up through the vanguard movement by shortening the various stages and establishing the socialist character of our revolution two years after the Revolution triumphed. In practice it really was already socialist in character—because we had taken the means of production and were aiming at the total seizure of these means. We were aiming at the total seizure of the means of man's exploitation of man and at the planning of all production processes for the purpose of distributing goods to everyone correctly and equitably. But these speeding-up processes leave many people by the wayside. Even now the old society and its ideas constantly influence people's way of thinking, and that is where the factor of the intensification of socialist awareness becomes so important.

A socialist society of the type that now exists in our country, and in many others where this system was established, is not achieved because of an explosion of prior social conditions. It does not come about, that is, through a mechanical change due to the existence of so many objective conditions that the transition is simply a matter of course.

Here in Cuba it was the vanguard that developed and guided the people, and this has been Fidel Castro's primary task during these four years of revolution. He has led our people, showing them at every turn what was the most important thing to do. He has taught them the lessons of dignity, of the spirit of sacrifice, and of courage—the lessons we have had to pass on to the whole world. And so the people, sometimes for emotional reasons, have become part of the formative process of socialism.

There are always laggards who remain behind, but our function is not to liquidate them—to crush them and force them to bow to an armed vanguard—but to educate them by leading them forward and getting them to follow us because of our example, or as Fidel called it, moral compulsion. These people have no desire to be doers, and they do not feel the need to follow the example of their best comrades, who work each day with enthusiasm, with fervor, and with joy.

A good example, like a bad one, is very contagious, and we have had to spread contagion with good examples. We must work on people's way of thinking by hammering away at their minds and demonstrating what we are capable of doing. We must demonstrate what a revolutionary movement is capable of when it is in power and is sure of its ultimate objective; when it has faith in the justice of its aims and the course it has followed; and when it is prepared, as all our people have been, to fight rather than give up a single one of our legitimate rights.

We must synthesize all this, explain it, and make it alive for each one of those who still do not feel it within them. There is also a need to gradually convert the latter.

It will be long and very hard, but this is where we must strike. We are almost as besieged as the Soviet Union was during those terrible, but at the same time wonderful, years in the history of humanity. But the Soviet Union exists now, and so does the camp of the socialist countries, an enormous block of people who are constantly adding new forces and new peoples to the socialist cause.

In Latin America we are isolated. The Organization of American States in one place, the United States in another, are getting ready, stirring up trouble in Guatemala or some other Latin American country. Airplanes suspiciously appear in territories whose governments are hostile to us, and letters and reports appear. And it is all the same face of the great imperialist conspiracy against the Cuban people.

Why? Because even if we have faults—and we know we do—if our four-year course produces great victories, it is such a great lesson for Latin America that the imperialists fear us. They fear us perhaps more than they do other more powerful nations.

Imperialism has its base in the Americas. American imperialism, which is the most powerful, is in the New World. Latin America speaks Spanish and understands us. Latin America, which admires us and sees in us a picture of what the future can be for all its peoples, is preparing for victory.

If there are guerrillas in Latin America—and both we and the Pentagon know there are—they were in no way created by us. We cannot create them, because we lack the strength, but we do look upon them with joy. We are enthusiastic about the triumphs of the Venezuelans and the spreading of the Venezuelan revolution. We are enthusiastic when we learn that in Colombia or Peru there are budding revolutions. We rejoice when cracks—still small, but systematic—develop in the scaffolding of imperial power.

There is, comrades, something that has produced very palpable results in Latin America. This something which speaks to them in their own language and explains clearly what must be done to achieve happiness is called the Cuban Revolution. It is because of this that we are really feared.

It is not conceit on our part. It is not false pride or the false claims of a small country: It is an objective analysis of the facts. All of us are responsible for their fear of us, and the imperialists hate us all. This should be the source of our pride: that they fear and hate us; that the Cuban Revolution is a terrible boil to Mr. Kennedy, which does not let him sleep; and that all Latin American puppets can read their future in the fate met by those we had here. Let them understand the extent and depth of the justice of the people when, rid of their shackles, they acquire power.

This is our definitive work and our great responsibility to all of Latin America and the world as well. At the end of last year we taught a lesson that the Americans never thought possible. And we are teaching it more and more by our deeds. This is the value it has in terms that transcend our own frontiers. We take greatest pride in the fact that a Cuban is respected, admired, loved—and sometimes feared or hated—everywhere in the world because of what the Revolution represents, because of its extent, and because of what it has achieved in four years.

In other words, comrades, we must prepare to multiply our achievements and decrease our errors. We must intensify the awareness of the masses and increase production. We must achieve more and more by our own efforts and grow accustomed to standing on our own in production as we have at many other difficult times. Help from friendly countries—generous, brotherly help, which has been given us many times—must be an element in our consolidation and the securing of our Revolution. But the basis of our strength must not be another country, however friendly and selfless it may be; no real strength can exist that does not stem from one's own sense of strength. It is when a nation acquires a sense of its strength and decides to struggle and move ahead that it is really strong. Then it can indeed face any enemy.

We have done it, and generally speaking, we can be very proud of what we have done. But we can still analyze things with cold objectivity. Just as you have analyzed your comrades and exercised your critical judgment of them, we must analyze our work with cold objectivity and criticize it whenever it is poor. So too when fundamental problems are not solved, or when there is a lapse into conformism and mechanical thinking and our work fails to be creative and vital.

All this is asked of you members of the Partido Unido de la Revolución, and it is also asked of those of you who still do not belong to the party.

We ask all our people to keep in step, and keep their vanguard contingent struggling against their many difficulties, moving rapidly so as to surpass the strongest contingent and all the forces of the people. That is their task.

It is now the duty of the comrades in the party to be the vanguard. Let them remember what Fidel told them: "The best will be there: the Camilos, men with self-confidence, men who sacrifice and are strong in spirit. . . ." But all our people must also become like those guerrillas who were disorganized at the beginning—who were afraid of the airplanes, the tanks, and the enemy soldiers—and yet ended by advancing through all Cuba and destroying a powerful army that had every weapon of destruction at its command but was immoral.

At the end, when victory was achieved, it was achieved because the vanguard was by then braver in every case—a little braver. But it was the entire army of rebellion that represented the people's courage. And every time its strength, its courage, and its determination to fight increased, the enemy yielded. It abandoned positions, lost faith, and disintegrated to the vanishing point.

This is our task. It is very difficult and very simple; it all depends on how we face it. It all depends on how we face the revolutionary situation and on what we are capable of doing, now that we are free as much as possible of the defects of the society which has died. OUR COUNTRY OR DEATH! VICTORY WILL BE OURS!

CHAPTER 19

On Production Costs[1]

ONE of the many problems a planned economy has to face is how to measure the economic performance of an enterprise under the new conditions created by the development of the socialist revolution.

The capitalist economy is regulated by the law of value, which expresses itself directly in the market. It is impossible to consider the law of value separately from the market. In other words, under capitalism the law of value is the law of the market. As the socialist society is built, many of the relations of production change with the change in the ownership of the means of production, and free competition, hitherto restricted only by the influence of the monopolies, disappears from the market, which now acquires new characteristics under the conscious influence of the socialist sector.

In the case of Cuba, the shortage of certain goods could have produced a rise in prices in the market until supply and demand reached a new level of coincidence. Instead, we established a strict price-freeze and maintained a system of rations in which the real value of the goods could not express itself in the market. Although rationing is a transitory stage, with the passage of time a planned economy in a given country begins to develop its own internal laws, distinct and apart from the laws of the outside world. A given price level is established through the interplay of raw material and other costs in the process of production and distribution.

When all products function in accordance with prices that have certain internal relationships among one another—relationships that differ from the relationships of these products in the capitalist market—a new price relationship is created that cannot be compared to the worldwide one. How can prices be made to coincide with value? How can a knowledge of the Law of Value be consciously wielded so as to achieve a balance between

[1] *Nuestra Industria Económica*, Año I, No. I, June 1963. Translated by Ray Agostini.

the underlying mercantile evaluation, on the one hand, and the faithful reflection of the true value on the other? This is one of the most serious problems confronting the socialist economy.

The Soviet Union and later other socialist countries decided on a system of planning which could be measured by broad economic results as reflected in financial terms. A loose relationship was allowed to exist between the various enterprises. This gave rise to what later became known as the self-financing enterprise.

Broadly speaking, self-financing is based on a network of financial controls of which the banks are the nerve center. Material incentives are used to encourage the maximum utilization of productive capacity, which, if achieved, brings greater benefits to the individual worker or the collective in the given enterprise. Under this system, loans made to the socialist enterprise have to be paid back with interest. This is meant to help accelerate the circulation of products.

At the very outset of the Revolution in Cuba, we started to centralize all the financial activities of the enterprises. This centralization allowed us to solve some difficult problems as they arose. Later on we felt it possible to develop more advanced methods of centralization, which would not be unusually bureaucratic, and which under certain conditions would be more efficient for industrial production. This system is based essentially on adapting the advanced methods of accounting, already in existence in capitalist enterprises, to a small country like ours, which has a good system of communications.

Under our system the banks will supply the various enterprises with an amount of money determined by the national budget, free of interest, since credit relations do not exist in these operations. Under this system, which is in operation only in certain branches of our economy, a product is seen as going through a long internal process of circulation through various steps within the socialist system. This product does not become a commodity until there is a change in ownership; that is, until it leaves the ownership of the state to become the property of a consumer.

The movement of a product from one enterprise to another, whether in the same or separate departments, will only be seen as a part of a process which adds value to the product, with the bank considered merely a cash register to keeps track of these movements. The enterprise does not have its own capital, and consequently its income is reintegrated into the national budget.

The workability of the system has been demonstrated. Nevertheless, certain weaknesses have been observed, which make it the target of serious objections.

These objections revolve primarily around the lack of direct material incentives and the bureaucratic tendencies engendered by this system.

In any case, these objections should not be discussed at this point. We would rather return to the question of measuring the economic performance of a budgeted enterprise. How should it be done, and under what premises? Here we consider the cost of production to be the primary factor that will allow the manager of a production unit, enterprise, or department to measure over-all immediate economic results.

We emphasize cost accounting because part of our theory is based on the fact that the relationship between production costs and the price structure in the socialist system is not necessarily a close one. For an underdeveloped nation like Cuba, which relies heavily on foreign trade, commercial relations with the rest of the world are of fundamental importance. For this reason we argue that under no circumstance should there be a separation between the general internal price structure and that of the world market. By the latter we understand of course the socialist world, where prices have a purely mathematical function, serving as measuring rods.

This is not to say that we have already found a criterion on which to base new investments, and that all we have to do is figure out present production costs, the possible cost of new investments, and our potential for capital accumulation, and on these factors decide what budget lines to establish. Things would not work out this way precisely because of the fact that in the world market the law of value expresses itself in relatively pure form, while in our market it comes under the influence of the socialist system and the amount of work which is socially necessary to produce certain items. This is to say nothing of the fact that we may want to lay stress on the development of a product which may not be very marketable but which in the long run may be of great benefit to the people. We must again stress that a given price may be set for consumers, which may have little to do with the internal prices of the enterprises regulated under this system. With this plan, we would immediately have a mirror in which to reflect the general progress of the economy at a given point. This type of organization, applied to certain branches of the economy, would allow us to develop an increasingly more accurate system for measuring economic performance.

The cost of production would be the real indicator of the performance of the enterprise. It would matter little whether costs were below or above the level of general prices in the socialist system, or in some cases below or above the level at which the product is sold to the consumer. What we are really interested in is the enterprise's success, over a long period of time, in lowering production costs. In this case the price would be an automatic reflection of the product's value in relation to world prices. It is necessary for us to work harder on these problems.

In this connection, many problems arise from the already existing disparity in the world market as regards prices and technological progress, as well as the effects of the monopolies, which force daily price fluctuations in the international market. Although we still have not completed our analysis of the problem, we feel we will be able to get around it. This could be done by establishing a general system based on a projected price average in the capitalist world market, with whatever corrections may be necessary as a result of the influence of the socialist market, which as far as international trade is concerned bears a close relationship to the capitalist market. To this would be added shipping costs, of course. All these prices would remain fixed during established periods of time.

If we were to take the prices of the principal products in our economy, and based on them, approximate the prices of all the other products, we would find the average level of prices in the world market. This would allow us to compare automatically the efficiency of all the branches of our economy against the world market.

We should note, however, that the price structure of the products would give a distorted image of national productivity, as it would only reflect an average of efficiency in the world market. This would bring about dangerous consumption tendencies, based on the prices of products that have a higher labor investment in them than otherwise denoted by world comparison.

This is a valid objection, and in order to plan properly it would be necessary to find an index number by which to designate the products according to their value. Since this system is based on a centrally guided economy, and a greater centralization of decision-making, one index would be sufficient to denote relative value. What we are really interested in is the general value of the production unit, which we continue to treat in a sketchy manner, without a really deep understanding.

It is necessary to work out a system of cost accounting that will reward and punish systematically the successes and failures in the struggle for lowering costs. It is also necessary to work out norms for consumption of raw materials, for indirect costs, unfinished products, inventories of raw materials, and finished products.

In modernizing our economy, we have to systematize the regulation of inventories and do an accurate analytical job on all the indicators previously mentioned,

In our system of accounting, we have divided costs into those relating to raw materials and other direct materials, indirect materials, labor costs, depreciation, and social security, the latter being paid by state enterprises on the basis of wage scales.

We have to work on each and every one of the aforementioned components. We should exclude from this analysis social security, for in the future, when all these methods are brought to perfection, the state will handle it by allocating in its budget a certain amount for social security, irrespective of the individual wages received by the workers.

As regards raw materials and other direct costs, we have to work toward making direct savings, bringing about technological changes, and avoiding waste. As regards indirect costs, we can make savings by reducing our consumption of electricity, fuel, etc., through reorganization or technological changes. And as far as labor costs are concerned, we can bring costs down by generally increasing productivity. As for depreciation, we have to develop more scientific methods of establishing depreciation rates, and at the same time we have to prolong the useful life of plant and equipment, through adequate maintenance.

No matter from what angle we look at it, everything is reduced to a common denominator: increasing productivity. This is fundamental to the construction of socialism and the building of communism.

Now, there are different areas in which we can establish the regulation of costs. First of all there is the area of administration. We need trained administrators who can adequately organize cost keeping and train the personnel in the immediate cost analysis, so that all these figures become a natural part of their daily work.

At this point we should expect many difficulties in this area. There is little tradition of economic analysis among our managers, added to which we find that their educational level is generally low. In addition, our entire economy is yet to be organized. However, serious work in this area will bear fruit in the short span of time, and that is why we have already begun to tackle this problem.

It must be clear that the analysis of production costs will not of necessity lead to the adoption of the measures needed to remove whatever deficiencies exist. There are certain very important objective facts that will make this impossible for a certain period of time: the poor organization of supplies, for which we are so dependent on foreign markets; the poor job we have done in the maintenance of plant and equipment, which has often led to unexpected halts in production; the lack of legal procedures governing relations among the enterprises, which causes serious disruptions in plans when sometimes an enterprise does not draw the supplies it has requested and abruptly changes its order. Suffice it to say that the general defects in planning and the obstacles in obtaining foreign supplies will keep the production units and enterprises subject to abrupt changes in cost levels for some time to come. But this should not worry us as much as not understanding these problems the minute they arise.

We must also work on the regulation of costs at the individual level. This means the control that the individual worker can bring about once adequate norms have been established to regulate the quality and quantity of the work. In considering quality, the saving of raw materials can become a tool that will bring about substantial results in a short time. This is one task in which we are making steady progress, although perhaps not as quickly as may be necessary.

We must also insist on the collective concern over costs. The collective in the production unit will bring this about once a system of production is established which has built-in incentives, which will focus the attention of the collective on reducing costs so as to gain greater benefits, the latter being of a social nature. This requires a deepening of political consciousness, together with a great leap forward in organization. This is a task for the party, which by taking up this problem and bringing it to the people, can, in a relatively short period of time, bring about a different attitude on the part of the workers towards the state administration. However, we cannot hope that changes in organization will proceed at the same speed as changes in political consciousness, so that we will have to resign ourselves to a period in which many adjustments will have to be made. We have in operation some pilot factories in which we are studying systems of collective incentives of a social nature which will have the effect of reducing costs. It must be established that this study has to be based on a plan of production which must be met, and that except where there is sufficient justification, the meeting of this plan of production is the key to measuring the performance of the collective and the incentives which are appropriate.

This general task is understood within the framework of the possibility of a centrally guided economy. However, this must not be taken to mean that all the decisions must be made at the highest level. Instead, we must establish varying levels of organization and decision-making, which will prevent the violation of the principles laid down and will force the adoption of whatever measures are necessary within that level of decision-making, without having to depend on other levels. The initial task of establishing clearly the relations among the various levels of decision-making, and what each level is required or forbidden to do, is mandatory for the correct functioning of the system.

All our efforts must be geared toward simplifying the administrative task of accounting and direction, so that the bodies concerned can begin to concentrate more on planning and technological development. Administration will be a mechanical task, free of serious problems, once all the criteria and all the methods and routines of accounting have been established by the progress of planning in all the sectors of the economy. When that point is reached, modern methods of planning will come into play, and it will then be possible to approximate the ideal state in which the economy will be governed by mathematical analysis through which we can decide how best to apportion our resources as between accumulation and consumption and among the various branches of production. Of course we must never forget that the human being, the *raison d'être* for the Revolution and for all our efforts, cannot be reduced to a mere formula, and that his requirements will become increasingly complex and will transcend the simple satisfaction of material needs. Automation will be brought to the various branches of production, which will greatly expand the worker's productivity and free him to devote more time to the highest level of cultural, sport, and scientific activities, and work will become a social necessity.

The posibility of this now distant future drawing closer to us will depend on the technical ability of the workers and experts to maintain the highest levels of service in every industry. It will depend on our ability to plan in such a way that the most felt needs of the population become wedded to the most vital needs of the economy so that we can produce the greatest possible benefits, while at the same time maintaining an adequate rate of economic growth. If we conceive of the economy's development in this manner, the function of regulation will be a simple one, which specialized bodies can perform with the aid of machines.

Today a large number of the technicians in our ministry are working under the constant pressure of having to solve the most routine tasks, however necessary the latter may be to the process of production. If they could be freed from this task and could dedicate themselves to research and generally creative tasks, great leaps in the quality of production would be seen immediately.

We have to work, therefore, toward making the job of administration one with clocklike precision, so that the greatest impetus to production may be brought about through the path of technological progress.

CHAPTER 20

On the Cuban Experience[1]

BEFORE we begin, I would like to explain what we mean by planification You have already heard it here from various qualified technicians, so I only want to raise the point briefly to reassert our train of thought. Planification, in its Marxist-Leninist sense, has both economic and political meaning. It is the way in which we develop a socialist society. This indicates something very important: If planification is to exist, there must first be a socialist will and the possibility of development in this path. If planification is to be meaningful, therefore, the popular forces must first act upon the means of production, seizing them and putting them at the disposal of the people.

The will to create is a characteristic of man. The will exists before the creation. It exists in consciousness before it realizes itself; that is to say, the concept of a socialist revolution precedes the concept of a socialist state.

I wanted to say these few words because it is from them that one can explain one of the errors we committed in our first attempts at planification. We had forgotten that the socialist revolution and the socialist state are two different things, and in doing so, we also forgot that planification and socialism must both obey certain conditions; to plan without socialism (as has been said here, and it is correct) is an impossibility. One can plan while constructing socialism, but always taking into account the fact that the planification must submit itself to objective conditions which are present at the moment of the plan's realization.

We have copied, automatically, from the experiences of brother countries, and this was a mistake, not of the gravest, but a mistake which slowed down the development of our forces and contributed dangerously to the development of one of the phenomena which we have had to fight a great deal during the socialist revolution: bureaucratism. This means that we

[1] Speech delivered in mid-1963 in Algiers in a closed seminar on planification. Also published in the now-defunct international magazine, *Révolution*, in October, 1963, No. 2. Translated by John Gerassi.

have had to learn from practice, by our errors, and while knocking our heads against the wall, that planification and socialism go together, and that one cannot plan everything when the economic conditions present do not allow it.

Allow me to make a short résumé of what was done in Cuba in 1959, very general because I have not brought here any documents to illustrate my points with exact statistics. Cuba's Revolution, a popular movement, destroyed the political and military power of the representatives of Yankee imperialism. But the revolutionary leaders consisted only of a group of combatants, high in their ideals, but insufficient in their knowledge.

The superstructure of the capitalist neocolonial state was intact; we had to work to destroy it and to rebuild our society on new bases. The financial agencies of the government were in the hands of future traitors who were already developing their slow-down policies in the revolutionary process. Applying their knowledge of the techniques of bourgeois finances, they set up constant obstacles to our development.

The old ministries were caves full of bureaucrats and parasites, without any internal life, without any harmony with their own government, without unity either among their own directors or in the fundamental line of the Revolution. These organs of bourgeois power existed in the center of the new state, and they were like cliffs in the sea, independent, isolated from the human tides which kept coming. We had to change the structures, and we began to do so, without a plan, without proposing any, or almost. The revolutionary group, with Fidel Castro at the head, issued first of all the Agrarian Reform Law. This law, indispensable, of which Mr. Kennedy still speaks today in his strange language of "alliance for progress," revealed a terrible instrument: the class struggle—and it pushed the Cuban Revolution to its maximum.

The big landowners, many of whom were North Americans, immediately sabotaged the Agrarian Reform Law. We faced an alternative which will confront you more than once in your revolutionary lives: a situation in which, once committed, it is hard to stop. But it is still more dangerous to go back, for it signifies the death of the Revolution. What to do in face of this choice? Of all the possible roads, the fairest and least dangerous was to go straight ahead. But since we were already advancing, we did so then in depth, violently. And what we could have imagined as an agrarian reform of bourgeois value, which would have given land to poor peasants, was transformed into a violent struggle, in the course of which were expropriated, without any compensation, all the lands of the big latifundists of Cuba. These allied themselves with the foreign enemy and took measures against us, confronting us from all sides.

Sometimes we felt the shock. We could only then respond with new blows. As in a boxing match, body to body, we exchanged blow for blow. Finally, the panorama cleared. The main means of production were in the hands of the people. The peasants organized themselves into cooperatives. More than 90 per cent of industry was nationalized. All foreign commerce was monopolized by the state. So were all major transportation networks. In the process we carried out an urban reform, giving houses to those who lived in them and forbidding all speculation on rents. We made considerable progress in public health and education.

But the struggle continued. The imperialist blockade was at its apex, and we saw ourselves forced to fight day after day just to give our people enough to eat, to maintain our industry, develop our fields, our commerce, to defend ourselves against sabotage from outlaw groups, from direct foreign aggression, their aerial bombardments, their daily violation of our sovereignty, and in addition, we had to smash reactionary opposition at home, expose traitors, and expel them from government. Sometimes they fled into exile, sometimes they were jailed, sometimes they were shot.

What was Cuba's economic structure like during those first years? A country of monoproduction, sugar; of monoculture, sugar cane; of monocommerce, the United States of America, which controlled 75 per cent of our imports and exports. The whole country was controlled by foreign capital, especially North American, which, when it installed industries, did so in such a way as to force us to depend on North American technology, North American raw materials, and North American spare parts. They profited from our effort and our cheap labor, and they exported their profits, with the okay of our customs, to their territory to the north.

Most of our technical cadre was trained in the United States and was influenced by their techniques. A country without industry, without agricultural development, with a stifling weight on its shoulders, with its monetary reserves convertible—all this is enough to show how great were our difficulties. Our lack of statistics on the economic past or present prevented us from elaborating a suitable plan of action. For a while we did not even have time to think about the best means of economic action, for we were in combat, body to body, with the enemy, anxious not to lose an inch of our newly won terrain, and having to defend ourselves constantly against new threats from the enemy.

Years passed. On April 15, 1961, American military planes, with Cuban insignia painted on their wings, bombed our ports in order to liquidate our small combat aerial force, and made believe to the world that the authors of the aggression were Cuban émigrés. The next day, at the funeral of the victims, our Prime Minister and secretary general of the United Party of the Socialist Revolution proclaimed before the world that the Cuban Revolution was socialist in character. Then there was the attempted invasion of the Bay of Pigs, and our victory. The blockades became harsher; imperialism tried to destroy us by all possible means. During last year's October [the 1962 missile] crisis, we gave the whole world a lesson in dignity; but before all this happened, we had to develop the economy of our country where every rock was foreign-owned, where technology came from a foreign country which waged war against us in order to seize our resources, not for the benefit of our people, but for the profit of American capital.

We had to keep our factories, our agriculture, and our transportation going—without credits, without insecticides, without raw materials, without spare parts, without technicians, without organization. During this time outlaws operated on our territory, supported by the United States, and committed acts of sabotage and aggression. The constant threat of invasion forced us to mobilize the Cuban people two or three times a year, thus paralyzing the country.

And yet that is how we forced our Revolution, rectifying our errors. These errors were of different types, essentially in the area of plantification. We did two contradictory things, impossible to harmonize: On the one hand we copied with exaggerated exactitude the techniques of planification of a brother country, from where specialists had come to help us; and on the other hand we continued to make snap decisions without taking time to analyze them, especially in their political ramifications, decisions which are necessary every day in the life of a government.

We are not backed by either statistics or historical experience. We have tried to act upon nature subjectively, as if our direct contact with it would accomplish what we were after, ignoring the objective experiences of other countries. When we used to say that there is no country in the world in the process of development that has a rise in revenue of 20 per cent a year, we told ourselves that we could do it. When we tackled the problem of growth in our country, we did not investigate what we had, what we could spend, and what could allow us to develop. We first calculated the possibilities of a 15 per cent growth, in order to see what we should do, and although it seems easy to establish what a developing country should produce, it is not the same thing for us, a monoculture country, with all the problems therein implied. Thus it was ridiculous to propose a 15 per cent growth.

We wanted to build schools, and we did; hospitals, and we did. We built roads and recreation centers, workers' centers. Salaries went up and simultaneously we talked of the development of the means of production. Planification was not possible because of the economic and political relationships of production. We could not force things, and naturally we have not achieved our plans. I will describe some specific cases so you may understand what took place in Cuba. We needed, for example, 22 million pairs of shoes. What is required for this product? So much leather, so many workers, so much technical skill in the tanneries, so much imports of raw material. All this can be obtained, but first of all we needed a plan for 22 million pairs of shoes.

Well, we knew we could not make it. Never had Cuban industry produced more than ten million. It is true that we may have had the installations, and the cattle we might have found, but a viable organization was necessary first, and we had not yet achieved it. We had only worked out, superficially, the final number and the main tasks. In reality we had neither enough cattle nor machinery for leather. The plan was a manifestation of absolute subjectivism, which referred especially to numbers in order to calculate our real possibilities, impossible to realize. It was all decisions made from the top.

But what happened to those made from below? Example: wood. How much wood was there? The chief of the wood department said, "There is so much, *X* amount," I don't remember the actual figure. We knew this was impossible, but they said it was so, affirmed it categorically. Thus Cuba, a traditional importer of wood, appeared in the plan as a potential exporter, without taking into account what the technicians at the base were suggesting. Result: We continue to import wood, but we import it badly, desperately seeking how to do it.

Our foreign commerce has totally changed directions, geographically. From 75 per cent with the United States, it has reached 75 per cent to 80 per cent with the socialist countries. This change has been positive for us in the social and political domain, but economically we needed a more complete organization. Before, hundreds of specialized importers asked for their products from the United States, and the next day, they arrived by ferryboat directly from Miami. In between there were neither stores nor warehouses.

All this system, without the specialists—enemy of the government—now had to melt itself into the Bank of Foreign Commerce. All this international shopping had to be carried out not in a day, by telephone, but with countries which are two months away, and which operate under a plan of their own, with internal and external short-range and long-range obligations, with different technology, equipment, and raw material. Better still, if you go today to one of our factories built by foreign capital, and you want to know what kind of steel is used for such-and-such a spare part, you will learn that the part has a catalogue number, and to order it you must ask for it by number, and that in this catalogue the transaction corresponds to a determined procedure. How do you ask for it from socialist countries? We first had to analyze the steel, sometimes actually have the part constructed for us specially, a task almost impossible, but one which our brother countries did repeatedly, out of solidarity. We had to import machinery to make the parts ourselves, though we lacked the qualified technicians, and we were unfamiliar with the nature of the materials. Such were our daily problems, and they still are in Cuba.

In setting up our plans, we committed errors in our conception of the development of industry and of agriculture, and in the balance of our economy. In industry, we evolved a plan based on the hope of becoming self-sufficient in a whole series of consumer products and of medium industry, which, however, could easily be obtained in friendly countries. We thus diminished our capacity of transformation without having fully used our own resources in raw materials. This policy has already been revised by the revolutionary government in respect to the development of natural resources, as much for our internal market as for foreign markets, and according to a technology that allows us to produce quality products at prices commensurate with the norms of international commerce.

In agriculture, we have committed the fundamental error of disdaining sugar, our national product, in trying to push through a diversification of the cane. This impoverished the cane; we must add to that an extraordinary drought which smothered us during two years, provoking a grave crisis in our production.

In the redistribution of wealth we gave too much importance at the beginning to satisfying social needs, to paying more equitable salaries, to increasing employment, without sufficiently taking into account the general state of our economy. The lack of standards of work in industry and agriculture made our workers alter their aspirations violently, which brought about the following phenomena: In a country where there are still unemployed, agriculture is short of labor, and each year we must appeal for voluntary workers to harvest the cane, and at certain times, to cultivate it, so as to augment its yield.

Without sufficient reserves, with such violent changes, our plan—perfect in its detail, dogmatic in its exigencies—was a brake on our Revolution. If today we posed anew the problem, how would we do it?

First of all we would try to know as much as possible about the actual situation, and without putting a stop to our efforts to find out all the possible facts of our reality, we would give to our figures and statistics a sense of national necessity, imposing a manner of work and thought based essentially on the knowledge derived from these facts and their analyses. We would undertake an examination as practical as possible of our economy and of our most urgent needs, taking into account our economic possibilities, the long-term credits we obtain from the socialist camp; and after this analysis we would make our decision on the means we would have to use to achieve our economic development, and to fulfill the social needs of our country. We would work out a general and flexible plan, allowing plenty of reserves for the unforeseen. From there, and within these limits, we would make up yearly plans.

Investments would be centralized to the fullest degree, without falling into bureaucratic petty details, and the socialization of the means of production would be carried out fundamentally in function of the cadre potential and of the general organization of the state apparatus, but also advancing without weakness in this domain.

I keep using the conditional. All this must take place in the framework of a violent class struggle in which the exploiters and their imperialist leaders take part and class struggle has a logic which does not always allow for the peaceful construction of a country.

This does not mean that we owe all our planification mistakes to our decisions. We owe them also to the action of imperialism, which forced upon us a process of acceleration way beyond the optimum possibilities of our cadre. Despite our errors we recorded considerable successes, and the errors committed have been rectified.

The two domains where the work of the revolutionary government saw itself crowned with success rapidly and efficiently were in education and public health. In education we have eliminated illiteracy, by establishing free and compulsory schooling, which includes all books and material through the third year of secondary school. At this moment we have some 100,000 scholarship students,[2] and among them, medical students who will work for the state in the future.

In public health we have built a large number of rural hospitals; we have launched national vaccination campaigns against polio; we have decided to send medical students to the countryside; we have developed auxiliary medical schools for nurses, technicians, radiologists, etc. Despite the departure for the United States of a great many doctors, a better distribution and utilization of all medical resources for the public has made it possible to bring medical attention to every sector of the population.

In the field of social security we have established new laws which guarantee the security of each worker, whatever his circumstances and whatever his ailment.

We have corrected our sugar policy by giving it the importance it deserves; we have set up norms on work and salaries in the industrial sector, and we are doing it in the agricultural sector. With USSR aid, we have begun to fight drought by establishing a very ambitious network of irrigation and dams; and especially, we have succeeded in making workers conscious that collective work is the motor of society, that this must be deemed the most important of all activities, besides that of defense in time of danger.

At the same time, various experiments have been undertaken in the economy with the idea of finding the best solution to the problems of creating a cadre within the principles of Marxism-Leninism.

In different villages of the interior we are putting into practice pilot plans of administration on local levels, working into them all public services, and this in some local industries, too. We have set up a committee of physical planfication dependent upon the Ministry of Construction, which coordinates its activities with the general planning boards; a plan to restructure the whole politico-administrative distribution, adapted to the economic necessities of the country, is being studied, and we have begun studies to give to planning an exact scientific character by using avant-garde mathematical methods in the economic field, such as linear programming, matrices of consumption of products, etc.

[2] *Becarios* or *becados* (both terms are used in Cuba) are students who are totally financed in housing, food, clothing, etc., by the government (ed.).

In administration there are two systems, each of which has its partisans and which are entrenched in different branches of the economy: There is the one we call the financial self-administration, and which in the USSR is called the Economic Calculus. There the government enterprise administers its own financial means and is financially controlled by the Central Bank. The other system is called Budgetary Calculus,[3] where the enterprise has no capital and is nothing more than a specialist in its administrative area, having to deal through the finance minister, who in turn, deals through the National Bank, for the monies necessary for the production of the item in question. The comparison between these two systems augments the possibilities of our cadre being able to distinguish the best road and contribute to a new confrontation of ideas which helps bring about a planification system less rigid, more accurate, and in the desired state of constant transformation.

The actual panorama of the Cuban economy is as follows: more than three-fourths of our foreign commerce is with the socialist camp; about three-fourths of our foreign earnings comes from sugar. Thus, the monoproductive structure of our economy has not improved after four years of revolution. But already we have set into motion the bases for an economy that would rest solidly on Cuban raw materials with a diversification of production and a degree of technical know-how that would allow us to be competitive in the world markets. Our agriculture, after its change of orientation, has made a good start, and we are realizing on all levels a diversification, while also developing and improving the fields of sugar cane. The tendency to nationalize all the means of production continues, but it is carried out as we triumph over the reactionary forces of the interior, in the rhythm that the revolution considers the fairest. To all the small owners of nationalized firms we are paying an indemnity. Sometimes, in the course of certain transitory moments of the class struggle, we must take such drastic measures as the nationalization of all commerce in a particular section of the country, where there were excessive outlaw activities, or the nationalization of all commerce of a particular branch, such as the food-stuff industry, which turned out to be particularly prone to speculation.

We could ask ourselves, in ending, what are the foreseen tasks of planification in Cuba? We consider our main task that of assuring ourselves with a statistical base complete enough to allow us to locate weaknesses in the economic machinery immediately, and accustom our cadre to act accordingly; we are working on this. But there is still much to do.

Next, once we know our errors, we must analyze them and deduce therefrom the conclusion that will be useful for the future, modifying our machinery so it may accomplish its real function in the economy and as a motor force at the same time.

To realize a plan for the future in accord with our possibilities, realistic,

[3] Or the Budgetary System. See Chapter 24 (ed.).

modest, corresponding exactly to the daily needs of our people, is to resolve, in part at least, one of the gravest problems facing a revolution. At the same time it is necessary to find the economic solution that would allow us to profit to the maximum from our own resources. It is necessary to derive the most from each invested peso, to use the reserves hidden in the bosom of our people and put them at the service of the people—these are tasks that only socialism can achieve.

We have the ambition to make of planning an instrument of automatic goal-setting, mathematically rigorous and as free as possible of the credits used for the research which are the basis of the future. Planification must transform itself with time into this political nerve center, into this mechanical instrument of action. The future lies in the great innovations which constantly change the face of the world. The future is in the development of chemistry and electronics, which will guarantee the kind of production that can satisfy all the needs of the people, and planification will be the discipline through which all the goods produced can be distributed and will be distributed equitably, between the productive sectors on the one hand, and the consuming sector on the other, in order to assure a continuous development and a maximum distribution of all kinds of products for the people.

For this youth that is growing up today, perhaps for our sons who will live communism, we seek the best road now. Through constant struggle and errors, experience makes both mistakes and regressions less regular and less grave. We are building socialism on our earth, and we are placing our small grain of sand at the service of the great aspiration of mankind—the elimination of exploitation of man by man. The most ferocious enemy of this aspiration is imperialism. We are fighting for the definite realization of communism—the society without classes.

This, briefly, is the disorganized synthesis of our experiences.

CHAPTER 21

Guerrilla Warfare: A Method[1]

GUERRILLA warfare has been waged innumerable times in history, under different conditions and with different ends in view. It has been waged recently in various people's wars of liberation where the vanguard of the people chose the path of irregular armed struggle against enemies of greater military potential. Asia, Africa, and America have been the scene of these actions when it was a matter of seizing power in the struggle against feudal, neocolonial, or colonial exploitation. In Europe it was conducted in conjunction with regular armies, whether of allies or fellow countrymen.

In the Americas, guerrilla warfare has been resorted to on various occasions. As the closest precedent, one might note the experience of César Augusto Sandino in his struggle against the Yankee expeditionary forces in Segovia, Nicaragua. Another precedent one might cite is the recent revolutionary war in Cuba. Since that time the problems of guerrilla warfare have been raised in discussions of theory within the progressive Latin American parties, and the possibility and advisability of its employment are the subject of heated debate. These notes will attempt to express our ideas on guerrilla warfare and what would be its correct employment.

Above all it must be made clear that this type of struggle is a method: a method for achieving a purpose. That purpose, indispensable and unavoidable for every revolutionary, is the conquest of political power. Therefore, in analyses of specific situations in the different Latin America countries the concept of the guerrilla force must be applied within the simplest terms of the struggle to achieve that purpose.

Almost immediately the question arises: Is the method of guerrilla warfare the only formula for seizing power in the whole Western Hemisphere, or in any case, the predominant one? Can it be simply one of various

[1] *Cuba Socialista*, Año III, No. 25, Sept. 1963. Translated by Leonard Mades.

means employed in the struggle? Or, taking an extreme position, the question is raised: Is the example of Cuba applicable to the other situations in the Hemisphere? In debates on the subject criticism is usually leveled at those who wish to wage a guerrilla war, on the grounds that they forget mass struggle; as if the two methods were incompatible! We reject the concept this position involves. A guerrilla war is a people's war, and it *is* a mass struggle. To attempt to conduct this type of war without the support of the populace is a prelude to inevitable disaster. The guerrilla force is the people's fighting vanguard, located in a specific part of a given territory, and it is armed and ready to carry out a series of military actions tending toward the only possible strategic aim: seizure of power. It is supported by the masses of peasants and workers of the region and the entire territory in question. Except on this basis, guerrilla warfare is unacceptable.

"In our Latin American situation, we believe that the Cuban Revolution made three fundamental contributions to the mechanics of revolutionary movements in the Americas. First, the people's forces can win a war against the army. Second, one need not always wait for the existence of all conditions favoring revolution; the insurrectionary nucleus can create them. Third, in underdeveloped Latin America, the arena of the armed struggle should be fundamentally the country (*Guerrilla Warfare*).[2]

Such are the contributions to the development of the revolutionary struggle in the Americas, and they can be applied to any of the Latin American countries where a guerrilla war is going to be fought.

> The Second Havana Declaration states: In our countries there is a combination of underdeveloped industry and an agrarian system that is feudal in character. It is for this reason that, hard as the living conditions of the urban population are, the rural population still lives under the most horrible conditions of oppression and exploitation. But it is also, with exceptions, the sector constituting an absolute majority, at times in excess of seventy per cent of the population of Latin America.
>
> Exclusive of the landowners, who often reside in cities, the rest of that great mass earns its living as farm laborers for wretched wages, or they till the soil under conditions of exploitation not exceeded by the Middle Ages. These are the circumstances which account for the fact that the rural poor constitute a tremendous potential revolutionary force.
>
> Armies, which are structured and equipped for conventional warfare, and are the force upon which the power of the exploiting classes rests, are absolutely powerless when they have to face irregular combat with peasants on the latter's home ground. They lose ten men for each revolutionary fighter who falls, and demoralization spreads among them rapidly when they have to face an invisible, invincible enemy who offers them no opportunity to display their tactics of the military academy or the military

[2] Guevara's book, published in English by Monthly Review Press (New York), 1963 (ed.).

fanfare they make such show of to repress students and workers in the cities.

The initial struggle by small nuclei of fighters is constantly fed by new forces. Mass action begins to unfold, the old order is gradually smashed into a thousand pieces, and it is at this moment that the working class and the urban masses decide to fight.

What is it that, from the very beginning of the struggle by these first nuclei, makes them invincible, regardless of the numbers, power, and resources of their enemies? Support by the people. And they can depend on this support by the masses to an ever greater extent.

But the peasant belongs to a class which, because of the uneducated state in which he is kept and the isolation in which he lives, needs the revolutionary leadership and policy provided by the working class and the revolutionary intellectuals. Without these he could not throw himself into the struggle and achieve victory.

Under present historical conditions in Latin America, the middle class of the nation cannot lead the antifeudal, anti-imperialist struggle. Experience demonstrates that in our nations this class, even when its interests run counter to those of Yankee imperialism, has been incapable of opposing the latter; it is paralyzed by fear of social revolution and frightened by the cry of the exploited masses.

Covering the full scope of these statements which constitute the crux of the declaration of revolution in the Americas, the Second Havana Declaration expresses the following in other paragraphs:

The subjective conditions in each country—the awareness factor, organization, leadership—can accelerate or slow down the revolution, depending on the greater or lesser degree of development. But sooner or later, in each period of history—when objective conditions ripen, awareness is achieved. and organization is acquired—leadership springs up, and revolution breaks out.

Whether the latter occurs along peaceful lines or comes into the world after a painful birth does not depend on the revolutionaries; it depends on the reactionary forces of the old society, which resist the emergence of the new one, engendered by the contradictions within the old. Revolution is to history what the doctor is to a new life he helps being into the world. The doctor does not use instruments to force a delivery unless it is necessary, but he uses them without hesitation whenever the need exists. It is a birth which brings hope of a better life to the enslaved and exploited masses.

In many Latin American countries revolution today is inevitable. This fact is not determined by the will of any individual. It is determined by the horrible conditions of exploitation under which the Latin American lives, the development of revolutionary awareness among the masses, the world crisis of imperialism, and the worldwide revolutionary movement of the subjugated peoples.

We shall base our analysis of the entire guerrilla warfare problem on these premises.

We have estabished that it is a method for struggling to achieve a purpose. What is of primary interest is an analysis of the purpose, and a determination as to whether the conquest of power can be achieved here in the Americas in some other way than armed struggle.

Peaceful struggle can be carried on through mass movements and can, under special crisis conditions, compel the governments to yield. In this case the forces of the people, which would establish the dictatorship of the proletariat, eventually hold power. This is correct theoretically. On analyzing the preceding in terms of the over-all Latin American picture, we have to come to the following conclusions:

In general, objective conditions exist in this hemisphere that drive the masses to violent actions against the government of the bourgeoisie and the landowners. Power crises and also subjective conditions exist in many other countries. Of course, in countries where all conditions are found, it would actually be criminal not to act to seize power. In those others in which this does not occur, it is right for other alternatives to appear and for the decision applicable in each country to arise out of theoretical discussion. The one thing history does not tolerate is errors on the part of analysts and executors of proletarian policy. No one can seek command of the vanguard party through an official diploma granted by a university. To be the vanguard party is to be at the head of the working class in the struggle for power, to know how to guide it toward seizure of that power, even leading it through shortcuts. This is the mission of our revolutionary parties, and analysis must be profound and exhaustive so as to prevent mistakes.

At the present time there exists in the Americas an unstable state of equilibrium between oligarchic dictatorship and pressure from the people. We classify it with the word *oligarchic* in an attempt to define the reactionary alliance between the middle classes of each country and the landowners, with a greater or lesser preponderance of feudal structures. These dictatorships occur within a certain framework of legality which they themselves appropriated in order to function more effectively during the entire unrestricted period of class domination. But we are going through a period in which popular pressures are very strong. They are knocking at the gates of bourgeois legality, and the latter must be violated by its own authors in order to hold back the impetus of the masses. But the brazen violations, which are contrary to all preestablished legislation—or legislation established a posteriori to justify actions already undertaken—increase tension among the people's forces. For this reason the oligarchic dictatorship tries to utilize old legal decrees in order to change the constitution and further stifle the proletariat without a direct clash. Nevertheless, this is where a contradiction arises. The people no longer tolerate the old, still less the new, coercive measures established by the dictatorship, and it tries to violate them. We must never forget the class, authoritative, and restrictive character of the bourgeois state. Lenin refers to the latter as follows:

> The state is a product and manifestation of the irreconcilable nature of class contradictions. The state arises in the place, at the moment, and in the degree to which class contradictions cannot, objectively, be reconciled. And, conversely, the existence of the state demonstrates that the class contradictions are irreconcilable [from *The State and Revolution*].

That is to say, we must not permit the word democracy, employed apologetically, to represent the dictatorship of the exploiting classes, to lose the profundity of its concept and acquire that of certain more or less optimum liberties granted the citizen. To struggle only to achieve restoration of a certain bourgeois legality, without, on the other hand, posing the problem of revolutionary power, is to struggle to return to a certain dictatorial order preestablished by the dominant social classes. It is, in any case, to struggle for the establishment of chains which merely allow the prisoner a lighter ball at the end.

Under these conditions of conflict, the oligarchy breaks its own contracts —its own appearance of "democracy"—and attacks the people, although it always tries to utilize the methods of the superstructure which it has created for oppression. At this stage the following dilemma is again presented: What is to be done? We reply: Violence is not the exclusive preserve of the exploiters; the exploited can use it, and what is more, should use it at the proper time. Martí said: "He who furthers an avoidable war in a country, and he who fails to further an unavoidable one, is a criminal."

Lenin, on the other hand, stated: "Social democracy has never approached war from a sentimental point of view, nor does it now. It absolutely condemns war as a violent means of settling differences among men, but it knows that wars are inevitable as long as society is divided into classes, as long as man exploits man. And in order to end this exploitation we shall be unable to avoid war, which, whenever and wherever it occurs, is started by the dominant oppressive exploiters themselves." He said this in 1905.

Later, in *The Military Program of the Proletarian Revolution,* where he profoundly analyzed the nature of the class struggle, he asserted:

> He who accepts the class struggle cannot help accepting civil wars, which in every class society represent the continuation, development, and recrudescence—natural and under certain circumstances inevitable—of the class struggle. All the great revolutions confirm this. To reject civil wars or to forget them would be to lapse into extreme opportunism and to deny the socialist revolution.

That is to say, we must not fear violence, the midwife of new societies. But that violence must break out at the precise moment when the leaders of the people have found circumstances favorable.

What will these conditions be? They depend, where subjective elements are concerned, on two factors which complement each other, and which in turn deepen in the course of the struggle: the awareness of the need for change and the certainty of the possibility of this revolutionary change. These, combined with the objective conditions—extremely favorable in almost all of Latin America for the development of the struggle—and with the firm will to achieve it, along with the new correlations of forces in the world, create the time for action.

However distant the socialist countries may be, their beneficent influence on the struggling peoples will always be felt, and their instructive example will give the latter greater strength. Fidel Castro said last July 26: "And the duty of the revolutionaries, above all at this moment, is to know how to be perceptive, to know how to grasp the changes which have occurred in the world in the correlation of forces, and to understand that this change facilitates the struggle of the different peoples. The duty of revolutionaries [of Latin American revolutionaries] does not consist in waiting for the change in the correlation of forces in order to perform the miracle of social revolutions in Latin America, but in taking full advantage of all the ways in which that change in the correlation of forces favors the revolutionary movement. Above all it consists in creating the revolutions!"

There are those who say: "Let us grant that revolutionary war is the proper means, in certain specific instances, of succeeding in seizing power. Where will we get the great leaders, the Fidel Castros, who will lead us to triumph?" Fidel Castro, like every human being, is a product of history. The military and political heads who lead insurrectionary struggles in Latin America, if they can possibly be united in one single person, will learn the art of war by the waging of war itself. There is no trade or profession that can be learned only from textbooks. Struggle, in this case, is the great teacher.

Naturally, the task will be neither simple nor free of grave peril throughout its course. During the development of the armed struggle two moments of extreme danger to the future of the revolution appear. The first of them arises during the preparatory stage, and the manner in which it is resolved is the measure of the will to fight and the clarity of purpose of the people's forces. When the bourgeois government advances against the people's positions, it is evident that a defensive operation must be undertaken against the enemy, who, at this moment of superiority, attacks. If the minimum objective and subjective conditions have already developed, the defense should be military. It should, however, be of such a type as not to make of the people's forces mere receivers of the enemy's blows. Nor should the defense installations simply be tranformed into a last refuge for the persecuted. The guerrilla force, a defensive device of the people at a given time, carries within it—and this must constantly be developed—the capacity to attack the enemy. This capacity is what determines, in time, its role as a catalyst of the people's forces. In other words the guerrilla force is not a form of passive self-defense. It is a defense involving attack, and from the moment it is established as such, it has as its ultimate aim the conquest of political power.

This moment is important. In social processes the difference between violence and nonviolence cannot be measured by the number of shots exchanged; it is a matter of concrete, fluctuating situations. And it is necessary to know how to see the moment when the people's forces, aware of their relative weakness—but, at the same time, aware of their strategic strength—must compel the enemy to take the necessary steps to prevent the situation from deteriorating. The oligarchic dictatorship-popular pressure equilibrium must be broken. Dictatorship constantly tries to operate without a show of force. Obliging it to drop its disguise, that is, show its true colors as the violent dictatorship of the reactionary classes, will contribute to its unmasking. This will deepen the struggle to the point of no return. The firm beginning of a long-range military action depends upon how the people's forces, embarked upon the task of compelling the dictatorship to show itself for what it is, fulfill their function, that is, whether they retreat or attack.

Eluding the other dangerous moment depends upon the power of the favorable development of the people's forces. Marx always recommended that, once the revolutionary process has started, the proletariat keep attacking without letup. A revolution that does not constantly expand is a revolution going backwards. The combatants, grown weary, begin to lose faith, and at such a time one of the maneuvers to which the bourgeoisie has us so accustomed can bear fruit.

These maneuvers can consist of elections in which power is handed over to another gentleman with a more mellifluous voice and a more angelic face than those of the dictator whose turn it had been. There can also be a *coup* executed by the reactionaries, who are generally led by the army and enjoy the direct or indirect support of the progressive forces. Other maneuvers are possible, but it is not our purpose to analyze tactical stratagems.

We wish to draw attention mainly to the maneuver of the military *coup* aimed upward. What can the army men give real democracy? What loyalty can be asked of them if they are mere instruments of domination by the reactionary classes and the imperialist monopolies, and as a caste which owes its existence to the weapons it possesses, they aspire only to the maintaining of their prerogatives?

When, in situations that are difficult for the oppressors, the army men conspire and overthrow a dictator (who has in reality already been defeated) it must be supposed that they do so because he is no longer capable of preserving their class privileges without extreme violence. This is something which, generally speaking, does not at this time suit the interests of the oligarchies.

This claim does not in any way mean that one should cast aside the utilization of soldiers as individual fighting men, separate from the social milieu in which they have acted and in fact rebelled against. And this utilization should take place within the framework of the revolutionary command, to which they will be subject as fighters and not as representatives of a caste.

In times long gone by, in the preface to the third edition of *The Civil War in France,* Engels said:

> The workers, after each revolution, were still armed. Therefore, the disarming of the workers was the first order of the bourgeoisie who headed the government. So it is that, after every revolution won by the workers, a new struggle took place that ended in the latter's defeat . . . [Quoted from Lenin, *The State and Revolution*].

This game of continual struggles, in which a formal change of any type is accomplished, but in which there is a strategic defeat, has been repeated for decades in the capitalist world. But yet the permanent deception of the proletariat in this respect has been going on periodically more than a century.

There is also the danger that, impelled by the desire to maintain for a time conditions that are more favorable for revolutionary action through the use of certain types of bourgeois legality, the leaders of progressive parties will be confused as to terminology—something very common in the course of the action—and forget the ultimate strategic objective: *the seizure of power.*

These two difficult revolutionary stages, which we have analyzed summarily, are avoided when the leading Marxist-Leninist parties are capable of seeing the implications of the moment clearly and of mobilizing the masses to the fullest, guiding them along the proper path to the revolution stemming from the fundamental contradictions.

In developing this subject, we have assumed that eventually the idea of armed struggle and the formula of guerrilla warfare as the method of combat will be accepted. Why do we believe that, under present conditions in this hemisphere, guerrilla warfare is the correct way? There are fundamental arguments, which, in our estimation, determine the necessity of guerrilla action in Latin America as the central axis of the struggle.

First, accepting as true the belief that the enemy will fight to continue in power, it is necessary to think of the destruction of the oppressor's army. To destroy it, a people's army must oppose it. This army is not created spontaneously; it must be equipped from the arsenal its enemy provides, and this means a hard and very long fight, in which the people's forces and their leaders, without adequate defense conditions and maneuverability, will always be exposed to attack by superior forces.

On the other hand, the guerrilla nucleus, based on territory favoring their struggle, guarantees the safety and permanence of the revolutionary command. The urban forces, commanded from the staff headquarters of the people's army, can carry out actions of incalculable importance. The possible destruction of these groups would not spell the end of the heart of the revolution, the leadership. From its rural fortress, the latter would continue to act as a catalyst of the revolutionary spirit of the masses and organize new forces for other battles.

Moreover, this is the area where the structuring of the future governmental apparatus, responsible for efficiently running the class dictatorship during the entire period of transition, will begin. The longer the struggle, the greater and more complex the administrative problems will be, and in their solution cadres will be trained for the difficult task of consolidation of power, and at a future stage, economic development.

Second, there is the general situation of the Latin American peasants and the more and more explosive nature of their struggle against the feudal structures, within the framework of a social situation involving an alliance between local and foreign exploiters.

To return to the Second Havana Declaration:

> The peoples of Latin America freed themselves from Spanish colonialism at the beginning of the last century, but they did not free themselves from exploitation. The feudal landowners assumed the authority of the Spanish rulers, the Indians continued in hard servitude, the Latin American continent continued to be in one form or another enslaved, and the slightest hopes of the people succumbed to the power of the oligarchies and the yoke of foreign capital. This has been the truth about Latin America, with this or that nuance, with this or that variation. Latin America today is under an imperialism that is much more fierce, much more powerful, and much more merciless than Spanish colonial imperialism.

And what is the attitude of Yankee imperialism in the face of the objective and historically inexorable reality of the Latin American revolution? Preparation for the waging of a colonial war with the peoples of Latin America; creation of the military machine, the political pretexts, and the pseudolegal instruments underwritten with the representatives of the reactionary oligarchies to put down, with bloodshed and fire, the struggle of the Latin American peoples.

This objective situation shows us the force that lies dormant, untapped, in our peasants, and the need to utilize it for the liberation of Latin America.

Third, there is the hemisphere-wide character of the struggle. Could this new stage in the emancipation of Latin America be conceived as the confrontation of two local forces struggling for power in a particular area? Not likely. The struggle between all the people's forces and all the forces of repression will be to the death. The paragraphs quoted above predict it too.

The Yankees will intervene because of common interests and because the struggle in Latin America is decisive. In fact they are intervening already in the preparation of a hemispheric fighting force. But henceforth they will do so with all their vigor. They will punish the people's forces with every weapon of destruction at their command. They will not allow revolutionary power to be consolidated, and if anyone succeeds in consolidating it they will return to the attack. They will not recognize him; they will attempt to divide the revolutionary forces; they will introduce saboteurs of every type; they will create frontier problems; they will pit other reactionary countries against the new government; they will try to snuff out by economic means—in a word, annihilate—the new government.

In view of this over-all Latin American picture, it is difficult for victory to be achieved and consolidated in one isolated country. The union of repressive forces must be met with the union of the forces of the people. In all countries in which oppression reaches unbearable levels, the banner of rebellion must be raised, and this banner will be, out of historic necessity, hemispheric in character. The mountain range of the Andes is called upon to be "the Sierra Maestra of [South] America," as Fidel said, and all the immense territories this continent embraces are destined to be the scene of the struggle to the death against imperialist power.

We cannot say when it will achieve these hemispheric characteristics nor how long the struggle will last. But we can predict its coming and its triumph, because it is the result of inevitable historic, economic, and political circumstances; its course cannot be halted. To initiate it when conditions are favorable, independently of the situation in the other countries, is the task of the revolutionary force in each country. The development of the struggle will determine the general strategy. The prediction as to the hemispheric character is the fruit of an analysis of the forces of each adversary, but this by no means excludes any independent outbreak. Just as the start of the struggle in one part of a country is destined to engender the full range of the struggle, the beginning of a revolutionary war contributes to the development of new conditions in neighboring countries.

The development of revolutions has been brought about normally by inversely proportional ebb and flow. The counterrevolutionary ebb corresponds to the revolutionary flow, and conversely, at times of revolutionary decline there is a counterrevolutionary ascendancy. At these times the situation of the people's forces becomes difficult, and they should resort to the best means of defense so as to suffer the fewest losses. The enemy is extremely strong, hemispheric. For this reason the relative weaknesses of the local bourgeoisies cannot be analyzed with a view to making decisions of limited scope. Still less could one think of the possible alliance of these oligarchies with the people under arms. The Cuban Revolution has sounded the alarm bell. The polarization of forces will become total: exploiters on one side and exploited on the other. The mass of the petty bourgeoisie will favor one side or the other, in accordance with its interests and the political success with which they are handled. Neutrality will constitute an exception. This is how the revolutionary war will be.

Let us think how a guerrilla nucleus could begin.

Relatively small nuclei of individuals choose places favorable for guerrilla warfare, whether with the intention of launching a counterattack or in order to provoke the enemy's full fury, and there they begin to operate. It is necessary to establish the following very clearly: At the beginning, the relative weakness of the guerrilla force is such that it must only work to establish itself in the area in order to become acquainted with the environment, establishing connections with the populace and reinforcing the places that may possibly be converted into their support bases.

There are three conditions of survival in a guerrilla force which begins its development on the basis expressed here: constant mobility, constant vigilance, constant distrust. Without the proper use of these three elements of military tactics, the guerrilla force is not likely to survive. It must be remembered that the heroism of the guerrilla fighter, at this time, consists of the scope of the objective established, and the enormous series of sacrifices that he will have to make in order to reach it.

These sacrifices will not be daily combat, face-to-face fighting with the enemy. They will take more subtle forms, which are more difficult for the mind and the body of the individuals in the guerrilla force to withstand.

The enemy army may punish them severely. At times they will be split up into groups, and those who fall prisoner will be tortured. They will be hounded like relentlessly pursued animals in the areas they have chosen for their operation. They will suffer the constant uneasiness of having enemies on the heels of their band, and they will constantly have to suspect all they encounter, since the frightened peasants will in some instances hand them over to the repressive troops in order to rid themselves of the latter by removing the reason for their presence. Their only alternatives will be death or victory, at times when death is a concept present a thousandfold, and victory, the myth of which only a revolutionary can dream.

This is the heroism of the guerrilla fighter. That is why it is said that merely to move is also a form of combat because to flee from combat at a certain time is nothing but one form of fighting. The plan, in the face of the enemy's general superiority, is to find a tactical means of achieving relative superiority in one chosen place, whether by being able to concentrate more troops than the enemy or by securing advantages arising out of the utilization of the terrain, thus upsetting the correlation of forces. Under these circumstances tactical victory is assured. If relative superiority is not clear, it is preferable not to engage in any action. One should not engage in any clash that does not produce victory, as long as one can choose the "how" and the "when."

In the framework of large-scale politico-military action, of which it is an element, the guerrilla force will keep growing and consolidating itself. Support bases, a fundamental element if the guerrilla force is to prosper, will then be established. These support bases are points the enemy cannot penetrate except at the cost of heavy losses. They are bastions of the revolution, a refuge and resource of the guerrilla force for the purpose of more and more distant and daring raids.

This point is reached if difficulties of a tactical and political nature have been surmounted simultaneously. The guerrilla fighters can never forget their function as the people's vanguard, or the mandate they embody, for which reason they must create the political conditions necessary for the establishment of revolutionary power based upon the total support of the masses. The great claims of the peasants must be satisfied to the degree and in the form that circumstances make advisable. The entire populace must be fashioned into a compact, resolute conglomerate.

If the military situation of the early stages will be difficult, no less delicate will the political one be. If one single military mistake can liquidate a guerrilla force, a political mistake can hold back its development for long periods. The struggle is politico-military. It is in this manner that it must be developed, and consequently, understood.

The guerrilla force, in its growth process, reaches a moment when its capacity for action covers a specific area for whose dimensions there is an excess of men and too great concentration in the region.

We then have the beehive effect. One of the leaders, an outstanding guerrilla fighter, jumps off to another region and repeats the chain of development of guerrilla warfare—subject, of course, to a central command.

Now then, it is necessary to point out that one cannot hope for victory without the formation of a people's army. The guerrilla forces can be expanded only up to a certain size. The people's forces, in the cities and in other vulnerable territories occupied by the enemy, will be able to inflict heavy damage on the latter, but the military potential of the reaction will still be intact. It must always be borne in mind that the end result must be the annihilation of the adversary. For this to come about all these new areas that are established, in addition to the areas that are penetrated behind the enemy's lines and the forces that operate in the principal cities, must not be independent but subject to a central command. It will not be possible to attempt to establish the closed hierarchical order that characterizes an army, but it will be possible to establish a strategic order. Within specific conditions of freedom of action, the guerrilla forces must carry out all strategic orders of the central command, which is installed in one of the areas—the safest and strongest—where it prepares the conditions for the fusion of the forces at a given time.

The guerrilla war, or war of liberation, will generally be in three stages. The first will be that of strategic defense, in which the small fleeing force wears down the enemy. The force is not dug in for a passive defensive action within a small radius; its defense consists, rather, of such limited attacks as it can launch. After this stage a point of equilibrium is reached at which the possibilities of enemy or guerrilla action are stabilized. The final stage is reached with the inundation of the repressive army, which leads to the seizure of the great cities, the great decisive battles, and the total annihilation of the adversary.

After attainment of the point of equilibrium, at which both forces respect each other, the guerrilla war acquires new characteristics as it goes through its development. The concept of the maneuver begins to be introduced: large columns that attack strongholds; a war of movement with the transfer of men and offensive weapons of relative power. But due to the capacity to resist and counterattack that the enemy still retains, this war of maneuver does not definitively replace the guerrilla forces. It is only a method of operation that they employ, an expansion of the guerrilla forces to the point where they finally crystallize into a people's army with an army corps. The guerrillas, in their "pure" state, will still precede action by the main forces, knocking out communications and sabotaging the enemy's entire defense establishment.

We predicted that the war would involve all of Latin America. This means it will also be prolonged. There will be many fronts, and it will cost much blood and countless lives over a long period. But there is something further. The phenomena of the polarization of forces occurring in the Americas—and the clear division that will be established between the exploiters and the exploited in future revolutionary wars—mean that, when seizure of power by the people's armed vanguard takes place, the country, or countries, that achieve this will have liquidated the imperialists and the homegrown exploiters along with the oppressor. The first stage of the socialist revolution will have crystallized. The people will be ready to stanch their wounds and begin to build socialism.

Are there other less cruel possibilities?

It was some time ago that the first distribution of the world took place, in which the lion's share of our continent fell to the United States. Today the imperialists of the Old World are developing anew, and the vigor of the European Common Market frightens the Americans themselves. All this could lead one to think that the possibility might exist of standing by as spectators of the interimperialist struggle and then making progress, perhaps in alliance with the strongest national bourgeoisies. Disregarding the fact that a passive policy never brings good results in the class struggle, and that alliances with the bourgeoisie—however revolutionary the latter may appear at a specific time—are only transitory in nature, there are reasons of time which lead one to decide on another course. The sharpening of the fundamental contradiction seems to be so rapid in Latin America that it disturbs the "normal" development of the contradictions in the imperialist camp in their struggle for markets.

The national bourgeoisies have joined American imperialism and must meet the same fate as the latter in each country. Even in cases where there are pacts or common contradictions shared by the national bourgeoisie and other imperialisms with American imperialism, this occurs within the framework of a fundamental struggle, which will, in the course of its development, necessarily encompass all the exploited and all the exploiters. The polarization of the opposing forces of class adversaries is, till now, swifter than the development of the contradictions among exploiters because of the division of the spoils. There are two factions; the choice becomes clearer for each individual and for each special stratum of the population.

The Alliance for Progress is an attempt to check the uncheckable.

But if the advance of the European Common Market, or of any other imperialist group, were swifter in Latin American markets than the development of the fundamental contradiction, all that would remain would be to introduce the people's forces like a wedge into the open breach. These forces would lead the entire struggle, using the new intruders with a clear awareness of what their eventual aims are.

Not a single position, weapon, or secret must be handed over to the class enemy, on pain of losing everything.

The Latin American struggle has started, in fact. Will its vortex be in Venezuela, Guatemala, Colombia, Ecuador? Will the present skirmishes be only signs of a restlessness that has not borne fruit? It does not matter what the results of today's struggles are. It does not matter, as far as the final result is concerned, whether one movement or another is momentarily defeated. What is definitive is the determination to fight (which matures from day to day), the awareness of the need for revolutionary change, and the certainty that the latter is possible.

This is a prediction. We make it out of the conviction that history will prove us right. Analysis of these objective and subjective factors in Latin America and the imperialist world indicates to us the certainty of these assertions based on the Second Havana Declaration.

CHAPTER 22

On Value[1]

In this issue of *Nuestra Industria Económica* we are reproducing the article by Alberto Mora which recently appeared under the title, "Concerning the Problem of the Operation of the Law of Value in the Cuban Economy at the Present Time," in the review *Comercio Exterior,* published by the Ministry of Foreign Commerce.

The article begins by saying: "Some comrades maintain that the Law of Value does not operate at present in the government sector of the Cuban economy." It is important to identify those charged with the assertion. "Some" has no first and last names, but the individuals at whom the criticism is directed do have them and are specific persons: the minister of industry, who signs this article, and comrade Luis Alvarez Rom, minister of finance, not to mention the others who might be criticized for following the vogue of the budgetary financing system.

We mention this first because it is a good idea to identify not only the concepts but also the people who defend them.

We should like to clarify three assertions made by Mora in his conclusions. It is our opinion that the most important subject to discuss in the article is not his disagreement with those who deny the operation of the Law of Value, but the way in which he defines value, since it is not in accord with Marx's ideas.

Mora states:

> In short, what is value? In my judgment, if we are going to assign any consistent meaning to the category, value, we cannot fail to appreciate that it encompasses (or, rather, expresses) a relationship. In the first place it is a measurement, and as such, expresses a relationship. In the second place, it is therefore a category created by man under specific circumstances and

[1] *Nuestra Industria Económica,* Año 1, No. 3, Oct. 1963. Translated by Leonard Mades.

with a specific purpose, which is circumscribed within the confines of the social relationships he has developed.

Let us analyze the paragraph. A few lines before, referring to value, Alberto Mora states: "But the measure of a thing is not the thing itself." Now he states: "In the first place, it is a measurement, and as such, expresses a relationship." This appears contradictory to us.

He then says: "In the second place, it is therefore a category created by man under specific circumstances and with a specific purpose. . . ." This is in flat contradiction to Marx's ideas on the economic laws of society. All Marx's work was devoted to delving into the essence of phenomena beneath the surface of their appearance and to demonstrating that the various fetishes acquired by humanity serve only to conceal its ignorance. It is our belief that if there is something man was incapable of doing it was to create value with fixed purposes. Value was caused to spring up by production relationships. Value exists objectively, and whether we recognize it or not, there is no variation in the reality of its existence or in the spontaneity of expression of capitalist relationships.

From Marx on, light has been shed on the intricate mechanism of the relationships of capitalist production, but this knowledge hardly changes reality. The only thing man can do is change society under specific conditions, not "invent" its laws.

Further on, Mora adds:

> Let it be remembered that only one type of work creates value: socially necessary work; that is, the application of limited available resources to the satisfaction of a socially recognized need. It is therefore precisely this relationship which is expressed by the category, value. It is this relationship which is, strictly speaking, value.

Let us note here that Mora attributes to the phrase "socially necessary" a meaning different from the one it has; namely, that of being necessary for society, whereas in reality it is expressed here as the measurement of work society as a whole needs to do in order to produce a value. Mora ends by stating that the relationship between needs and resources is value.

It is evident that if society does not recognize the utility of the product, the latter will have no exchange value (hence, perhaps, Mora's conceptual error in referring to socially necessary work) but it is no less evident that Marx identifies the idea of value with that of abstract work. The search for a measurement of work is identified with the search for a measurement of value. We read the following in *Das Kapital:* "Therefore, an object-value, a possession, contains a value only because it is the embodiment or materialization of abstract human work. How is the amount of this value measured? By the amount of material that creates value, that is, the amount of work that it involves."

It follows that without object-value, value does not exist, just as object-value without value is inconceivable (except for some natural forces) because of the dialectical interrelation that exists between the two.

The idea that the relationship, need-resource, is implicit in the concept of value might be closer to reality. This seems logical, since this formula can be interchanged with that of supply-demand, which exists in the market, and which constitutes one of the links in the operation of the Law of Value or of the value of relationship.

We have devoted this much space to the first objection we consider important because of how dangerous it would be to merely give the outlines of this problem, carrying it to the point of a simple enunciation of the law of supply and demand.

Coming to the beginning of the first paragraph of the article on which we are commenting, we shall say that this appraisal is not exact. We approach the problem of value from another angle. I shall refer to the article published in *Nuestra Industria Económica*, number 1.[2] I said there:

> When all products function in accordance with prices that have certain internal relationships among one another—relationships which differ from the relationships of these products in the capitalist market—a new price relationship is created that cannot be compared to the worldwide one. How can prices be made to coincide with value? How can a knowledge of the Law of Value be consciously wielded so as to achieve a balance between the underlying mercantile evaluation on the one hand, and the faithful reflection of the true value on the other? This is one of the most serious problems confronting the socialist economy.

In other words the operation of the Law of Value is not being contested; the observation is being made that this law exists in its most developed form throughout the capitalist market, and that the variations introduced into the market by the socialization of the means of production and of the distribution system bring changes that impede immediate clarification of its operation.

We maintain that the Law of Value governs mercantile relationships in the capitalist world, and that, as a consequence, to the extent that markets are distorted due to whatever cause, operation of the Law of Value will undergo certain distortions.

The way and the degree to which this occurs has not been studied in the same depth that Marx carried out his study of capitalism. He and Engels did not foresee that the period of transition might begin in economically backward countries. Consequently they neither studied nor pondered the economic characteristics of that phase.

Lenin, despite his genius, did not have the time to devote long studies, to

[2] See Chapter 19 (ed.).

devote his whole life, as did Marx, to the economic problems of this transition stage in which a new society emerges from capitalism (without having completed its development so that the remains of feudalism are still found) and establishes the concentration of ownership of the means of production in the hands of the people.

This is a reality the possibility of which was foreseen by Lenin in his studies of the uneven development of capitalism, the beginning of imperialism, and the theory of the breaking away of the weakest links in the system during times of such social unpheavals as war. He himself proved, by the Russian Revolution and the creation of the first socialist state, that this was feasible. However, he had no time to continue his research, since he devoted himself entirely to the consolidation of power and to participation in the revolution, as he announced in the abrupt ending to his book *The State and Revolution.* (Lenin's entire works on the economics of the period of transition serve us as a highly valuable introduction to the subject, but they lack the development and depth that time and experience would have given them.)

In his conclusions comrade Mora states categorically: "Under socialism the Law of Value continues to operate, although it is not the only criterion governing production. Under socialism the Law of Value operates throughout the plan."

We are not so sure of this. Assuming a plan is drawn up that is harmonious in all respects, it must be assumed that it should have some means of analysis other than the one its evaluation permits. It does not seem to me that it can be any other than the results it produces. But the results are the *a posteriori* proof that everything is either going well or not going well (with respect to the Law of Value, that is, since there can be defects of some other origin). We would have to begin to minutely study the weak points in order to try to take practical measures, again *a posteriori,* to correct the situation by means of trial and error. In any case, the balance between the mercantile evaluation and effective demand would be the control pattern; analysis of unsatisfied needs would shed no light, since by definition conditions do not exist that would give man what he demands in this period.

Let us assume something more concrete, namely that measures must be taken to meet a given situation, or that money must be spent on the correction of great imbalances in domestic production or on investments that will use up part of our capacity to produce consumer goods—investments necessary because of their strategic importance (I do not refer to military considerations alone but to economic ones as well). Tensions will then be created which it will be necessary to correct by administrative measures in order to prevent runaway prices, and new relationships will be created, which will obscure the operation of the Law of Value more and more.

One can always calculate effects. The capitalist nations occasionally do it in their studies. But there will be a dimmer and dimmer reflection in the plan of the Law of Value. This is our opinion on the subject.

We should also like to refer to another part of the above article, in which the following is stated:

> When some comrades deny that the Law of Value operates in the relationships among enterprises within the government sector, they argue that the government sector is a single ownership and that the enterprises are the property of society. This, of course, is true. But economically it is an incorrect judgment. Government ownership is still not fully developed ownership by society. This will be achieved only with communism.

And then the article says: "It is sufficient simply to note the relationships among the government enterprises and see how contradictions arise from them, one contradicting the other, in order to realize that in Cuba at the present time the entire government sector in no way constitutes a single great enterprise."

Alberto Mora refers to some talks we have had, to a personal intervention in the closing of the academic year at the School of Administration, and to an unpublished pamphlet by comrade Alvarez Rom, in which reference is made to the subject as an aspiration of Lenin's. In the pamphlet attention is devoted to treatment of the factories as shops, pertaining to the consolidated enterprise and to the aspiration, consistent with the development of the economy, of making all relationships what they will be in a great single factor.

We should like to point out that, although it is true that contradictions among different enterprises exist—and we shall not cite enterprises of the economy in general but those administered by the Ministry of Industry—it is no less true that contradictions exist among an enterprise's factories or among a factory's shops. Sometimes, as in the case of the workers of a brigade working during hours that call for premium pay, the contradictions are expressed in a practical example when the brigade refuses to permit one of its workers to give up an hour's production in order to teach some other comrades, due to the fact that it lowers the group's productivity, and consequently, its pay. Nevertheless we are building socialism, liquidating man's exploitation of man.

Do not similar things occur under capitalism in a factory's shops that are independent of one another? Can it be perchance that the two systems have contradictions of a similar type?

The contradictions among men are constantly reflected in the socialist world. But when the men are not guilty of extreme lack of understanding or unrevolutionary behavior, they are contradictions which are not antagonistic and can be resolved within the bounds the society sets for its actions. We agree that the government sector still does not in any way constitute a single great enterprise, the causes being organizational defects, the lack of development of our society, and the existence of two financial systems. The main basis of our expressing our concept of a single enterprise was the definition Marx gives of goods: "In order to be goods, the product has to pass into the hands of a second party, the one who consumes it, by means of an act of exchange." We also based our statement on Engels's annotation explaining that Marx introduces the concept of goods in order to avoid the error of those who consider goods to be any product consumed by a party other than the person himself who produced it, and that Marx explains that taxes are not goods because no exchange is involved.

Engels gives an example drawn from feudal society, but could this concept of goods, with its corresponding examples, not be valid in our present time in which socialism is being built?

We believe that transfer from one shop to another, or from one enterprise to another, in the budget system we have developed, cannot be considered an act of exchange. It is simply an act of creation or aggregation of new values through work. In other words, if by goods is meant that product that changes hands through an act of exchange, and if all factories are government property under the budget system (in which this phenomenon does not occur), then the product will acquire the characteristics of goods when it reaches the market and passes into the hands of the consuming public.

Our opinion regarding costs is reflected in the article already mentioned, which appeared in this review under my signature. We refer the interested reader to it. As for the size of Cuba, if we apply Mora's criterion we can propose to him that he divide his ministry into nine autonomous ministries, one to the floor, in view of its exaggerated size. If he does not believe this, let him try going up to his office by the stairway and he will be convinced of the truth of the assertion. If he uses the telephone, the elevator, and the intercommunication system, it is because they exist for this purpose. Distances in Cuba are measured by technical means of modern communication, not by the time our ancestors took to move from one place to another. So much for discrepancies.

We want to state that this dispute, which begins with our reply, can have great educational value for us, to the degree that we are capable of carrying it on in the most rigorously scientific way possible and with the greatest equanimity. We do not run from confrontations, but since we are in the middle of an argument which reaches the upper levels of government and the party, where two schools of thought prevail about the financial system, we believe that concern for the form and method of argument is important.

We salute comrade Mora for the initiative he has displayed in appearing in the public forum with his charges, even if it is always better to give things their names. We also congratulate him on the quality of the Ministry of Foreign Trade's review, a quality we shall try to achieve with our modest publication.

CHAPTER 23

On Solidarity with Vietnam[1]

Comrades of the Liberation Front of South Vietnam,
Comrade Ambassador of the Republic of Vietnam.

The revolutionary government and the United party of the Revolution have elected me, in its name and in the name of the Cuban people, to hail the struggle for liberation of the South Vietnamese people on the third anniversary of this armed struggle for liberation.

The struggle of the South Vietnamese people has been going on for many years, if we do not consider the Vietnamese people under the artificial division laid down by the Geneva accords. It was when all Vietnam still belonged to French colonial power, and was known in the West as Indochina, that the popular forces began their long struggle for liberation.

Just when we in America were witnessing the fall of the only true democracy that then existed on our continent, in mid-1954,[2] news of the triumph of the popular forces at Dien Bien Phu began to arrive. It was like a warning to the imperialists that a partial victory in one given part of the world by no means meant victory for imperialism. And it was also a voice of hope for the oppressed of the world, insofar as one partial defeat of popular forces by no means should lead to total frustration of peoples longing for freedom. A few months later the French colonial troops, convinced of the uselessness of a battle in which the whole French people was being used up, arrived at the decision to end the battle, and in Geneva an accord was signed, by which Vietnam was to be divided into two parts. This accord was similar in its essential characteristics to the one which years before had divided the Korean people into two halves.

[1] Speech delivered at the Ministry of Industry, November 20, 1963, reproduced in *Obra Revolucionaria,* Año 1963, No. 34. Translated by Judith Mauleón.

[2] Guatemala, where the popular elected nationalist-reformist regime of Jacóbo Arbenz was overthrown by the CIA-financed and led forces of Col. Castillo Armas, invading from Nicaragua (ed.).

But in this second agreement general elections were scheduled, through which the Vietnamese people could decide their own destiny. French imperialism, while completely withdrawing from that Asian area, was giving its place up to North American imperialism. And the North Americans soon realized that any free popular manifestation could only result in the complete loss of its possessions in Southeast Asia, an area considered strategic by them.

In this way, the Geneva accords were violated. In this way the will of the Vietnamese people was violated, and the U.S. began to prepare for the long war of extermination which they now foresaw.

The people of South Vietnam waited awhile. Between 1954, when the war ended, and 1960, when it began again, there were many peaceful demonstrations of peaceful struggle to gain respect for the united will of a people. The moment arrived in which it was clear that the only recourse was to take up arms again. And we say that this was the only recourse, although this kind of people's war, with small armies and great unarmed support against colonial powers with all the means of destruction at hand, means great losses for the people, and a real holocaust of popular forces before achieving final liberation. But there was no other way, and thus began once again the battle in South Vietnam.

During that time, once again in America, it was being proclaimed to all the peoples of the world that the American people were not sleeping, and had not given up completely on their liberation. Thus the Cuban Revoltion began to be one of North America's most serious problems, as they themselves confess publicly.

Around that same time, the war of liberation of the people of Algeria was also coming to a head. The result, a few years later, was to be the Evian accords and the liberation of the Algerian people and its present socialist government. America, Asia, and Africa—the three oppressed continents—were showing signs that they would not admit much longer the presence of colonial powers in any of these continents.

Since then new wars of liberation have broken out: in Laos an unstable situation persists, after Laos succeeded in at least thwarting imperialist intentions; in Angola and Portuguese Guinea there are direct battles of guerrilla warfare; and on our continent—at present in Nicaragua, Honduras, Guatemala, Santo Domingo, Colombia, Venezuela, and Paraguay—the popular forces are showing their vitality and in addition, the impotence of the armies formed to repress the people and oppose their freedom.

In the last months of this year great victories have been won by the popular Venezuelan forces on this continent and by the army of liberation in South Vietnam. Eight thousand casualties inflicted on the enemy in the latest encounters—consisting of four thousand prisoners and deserters and four thousand dead and wounded—show the power possessed by the movement in South Vietnam. The mountain bases of the north are virtually liberated, and the armed forces of South Vietnam are moving toward the plains and the capital, Saigon, weakening more and more the strength of the South Vietnamese puppets.

We cannot say how long this struggle will last. They are very long struggles, or almost always very slow processes, of great sacrifices, but they gain, in geometric progression, the forces of the people, and as soon as the correlation of forces offers a small margin to the people's party, the solutions come quickly.

This is the way it happened in our Cuba, this is the way it happened in North Vietnam, this is the way it happened in the long war for independence that resulted in the establishment of the Chinese People's Republic.

At a given moment the popular forces attain such a strength that they immediately take the offensive on grand scale, transform their guerrilla forces into regular or semiregular armies, move from simple guerrilla action to that of a column, to operational tactics, and soon destroy the oppressive power.

We do not know when we will be able to hail the total liberation of South Vietnam. We can never say when freedom will be attained by each of the peoples who are struggling today, weapons in hand, for their freedom. We do know that the result will be, without fail, the liberty of all peoples. And when they strike for their freedom with more energy, more enthusiasm, and more faith, they shorten the time they will have to endure the attacks of the oppressive power.

In South Vietnam, a few months ago, conditions were created in which the United States decided to put a new team in power. The dictator for the day did not accept this, and once again the United States demonstrated what happens to puppets who do not obey orders. And according to the broadcasts of the North American information agencies, dictator Ngo Dinh Diem and his brother underwent what was then known as "accidental suicide," more or less the same fate that befell Trujillo in our area when he also refused to lend himself to one of those transactions that imperial power opportunistically conducts when its team is losing.

This shows, nevertheless, that the situation is getting out of hand for the oppressive forces in South Vietnam, and the comrades of the National Liberation Front have said it clearly. There are three roads: This present one, that of using South Vietnamese nationals as troops, and only a special team of advisors in battle, repression, and torture, shows itself as impossible to maintain. This presents the alternative of moving to direct invasion of South Vietnam, and mass use of Yankee expeditionary forces.

Of course that will make the struggle harder, but its meaning for the world will be clearer. If today, when the victories are being celebrated and eight thousand casualties are announced in the South Vietnamese army of repression, it might be asked how many of those eight thousand included innocent men, men of the people who for one reason or another were grabbed up to fight against freedom, as happened so many times in Cuba, where Batista's soldiers, who joined the army because they had no place else to work, had to give their lives in the attempt to halt the progress of the revolutionary struggle. If the Yankee interventionist troops were to penetrate *en masse* into South Vietnam, the Vietnamese would know very well at whom to shoot and why. The whole world would understand much better who is the enemy, and would be able to identify him more quickly. The Yankees know that, too.

When today we enthusiastically raise the flag of South Vietnam, we do not do it just for proletarian internationalism or because of the craving for justice that the Revolution has instilled in all of us. We also do it because that battlefront is most important for the future of all America.

There in Vietnam are being trained the troops that one day will be able to defeat our guerrillas—ours in all America. There are being tested the new weapons of extermination and the most modern techniques to fight against the people's freedom. At this moment Vietnam is the great laboratory of Yankee imperialism for preparing all their equipment for a battle, perhaps more awesome, maybe more important, which will have to take place in the back yard of their colonial possessions on the whole American continent.

They know that the victorious end of this battle will also spell the end of North American imperialism. That is why they pay so much attention to it, not to mention, in addition, the strategic importance of South Vietnam as a base of operations against the entire socialist block in Asia. These two strategic characteristics classify South Vietnam as one of the serious problems facing the new Yankee administration, which at this very moment is no doubt making a careful analysis of what to do.

It is natural that no one thinks that a real and democratic formula for peace is being worked out and that the Vietnamese people are going to be able to achieve their victory, to unite as a nation and build socialism, as did their brothers in the north, on the bases of backwardness inherited from colonialism and destroyed riches inherited from war. They require other tactics and in another strategic sense. What will be their decision? We do not know this yet, but we foresee a long struggle and great suffering for the heroic people of South Vietnam, the same things one can foresee for all people who are struggling for their freedom.

However, the living presence of the liberation forces of Vietnam, their constant successes, their continual advancement toward the better-defended zones of the enemy, are an example taken by all peoples. Our mission here, in Cuba, is to take this living example; to make our people feel it deeply because of what it represents as a just cause and as an integral part of the great brotherhood of oppressed peoples of the world, and in addition, to carry this example, by any means, to oppressed America, to show how in all continents it is possible to struggle for the emancipation of people. And demonstrate something else to our peoples of America: that when peaceful conditions of struggle are exhausted, when the reactionary powers deceive the people time and time again, not only *may* we wave the banner of revolution, but we *must* wave the banner of revolution.

We are not speaking of specific countries. We are speaking of concrete situations. The form, the way, and the day will be determined by the popular forces of each country. But the examples are there, living demonstrations of how, despite chemical warfare, despite the new methods of destruction, tested day by day by the Yankees themselves, the struggle can be successful. And if we pause a moment before the map of Vietnam—small as it is—and we pause later before the thirteen million square miles of our immense America, we will clearly see that the struggle can be carried out very easily.

Many peoples of America are ready for revolution, not only those who today have already begun their struggle. There are some who have not yet begun, and who, nevertheless, are patiently sharpening their machetes because they know the time is drawing near. They know that North American imperialism will intervene in America, but they also know that the more fronts open simultaneously, the more difficult the struggle will be. Today we are no longer dealing with countries—as Cuba is not a country in this part of the world—but a part of a single country, and in addition a symbol for all America.

Thus each people which begins its struggle also begins to dig the grave of imperialism and should merit all our support and all our applause.

Today they are trying to destroy Cuba in order to destroy the "bad example," no doubt thinking that if they succeed, they will undo all that this government has done, all the social progress and all the representatives of this government. We know this very well. This is why it is a struggle unto death. The South Vietnamese people know it too. There is no choice but victory or destruction, with years and years of imperialist power trampling on oppressed countries.

That is why one should think clearly: the battle should be well planned, but once begun, it must continue to the end. There cannot be negotiations or halfway terms. There cannot be truces which half-guarantee the stability of a country. The victory must be total. With these feelings our people are ready for battle. With these same feelings the Algerian people fought for seven years. And with this same conviction the Vietnamese people are struggling. But they have even more advantages. They have the encouragement and support of their brothers in North Vietnam, they have, nearer than anyone else, the example of the real meaning of incessant struggle of a people for its freedom, that of their brothers who fought nine years to shake off the French yoke, and they have the example of the present situation in North Vietnam, as opposed to the suffering of South Vietnam.

Because of all this their faith must be even deeper, their confidence in triumph even greater. Because of all this we know—as the comrade delegate has said—that whatever the result, whatever the method used by North American imperialism, the final result will be the victory of South Vietnam and the reunification of the entire country.

At the close of these celebrations in this week of commemoration of the third anniversary of the establishment of the National Liberation Front, we hail our brothers in South Vietnam as brothers in battle, as a fellow example in these difficult moments in world history, and even more, as our allies, as front-line soldiers in the front trenches of the world proletariat against imperialism.

For all these reasons, when we join together to hail the Vietnamese people, we are hailing a true brother; we are embracing men who in a distant region of the world are fighting for our security and are fighting for the common desires which unite the peoples of the three oppressed continents of the present: Asia, Africa, and our America.

Comrades, permit me to end these words of greeting with the call that today has been repeated so many times:

Long live the people of South Vietnam!
Long live their revolutionary army!
Long live proletarian internationalism!
Death to imperialism!
Freedom or death!

CHAPTER 24

On the Budgetary System of Financing[1]

THE subject has already been discussed to a degree, but not sufficiently, and I consider it imperative to analyze it more thoroughly, so as to give a clear idea of its scope and methodology.

It has its official sanction in the *Law regulating the budgetary system of financing government-operated enterprises,* and it has been tried out in the internal workings of the Ministry of Industry. Its history is short, dating back only as far as 1960, when it begins to show some consistent use. But our purpose is not to analyze its development but the system just as it exists now, with the understanding that its evolution has far from ended.

What we are interested in is a comparison with so-called economic forecasting.[2] Within this system we emphasize the self-motivation aspect, because it is a fundamental characteristic of differentiation. We also emphasize the attitude toward material incentives, since they are the foundation upon which financial self-motivation is established.

The explanation of differences is difficult because the latter are often obscure and subtle. It is also difficult because the budgetary system of financing has not been studied thoroughly enough to permit the propounding of it to compete in clarity with the propounding of economic forecasting.

We shall begin with some quotations. The first is from Marx's *Economico-Philosophic Manuscripts,* dating back to the period of "the young Marx." Even in his language, at this time, the influence of the philosophic ideas that contributed to his development was very evident,

1 *Nuestra Industria Económica,* Año 2, No. 5, February 1964. Translated by Leonard Mades.

2 Or "Economic Calculus," or the Self-Financing Enterprise System, which is applied in European Socialist countries and in most Cuban enterprises—but not those dependent upon Che's Ministry of Industry, where the emphasis is budgetary financing and moral incentives (ed.).

and his ideas on economics were less precise. Nevertheless, Marx was in the prime of life and had already embraced the cause of the poor and explained it philosophically, although without the rigorous scientific method of *Das Kapital.* He thought like a philosopher; therefore, he referred more specifically to man as a human individual and to the problems of his liberation as a social being. He did not yet undertake an analysis of the inevitability of the cracking of the social structures of his age and the subsequent period of transition, the dictatorship of the proletariat. In *Das Kapital* Marx emerges as the scientific economist who minutely analyzes the transitory character of the various social eras and their connection with production relationships. He does not permit philosophical disquisitions to enter into the discussion.

The influence of this monument of human intelligence is such that it has frequently made us forget the humanist character—humanist in the best sense of the word—of his concerns. The mechanics of production relationships and their consequence, the class struggle, to a certain extent obscure the objective fact that it is men who are the actors on the stage of history. Right now we are interested in man. The fact that the quotation belongs to his youth does not lessen its value as an expression of the philosopher's thought.

> . . . Communism as the positive transcendence of private property, as human self-estrangement, and therefore, as the real appropriation of the human essence by and for man; communism, therefore, as the complete return of man to himself as a social (*i.e.,* human) being—a return become conscious, and accomplished within the entire wealth of previous development. This communism, as fully developed naturalism, equals humanism, and as fully developed humanism, equals naturalism; it is the genuine resolution of the conflict between man and nature and between man and man—the true resolution of the strife between existence and essence, between objectification and self-confirmation, between freedom and necessity, between the individual and the species. Communism is the riddle of history solved, and it knows itself to be that solution.[3]

The word *consciousness* is underlined because Marx considered it basic to the statement of the problem. Marx thought about the liberation of man and saw communism as the resolution of the contradictions which have produced his alienation. But he saw it as a conscious act. In other words, communism cannot be looked at merely as the result of the class contradictions in a highly developed society—contradictions that will be resolved in a period of transition leading to the final goal. Man is the conscious actor of history. Without this *consciousness,* which encompasses his awareness as a social being, there can be no communism.

[3] Karl Marx, *Economic and Philosophic Manuscripts of 1844* (New York, International Publishers, 1964), p. 135.

During the writing of *Das Kapital* Marx did not abandon his militant attitude. When in 1875 the Congress of Gotha met for the purpose of unifying the existing labor organizations in Germany (Social Democratic Workers Party and General Association of German Workers) and the program named after the congress was drawn up, his reply was *The Gotha Program*.

This work, written in the midst of his fundamental work and with a clearly polemical orientation, is important because Marx deals in it, even if in passing, with the subject of the period of transition. In his analysis of point three of the Gotha Program he expatiates somewhat on some of the most important matters pertaining to this period—a period he considered to be the result of the cracking of the developed capitalist system. In this period the use of money is not foreseen but individual rewards for work are, because:

> What we have to deal with here is a communist society, not as it had *developed on a basis of its own,* but on the contrary as *it emerges from capitalist society,* which is thus in every respect tainted economically, morally, and intellectually, with the hereditary diseases of the old society from whose womb it is emerging. In this way the individual producer receives back again from society, with deductions, exactly what he gives. What he has given to society is his individual amount of labour.[4]

Marx could only intuit the development of the worldwide imperialist system. Lenin listens to its heartbeat and gives his diagnosis:

> The inequality of economic and political development is an absolute law of capitalism. From this we deduce that it is possible for the victory of socialism to begin in some capitalist countries, or even in only one capitalist country. The triumphant proletariat of that country, after expropriating the capitalists and organizing socialist production within its boundaries, will confront the rest of the world—the capitalist world—attracting to its side the oppressed classes of the other countries, arousing in them rebellion against the capitalists, using, if necessary, even the force of arms against the exploiting classes of their states.
>
> The political form of society in which the proletariat triumphs, overthrowing the bourgeoisie, will be the democratic republic, which will centralize more and more the forces of the proletariat of that nation or those nations in the struggle against the states that have not become socialist. It is impossible to suppress classes without a dictatorship of the oppressed class, the proletariat. The free union of nations in socialism is impossible without a tenacious, more or less prolonged struggle of the socialist republics against the backward states.[5]

[4] Karl Marx, *Critique of the Gotha Programme* (New York, International Publishers, 1933), p. 29.

[5] Lenin, *On the Watchword of the United States of Europe*. Retranslated from the Spanish text.

Not many years later Stalin systematized the idea to the point of considering the possibility of socialist revolution in the colonies.

> The third contradiction is the contradiction between the handful of ruling "civilized" nations and the hundreds of millions of the colonial and dependent peoples of the world. Imperialism is the most barefaced exploitation and the most inhuman oppression of hundreds of millions of people inhabiting vast colonies and dependent countries. The purpose of this exploitation and of this oppression is to squeeze out super-profits. But in exploiting these countries imperialism is compelled to build railroads, factories and mills there, to create industrial and commercial cities. The appearance of a class of proletarians, the emergence of a native intelligentsia, the awakening of national consciousness, the growth of the movement for emancipation—such are the inevitable results of this "policy." The growth of the revolutionary movement in all colonies and dependent countries without exception clearly testifies to this fact. This circumstance is of importance for the proletariat in that it radically undermines the position of capitalism by converting the colonies and dependent countries from reserves of imperialism into reserves of the proletarian revolution.[6]

Lenin's theses are proven by practice, that is, by his triumph in Russia that gave birth to the U.S.S.R.

We are witnessing a new phenomenon: the appearance of socialist revolution in a single country that is economically backward, occupies an area of 22,000,000 square kilometers, has a low population density, suffers from increased poverty due to war, and, as though this were not enough, is attacked by the imperialist powers.

After a period of wartime communism, Lenin set down the principles of the NEP, and with it the principles of the development of Soviet society up until our own day.

It is necessary to point out here what the situation in the Soviet Union was, and for that purpose there is no one better than Lenin:

> Thus, in 1918 I was of the opinion that with regard to the economic situation then obtaining in the Soviet Republic, state capitalism would be a step forward. This sounds very strange, and perhaps even absurd, for already at that time our Republic was a socialist republic and we were every day hastily—perhaps too hastily—adopting various new economic measures which could not be described as anything but socialist measures. Nevertheless, I then held the view that in relation to the economic situation then obtaining in the Soviet Republic state capitalism would be a step forward, and I explained my idea simply by enumerating the elements of the economic system of Russia. In my opinion these elements were the following: (1) patriarchal, *i.e.*, the most primitive form of agriculture; (2)

[6] Joseph Stalin, "Foundations of Leninism," *The Historical Roots of Leninism* (New York, International Publishers, 1939), p. 14.

small commodity production (this includes the majority of the peasants who trade in grain); (3) private capitalism; (4) state capitalism; and (5) socialism. All these economic elements were present in Russia at that time. I set myself the task of explaining the relationship of these elements to one another, and whether one of the non-socialist elements, namely, state capitalism, should not be rated higher than, regarded as superior to, socialism in a republic which declares itself a socialist republic. But the fact will become intelligible if you recall that we definitely did not regard the economic system of Russia as something homogeneous and highly developed; we were fully aware that in Russia we had patriarchal agriculture, *i.e.*, the most primitive form of agriculture, alongside the socialist form. What role could state capitalism play in these circumstances? . . .

Now that I have emphasised the fact that as early as 1918 we regarded state capitalism as a possible line of retreat, I shall deal with the results of our New Economic Policy. I repeat: At that time it was still a very vague idea, but in 1921, after we had passed through the most important stage of the Civil War—and passed through it victoriously—we felt the impact of a grave—I think it was the gravest—internal political crisis in Soviet Russia. This internal crisis brought to light discontent, not only among a considerable section of the peasantry, but also among the workers. This was the first, and I hope, the last time in the history of Soviet Russia that feeling ran against us among large masses of peasants, not consciously but instinctively. What gave rise to this peculiar, and for us, of course, very unpleasant, situation? The reason for it was that in our economic offensive we had run too far ahead, that we had not provided ourselves with adequate resources, that the masses sensed what we ourselves were not then able to formulate consciously but what we admitted soon after, a few weeks later, namely that the direct transition to purely socialist forms, to purely socialist distribution, was beyond our available strength, and that if we were unable to effect a retreat so as to confine ourselves to easier tasks, we would face disaster.[7]

As can be seen, the economic and political situation in the Soviet Union necessitated the cutback of which Lenin spoke. One can characterize that whole policy by the Soviet Union as a tactic closely linked to the country's historical situation, for which reason not all his statements should be considered universally valid. It seems to us that two factors of extraordinary importance for their introduction in other countries must be considered:

(1) The characteristics of Czarist Russia during the revolutionary period, including the following: the development of technology at all levels; the special character of the people; the general conditions in the country, to which must be added the destruction wrought by a world war and the devastation caused by the White hordes and the imperialist invaders.

(2) The general characteristics of the period with respect to economic administrative and control techniques.

[7] V. I. Lenin, *Selected Works* (Moscow, Progress Publishers, 1967), Vol. III, pp. 716, 718.

Oscar Lange, in his article, "Present Economic Problems in Poland," says the following:

> Bourgeois economics has still another function. The bourgeoisie and the monopolies do not, merely as an aid to the apologetics of the capitalist system, devote large sums to the establishment of institutions of higher learning and institutes of scientific analysis in the field of the economic sciences. They expect something more from economists; they expect help with the solution of the numerous problems connected with economic policy.
>
> In the period of free-enterprise capitalism, the tasks in this field were limited; they had to do only with financial management, monetary policy, credit, tariff policy, transportation, etc. But under the conditions of monopolistic capitalism—especially under the conditions stemming from state capitalism's increasing entry into economic life—problems of this type are growing. One of these concerns market analysis to facilitate the price policy of the great monopolies. Another is related to such methods as a complex of centrally controlled industrial enterprises as reciprocal accounting systems among these enterprises; the programmed interlocking of their activitites, development, and location; and amortization and investment policy.
>
> It is out of all this that the problems relating to the capitalist state's activity at the present time arise. It is analogous to such policies of nationalized industries as those pertaining to investment and location (in the energy field, for example) and to politico-economic participation in the national economy as a whole.
>
> To all these problems must be added a series of technical and economic procedures we can utilize, in part, in the process of establishing the socialist system. They can be employed in fields like market analysis; programming of enterprises forming a group; internal accounting procedures within each factory or group; and amortization and other such policies. No doubt, in fact, the workers of the future will use them when the transition to socialism takes place in those countries that are now capitalist.[8]

It should be noted that Cuba had neither made its transition nor even begun its revolution when this was written. Many of the technical advances Lange describes existed in Cuba, that is, the conditions in Cuban society at that time permitted centralized control over some enterprises whose headquarters were Havana or New York. The Empresa Consolidada del Petróleo, whose establishment dates back to the unification of the three existing imperialist refineries (Esso, Texaco, and Shell), maintained—and in some cases perfected—its control systems, and it is considered a model at this Ministry. In those enterprises in which there existed no tradition of centralization or conditions made it impractical, the conditions were created, based upon the nation's experience. Such was the case of the Empresa

[8] Quotation, which is not footnoted in the Spanish, is retranslated.

Consolidada de la Harina, which took first place among the enterprises under the jurisdiction of the Vice Ministry of Light Industry.

Although practice during the early days of industrial management fully convinces us of the impossibility of rationally following another course, it would be idle at this time to discuss whether the organizational measures that were taken would have produced similar or better results than the introduction of self-motivation at the unit level. The important thing is that it could be accomplished under very difficult conditions and that centralization made possible the liquidation—in the case of the shoe industry, for example—of a great number of annoying incompetents. It also made it possible to assign six thousand workers to other branches of industry.

By the previous quotations we have attempted to define the points we consider basic to an understanding of the system:

First: Communism is a goal which man achieves consciously; therefore, education—and the eradication of the scars left by the old society in the minds of the people—is extremely important. We must never forget, of course, that without parallel progress in production a communist society cannot be achieved.

Second: From the point of view of technology, we must borrow the most advanced forms wherever they can be found as long as they can be adapted to the new society. We can borrow the technology used by the imperialist camp in the petrochemical industry without fear of being infected by bourgeois ideology. In the area of norms of management and control of production, the same rule applies.

Without trying to be too pretentious we could paraphrase Marx's characterization of Hegel's dialectics and say that some of the techniques of capitalism can be turned to rights.

An analysis of the accounting techniques regularly used today in socialist countries shows us that theirs and ours are separated by a difference of concept comparable to the one separating competitive capitalism from monopolistic capitalism. After all, prior techniques served as the foundation of the development of both systems, which were "set upon the base." But from then on their paths separate; socialism has its own production relationships, and therefore, its own requirements.

Technically, then, we can say that the forerunner of the budgetary system of financing is imperialist monopoly as it existed in Cuba after having undergone the variations inherent in the long process of development of the technology of management and control—a process that extends from the earliest days of the monopolistic system to our times, in which it reaches its highest level. When the monopolists withdrew, they took their top men, and some on the intermediate level, with them. At the same time our immature concept of the revolution led us to destroy things merely because they were capitalist. This is why our system has still not attained the degree of efficiency that characterized the Cuban branches of the monopolies with respect to the management and control of production. We are heading in that direction as we clear away any dead leaves left over from the past.

There are differences of varying degrees between economic forecasting and the budgetary system of financing. We shall try to divide them into two large groups and explain them briefly. There are differences of a methodological nature—practical, we would say—as well as differences of a more profound nature, but whose nature can cause analysis to seem useless if one does not proceed with great caution.

It is necessary to make it clear now that what we seek is a more efficient way of achieving communism. There is no argument about principle. Economic forecasting has demonstrated its practical effectiveness, and starting from the same base, the same objectives are established. We believe that our system's plan of action, if properly developed, can increase the effectiveness of economic management by the socialist government, intensify the consciousness of the masses, and create greater cohesion in the world socialist system, on the basis of concerted action.

The most immediate difference arises when we speak of enterprises. To us an enterprise is a conglomerate of factories or units that have a similar technological basis, a common destination for their production, or in some cases the same limited geographical area. For the purpose of economic forecasting an enterprise is a unit of production with its own legal personality. A community sugar mill is an enterprise according to that method; to us, all the community sugar mills and other units connected with sugar constitute the Empresa Consolidada del Azúcar. In the U.S.S.R. recently there were experiments of this type adapted to the special conditions in this sister country. (See "Los combinados de empresas soviéticas: La nueva forma de administración de las industrias," I. Ivonin, *Nuestra Industria: Revista Económica,* No. 4.)

Another difference is the way money is used. In our system it only operates as arithmetic money, as a price reflection of the operation of the enterprise. It will be analyzed by the central bodies in order to exercise control over its operation. In economic forecasting it is not only this but also a means of payment that functions as an indirect instrument of control, since these funds make possible the operation of the unit. Its relations with the banks are similar to those of a private producer in contact with capitalist banks to which they must exhaustively explain their plans and prove their solvency. Naturally, in this case what operates is not any arbitrary decision but adherence to a plan, and relations are maintained among state organizations.

In accordance with the method of using money, our enterprises do not have their own funds. Separate accounts exist at the bank for the purpose of withdrawals and deposits. The enterprise can withdraw funds, according to the plan, from the general expense account and from the special account for payment of salaries. However, when a deposit is made it automatically becomes the state's.

The majority of the enterprises of our sister countries have their own funds in the banks, which they reinforce with credits on which they pay interest. It must never be forgotten that these funds of their own belong, as the credits do, to society, and that their movement expresses the financial status of the enterprise.

As for work methods, enterprises under the economic forecasting system use overtime work as well as piecework or work paid by the hour (by the job). We are trying to institute overtime work at all our factories, with rewards up to the highest rate of pay for overfulfillment of quotas. We shall elaborate on this later.

Under a fully developed system of economic forecasting there is a rigorous method of carrying on transactions. Based upon a legal scaffolding established after years of experience, there are monetary penalties for nonfulfillment of quotas. In our country such a structure still does not exist even for self-managed organizations like the INRA, and it becomes particularly difficult to establish it due to the coexistence of two systems that are so dissimilar. For now we have the Arbitration Commission, which lacks executive powers, but the importance of which is gradually growing and may be the foundation of our legal structure in the future. Internally, among organizations under the system of budgetary financing, decision-making is easy. Administrative measures are taken if the control accounts are well operated and up to date (something already happening in the majority of the enterprises under this Ministry).

On the basis that under both systems the general plan of the government is the supreme authority, adherence to which is compulsory, operating analogies and differences can be analyzed by saying that self-management is based upon over-all centralized control and a more marked decentralization. Indirect control is exercised by the bank by means of the ruble, and the monetary result of the operation serves as a measurement for the purpose of rewards.

Interest in material gain is the great lever that moves the workers individually and collectively.

The budgetary system of financing is based upon centralized control of the enterprise's activity. Its plan and economic operation are controlled by central organizations directly. It has no funds of its own; nor does it receive bank credits. It uses, on an individual basis, material incentives, that is, individual monetary rewards and punishments. When opportune, it will use collectives, but direct material incentives are limited by the method of payment of the weekly wage.

We now come smack up against the more subtle contradictions, which should be better explained. The theme of material incentives versus moral incentives has given rise to many discussions among those interested in these matters. One thing must be made very clear: We do not deny the objective need for material incentives, but we certainly are unwilling to use them as a fundamental driving force. We believe that, in economics, this kind of force quickly becomes an end in itself and then exercises its power over the relationships among men. It must not be forgotten that it comes from capitalism and is destined to die under socialism.

"How shall we make it die? Little by little, by means of the gradual increase of consumer goods for the people, which increase makes these incentives unnecessary," they reply to us. We see too rigidly mechanical a way of thinking in this notion. *Consumer goods:* This is the watchword and the great molder, in short, of conscience, according to the proponents of the other system. In our estimation, direct material incentives and conscience are contradictory terms.

This is one of the points over which our disagreements acquire specific dimensions. It is no longer a matter of nuances. To the supporters of financial self-management, direct material incentives—projected into the future and accompanying society during the different stages in the creation of a communist society—do not contradict the "development" of conscience. For us, they do. It is because of this that we are struggling against their predominance because it would mean retardation of the development of socialist morality.

If material incentives are opposed to the development of conscience, but are a great force for achieving improvements in production, are we to understand that preferential attention to the development of conscience retards production? In terms of comparison, it is possible in a given period, although no one has made the pertinent calculations. We maintain that in a relatively short time the development of conscience does more for the development of production than material incentives do. We base this on the general projection of the development of society necessary to achieve a communist society, which presupposes that work ceases to be a painful necessity and changes into a pleasant imperative. Because it is loaded with subjectivism, the statement requires confirmation by experience, and that is what we are witnessing. If in the course of that experience it were demonstrated that it is a dangerous deterrent to development of productive forces, we would have to decide to follow a healthy course and return to well-traveled roads. Until now this has not happened, and the method, with the improvement practice is providing, is acquiring more and more consistency and demonstrating its inner coherence.

What, then, is the correct way of handling material incentives? We believe that their existence, whether as a collective expression of the interests of the masses or as an individual presence, is a reflection of the habits of the old society in the minds of the workers. We do not as yet have a well-defined idea of how to treat material incentives in a collective manner, due to insufficiencies in the planning apparatus, which prevent us from having absolute faith in it and from being able until now to structure a method that would permit us to steer clear of difficulties. We see the greatest danger in the antagonism that is being created between the government administration and the production organizations. The antagonism has been analyzed by the Soviet economist Liberman, who comes to the conclusion that the methods of collective incentives must be changed in such a manner as to abandon the old formula of rewards based upon the fulfillment of quotas and to go on to other more advanced ones.

Even if we are not in agreement with him on the emphasis he gives to material incentives (as a lever), his preoccupation with the aberrations that the concept "fulfillment of quota" has developed, as the years have gone by, seems correct to us. The relationships between the enterprises and the central organizations acquire quite contradictory forms, and the methods used by the enterprises to obtain benefits sometimes take on characteristics that depart considerably from the image of socialist morality.

We believe that in a certain way the possibilities of development the new production relationships offer for orienting the evolution of man in the direction of "The kingdom of liberty" are being wasted. We gave a detailed account of precisely this in our definition of the fundamental arguments of the system of interrelationships that exist between education and the development of production. We can embark upon the task of creating the new conscience because we are witnessing new types of production relationships, and although in a general historical sense conscience is a product of production relationships, consideration must be given to the characteristics of the present period, whose fundamental contradiction (on a worldwide plane) is the one existing between imperialism and socialism. Socialist ideas affect the conscience of the peoples of the entire world. Therefore a development consistent with the particular status of the productive forces in a given country can take the lead.

In the U.S.S.R. of the early days, the socialist state characterized the regime in spite of the existence within it of relationships of a much more backward type. Under capitalism there are remainders of the feudal period, but capitalism is the system that characterizes a capitalist country after this system has triumphed in the fundamental aspects of its economy. In Cuba, the development of the contradictions between two world systems permitted the establishment of the socialist character of the revolution. It was a character given it by a conscious act, thanks to the knowledge acquired by its leaders, to the intensification of the conscience of the masses, and to the correlation of world forces.

If all this is possible, why not think of the role of education as a pertinacious assistant of the socialist state in its task of eliminating the old defects of a society that has died and carries its old production relationships to the grave?

> Infinitely stereotyped, for instance, is the argument they learned by rote during the development of Western European Social Democracy, namely, that we are not yet ripe for socialism, that as certain "learned" gentlemen among them put it, the objective economic premises for socialism do not exist in our country. It does not occur to any of them to ask: but what about a people that found itself in a revolutionary situation such as that created during the first imperialist war? Might it not, influenced by the hopelessness of its situation, fling itself into a struggle that would offer it at least some chance of securing conditions for the further development of civilization that were somewhat unusual?
>
> "The development of the productive forces of Russia has not attained the level that makes socialism possible." All the heroes of the Second International, including, of course, Sukhanov, beat the drums about this proposition. They keep harping on this incontrovertible proposition in a thousand different keys, and think that it is the decisive criterion of our revolution.
>
> But what if the situation, which drew Russia into the imperialist world war which involved every more or less influential Western European country, and made her a witness of the eve of the revolutions maturing or partly already begun in the East, gave rise to circumstances that put Russia and her development in a position which enabled us to achieve precisely that combination of a "peasant war" with the working-class movement suggested in 1856 by no less a Marxist than Marx himself as a possible prospect for Prussia?
>
> What if the complete hopelessness of the situation, by stimulating the efforts of the workers and peasants tenfold, offered us the opportunity to create the fundamental requisites of civilization in a different way from that of the Western European countries? Has that altered the basic relations between the basic classes of all the countries that are being, or have been, drawn into the general course of world history?
>
> If a definite level of culture is required for the building of socialism (although nobody can say just what that definite "level of culture" is, for it differs in every Western European country), why cannot we begin by first achieving the prerequisites for that definite level of culture in a revolutionary way, and *then*, with the aid of the workers' and peasants' government and the Soviet system, proceed to overtake the other nations?[9]

As for the presence of material incentives on an individual basis, we recognize it though we fight against it and try to speed up its elimination by means of education. We apply it to the rules governing overtime work and to the punishment for noncompliance.

The subtle difference between the adherents of self-motivation and us on the subject consists of the arguments for paying a wage based upon rewards and punishments. The production quota is the average amount of work a

[9] V. I. Lenin, *Selected Works* (Moscow, Progress Publishers, 1967), Vol. III, pp. 776–777.

product creates in a given time, just as the average output produced by use of equipment under given conditions is the delivery of a work quota made to society by one of its members. It is the fulfillment of his social duty. If the quotas are overfulfilled, there is a greater benefit to society, and it can be assumed that the worker who creates it fulfills his duties better and therefore deserves some material reward. We accept this conception as a necessary evil in a period of transition, but we do not agree that the maxim "from each according to his capacity, to each according to his work" be interpreted as total payment (bonus pay) for the overfulfillment of a given quota. There are cases in which the pay exceeds the percentage of fulfillment so as to provide special incentives for individual productivity. Marx explains very clearly in *The Gotha Program* that a considerable part of the worker's pay is assigned to items that are far removed from the immediate account:

> Let us take the words "proceeds of labour" in the sense of the product of labour, thus the co-operative proceeds of labour is the *total social product.*
>
> But from this must be deducted: firstly: Reimbursement for the replacement of the means of production used up:
>
> Secondly: an additional portion for the extension of production.
>
> Thirdly: reserve or insurance funds to provide against misadventures, disturbances through natural events and so on.
>
> These deductions from the "whole proceeds of labour" are an economic necessity and their magnitude can be determined by existing means and forces and partly through the calculation of probabilities, but they are under no circumstances calculable by equity.
>
> There is left the other portion of the total product which is meant to serve definitely as means of consumption.
>
> But before this can go for individual consumption there has to be taken from it yet:
>
> *Firstly: the general costs of administration not appertaining to production.*
>
> This proportion will of course be considerably lessened in comparison with what it represents in society as it is at present and will diminish in proportion to the development of the new society.
>
> *Secondly: what is destined for the satisfaction of communal needs,* such as schools, health services, etc.
>
> This proportion will of course increase in comparison with the expenditure on the same objects in existing society and will grow in proportion to the development of the new society.
>
> *Thirdly: funds for those unable to work,* etc., in short, what comes under the heading of so-called official poor relief to-day.
>
> Now at last we come to the "distribution" which the programme, under the influence of Lassalle, alone has in sight with its limited outlook, to wit, the portion of the means of consumption which is divided among the individual producers of the co-operative commonwealth.

> The whole "proceeds of labour" have already changed in our hands into "part of the proceeds" even if what is taken away from the producer as a private individual is given back to him directly or indirectly in his capacity as member of the co-operative commonwealth.
>
> As the phrase "the whole proceeds of labour" disappears, so does now the phrase "the proceeds of labour."[10]

Nonfulfillment of a quota means nonfulfillment of one's social duty. Society therefore punishes the offender by deducting part of his wages. The quota is not merely a guidepost which establishes a possible measurement or convention for calculating amounts of work; it is the expression of a moral obligation on the part of the worker. It is his social duty. This is where administrative control activity must combine with ideological control. The important role of the party in the coordination of production consists of the party's function as the latter's driving force and its utilization of every type of example set by its militants so that productive work, training, and participation in the economic affairs of the unit will be an integral part of the workers' lives and turn into an irreplaceable habit.

A profound difference—at least in the strict sense of the terms employed—exists between the conception of the Law of Value (and the possibility of its deliberate use, posed by the proponents of economic forecasting), on the one hand; and on the other, the conception we have.

The Manual of Political Economy says:

"Under capitalism, the Law of Value operates like a blind spontaneous force which rules over men. By contrast, under a socialist economy there is an awareness of the Law of Value; the state keeps it in mind and *uses* it in its policies relating to the planned control of the economy.

"A knowledge of the operation of the Law of Value, and its *intelligent use*, are bound to help the heads of the economy channel production along rational lines, systematically improve work methods, and make use of untapped reserves so as to increase as well as better production."[11]

All this shows us that the amount of reserve funds depends on a series of politico-economic or politico-administrative decisions. As all existing wealth in the reserve always results from unrewarded work, we must assume that decisions regarding the funds analyzed by Marx permit changes of payment, that is variations in the volume of work that is not rewarded directly. To all this it must be added that there does not exist—if it exists, it is not known—a mathematical method for determining the "fairness" of the reward for overfulfillment. The same is true of the base salary. Therefore, it must be based fundamentally on the new social relationships—on the legal structure that authorizes the method of distribution of a part of the individual worker's labor by the community.

Our methods system has the merit that it makes professional qualifica-

[10] Karl Marx, *Critique of the Gotha Programme* (unspecified in Guevara's original, but in the 1933 International Publishers [N.Y.] edition, pp. 27–28).

[11] No source given in the original; retranslated herein.

tions obligatory for promotion from one position to another. In time this will produce a considerable rise in the level of our technology.

The words we have *underlined* indicate the spirit of the quoted paragraphs.

The Law of Value would operate as a force, which, because it is blind but known to us, is pliable or usable by man. But this law has some characteristics. First, it is conditioned by the existence of a mercantile society. Second, its results are not susceptible to *a priori* measurement and must be expressed in the market, where there is an interchange between producers and consumers. Third, it is completely coherent with respect to world markets, and changes and distortions in some branches of production are reflected in the total result. Fourth, given its character of an economic law, it operates fundamentally as a tendency, and in periods of transitions, its tendency should logically be to disappear.

A few paragraphs further on, the *Manual* states: "The socialist state uses the Law of Value by exercising, through the financial and credit system, control over production and distribution of the social product. Controlling the Law of Value and using it in accordance with a plan represent an enormous advantage socialism has over capitalism. Thanks to control over this law, its operation in the socialist economy does not entail the squandering of social labor that is inseparable from the anarchy that characterizes production under capitalism.

The Law of Value and the elements related to it—money, prices, trade, credit, finances—are successfully utilized by the U.S.S.R., and countries under people's democracy, in the interests of establishing socialism and communism. They are utilized by them in national economic planning too."[12]

This can only be considered exact with regard to the total amount of values produced for the direct use of the people and to the respective funds available for their acquisition—something any capitalist minister of finance could accomplish with relatively balanced finances. Within this framework every partial distortion of the law is possible.

Further on, the author states:

"Production for profit, the Law of Value, and money will disappear only when the higher stage of communism is reached. But in order to create the conditions which can make possible the elimination of production for profit and the circulation of money when the higher stage of communism is reached, it is necessary to *develop* and use the Law of Value as well as the monetary and commercial relationships while a communist society is being established."[13]

Why *develop?* We can understand that for a certain time the categories of capitalism will be retained and that this period of time cannot be ascer-

[12] *Ibid.*
[13] *Ibid.*

tained beforehand, but the characteristics of the period of transition are those of a society which is eliminating its old ties in order to rapidly enter a new era. The tendency should be, in our opinion, to eliminate the old categories as vigorously as possible. These include the market, money, and consequently the motive force of material incentives, or rather, the conditions which bring the categories into being. For it to be otherwise would lead to the assumption that the task of creating a socialist society in a backward one is in the nature of a historical accident and that its leaders, in order to excuse the *error*, should devote themselves to consolidating all categories belonging to the intermediate society. All that would remain would be the distribution of income in accordance with work and the tendency to eliminate man's exploitation of man, as fundamentals of the new society. This seems sufficient in itself as a factor in the development of the gigantic change of conscience that is necessary in order to be able to face the transition. The change must occur as the result of the multifaceted action of all the new relationships, education, and socialist morality. It must replace the individualistic conception that direct material incentives instill in the minds of men, checking man's development as a social being.

We shall now summarize the ways in which we differ. We believe the Law of Value still exists, in part due to the remains of the mercantile society, which is still reflected in the governmental supplier and the consumer. We believe that, particularly in a society like ours with highly developed foreign trade, the Law of Value on an international scale must be recognized as a fact that governs business transactions even within the socialist block. We recognize the necessity for this trade to assume a higher form now in the countries of the new society. By interchange we must avoid the widening of the differences between the developed countries and the more backward ones. In other words, it is necessary to find ways of trading that permit the financing of industrial investments in the developing countries, even if this violates the existing price systems in the capitalist world market. This will permit the more even advancement of the whole socialist block, and it will have the natural consequences of smoothing the rough spots and bringing greater cohesion to the spirit of proletarian internationalism. The recent agreement between the U.S.S.R. and Cuba is a sample of the steps that can be taken in this direction.

We deny the possibility of the deliberate use of the Law of Value, and we base our opinion on the nonexistence of a free market, which automatically expresses the contradiction between producers and consumers. We deny the existence of the category *goods* in the relationships among state enterprises, and we consider all such establishments to be part of the single great enterprise that is the state (although in practice this is still not the case in our country). The Law of Value and planning are two terms that are linked by a contradiction and its resolution. We can therefore state that centralized planning is the way of life in a socialist society. It is what defines it and is the point at which man's mind succeeds in finally synthesizing and directing the economy toward its goal, which is the complete liberation of the human being within the framework of communist society.

There still are profound differences between us with respect to the theory of the establishment of prices. In self-management, prices are established "in accordance with the Law of Value," but there is no explanation (as far as we know) of which expression of the Law of Value is applied. The principle of socially necessary work in the production of a given article is recognized. However, no attention is paid to the fact that socially necessary work is an economico-historic concept and that it is therefore changeable on the local or national level as well as the international one. The continual advances in technology, the consequence of competition in the competitive capitalist world, decrease the expenditure of necessary work, and therefore, the value of the product.

A closed society can ignore changes for a specified time, but it will always have to return to these international relationships in order to establish their value. If a particular society remains ignorant of these changes for a long time, without developing new and exact methods to replace the old ones, it will create inner interconnections that shape their own value scheme. This scheme will be consistent within itself, but contrary to the tendencies of the most highly developed technology. Such is the case of steel and plastics. This can cause relative backwardness of some importance, and in any case, distortions of the Law of Value on an international scale, which will make it impossible to compare economies.

The "circulation tax" is an accounting fiction by means of which certain income levels of enterprises are maintained by making products more expensive for the consumer in such a way that supply is made level with the amount of solvent demand. We believe that it is an imposition of the system but not an absolute necessity, and we are working on methods that take all these aspects into account.

We consider an over-all stabilization of the mercantile fund and solvent demand necessary. The Ministry of Internal Commerce would be in charge of equalizing the purchasing power of the people and the prices of the goods offered, always bearing in mind that a whole series of articles that are basic necessities for man should be offered at low prices. This, even though in the case of other less important articles excessively high prices are charged with a manifest ignorance of the Law of Value in each specific instance.

Thus a serious problem arises. What criterion for the establishment of real prices should the economy employ in its analysis of production relationships? It could be analysis of the amount of work necessary in terms of Cuba. This would bring immediate distortions and a loss of vision with respect to world problems, because of the necessary automatic interrelationships that would be created. On the other hand, the world price could be employed. This would cause a loss of vision with respect to domestic problems, since in no branch of industry is our work on a level of productivity acceptable by world standards.

We suggest, as a first approach to the problem, that consideration be given to price indexes based on the following:

All imported raw materials will have a fixed, stable price, based upon an average international market price plus a few points to cover the cost of transportation and the facilities of the Ministry of Foreign Commerce. All Cuban raw materials would have the price of their real cost of production in terms of money. To each group of raw materials we would assign the estimated labor costs plus depreciation of the basic means for producing them. That would be the price of the products supplied by one enterprise to another and to the domestic market. But prices would constantly be affected by the indexes that express the price of the articles in the world market plus the costs of transportation and of the Ministry of Foreign Trade. Those enterprises that operate under the system of budgetary financing would operate on the basis of estimated costs and would not make any profit. All profit would be made by MINCIN.[14] Naturally, this refers to that part of the social product that is created in the form of goods, and it is fundamental as the basis of consumption. The indexes will tell us—the central agency and the enterprise, that is—what our real assets are and would prevent our making wrong decisions. The people would in no way suffer as a result of all these changes, since the prices of the goods they purchase are independently fixed, with an eye to demand and the vital necessity of each product.

For example, in order to calculate the amount of an investment we would calculate the amount for raw material and directly imported equipment, the expense of the construction and installation of equipment, and the cost of planned salaries. We would allow for real contingencies and a certain margin for the cost of the construction equipment. This could give us, as the investment was completed, three figures: first, the real cost of the operation in money; second, what the operation should have cost according to our plans; third, what it should cost in terms of world production. The difference between the first and the second would be charged to the inefficiency of the construction equipment. The difference between the second and the third would be the index of our lag in the sector involved.

This permits us to make fundamental decisions concerning the use of other materials such as cement, iron, plastics; roofs made of fibercement, aluminum, or zinc; iron, lead, or copper piping; wood, iron, aluminum, or other types of windows.

All decisions could depart from the mathematical optimum when there were political reasons, reasons relating to foreign trade, etc., but we would always have before our eyes a reflection of the real response of the world to our work. Prices will never be separate from their world levels, which will fluctuate in certain years in accordance with technological advances. They

[14] Ministry of Internal Commerce (ed.).

will also fluctuate where the socialist market and the international division of labor will have greater and greater preeminence, once a world socialist price system that is more logical than the one used at present is achieved.

We could go on expatiating on this very interesting subject, but it is preferable to outline a few primary ideas here and explain that all this requires subsequent elaboration.

With regard to collective rewards for the management of the enterprise, we wish to refer first of all to the experiments described by Fikriat Tabeiev, "Investigación económica y dirección de la economía" in No. 11, 1963 of the *Revista Internacional*,[15] where he says:

> What then shall the fundamental and decisive index for evaluating the work of the enterprises be? Economic research has led to several proposals in this regard.
>
> Some economists propose as the index the standard of accumulation; others, the cost of labor, etc. The Soviet press has expressed in its pages the broad discussion aroused by an article by Professor Liberman, in which he proposes as the fundamental exponent of the work of the enterprise the income level, the standard of accumulation, and profit. We believe that, in judging the operation of an enterprise, it is necessary above all to bear in mind the contribution made by the personnel of the same to the particular product involved. This, which in the final analysis does not rule out the struggle for sufficiently high income, permits better concentration of the enterprise's personnel on perfecting the productive process.
>
> The social organizations of Tartary have proposed the standard of value of the manufacturing process of each part of the article manufactured. In order to demonstrate the possibility of putting this proposal into practice, an economic experiment has been conducted. In 1962 the standards of value of the manufacturing process for production at all branches of Tartary's industry were designated and approved. This year constituted a transition period during which the new index was used in planning, in conjunction with the index of over-all production. The index based upon the standard of value of the manufacturing process expresses technically justified expenses in which are included the salaries and bonuses received by the workers, in addition to plant expenses and those of the entire factory with regard to the production of each article.
>
> It is necessary to point out that the application of this index has nothing to do with the "infernal" accounting systems used in capitalist countries. We are consistently orienting ourselves toward rational organization of work processes rather than intensification of work on a disproportionate scale. All work devoted to establishment of work standards is done with the direct participation of the personnel of the enterprises and social organizations, particularly unions.
>
> Unlike the index of over-all production, the standard of value of the

[15] This article was not carried in the English edition, thus the quotes herein have been retranslated (ed.).

manufacturing process does not include the vast majority of material expenses—prior work built into the product by other enterprises—nor does it include profit. In other words it does not include those components of the value of the over-all mercantile production which diminish the value of the true volume of the enterprise's production.

As a truer reflection of the work invested in the manufacture of each article, the index that expresses the standard of value of the manufacturing process permits more exact identification of the operations relating to increased yield, lowered costs, and profit from the product in question. This index is also the one best suited from the point of view of planning within the factory and organization of economic forecasting within the enterprise. Moreover, it permits comparison with labor's productivity in related enterprises.

We think this Soviet experiment is very worth studying and is consistent, in some respects, with our thesis.

In order to summarize our ideas on the budgetary system of financing, we should begin by explaining that it is a total concept. Its objective operation would begin when it entered into all aspects of the economy, in a single whole that, starting with political decisions and going through JUCEPLAN,[16] would reach the enterprises and units through ministerial channels. There it would merge with the people, to return to the organ of policymaking, thus describing a gigantic even circle. Within the circle certain production rates could change more or less automatically, because production controls would permit it.

The ministries would have the specific responsibility of drawing up and supervising the plans—something the enterprises and units would also do—in accordance with levels of decision that could be more or less elastic. The degree of flexibility would depend on the organizational thoroughness that has been attained, the type of production, and the period involved. JUCEPLAN would be responsible for the over-all central controls of the economy and would be assisted in its function by the Ministry of Finance (in all financial control) and by the Ministry of Labor (in planning related to the work force).

As all this does not happen at present, we shall describe our present situation, with all its limitations and small triumphs. We shall also describe its defeats—some of them justified or justifiable, some the product of our inexperience, and others the result of our gross failings.

JUCEPLAN provides only the general outlines of the plan and the control figures for those products that are designated as basic, and over which it keeps a more or less strict control. The central organizations, among which we include the Ministry of Industry, exercise control over so-called centralized products by means of an agreement with the various

[16] Junta Central de Planificación, the central planning board (ed.).

enterprises. Once the plan is established and made compatible, contracts are signed—sometimes this is done on a preliminary basis—and work begins.

The central office of the Ministry is responsible for insuring the filling of production quotas at the enterprise level. The enterprise is responsible for insuring the filling of quotas at the unit level. The main thing is that the accounting system be consolidated at these two points: the enterprise and the Ministry. The basic means of production and the inventories should be controlled from a central point so that those resources that, because of certain circumstances, remain idle at any particular unit can be moved easily to any other. The Ministry also has authority to move the basic means of production from one enterprise to another. The funds do not have a commercial character. They are merely entered on the books as debits or credits. Part of production is delivered directly to the people through MINCIN, and part to the units that produce other articles for which ours are intermediate products.

Our fundamental concept is that in this entire process the product keeps acquiring value because of the work that goes into it. However, there is no need of commercial relationships; the contracts covering delivery and the corresponding purchase orders—or the document which must be requested at any particular step—only mean that one has fulfilled his duty to produce and deliver a particular product. Acceptance of an article on the part of an enterprise would mean (in somewhat idealistic terms at present, one must recognize) acceptance of the quality of the product. The latter becomes merchandise when there is a legal change of ownership—when it is consumed by an individual. The means of production for other enterprises do not constitute merchandise, but a value must be placed on them in accordance with the indexes that we suggested earlier. There must be a comparison with the amount of work necessary to fill the quota assigned to consumption, so as to be able to establish the price of the basic means or raw material involved.

Quality, quantity, and variety should be achieved in accordance with quarterly plans. The unit, in accordance with its work quotas, would pay the workers their wages directly. We have omitted one of the points that have not been covered yet: the method of rewarding the workers of a unit as a group for any particularly brilliant performance or performance more brilliant than the average of the economy as a whole. Nor have we touched on the matter of whether or not to punish other factories, which have been incapable of adequately doing their part.

What is happening today? One of the most serious things happening is that the factory never receives supplies in the manner or at the time required. Thus it does not carry out its production plans. But what is worse is that in many cases it receives raw materials for some other manufacturing process. This leads to technological changes, which incur direct production costs beyond those related to manpower and investment, in some cases. They often undo every plan and thus force frequent changes.

At the present time, at the ministerial level, we have had to be merely passive toward these irregularities or function as recorders of the same. But we are entering a phase in which we shall be able to take action with respect to certain aspects of the plan, at least so as to be able to require that any distortion of the plan be foreseen mathematically and thus be controlled. We still do not have the automatic devices necessary to insure that all controls are maintained accurately and that indexes can be analyzed. We do not have sufficient analytical capacity. Nor do we have sufficient ability to furnish indexes or correct figures for interpretation.

The enterprises are in direct communication with the factories, sometimes by telephone or telegraph or through some provincial delegate. In other instances communication is through the Ministry's delegations, who exercise control. In the municipalities or economico-political places of this type, the so-called CILOS, which are nothing but an assembly of unit administrators responsible for analyzing unit problems and deciding about minor mutual assistance involving considerable bureaucratic red tape. In some cases they can lend basic means of production, but it must always be taken into account that it is necessary to consult with the particular enterprise before final transfers of equipment can be made.

At the beginning of each month production statistics are sent to the ministry, where they are analyzed at even the highest levels, and basic measures are taken to correct defects. During the days following, other more elaborate statistics are furnished, which also permit the taking of concrete measures at different levels in order to solve problems.

What are the fundamental weaknesses of the system? We believe that its immaturity must take first place. In the second place there is the scarcity of cadres who are really qualified at all levels. In the third place there is a lack of complete dissemination of the entire system with its devices for making the people understand it better. We can also cite the lack of a central planning agency that can function uniformly and with an absolutely hierarchical order. This could facilitate the work. We shall cite the shortcomings of supply, materials, and transport. At times these shortcomings compel us to accumulate products. Sometimes they prevent us from producing. There are shortcomings in all our resources relating to quality control and to our relationships with distribution organizations, particularly MINCIN. Actually these relationships should be very close, very harmonious, and very closely defined. There are shortcomings in our relationships with some supply organizations, particularly MINCEX[17] and INRA.[18] It is still difficult to specify which shortcomings are the result of weaknesses inherent in the system and which others are due substantially to our present degree of organization.

[17] Ministry of External (Foreign) Commerce (ed.).
[18] Agrarian Reform Institute (ed.).

Neither the factory nor the enterprise at this time has any material incentives of a collective nature, which is due not to any central idea of the whole scheme but to our not having achieved sufficiently thorough organization till now to permit us to provide incentives on some basis other than the simple execution or nonexecution of the enterprise's main plans. The reason is the one we have already indicated.

The system is accused of a tendency toward bureaucracy, and one of the points on which we must constantly insist has to do with placing the entire administrative setup on a rational basis so as to reduce this bureaucracy to the minimum. Well then, from the point of view of objective analysis, it is evident that much less bureaucracy will exist if we can provide greater centralization in the recording of information and control of the enterprise and the unit. In this way, if each enterprise could centralize all its administrative activities, its bureaucracy could be reduced at the unit level to a small managerial nucleus and a collector of information to be passed on to the central organization.

Although this is impossible at the present time, we have to proceed with the establishment of units of optimum size. This is something which is very much facilitated by the system if we establish work regulations calling for one single salary level so as to demolish the narrow ideas about the enterprise as a center of individual action and orient ourselves more in the direction of society as a whole.

In our opinion, this system has the following advantages:

First, in tending toward centralization it tends toward a more rational utilization of national funds.

Second, it tends toward greater rationality in the entire administrative setup of the state.

Third, this same tendency toward centralization makes obligatory the creation of larger units, within proper limits, that save manpower and increase the workers' productivity.

Fourth, once it is integrated into a single system of quotas it makes one great government enterprise of the ministry, to name an example, and of all ministries, if possible. Within this enterprise there can be movement from one part to another and advancement within the various branches or elsewhere, without salary problems. Wages will simply conform to a national pay scale.

Fifth, with building organizations provided for in a budget, there can be considerable simplification of the control of investments. The contracting investor will look after the physical assets, and the Ministry of Finance will provide the financial supervision.

It is important to point out that we are instilling in the worker the general idea of cooperation among all, the idea of belonging to a large aggregate which is the people of the country. We are promoting the development of his awareness of his social duty.

The following quotation from Marx is interesting, because stripped of the words that presuppose the capitalist system, it explains the process of the formation of work traditions, and on that account can provide us with a background for the creation of a socialist society:

> . . . It is not a case of two independent forces working on one another. Les dés sont pipés. Capital works on both sides at the same time. If its accumulation, on the one hand, increases the demand for labour, it increases on the other the supply of labourers by the "setting free" of them, whilst at the same time the pressure of the unemployed labour, and therefore makes the supply of labour, to a certain extent, independent of the supply of labourers. The action of the law of supply and demand of labour on this basis completes the despotism of capital. As soon, therefore, as the labourers learn the secret, how it comes to pass that in the same measure as they work more, as they produce more wealth for others, and as the productive power of their labour increases, so in the same measure even their function as a means of the self-expansion of capital becomes more and more precarious for them; as soon as they discover that the degree of intensity of the competition among themselves depends wholly on the pressure of the relative surplus-population; as soon as, by Trades' Unions, etc., they try to organise a regular co-operation between employed and unemployed in order to destroy or to weaken the ruinous effects of this natural law of capitalistic production on their class, so soon capital and its sycophant, political economy, cry out at the infringement of the "eternal" and so to say "sacred" law of supply and demand. Every combination of employed and unemployed disturbs the "harmonious" action of this law. But, on the other hand, as soon as (in the colonies, *e.g.*) adverse circumstances prevent the creation of an industrial reserve army and, with it, the absolute dependence of the working class upon the capitalist class, capital, along with its commonplace Sancho Panza, rebels against the "sacred" law of supply and demand, and tries to check its inconvenient action by forcible means and State interference.[19]

The forces of production are developing and production relationships are changing. Everything awaits the direct impact of the worker's state on the people's consciousness.

As for material incentives, what we want to achieve with this system is the changing of the lever into something that forces the individual, as an individual, or forces the group to struggle desperately along with others in order to insure certain production or distribution conditions which will place him in a privileged position. We must make social duty the fundamental basis for all of the worker's labor, but we must watch his labor with an awareness of his weaknesses. We must reward or punish by applying material incentives or deterrents of an individual or collective type accord-

[19] Karl Marx, *Capital* (New York, International Publishers, 1947), Vol. I, pp. 654–655. (In the original, Che eliminated the French phrases and esoteric references.)

ing to whether the worker or the production unit is able to do his social duty. Moreover, compulsory training as a requirement for promotion, when we can put it into practice on a national scale, can stimulate a general interest in study on the part of the entire mass of the nation's workers. We refer to training without limitation by any local situation, since the work area is the entire country, and this therefore stimulates a very great tendency toward technical perfection.

We must also consider the fact that, through a policy of subsidies, student workers being trained for other more interesting jobs can easily withdraw from work. They can go to other parts of the country to establish factories with a greater productive capacity that is more in accord with the central idea of passing over into communism, the form of society with large-scale production and the satisfaction of man's basic needs.

It remains for us to stress the educational role the party must play in the transformation of the work center into the collective expression of the aspirations of the workers and of their concerns—into the place where their desire to serve society is molded.

We may also suppose that the work center will be the basis of the political nucleus of the future society, whose suggestions, when transferred to more complex political organizations, will permit the party and the government to make the fundamental decisions for the economy and the cultural life of the individual.

CHAPTER 25

On Development[1]

THE delegation of Cuba, an island nation situated at the mouth of the Gulf of Mexico in the Caribbean Sea, is addressing you. It addresses you under the protection of its rights, on many grounds, to come to this forum and proclaim the truth about itself. It addresses you first of all, as a country that is building socialism; as a country belonging to the group of Latin American nations, even though decisions contrary to law have temporarily severed it from the regional organization, owing to the pressure exerted and the action taken by the United States of America. Its geographical position indicates it is an underdeveloped country that addresses you, one which has borne the scars of colonialist and imperial exploitation and which knows from bitter experience the subjection of its markets and its entire economy, or what amounts to the same thing, the subjection of its entire governmental machinery to a foreign power. Cuba also addresses you as a country under attack.

All these features have given our country a prominent place in the news throughout the world, in spite of its small size, its limited economic importance, and its meager population.

At this conference, Cuba will express its views from the various standpoints which reflect its special situation in the world, but it will base its analysis on its most important and positive attribute: that of a country which is building socialism. As an underdeveloped Latin American country, it will support the main demands of its fraternal countries, and as a country under attack it will denounce from the very outset all the machinations set in train by the coercive apparatus of that imperial power, the United States of America.

We preface our statement with these words of explanation because our

[1] Speech delivered March 25, 1964 at the plenary session of the United Nations Conference on Trade and Development (UNCTAD) at Geneva, Switzerland, at which Guevara headed the Cuban delegation. Official Cuban Government translation.

country considers it imperative to define accurately the scope of the conference, its meaning, and its possible importance.

We come to this meeting seventeen years after the Havana Conference, where the intention was to create a world order that suited the competitive interests of the imperialist powers. Although Cuba was the site of that Conference, our revolutionary government does not consider itself bound in the slightest by the role then played by a government subordinated to imperialist interests, nor by the content or scope of the so-called Havana Charter.

At that conference, and at the previous meeting at Bretton Woods, a group of international bodies were set up whose activities have been harmful to the interests of the dependent countries of the contemporary world. And even though the United States of America did not ratify the Havana Charter because it considered it too "daring," the various international credit and financial bodies and the General Agreement on Tariffs and Trade which were the tangible outcome of those two meetings, have proved to be effective weapons for defending its interests, and what is more, weapons for attacking our countries.

These are subjects which we must deal with at length later on.

Today the conference agenda is broader and more realistic because it includes, among others, three of the crucial problems facing the modern world: the relations between the camp of the socialist countries and that of the developed capitalist countries; the relations between the underdeveloped countries and the developed capitalist powers; and the great problem of development for the dependent world.

The participants at this new meeting far outnumber those who met at Havana in 1947. Nevertheless, we cannot say with complete accuracy that this is the forum of the peoples of the world. The result of the strange legal interpretations which certain powers still use with impunity is that countries of great importance in the world are missing from this meeting: for example the People's Republic of China, the sole lawful representative of the most populous nation on earth, whose seats are occupied by a delegation which falsely claims to represent that nation, and which, to add to the anomaly, even enjoys the right of veto in the United Nations.

It should also be noted that delegations representing the Democratic Republic of Korea and the Democratic Republic of Vietnam, the genuine governments of those nations, are absent, while representatives of the governments of the southern parts of both those divided states are present; and to add to the absurdity of the situation, while the German Democratic Republic is unjustly excluded, the Federal Republic of Germany is attending this conference and is given a Vice Presidency. And while the socialist republics I mentioned are not represented here, the government of the Union of South Africa, which violates the Charter of the United Nations by the inhuman and fascist policy of *apartheid* embodied in its national laws, and which defies the United Nations by refusing to transmit information on the territories which it holds in trust, makes bold to occupy a seat in this hall.

Because of these anomalies the conference cannot be defined as the forum of the world's peoples. It is our duty to point this out and draw it to the attention of the participants, because so long as this situation persists, and justice remains the tool of a few powerful interests, legal interpretations will continue to be made to suit the convenience of the oppressor powers and it will be difficult to relax the prevailing tension: a situation which entails real dangers for mankind. We also stress these facts in order to call attention to the responsibilities incumbent upon us and to the consequences that may result from the decisions taken here. A single moment of weakness, wavering, or compromise may discredit us in the eyes of history, just as we, the member states of the United Nations, are in a sense accomplices and bear on our hands the blood of Patrice Lumumba, Prime Minister of the Congolese, who was wretchedly murdered at a time when United Nations troops were presumably guaranteeing the stability of his regime. What is worse, those troops had been expressly requested by the martyr, Patrice Lumumba.

Events of such gravity, or other similar events, or those which have negative implications for international relations and which jeopardize our prestige as sovereign nations, must not be allowed to happen at this conference.

We live in a world that is deeply and antagonistically divided into groupings of nations very dissimilar in economic, social, and political outlook. In this world of contradictions, the one existing between the socialist countries and the developed capitalist countries is spoken of as the fundamental contradiction of our time. The fact that the cold war, conceived by the warmongering West, has shown itself lacking in practical effectiveness and in political realism is one of the factors that have led to the convening of this conference. But while that is the most important contradiction, it is nevertheless not the only one; there is also the contradiction between the developed capitalist countries and the world's underdeveloped nations; and at this Conference on Trade and Development, the contradictions existing between these groups of nations are also of fundamental importance. In addition there is the inherent contradiction between the various developed capitalist countries, which struggle unceasingly among themselves to divide up the world and to gain a firm hold on its markets so that they may enjoy an extensive development based, unfortunately, on the hunger and exploitation of the dependent world.

These contradictions are important; they reflect the realities of the world today, and they give rise to the danger of new conflagrations, which, in the atomic age, could spread throughout the world.

If at this egalitarian conference, where all nations can express, through their votes the hopes of their peoples, a solution satisfactory to the majority can be reached, a unique step will have been taken in the history of the world. However, there are many forces at work to prevent this from happening. The responsibility for the decisions to be taken devolves upon the representatives of the underdeveloped peoples. If all the peoples who live under precarious economic conditions, and who depend on foreign powers for some vital aspects of their economy and for their economic and social structure, are capable of resisting the temptations, offered coldly although in the heat of the moment, and impose a new type of relationship here, mankind will have taken a step forward.

If, on the other hand, the groups of underdeveloped countries, lured by the siren song of the vested interests of the developed powers which exploit their backwardness, contend futilely among themselves for the crumbs from the tables of the world's mighty, and break the ranks of numerically superior forces; or if they are not capable of insisting on clear agreements, free from escape clauses open to capricious interpretations; of if they rest content with agreements that can simply be violated at will by the mighty, our efforts will have been to no avail, and the long deliberations at this conference will result in nothing more than innocuous files in which the international bureaucracy will zealously guard the tons of printed paper and kilometers of magnetic tape recording the opinions expressed by the participants. And the world will remain as it is.

Such is the nature of this conference. It will have to deal not only with the problems involved in the domination of markets and the deterioration in the terms of trade but also with the main reason for this state of world affairs: the subordination of the national economies of the dependent countries to other more developed countries, which, through investment, hold sway over the main sectors of their economies.

It must be clearly understood, and we say it in all frankness, that the only way to solve the problems now besetting mankind is to eliminate completely the exploitation of dependent countries by developed capitalist countries, with all the consequences that this implies. We have come here fully aware that what is involved is a discussion between the representatives of countries which have put an end to the exploitation of man by man, of countries which maintain such exploitation as their working philosophy, and of the majority group of the exploited countries. We must begin our discussion by acknowledging the truth of the above statements.

Even when our convictions are so firm that no arguments can change them, we are ready to join in constructive debate in a setting of peaceful coexistence between countries with different political, economic, and social systems. The difficulty lies in making sure that we all know how much we can hope to get without having to take it by force, and where to yield a privilege before it is inevitably wrung from us by force. The conference has to proceed along this difficult, narrow road; if we stray, we shall find ourselves on barren ground.

We announced at the beginning of this statement that Cuba would speak here also as a country under attack. The latest developments, which have made our country the target of imperialist wrath and the object of every conceivable kind of repression and violation of international law, from before the time of Playa Girón till now, are known to all. It was no accident that Cuba was the main scene of one of the incidents that have most gravely endangered world peace, as a result of legitimate action taken by Cuba in exercise of its right to adopt the principles of its own people.

Acts of aggression by the United States against Cuba began virtually as soon as the Revolution had been won. In the first stage they took the form of direct attacks on Cuban centers of production.

Later, these acts took the form of measures aimed at paralyzing the Cuban economy; about the middle of 1960 an attempt was made to deprive Cuba of the fuel needed to operate her industries, transport, and power stations. Under pressure from the Department of State, the independent United States oil companies refused to sell petroleum to Cuba or to provide Cuba with tankers to ship it in. Shortly afterward efforts were made to deprive Cuba of the foreign exchange needed for its external trade; a cut of 700,000 short tons in the Cuban sugar quota in the United States was made by President Eisenhower on July 6, 1960, and the quota was abolished altogether on March 31, 1961, a few days after the announcement of the Alliance for Progress and a few days before Playa Girón. In an endeavor to paralyze Cuban industry by cutting off its supplies of raw materials and spare machine parts, the United States Department of Commerce issued on October 19, 1960, an order prohibiting the shipment of many products to our island. This ban on trade with Cuba was progressively intensified until on February 3, 1962, the late President Kennedy placed an embargo on all United States trade with Cuba.

After all these acts of aggression had failed, the United States went on to subject our country to economic blockade with the object of stopping trade between other countries and our own. Firstly, on January 24, 1962, the United States Treasury Department announced a ban on the importation into the United States of any article made wholly or partly from products of Cuban origin, even if it was manufactured in another country. A further step, equivalent to setting up a virtual economic blockade, was taken on February 6, 1963, when the White House issued a communiqué announcing that goods bought with United States Government funds would not be shipped in vessels flying the flag of foreign countries which had traded with Cuba after January 1, of that year. This was the beginning of the blacklist, which now includes over 150 ships belonging to countries that have not yielded to the illegal United States blockade. A further measure to obstruct Cuba's trade was taken on July 8, 1963, when the United States Treasury Department froze all Cuban property in United States territory and prohibited the transfer of dollars to or from Cuba, together with other kinds of dollar transaction carried out through third countries. Obsessed with the desire to attack us, the United States specifically excluded our country from the supposed benefits of the Trade Expansion Act. Acts of aggression have continued during the current year. On February 18, 1964, the United States announced the suspension of its aid to the United Kingdom, France, and Yugoslavia, because these countries were still trading with Cuba. Secretary of State Dean Rusk said that, "there could be no improvement in relations with Communist China while that country incited and supported acts of aggression in Southeast Asia, or in relations with Cuba while it represented a threat to the Western Hemisphere." That threat, he went on, could be ended to Washington's satisfaction only with the overthrow of the Castro regime by the Cuban people. They regarded that regime as temporary.

Cuba summons the delegation of the United States Government to say whether the actions foreshadowed by the Secretary's statement and others like it, and the incidents we have described are or are not at odds with coexistence in the world today, and whether, in the opinion of that delegation, the successive acts of economic aggression committed against our island and against other countries which trade with us are legitimate. I ask whether that attitude is or is not at odds with the principle of the organization that brings us together—that of practicing tolerance between states—and with the obligation laid by that organization upon countries that have ratified its Charter to settle their disputes by peaceful means. I ask whether that attitude is or is not at odds with the spirit of this meeting in favor of abandoning all forms of discrimination and removing the barriers between countries with different social systems and at different stages of development. And I ask this conference to pass judgement on the explanation, if the United States delegation ventures to make one. We, for our part, maintain the only position we have ever taken in the matter: We are ready to join in discussions provided that no prior conditions are imposed.

The period that has elapsed since the Havana Charter was signed has been marked by events of undeniable importance in the field of trade and economic development. In the first place we have to note the expansion of the socialist camp and the collapse of the colonial system. Many countries, covering an area of more than thirty million square kilometres and with one-third of the world's population, have chosen as their system of development the construction of the communist society, and as their working philosophy, Marxism-Leninism. Others, without directly embracing the Marxist-Leninist philosophy, have stated their intention of laying the foundations on which to build socialism. Europe, Asia, and now Africa and America, are continents shaken by the new ideas abroad in the world.

The countries in the socialist camp have developed uninterruptedly at rates of growth much faster than those of the capitalist countries in spite of having started out, as a general rule, from fairly low levels of development and of having had to withstand wars to the death and rigorous blockades.

In contrast with the surging growth of the countries in the socialist camp and the development taking place, albeit much more slowly, in the majority of the capitalist countries, is the unquestionable fact that a large proportion of the so-called underdeveloped countries are in total stagnation, and that in some of them the rate of economic growth is lower than that of population increase.

These characteristics are not fortuitous; they correspond strictly to the nature of the developed capitalist system in full expansion, which transfers to the dependent countries the most abusive and barefaced forms of exploitation.

Since the end of the last century this aggressive expansionist trend has been manifested in countless attacks on various countries on the more underdeveloped continents. Today, however, it mainly takes the form of control exercised by the developed powers over the production of and trade in raw materials in the dependent countries. In general it is shown by the dependence of a given country on a single primary commodity, which sells only in a specific market in quantities restricted to the needs of that market.

The inflow of capital from the developed countries is the prerequisite for the establishment of economic dependence. This inflow takes various forms: loans granted on onerous terms; investments that place a given country in the power of the investors; almost total technological subordination of the dependent country to the developed country; control of a country's foreign trade by the big international monopolies; and in extreme cases, the use of force as an economic weapon in support of the other forms of exploitation.

Sometimes this inflow takes very subtle forms, such as the use of international financial credit and other types of organizations. The International Monetary Fund, the International Bank for Reconstruction and Development, GATT,[2] and on the American continent, the Inter-American Development Bank are examples of international organizations placed at the service of the great capitalist colonialist powers—essentially at the service of United States imperialism. These organizations make their way into domestic economic policy, foreign trade policy, and domestic and external financial relations of all kinds.

The International Monetary Fund is the watchdog of the dollar in the capitalist camp; the International Bank for Reconstruction and Development is the instrument for the infiltration of United States capital into the underdeveloped world, and the Inter American Development Bank performs the same sorry function on the American continent. All these organizations are governed by rules and principles which are represented as safeguards of equity and reciprocity in international economic relations, whereas in reality they are merely hocus-pocus masking the subtlest kinds of instruments for the perpetuation of backwardness and exploitation. The

[2] General Agreement on Trade and Tariffs (ed.).

International Monetary Fund, which is supposed to watch over the stability of exchange rates and the liberalization of international payments, merely denies the underdeveloped countries even the slightest means of defense against the competition of invading foreign monopolies.

While launching so-called austerity programs and opposing the forms of payment necessary for the expansion of trade between countries faced with a balance of payments crisis and suffering from severe discriminatory measures in international trade, it strives desperately to save the dollar from its precarious situation, without going to the heart of the structural problems which afflict the international monetary system and which impede a more rapid expansion of world trade.

GATT, for its part, by establishing equal treatment and reciprocal concessions between developed and underdeveloped countries, helps to maintain the *status quo* and serves the interests of the former group of countries, and its machinery fails to provide the necessary means for the elimination of agricultural protectionism, subsidies, tariffs, and other obstacles to the expansion of exports from the dependent countries. Even more, it now has its so-called "Programme of Action," and by a rather suspicious coincidence, the "Kennedy Round" is just about to begin.

In order to strengthen imperialist domination, the establishment of preferential areas has been adopted as a means of exploitation and neocolonial control. We can speak in full knowledge of this, for we ourselves have suffered the effects of preferential Cuban-United States agreements which shackled our trade and placed it at the disposal of the United States monopolies.

There is no better way to show what those preferences meant for Cuba than to quote the views of Sumner Welles, the United States Ambassador, on the Reciprocal Trade Agreement which was negotiated in 1933 and signed in 1934: ". . . the Cuban Government in turn would grant us a practical monopoly of the Cuban market for American imports, the sole reservation being that in view of the fact that Great Britain was Cuba's chief customer for that portion of sugar exports which did not go to the United States, the Cuban Government would desire to concede certain advantages to a limited category of imports from Great Britain.

". . . Finally, the negotiation at this time of a reciprocal trade agreement with Cuba, along the lines above indicated, will not only revive Cuba but will give us practical control of a market we have been steadily losing for the past ten years, not only for our manufactured products but for our agricultural exports as well, notably in such categories as wheat, animal fats, meat products, rice, and potatoes [telegram from Ambassador Welles to the Secretary of State of the United States, sent on May 13, 1933 at 6 P.M. and reproduced on pages 289 and 290 of Volume V (1933) of the official publication *Foreign Relations of the United States*. The results of the so-called Reciprocal Trade Agreement confirmed the view of Ambassador Welles.

Cuba had to vend its main product, sugar, all over the world in order to obtain foreign currency with which to achieve a balance of payments with the United States, and the special tariffs which were imposed prevented producers in European countries, as well as our own national producers, from competing with those of the United States.

It is necessary only to quote a few figures to prove that it was Cuba's function to seek foreign currency all over the world for the United States. During the period 1948 to 1957, Cuba had a persistent debit balance of trade with the United States, totaling 382.7 million pesos, whereas its trade balance with the rest of the world was consistently favorable, totaling 1,274.6 million pesos. The balance of payments for the period 1948-1958 tells the story even more eloquently: Cuba had a positive balance of 543.9 million pesos in its trade with countries other than the United States, but lost this to its rich neighbor with which it had a negative balance of 952.1 million pesos, with the result that its foreign currency reserves were reduced by 408.2 million pesos.

The so-called Alliance for Progress is another clear demonstration of the fraudulent methods used by the United States to maintain false hopes among nations, while exploitation grows more acute.

When Fidel Castro, our Prime Minister, indicated at Buenos Aires in 1959, that a minimum of 3 billion dollars a year of additional external income was needed to finance a rate of development which would really reduce the enormous gap separating Latin America from the developed countries, many thought that the figure was exaggerated. At Punta del Este, however, 2 billion dollars a year was promised. Today it is recognized that merely to offset the loss caused by the deterioration in the terms of trade in 1961 (the last year for which figures are available), 30 per cent a year more than the hypothetical amount promised will be required. The paradoxical situation now is that, while the loans are either not forthcoming or are made for projects which contribute little or nothing to the industrial development of the region, increased amounts of foreign currency are being transferred to the industrialized countries. This means that the wealth created by the labor of peoples who live for the most part in conditions of backwardness, hunger, and poverty is enjoyed in United States imperialist circles. In 1961, for instance, according to ECLA[3] figures, there was an outflow of 1.735 billion dollars from Latin America, in the form of interest on foreign investments and similar payments, and of 1.456 billion dollars in payments on foreign short-term and long-term loans. If we add to this the indirect loss of purchasing power of exports (or deterioration in the terms of trade), which amounted to 2.66 billion dollars in 1961, and 400 million dollars for the flight of capital, we arrive at a total of 6.2 billion dollars, or more than three "Alliances for Progress" a year. Thus, assuming that the situation has not deteriorated further in 1964, the Latin American countries participating in the Alliance for

[3] Economic Commission on Latin America, a UN Agency (ed.).

Progress will lose directly or indirectly, during the three months of this conference, almost 1.6 billion dollars of the wealth created by the labor of their peoples. On the other hand, of the 2 billion dollars pledged for the entire year, barely half can be expected, on an optimistic estimate, to be forthcoming.

Latin America's experience of the real results of this type of "aid," which is represented as the surest and most effective means of increasing external income, better than the direct method—that of increasing the volume and value of exports, and modifying their structure—has been a lamentable one. For this very reason it may serve as a lesson for other regions and for the underdeveloped world in general. At present that region is virtually at a standstill so far as growth is concerned; it is also afflicted by inflation and unemployment, is caught up in the vicious circle of foreign indebtedness, and is racked with tensions which are sometimes discharged by armed conflict.

Cuba has drawn attention to these facts as they emerged, and has predicted the outcome, specifying that it rejected any implication in it other than that emanation from its example and its moral support; and events have proved it to be right. The Second Declaration of Havana is proving its historical validity.

These phenomena, which we have analyzed in relation to Latin America, but which are valid for the whole of the dependent world, have the effect of enabling the developed powers to maintain trade conditions that lead to a deterioration in the terms of trade between the dependent countries and the developed countries.

This aspect—one of the more obvious ones, which the capitalist propaganda machinery has been unable to conceal—is another of the factors that have led to the convening of this conference.

The deterioration in the terms of trade is quite simple in its practical effect: the underdeveloped countries must export raw materials and primary commodities in order to import the same amount of industrial goods. The problem is particularly serious in the case of the machinery and equipment which are essential to agricultural and industrial development.

We submit a short tabulation, indicating, in physical terms, the amount of primary commodities needed to import a thirty to thirty-nine horsepower tractor in the years 1955 and 1962. These figures are given merely to illustrate the problem we are considering. Obviously, there are some primary commodities for which prices have not fallen and may indeed have risen somewhat during the same period, and there may be some machinery and equipment which have not risen in relative cost as substantially as that in our example. What we give here is the general trend.

We have taken several representative countries as producers of the raw materials or primary commodities mentioned. This does not mean, however, that they are the only producers of the item or that they produce nothing else.

QUANTITY OF PRIMARY COMMODITIES NEEDED TO PURCHASE A 30–39 H.P. TRACTOR
(Commodity data: FINANCIAL STATISTICS)

COMMODITY	UNIT OF MEASUREMENT	COUNTRY	% OF NATIONAL EXPORTS WHICH THE COMMODITY REPRESENTS	1955	1962	INCREASE	PERCENTAGE INCREASE
Cocoa	Met. Tons	Ghana	67	3.06	7.14	4.08	133
Coconut oil	" "	Philippines	35	11.21	13.63	2.42	21
Coffee	" "	Brazil	46	2.38	4.79	2.41	101
Copper	" "	Rhodesia	58	4.23	5.45	1.22	28
Cotton (Karmak)	" "	United Arab Republic	71	2.11	3.41	1.30	61
Petroleum	Barrels	Venezuela	92	938	1118	180	19
Rice	Met. Tons	Burma	71	26.35	32.57	6.22	23
Rubber	" "	Malaysia	66	3.27	5.55	2.28	70
Tea	" "	Ceylon	60	1.89	2.93	1.04	55
Tobacco	" "	Turkey	26	1.77	2.90	1.13	63
Wool	" "	Uruguay	55	1.94	2.59	0.58	20

(Price: FAO/Production Yearbook)

Many underdeveloped countries, on analyzing their troubles, arrive at what seems a logical conclusion. They say that the deterioration in the terms of trade is an objective fact and the underlying cause of most of their problems and is attributable to the fall in the prices of the raw materials which they export and the rise in the prices of manufactures which they import—I refer here to world market prices. They also say, however, that if they trade with the socialist countries at the prices prevailing in those markets, the latter countries benefit from the existing state of affairs because they are generally exporters of manufactures and importers of raw materials. In all honesty, we have to recognize that this is the case, but we must also recognize that the socialist countries did not cause the present situation—they absorb barely 10 per cent of the underdeveloped countries' primary commodity exports to the rest of the world—and that, for historical reasons, they have been compelled to trade under the conditions prevailing in the world market, which is the outcome of imperialist domination over the internal economy and external markets of the dependent countries. This is not the basis on which the socialist countries organize their long-term trade with the underdeveloped countries. There are many examples to bear this out, including, in particular, Cuba. When our social structure changed and our relations with the socialist camp attained a new level of mutual trust, we did not cease to be underdeveloped, but we established a new type of relationship with the countries in that camp. The most striking example of this new relationship are the sugar price agreements we have concluded with the Soviet Union, under which that fraternal country has undertaken to purchase increasing amounts of our main product at fair and stable prices, which have already been agreed up to the year 1970.

Furthermore, we must not forget that there are underdeveloped countries in a variety of circumstances and that they maintain a variety of policies toward the socialist camp. There are some, like Cuba, which have chosen the path of socialism; there are some which are developing in a more or less capitalist manner and are beginning to produce manufactures for export; there are some which have neocolonial ties; there are some which have a virtually feudal structure; and there are others which, unfortunately, do not participate in conferences of this type because the developed countries have not granted the independence to which their people aspire. Such is the case of British Guiana, Puerto Rico, and other countries in Latin America, Africa, and Asia. Except in the first of these groups, foreign capital has made its way into these countries in one way or another, and the demands that are today being directed to the Socialist countries should be placed on the correct footing of negotiation. In some cases this means negotiation between underdeveloped and developed country; almost always, however, it means negotiation between one country subject to discrimination and another in the same situation. On many occasions these same countries demand unilateral preferential treatment from all the developed countries without exception: *i.e.*, including in this category the socialist countries. They place all kinds of obstacles in the way of direct trading with these states. There is a danger that they may seek to trade through national subsidiaries of the imperialist powers—thus giving the latter the chance of spectacular profits—by claiming that a given country is underdeveloped and therefore entitled to unilateral preferences.

If we do not want to wreck this conference, we must abide strictly by principles. We who speak for underdeveloped countries must stress the right on our side; in our case, as a socialist country, we can also speak of the discrimination that is practiced against us, not only by some developed capitalist countries but also by underdeveloped countries, which consciously or otherwise, are serving the interests of the monopoly capital that has taken over basic control of their economy.

We do not regard the existing terms of world trade as just, but this is not the only injustice that exists. There is direct expolitation of some countries by others; there is discrimination among countries by reason of differences in economic structure; and, as we already pointed out, there is the invasion of foreign capital to the point where it controls a country's economy for its own ends. To be logical, when we address requests to the developed socialist countries, we should also specify what we are going to do to end discrimination and at least specify the most obvious and dangerous forms of imperialist penetration.

We all know about the trade discrimination practiced by the leading imperialist countries against the socialist countries with the object of hampering their development. At times it has been tantamount to a real blockade, such as the almost absolute blockade maintained by United States imperialism against the German Democratic Republic, the People's Republic of China, the Democratic Republic of Korea, the Democratic Republic of Vietnam, and the Republic of Cuba. Everyone knows that that policy has failed, and that other powers which originally followed the lead of the United States have gradually parted company from it in order to secure their own profits. The failure of this policy is by now only too obvious.

Trade discrimination has also been practiced against dependent and socialist countries, the ultimate object being to ensure that the monopolies do not lose their sphere of exploitation and at the same time to strengthen the blockade of the socialist camp. This policy, too, is failing, and the question arises whether there is any point in remaining bound to foreign interests which history has condemned, or whether the time has come to break through all the obstacles to trade and expand markets in the socialist area.

The various forms of discrimination which hamper trade, and which make it easier for the imperialists to manipulate a range of primary commodities and a number of countries producing those commodities, are still being maintained. In the atomic era it is simply absurd to classify such products as copper and other minerals as strategic materials and to obstruct trade in them; yet this policy has been maintained, and is being maintained to this day. There is also talk of so-called incompatibilities between state monopoly of foreign trade and the forms of trading adopted by the capitalist countries; and on that pretext discriminatory relations, quotas, etc., are established—maneuvers in which GATT has played a dominant role under the official guise of combating unfair trade practices. Discrimination against state trading not only serves as a weapon against the socialist countries but is also designed to prevent the underdeveloped countries from adopting any of the most urgent measures needed to strengthen their negotiating position on the international market and to counteract the operations of the monopolies.

The suspension of economic aid by international agencies to countries adopting the socialist system of government is a further variation on the same theme. For the International Monetary Fund to attack bilateral payments agreements with socialist countries and impose on its weaker members a policy of opposition to this type of relations between peoples has been a common practice in recent years.

As we have already pointed out, all these discriminatory measures imposed by imperialism have the dual object of blockading the socialist camp and strengthening the exploitation of the underdeveloped countries.

It is incontrovertible that present-day prices are unfair; it is equally true that prices are conditioned by monopolist limitation of markets and by the establishment of political relationships that make free competition a term of one-sided application; free competition for the monopolies; a free fox among free chickens! Quite apart from such agreements as may emanate from this conference, the opening up of the large and growing markets of the socialist camp would help to raise the prices of raw materials. The world is hungry but lacks the money to buy food; and paradoxically, in the underdeveloped world, in the world of the hungry, possible ways of expanding food production are discouraged in order to keep prices up, in order to be able to eat. This is the inexorable law of the philosophy of plunder, which must cease to be the rule in relations between peoples.

Furthermore it would be feasible for some underdeveloped countries to export manufactured goods to the socialist countries, and even for long-term agreements to be concluded so as to enable some nations to make better use of their natural wealth and specialize in certain branches of industry that would enable them to participate in world trade as manufacturing countries. All this can be supplemented by the provision of long-term credits for the development of the industries, or branches of industry, we are considering; it must always be borne in mind, however, that certain measures in respect to relations between socialist countries and underdeveloped countries cannot be taken unilaterally.

It is a strange paradox that, while the United Nations is forecasting in its reports adverse trends in the foreign trade of the underdeveloped countries, and while Mr. Prebisch, the secretary-general of the conference, is stressing the dangers that will arise if this state of affairs persists, there is still talk of the feasibility—and in some cases, such as that of the so-called strategic materials, the necessity—of discriminating against certain states because they belong to the socialist countries' camp.

All these anomalies are possible because of the incontrovertible fact that, at the present stage of human history, the underdeveloped countries are the battleground of economic systems that belong in different eras. In some of these countries, feudalism still exists; in others a nascent, still weak *bourgeoisie* has to stand the dual pressure of imperialist interests and of its own proletariat, who are fighting for a fairer distribution of income. In the face of this dilemma a certain section of the national *bourgeoisie* in some countries have maintained their independence or have found a certain form of common action with the proletariat, while the other part has made common cause with imperialism; they have become its appendages, its agents, and have imparted the same character to the governments representing them.

We must sound a warning that this type of dependence, skillfully used, may endanger the achievement of solid progress at the conference; but we must also point out that such advantages as these governments may gain today, as the price of disunity, will be repaid with interest tomorrow, when in addition to facing the hostility of their own peoples, they will have to stand up alone to the monopolist offensive whose only law is maximum gain.

We have made a brief analysis of the causes and results of the contradictions between the socialist camp and the imperialist camp and between the camp of the exploited and that of the exploiting countries; here are two clear and present dangers to the peace of the world. It must also be pointed out, however, that the growing boom in some capitalist countries, and their inevitable expansion in search of new markets, have led to changes in the balance of forces among them and set up stresses that will need careful attention if world peace is to be preserved. It should not be forgotten that the last two world conflagrations were sparked off by clashes between developed powers that found force to be the only way out. On every hand we observe a series of phenomena which demonstrate the growing acuteness of this struggle.

This situation may involve real dangers to world peace in time to come, but now, today, it is exceedingly dangerous to the smooth progress of this very conference. There is a clear distribution of spheres of influence between the United States and other developed capitalist powers, embracing the underdeveloped continents, and in some cases, Europe as well. If these influences grow so strong as to turn the exploited countries into a field of battle waged for the benefit of the imperialist powers, the conference will have failed.

Cuba considers that, as is pointed out in the joint statement of the underdeveloped countries, the trade problems of our countries are well known and what is needed is that clear principles be adopted and practical action taken to usher in a new era for the world. We also consider that the statement of principles submitted by the U.S.S.R. and other socialist countries forms the right basis on which to start discussion, and we endorse it fully. Our country also supports the measures formulated at the meeting of experts at Brasilia, which would give coherence to the principles we advocate, and which we shall go on to expound.

Cuba wishes to make one point clear at the outset: We must not come here to plead for aid, but to demand justice; but not a justice subject to the fallacious interpretations we have so often seen prevail at international meetings; a justice which, even though the peoples cannot define it in legal terms but the desire for which is deeply rooted in spirits oppressed by generations of exploitation.

Cuba affirms that this conference must produce a definition of international trade as an appropriate tool for the speedier economic development of the underdeveloped peoples and of those subjected to discrimination, and that this definition must make for the elimination of all forms of discrimination and all differences, even those emanating from allegedly equal treatment. Treatment must be equitable, and equity, in this context, is not equality; equity is the inequality needed to enable the exploited peoples to attain an acceptable standard of living. Our task here is to lay a foundation on which a new international division of labor can be instituted by making full use of a country's entire natural resources and by raising the degree of processing of those resources until the most complex forms of manufacture can be undertaken.

In addition the new division of labor must be approached by restoring to the underdeveloped countries the traditional export markets that have been snatched from them by artificial measures for the protection and encouragement of production in the developed countries; and the underdeveloped countries must be given a fair share of future increases in consumption.

The conference will have to recommend specific methods of regulating the use of primary commodity surpluses so as to prevent their conversion into a form of subsidy for the exports of developed countries to the detriment of the traditional exports of the underdeveloped countries, or their use as an instrument for the injection of foreign capital into an underdeveloped country.

It is inconceivable that the underdeveloped countries, which are sustaining the vast losses inflicted by the deterioration in the terms of trade and which, through the steady drain of interest payments, have richly repaid the imperialist powers for the value of their investments, should have to bear the growing burden of indebtedness and repayment, while even more rightful demands go unheeded. The Cuban delegation proposes that, until such time as the prices for the underdeveloped countries' exports reach a level which will reimburse them for the losses sustained over the past decade, all payments of dividends, interest, and amortization should be suspended.

It must be made crystal clear that foreign capital investment dominating any country's economy, the deterioration in terms of trade, the control of one country's markets by another, discriminatory relations, and the use of force as an instrument of persuasion, are a danger to world trade and world peace.

This conference must also establish in plain terms the right of all peoples to unrestricted freedom of trade, and the obligation of all states signatories of the agreement emanating from the conference to refrain from restraining trade in any manner, direct or indirect.

The right of all countries freely to arrange the shipment of their goods by sea or air and to move them freely throughout the world without let or hindrance will be clearly laid down.

The application of economic measures, or the incitement to apply economic measures, used by a state to infringe the sovereign freedom of another state and to obtain from it advantages of any nature whatsoever, or to bring about the collapse of its economy, must be condemned.

In order to achieve the foregoing, the principle of self-determination embodied in the Charter of the United Nations must be fully implemented and the right of states to dispose of their own resources, to adopt the form of political and economic organization that suits them best, and to choose their own lines of development and specialization in economic activity, without incurring reprisals of any kind whatsoever, must be reaffirmed.

The conference must adopt measures for the establishment of financial, credit, and tariff bodies, whose rules are based on absolute equality and on justice and equity, to take the place of the existing bodies, which are out of date from the functional point of view and reprehensible from the standpoint of specific aims.

In order to guarantee to a people the full disposal of their resources, it is necessary to condemn the existence of foreign bases, the presence, temporary or otherwise, of foreign troops in a country without its consent, and the maintenance of colonialism by a few developed capitalist powers.

For all these purposes the conference must reach agreement and lay a firm foundation for the establishment of an International Trade Organization, to be governed by the principle of the equality and universality of its members, and to possess sufficient authority to take decisions binding on all signatory states, abolishing the practice of barring such forums to countries which have won their liberation since the establishment of the United Nations and whose social systems are not to the liking of some of the mighty ones of this world.

Only the establishment of an organization of the type mentioned, to take the place of existing bodies that are mere props for the *status quo* and for discrimination, and not compromise formulae, which merely enable us to talk ourselves to a standstill about what we already know, will guarantee compliance with new rules of international relations and the attainment of the desired economic security.

At all relevant points, exact time-limits must be laid down for the completion of the measures decided upon.

These, gentlemen, are the most important points which the Cuban delegation wished to bring to your attention. It should be pointed out that many of the ideas which are now gaining currency upon being expressed by international bodies, in the precise analysis of the present situation of the developing countries submitted by Mr. Prebisch, the secretary-general of the conference, and many of the measures approved by other states—trading with socialist countries, obtaining credits from them, the need of basic social reforms for economic development, etc.—have been formulated and put into practice by Cuba during the revolutionary government's five years in office, and have exposed it to unjust censure and acts of economic and military aggression approved by some of the countries which now endorse those ideas.

Suffice it to recall the criticism and censure aimed at Cuba for having established trade relations and cooperation with countries outside our hemishpere, and its *de facto* exclusion, to this day, from the Latin American regional group which meets under the auspices of the Charter of Alta Gracia, namely the Organization of American States, from which Cuba is barred.

We have dealt with the basic points concerning foreign trade, the need for changes in the foreign policy of the developed countries in their relations with the underdeveloped countries, and the need to reconstruct all international credit, financial and similar bodies; but it must be emphasized that these measures are not sufficient to guarantee economic development, and that other measures—which Cuba, an underdeveloped country, has put into practice—are needed as well. As a minimum, exchange control must be established, prohibiting remittances of funds abroad or restricting them to an appreciable degree; there must be state control of foreign trade, and land reform; all natural resources must be returned to the nation; and technical education must be encouraged, together with other measures of internal reorganization which are essential to a faster rate of development.

Out of respect for the wishes of the governments represented here, Cuba has not included among the irreducible minimum measures the taking over by the state of all the means of production, but it considers that this measure would contribute to a more efficient and swifter solution to the serious problems under discussion.

And the imperialists? Will they sit with their arms crossed? No!

The system they practice is the cause of the evils from which we are suffering, but they will try to obscure the facts with spurious allegations, of which they are masters. They will try to compromise the conference and sow disunity in the camp of the exploited countries by offering them pittances.

They will try everything in an endeavor to keep in force the old international bodies which serve their ends so well, and will offer reforms lacking in depth. They will seek a way to lead the conference into a blind alley, so that it will be suspended or adjourned; they will try to rob it of importance by comparison with other meetings convened by themselves, or to see that it ends without achieving any tangible results.

They will not accept a new international trade organization; they will threaten to boycott it, and will probably do so.

They will try to show that the existing international division of labor is beneficial to all, and will refer to industrialization as a dangerous and excessive ambition.

Lastly, they will allege that the blame for underdevelopment rests with the underdeveloped.

To this we can reply that to a certain extent they are right, and they will be all the more so if we show ourselves incapable of joining together, in wholehearted determination, in a united front of victims of discrimination and exploitation.

The questions we wish to ask this assembly are these: Shall we be able to carry out the task history demands of us? Will the developed capitalist countries have the political acumen to accede to minimum demands?

If the measures here indicated cannot be adopted by this conference, and all that emerges once again is a hybrid document crammed with vague statements and escape clauses; and unless, at the very least, the economic and political barriers to trade among all regions of the world, and to international cooperation, are removed, the underdeveloped countries will continue to face increasingly difficult economic situations and world tension could mount dangerously. A world conflagration could be sparked off at any moment by the ambition of some imperialist country to destroy the socialist countries' camp, or in the not too distant future, by intractable contradictions between the capitalist countries. In addition, however, the feeling of revolt will grow stronger every day among the peoples subjected to various degrees of exploitation, and they will take up arms to gain by force the rights which reason alone has not won them.

This is happening today among the peoples of so-called Portuguese Guinea and Angola, who are fighting to free themselves from the colonial yoke, and with the people of South Vietnam who, weapons in hand, stand ready to shake off the yoke of imperialism and its puppets.

Let it be known that Cuba supports and applauds those people who, having exhausted all possibilities of a peaceful solution, have called a halt to exploitation, and that their magnificent defiance has won our militant solidarity. Having stated the essential points on which our analysis of the present situation is based, having put forward the recommendations we consider pertinent to this conference, and our views on what the future holds if no progress is made in trade relations between countries—an appropriate means of reducing tension and contributing to development—we wish to place on record our hope that the constructive discussion we spoke of will take place.

The aim of our efforts is to bring about a discussion from which everyone will gain and to rally the underdeveloped countries of the world to unity, so as to present a cohesive front. We place our hopes also in the success of this conference, and join our hopes, in friendship, to those of the world's poor, and to the countries in the socialist camp, putting all our meager powers to work for its success.

CHAPTER 26

On Creating a New Attitude[1]

I BELIEVE today, on this occasion in celebration of such significant and revolutionary action when the Ministry of Industry is so proud of having always been first in the intensification of the revolutionary conscience through collective work, work of a social and voluntary nature, it is necessary to make some preliminary consideration of what work is in socialism.

If you will allow me, I am going to "push" on you a short poem. Don't worry; it is not of my own inspiration, as they say! It is a poem, or only a few verses of a poem, of a desperate man. It is a poem written by an old poet who is approaching the end of his life, who is more than eighty years old, and who, years ago, saw the fall of the political cause defended by the Spanish Republic, who since then has continued to live in exile and who today lives in Mexico. In the last book which he published a few years ago, he has some interesting verses. He says:

> But man is a child, laborious and stupid,
> Who has turned work into tiresome toil.
> He has turned the drum stick into a hoe,
> And instead of spreading over the earth a song of happiness,
> He began to dig . . .

And further on it says, more or less, because I don't have a good memory:

> I mean that no one has been able to dig the rhythm of the sun,
> And that no one yet has cut an ear of corn with love and grace.[2]

[1] Speech delivered to a workers' rally on August 15, 1964, at the *Salón* Theatre in Havana, reproduced in *Obra Revolucionaria,* Año 1964, No. 21. Translated by Sharon Duncan Ataman.

[2] The lines quoted are from Leon Felipe's "Juegos" in *El Ciervo* (ed.).

This is precisely the attitude of a defeated man in another world, another world which we have already left behind through our attitude toward work, through our desire to return to nature, to change daily chores into a meaningful play. I quote those words because today we could tell that great desperate poet to come to Cuba to see how man, after passing through all the stages of capitalist alienation, and after being considered a beast of burden harnessed to the yoke of the exploiter, has rediscovered his way and has found his way back to play. Today in our Cuba, everyday work takes on new meaning. It is done with new happiness.

And we could invite him to our cane fields so that he might see our women cut the cane with love and grace, so that he might see the virile strength of our workers cutting the cane with love, so that he might see a new attitude toward work, so that he might see that what enslaves man is not work but rather his failure to possess the means of production. When society arrives at a certain stage in its development and is capable of initiating the harsh struggle, of destroying the oppressive power, of destroying its strong arm—the army—and of taking power, then man once again regains the old sense of happiness in work, the happiness of fulfilling a duty, of feeling himself important within the social mechanism. He becomes happy to feel himself a cog in the wheel, a cog which has its own characteristics and is necessary although not indispensable, to the production process, a conscious cog, a cog which has its own motor, and which constantly tries to push itself harder and harder to carry to a happy conclusion one of the premises of the construction of socialism—creating a sufficient quantity of consumer goods for the entire population.

And together with that, together with work which every day is fulfilling the task of creating new riches to distribute throughout the society, the man who works with that new attitude is perfecting himself.

Therefore, we say that voluntary work ought not to be viewed for the economic importance it has today for the state. Fundamentally, voluntary work is the factor that develops the conscience of the workers more than any other; and still more so when those workers carry out their work in places that are not habitual for them. Our administrative workers and technicians know the fields of Cuba and know the factories of our industry by having done voluntary work in them, at times under very difficult conditions. As a result, a new cohesion and comprehension is established between the two sectors, which the capitalist technique of production always keeps separate and in rivalry because it is part of the capitalist effort of constant division to keep a large army of unemployed, desperate people ready to fight for a crust of bread, despite all long-term goals and at times despite all principles.

Voluntary work, then, is changed into a vehicle of union and of comprehension between our administrative workers and the manual workers. It is a way of preparing the road toward a new stage of our society, a new stage of society where classes will not exist, and therefore, where there will be no difference between a manual worker and an intellectual worker, between worker and peasant.

For that reason we defend it so earnestly. For that reason we try to be faithful to the principle that the leaders should be examples of revolutionary commitment, as Fidel has so often insisted.

And we have come to this meeting also, with comrade Borrego, to receive our diplomas. This is not a childish act, and it is not an act of demagoguery; it is simply the necessary demonstration of the fact that, since we talk constantly of the imperative necessity of creating a new society to develop the country so that it can defend itself against the enormous difficulties and the great dangers which lie ahead, we can prove that we are conscious of and consistent with what we say. If so, then, we have the right to ask something more of our people.

Because the difficult days still have not passed, not even remotely—they have not passed in the matter of economy, and much less have they passed in terms of threats of foreign aggression—these are truly difficult days, but worthy of being lived through. All the underdeveloped peoples, as they are called, the exploited and dependent peoples, the people against whom the imperialists hurl blockades, monopolies and exploiting armies, extracting the last drop of richness, these people are awakening and struggling. And that struggle is a danger for us.

We are blamed for it. We are condemned in meetings of the colonial ministries. But the name of Cuba is on the lips of the revolutionaries of the entire world. The name of Cuba transcends our frontiers and has done so for some years; and not only as an example and as a hope for Latin America, but also for other regions of the world of which our country, submerged in exploitation, in ignorance, scarcely knew.

But today our whole country knows that Vietnam exists, knows that that country—first exploited, now divided—struggles with all its forces united against imperialist oppression, knows that that parallel which artificially divides the country will be only a souvenir of history within a short time.

Our country, which was ignorant of geography and scarcely had the vaguest idea of the existence of a French colony called Indochina, in the confines of Asia, in the Antipodes, today knows of all the heroic achievements of our Vietnamese brothers. And over there in Vietnam we have seen how, a few days ago, the batallion or the brigade known as "Playa Girón" intervened heroically, as the combatants in Vietnam always do. Playa Girón is a symbol for all the oppressed peoples. Playa Girón represents the first defeat of imperialism in Latin America, but it also represents one of the first defeats of imperialism on a world scale. And the countries are picking up its name.

And because of what happened in Vietnam we can be proud of the fact that that name, for us already historic, is the name of a combat brigade of heroic fighters.

And so our name and the name of our commander in chief have appeared in the presses of the whole world, and many humble people submerged in ignorance, in centuries of oppression, identify with us.

That has occurred many times on trips we have had to make because of government work. And that is our great pride, that is what repays the people for all the poverty of the blockade, for all the threats of invasion, for all the difficulties beyond the primary one of building socialism. Despite these difficulties we forge ahead, we become better every day, independent of the fact that political situations are constantly changing and the economic situation does not follow a straight ascending line, and there are waverings, good and bad years, good and bad cane harvests. Despite this, despite the material and concrete aspect of any given year, our people acquire a greater degree of conscience every single day.

And our work, our work as combatants in production, is to make our conscience develop more every day on this road along which we travel. We must do it so well that every worker loves his factory, but at the same time knowing that if the price for keeping his factory, his work, or his own life intact is to fall on his knees and beg, that he will never pay it, that such a price will never be paid by the people of Cuba.

We have come here to celebrate the awarding of communist certificates of peaceful work, of creative work. I do not know by what mental mechanism we immediately got to talk of bullets, of battles, or our decision to keep ourselves free no matter what happens. The fact is that the two are very much related: The fact is that it is our struggle which permits us today to enjoy constructive peace, and total peace is our aspiration, complete peace, the peace of all peoples who have left behind the system of exploitation, who have passed on to superior stages of society. But if someone tries to prevent Cuba's reality from being reproduced in other countries of the world, then it is permissible to forfeit peace for a moment and win peace with arms.

And this is what the Vietnamese comrades are doing. This is what they are doing day after day, no matter what the provocations, no matter that their sky is violated by Yankee planes which attack their ships, destroy their economy, bombarding it mercilessly. It is no longer a matter of a despotic giant attacking something undefendable; it is no longer a matter of the principles of centuries or even of those principles of the end of the last century, when the single mouth of the yankee cannon imposed respect and changed governments. Now the forces of the people are answering.

For a time, some of the economy of Vietnam will be destroyed. We recognize that; we know that some day it is possible that a similar attack, launched under an imagined provocation, may fall on our land. And so what if it does? One must pay any price for the right to keep our flag waving high and the right to build socialism according to the will of our people!

I would ask you, comrades, who—among you who are here—who with more right could show a certificate of communist work? [Crowd yells: Fidel] Among those who are here I said—who other than a worker who, for many years in the mountains of his native province, watched his comrades die of hunger, fighting from day to day, from moment to moment. In those days he knew neither how to read nor write, living through years of hunger and misery, seeing how imperialism, colonialism, destroyed entirely the little he was able to create, seeing his relatives die, sometimes of hunger, other times victims of enemy shrapnel. Many of you have read that history. Because of it, constructive communist work is linked to communist faith and the decision to create a better world and break down all the barriers. And among us there is no one who deserves this certificate with greater justice than comrade Noup, worthy representative of his people. [Applause and shouts of "Cuba, Vietnam, united we shall conquer," as he hands Noup his certificate of communist achievement.]

Very well, comrades, we shall say a few things about the meaning, with some numbers, of the competition which I summarize here today. The hours worked were 1,683,000. If we divide these hours into eight normal hours of work, it means that 21,037 days—that is several years of work—were done voluntarily.

Let us see another example of what a man can do, a man who indeed can cut cane with love and grace. We analyzed the record of comrade Arnet, and since our spirit is still—yes, still and for a long time—a little bit distrustful, we began to do some calculations. One thousand six hundred and seven hours, divided by eight work hours, are two hundred work days. Six months are 182 working days. That is to say that this comrade has worked much more than a working day of eight extra hours over and above his normal work. Then we decided to make an inspection. The inspection confirmed the absolute honesty of comrade Arnet; but I think he got a little angry, because he told me he was working to finish the Revolution, and not to win prizes, and the fact of whether they were more or less hours didn't matter to him at all, and that he simply dedicated those hours to the Revolution. For example, for some years now he has worked all through his vacations. He did this also because of a variety of skills he has acquired —because he already has quite a few years behind him, right? How many? Forty-nine—he works in carpentry, electricity, plumbing, mechanics, painting, in voluntary hours. What is more, it gave me great satisfaction to see that comrade Arnet is of my own mold, of those whom it hurts greatly to spend a cent. Listen to this part of the inspection data! It says: "He did the masonry and installation of two bathrooms and a shower room, painted the whole unit by himself, and to avoid expenses he considered unnecessary, refused to rent scaffolding and made it himself, using two rolls of paper as a base. On the paper rolls he put two planks, and on top of that he put a table, and on the table, a ladder, climbing up the ladder with a large paint brush on a stick, with which he was able to reach the highest part of the wall." And the whole story of the 1,600 hours that comrade worked is the same.

We know—and we know it through our own experience—that to work two hundred and forty hours is tiring. We cannot hope that all the comrades have the same efficiency, although there are some who put in around a thousand hours also: the comrade from electricity, comrade Manuel Fumero, worked nine hundred one hours. But what we want is for this to serve as an example, that more people become enthusiastic and more people contribute to the voluntary work.

And once more I say it: The economic magnitude of what is accomplished does not interest us. Definitely, all that which economically can be achieved here—lower costs, increased production—is only to be able to distribute among you, among the people in general. No one gets a cent more than the other man because of the fact that he works voluntarily. This effort is awarded to the collectivity.

But we want the effort to increase so that more people who are not capable of going the limit of the two hundred and forty hours, which means one entire month of normal work of eight hours in the semester, can also participate in voluntary work, each time accomplishing a larger task, so that a good number of hours may be worked by men in each branch. For what purpose? Again, so that each one may acquire more conscience. Of course, this is an efficacious thing for production because of what it directly signifies, and also for what it means as an example, as development of conscience.

Comrade Arnet—to tell it once more—also boasted that his factory, for entire months, had no absenteeism. Besides, the cleanliness, the maintenance in that factory is exemplary. It is very small, too. Now Comrade Arnet, because of the inveterate bad habit we have, has been acting as shop foreman some time now; so we have removed a great comrade from production and have taken some hours away from him so that he might manage the shop. I say inveterate bad habit because the task of direction is a difficult task, which must be analyzed well and which does not always correspond to the spirit, to the way of working, to the idiosyncrasies of an exemplary worker. There are great workers who cannot be great administrators, because that is a different job. Manual work is concrete; the work of direction is abstract. But naturally, since no one is arguing about merits, the only thing that interests us is that Comrade Arnet continues to constantly inspire the rest of the employees to outdo themselves. Already the comrade from electricity told me that he, this semester, is "laying" for him; I do not know if Arnet, now that he is an administrator, is going to slow his pace a little, but he already has a good contender there.

And this kind of competition is what is becoming a game. Let it improve. Let the number of workers who consciously participate in it increase every day, because each hour that is given is one conscious hour. The other hours are involved in the mechanism of social relations and are more or less unconscious hours.

For that reason we were discussing with some ministers the necessity of encouraging naturally, voluntarily, those who consider this so. We got together with Comrade Borrego, from the Ministry of Sugar Industry, with Comrade Yabur, from the Ministry of Justice, which is very good for manual labor because it already has achieved complete harmony between nonproductive work, service work, intellectual work, and productive work. Guided by the CTC, which trained and directed the Ministry, among the four of us, we composed a composite memorandum.

This memorandum is a call to other departments who want to do it, who want to participate in what can be a contest, or can become a competition among departments. Already Comrade Borrego, like a prodigal son of the Ministry of Industry, has challenged his parents and has established a tremendous threat of voluntary batallions.

The memorandum reads as follows:

On voluntary work.

"FIRST: In socialism the incessant increment of the production of material goods to assure the maximum satisfaction of the always-increasing necessities of the society requires of the workers in this undertaking their enthusiastic and dedicated participation.

SECOND: Voluntary work is the genuine expression of the communist attitude toward work in a society where the fundamental means of production belong to the society; it is the example of men who love the proletarian cause and who subordinate to that cause their moments of recreation and rest in order to unselfishly fulfill the tasks of the Revolution.

Voluntary work is a creative school of conscience. It is the endeavor realized within society and for society as an individual and collective contribution, and thus continues the intensification of conscience which allows us to accelerate the process of transition toward communism.

In order to organize voluntary work on a national scale in the departments that subscribe to this joint memorandum and the participation of all their workers, thus assuring the fulfillment of the agreements that may be adopted, and in order to exhort all the workers of the nation to become a part of the Red Battalions of voluntary work, the above-mentioned departments formulate the following proposition:

That the Red Battalions already integrated and those that will be formed in the future, based on the experience acquired during a year with favorable balance in voluntary work throughout the Red Battalions, adopt regulations relevant to their organization on the following bases:

ON VOLUNTARY WORK: Voluntary work is that which is done outside normal working hours without receiving additional economic remuneration. The work may be done within or outside one's work center.

ON THE BATTALIONS: Composition: the Battalion will be composed of the following: A chief, a responsible brigade general, and as many brigade chiefs as the Battalion has brigades. The number of members of each brigade will be determined by the nature of the work to be done or the organization of the Battalion.

CLASSIFICATION OF THE MEMBERS: Three categories will exist, as follows: a vanguard member, who will be the one who accumulates 240 hours or more in a semester; a distinguished member, the one who accumulates 160 hours in a semester; a member, the one who turns in a minimum of 80 hours.

ON THE ORGANIZATION OF WORK: Good organization of the voluntary work is the fundamental requisite of the development of this activity; therefore, the following aspects should be considered: productive agricultural or industrial work; unremunerated educational work; technical work. The category of technical work will be given to the brigade of technicians that is created at a specific time for the accomplishment of a specific task.

ON THE COMPETITION AND CONTROL OF THE BATTALIONS: Each Battalion, together with its Syndicate, will establish competition records of an individual or collective type, as much within its own Battalion as with other Battalions.

To classify the work of the Battalion, in proportion to its contribution to the development of the communist society, the strictest control over the results of the completed work will be exerted.

ON THE RECOGNITIONS: In addition to a distinctive badge, vanguard members will be given a certificate of communist work, signed by the Minister of his branch and the Secretary General of the Revolutionary CTC. The distinguished members will be awarded a diploma classifying them as such, with the indicated signatures. And the members will be awarded an accreditative diploma of such condition. All these recognitions will be awarded for each semester worked.

ON THE REGULATIONS OF THE BATTALIONS: Each Battalion, together with its Syndicate, will make up the regulations by which it will be governed, including fundamentally the following: (a) manner of entrance, (b) duties of the responsible people and members of the Battalion, (c) discipline which should be observed, (d) quality of the work, (e) divulgence of the results of the work.

The regulations will be submitted for the approval of the Revolutionary CTC to give them form, so that they will be more or less similar.

And then, it says below, like the Havana Declaration—"and with the approval of this General Assembly of Voluntary Workers, in the Salón Teatro of our Central Syndicate of Cuban Workers, the fifteenth of August, nineteen hundred and sixty-four, signed by the respective divisions: Ministry of Industry, Ministry of Sugar, Ministry of Justice, Central Syndicate of Revolutionary Cuban Workers."

Do you agree? [Applause and shouts of *"yes!"*]

A reminder, comrades: The categories of distinguished member and member are made so that other comrades may join the Battalion of voluntary workers. It is not so that you may sit back and lose your classification. You have to keep yourself there as a worker of the vanguard; we all have to. Already we have a certificate, and we shall have to continue getting them every semester within the shortest period of time.

Very well: We have acquired a great experience, we have seen the great possibility that there is for development of this kind of work; but we have also seen how the lack of interest and the lack of comprehension of the problem decrease the work.

Light Mechanics was the first branch that began with this kind of work: It had that initiative more than a year ago. Again the Light Mechanics branch is the winner. In addition, a project of that branch, the Recovery of Raw Materials, which had particular motivation, has forty-seven man hours accumulated this semester. That is if we divided the total of the hours worked by the total number of people in the project, the result would be that each of them has worked 47 voluntary hours. Of course, it is not so, because there are many who don't work and others who work much more, but these averages are very interesting and very superior, naturally, to those of all the other projects.

Now we come to the negative part of all this, the negative aspect. For example, the projects and institutes that did not obtain any communist certificate of voluntary work. And here the project directors have a lot to do with it. In some specific cases there are problems of raw materials, very serious problems, and the projects have their production very limited. But the project is made up of a number of factories: There is always work to be done, even voluntary work, to paint the factory, to keep it clean, many things. The problem is not that the workers of these projects are uninterested. The problem is that they have not been correctly motivated.

The director of the project, on one hand, and the union, on the other, have to function together as a team in order to show the masses what is to be done, and to communicate their enthusiasm, so that they, the workers, will take on voluntary work.

These projects are: machinery construction, the automator, and metals conformation. Agapito was saying—where is Agapito?—that he has brought a flock of people; he has three projects in the branch.

The consolidated project of mining also has given none, neither have the Institutes of Technological Investigations for the Development of Machinery, the Research Institute of Mining and Metallurgy, nor the Institute for the Development of the Chemical Industry.

Only one provincial delegation won the communist certificate of voluntary work. That was the Matanzas delegation, with one worker.

Among those who obtained it, the Consolidated Project of Basic Chemistry is the one that had the least: only one comrade, and he is administrative.

The total of the workers in the Ministry of Industry who attained certificates of voluntary work was 1,002. At the beginning there were nineteen hundred and some; more appeared at the end. These are the negative things. Because all is voluntary work, it is all an expression of the enthusiasm of the people. But without control we cannot build socialism, and in addition, voluntary work must be well controlled, not bureaucratically, but controlled well.

We hope that this next semester many more Red Battalions will be formed and also, in spite of the fact that we do not have the harvest where one can work and accumulate hours, that this next semester we shall have more voluntary workers who have put in the 240 hours, that is the certificate of communist work which is still in force.

We understand that with this organization we can increase the incorporation of more comrades to work. In that way we shall be able to increase our work even more. I have repeated it with insistence tonight: Our greatest necessity is to increase voluntary work for its educational value. And meanwhile, of course, we shall continue our tasks, the extremely difficult task of completing production plans, with which we always stumble upon an enormous number of problems. In only one month of the history of the Ministry of Industry has the entire Ministry fulfilled its plan of production 100 per cent. [Applause]

Why do you applaud? Only one month was it fulfilled and you applaud! What would you do if it had been fulfilled every month?

O.K. There is one interesting thing. That month in which it was fulfilled was this past month, the month of July, that is to say, a month when there was motivation to reach the goals and everybody put his shoulder to the wheel.

Once upon a time we said it was necessary to inspire that creative spirit in the workers to help the technicians and also the administrators to improve the quality of their work. It would also help to draw out all that great potential wealth, which at times is to be found in the ground and at times in our warehouses, and which we cannot put together for lack of raw materials, for lack of adequate technology, for lack of organization, and which prevents us from perfectly completing our tasks. Of course there is the imperialist blockade, and that will continue to be a problem for some time, until they get tired, or until something else occurs to them. But that should serve only the more to provide a new stimulus to our work, to inspire us to create our own work force, our own commodities as substitutes, our own technology, and to depend less and less on the capitalist area, which is not a very trustworthy area for us, because they are always subject to enormous political pressures and constantly have some problem or other.

A few days ago you saw the government of Chile, which had voted against the OAS, break off relations with us, because of pressure from the

United States or perhaps because of some internal maneuver, definitely despite the fact that it had previously maintained a correct judicial attitude. But it is a bourgeois government and besides, it is tied to the blockade decreed by imperialism.

And this can happen with one country or another. So we must have a very solid basis here, which will let us take maximum advantage of world trade but never leave us dependent on it. What I mean is that it will permit us, for example, to have relations with all the countries with whom we now have relations, and to expand them, but those relations must have nothing to do—since they cannot—with problems of conscience or problems of principles of the Revolution.

Once, some time ago, the French government was very angry with us because we supported Algeria; we recognized the Algerian government-in-arms. At that moment France was also somewhat involved in the imperialist blockade. Later the French government acquired a greater degree of understanding. Algeria was liberated; historically, it was destined to be liberated; there could be no other solution than the liberation of Algeria. And everything and everyone against the liberation was for plunging a heroic people into disgrace and for sending many French soldiers to their death. The problem was solved in the best possible way. Today Algeria and France maintain good relations; and we maintain unimprovable relations with the brother country of Algeria and also good relations with France.

But we have to be prepared not to depend on the good will of anyone. And to that end it is necessary to study, it is necessary to prepare oneself, because without an adequate technological base, our efforts, however great they may be, however heroic they may be, will not permit us to progress with sufficient rapidity.

And it is necessary, as always, to maintain that order which for a long time has been the watchword of the Young Communists: study, work, and the gun. That is, it is necessary always to preserve like three banners that motto of three words, because the three have importance every minute. And in order to be able to keep our right to live and to speak with the authority of a revolutionary country, we must have all three: work, directing the construction of socialism; study, in order to daily increase our knowledge and our capacity to act; and the gun, obviously, to defend the Revolution.

It does not matter if these are the times when the bad winds blow, when the threats increase from day to day, when the pirate attacks are unleashed against us and against other countries of the world. It does not matter if we are threatened with Johnson or Goldwater, that is to say with "Jane, or her sister"; it does not matter that every day imperialism is more aggressive. The people have decided to fight for their liberty and to keep the liberty they have won. They will not be intimidated by anything. And together we shall build a new life, together—because we are together—we here in

Cuba, in the Soviet Union, or over there in the People's Republic of China, or in Vietnam fighting in southern Asia.

For some time now imperialist aggressiveness has been increasing. But why should one not think that they are right? And they are right because it is very difficult for them to strive against all the countries about to liberate themselves. They try to bury any liberation movement in blood. Nevertheless, here in Latin America today there are at least two established movements which are fighting and which are inflicting defeat after defeat on imperialism; they are the movements of the peoples of Guatemala and Venezuela.

And what is happening in Africa? Africa, where scarcely a couple of years ago the Prime Minister of the Congo was murdered and quartered, where the North American monopolies were established and then began the battle for the Congo? Why? Because there is copper, because there are radioactive minerals, because the Congo contains extraordinarily strategic riches. For that reason they assassinated a leader who had the naïveté to believe in right, without realizing that right must be united to force. And thus he was made a martyr of his people.

But his people took up that cause. And today North American troops must go to the Congo. For what purpose? To get involved in another Vietnam, to suffer inevitably another defeat. No matter how long a time passes, the defeat will come. And the people of Africa, the Mediterranean people of Africa, today are making great extensions of territory—of an immense territory—and preparing themselves for a struggle which will be long but which will be triumphant.

And likewise in the northeast of Africa, there is a small country, rarely mentioned in cables, the so-called Portuguese Guinea. More than half of that territory is already controlled by the Liberation Forces of Guinea, and inevitably it will liberate itself, as Angola will be liberated, as Zanzibar was liberated, whom the imperialists say had the help of Cuban troops. Zanzibar is our friend, and we gave them our small bit of assistance, our fraternal assistance, our revolutionary assistance at the moment when it was necessary. And in Asia, Laos, and Vietnam, they also fight for their liberation and there, also, North American imperialism is the aggressor.

In every place where the people are liberating themselves, there is imperialism. That ought not to frighten us. There can be terrible consequences for the world if they should err; but we cannot let ourselves be frightened by the possibility that they will err. If they make a mistake, thousands of beings will die everywhere, but the responsibility will be theirs, and their people will also suffer. And when I say their people, I am at this moment thinking of what the leaders of North America must think of their people, the small elite around them who also will suffer the consequences of an atomic war.

But that should not worry us. It should not worry us whether it is

Johnson or Goldwater. We should not worry about the actions of the enemy except when they represent a general threat to world peace, and this threat ought to worry everyone in the world. But we as a country know we depend on the great strength of all the countries of the world that make up the socialist block and of the peoples who fight for their liberation, and on the strength and cohesion of our people, on the decision to fight to the last man, to the last woman, to the last human being capable of firing a gun.

That guarantee of our people is what makes imperialism know that in spite of our smallness, of our lack of physical strength to defend ourselves, they cannot toy with us.

And we can be proud of representing what we represent to the movements of the world. But without excessively boasting of ourselves, and without putting too much faith in our strength, we must know how to measure exactly the magnitude of our strength, and never allow ourselves to be provoked.

We must do what Fidel recommended a few days ago: have a cool head, one that has valor and intelligence together, but not let either of the two be greater than the other, let the two always be united. And thus we shall be able to continue holding and consolidating our position as a country which speaks to the world with its own voice and has something to say to the world, as a country which is united in a great fraternity of socialist countries, which proclaims it with pride, and which proclaims with pride—in Spanish, in Latin America, some 150 kilometers from the North American beaches—its boast of being the first country to construct socialism in Latin America.

And you, comrades, you who are the vanguard of the vanguard, who have demonstrated your spirit of sacrifice toward work, your communist spirit, your new attitude toward life, ought always to be worthy of Fidel's words, which you inserted in one of the boxes in this precinct: "What we were at a time of mortal danger, may we also learn to be in production; may we learn to be workers of Liberty or Death!"

CHAPTER 27

The Cuban Economy[1]

To write for a journal of this type is a most difficult task for a revolutionary politician who wishes to defend the views that have guided his actions and to make a cool analysis of the causes of the present state of the world which have a bearing on the stiuation in his own country. It is difficult to do this without making statements that may shock, given the extreme differences of opinion which separate us. However, I shall try. I apologize in advance if I do not make myself clear, but I do not apologize for what I intend to say.

The Paris Peace Treaty of 1898 and the Platt Amendment of 1901 were the signs under which our new Republic was born. In the first, the settlement of accounts after the war between two Powers led to the withdrawal of Spain and the intervention of the United States. On the island, which had suffered years of cruel struggle, the Cubans were only observers; they had no part in the negotiations. The second, the Platt Amendment, established the right of the United States to intervene in Cuba whenever her interests demanded it.

In May 1902 the political-military oppression of the United States was formally ended, but her monopolistic power remained. Cuba became an economic colony of the United States and this remained its main characteristic for half a century.

In a country generally laid waste the imperialists found an interesting phenomenon: a sugar industry in full capitalistic expansion.

The sugar cane has been part of the Cuban picture since the 16th century. It was brought to the island only a few years after the discovery of America; however, the slave system of exploitation kept the cultivation on

[1] Written for and at the invitation of *International Affairs* (Vol. 40, No. 4, October 1964), whose permission to reprint is herewith gratefully acknowledged. The article also appeared in Spanish in *Nuestra Industria Económica,* Año 2, No. 10, December 1964.

a subsistence level. Only with the technological innovations which converted the sugar mill into a factory, with the introduction of the railway and the abolition of slavery, did the production of sugar begin to show a considerable growth, and one which assumed extraordinary proportions under Yankee auspices.

The natural advantages of the cultivation of sugar in Cuba are obvious; but the predominant fact is that Cuba was developed as a sugar factory of the United States.

The American banks and capitalists soon controlled the commercial exploitation of sugar and, furthermore, a good share of the industrial output and of the land. In this way, a monopolistic control was established by U.S. interests in all aspects of a sugar production which soon became the predominant factor in our foreign trade, due to the rapidly developing monoproductive characteristics of the country.

Cuba became the sugar producing and exporting country *par excellence,* and if she did not develop even further in this respect, the reason is to be found in the capitalist contradictions which put a limit to a continuous expansion of the Cuban sugar industry, which depended almost entirely on American capital.

The American Government used the quota system on imports of Cuban sugar, not only to protect her own sugar industry, as demanded by her own producers, but also to make possible the unrestricted introduction into our country of American manufactured goods. The preferential treaties of the beginning of the century gave American products imported into Cuba a tariff advantage of 20 per cent over the most favoured of the nations with whom Cuba might sign trade agreements. Under these conditions of competition, and in view of the proximity of the United States, it became almost impossible for any foreign country to compete with American manufactured goods.

The U.S. quota system meant stagnation for our sugar production; during the last years the full Cuban productive capacity was rarely utilised to the full; but the preferential treatment given to Cuban sugar by the quota also meant that no other export crops could compete with it on an economic basis.

Consequently, the only two activities of our agriculture were cultivation of sugar cane and the breeding of low-quality cattle on pastures which at the same time served as reserve areas for the sugar plantation owners.

Unemployment became a constant feature of life in rural areas, resulting in the migration of agricultural workers to the cities. But industry did not develop either; only some public service undertakings under Yankee auspices (transportation, communications, electrical energy).

The lack of industry and the great part played by sugar in the economy resulted in the development of a very considerable foreign trade which bore all the characteristic marks of colonialism: primary products to the metropolis, manufactured goods to the colony. The Spanish empire had followed the same pattern, but with less ability.

Other exports were also primary products, but their proportion only reached 20 per cent. of Cuba's total exports. They were: tobacco, principally in leaves; coffee—only occasionally, due to the small production; raw copper and manganese; and, during later years, semiprocessed nickel.

Such was the picture of the Cuban economy: in effect, a monoproductive country (sugar) with one particular export and import market (the United States), and vitally dependent on its foreign trade.

Under these conditions a *bourgeoisie* dependent on imports came into being and grew to be one of the greatest obstacles to the industrialisation of the country. Only in later years did the *bourgeoisie* ally itself with American manufacturing interests, creating industries which used American equipment, raw materials, technology and a cheap native labour force. The profits of those industries went to the country of the monopolies, either to the parent companies or to the American banks which the native capitalists considered the safest place for deposits.

This twisted development brought with its great unemployment, great poverty, great parasitic strata, and the division of the working class through the appearance of a labour aristocracy made up of the workers of the imperialist enterprises, whose wages were much higher than those of the workers who sold their labour to the small native capitalists, and, naturally, infinitely higher than those of the part-time employed and totally unemployed.

The "American way of life" came to our defenceless society through the penetration of the monopolies; and the importation of luxury articles accounted for a great percentage of our trade while the sugar market stagnated and with it the possibility of acquiring precious foreign exchange. The deficit in our balance of payments became yearly greater, consuming the reserves accumulated during the Second World War.

With the exception of the two years 1950 and 1957, during which sugar prices jumped temporarily due to the war in Korea and the tense military situation in the Near East, our terms of trade showed a constant decrease during the decade following 1948. (A sad fate; only war could give the people of Cuba relative well-being.)

In that decade the flow of our exports had become stagnant and the terms of trade downward; the Cuban standard of living was bound to decline if remedial measures were not taken. And they were "taken," chiefly in the shape of budgetary increases for public works and the creation of state credit organisations to encourage private investment in industry.

Never have the state stabilisation measures recommended by the Keynesian economists been so openly employed to conceal embezzlement of public funds and the illegal enrichment of politicians and their allies. The national debt rose considerably. Expensive roads and highways were built, as well as tunnels and enormous hotels in Havana and the great towns; but none of these works was of any real economic utility nor did any of them constitute the most appropriate action to be taken in an underdeveloped country.

A number of industries were created which by their characteristics could be divided into two groups: the first consisted of factories of relatively high technical standard, the property of American enterprises which used the few credit resources of a poor and economically very underdeveloped country to increase their foreign assets; the other, of a number of factories with obsolete equipment and uneconomic methods, which from the very beginning required state protection and subsidies. It was this group that served as a means of enrichment for politicians and their capitalistic associates; they made enormous commissions on the purchases of equipment.

In 1958, Cuba had a population of 6.5 m. with a *per capita* income of about $350 (calculating the national income according to capitalist methods); the labour force comprised one third of the total population, and one fourth of it was virtually unemployed.

Although great areas of fertile land were lying waste, and rural labour was far from being fully utilised, imported foodstuffs and textile fibres of agricultural origin amounted to 28 per cent of the country's total imports. Cuba had a coefficient of 0.75 head of cattle per inhabitant, a figure exceeded only by the great cattle-breeding countries. Nevertheless, the exploitation of this great number of cattle was so inefficient that it was necessary to import cattle products.

In 1948, imports amounted to 32 per cent of the national income; 10 years later the figure had risen to 35 per cent. Exports provided 90 per cent of the total income of foreign currencies. On the other hand, profits on foreign capital transferred abroad absorbed up to 9 per cent of the foreign currency income on the trade balance.

Due to the constant deterioration of the terms of trade and the transfer of profits abroad, the Cuban trade balance showed a total deficit of $600 m. for the period 1950-58, the effect of which was to reduce the available foreign currency reserves to $70 m. This reserve represented 10 per cent of the average annual imports during the last three years.

The two main economic problems of the Cuban Revolution during its first months were unemployment and a shortage of foreign currencies. The first was an acute political problem, but the second was more dangerous, given the enormous dependence of Cuba on foreign trade.

The Revolutionary Government's economic policy was directed primarily towards solving these two problems. It is therefore appropriate to make a short analysis of the actions taken and the errors made during the first months.

The agrarian reform implied such a profound institutional change that it became immediately possible to make an effort towards the elimination of the obstacles that had prevented the utilisation of human and natural resources in the past.

Because of the predominant part which had been played by the *latifundia* in agricultural production, and the enormous size of the sugar cane plantations organised along capitalistic lines, it was relatively easy to convert this type of rural property into state farms and co-operatives of considerable size. Cuba thus avoided the slow-moving development characteristic of other agrarian revolutions: the division of land into a fantastic number of small farms, followed by the grouping of such small units to enable more modern techniques, feasible only on certain levels of production, to be applied.

What was the economic policy followed in agriculture after the transfer of the large estates? As a natural part of this process, rural unemployment disappeared and the main efforts were directed towards self-sufficiency as regards the greater part of foodstuffs and raw materials of vegetable or animal origin. The trend in the development of agriculture can be defined in one word: diversification. In its agricultural policy the Revolution represented the antithesis of what had existed during the years of dependence on imperialism and of exploitation by the land-owning class. Diversification versus monoculture; full employment versus idle hands; these were the major transformations in the rural areas during those years.

It is well known that, nevertheless, serious agricultural problems immediately arose, and these have only begun to be solved during recent months. How can we explain the relative scarcity of some agricultural products, and particularly the decline in sugar production, when the Revolution began by incorporating all the idle rural productive factors in the agricultural process, thus greatly increasing its potentialities? We believe we committed two principal errors.

Our first error was the way in which we carried out diversification. Instead of embarking on diversification by degrees we attempted too much at once. The sugar cane areas were reduced and the land thus made available was used for cultivation of new crops. But this meant a general decline in agricultural production. The entire economic history of Cuba had demonstrated that no other agricultural activity would give such returns as those yielded by the cultivation of the sugar cane. At the outset of the Revolution many of us were not aware of this basic economic fact, because a fetishistic idea connected sugar with our dependence on imperialism and with the misery in the rural areas, without analysing the real causes: the relation to the uneven trade balance.

Unfortunately, whatever measures are taken in agriculture, the results do not become apparent until months, sometimes years, afterwards. This is particulary true as regards sugar cane production. That is why the reduction of the sugar cane areas made between the middle of 1960 and the end of 1961—and, let us not forget the two years of drought—has resulted in lower sugar cane harvests during 1962 and 1963.

Diversification on a smaller scale could have been achieved by utilising the reserves of productivity existing in the resources assigned to the various traditional types of cultivation. This would have permitted the partial use of idle resources for a small number of new products. At the same time, we could have taken measures to introduce more modern and complex techniques requiring a longer period of assimilation. After these new technical methods had begun to bear fruit in the traditional fields, particularly in those related to exports, it would have been practicable to transfer resources from these fields to the areas of diversification without prejudice to the former.

The second mistake made was, in our opinion, that of dispersing our resources over a great number of agricultural products, all in the name of diversification. This dispersal was made, not only on a national scale but also within each of the agricultural productive units.

The change made from monoculture to the development of a great number of agricultural products implied a drastic transformation within relatively few months. Only a very solid productive organisation could have resisted such rapid change. In an underdeveloped country, in particular, the structure of agriculture remains very inflexible and its organisation rests on extremely weak and subjective foundations. Consequently, the change in the agricultural structure and diversification, coming simultaneously, produced a greater weakness in the agricultural productive organisation.

Now that the years have passed, conditions have changed and the pressure of the class struggle has lessened, and so it is fairly easy to make a critical assessment of the analysis made during those months and years. It is for history to judge how much was our fault and how much was caused by circumstances.

At any rate, hard facts have shown us both the errors and the road towards their correction, which is the road the Cuban Revolution is at present following in the agricultural sector. Sugar now has first priority in the distribution of resources, and in the assessment of those factors which contribute to the most efficient use of those resources. The other sectors of agricultural production and their development have not been abandoned, but adequate methods have been sought to prevent a dispersal of resources of which the effect would be to hinder the obtaining of maximum yields.

In the industrial sector our policy is directed towards the same two objectives: the solution of the two problems of unemployment and scarcity of foreign exchange. The agrarian reform, the revolutionary measures as regards redistribution of income, and the increase in employment observed in other sectors of the economy and in industry itself, extended the national market considerably. This market was further strengthened by the establishment of a government monopoly of foreign trade, and by the introduction of a protectionist policy as regards the importation of goods which, without any disadvantage to the national consumer, can be manufactured in Cuba.

What industry there was in Cuba only worked to a fraction of its capacity, due to the competition of American goods, many of which entered the country practically duty free, and also to the fact that national demand was limited by the concentration among the parasitic classes of a large part of the national income.

Immediately after the Revolution the explosive increase of demand permitted a higher degree of utilisation of our industrial capacity, and nationally-produced articles accounted for a greater share of total consumption. This industrial growth, however, aggravated the problem of the balance of payments, for an extraordinarily high percentage of the costs of our industry—which was nationally integrated only to a small degree—was represented by the importation of fuel, raw materials, spare parts and equipment for replacement.

The problem of the balance of payments, and that of urban unemployment, made us follow a policy aimed at an industrial development which would eliminate these defects. Here, too, we both achieved successes and committed errors. Already during the first years of the Revolution we ensured the country's supply of electric power, acquiring from the socialist countries new plant-capacities which will meet our needs until 1970. New industries have been created, and many small and medium-sized production units in the mechanical field have been re-equipped. One result of these measures was that our industry could be kept running when the American embargo on spare parts hit us hardest. Some textile factories, some extractive and chemical installations and a new and vigorous search for fresh mineral resources have all contributed to successes in the more efficient use of native natural resources and raw materials.

I have spoken of certain achievements in the industrial field during the first years, but it is only just that I should also mention the errors made. Fundamentally, these were caused by a lack of precise understanding of the technological and economic elements necessary in the new industries installed during those years. Influenced by existing unemployment and by the pressure exerted by the problems in our foreign trade, we acquired a great number of factories with the dual purpose of substituting imports and providing employment for an appreciable number of urban workers. Later we found that in many of these plants the technical efficiency was insufficient when measured by international standards, and that the net result of the substitution of imports was very limited, because the necessary raw materials were not nationally produced.

We have rectified this type of error in the industrial sector. In planning new industries we are evaluating the maximum advantages which they may bring to our foreign trade through use of the most modern technical equipment at present obtainable, taking into consideration the particular conditions of our country.

So far the industrial development achieved can be described as satisfactory, if we take into account the problems caused by the American blockade and the radical changes which have occurred in only three years as regards our foreign sources of supply. Last year our sugar production fell from 4.8 m. metric tons to 3.8 m., but this was offset by an increase, in general terms, of 6 per cent in the rest of industry. This year, 1964, given the greater strength of our internal productive organisation and our greater experience in commercial relations with our new sources of supply, the industrial advance should be still greater.

The transformations so far made in the Cuban economy have produced great changes in the structure of our foreign trade. As regards exports the changes have been limited chiefly to the opening up of new markets, with sugar continuing to be the main export article. On the other hand, the composition of our imports has changed completely during these five years. Imports of consumer goods, particularly durables, have decreased substantially in favour of capital equipment, while a small decrease can be noted in the import of intermediate goods. The policy of substitution of imports is showing slow but tangible results.

The economic policy of the Revolution having attained a certain integral strength, it is clear that imports of durable consumer goods will once more increase, to satisfy the growing needs of modern life. The plans being made for the future provide for both an absolute and a relative increase in the importation of these articles, taking into account the social changes which have occurred. It will be unnecessary, for example, to import Cadillacs and other luxury cars, which in former years were paid for to a great extent with the profits derived from the labour of the Cuban sugar worker.

This is only one aspect of the problems connected with the future development of Cuba which are at present being studied. The policy we shall follow in years to come will largely depend on the flexibility of our foreign trade, and on the extent to which it will permit us to take full advantage of opportunities which may present themselves. We expect the Cuban economy to develop along three principal lines between now and 1970.

Sugar will continue to be our main earner of foreign exchange. Future development implies an increase of 50 per cent in present productive capacity. Simultaneously a qualitative advance will take place in the sugar sector, consisting of a substantial increase in the yield per unit of land under cultivation, and an improvement in technology and equipment. That improvement will tend to make up for the ground lost through inefficiency during the last 10-15 years. During that period the complete lack of expansion of our market led to technological stagnation. With the new possibilities which have opened up in the socialist countries, the panorama is changing rapidly.

One of the main bases for the development of our sugar industry, as well as for the development of the country as a whole, is the agreement recently signed between the U.S.S.R. and Cuba. This guarantees to us future sales of enormous quantities of sugar at prices much above the average of those paid in the American and world markets during the last 20 years. Apart from this and other favourable economic implications, the Agreement signed with the U.S.S.R. is of political importance inasmuch as it provides an example of the relationship that can exist between an underdeveloped and a developed country when both belong to the socialist camp, in contrast to the commercial relations between the underdeveloped countries exporting raw materials and the industrialised capitalist countries—in which the permanent tendency is to make the balance of trade unfavourable to the poor nations.

The second line of industrial development will be nickel. The deposits in north-eastern Cuba offer great possibilities for making this part of the island the future centre of the metallurgical industry. The capacity of the nickel smelting works will be increased, making Cuba the second or third largest producer in the world of this strategic metal.

The third line of this future development will be the cattle industry. The large number of cattle, great indeed in proportion to the size of the population, offers rich possibilities for the future. We estimate that within about 10 years our cattle industry will be equalled in importance only by the sugar industry.

As I have indicated, the role played by foreign trade in the Cuban economy will continue to be of basic importance, but there will be a qualitative change in its future development. None of the three principal lines of development will imply an effort to substitute imports, with the exception of the cattle industry, during the first years. After these first years the character of our new economic development will be fully reflected in our exports, and although the policy of substitution of imports will not be abandoned, it will be balanced by exports. For the decade following 1970 we are planning a more accelerated process of substitution of imports. This can only be achieved on the basis of an industrialisation programme of great scope. We shall create the necessary conditions for such a programme, making full use of the opportunities offered to an underdeveloped economy by our external trade.

Has the indisputable political importance in the world achieved by Cuba any economic counterpart? If so, should that importance lead to the contemplation of more serious economic relations with other countries, materialising in trade? In such an event, how would we build up this trade which has been greatly reduced due to the American blockade?

In considering these questions I leave aside reasons of a utilitarian nature which might lead me to make an apology for international trade, for it is evident that Cuba is interested in an active, regular and sustained interchange of trade with all countries of the world. What I am trying to do is to present an exact picture of the present situation. The American Government is obsessed by Cuba, and not only because of its abnormal colonialist mentality. There is something more. Cuba represents, in the first place, a clear example of the failure of the American policy of aggression on the very doorstep of the continent. Further, Cuba provides an example for the future socialist countries of Latin America and so an unmistakable warning of the inevitable reduction of the field of action of U.S. finance capital.

American imperialism is weaker than it seems; it is a giant with feet of clay. Although its present great potentialities are not seriously affected by violent internal class struggles leading to the destruction of the capitalist system, as foreseen by Marx, those potentialities are fundamentally based on a monopolistic extra-territorial power exercised by means of an unequal interchange of goods and by the political subjection of extensive territories. On these fall the full weight of the contradictions.

As the dependent countries of America and other regions of the world cast off the monopolistic chains, and establish more equitable systems and more just relations with all the countries of the world, the heavy contributions made by them to the living standard of the imperialist Powers will cease, and of all the capitalist countries the United States will then be the most seriously affected. This will not be the only outcome of an historical process; displaced finance capital will be forced to seek new horizons to make good its losses and, in this struggle, the most wounded, the most powerful and the most aggressive of all the capitalist Powers, the United States, will employ her full strength in a ruthless competition with the others, adopting, perhaps, unexpected methods of violence in her dealings with her "allies" of today.

Thus the existence of Cuba represents not only the hope of a better future for the peoples of America but also the prospect of a dangerous future for the seemingly unshakable monopolistic structure of the United States. The American attempt to strangle Cuba implies a desire to stop history; but if, in spite of all kinds of aggression, the Cuban state remains safe, its economy becoming increasingly strong and its foreign trade more important, then the failure of this policy will be complete and the move towards peaceful co-existence will become more rapid.

New relations based on mutual interests will be established. These will benefit the socialist bloc and the countries now liberating themselves. Yet the great capitalist countries, including England, facing serious economic problems and limitations of markets, could have the opportunity to lead this new interchange, as France has already tried to do to a certain extent.

To such countries the Cuban market, although not unimportant, may not be worth a break with the United States, but Latin America as a whole is a gigantic potential market of 200 million people. It is useless to close one's eyes to the reality that this continent will continue its struggle for liberation, and that it will ultimately, if gradually, establish either groups or a bloc of countries free of imperialism and with internal systems related to socialism. Therefore, the capitalist countries should decide whether it is worthwhile to use Cuba as a means of testing a situation which may prove to be of great advantage even if it represents a danger to the future of the capitalistic system.

The alternatives are clear, and in our opinion they imply the need for serious decisions: one can be an ally of the United States until the collapse of a policy of oppression and aggression and then fall victim to the same internal and external problems as will afflict the United States when that moment arrives; or one can break that alliance, which in any case is already beginning to crack in relation to Cuba, in order to help—by means of trade—the rapid development of the countries which are liberating themselves, thus not only giving greater hopes to those peoples still fighting for liberation, but simultaneously creating conditions which will bring closer the disappearance of capitalism.

We think this is the great dilemma now facing countries like England. Cuba is part of that dilemma in her role as a catalysing agent of the revolutionary ideas of a continent, and as the pioneer of these ideas.

It is not for us to say what final decision should be taken. We simply state the alternatives.

CHAPTER 28

"Camilo"[1]

MEMORY is a way of reviving the past, the dead. To remember Camilo is to remember things which are past or dead, and yet Camilo is a living part of the Cuban Revolution, immortal by his very nature. I would like simply to give our comrades of the rebel army an idea of who this invincible guerrilla fighter was. I am able to do so, since from the sad hours of the first setback at Alegría del Pío on we were always together, and it is my duty to do so, because far more than a comrade in arms, in joys and victories, Camilo was a real brother. I never got to know him in Mexico, as he joined us at the last minute. He had come from the United States without any previous recommendation, and we did not have any confidence in him—or in anyone else, in fact—in those risky days. He came on the *Granma,* just one among the eighty-two who crossed the sea at the mercy of the elements to carry out a feat that was to shake the entire continent. I realized what he was like, before I actually got to know him, through hearing a representative exclamation of his during the disastrous battle of Alegría del Pío. I was wounded, stretched out in a clearing, next to a comrade covered with blood who was firing his last rounds, ready to die fighting. I heard someone cry weakly: "We're lost. Let's surrender." And a clear voice from somewhere among the men shouted in reply: "Nobody surrenders here!" followed by a four-letter word.

The battle ended, we survived, and I went on breathing, thanks to the help of Comrade Almeida. Five of us wandered around the steep cliffs near Cabo Cruz. One clear, moonlit night we came upon three other comrades sleeping peacefully, without any fear of the soldiers. We jumped them, believing them to be enemies. Nothing happened, but the incident served later as a base for a mutual joke between us: the fact that I was among those who had caught them by surprise, and the fact that it was I who had

[1] Unfinished, written in October 1964, published in *Granma*, English Edition, Havana, November 12, 1967, p. 2.

to raise the white flag so that they would not shoot us, mistaking us for Batista soldiers.

And so then there were eight of us. Camilo was hungry and wanted to eat; he didn't care what or where, he simply wanted to eat. This led to some serious disagreements with him, because he continually wanted to approach bohíos to ask for food. Twice, for having followed the advice of "the hungry ones," we nearly fell into the hands of enemy soldiers who had killed dozens of our comrades. On the ninth day "the hungry ones" won out, and we approached a bohío, ate, and all got sick. And among the sickest was, naturally, Camilo, who, like a hungry lion, had gulped down an entire kid.

During that period I was more a medic than a soldier. I put Camilo on a special diet and ordered him to stay behind in the bohío, where he would receive proper attention. That trouble passed, and we were together again, and the days lengthened into weeks and months during which many comrades were killed. Camilo showed his mettle, earning the rank of lieutenant of the vanguard of our one and only beloved column, which would later be called the José Martí Column number one, under Fidel's personal command. Almeida and Raúl were captains; Camilo, lieutenant of the vanguard; Efigenio Ameijeiras, leader of the rear guard; Ramiro Valdés, lieutenant in one of Raúl's platoons; and Calixto, soldier in another platoon. In other words all our forces were born there, where I was the group's lieutenant medic. Later, following the battle of Uvero, I was given the rank of captain, and a few days later, the rank of major and the command of a column. One day Camilo was made captain of the column which I commanded, the Fourth Column. We bore that number to deceive the enemy, as actually there were only two. And it was there that Camilo began his career of exploits, and it was with untiring effort and extraordinary zeal that, time and again, he hunted down enemy soldiers. Once he shot a soldier of the enemy's scout at such close range that he caught the man's rifle before it even hit the ground. Another time he planned to let the first of the enemy soldiers go by until he was abreast of our troop, and then open flank fire. The ambush never materialized because someone in our group got nervous and opened fire before the enemy got close enough. By then Camilo was "Camilo, Lord of the Vanguard," a real guerrilla fighter who was able to assert himself through his own colorful way of fighting.

I recall my anxiety during the second attack on Pino del Agua, when Fidel ordered me to stay with him and gave Camilo the responsibility of attacking one of the enemy's flanks. The idea was simple. Camilo was to attack and take one end of the enemy camp and then surround it. The firing started, and he and his men took the sentry post and continued advancing, entering the settlement, killing or taking prisoner every soldier in their path. The town was taken house by house until finally the enemy organized its resistence and the barrage of bullets began to take its toll among our ranks. Valuable comrades, among them Noda and Capote, lost their lives in this battle.

An enemy machine gunner advanced, surrounded by his men, but at a given moment he found himself amidst a veritable storm of gunfire. The machine gunner's assistants were killed, and the soldier manning the gun dropped it and fled. It was dawn. The attack had begun at night. Camilo hurled himself across the machine gun to seize and defend it, and was shot twice. A bullet pierced his left thigh, and another hit him in the abdomen. He got away and his comrades carried him. We were two kilometers away, with the enemy between us. We could hear machine gun bursts and shouting: "There goes Camilo's gun!" "That's Camilo firing!" and vivas for Batista. We all thought that Camilo had been killed. Later we praised his luck that the bullet had entered and left his abdomen without hitting his intestines or any vital organ. Then came the tragic day of April 9, and Camilo, the trailblazer, went to the Oriente plains and became a legend, striking terror into the heart of the enemy forces mobilized in the Bayamo area. Once he was surrounded by six hundred men, and there were only twenty in the rebel force. They resisted an entire day against an enemy advance that included two tanks, and at night they made a spectacular escape.

Later came the offensive, and in the face of imminent danger and the concentration of forces Camilo was called, as he was the man Fidel trusted to leave in his place when he went to a specific front. Then came the marvelous story of the invasion and his chain of victories on the plains of Las Villas—a difficult feat, as the terrain afforded little natural protection. These actions were magnificent for their audacity, and at the same time one could already see Camilo's political attitude, his decision regarding political problems, his strength and his faith in the people. Camilo was happy, down-to-earth, and a joker. I remember that in the Sierra a peasant, one of our great magnificent, anonymous heroes, had been nicknamed by Camilo, who accompanied this with an ugly gesture. One day the peasant came to see me as head of the column, complaining that he should not be insulted and that he was no ventriloquist. As I did not understand, I went to speak with Camilo so that he could explain the man's strange attitude. What happened was that Camilo had looked at the man with an air of disrespect and called him a ventriloquist, and as the peasant did not know what a ventriloquist was, he was terribly offended.

Camilo had a little alcohol burner and he used to cook cats and offer them as a delicacy to new recruits who joined us. It was one of the many tests of the Sierra, and more than one failed this preliminary "examination" when he refused to eat the cat proffered. Camilo was a man of anecdotes, a million anecdotes. They were a part of his nature. His appreciation of people and his ability to get along with them were a part of his personality. These qualities, which today we sometimes forget or overlook, were present in all his actions, something precious that few men can attain. It is true, as Fidel has said, that he had no great amount of "book learning," but he had the natural intelligence of the people who had chosen him from among thousands to place him in that privileged place earned by his audacity, his tenacity, his intelligence, and devotion. Camilo was uncompromisingly loyal to two things, and with the same results: He had unlimited loyalty and devotion to Fidel and the people. Fidel and the people march together, and Camilo's devotion was projected toward them both.

Who killed Camilo? Who killed the man who, in the lives of others like him, lives on in the people? Such men do not die so long as the people do not authorize it. The enemy killed him, killed him because they wanted him to die, because there are no completely safe airplanes, because pilots are not able to acquire all the necessary experience, because he was overloaded with work and had to be in Havana as quickly as possible. He was killed by his drive. Camilo did not measure danger. He utilized it as a game, he played with it, he courted it, he attracted and handled it, and with his guerrilla mentality, a mere cloud could not detain or deviate him from the line he was following. It happened at a time everyone knew him, admired and loved him; it could have happened before, and then his story would have been known only as that of a mere guerrilla captain. There will be many Camilos, as Fidel has said; and there have been Camilos, I can add—Camilos who died before completing the magnificent work he had managed to complete so as to enter the pages of history. Camilo and the other Camilos—the ones who fell early and those still to come—are the index of the people's strength; they are the most complete expression of the heights that can be reached by a nation fighting to defend its purest ideals and with complete faith in the fulfillment of its noblest goals. There is too much to be said to allow me to put his essence into a lifeless mold, which would be equivalent to killing him. It is better to leave it like this, in general descriptive terms, without spelling out in black and white his socio-economic ideology, which was not precisely defined. But we must always bear in mind that there was never a man—not even before the Revolution—comparable to Camilo: a complete revolutionary, a man of the people, an artist of the Revolution, sprung from the heart of the Cuban nation. His mind was incapable of the slightest slackening or disappointment. He is an object of daily remembrance; he is the one who did this or that, something by Camilo; he who left his exact and indelible imprint on the Cuban Revolution, who is present among those who fell early in their revolutionary careers and those heroes who are yet to come. In his constant and eternal rebirth, Camilo is the image of the people.

CHAPTER 29

Colonialism Is Doomed[1]

THE Cuban delegation to this assembly has pleasure, first of all, in fulfilling the pleasant duty of welcoming three new nations to the large number of nations whose representatives are discussing the problems of the world. We therefore greet through their Presidents and Prime Ministers the people of Zambia, Malawi, and Malta, and express the hope that from the outset these countries will be added to the group of nonaligned countries which struggle against imperialism, colonialism, and neocolonialism.

We also wish to convey our congratulations to the President of this assembly whose elevation to so high a post is of special significance since it reflects this new historic stage of resounding triumphs for the peoples of Africa, until recently subject to the colonial system of imperialism, and who, today, for the great part in the legitimate exercise of self-determination, have become citizens of sovereign states. The last hour of colonialism has struck, and millions of inhabitants of Africa, Asia, and Latin American rise to meet a new life, and assert their unrestricted right to self-determination and to the independent development of their nations.

We wish you, Mr President, the greatest success in the tasks entrusted to you by member states.

Cuba comes here to state its position on the most important controversial issues and will do so with the full sense of responsibility which the use of this rostrum implies, while at the same time responding to the unavoidable duty of speaking out, clearly and frankly.

We should like to see this assembly shake itself out of complacency and move forward. We should like to see the committees begin their work and not stop at the first confrontation. Imperialism wishes to convert this meeting into an aimless oratorical tournament, instead of using it to solve the

[1] Speech delivered before the General Assembly of the United Nations on December 11, 1964; Havana, Ministry of External Relations, Information Department. Official Cuban Government translation.

grave problems of the world. We must prevent their doing so. This assembly should not be remembered in the future only by the number nineteen which identifies it. We feel that we have the right and the obligation to try to make this meeting effective because our country is a constant point of friction; one of the places where the principles supporting the rights of small nations to sovereignty are tested day by day, minute by minute; and at the same time our country is one of the barricades of freedom in the world, situated a few steps away from United States imperialism, to show with its actions, its daily example, that peoples can liberate themselves, can keep themselves free, in the existing conditions of the world.

Of course, there is now a socialist camp which becomes stronger day by day and has more powerful weapons of struggle. But additional conditions are required for survival: the maintenance of internal cohesion, faith in one's destiny, and the irreversible decision to fight to the death for the defense of one's country and revolution. These conditions exist in Cuba.

Of all the burning problems to be dealt with by this assembly, one which has special significance for us and whose solution we feel must be sought first, so as to leave no doubt in the minds of anyone, is that of peaceful coexistence among states with different economic and social systems. Much progress has been made in the world in this field. But imperialism, particularly United States imperialism, has tried to make the world believe that peaceful coexistence is the exclusive right of the great powers on earth. We repeat what our President said in Cairo, and which later took shape in the Declaration of the Second Conference of Heads of State or Government of Non-Aligned Countries: that there cannot be peaceful coexistence only among the powerful if we are to ensure world peace. Peaceful coexistence must be practiced by all states, independent of size, of the previous historic relations that linked them, and of the problems that may arise among some of them at a given moment.

At present the type of peaceful coexistence to which we aspire does not exist in many cases. The kingdom of Cambodia, merely because it maintained a neutral attitude and did not submit to the machinations of United States imperialism, has been subjected to all kinds of treacherous and brutal attacks from the Yankee bases in South Vietnam.

Laos, a divided country, has also been the object of imperialist aggression of every kind. The conventions concluded at Geneva have been violated, its peoples have been massacred from the air, and part of its territory is in constant danger from cowardly attacks by imperialist forces.

The Democratic Republic of Vietnam, which knows of the histories of aggressions as few people on earth, once again has seen its frontier violated, its installations attacked by enemy bomber and fighter planes, its naval posts attacked by the United States warships violating territorial waters.

At this moment, there hangs over the Democratic Republic of Vietnam the threat that the United States warmongers may openly extend to its territory the war that, for many years, they have been waging against the people of South Vietnam.

The Soviet Union and the People's Republic of China have given serious warning to the United States. Not only the peace of the world is in danger in this situation, but also the lives of millions of human beings in this part of Asia are being constantly threatened and subjected to the whim of the United States invader.

Peaceful coexistence has also been put to the test in a brutal manner in Cyprus, due to pressures from the Turkish Government and NATO, compelling the people and the government of Cyprus to make a firm and heroic stand in defense of their sovereignty.

In all these parts of the world imperialism attempts to impose its version of what coexistence should be. It is the oppressed peoples in alliance with the socialist camp which must show them the meaning of true coexistence, and it is the obligation of the United Nations to support them.

We must also say that it is not only in relations between sovereign states that the concept of peaceful coexistence must be clearly defined. As Marxists we have maintained that peaceful coexistence among nations does not encompass coexistence between the exploiters and the exploited, the oppressor and the oppressed.

Furthermore, a principle proclaimed by this Organization is that of the right to full independence of all forms of colonial oppression. That is why we express our solidarity with the colonial peoples of so-called Portuguese Guinea, Angola, and Mozambique, who have been massacred for the crime of demanding their freedom, and we are prepared to help them to the extent of our ability in accordance with the Cairo Declaration.

We express our solidarity with the people of Puerto Rico and its great leader, Pedro Albizu Campos, who has been set free in another act of hypocrisy, at the age of seventy-two, after spending a lifetime in jail, now paralytic and almost without the ability to speak. Albizu Campos is a symbol of the still unredeemed but indomitable America. Years and years of prison, almost unbearable pressures in jail, mental torture, solitude, total isolation from his people and his family, the insolence of the conqueror and lackeys in the land of his birth—nothing at all broke his will. The delegation of Cuba, on behalf of its people, pays a tribute of admiration and gratitude to a patriot who bestows honor upon America.

The North Americans, for many years, have tried to convert Puerto Rico into a reflection of hybrid culture—the Spanish language with an English inflection, the Spanish language with hinges on its backbone, the better to bend before the United States soldier. Puerto Rican soldiers have been used as cannonfodder in imperialist wars, as in Korea, and even been made to fire at their own brothers, as in the massacre perpetrated by the United States Army a few months ago against the helpless people of Panama—one of the most recent diabolical acts carried out by Yankee imperialism. Yet despite that terrible attack against its will and its historic destiny, the people of Puerto Rico have preserved their culture, their Latin character, their national feelings, which in themselves give proof of the implacable will for independence that exists among the masses on the Latin American island.

We must also point out that the principle of peaceful coexistence does not imply a mockery of the will of the peoples, as is happening in the case of so-called British Guiana, where the government of Prime Minister Cheddi Jagan has been the victim of every kind of pressure and maneuver, while the achievement of independence has been delayed by the search for methods that would allow for the flouting of the will of the people while ensuring the docility of a Government different from the present one, put in by underhanded tactics, and then to grant an important "freedom" to this piece of American soil. Whatever roads Guiana may be compelled to follow to obtain independence, the moral and militant support of Cuba goes to its people.

Furthermore, we must point out that the islands of Guadaloupe and Martinique have been fighting for a long time for their autonomy without obtaining it. This state of affairs must not continue.

Once again we raise our voice to put the world on guard against what is happening in South Africa. The brutal policy of apartheid is being carried out before the eyes of the whole world. The peoples of Africa are being compelled to tolerate in that continent the concept, still official, of the superiority of one race over another and in the name of that racial superiority the murder of people with impunity. Can the United Nations do nothing to prevent this? I should like specifically to refer to the painful case of the Congo, unique in the history of the modern world, which shows how, with absolute impunity, with the most insolent cynicism, the rights of peoples can be flouted. The prodigious wealth of the Congo, which the imperialist nations wish to maintain under their control, is the direct reason for this. In his speech on his first visit to the United Nations, our comrade Fidel Castro said that the whole problem of coexistence among peoples was reduced to the undue appropriation of another's wealth. He said, "When this philosophy of despoilment disappears, the philosophy of war will have disappeared."

The philosophy of despoilment not only has not ceased, but rather it is stronger than ever, and that is why those who used the name of the United Nations to commit the murder of Lumumba, today, in the name of the defense of the white race, are assassinating thousands of Congolese. How can one forget how the hope that Patrice Lumumba placed in the United Nations was betrayed? How can one forget the machinations and maneuvers which followed in the wake of the occupation of that country by United Nations troops under whose auspices the assassins of this great

African patriot acted with impunity? How can we forget that he who flouted the authority of the United Nations in the Congo, and not exactly for patriotic reasons, but rather by virtue of conflicts between imperialists, was Moise Tshombe, who initiated the secession in Katanga with Belgian support? And how can one justify, how can one explain, that at the end of all the United Nations activities there, Tshombe, dislodged from Katanga, returned as lord and master of the Congo? Who can deny the abject role that the imperialists compelled the United Nations to play?

To sum up, dramatic mobilizations were made to avoid the secession of Katanga, but today that same Katanga is in power! The wealth of the Congo is in imperialist hands and the expenses must be paid by honest nations. The merchants of war certainly do good business. That is why the government of Cuba supports the just attitude of the Soviet Union in refusing to pay the expenses of this crime.

And as if this were not enough, we now have flung in our faces recent events which have filled the world with horror and indignation. Who are the perpetrators? Belgian paratroopers transported by United States planes, who took off from British bases. We remember as if it were yesterday that we saw a small country in Europe, a civilized and industrious country, the kingdom of Belgium, invaded by the hordes of Hitler. We learned with bitterness that these people were being massacred by the German imperialists, and our sympathy and affection went out to them. But the other side of the imperialist coin many did not then perceive. Perhaps the sons of Belgian patriots who died defending their country are now assassinating thousands of Congolese in the name of the white race, just as they suffered under the German heel because their blood was not purely Aryan. But the scales have fallen from our eyes and they now open upon new horizons, and we can see what yesterday, in our conditions of colonial servitude, we could not observe—that "Western civilization" disguises under its showy front a scene of hyenas and jackals. That is the only name that can be applied to those who have gone to fulfill "humanitarian" tasks in the Congo. Bloodthirsty butchers who feed on helpless people! That is what imperialism does to men; that is what marks the "white" imperialists.

The free men of the world must be prepared to avenge the crime committed in the Congo. It is possible that many of those soldiers who were converted into "supermen" by imperialist machinery, believe in good faith that they are defending the rights of a superior race, but in this assembly those peoples whose skins are darkened by a different sun, colored by different pigments, constitute the majority, and they fully and clearly understand that the difference between men does not lie in the color of their skins, but in the ownership of the means of production and in the relationship of production.

The Cuban delegation extends greetings to the peoples of Southern Rhodesia and Southwest Africa, oppressed by white colonialist minorities, to the peoples of Basutoland, Bechuanaland, Swaziland, French Somaliland, the Arabs of Palestine, Aden, and the Protectorates, Oman, and to all peoples in conflict with imperialism and colonialism; and we reaffirm our support.

I express also the hope that there will be a just solution to the conflict facing our sister republic of Indonesia in its relations with Malaysia.

One of the essential items before this conference is general and complete disarmament. We express our support of general and complete disarmament. Furthermore, we advocate the complete destruction of thermonuclear devices and the holding of a conference of all the nations of the world toward the fulfillment of this aspiration of all people. In his statement before this assembly, our Prime Minister said that arms races have always led to war. There are new atomic powers in the world, and the possibilities of a confrontation are grave.

We feel that a conference is necessary to obtain the total destruction of thermonuclear weapons and as a first step, the total prohibition of tests. At the same time there must be clearly established the obligation of all states to respect the present frontiers of other states and to refrain from indulging in any aggression even with conventional weapons.

In adding our voice to that of all peoples of the world who plead for general and complete disarmament, the destruction of all atomic arsenals, the complete cessation of thermonuclear devices and atomic tests of any kinds, we feel it necessary to stress, furthermore, that the territorial integrity of nations must be respected and the armed hand of imperialism, no less dangerous with conventional weapons, must be held back. Those who murdered thousands of defenseless citizens in the Congo did not use the atomic weapons. They used conventional weapons, and it was these conventional weapons, used by imperialists, which caused so many deaths.

Even if the measures advocated here were to become effective, thus making it unnecessary to say the following, we must still point out that we cannot adhere to any regional pact for denuclearization so long as the United States maintains aggressive bases on our territory, in Puerto Rico and in Panama, and in other American states where it feels it has the right to station them without any restrictions on conventional or nuclear weapons.

However, we feel we must be able to provide for our own defense in the light of the recent resolution of the Organization of American States against Cuba, which on the basis of the Treaty of Rio might permit aggression.

If such a conference to which we have just referred should achieve all these objectives—which unfortunately, would be rather difficult to do—it would be one of the most important developments in the history of mankind. To ensure this, the People's Republic of China must be represented, and that is why such a conference must be held. But it would be much simpler for the peoples of the world to recognize the undeniable truth that the People's Republic of China exists, that its rulers are the only representatives of the Chinese people, and to give it the place it deserves, which is, at present, usurped by a clique who control the province of Taiwan with United States aid.

The problem of the representation of China in the United Nations cannot, in any way, be considered as a case of a new admission to the organization, but rather as the restitution of their legitimate rights to the people of the People's Republic of China.

We repudiate strongly the concept of "two Chinas." The Chiang Kaishek clique of Taiwan cannot remain in the United Nations. It must be expelled and the legitimate representative of the Chinese people put in.

We warn, also, against the insistence of the United States Government on presenting the problem of the legitimate representation of China in the United Nations as an "important question" so as to require a two-thirds majority of members present and voting.

The admission of the People's Republic of China to the United Nations is, in fact, an important question for the entire world, but not for the mechanics of the United Nations where it must constitute a mere question of procedure.

Thus will justice be done, but almost as important as attaining justice would be the fact that it would be demonstrated, once and for all, that this august Assembly uses its eyes to see with, its ears to hear with, and its tongue to speak with; and has definite standards in making its decisions.

The proliferation of atomic weapons among the member States of NATO, and especially the possession of these devices of mass destruction by the Federal Republic of Germany, would make the possibility of an agreement on disarmament even more remote, and linked to such an agreement is the problem of the peaceful reunification of Germany. So long as there is no clear understanding, the existence of two Germanies must be recognized: that of the Democratic Republic of Germany and the Federal Republic. The German problem can only be solved with the direct participation of the Democratic Republic of Germany with full rights in negotiations.

We shall touch lightly on the questions of economic development and international trade which take up a good part of the agenda. In this year, 1964, the Conference of Geneva was held, where a multitude of matters related to these aspects of international relations was dealt with. The warnings and forecasts of our delegation were clearly confirmed to the misfortune of the economically dependent countries.

We wish only to point out that insofar as Cuba is concerned, the United States of America has not implemented the explicit recommendations of that conference, and recently the United States Government also prohibited the sale of medicine to Cuba, thus divesting itself, once and for all, of the mask of humanitarianism with which it attempted to disguise the aggressive nature of its blockade against the people of Cuba.

Furthermore, we once more state that these colonial machinations, which impede the development of the peoples, are not only expressed in political relations. The so-called deterioration of the terms of trade is nothing less than the result of the unequal exchange between countries producing raw materials and industrial countries which dominate markets and impose a false justice on an inequitable exchange of values.

So long as the economically dependent peoples do not free themselves from the capitalist markets, and as a bloc with the socialist countries, impose new terms of trade between the exploited and the exploiters, there will be no sound economic development, and in certain cases there will be retrogression, in which the weak countries will fall under the political domination of imperialists and colonialists.

Finally, it must be made clear that in the area of the Caribbean, maneuvers and preparations for aggression against Cuba are taking place; off the coast of Nicaragua above all, in Costa Rica, in the Panama Canal Zone, in the Vieques Islands of Puerto Rico, in Florida, and possibly in other parts of the territory of the United States, and also, perhaps, in Honduras, Cuban mercenaries are training, as well as mercenaries of other nationalities, with a purpose that cannot be peaceful.

After an open scandal, the government of Costa Rica, it is said, has ordered the elimination of all training fields for Cuban exiles in that country. No one knows whether this attitude is sincere, or whether it it simply a maneuver, because the mercenaries training there were about to commit some offense. We hope that full cognizance will be taken of the actual existence of those bases for aggression, which we denounced long ago, and that the world will think about the international responsibility of the government of a country which authorizes and facilitates the training of mercenaries to attack Cuba.

We must point out that news of the training of mercenaries at different places in the Caribbean and the participation of the United States Government in such acts is news that appears openly in United States newspapers. We know of no Latin American voice that has been lifted officially in protest against this. This shows the cynicism with which the United States moves its pawns.

The shrewd foreign ministers of the OAS had eyes to "see" Cuban emblems and find "irrefutable proof" in the Yankee weapons in Venezuela, but do not see the preparations for aggression in the United States, just as they did not hear the voice of President Kennedy, who explicitly declared himself to be the aggressor against Cuba at Playa Girón. In some cases it is a blindness provoked by the hatred of the ruling classes of the Latin American people against our revolution; in others, and these are even more deplorable, it is the result of the blinding light of Mammon.

As everyone knows, after the terrible upheaval called the "Caribbean crisis," the United States undertook certain given commitments with the Soviet Union which culminated in the withdrawal of certain types of weapons that the continued aggressions of that country—such as the mercenary attack against Playa Girón and threats of invasion against our country—had compelled us to install in Cuba as a legitimate act of defense.

The Americans claimed, furthermore, that the United Nations should inspect our territory, which we refused and refuse emphatically since Cuba does not recognize the right of the United States, or of anyone else in the world, to determine what type of weapons Cuba may maintain within its borders.

In this connection, we would only abide by multilateral agreements, with equal obligations for all the parties concerned. Fidel Castro declared that "so long as the concept of sovereignty exists as the prerogative of nations and of independent peoples, and as a right of all peoples, we shall not accept the exclusion of our people from that right; so long as the world is governed by these principles, so long as the world is governed by those concepts which have universal validity because they are universally accepted by peoples, we shall not accept the attempt to deprive us of any of those rights and we shall renounce none of those rights."

The Secretary-General of the United Nations, U Thant, understood our reasons. Nevertheless, the United States presumed to establish a new prerogative, an arbitrary and illegal one; that of violating the air space of any small country. Thus, we see flying over our country U-2 aircraft and other types of espionage apparatus which fly over our airspace with impunity. We have issued all the necessary warnings for the cessation of the violation of our airspace as well as the provocations of the American navy against our sentry posts in the zone of Guantánamo, the "buzzing" by aircraft over our ships or ships of other nationalities in international waters, the piratical attacks against ships sailing under different flags, and the infiltration of spies, saboteurs and weapons in our island.

We want to build socialism; we have declared ourselves partisans of those who strive for peace; we have declared ourselves as falling within the group of nonaligned countries, although we are Marxist-Leninists, because the nonaligned countries, like ourselves, fight imperialism. We want peace; we want to build a better life for our people, and that is why we avoid answering, so far as possible, the planned provocations of the Yankee. But we know the mentality of United States rulers; they want to make us pay a very high price for that peace. We reply that price cannot go beyond the bounds of dignity.

And Cuba reaffirms once again the right to maintain on its territory the weapons it wishes and its refusal to recognize the right of any power on earth—no matter how powerful—to violate our soil, our territorial waters, or our airspace.

If, in any assembly, Cuba assumes obligations of a collective nature, it will fulfill them to the letter. So long as this does not happen, Cuba maintains all its rights, just as any other nation.

In the face of the demands of imperialism our Prime Minister posed the five necessary points for the existence of a sound peace in the Caribbean. They are as follows:

1. Cessation of the economic blockade and all economic and trade pressure by the United States in all parts of the world against our country.

2. Cessation of all subversive activities, launching and landing of weapons, and explosives by air and sea, organization of mercenary invasions, infiltration of spies and saboteurs, all of which acts are carried out from the territory of the United States and some accomplice countries.

3. Cessation of piratical attacks carried out from existing bases in the United States and Puerto Rico.

4. Cessation of all the violations of our airspace and our territorial waters by aircraft and warships of the United States.

5. Withdrawal from the Guantánamo naval base and restitution of the Cuban territory occupied by the United States.

None of these fundamental demands has been met, and our forces are still being provoked from the naval base at Guantánamo. That base has become a nest of thieves and the point from which they are introduced into our territory.

We would bore this assembly were we to give a detailed account of the large number of provocations of all kinds. Suffice it to say that including the first day of December, the number amounts to 1,323 in 1964 alone. The list covers minor provocations such as violation of the dividing line, launching of objects from the territory controlled by the North Americans, the commission of acts of sexual exhibitionism by North Americans of both sexes, verbal insults, others which are graver such as shooting off small-caliber weapons, the manipulation of weapons directed against our territory and offenses against our national emblem. The more serious provocations are those of crossing the dividing line and starting fires in installations on the Cuban side, seventy-eight rifle shots this year and the death of Ramon Lopez Pena, a soldier, from two shots fired from the United States post three and a half kilometers from the coast on the northern boundary.

This grave provocation took place at 19:07 hours on July 19, 1964, and our Prime Minister publicly stated on July 26 that if the event were to recur, he would give orders for our troops to repel the aggression. At the same time orders were given for the withdrawal of the advance line of Cuban forces to positions farther away from the dividing line and construction of the necessary housing.

One thousand three hundred and twenty-three provocations in 340 days amount to approximately four per day. Only a perfectly disciplined army with a morale such as ours could resist so many hostile acts without losing its self-control.

Forty-seven countries which met at the Second Conference of Heads of State or Government of the nonaligned countries at Cairo unanimously agreed that:

> Noting with concern that foreign military bases are, in practice, a means of bringing pressure on nations and retarding their emancipation and development, based on their own ideological, political, economic and cultural ideas . . . declares its full support to the countries which are seeking to secure the evacuation of foreign bases on their territory and calls upon all States maintaining troops and bases in other countries to remove them forthwith.
>
> The Conference considers that the maintenance at Guantánamo (Cuba) of a military base of the United States of America, in defiance of the will of the Government and people of Cuba and in defiance of the provisions embodied in the Declaration of the Belgrade Conference, constitutes a violation of Cuba's sovereignty and territorial integrity.
>
> Noting that the Cuban Government expresses its readiness to settle its dispute over the base at Guantánamo with the United States on an equal footing, the Conference urges the United States Government to negotiate the evacuation of their base with the Cuban Government.

The government of the United States has not responded to the above request of the Cairo Conference and presumes to maintain indefinitely its occupation by force of a piece of our territory from which it carries out acts of aggression such as those we mentioned earlier.

The Organization of American States—also called by some people the United States Ministry of Colonies—condemned us vigorously, although it had excluded us from its midst, and ordered its members to break off diplomatic and trade relations with Cuba. The OAS authorized aggression against our country at any time and under any pretext and violated the most fundamental international laws, completely disregarding the United Nations. Uruguay, Bolivia, Chile, and Mexico opposed that measure, and the government of the United States oi Mexico refused to comply with the sanctions that had been approved. Since ιhen we have no relations with any Latin American countries other than Mexico; thus the imperialists have carried out one of the stages preliminary to a plan of direct aggression.

We want to point out once again that our concern over Latin America is based on the ties that link us; the language we speak, our culture, and the common master we shared. But we have no other reason for desiring the liberation of Latin America from the colonial yoke of the United States. If any of the Latin American countries here decides to [resume relations it must be on the] basis of equality and not with the assumption that it is a gift to our government that we be recognized as a free country in the world, because we won the recognition of our freedom with our blood in the days of our struggles for liberation. We acquired it with our blood in the defense of our shores against Yankee invasion.

Although we reject any attempt to attribute to us interference in the internal affairs of other countries, we cannot deny that we sympathize with those people who strive for their freedom, and we must fulfill the obligation of our government and people to state clearly and categorically to the world that we morally support and feel as one with people everywhere who struggle to make a reality of the rights of full sovereignty proclaimed in the United Nations Charter.

It is the United States of America which intervenes. It has done so throughout the history of America. Since the end of the last century Cuba has known very well the truth of the matter; but it is known, too, by Venezuela, Nicaragua, Central America in general, Mexico, Haiti, and Santo Domingo. In recent years, besides our peoples, Panama has also known direct aggression, when the marines of the Canal opened fire against the defenseless people; Santo Domingo, whose coast was violated by the Yankee fleet to avoid an outbreak of the righteous fury of the people after the death of Trujillo; and Colombia, whose capital was taken by assault as a result of a rebellion provoked by the assassination of Gaitán.

There are masked interventions through military missions which participate in internal repression, organizing forces designed for that purpose in many countries, and also in *coups d'état* which have been so frequently repeated on the American continent during the past few years. Specifically, United States forces took part in the repression of the peoples of Venezuela, Colombia, and Guatemala, who carry on an armed struggle for their freedom. In Venezuela not only do the Americans advise the army and the police, but they also direct acts of genocide from the air against the peasant population in vast rebel-held areas, and the United States companies established there exert pressures of every kind to increase direct interference.

The imperialists are preparing to repress the peoples of America and are setting up an "international" [network] of crime. The United States interfered in America while invoking the "defense of free institutions." The time will come when this assembly will acquire greater maturity and demand guarantees from the United States Government for the lives of the Negro and Latin American population who reside in that country, most of whom are native-born or naturalized United States citizens.

How can they presume to be the "guardians of liberty" when they kill their own children and discriminate daily against people because of the color of their skin; when they not only free the murderers of colored people, but even protect them, while punishing the colored population because they demand their legitimate rights as free men? We understand that today the assembly is not in a position to ask for explanations of these acts, but it must be clearly established that the government of the United

States is not the champion of freedom, but rather the perpetrator of exploitation and oppression of the peoples of the world, and of a large part of its own population.

To the equivocating language with which some delegates have painted the case of Cuba and the Organization of American States, we reply with blunt words, that the governments pay for their treason.

Cuba, a free and sovereign state, with no chains binding it to anyone, with no foreign investments on its territory, with no proconsuls orienting its policy, can speak proudly in this assembly, proving the justice of the phrase by which we will always be known, "Free Territory of America."

Our example will bear fruit in our continent, as it is already doing to a certain extent already in Guatemala, Colombia, and Venezuela. The imperialists no longer have to deal with a small enemy, a contemptible force, since the people are no longer isolated.

As laid down in the Second Declaration of Havana:

> No people of Latin America is weak, because it is part of a family of 200 million brothers beset by the same miseries, who harbor the same feelings, have the same enemy, while they all dream of the same better destiny and have the support of all honest men and women in the world.
>
> Future history will be written by the hungry masses of Indians, of landless peasants, of exploited workers; it will be written by the progressive masses, by the honest and brilliant intellectuals who abound in our unfortunate lands of Latin America, by the struggle of the masses and of ideas; an epic that will be carried forward by our peoples who have been ill-treated and despised by imperialism, our peoples who have until now gone unrecognized but who are awakening. We were considered an impotent and submissive flock; but now they are afraid of that flock, a gigantic flock of 200 million Latin Americans, which is sounding a warning note to the Yankee monopolist capitalists.
>
> The hour of vindication, the hour it chose for itself, is now striking from one end to the other of the continent. That anonymous mass, that colored America, sombre, adamant, which sings throughout the continent the same sad, mournful song; now that mass is beginning definitely to enter into its own history, it is beginning to write it with its blood, to suffer and to die for it. Because now, in the fields, and in the mountains of America, in its plains and in its forests, in the solitude, and in the bustle of cities, on the shores of the great oceans and rivers, it is beginning to shape a world full of quickening hearts, who are ready to die for what is theirs, to conquer their rights which have been flouted for almost 500 years. History will have to tell the story of the poor of America, of the exploited of Latin America, who have decided to begin to write for themselves, forever, their own odyssey. We see them already walking along those roads, on foot, day after day, in long and endless marches, hundreds of kilometers, until they reach the ruling "Olympus" and wrest back their rights. We see them armed with stones, with sticks, with machetes, here, there, everywhere,

daily occupying their lands, and taking root in the land that is theirs and defending it with their lives; we see them carrying banners, their banners running in the wind in the mountains and on the plains. And that wave of heightening fury, of just demands, of rights that have been flouted, is rising throughout Latin America, and no one can stem that tide; it will grow day by day because it is made up of the great multitude in every respect, those who with their work create the riches of the earth, and turn the wheel of history, those who are now awakening from their long, stupefying sleep.

For this great humanity has said "enough" and has started to move forward. And their march, the march of giants, cannot stop, will not stop until they have conquered their true independence, for which many have already died, and not uselessly. In any event, those who die will die like those in Cuba, at Playa Girón; they will die for their never-to-be-renounced, their only true independence."

This new will of a whole continent, America, shows itself in the cry proclaimed daily by our masses as the irrefutable expression of their decision to fight, to grasp and deter the armed hand of the invader. It is a cry that has the understanding and support of all the peoples of the world and especially of the socialist camp, headed by the Soviet Union.

That cry is: "Our country or death."

CHAPTER 30

On Our Common Aspiration—The Death of Imperialism and the Birth of a Moral World[1]

DEAR BROTHERS:

Cuba comes to this conference as the lone voice of the peoples of Latin America. As we emphasized on other occasions, it does so also in its capacity as an underdeveloped country, which at the same time is building socialism. It is no accident that our delegation has been permitted to state the point of view of these countries before the family of Asian and African peoples. Our common aspiration, the defeat of imperialism, unites us in our march toward the future; our common history of struggle against the same enemy has united us along that road.

This is an assembly of the peoples engaged in a struggle which is being maintained on two fronts of equal importance and demands our total effort. The struggle against imperialism—to be rid of colonial or neocolonial bondage—that is being carried on by means of political weapons and weapons of war, or a combination of both, is not unconnected with the struggle against backwardness and poverty. Both are stages in a single journey toward the creation of a new society that is rich and just at the same time. It is imperative to obtain political power and liquidate the oppressive classes, but afterward we must face the second stage of the struggle, which assumes characteristics that are, if that is possible, more difficult than the previous one.

Since monopolistic capital took over the world, it has kept most of humanity in poverty while dividing up the profits among the group of the stronger countries. The standard of living of these countries is based upon the misery of ours. To raise the standard of living of the underdeveloped countries it is therefore necessary to fight against imperialism. Each time a

[1] Speech delivered February 26, 1965, in Algiers during the Afro-Asian Solidarity Conference (Feb. 22–27, 1965) and published in both *Nuestra Industria Económica*, Año 3, No. 13, June 1965, and in *Política Internacional*, Año 3, No. 9, 1965. Translated by Leonard Mades.

country splits off from the imperialist tree, it is not only winning a partial victory against the fundamental enemy, but also contributing to that enemy's real debilitation and taking a step toward final victory.

There are no frontiers in this struggle to the death. We cannot remain indifferent in the face of what occurs in any part of the world. A victory for any one country against imperialism is our victory, just as a defeat for any one country is a defeat for all. The practice of proletarian internationalism is not only a duty of the countries which are struggling to insure a better future; it is also an unavoidable necessity. If the imperialist enemy, American or any other, acts against the underdeveloped peoples and the socialist countries, an elementary logic determines the need for an alliance of the underdeveloped peoples and the socialist countries. If there were no other factor favoring unity, the common enemy would have to constitute it.

Of course these unions cannot be established spontaneously, without discussion and without an occasionally painful birth. Each time a country is liberated, as we have said, it is a defeat for the world imperialist system, but we must agree that the breaking away does not occur because of the mere fact of a declaration of independence or the winning of an armed victory in a revolution. It occurs when imperialist economic rule over a people ceases. Therefore, the socialist countries are vitally interested in these separations really occurring, and it is our international duty, a duty imposed by the ideology from which we take our direction, to contribute with our efforts to the achievement of the liberation in the quickest, most thoroughgoing way possible.

One conclusion must be drawn from all this: The development of the countries that now set out on the road to liberation must cost the socialist countries something. We say it in this manner without the least desire to blackmail anyone or be spectacular. Nor do we say it to make the quest for a closer bond among the Afro-Asian peoples as a whole easier; it is a profound conviction. Socialism cannot exist if a change does not take place, in man's consciousness, that evokes a new fraternal attitude toward humanity. Such a change must be of an individual nature, in the society in which socialism is being built or has already been built, as well as of a worldwide nature in relation to all the peoples who suffer from imperialist oppression.

We believe that it is in this spirit that responsibility for helping dependent countries must be faced and that there must be no talk of developing mutually profitable trade based upon the prices that the Law of Value and international unequal exchange relations impose upon backward countries.

How can selling, at world market prices, the raw materials that cost the backward countries sweat and unlimited suffering, and buying at world market prices the machinery produced in the great present-day automated factories, mean "mutual profit"?

If we establish this type of relationship between the two groups of nations, we must agree that the socialist countries are, in a way, accomplices of imperialist exploitation. It can be argued that the amount of interchange with the underdeveloped countries constitutes an insignificant part of the foreign trade of these countries. It is very true, but it does not eliminate the immoral nature of the interchange.

The socialist countries have the moral duty to liquidate their tacit complicity with the exploiting nations of the West. The fact that the volume of trade is small today means nothing. In 1959 Cuba occasionally sold sugar to a socialist-bloc country, especially through brokers of English or other nationality, and today 80 per cent of its trade is carried on in that area. All its vital supplies come from the socialist camp, and as a matter of fact Cuba has joined that camp. We cannot say that joining it has occurred merely because of the increase in trade, nor that the trade has increased because of Cuba's having broken the old structures and turned toward the socialist form of development; both extremes meet, and both are interrelated.

We did not, when we set forth upon the course that will end in communism, foresee every step as the logical product of an ideological development which proceeds with a fixed objective in view. The truths of socialism, as well as the raw truths of imperialism, were forging our people and showing them the way that we then consciously adopted. The peoples of Africa and Asia who move toward their final liberation will have to take the same path. They will take it sooner or later, even if their socialism today has no clear definition. There is no other valid definition of socialism for us than the abolition of man's exploitation of man. As long as this does not take place, a nation is in the building stage of a socialist society, and if, instead of this phenomenon occurring, the task of eliminating exploitation stagnates or even loses ground, it is invalid to even speak of building socialism.

We must prepare the conditions necessary for our brothers to set out directly and consciously on the road to final elimination of exploitation, but we cannot invite them to set out upon it if we are accomplices in that exploitation. If we were asked what were the ways to establish fair prices, we would be unable to answer. We do not know all sides of this question; we only know that, after political discussions, the Soviet Union and Cuba have signed agreements that are advantageous to us and through which we shall succeed in selling as many as five million tons at fixed prices higher than the normal ones in the so-called free-world sugar market. The Chinese People's Republic also maintains these purchase prices.

This is only an antecedent; the real task consists of fixing prices that permit development. A great change of point of view will consist in changing the order of international relations. Foreign trade must not be what determines policy; on the contrary, the former must be subordinate to a fraternal policy toward the different peoples.

We shall briefly analyze the problem of long-term credits for the development of basic industries. It frequently happens that beneficiary countries prepare to establish industrial bases that are disproportionate to their present capacity and whose products will not be consumed domestically, in addition to which the nation's reserves will be committed by the effort. Our reasoning is that investments by socialist states in their own territory are a direct burden on the government budget and are not recovered except through utilization of the products throughout the complete manufacturing process until the very end of production. Our proposal is that thought be given to the possibility of making investments of this type in underdeveloped countries.

In this way one could set in motion an immense force that has lain beneath the surface of our continents—which have been miserably exploited but never been helped in their development—and begin a new era of authentic international division of labor based not on the history of what has been done until now but on the future history of what can be done.

The countries in whose territories the new investments were made would have all the rights over them that are inherent in sovereign ownership, without any payment or credit whatever being involved. The owners would be required to supply fixed quantities of products to the investing countries for a specified number of years at a specified price.

It is worthwhile to also study ways of financing the local part of the costs a country making investments of this nature must bear. One form of help, which does not entail distributions in freely convertible foreign exchange, could be to supply easily salable products to the governments of the underdeveloped countries by means of long-term credits.

Another problem that is difficult to solve is that of acquiring technical skills. The shortage of technically trained people from which we developing countries suffer is well known to all. There is a lack of educational institutions and teaching personnel. At times there is the lack of a real awareness of our needs and of a determination to carry out a policy of technical, cultural, and ideological development to which a top priority is assigned.

The socialist countries must supply the help needed to establish technical schools, insist on the primary importance of this fact, and furnish the teaching personnel who will make up for the present shortage. It is necessary to insist further on this last point: The experts who come to our countries must be exemplary. They are comrades who will have to face an unfamiliar environment that is often hostile to technology, that speaks a different language, and has totally different habits. The experts who face the difficult task must be, above all, Communists in the deepest and most noble sense of the word. With that quality alone, in addition to a minimum of organization and flexibility, marvels will be accomplished.

We know that it can be achieved because sister countries have sent us a certain number of experts who have done more for the development of our country than ten institutes, and they have contributed more to our friendship than ten ambassadors or a hundred diplomatic receptions.

If we could really put into practice the points that we have noted and could also place within the reach of the underdeveloped countries all the technology of the advanced ones, without following present patent procedures covering discoveries in both groups of countries, we could make much progress with our common task.

Imperialism has been defeated in many limited battles, but it is a considerable force in the world. One cannot aspire to its defeat except through effort and sacrifice by all.

Nevertheless, the whole of the proposed measures cannot be carried out unilaterally. The development of the underdeveloped countries must involve expense to the socialist countries. Agreed, but the forces of the underdeveloped countries must gird themselves and firmly take the path of building a new society—call it what one will—in which the machine, the instrument of work, is not an instrument of man's exploitation of man. Nor can they hope to enjoy the confidence of socialist countries when they waver between capitalism and socialism and try to use both forces as opposing elements in order to derive certain advantages from that competition. A new policy of absolute reliability must govern relations between the two groups of societies. It is well to emphasize once more that the means of production should preferably be in the hands of the state so that the signs of exploitation can gradually disappear.

On the other hand, development must not be left to the most complete improvisation; the building of the new society must be planned. Planning is one of the laws of socialism, and without it the system will not exist. Without correct planning, no adequate guarantee can exist that all economic sectors of any country will be harmoniously linked so as to permit the forward strides that this era we live in demands. Planning is not an isolated problem of each one of our countries. They are small and misshapen in their development, and while they possess a few raw materials or produce a few manufactured or semi-manufactured products, they lack the majority of the others. The planning will have to tend from the very beginning toward a certain regional unity in order to sink into the countries' minds and thus achieve an integration based upon authentic mutual profit.

We believe the present path is full of dangers—dangers that are neither invented nor envisioned in the distant future by some superior mind; they are the inevitable result of the realities that beset us. The struggle against colonialism has reached its final stages, but in the present period, colonial status is only a manifestation of imperialist domination. By definition, as long as imperialism exists it will exert its domination over other countries. This domination is called neocolonialism today.

Neocolonialism developed first in South America, throughout an entire continent, and today it is beginning to make itself felt with increasing intensity in Africa and Asia. Its method of penetration and development has distinct characteristics. One of these is the brutal one with which we became acquainted in the Congro. Brute force, without hesitation or subterfuge of any kind, is its ultimate weapon. There is another that is more subtle: penetration of countries that liberate themselves politically, ties with the nascent native bourgeoisies, development of a parasitic middle class that is in close alliance with big-city interests on the basis of a certain transitory prosperity or minor improvement in the people's standard of living due to the fact that in very backward countries the mere transition from feudal relationships to capitalist relationships means a big advance, apart from the tragic consequences they bring for the workers in the long run.

Neocolonialism has shown its claws in the Congo—a sign not of power but of weakness. It has had to resort to its ultimate weapon, force, as an economic argument, which provokes contrary reactions of great intensity. But force is being shown in another series of Asian and African countries in a much more subtle form, and we are witnessing what has been called the South Americanization of these continents, that is, the development of a parasitic bourgeoisie. The latter adds nothing to the wealth of the nation; it even deposits its huge ill-gotten gains in capitalist banks outside the country and enters into agreements with the foreigner in order to reap more profit, with an absolute scorn for the welfare of its country's people.

There are also other dangers, such as competition among sister countries that are friends politically and sometimes neighbors but try to develop the same investments at the same time and in markets that often do not permit it. This competition has the defect of wasting energies that could be used to complement each other economically on a much vaster scale and permit the operation of imperialist monopolies.

On occasion, in the face of the real impossibility of making a particular investment with the help of the socialist camp, an investment is made through agreements with the capitalists. And these capitalist investments not only have the disadvantage of the manner in which loans are made, but also attendant disadvantages of great importance, such as the establishment of mixed companies with a dangerous partner. As the investments are generally parallel to those of other countries, this tends toward divisions among friendly countries, due to economic competition, and creates the danger of corruption arising out of the constant presence of capitalism, which is adept at presenting an image of development and well-being that beclouds the understanding of many people.

Later on the decline of market prices is the consequence of the saturation of products of a similar nature. The countries affected are compelled to request new loans or allow supplementary investments to maintain their competitiveness. The decline of the economy in the hands of the monopolies, and a slow but sure return to the past, is the final consequence of such a policy. In our judgment the only safe way to handle investments with the participation of imperialist powers is the direct participation of the state as the purchaser of all goods, and the limitation of imperialist freedom to supply contracts. In this way the imperialists will not get past the street door of our house. And here it is indeed legitimate to profit by inter-imperialist contradictions in order to obtain less onerous conditions.

It is necessary to be alert to the "disinterested" economic, cultural, and other such aid that imperialism extends either directly or through puppet states that are more acceptable in certain parts of the world.

If all the dangers noted here are not seen in time, the path to neocolonialism may be embarked upon in countries that have begun their task of national liberation with faith and enthusiasm. Domination by the monopolies may be established by subtle means that are so gradual that it is very difficult to perceive their effects until they are felt in all their brutality.

There is a whole great task to be performed. Immense problems are presented to our two worlds, the world of the socialist countries and this one which is known as the third world. They are problems that are directly related to man and his well-being and to the struggle against the main culprits guilty of our backwardness. All we countries and peoples who are aware of our duties and of the dangers that the situation entails must take definite steps to solve these problems so that our friendship can be cemented on two planes, the economic and the political, which can never be separate. We must form a large compact bloc that will in turn help other countries liberate themselves not only from imperialist political power but from imperialist economic power as well. The question of armed liberation from an oppressive political power must be handled in accordance with the rules of proletarian internationalism. If it is absurd to think the head of a business enterprise in a socialist country that is at war will hesitate to send the tanks he produces to a front where there is no guarantee of payment, no less absurd must it seem to investigate the possibility of payment by a country that is struggling to liberate itself or is in need of those arms for the defense of its liberty. Arms must not be like merchandise in our worlds; they should be delivered without any cost whatever and in the quantities necessary and possible to the peoples who request them for use against the common enemy. This is the spirit in which the U.S.S.R. and the Chinese People's Republic have offered us their military aid. We are socialists and are our own guarantee of the utilization of these arms, but we are not the only ones, and all must receive the same treatment.

The ominous American imperialist attack on Vietnam or the Congo must be answered with the supplying of these sister countries with all the weapons of defense they need and with the offer of our complete and absolutely unconditional solidarity.

In the economic sphere, we must win the battle of development by using the most advanced technology possible. We cannot start at the bottom of humanity's long ascent from feudalism to the atomic age of automation; it would be a course involving enormous sacrifices and it would, in part, be useless. Technology must be adopted at its present level; there must be the great technical leap forward in order to diminish the difference which exists today between the more developed countries and us. This technology must be in the great factories and also in a suitably developed agriculture. Above all it must rest upon a foundation of a technical and ideological culture that has sufficient strength and mass basis to permit the continuous supplying of the institutes and research facilities that must be established in each country. It must also furnish the men who will employ present technology and be capable of adapting to the newly acquired technological knowledge.

These cadres must be clearly aware of their duty to the society in which they live. There cannot be a proper technical culture if it is not supplemented by an ideological culture. In the majority of our countries it will not be possible to have an adequate base under our industrial development, which is the one that determines the development of modern society, if we do not begin by assuring the people of the food they need, the most essential consumer goods, and an adequate education.

It is necessary to spend a good part of the national income on the so-called nonproductive investments in education, and we must give preferential attention to the development of agricultural productivity. The latter has reached really incredible levels in many capitalist countries, giving rise to the absurdity of overproduction crises and the dumping of grains and other food products or industrial raw materials originating in developed countries. This while there is an entire world suffering from hunger while possessing sufficient land and manpower to produce several times what the whole world needs to feed itself.

Agriculture must be considered a fundamental pillar of development. Toward this end changes in the agricultural structure, and adaptation to the new technological possibilities and the new tasks arising from the elimination of the exploitation of men, must constitute basic features of labor.

Before making costly decisions that could cause irreparable damage, it is necessary to make a careful survey of the territory of the nation; this constitutes one of the preliminary steps in economic research and is an elementary requirement of correct planning.

We warmly support Algeria's proposal regarding the institutionalization of our relations. We wish only to present some supplementary considerations.

First: For our union to be the instrument of the struggle against imperialism, the participation of the Latin American countries and of the alliance of socialist countries is necessary.

Second: We guard the revolutionary character of the union. Admission into it must be denied to governments or movements that are not identified with the general aspirations of our peoples, and machinery must be established that would permit the separation of any who deviate from the right path, be they governments or popular movements.

Third: We must protect the establishment of new relations on a basis of equality between our countries and the capitalist ones. A revolutionary jurisprudence must be established that will assist us in the event of conflict and give new content to relations between ourselves and the rest of the world.

We speak a revolutionary language and struggle earnestly for the triumph of the revolutionary cause, but we often are ourselves enmeshed in international law that was created as a result of the conflicts among imperialist powers and not as a result of disputes among free, just peoples. Our peoples, for example, suffer from the grievous pressure of foreign bases established on our territory or must bear the heavy burden of foreign debts of incredible magnitude.

The history of these trials is well known to all. Puppet governments, governments weakened by a long struggle for liberation or by the development of capitalist laws of the market place, have permitted the signing of agreements which menace our internal stability and compromise our future.

It is time to throw off the yoke, compel renegotiation of oppressive external debts, and force the imperialists to abandon their bases for aggression.

I would not want to conclude these words, this repetition of concepts that are familiar to you all, without calling the attention of this seminar to the fact that Cuba is not the only Latin American country; it just happens to be the one that has the opportunity to speak to you today. Other countries are shedding their blood to acquire the rights we now have. Here and at all conferences, wherever they may be held, we should—along with our greeting to the heroic peoples of Vietnam, Laos, "Portuguese" Guinea, South Africa, or Palestine—extend to all exploited countries struggling for emancipation our friendly voice, our hand, and our encouragement; to our brothers in Venezuela, Guatemala, and Colombia who, having taken up arms today, are saying a final *"No!"* to the imperialist enemy.

There are few places from which to encourage them that are as symbolic as Algiers, one of the most heroic capitals of liberty. Let the magnificent Algerian people—trained like few others by the sufferings endured in their achievement of independence, under the determined leadership of their party and with our dear comrade Ahmed Ben Bella at their head—serve as an inspiration to us in this battle without quarter against world imperialism.

CHAPTER 31

Man and Socialism in Cuba[1]

DEAR COMRADE:

I am finishing these notes while traveling through Africa, moved by the desire to keep my promise, although after some delay. I should like to do so by dealing with the topic that appears in the title. I believe it might be of interest to Uruguayan readers.

It is common to hear how capitalist spokesmen use as an argument in the ideological struggle against socialism the assertion that such a social system, or the period of building socialism upon which we have embarked, is characterized by the extinction of the individual for the sake of the state. I will make no attempt to refute this assertion on a merely theoretical basis, but will instead establish the facts of the Cuban experience and add commentaries of a general nature. I shall first broadly sketch the history of our revolutionary struggle both before and after taking of power.

As we know, the exact date of the beginning of the revolutionary actions which were to culminate on January 1, 1959, was July 26, 1953. A group of men led by Fidel Castro attacked the Moncada military garrison in the province of Oriente, in the early hours of the morning of that day. The attack was a failure. The failure became a disaster and the survivors were imprisoned, only to begin the revolutionary struggle all over again, once they were amnestied.

During this process, which contained only the first seeds of socialism, man was a basic factor. Man—individualized, specific, named—was trusted and the triumph or failure of the task entrusted to him depended on his capacity for action.

Then came the stage of guerrilla warfare. It was carried out in two different environments: the people, an as yet unawakened mass that had to be mobilized, and its vanguard, the guerrilla, the thrusting engine of mo-

[1] Letter to Carlos Quijano, editor-publisher of the Uruguayan weekly, *Marcha*, written early in 1965, then published in Cuba as "El socialismo y el hombre en Cuba," Havana: Ediciones R. Official government translation by Margarita Zimmermann.

bilization, the generator of revolutionary awareness and militant enthusiasm. This vanguard was the catalyst which created the subjective condition necessary for victory. The individual was also the basic factor in the guerrilla, in the framework of the gradual proletarianization of our thinking, in the revolution taking place in our habits and in our minds. Each and every one of the Sierra Maestra fighters who achieved a high rank in the revolutionary forces has to his credit a list of noteworthy deeds. It was on the basis of such deeds that they earned their rank.

It was the first heroic period in which men strove to earn posts of greater responsibility, of greater danger, with the fulfillment of their duty as the only satisfaction. In our revolutionary educational work we often return to this instructive topic. The man of the future could be glimpsed in the attitude of our fighters.

At other times of our history there have been repetitions of this utter devotion to the revolutionary cause. During the October Crisis and at the time of the hurricane Flora, we witnessed deeds of exceptional valor and self-sacrifice carried out by an entire people. One of our fundamental tasks from the ideological standpoint is to find the way to perpetuate such heroic attitudes in everyday life.

The revolutionary government was established in 1959 with the participation of several members of the "sell-out" bourgeoisie. The presence of the rebel army constituted the guarantee of power as the fundamental factor of strength.

Serious contradictions arose which were solved in the first instance in February 1959, when Fidel Castro assumed the leadership of the government in the post of Prime Minister. This process culminated in July of the same year with the resignation of President Urrutia in the face of mass pressure.

With clearly defined features, there now appeared in the history of the Cuban Revolution a personage which will systematically repeat itself: the masses.

This multifacetic being is not, as it is claimed, the sum total of elements of the same category (and moreover, reduced to the same category by the system imposed upon them) and which acts as a tame herd. It is true that the mass follows its leaders, especially Fidel Castro, without hesitation, but the degree to which he has earned such confidence is due precisely to the consummate interpretation of the people's desires and aspirations, and to the sincere struggle to keep the promises made.

The mass participated in the agrarian reform and in the difficult undertaking of the management of the state enterprises; it underwent the heroic experience of Playa Girón; it was tempered in the struggle against the groups of bandits armed by the CIA; during the October Crisis it lived one of the most important definitions of modern times, and today it continues the work to build socialism.

Looking at things from a superficial standpoint, it might seem that those who speak of the submission of the individual to the state are right; with incomparable enthusiasm and discipline, the mass carries out the tasks set by the government whatever their nature: economic, cultural, defense, sports, etc. The initiative generally comes from Fidel or the high command of the revolution: It is explained to the people, who make it their own. At times local experiences are taken up by the party and the government and are thereby generalized, following the same procedure.

However, the state at times makes mistakes. When this occurs, the collective enthusiasm diminishes palpably as a result of a quantitative diminishing that takes place in each of the elements that make up the collective, and work becomes paralyzed until it finally shrinks to insignificant proportions; this is the time to rectify.

This was what happened in March 1962 in the presence of the sectarian policy imposed on the party by Anibal Escalante.

This mechanism is obviously not sufficient to ensure a sequence of sensible measures; what is missing is a more structured relationship with the mass. We must improve this connection in the years to come, but for now, in the case of the initiatives arising on the top levels of government, we are using the almost intuitive method of keeping our ears open to the general reactions in the face of the problems that are posed.

Fidel is a past master at this; his particular mode of integration with the people can only be appreciated by seeing him in action. In the big public meetings one can observe something like the dialogue of two tuning forks whose vibrations summon forth new vibrations each in the other. Fidel and the mass begin to vibrate in a dialogue of growing intensity which reaches its culminating point in an abrupt ending crowned by our victorious battle cry.

What is hard to understand for anyone who has not lived the revolutionary experience is that close dialectical unity which exists between the individual and the mass, in which both are interrelated, and the mass, as a whole composed of individuals, is in turn interrelated with the leader.

Under capitalism certain phenomena of this nature can be observed with the appearance on the scene of politicians capable of mobilizing the public, but if it is not an authentic social movement, in which case it is not completely accurate to speak of capitalism, the movement will have the same life span as its promoter or until the rigors of capitalist society put an end to popular illusions. Under capitalism man is guided by a cold ordinance which is usually beyond his comprehension. The alienated human individual is bound to society as a whole by an invisible umbilical cord: the law of value. It acts upon all facets of his life, shaping his road and his destiny.

The laws of capitalism, invisible and blind for most people, act upon the individual without his awareness. He sees only the broadness of horizon that appears infinite. Capitalist propaganda presents it in just this way, and attempts to use the Rockefeller case (true or not) as a lesson in the prospects for success. The misery that must be accumulated for such an example to arise and the sum total of baseness contributing to the formation of a fortune of such magnitude do not appear in the picture, and the popular forces are not always able to make these concepts clear. (It would be fitting at this point to study how the workers of the imperialist countries gradually lose their international class spirit under the influence of a certain complicity in the exploitation of the dependent countries and how this fact at the same time wears away the militant spirit of the masses within their own national context, but this topic is outside the framework of the present note.)

In any case we can see the obstacle course which may apparently be overcome by an individual with the necessary qualities to arrive at the finish line. The reward is glimpsed in the distance and the road is solitary. Furthermore, it is a race of wolves: He who arrives does so only at the expense of the failure of others.

I shall now attempt to define the individual, the actor in this strange and moving drama that is the building of socialism, in his twofold existence as a unique being and a member of the community.

I believe that the simplest approach is to recognize his unmade quality: he is an unfinished product. The flaws of the past are translated into the present in the individual consciousness and constant efforts must be made to eradicate them. The process is twofold: On the one hand society acts upon the individual by means of direct and indirect education, while on the other hand the individual undergoes a conscious phase of self-education.

The new society in process of formation has to compete very hard with the past. This makes itself felt not only in the individual consciousness, weighed down by the residues of an education and an upbringing systematically oriented toward the isolation of the individual, but also by the very nature of this transition period, with the persistence of commodity relations. The commodity is the economic cell of capitalist society: As long as it exists, its effects will make themselves felt in the organization of production and therefore in man's consciousness.

Marx's scheme conceived of the transition period as the result of the explosive transformation of the capitalist system torn apart by its inner contradictions: Subsequent reality has shown how some countries, the weak limbs, detach themselves from the imperialist tree, a phenomenon foreseen by Lenin. In those countries capitalism has developed sufficiently to make its effects felt upon the people in one way or another, but it is not its own inner contradictions that explode the system after exhausting all of its possibilities. The struggle for liberation against an external oppressor, the misery which has its origin in foreign causes, such as war, whose consequences make the privileged classes fall upon the exploited, the liberation movements aimed at overthrowing neocolonial regimes, are the customary factors in this process. Conscious action does the rest.

In these countries there still has not been achieved a complete education for the work of society, and wealth is far from being within the reach of the masses through the simple process of appropriation. Underdevelopment and the customary flight of capital to "civilized" countries make impossible a rapid change without sacrifices. There still remains a long stretch to be covered in the building of the economic base, and the temptation to follow the beaten paths of material interest as the lever of speedy development is very great.

There is a danger of not seeing the forest because of the trees. Pursuing the chimera of achieving socialism with the aid of the blunted weapons left to us by capitalism (the commodity as the economic cell, profitability and individual material interest as levers, etc.), it is possible to come to a blind alley. And the arrival there comes about after covering a long distance where there are many crossroads and where it is difficult to realize just when the wrong turn was taken. Meanwhile, the adapted economic base has undermined the development of consciousness. To build communism, a new man must be created simultaneously with the material base.

That is why it is so important to choose correctly the instrument of mass mobilization. That instrument must be fundamentally of a moral character, without forgetting the correct use of material incentives, especially those of a social nature.

As I already said, in moments of extreme danger it is easy to activate moral incentives: To maintain their effectiveness, it is necessary to develop a consciousness in which values acquire new categories. Society as a whole must become a huge school.

The broad characteristics of the phenomenon are similar to the process of formation of capitalist consciousness in the system's first stage. Capitalism resorts to force, but it also educates people in the system. Direct propaganda is carried out by those who are entrusted with the task of explaining the inevitability of a class regime, whether it be of divine origin or due to the imposition of nature as a mechanical entity. This placates the masses, who see themselves oppressed by an evil against which it is not possible to struggle.

This is followed by hope, which differentiates capitalism from the previous caste regimes that offered no way out. For some the caste formula continues in force: The obedient are rewarded by the *post mortem* arrival in other wonderful worlds where the good are requited, and the old tradition is continued. For others, innovation: The division in classes is a matter of fate, but individuals can leave the class to which they belong through work, initiative, etc. This process, and that of self-education for success, must be deeply hypocritical: It is the interested demonstration that a lie is true.

In our case, direct education acquires much greater importance. Explanations are convenient because they are genuine; subterfuges are not needed. It is carried out through the State's educational apparatus in the form of general, technical, and ideological culture, by means of bodies such as the Ministry of Education and the party's information apparatus. Education takes among the masses, and the new attitude that is praised tends to become habit; the mass gradually takes it over and exerts pressure on those who have still not become educated. This is the indirect way of educating the masses, as powerful as the other, structured, one.

But the process is a conscious one: The individual receives the impact of the new social power and perceives that he is not completely adequate to it. Under the influence of the pressure implied in indirect education, he tries to adjust to a situation that he feels to be just and whose lack of development has kept him from doing so thus far. He is educating himself.

We can see the new man who begins to emerge in this period of the building of socialism. His image is as yet unfinished. In fact it will never be finished, since the process advances parallel to the development of new economic forms. Discounting those whose lack of education makes them tend toward the solitary road, toward the satisfaction of their ambitions, there are others who, even within this new picture of over-all advances, tend to march in isolation from the accompanying mass. What is important is that people become more aware every day of the need to incorporate themselves into society and of their own importance as motors of that society.

They no longer march in complete solitude along lost roads toward far-off longings. They follow their vanguard, composed of the party, of the most advanced workers, of the advanced men who move along bound to the masses and in close communion with them. The vanguards have their eyes on the future and its recompenses, but the latter are not envisioned as something individual; the reward is the new society, where human beings will have different characteristics: the society of communist man.

The road is long and full of difficulties. At times the route strays off course, and it is necessary to retreat; at times, a too rapid pace separates us from the masses, and on occasions the pace is slow, and we feel upon our necks the breath of those who follow upon our heels. Our ambition as revolutionaries makes us try to move forward as far as possible, opening up the way before use, but we know that we must be reinforced by the mass, while the mass will be able to advance more rapidly if we encourage it by our example.

In spite of the importance given to moral incentives, the existence of two principal groups (excluding, of course, the minority fraction of those who do not participate for one reason or another in the building of socialism) is an indication of the relative lack of development of social consciousness. The vanguard group is ideologically more advanced than the mass; the latter is acquainted with the new values, but insufficiently. While in the former a qualitative change takes place which permits them to make sacrifices as a function of their vanguard character, the latter see only by halves and must be subjected to incentives and pressures of some intensity; it is the dictatorship of the proletariat being exercised not only upon the defeated class but also individually upon the victorious class.

To achieve total success, all of this involves the necessity of a series of mechanisms, the revolutionary institutions. The concept of institutionalization fits in with the images of the multitudes marching toward the future as that of a harmonic unit of canals, steps, well-oiled apparatuses that make the march possible, that permit the natural selection of those who are destined to march in the vanguard and who dispense rewards and punishments to those who fulfill their duty or act against the society under construction.

The institutionality of the Revolution has still not been achieved. We are seeking something new that will allow a perfect identification between the government and the community as a whole, adapted to the special conditions of the building of socialism and avoiding to the utmost the commonplaces of bourgeois democracy transplanted to the society in formation (such as legislative houses, for example). Some experiments have been carried out with the aim of gradually creating the institutionalization of the Revolution, but without too much hurry. We have been greatly restrained by the fear that any formal aspect might make us lose sight of the ultimate and most important revolutionary aspiration: to see man freed from alienation.

Notwithstanding the lack of institutions, which must be overcome gradually, the masses now make history as a conscious aggregate of individuals who struggle for the same cause. In spite of the apparent standardization of man in socialism, he is more complete; his possibilities for expressing himself and making himself heard in the social apparatus are infinitely greater, in spite of the lack of a perfect mechanism to do so.

It is still necessary to accentuate his conscious, individual and collective, participation in all the mechanisms of direction and production and associate it with the idea of the need for technical and ideological education, so that the individual will realize that these processes are closely interdependent and their advances are parallel. He will thus achieve total awareness of his social being, which is equivalent to his full realization as a human being, having broken the chains of alienation.

This will be translated concretely into the reappropriation of his nature through freed work and the expression of his own human condition in culture and art.

In order for it to develop in culture, work must acquire a new condition; man as commodity ceases to exist, and a system is established that grants a quota for the fulfillment of social duty. The means of production belong to society, and the machine is only the front line where duty is performed. Man begins to free his thought from the bothersome fact that presupposed the need to satisfy his animal needs by working. He begins to see himself portrayed in his work and to understand its human magnitude through the created object, through the work carried out. This no longer involves leaving a part of his being in the form of labor power sold, which no longer belongs to him; rather it signifies an emanation from himself, a contribution to the life of society in which he is reflected, the fulfillment of his social duty.

We are doing everything possible to give work this new category of social duty and to join it to the development of technology, on the one hand, which will provide the conditions for greater freedom, and to voluntary work on the other, based on the Marxist concept that man truly achieves his full human condition when he produces without being compelled by the physical necessity of selling himself as a commodity.

It is clear that work still has coercive aspects, even when it is voluntary: Man has still not transformed all the coercion surrounding him into conditioned reflexes of a social nature, and in many cases he still produces under the pressure of the environment (Fidel calls this moral compulsion). He is still to achieve complete spiritual recreation in the presence of his own work, without the direct pressure of the social environment but bound to it by new habits. That will be communism.

The change in consciousness does not come about automatically, just as it does not come about automatically in the economy. The variations are slow and not rhythmic; there are periods of acceleration, others are measured and some even involve a retreat.

We must also consider, as we have pointed out previously, that we are not before a pure transition period such as that envisioned by Marx in the "Critique of the Gotha Program," but rather a new phase not foreseen by him: the first period in the transition to communism or in the building of socialism.

Elements of capitalism are present within this process, which takes place in the midst of violent class struggle. These elements obscure the complete understanding of the essence of the process.

If to this be added the scholasticism that has held back the development of Marxist philosophy and impeded the systematic treatment of the period, whose political economy has still not been developed, we must agree that we are still in diapers. We must study all the primordial features of the period before elaborating a more far-reaching economic and political theory.

The resulting theory will necessarily give preeminence to the two pillars of socialist construction: the formation of the new human being and the development of technology. We still have a great deal to accomplish in both aspects, but the delay is less justifiable as far as the conception of technology as the basis is concerned: Here, it is not a matter of advancing blindly, but rather of following for a sizable stretch the road opened up by the most advanced countries of the world. This is why Fidel harps so insistently on the necessity of the technological and scientific formation of all of our people and especially of the vanguard.

In the field of ideas that lead to nonproductive activities, it is easier to see the division between material and spiritual needs. For a long time man has been trying to free himself from alienation through culture and art. He dies daily in the eight and more hours during which he performs as a commodity to resuscitate in his spiritual creation. But this remedy itself bears the germs of the same disease: He is a solitary being who seeks communion with nature. He defends his environment-oppressed individuality and reacts to esthetic ideas as a unique being whose aspiration is to remain immaculate.

It is only an attempt at flight. The law of value is no longer a mere reflection of production relations; the monopoly capitalists have surrounded it with a complicated scaffolding which makes of it a docile servant, even when the methods used are purely empirical. The artist must be educated in the kind of art imposed by the superstructure. The rebels are overcome by the apparatus, and only exceptional talents are able to create their own work. The others become shame-faced wage-workers, or they are crushed.

Artistic experimentation is invented and is taken as the definition of freedom, but this "experimentation" has limits which are imperceptible until they are clashed with, that is, when the real problems of man and his alienated condition are dealt with. Senseless anguish or vulgar pastimes are comfortable safety valves for human uneasiness; the idea of making art a weapon of denunciation and accusation is combatted.

If the rules of the game are respected, all honors are obtained—the honors that might be granted to a pirouette-creating monkey. The condition is not attempting to escape from the invisible cage.

When the Revolution took power, the exodus of the totally domesticated took place; the others, revolutionaries or not, saw a new road. Artistic experimentation took on new force. However, the routes were more or less traced, and the concept of flight was the hidden meaning behind the word freedom. This attitude, a reflection in consciousness of bourgeois idealism, was frequently maintained in the revolutionaries themselves.

In countries that have gone through a similar process, endeavors were made to combat these tendencies with an exaggerated dogmatism. General culture became something like a taboo, and a formally exact representation of nature was proclaimed as the height of cultural aspiration. This later became a mechanical representation of social reality created by wishful thinking: the ideal society, almost without conflict or contradictions, that man was seeking to create.

Socialism is young and makes mistakes. We revolutionaries often lack the knowledge and the intellectual audacity to face the task of the development of the new human being by methods different from the conventional ones, and the conventional methods suffer from the influence of the society that created them (once again the topic of the relation between form and content appears). Disorientation is great and the problems of material construction absorb us. There are no artists of great authority who also have great revolutionary authority.

The men of the party must take this task upon themselves and seek the achievement of the principal aim: to educate the people.

What is then sought is simplification, what everyone understands, that is, what the functionaries understand. True artistic experimentation is obliterated and the problem of general culture is reduced to the assimilation of the socialist present and the dead (and therefore not dangerous) past. Socialist realism is thus born on the foundation of the art of the last century.

But the realistic art of the nineteenth century is also class art, perhaps more purely capitalist than the decadent art of the twentieth century, where the anguish of alienated man shows through. In culture, capitalism has given all that it had to give and all that remains of it is the foretaste of a bad-smelling corpse; in art, its present decadence. But why endeavor to seek in the frozen forms of socialist realism the only valid recipe? "Freedom" cannot be set against socialist realism because the former does not yet exist: It will not come into being until the complete development of the new society. But let us not attempt to condemn all post-midnineteenth-century art forms from the pontifical throne of realism-at-all-costs. That would mean committing the Proudhonian error of the return to the past, and straitjacketing the artistic expression of the man who is born and being formed today.

An ideological and cultural mechanism must be developed which will permit experimentation and clear out the weeds that shoot up so easily in the fertilized soil of state subsidization.

The error of mechanical realism has not appeared (in Cuba), but reather the contrary. This is so because of the lack of understanding of the need to create a new human being who will represent neither nineteenth-century ideas nor those of our decadent and morbid century. It is the twenty-first-century man whom we must create, although this is still a subjective and unsystematic aspiration. This is precisely one of the basic points of our studies and work; to the extent that we make concrete achievements on a theoretical base or vice versa, that we come to broad theoretical conclusions on the basis of our concrete studies, we will have made a valuable contribution to Marxism-Leninism, to the cause of mankind.

The reaction against nineteenth-century man has brought a recurrence of twentieth-century decadence. It is not a very serious error, but we must overcome it so as not to leave the doors open to revisionism.

The large multitudes of people are developing themselves, the new ideas are acquiring an adequate impetus within society, the material possibilities of the integral development of each and every one of its members make the task ever more fruitful. The present is one of struggle; the future is ours.

To sum up, the fault of many of our intellectuals and artists is to be found in their "original sin": They are not authentically revolutionary. We can attempt to graft elm trees so they bear pears, but at the same time we must plant pear trees. The new generations will arrive free of "original sin." The likelihood that exceptional artists will arise will be that much greater because of the enlargement of the cultural field and the possibilities for expression. Our job is to keep the present generation, maladjusted by its conflicts, from becoming perverted and perverting the new generations. We do not want to create salaried workers docile to official thinking or "fellows" who live under the wing of the budget, exercising freedom in quotation marks. Revolutionaries will come to sing the song of the new man with the authentic voice of the people. It is a process that requires time.

In our society the youth and the party play a big role. The former is particularly important because it is the malleable clay with which the new man, without any of the previous defects, can be formed.

Youth receives treatment in consonance with our aspirations. Education is increasingly integral, and we do not neglect the incorporation of the students into work from the very beginning. Our scholarship students do physical work during vacation or together with their studies. In some cases work is a prize, while in others it is an educational tool; it is never a punishment. A new generation is being born.

The party is a vanguard organization. The best workers are proposed by their comrades for membership. The party is a minority, but the quality of its cadres gives it great authority. Our aspiration is that the party become a mass one, but only when the masses reach the level of development of the vanguard, that is, when they are educated for communism. Our work is aimed at providing that education. The party is the living example; its cadres must be full professors of assiduity and sacrifice; with their acts they must lead the masses to the end of the revolutionary task, which means years of struggle against the difficulties of construction, the class enemies, the defects of the past, imperialism.

I should now like to explain the role played by the personality, the man as the individual who leads the masses that make history. This is our experience, and not a recipe.

Fidel gave impulse to the Revolution in its first years, he has always given it leadership and set the tone, but there is a good group of revolutionaries developing in the same direction as Fidel and a large mass that follows its leaders because it has faith in them. It has faith in them because these leaders have known how to interpret the longings of the masses.

It is not a question of how many kilograms of meat are eaten or how many times a year someone may go on holiday to the seashore or how many pretty imported things can be bought with present wages. It is rather that the individual feels greater fulfillment, that he has greater inner wealth and many more responsibilities. In our country the individual knows that the glorious period in which it has fallen to him to live is one of sacrifice; he is familiar with sacrifice.

The first came to know it in the Sierra Maestra and wherever there was fighting; later we have known it in all Cuba. Cuba is the vanguard of America and must make sacrifices because it occupies the advance position, because it points out to the Latin American masses the road to full freedom.

Within the country, the leaders have to fulfill their vanguard role; and it must be said with complete sincerity that in a true revolution, to which you give yourself completely without any thought for material retribution, the task of the vanguard revolutionary is both magnificent and anguishing.

Let me say, with the risk of appearing ridiculous, that the true revolutionary is guided by strong feelings of love. It is impossible to think of an authentic revolutionary without this quality. This is perhaps one of the great dramas of a leader; he must combine an impassioned spirit with a cold mind and make painful decisions without flinching. Our vanguard revolutionaries must idealize their love for the people, for the most hallowed causes, and make it one and indivisible. They cannot descend, with small doses of daily affection, to the terrain where ordinary men put their love into practice.

The leaders of the Revolution have children who do not learn to call their father with their first faltering words; they have wives who must be part of the general sacrifice of their lives to carry the Revolution to its destination; their friends are strictly limited to their comrades in revolution. There is no life outside the Revolution.

In these conditions the revolutionary leaders must have a large dose of humanity, a large dose of a sense of justice and truth, to avoid falling into dogmatic extremes, into cold scholasticism, into isolation from the masses. They must struggle every day so that their love of living humanity is transformed into concrete deeds, into acts that will serve as an example, as a mobilizing factor.

The revolutionary, ideological motor of the Revolution within his party, is consumed by this uninterrupted activity that ends only with death, unless construction be achieved on a worldwide scale. If his revolutionary eagerness becomes dulled when the most urgent tasks are carried on a local scale, and if he forgets about proletarian internationalism, the revolution that he leads ceases to be a driving force and it sinks into a comfortable drowsiness which is taken advantage of by imperialism, our irreconcilable enemy, to gain ground. Proletarian internationalism is a duty, but it is also a revolutionary need. This is how we educate our people.

It is evident that there are dangers in the present circumstances. Not only that of dogmatism, not only that of the freezing up of relations with the masses in the midst of the great task; there also exists the danger of weaknesses in which it is possible to incur. If a man thinks that in order to devote his entire life to the Revolution, he cannot be distracted by the worry that one of his children lacks a certain article, that the children's shoes are in poor condition, that his family lacks some necessary item; with this reasoning, the seeds of future corruption are allowed to filter through.

In our case we have maintained that our children must have, or lack, what the children of the ordinary citizen have or lack; our family must understand this and struggle for it. The Revolution is made by man, but man must forge his revolutionary spirit from day to day.

Thus we go forward. Fidel is at the head of the immense column—we are neither ashamed nor afraid to say so—followed by the best party cadres, and right after them, so close that their great strength is felt, come the people as a whole, a solid bulk of individualities moving toward a common aim; individuals who have achieved the awareness of what must be done; men who struggle to leave the domain of necessity and enter that of freedom.

That immense multitude is ordering itself; its order responds to an awareness of the need for order; it is no longer a dispersed force, divisible in thousands of fractions shot into space like the fragments of a grenade, trying by any and all means, in a fierce struggle with their equals, to achieve a position that would give them support in the face of an uncertain future.

We know that we have sacrifices ahead of us and that we must pay a price for the heroic fact of constituting a vanguard as a nation. We, the leaders, know that we must pay a price for having the right to say that we are at the head of the people that is at the head of America.

Each and every one of us punctually pays his share of sacrifice, aware of being rewarded by the satisfaction of fulfilling our duty, aware of advancing with everyone toward the new human being who is to be glimpsed on the horizon.

Allow me to attempt to come to some conclusions:

We socialists are more free because we are more fulfilled: We are more fulfilled because we are more free.

The skeleton of our complete freedom is formed, but it lacks the protein substance and the draperies. We will create them.

Our freedom and its daily sustenance are the color of blood and swollen with sacrifice.

Our sacrifice is a conscious one: It is in payment for the freedom we are building.

The road is long and in part unknown; we are aware of our limitations. We will make the twenty-first-century man; we ourselves.

We will be tempered in daily actions, creating a new human being with a new technology.

The personality plays the role of mobilization and leadership in so far as it incarnates the highest virtues and aspirations of the people and does not become detoured.

The road is opened up by the vanguard group, the best among the good, the party.

The basic raw material of our work is the youth: In it we place our hopes and we are preparing it to take the banner from our hands.

If this faltering letter has made some things clear, it will have fulfilled my purpose in sending it.

Accept our ritual greetings, as a handshake or an "Ave María Purísima."

Patria o muerte

CHAPTER 32

Socialist Planning[1]

In issue Number Thirty-two of the review, *Cuba Socialista,* an article appeared by Comrade Charles Bettelheim, entitled "Forms and Methods of Socialist Planning and the Level of Development of Productive Forces." This article touches on points of real interest, but it is especially important for us because it was written in defense of the so-called Economic Calculus and of the categories which this system implies exist within the socialist sector—categories such as money as a function of means of payment, credit, goods, etc.

We believe that two fundamental errors have been made in this article, and we will try to point them out.

The first refers to the interpretation of the necessary correlation that must exist between the productive forces and the relationships of production.[2] To illustrate this point, Comrade Bettelheim draws from the Marxist classics.

Productive forces and social relationships of production are two mechanisms which go hand in hand in all the mediating processes of social development. When are the relationships of production no longer a faithful reflection of the development of the productive forces? At the moment when a new society appears to smash the old one, and while the old society is breaking up; when the new one, whose relationships of production have yet to be established, is struggling to consolidate itself and destroy the old superstructure. Thus, when analyzed correctly, the productive forces and the relationships of production will not, at a given historical moment, exactly correspond to one another. This is precisely the theory that allowed Lenin to declare that the October Revolution was socialist, and at another

[1] *Nuestra Industria Económica,* Año 3, No. 12, April, 1965. Translated by Morton Marks and Robert Novick.

[2] Marxist language for the relationships among men in their role as producers (ed.).

time to say that it could adopt state capitalism and exercise caution in dealing with the peasantry. The reason for Lenin's statement is found in his great discovery of the development of the world-wide system of capitalism.

Bettelheim states:

> . . . the decisive factor in changing the behavior of man consists in the changes brought to production and its organization. Education has as its essential mission the task of erasing attitudes and behavior patterns inherited from the past which still survive in our time, and of assuring the learning of new standards of conduct imposed by the development of the productive forces.

Lenin says:

> "The development of the productive forces of Russia has not attained the level that makes socialism possible." All the heroes of the Second International, including, of course, Sukhanov, beat the drums about this proposition. They keep harping on this incontrovertible proposition in a thousand different keys, and think that it is the decisive criterion of our revolution.
>
> But what if the situation, which drew Russia into the imperialist world war which involved every more or less influential Western European country, and made her a witness of the eve of the revolutions maturing or partly already begun in the East, gave rise to circumstances that put Russia and her development in a position which enabled us to achieve precisely that combination of a "peasant war" with the working-class movement suggested in 1856 by no less a Marxist than Marx himself as a possible prospect for Prussia?
>
> What if the complete hopelessness of the situation, by stimulating the efforts of the workers and peasants tenfold, offered us the opportunity to create the fundamental requisites of civilization in a different way from that of the Western European countries? Has that altered the basic relations between the basic classes of all the countries that are being, or have been, drawn into the general course of world history?
>
> If a definite level of culture is required for the building of socialism (although nobody can say just what that definite "level of culture" is, for it differs in every Western European country), why cannot we begin by first achieving the prerequisites for that definite level of culture in a revolutionary way, and *then*, with the aid of the workers' and peasants' government and the Soviet system, proceed to overtake the other nations?[3]

As capitalism expanded into a worldwide system, and as the relationships of exploitation developed, not only among the individual members of a people, but among whole peoples, the worldwide system of capitalism,

[3] V. I. Lenin, *Selected Works* (Moscow, Progress Publishers, 1967), Vol. III, pp. 776–777. Che quotes these same paragraphs in Chapter 24 (ed.).

which has become imperialism, entered into conflict and hence could be broken at its weakest link. This was czarist Russia after the first World War and the beginning of the Revolution, in which coexisted the five economic points that Lenin enumerated: the most primitive patriarchal agriculture, petty capitalist production, private capitalism, state capitalism, and socialism.

Lenin pointed out that all these types appeared in Russia immediately after the Revolution. What stands out, however, is the generally socialist nature of the system, although the development of the productive forces at certain points may not have reached its full capacity. Evidently, when the lag is very great, the proper Marxist action must be to make as much accommodation as possible to the spirit of the new age, leading to the elimination of man's exploitation of man within the concrete situation of the country. This is what Lenin did in a Russia newly freed from Czarism, and he applied it as a standard for the Soviet Union.

We believe that the entire argument, at that time absolutely valid and extraordinary in its keenness, is applicable to concrete situations at particular historical moments. But since then, tremendously important events have taken place, such as the establishment of the worldwide socialist system, with about a billion inhabitants, one third of the world's population. The steady advance of the whole socialist system influences the consciousness of peoples at every level, and as a result, produces in Cuba at one moment in its history, a definition of the socialist revolution, a definition that did not precede by any means the fact that there already existed the economic bases for that definition.

How can we produce the transition to socialism in a country colonized by imperialism, without any development of its basic industries, in a situation of monopoly production and dependent on a single market?

The following statements may be applicable: One might declare, along with the theoreticians of the Second International, that Cuba has broken all the laws of dialectics, of historical materialism, and of Marxism, and that it is therefore not a socialist country and must return to its former condition.

Or, instead of that, one can be more realistic and seek within the relationships of production the internal motivation which has led to the present Revolution. But naturally, this would only demonstrate that there are many countries in Latin America and in other parts of the world where revolution is much more feasible than it was in Cuba.

There is still a third explanation, which is correct in our judgment. Within the great framework of the worldwide capitalist system, struggling against socialism, one of its weak links can be broken. In this particular case we mean Cuba. Taking advantage of unusual historical circumstances and following the skillful leadership of their vanguard, the revolutionary forces take over at a particular moment. Then, assuming that the necessary objective conditions already exist for the socializaton of labor, they skip stages, declare the socialist nature of the revolution, and begin to build socialism.

This is the dynamic dialectical manner in which we view and analyze the problem of the necessary correlations between the relationships of production and the development of the productive forces. Once the fact of the Cuban Revolution is established, which cannot escape analysis or be ignored when our history is studied, we come to the conclusion that a socialist revolution has been accomplished in Cuba, and that therefore, the conditions for it did exist. To realize a revolution without the necessary conditions, to come to power and declare socialism through magical means, is something not anticipated by any theory, and is something that comrade Bettelheim would deny.

If the concrete fact of the birth of socialism is established under these new conditions. it is because the development of the productive forces has clashed with the relationships of production prior to the time that could reasonably have been expected in an isolated capitalist country. What has happened? The vanguard of the revolutionary movement, increasingly influenced by Marxist-Leninism, is capable of consciously anticipating a whole series of steps leading toward realizing and hastening the course of events, but hastening them within the limits of what is objectively possible.

We strongly insist on this point because its denial is one of the basic errors in Bettelheim's argument.

If we start with the concrete fact that a revolution can be accomplished only when there are fundamental contradictions between the development of the productive forces and the relationships of production, we must further admit that this fact imparts socialist characteristics to the Cuban Revolution. This is so, even though, when objectively analyzed, there are numerous forces still in an embryonic state. But if under these conditions the Revolution is successful, how does one utilize the argument of the tight and obligatory agreement between productive forces and relationships of production, in order to defend, for example, Economic Calculus, and to attack the system of Consolidated Enterprises which we ourselves practice? To say that the Consolidated Enterprise system is an aberration is roughly equivalent to saying that the Cuban Revolution is an aberration. They are similar concepts and stem from the same analysis. Comrade Bettelheim has never said that the Cuban Revolution is not authentic, but he does say that our present relationships of production do not correspond to the development of productive forces, and therefore he predicts great failures.

Comrade Bettelheim's error stems from his failure to apply dialectical thought in these two areas which are of different magnitude, but show the same tendency. The consolidated enterprises were born, have been developed, and continue to develop because it was possible; this is a practical truth. Whether the administrative method is the most suitable is finally of little importance, because the differences between methods are basically quantitative. Hopes for our system are aimed toward the future, toward a more accelerated development of consciousness, and through consciousness, of the productive forces.

Comrade Bettelheim denies the activity of consciousness, basing himself on Marx's argument that consciousness is a product of the social milieu, and not the other way around. We can use the Marxist argument in our debate with Bettelheim, and tell him that it is a valid argument, but that in the present era of imperialism, consciousness takes on worldwide characteristics. The present consciousness results from the development of all productive forces in the world, and from the teachings and examples given by the Soviet Union and the other socialist countries to the masses all over the world.

It should be considered that the consciousness of those men in the vanguard of a particular country, when it is based on the general development of productive forces, can determine the proper means for bringing about a triumphant socialist revolution, although at their level the contradictions do not objectively exist between the development of productive forces and the relationships of production, which would make a revolution essential or possible (regarding the country as a unique and isolated entity).

This is our conclusion so far. The second serious mistake committed by Bettelheim is his insistence upon granting independent existence to the juridical structure. His analysis constantly refers to the need for taking into account the relationships of production for the legal establishment of ownership. To believe that legal ownership, or rather the superstructure of a particular state at a particular moment, has been imposed against the realities of the relationships of production is to deny the determinism on which he relied when he argued that consciousness is a social product. Naturally, all these processes are historical, and not physiochemical, lasting thousandths of a second. They are realized throughout the long course of human history. There are many aspects of juridical relationships that do not correspond to the relationships of production, which at the time characterize the country. This means only that such aspects will be destroyed in time, when the new relationships are imposed on the old ones. Thus, it is possible to change the superstructure without first having changed the relationship of production.

Comrade Bettelheim insists again and again that the nature of the relationships of production is determined by the level of development of the productive forces, and that the ownership of the means of production is the juridical and abstract expression of some relationships of production. He avoids the fundamental fact that this is perfectly suited to a general situation (whether world wide or in one country), but that one cannot establish the microscopic correspondence that he is trying to achieve between the level of development of the productive forces and the juridical relationship of ownership in every region or in every situation.

He attacks those economists who claim to see an expression of socialism in the people's ownership of the means of production, saying that these institutional relationships do not form the basis for anything. In a sense, he could be right, with respect to the word "basis," but the essential thing is that the relationships of production and the development of productive forces clash at a particular moment. That clash is not mechanically determined by an accumulation of economic forces, from the standpoint of economic development, not by violence between social classes, from the political and historical standpoint. That is, one can never separate economic analysis from the historical fact of the class struggle (until the perfect society is achieved). For man, who is the living expression of the class struggle, the juridical basis that represents the superstructure of the society in which he lives has concrete characteristics and expresses a palpable truth. The relationships of production, the development of productive forces, are economic-technological phenomena which accumulate in the course of history. Social ownership is the living expression of these relationships, just as concrete goods are the expression of the relationships among men. Goods exist because capitalist society exists, wherein the division of labor is based on private property. Socialism exists because there is a new kind of society, wherein the expropriators have been expropriated, and social ownership has replaced the old individual capitalistic form.

This is the general line that the period of transition should follow. The distinctions between this or that level of society have interest only for certain concrete analysis. But theoretical analysis should include also the great framework that delimits the new relationships among men in a society on the road to socialism.

Starting from these two fundamental conceptual errors, Bettelheim defends the obligatory identity in the development of productive forces in each given moment and each given place and in the relationships of production. At the same time he transplants these same relationships to the level of juridical expression. What is the conclusion?

Bettelheim says:

> Under these conditions, any line of reasoning that begins from the general notion of "state ownership" to designate the different forms of socialist ownership, and attempts to reduce it to a single reality, comes up against insurmountable difficulties, especially when it attempts to analyze the circulation of goods within the socialist sector of the State, socialist trade, the role of money, etc.

And then, analyzing Stalin's division of two forms of ownership, he states:

This juridical point of departure and the analyses that derive from it tend to deny the presently necessary capitalist category of exchange among State socialist enterprises, and tend, on a theoretical level, to render incomprehensible the nature of purchase and sale undertaken among State enterprises, the nature of money, of prices, of financial calculation, of financial autonomy, etc. These categories are thus deprived of any real social content. They appear as abstract forms or as technical procedures that are more or less arbitrary, and not as the expression of these objective economic laws, whose need was pointed out by Stalin himself."

For us, Comrade Bettelheim's article (in spite of the fact that it takes issue with some of the ideas that we have expressed on various occasions) is of real importance, since it comes from a highly learned Marxist economist and theoretician. Starting from a de facto situation, he makes, in our opinion, an ill-conceived defense of the use of the categories inherent in capitalism during the period of transition and of the need for individualized ownership within the socialist sector. He reveals that the detailed analysis of the processes of production and of social ownership is incompatible (following the Marxist line, which we would call orthodox) with the maintenance of these categories, and points out that there is something incomprehensible here.

We hold exactly the same opinion, except that our conclusion is different: We believe that the inconsistency among defenders of Economic Calculus stems from the fact that in following the line of Marxist analysis up to a certain point, they have to make a leap (omitting the "missing link") to shift to a new position from which to continue their line of reasoning. Concretely, the defenders of Economic Calculus have never correctly explained how the essential concept of goods within the state sector is supported, or how one makes "intelligent" use of the Law of Value in the socialist sector with distorted markets.

Noting the inconsistency, Comrade Bettelheim marshals his terms and begins the analysis where it should really end—with the judicial relationships actually existing in the socialist countries and the categories that survive—stating the truth that these juridical and capitalist categories do exist; and from this he concludes pragmatically that if they exist, it is because they are necessary. Beginning here, he moves backward analytically to reach the point where theory and practice clash. At this point he gives a new interpretation to the theory, submits it to analysis by Marx and Lenin, and draws his own conclusions on the erroneous premises we have pointed out, thus permitting himself a consecutive argument throughout the article.

He forgets, however, that the period of transition is historically young. At the moment when man fully understands economic facts and controls them by means of planning, he is subject to inevitable errors of judgment. Why think that what "is" in the period of transition, necessarily "should be"? Why reason that the blows dealt by reality to certain daring actions are the exclusive result of such daring? Are they not also, partially or totally, due to technical administrative faults?

Here, it seems to us, Bettelheim is discounting the importance of socialist planning, with all the technical difficulties it may have, when he argues:

> This leads to the impossibility of proceeding in a satisfactorily efficient manner with a full *a priori* division of goods and the means of production, and of proceeding with the need for socialist trade and state commercial agencies. Here lies the origin of the role of money at the very center of the socialist sector. The role of the Law of Value and the price system should reflect not only the social cost of different goods, but it should also express the relationship between supply and demand. Eventually, the balance between supply and demand should be assured, when planning has not been able to assure it *a priori,* and when the implementation of administrative measures (in order to realize this balance) would compromise the development of the productive forces.

Considering our weaknesses (in Cuba), we nevertheless have made an attempt at a fundamental definition:

> We deny the possibility of the deliberate use of the Law of Value, and we base our opinion on the nonexistence of a free market which automatically expresses the contradiction between producers and consumers. We deny the existence of the category, "goods" in the relationships among state enterprises, and we consider all such establishments to be part of the single great enterprise that is the state (although in practice this has not yet been achieved in our country). The Law of Value and planning are two terms that are linked by a contradiction and its resolution. We can therefore state that centralized planning is the way of life in a socialist society. It is what defines it and is the point at which man's mind succeeds in finally synthesizing and directing the economy toward its goal, which is the complete liberation of the human being within the framework of communist society.[4]

To relate the unit of production (for Bettelheim, the economic entity) to the physical level of integration is to carry the mechanism to its final extreme, and denies us the possibility of accomplishing what technically the North American monopolies have already done in many branches of Cuban industry. This shows too little confidence in our powers and abilities.

What could then be called a unit of production (and that is what constitutes a true economic entity) would evidently vary according to the level of development of the productive forces. In certain branches of production,

[4] *Nuestra Industria Económica*, Año 2, No. 5, Feb. 1964. See Chapter 24, in this volume.

where the integration of activities is sufficiently advanced, the branch itself can constitute a "unit of production." This could be the case, for example, in the electrical industry on the basis of its in interconnections, because it permits centralized management of the entire industry.

As our system develops pragmatically, we are able to locate certain of these problems, and we can try to resolve them, following as much as possible the great ideas of Marx and Lenin. This brought us to seek a solution to the contradiction in Marxist political economy during the period of transition. When we try to overcome the contradictions, which are only temporary obstacles blocking socialist development, because socialist society does in fact exist, we investigate the organizational methods best suited to theory and practice, which would permit us to advance toward the new society through the development of conscience and production. This is where we are today.

To conclude:

1. We believe that Bettelheim makes two gross methodological errors: (a) He mechanically translates the concept of the necessary correspondence between the relationships of production and the development of productive forces (which are of universal validity) into the "microcosmos" of the relationships of production in specific features of a given country during the period of transition; thus he extracts apologetic conclusions, tinged with pragmatism, for the so-called Economic Calculus; (b) he makes the same mechanical analysis for the concept of property.

2. Therefore, we do not agree with his opinion that financial self-management or autonomy "are tied at a certain level in the productive forces." This opinion is the result of his faulty analytic methods.

3. We deny his concept of centralized management, which he bases on the physical centralization of production (in his example of an interconnected electrical network), and we instead apply it to a centralization of the principal economic decisions.

4. We do not find correct his explanation for the necessary unrestricted operation of the Law of Value and other capitalist categories during the period of transition, although we do not deny the possibility of using elements of this Law for similar purposes (cost and yield expressed in monetary terms).

5. For us, "centralized planning is the way of life in a socialist society," etc., and therefore, we attribute to it a much greater conscious power of decision than does Bettelheim.

6. We ascribe great theoretical importance to the examination of the inconsistencies between the classical Marxist method of analysis and the survival of the categories within the socialist sector, a matter which should be studied in great detail.

7. To the defenders of Economic Calculus, the following is appropriate: "God protect me from my friends, so that I may protect myself from my enemies."

CHAPTER 33

Letter to Fidel[1]

Havana, Year of Agriculture

FIDEL:

At this moment I remember so many things: when I met you at Maria Antonia's house; when you asked me to come; all the excitement of getting ready.

One day they came and asked who was to be notified in case of death, and the real possibility of this struck us all. Later we learned that it *was* real, that in revolution (if it is a genuine one) you either win or die. Many comrades have fallen along the path to victory.

Today everything seems less dramatic, because we are more mature, but the fact repeats itself. I feel I have fulfilled that part of my duty which bound me to the Cuban Revolution on its own territory, and I bid farewell to you, to the comrades, and to your people, who are now mine.

I formally renounce my duties in the national leadership of the party, my post as minister, my rank of major, and my Cuban citizenship. I have no legal ties to Cuba, only ties of a different kind which cannot be dissolved as official positions can.

When I look back over the past, I believe I have worked with honesty and dedication to assure the triumph of the Revolution. My only serious mistake was not to have trusted you more from the first days in the Sierra Maestra, and not to have understood soon enough your qualities as a leader and a revolutionary. I have lived through some magnificent days, and at your side I have felt the pride of belonging to our people during those radiant yet sad days of the Caribbean crisis. Not often has a statesman acted more brilliantly than you did during those days, and I am also proud of having followed you unhesitatingly, identifying with your way of thinking, and realizing the dangers and principles of our position.

1 Written in mid-1965 and read by Fidel during an October 3, 1965, speech. Reproduced by the Comité para la Defensa de la Revolución as a record in 1967. Translated by Judith Mauleón.

Other nations are calling for the aid of my modest efforts. I can do what you are unable to do because of your responsibility as Cuban Leader. The time has come for our separation.

I want it to be known that I do this with a mixture of joy and sorrow: Here I leave behind the purest of my hopes for building, and the dearest of my loved ones, and I leave a people that has accepted me as its son. This deeply hurts a part of my spirit. In new fields of battle I will bear the faith you instilled in me, the revolutionary spirit of my people, the feeling that I am fulfilling the most sacred of duties: to fight against imperialism wherever it may be. This comforts me and more than compensates for any regrets.

Once again, let me say that I absolve Cuba from any responsibility, except for that which stems from the example it has set. If my final hour comes under distant skies, my last thoughts will be for this people and especially for you. I thank you for your teachings and your example, and will try to be faithful up to the final consequences of my acts. I have always identified myself with the foreign policy of our Revolution, and I continue to do so. Wherever I may be, I will remain conscious of the responsibility of being a Cuban revolutionary, and will act as such. I have left no material possessions to my wife and children, and I do not regret it; I am happy it is this way. I ask nothing for them, since the state will provide for their needs and their education.

There are many things I would like to say to you and to our people, but I feel it is unnecessary; words cannot express what I would want them to, and it is not worth wasting paper.

Ever onward to victory. Liberty or Death!

I embrace you with all my revolutionary fervor.

"Che"

CHAPTER 34

Letter to His Family[1]

DEAR FOLKS:

Once again I feel Rocinante's bony ribs beneath my legs. Again I begin my journey, carrying my shield.

Almost ten years ago I wrote you another letter of farewell. As I recall, I regretted not being a better soldier and a better doctor. I no longer care about the latter, but I'm not such a bad soldier, now.

In essence nothing has changed, except that I am much more conscious; my Marxism has been deepened and purified. I believe in armed struggle as the only solution for people who are fighting for freedom, and I act according to this belief.

Many will call me an adventurer, and I am, but of a different kind—one who risks his skin in order to prove his convictions.

Perhaps this will be my last letter. It is not my intention, but it is within the realm of logical probability. If so, I send you a last embrace.

I have loved you very much, only I have not known how to express this love; I am extremely set in my ways, and I think at times you have not understood me. Understanding me has not been easy, but just for today, believe me.

My will, which I have perfected with an artist's care, will now hold up my shaky legs and exhausted lungs. I will do it.

Give an occasional thought to this little twentieth-century *condottiere*. Kisses for Celia, Roberto, Juan Martín, Pototín, for Beatriz, for everyone.

And for you, an embrace from your recalcitrant prodigal son,

Ernesto

[1] Written in mid-1965 and reproduced by *Juventud Rebelde*, June 24, 1967. Translated by Judith Mauleón.

CHAPTER 35

Message to the Tricontinental: "Create two, three . . . many Vietnams"[1]

Now is the time of the furnaces, and only light should be seen.

JOSÉ MARTÍ

TWENTY-ONE years have already elapsed since the end of the last world conflagration; numerous publications, in every possible language, celebrate this event, symbolized by the defeat of Japan. There is a climate of apparent optimism in many areas of the different camps into which the world is divided.

Twenty-one years without a world war, in these times of maximum confrontations, of violent clashes and sudden changes, appears to be a very high figure. However, without analyzing the practical results of this peace (poverty, degradation, increasingly larger exploitation of enormous sectors of humanity) for which all of us have stated that we are willing to fight, we would do well to inquire if this peace is real.

It is not the purpose of these notes to detail the different conflicts of a local character that have been occurring since the surrender of Japan, neither do we intend to recount the numerous and increasing instances of civilian strife which have taken place during these years of apparent peace. It will be enough just to name, as an example against undue optimism, the wars of Korea and Vietnam.

In the first one, after years of savage warfare, the Northern part of the country was submerged in the most terrible devastation known in the annals of modern warfare: riddled with bombs; without factories, schools or hospitals; with absolutely no shelter for housing ten million inhabitants.

Under the discredited flag of the United Nations, dozens of countries

[1] Pamphlet, published in English by the Executive Secretariat of the Organization of the Solidarity of the Peoples of Africa, Asia, and Latin America (OSPAAAL), Havana, April 16, 1967.

under the military leadership of the United States participated in this war with the massive intervention of U.S. soldiers and the use, as cannon fodder, of the South Korean population that was enrolled. On the other side, the army and the people of Korea and the volunteers from the Peoples' Republic of China were furnished with supplies and advise by the Soviet military apparatus. The U.S. tested all sort of weapons of destruction, excluding the thermonuclear type, but including, on a limited scale, bacteriological and chemical warfare.

In Vietnam, the patriotic forces of that country have carried on an almost uninterrupted war against three imperialist powers: Japan, whose might suffered an almost vertical collapse after the bombs of Hiroshima and Nagasaki; France, who recovered from that defeated country its Indo-China colonies and ignored the promises it had made in harder times; and the United States, in this last phase of the struggle.

There were limited confrontations in every continent although in Our America, for a long time, there were only incipient liberation struggles and military coups d'Etat until the Cuban revolution resounded the alert, signaling the importance of this region. This action attracted the wrath of the imperialists and Cuba was finally obliged to defend its coasts, first in Playa Girón, and again during the Missile Crisis.

This last incident could have unleashed a war of incalculable proportions if a U.S.-Soviet clash had occurred over the Cuban question.

But, evidently, the focal point of all contradictions is at present the territory of the peninsula of Indo-China and the adjacent areas. Laos and Vietnam are torn by a civil war which has ceased being such by the entry into the conflict of U.S. imperialism with all its might, thus transforming the whole zone into a dangerous detonator ready at any moment to explode.

In Vietnam the confrontation has assumed extremely acute characteristics. It is not out intention, either, to chronicle this war. We shall simply remember and point out some milestones.

In 1954, after the annihilating defeat of Dien-Bien-Phu, an agreement was signed at Geneva dividing the country into two separate zones; elections were to be held within a term of 18 months to determine who should govern Vietnam and how the country should be reunified. The U.S. did not sign this document and started maneuvering to substitute the emperor, Bao-Dai, who was a French puppet, for a man more amiable to its purposes. This happened to be Ngo-Din-Diem, whose tragic end—that of an orange squeezed dry by imperialism—is well known by all.

During the months following the agreement, optimism reigned supreme in the camp of the popular forces. The last pockets of the anti-French resistance were dismantled in the South of the country—and they awaited the fulfillment of the Geneva agreements. But the patriots soon realized there would be no elections—unless the United States felt itself capable of imposing its will in the polls, which was practically impossible even resorting to all its fraudulent methods. Once again the fighting broke out in the South and gradually acquired full intensity. At present the U.S. army has increased to over half a million invaders while the puppet forces decrease in number and, above all, have totally lost their combativeness.

Almost two years ago the United States started bombing systematically the Democratic Republic of Vietnam, in yet another attempt to overcome the belligerance [sic] of the South and impose, from a position of strength, a meeting at the conference table. At first, the bombardments were more or less isolated occurrences and were adorned with the mask of reprisals for alleged provocations from the North. Later on, as they increased in intensity and regularity, they became one gigantic attack carried out by the air force of the United States, day after day, for the purpose of destroying all vestiges of civilization in the Northern zone of the country. This is an episode of the infamously notorious "escalation."

The material aspirations of the Yankee world have been fulfilled to a great extent, regardless of the unflinching defense of the Vietnamese anti-aircraft artillery, of the numerous planes shot down (over 1,700) and of the socialist countries aid in war supplies.

There is a sad reality: Vietnam—a nation representing the aspirations, the hopes of a whole world of forgotten peoples—is tragically alone. This nation must endure the furious attacks of U.S. technology, with practically no possibility of reprisals in the South and only some of defense in the North—but always alone.

The solidarity of all progressive forces of the world towards the people of Vietnam today is similar to the bitter irony of the plebeians coaxing on the gladiators in the Roman arena. It is not a matter of wishing success to the victim of aggression, but of sharing his fate; one must accompany him to his death or to victory.

When we analyze the lonely situation of the Vietnamese people, we are overcome by anguish at this illogical moment of humanity.

U.S. imperialism is guilty of aggression—its crimes are enormous and cover the whole world. We already know all that, gentlemen! But this guilt also applies to those who, when the time came for a definition, hesitated to make Vietnam an inviolable part of the socialist world; running, of course, the risks of a war on a global scale—but also forcing a decision upon imperialism. And the guilt also applies to those who maintain a war of abuse and snares—started quite some time ago by the representatives of the two greatest powers of the socialist camp.

We must ask ourselves, seeking an honest answer: Is Vietnam isolated, or is it not? Is it not maintaining a dangerous equilibrium between the two quarrelling powers?

And what great people these are! What stoicism and courage! And what a lesson for the world is contained in this struggle! Not for a long time shall we be able to know if President Johnson ever seriously thought of bringing about some of the reforms needed by his people—to iron out the barbed class contradictions that grow each day with explosive power. The truth is that the improvements announced under the pompous title of the "Great Society" have dropped into the cesspool of Vietnam.

The largest of all imperialist powers feels in its own guts the bleeding inflicted by a poor and underdeveloped country; its fabulous economy feels the strain of the war effort. Murder is ceasing to be the most convenient business for its monopolies. Defensive weapons, and never in adequate number, is all these extraordinary soldiers have—besides love for their homeland, their society, and unsurpassed courage. But imperialism is bogging down in Vietnam, is unable to find a way out and desperately seeks one that will overcome with dignity this dangerous situation in which it now finds itself. Furthermore, the Four Points put forward by the North and the Five Points of the South now corner imperialism, making the confrontation even more decisive.

Everything indicate [sic] that peace, this unstable peace which bears that name for the sole reason that no worldwide conflagration has taken place, is again in danger of being destroyed by some irrevocable and unacceptable step taken by the United States.

What role shall we, the exploited people of the world, play? The peoples of the three continents focus their attention on Vietnam and learn their lesson. Since imperialists blackmail humanity by threatening it with war, the wise reaction is not to fear war. The general tactics of the people should be to launch a constant and a firm attack in all fronts where the confrontation is taking place.

In those places where this meager peace we have has been violated, which is our duty? To liberate ourselves at any price.

The world panorama is of great complexity. The struggle for liberation has not yet been undertaken by some countries of ancient Europe, sufficiently developed to realize the contradictions of capitalism, but weak to such a degree that they are unable either to follow imperialism or even to start on its own road. Their contradictions will reach an explosive stage during the forthcoming years—but their problems and, consequently, their own solutions are different from those of our dependent and economically underdeveloped countries.

The fundamental field of imperialist exploitation comprises the three underdeveloped continents: America, Asia, and Africa. Every country has also its own characteristics, but each continent, as a whole, also presents a certain unity.

Our America is integrated by a group of more or less homogeneous countries and in most parts of its territory U.S. monopolist capitals maintain an absolute supremacy. Puppet governments or, in the best of cases, weak and fearful local rulers, are incapable of contradicting orders from their Yankee master. The United States has nearly reached the climax of its political and economic domination; it could hardly advance much more; any change in the situation could bring about a setback. Their policy is to maintain that which has already been conquered. The line of action, at the present time, is limited to the brutal use of force with the purpose of thwarting the liberation movements, no matter of what type they might happen to be.

The slogan "we will not allow another Cuba" hides the possibility of perpetrating aggressions without fear of reprisal, such as the one carried out against the Dominican Republic or before that the massacre in Panama —and the clear warning stating that Yankee troops are ready to intervene anywhere in America where the ruling regime may be altered, thus endangering their interests. This policy enjoys an almost absolute impunity: the OAS is a suitable mask, in spite of its unpopularity; the inefficiency of the UN is ridiculous as well as tragic; the armies of all American countries are ready to intervene in order to smash their peoples. The International of Crime and Treason has in fact been organized. On the other hand, the autochthonous bourgeoisies have lost all their capacity to oppose imperialism—if they ever had it—and they have become the last card in the pack. There are no other alternatives; either a socialist revolution or a make-believe revolution.

Asia is a continent with many different characteristics. The struggle for liberation waged against a series of European colonial powers resulted in the establishment of more or less progressive governments, whose ulterior evolution have brought about, in some cases, the deepening of the primary objectives of national liberation and in others, a setback towards the adoption of pro-imperialist positions.

From the economic point of view, the United States had very little to lose and much to gain from Asia. These changes benefited its interests; the struggle for the overthrow of other neocolonial powers and the penetration of new spheres of action in the economic field is carried out sometimes directly, occasionally through Japan.

But there are special political conditions, particularly in Indo-China, which create in Asia certain characteristics of capital importance and play a decisive role in the entire U.S. military strategy.

The imperialists encircle China through South Korea, Japan, Taiwan, South Vietnam and Thailand at least.

This dual situation, a strategic interest as important as the military encirclement of the Peoples' Republic of China and the penetration of these great markets—which they do not dominate yet—turns Asia into one of the most explosive points of the world today, in spite of its apparent stability outside of the Vietnamese war zone.

The Middle East, though it geographically belongs to this continent, has its own contradictions and is actively in ferment; it is impossible to foretell how far this cold war between Israel, backed by the imperialists, and the progressive countries of that zone will go. This is just another one of the volcanoes threatening eruption in the world today.

Africa offers an almost virgin territory to the neocolonial invasion. There have been changes which, to some extent, forced neocolonial powers to give up their former absolute prerogatives. But when these changes are carried out uninterruptedly, colonialism continues in the form of neocolonialism with similar effects as far as the economic situation is concerned.

The United States had no colonies in this region but is now struggling to penetrate its partners' fiefs. It can be said that following the strategic plans of U.S. imperialism, Africa constitutes its long range reservoir; its present investments, though, are only important in the Union of South Africa and its penetration is beginning to be felt in the Congo, Nigeria and other countries where a violent rivalry with other imperialist powers is beginning to take place (in a pacific manner up to the present time).

So far it does not have there great interests to defend except its pretended right to intervene in every spot of the world where its monopolies detect huge profits or the existence of large reserves of raw materials.

All this past history justifies our concern regarding the possibilities of liberating the peoples within a long or a short period of time.

If we stop to analyze Africa we shall observe that in the Portuguese colonies of Guinea, Mozambique and Angola the struggle is waged with relative intensity, with a concrete success in the first one and with variable success in the other two. We still witness in the Congo the dispute between Lumumba's successors and the old accomplices of Tshombe, a dispute which at the present time seems to favor the latter: those who have "pacified" a large area of the country for their own benefit—though the war is still latent.

In Rhodesia we have a different problem: British imperialism used every means within its reach to place power in the hands of the white minority, who, at the present time, unlawfully holds it. The conflict, from the British point of view, is absolutely unofficial; this Western power, with its habitual diplomatic cleverness—also called hypocrisy in the strict sense of the word—presents a facade of displeasure before the measures adopted by the government of Ian Smith. Its crafty attitude is supported by some Commonwealth countries that follow it, but is attacked by a large group of countries belonging to Black Africa, whether they are or not servile economic lackeys of British imperialism.

Should the rebellious efforts of these patriots succeed and this movement receive the effective support of neighboring African nations, the situation in Rhodesia may become extremely explosive. But for the moment all these problems are being discussed in harmless organizations such as the UN, the Commonwealth and the OAU.

The social and political evolution of Africa does not lead us to expect a continental revolution. The liberation struggle against the Portuguese should end victoriously, but Portugal does not mean anything in the imperialist field. The confrontations of revolutionary importance are those which place at bay all the imperialist apparatus; this does not mean, however, that we should stop fighting for the liberation of the three Portuguese colonies and for the deepening of their revolutions.

When the black masses of South Africa or Rhodesia start their authentic revolutionary struggle, a new era will dawn in Africa. Or when the impoverished masses of a nation rise up to rescue their right to a decent life from the hands of the ruling oligarchies.

Up to now, army putsches follow one another; a group of officers succeeds another or substitute a ruler who no longer serves their caste interests or those of the powers who covertly manage him—but there are no great popular upheavals. In the Congo these characteristics appeared briefly, generated by the memory of Lumumba, but they have been losing strength in the last few months.

In Asia, as we have seen, the situation is explosive. The points of friction are not only Vietnam and Laos, where there is fighting; such a point is also Cambodia, where at any time a direct U.S. aggression may start, Thailand, Malaya, and, of course, Indonesia, where we can not assume that the last word has been said, regardless of the annihilation of the Communist Party in that country when the reactionaries took over. And also, naturally, the Middle East.

In Latin America the armed struggle is going on in Guatemala, Colombia, Venezuela and Bolivia; the first uprisings are cropping up in Brazil [*sic*]. There are also some resistance focuses which appear and then are extinguished. But almost all the countries of this continent are ripe for a type of struggle that, in order to achieve victory, can not be content with anything less than establishing a government of socialist tendencies.

In this continent practically only one tongue is spoken (with the exception of Brazil, with whose people, those who speak Spanish can easily make themselves understood, owing to the great similarity of both languages). There is also such a great similarity between the classes in these countries, that they have attained identification among themselves of an *international americano* type, much more complete than in the other continents. Language, habits, religion, a common foreign master, unite them. The degree and the form of exploitation are similar for both the exploiters and the men they exploit in the majority of the countries of Our America. And rebellion is ripening swiftly in it.

We may ask ourselves: how shall this rebellion flourish? What type will it be? We have maintained for quite some time now that, owing to the similarity of their characteristics, the struggle in Our America will achieve, in due course, continental proportions. It shall be the scene of many great battles fought for the liberation of humanity.

Within the frame of this struggle of continental scale, the battles which are now taking place are only episodes—but they have already furnished their martyrs, they shall figure in the history of Our America as having given their necessary blood in this last stage of the fight for the total freedom of man. These names will include Comandante Turcios Lima, padre Camilo Torres, Comandante Fabricio Ojeda, Comandantes Lobatón and Luis de la Puente Uceda, all outstanding figures in the revolutionary movements of Guatemala, Colombia, Venezuela and Peru.

But the active movement of the people creates its new leaders; César Montes and Yon Sosa raise up their flag in Guatemala; Fabio Vázquez and Marulanda in Colombia; Douglas Bravo in the Western part of the country and Américo Martín in El Bachiller, both directing their respective Venezuelan fronts.

New uprisings shall take place in these and other countries of Our America, as it has already happened in Bolivia, and they shall continue to grow in the midst of all the hardships inherent to this dangerous profession of being modern revolutionaries. Many shall perish, victims of their errors; others shall fall in the touch battle that approaches; new fighters and new leaders shall appear in the warmth of the revolutionary struggle. The people shall create their warriors and leaders in the selective framework of the war itself—and Yankee agents of repression shall increase. Today there are military aids in all the countries where armed struggle is growing; the Peruvian army apparently carried out a successful action against the revolutionaries in that country, an army also trained and advised by the Yankees. But if the focuses of war grow with sufficient political and military insight, they shall become practically invincible and shall force the Yankees to send reinforcements. In Peru itself many new figures, practically unknown, are now reorganizing the guerrilla. Little by little, the obsolete weapons, which are sufficient for the repression of small armed bands, will be exchanged for modern armaments and the U.S. military aids will be substituted by actual fighters until, at a given moment, they are forced to send increasingly greater number of regular troops to ensure the relative stability of a government whose national puppet army is desintegrating before the impetuous attacks of the guerrillas. It is the road of Vietnam; it is the road that should be followed by the people; it is the road that will be followed in Our America, with the advantage that the armed groups could create Coordinating Councils to embarrass the repressive forces of Yankee imperialism and accelerate the revolutionary triumph.

America, a forgotten continent in the last liberation struggles, is now beginning to make itself heard through the Tricontinental and, in the voice of the vanguard of its peoples, the Cuban Revolution, will today have a task of much greater relevance: creating a Second or a Third Vietnam, or the Second *and* Third Vietnam of the world.

We must bear in mind that imperialism is a world system, the last stage of capitalism—and it must be defeated in a world confrontation. The strategic end of this struggle should be the destruction of imperialism. Our share, the responsibility of the exploited and underdeveloped of the world is to eliminate the foundations of imperialism: our oppressed nations, from where they extract capitals, raw materials, technicians and cheap labor, and to which they export new capitals—instruments of domination—arms and all kinds of articles; thus submerging us in an absolute dependance [*sic*].

The fundamental element of this strategic end shall be the real liberation of all people, a liberation that will be brought about through armed struggle in most cases and which shall be, in Our America, almost indefectibly, a Socialist Revolution.

While envisaging the destruction of imperialism, it is necessary to identify its head, which is no other than the United States of America.

We must carry out a general task with the tactical purpose of getting the enemy out of its natural environment, forcing him to fight in regions where his own life and habits will clash with the existing reality. We must not underrate our adversary; the U.S. soldier has technical capacity and is backed by weapons and resources of such magnitude that render him frightful. He lacks the essential ideologic motivation which his bitterest enemies of today—the Vietnamese soldiers—have in the highest degree. We will only be able to overcome that army by undermining their morale—and this is accomplished by defeating it and causing it repeated sufferings.

But this brief outline of victories carries within itself the immense sacrifice of the people, sacrifices that should be demanded beginning today, in plain daylight, and which perhaps may be less painful than those we would have to endure if we constantly avoided battle in an attempt to have others pull our chestnuts out of the fire.

It is probable, of course, that the last liberated country shall accomplish this without an armed struggle and the sufferings of a long and cruel war against the imperialists—this they might avoid. But perhaps it will be impossible to avoid this struggle or its effects in a global conflagration; the suffering would be the same, or perhaps even greater. We cannot foresee the future, but we should never give in to the defeatist temptation of being the vanguard of a nation which yearns for freedom, but abhors the struggle it entails and awaits its freedom as a crumb of victory.

It is absolutely just to avoid all useless sacrifices. Therefore, it is so important to clear up the real possibilities that dependent America may have of liberating itself through pacific means. For us, the solution to this question is quite clear: the present moment may or may not be the proper one for starting the struggle, but we cannot harbor any illusions, and we have no right to do so, that freedom can be obtained without fighting. And these battles shall not be mere street fights with stones against tear-gas bombs, or of pacific general strikes; neither shall it be the battle of a furious people destroying in two or three days the repressive scaffolds of the ruling oligarchies; the struggle shall be long, harsh, and its front shall be in the guerrilla's refuge, in the cities, in the homes of the fighters—where the repressive forces shall go seeking easy victims among their families—in the massacred rural population, in the villages or cities destroyed by the bombardments of the enemy.

They are pushing us into this struggle; there is no alternative: we must prepare it and we must decide to undertake it.

The beginnings will not be easy; they shall be extremely difficult. All the oligarchies' powers of repression, all their capacity for brutality and demagoguery will be placed at the service of their cause. Our mission, in the first hour, shall be to survive; later, we shall follow the perennial example of the guerrilla, carrying out armed propaganda (in the Vietnamese sense, that is, the bullets of propaganda, of the battles won or lost—but fought—against the enemy). The great lesson of the invincibility of the guerrillas taking root in the dispossessed masses. The galvanizing of the national spirit, the preparation for harder tasks, for resisting even more violent repressions. Hatred as an element of the struggle; a relentless hatred of the enemy, impelling us over and beyond the natural limitations that man is heir to and transforming him into an effective, violent, selective and cold killing machine. Our soldiers must be thus; a people without hatred cannot vanquish a brutal enemy.

We must carry the war into every corner the enemy happens to carry it: to his home, to his centers of entertainment; a total war. It is necessary to prevent him from having a moment of peace, a quiet moment outside his barracks or even inside; we must attack him wherever he may be; make him feel like a cornered beast wherever he may move. Then his moral fiber shall begin to decline. He will even become more beastly, but we shall notice how the signs of decadence begin to appear.

And let us develop a true proletarian internationalism; with international proletarian armies; the flag under which we fight would be the sacred cause of redeeming humanity. To die under the flag of Vietnam, of Venezuela, of Guatemala, of Laos, of Guinea, of Colombia, of Bolivia, of Brazil—to name only a few scenes of today's armed struggle—would be equally glorious and desirable for an American, an Asian, an African, even a European.

Each spilt drop of blood, in any country under whose flag one has not been born, is an experience passed on to those who survive, to be added later to the liberation struggle of his own country. And each nation liberated is a phase won in the battle for the liberation of one's own country.

The time has come to settle our discrepancies and place everything at the service of our struggle.

We all know great controversies rend the world now fighting for freedom; no one can hide it. We also know that they have reached such intensity and such bitterness that the possibility of dialogue and reconciliation seems extremely difficult, if not impossible. It is a useless task to search for means and ways to propitiate a dialogue which the hostile parties avoid. However, the enemy is there; it strikes every day, and threatens us with new blows and these blows will unite us, today, tomorrow, or the day after. Whoever understands this first, and prepares for this necessary union, shall have the people's gratitude.

Owing to the virulence and the intransigence with which each cause is defended, we, the dispossessed, cannot take sides for one form or the other of these discrepancies, even though sometimes we coincide with the contentions of one party or the other, or in a greater measure with those of one part more than with those of the other. In time of war, the expression of current differences constitutes a weakness; but at this stage it is an illusion to attempt to settle them by means of words. History shall erode them or shall give them their true meaning.

In our struggling world every discrepancy regarding tactics, the methods of action for the attainment of limited objectives should be analyzed with due respect to another man's opinions. Regarding our great strategic objective, the total destruction of imperialism by armed struggle, we should be uncompromising.

Let us sum up our hopes for victory: total destruction of imperialism by eliminating its firmest bulwark: the oppression exercized by the United States of America. To carry out, as a tactical method, the peoples gradual liberation, one by one or in groups: driving the enemy into a difficult fight away from its own territory; dismantling all its sustenance bases, that is, its dependent territories.

This means a long war. And, once more we repeat it, a cruel war. Let no one fool himself at the outstart and let no one hesitate to start out for fear of the consequences it may bring to his people. It is almost our sole hope for victory. We cannot elude the call of this hour. Vietnam is pointing it out with its endless lesson of heroism, its tragic and everyday lesson of struggle and death for the attainment of final victory.

There, the imperialist soldiers endure the discomforts [*sic*] of those who, used to enjoying the U.S. standard of living, have to live in a hostile land with the insecurity of being unable to move without being aware of walking on enemy territory:—death to those who dare take a step out of their fortified encampment. The permanent hostility of the entire population. All this has internal repercussion in the United States; propitiates the resurgence of an element which is being minimized in spite of its vigor by all imperialist forces: class struggle even within its own territory.

How close we could look into a bright future should two, three or many Vietnams flourish throughout the world with their share of deaths and their immense tragedies, their everyday heroism and their repeated blows against imperialism, impelled to disperse its forces under the sudden attack and the increasing hatred of all peoples of the world!

And if we were all capable of uniting to make our blows stronger and infallible and so increase the effectiveness of all kinds of support given to the struggling people—how great and close would that future be!

If we, in a small point of the world map, are able to fulfill our duty and place at the disposal of this struggle whatever little of ourselves we are permitted to give: our lives, our sacrifice, and if some day we have to breathe our last breath on any land, already ours, sprinkled with our blood, let it be known that we have measured the scope of our actions and that we only consider ourselves elements in the great army of the proletariat but that we are proud of having learned from the Cuban Revolution, and from its maximum leader, the great lesson emanating from his attitude in this part of the world: "What do the dangers or the sacrifices of a man or of a nation matter, when the destiny of humanity is at stake."

Our every action is a battle cry against imperialism, and a battle hymn for the people's unity against the great enemy of mankind: the United States of America. Wherever death may surprise us, let it be welcome, provided that this, our battle cry, may have reached some receptive ear and another hand may be extended to wield our weapons and other men be ready to intone the funeral dirge with the staccato singing of the machine-guns and new battle cries of war and victory.

APPENDIX I

The Government of Cuba, Council of Ministers' Resolution of October 15, 1967

WHEREAS: The heroic Major Ernesto Guevara died fighting for the liberation of the peoples of America at the head of the Liberation Army of Bolivia;

WHEREAS: The people of Cuba will always remember the extraordinary service rendered by Major Ernesto Guevara, both in our War of Liberation and in the consolidation and advancement of our Revolution;

WHEREAS: His conduct embodies the spirit of internationalism which inspires the united struggle of the peoples;

WHEREAS: His untiring revolutionary activity, which knew no frontiers, his Communist thinking and his unbreakable determination to fight until victory or death in defense of the national and social liberation of the peoples of the hemisphere and against imperialism constitute an example of revolutionary conviction and heroism that shall last forever . . .

THEREFORE: The Council of Ministers resolves the following:

FIRST: That for 30 days, beginning with the signing of this resolution, the national flag be flown at half-mast, and for three days, starting today at 12:00 midnight, all public entertainment be suspended;

SECOND: That the day of his heroic death in combat be declared a national memorial day, establishing to that effect the 8th of October as "The Day of the Heroic Guerrilla";

THIRD: That as many activities be carried out as may be conducive to perpetuating his life and his example in the memory of future generations.

APPENDIX II

Che Guevara[1]

Como si San Martín la mano pura
a Martí familiar tendido hubiera,
como si el Plata vegetal viniera
con el Cauto a juntar agua y ternura.

asi Guevara, el gaucho de voz dura,
brindó a Fidel su sangre guerrillera
y su ancha mano fue más compañera
cuando fue nuestra noche más oscura.

Huyó la muerte. De su sombra impura,
del puñal, del veneno, de la fiera,
sólo el recuerdo bárbaro perdura.

Hecha de dos un alma brilla entera,
como si San Martín la mano pura
a Martí familiar tendido hubiera.

Nicolás Guillén
1959

[1] Original Spanish published in *Granma,* lunes 16 de octubre, 1967; English version published in *Granma,* weekly English edition, Oct. 29, 1967.

Che Guevara

As if San Martín's hand, noble and pure,
Were extended to his brother, Martí,
And the plant-banked Plata streamed through the sea,
To join the Cauto's love-swept overture.

Guevara, strong-voiced gaucho, moved to assure
His guerrilla blood to Fidel's stout company,
Held out his comrade hand, stalwartly,
When our night was blackest, most obscure.

Death retreated. From its shadows faded impure
Traces of daggers, of poison, of brutally
Warped beasts, and only sad memories endure.

A single soul, fused from two, shines passionately,
As if San Martín's hand, noble and pure,
Were extended to his brother, Martí.

APPENDIX III

Che Comandante[1]

No porque hayas caído
tu luz es menos alta.
Un caballo de fuego
sostiene tu escultura guerrillera
entre el viento y las nubes de la Sierra.
No por callado eres silencio.
Y no porque te quemen,
porque te disimulen bajo tierra,
porque te escondan
en cementerios, bosques, páramos,
van a impedir que te encontremos,
che Comandante
amigo.

Con sus dientes de júbilo
Norteamérica ríe. Mas de pronto
revuélvese en su lecho
de dólares. Se le cuaja
la risa en una máscara,
y tu gran cuerpo de metal
sube, se disemina
en las guerrillas como tábanos,
y tu ancho nombre herido por soldados
ilumina la noche americana
como una estrella súbita, caída
en medio de una orgía.
Tú lo sabías, Guevara,

[1] Written October 15, 1967, and printed in *Granma*, Año 2, No. 43, October 29, 1967 in original Spanish and in English, translated by the *Granma* staff, in the weekly edition of the same date.

pero no lo dijiste por modestia,
por no hablar de ti mismo,
che Comandante,
amigo.

Estás en todas partes. En el indio
hecho de sueño y cobre. Y en el negro
revuelto en espumosa muchedumbre,
y en el ser petrolero y salitrero.
Y en terrible desamparo
de la banana, y en la gran pampa de las pieles,
y en el azúcar y en la sal y en los cafetos,
tú, móvil estatua de tu sangre como te derribaron,
vivo, como no te querían,
che Comandante,
amigo.

Cuba te sabe de memoria. Rostro
de barbas que clarean. Y marfil
y aceituna en la piel de santo joven.
Firme la voz que ordena sin mandar,
que manda compañera, ordena amiga,
tierna y dura de jefe camarada.
Te vemos cada día ministro,
cada día soldado, cada día
gente llana y difícil
cada día.
Y puro como un niño
o como un hombre puro,
che Comandante,
amigo.

Pasas en tu descolorido, roto, agujereado traje de campaña.
El de la selva, como antes
fue el de la Sierra. Semidesnudo
el poderoso pecho de fusil y palabra,
de ardiente vendaval y lenta rosa.
No hay descanso.

¡Salud Guevara!
O mejor todavia desde el hondón americano:
Espéranos. Partiremos contigo. Queremos
morir para vivir como tú has muerto,
para vivir como tú vives,
che Comandante,
amigo.

Nicolás Guillén

Che Commander

Your light has not been quenched
Though you have fallen.
You move, guerrilla,
A figure on a flaming steed
Through the mountains, wind, and clouds.
Silenced, you are not silent.
And though they burn your body,
Though they hide you away
In graveyards, forests, cold uplands,
They cannot keep us from you
Che commander
Friend and brother.

The USA flashes
Its jubilant teeth. But
Soon it is tossing and turning
About on its dollar-strewn couch.
Its smile freezes into a mask,
To see your figure, tempered steel,
Climb the hills. Around you
Come guerrillas, mountain gadflies.
And your great heart, shattered by soldiers,
Shines forth into the night of America
Like a sudden star, exploding,
And falling amidst their orgies.
You knew this, Guevara,
But modesty forbade you to say it,
To speak of yourself.
Che commander
Friend and brother.

There is no place
Which does not hold you.
You are in the Indian,
Dreams and copper
In the Negro, surging up,
Wave after wave of rebellion,
In the souls damped down
By oil and saltpeter,
In the desolate earth of the banana,
And the pampas of hides, never-ending,
And in sugar and salt and coffee trees,
You, whose blood sprang up
An animated monument
A second after dying,
Alive, against all their wishes,
Che commander
Friend and brother.

Cuba knows you all in all by heart,
The bearded face of radiance,
Young saint painted in ivory and olive.
Firm the voice which commands
But never overbears;
Orders given by a friend, a companion,
Tender and hard the comrade commander.
Every day we still can see you,
Minister, soldier still, every day
Intransigent and frank, every day
Pure as a child
And as a man, still pure,
Che commander
Friend and brother.

You move on in your discolored, rent, threadbare battle-clothes,
A figure threading through Jungle, as before
Through the Sierra, broad chest half bared to the elements,
Respiring words and weapons,
Burning sea wind and slow-blooming rose.
There is no rest for you. Good heart, Guevara!
Or better yet, from the deep heart
Of America: Wait for us!
We will set off with you.

We would die, then, to live
As you have died, as you still live.
Che commander
Friend and brother.

Nicolás Guillén
October 15, 1967

APPENDIX IV

"To Che and to the Heroes Who Fought and Died with Him We Say: Ever Onward to Victory!"[1]

Revolutionary Comrades:

I first met Che one day in July or August, 1955. And in one night—as he recalls in his writings—he became one of the future expeditionaries of the Granma, although at that time the expedition possessed neither ship nor arms nor troops. And that was how, together with Raúl, Che became one of the first two on the Granma list. And twelve years have passed since then; they have been twelve years filled with struggle and historical significance. During this time death has cut down many brave and invaluable men, but at the same time throughout those years of our Revolution, extraordinary persons have arisen, forged from among men of the Revolution, and between those men and the people bonds of affection and of friendship have emerged which surpass all description.

Tonight we are meeting to try to express, in some degree, our feelings toward him who was one of the closest, the most admired, the most beloved, and without doubt, the most extraordinary of our revolutionary comrades; to express our feelings for him and for the heroes who have fought with him and fallen with him, his internationalist army that has been writing a glorious and never-to-be-effaced historical epic.

Che was one of those people who is liked immediately for his simplicity, his character, his naturalness, his comradely attitude, his personality, his originality, even when one had not yet learned of his other characteristic and unique virtues.

In those first days he was our troop doctor. And so our bonds of friendship and warm feelings for him were ever increasing.

He was filled with a profound spirit of hatred and loathing for imperialism, not only because his political awareness was already considerably

[1] Eulogy delivered by Major Fidel Castro Ruz, in memory of Major Ernesto Che Guevara, at the Plaza de la Revolución, on October 18, 1967. Reprinted in *Granma*, English Edition, Havana, October 29, 1967.

developed, but also because shortly before he had had the opportunity of witnessing the criminal imperialist intervention in Guatemala through the mercenaries who aborted the Revolution in that country. A man like Che did not require elaborate arguments. It was sufficient for him to know that there were men determined to struggle against that situation, arms in hand; it was sufficient for him to know that those men were inspired by genuinely revolutionary and patriotic ideals. That was more than enough. And so, one day at the end of November, 1956, he set out on the expedition toward Cuba with us. I recall that that trip was very hard for him, since because of the circumstances under which it was necessary to organize the departure, he could not even provide himself with the medicine he needed, and throughout the trip, he suffered from a severe attack of asthma without anything to alleviate it, but also without ever complaining. We arrived, set out on our first march, suffered our first setback, and at the end of some weeks, as you all know, a group of those who had survived from the expedition of the Granma was able to reunite. Che continued to be the doctor of our troop.

We came through the first battle victorious, and Che was already a soldier of our troop, and at the same time still our doctor. We came through the second victorious battle, and Che was not only a soldier but the most outstanding soldier in that battle, carrying out for the first time one of those singular feats that characterized him in all military action. Our forces continued to develop, and we faced another battle of extraordinary importance at that moment. The situation was difficult. The information we had was erroneous in many respects. We were going to attack, in full daylight, at dawn, a strongly defended, well-armed position at the edge of the sea. Enemy troops were at our rear, not very distant, and in that confused situation it was necessary to ask the men to make a supreme effort. Comrade Juan Almeida had taken on one of the most difficult missions, but one of our flanks remained completely without forces; one of the flanks was left without an attacking force, placing the operation in danger. And at that moment, Che, who was still functioning as our doctor, asked for two or three men, among them one with a machine gun, and in a matter of seconds, rapidly set off to assume the mission of attack from that direction.

On that occasion he was not only an outstanding combatant but also an outstanding doctor, attending the wounded comrades and at the same time attending the wounded enemy soldiers. After all the weapons had been captured and it became necessary to abandon that position, undertaking a long return march under the harassment of diverse enemy forces, it was necessary for someone to stay behind with the wounded, and Che stayed with the wounded. Aided by a small group of our soldiers, he took care of them, saved their lives and later rejoined the column with them.

From that time forward, he stood out as a capable and valiant leader of that type of men who, when a difficult mission is pending, do not wait to be asked to carry it out.

Thus it was at the battle of El Uvero, but he had acted in a similar way on a not previously mentioned occasion in the first days when, following a betrayal, our little troop was attacked by surprise by a number of airplanes and we were forced to retreat under bombardment. We had already walked some distance when we remembered some rifles of some farmer-soldiers who had been with us in the first actions, and had then asked permission to visit their families at a time when there was still not much discipline in our embryonic army. And right then it was thought that possibly the rifles were lost. I recall that the problem was not brought up again, and during the bombardment, Che volunteered and having done so, quickly went out to recover those rifles.

This was one of his principal characteristics: his willingness to instantly volunteer for the most dangerous mission. And naturally this aroused admiration, and twice the usual admiration for a fellow combatant, fighting alongside us, who had not been born here, a man of profound ideas, a man in whose mind stirred the dream of struggle in other parts of the continent and who was, nonetheless, so altruistic, so disinterested, so willing to always do the most difficult things, to constantly risk his life.

And that was how he won the rank of major and leader of the second column, organized in the Sierra Maestra. Thus his prestige began to increase, and he began to gain fame as a magnificent combatant who was to reach the highest posts in the course of the war. Che was an incomparable soldier. Che was an incomparable leader. Che was, from a military point of view, an extraordinarily capable man, extraordinarily courageous, extraordinarily aggressive. If, as a guerrilla, he had his Achilles' heel, it was this excessively aggressive quality, his absolute contempt for danger.

The enemy believes it can draw certain conclusions from his death. Che was a master of warfare! He was a virtuoso in the art of guerrilla struggle! And he showed that an infinite number of times. But he showed it especially in two extraordinary deeds. One of these was in the invasion, in which he led a column, a column pursued by thousands of enemy soldiers over flat and absolutely unknown terrain, carrying out, together with Camilo, an extraordinary military accomplishment. He also showed it in his lightning campaign in Las Villas Province, especially in the audacious attack on the city of Santa Clara, entering with a column of barely three hundred men, a city defended by tanks, artillery, and several thousand infantry soldiers.

Those two heroic deeds stamped him as an extraordinarily capable leader, as a master, as a virtuoso in the art of revolutionary war. However, now after his heroic and glorious death, some attempt to deny the truth or value of his concepts, his guerrilla theories.

The master may die, especially when he is a virtuoso in an art as dangerous as revolutionary struggle, but what will surely never die is the art to which he dedicated his life, his intelligence.

What is so strange about the fact that this master died in combat? What is stranger is that he did not die in combat on one of the innumerable occasions when he risked his life during our revolutionary struggle. And many times it was necessary to take steps to keep him from losing his life in actions of minor significance.

And so it was in combat, in one of the many battles he fought, that he lost his life. We do not have sufficient evidence to enable us to make deductions about what circumstances preceded that combat, to imagine how far he may have acted in an excessively aggressive way, but—we repeat—if, as a guerrilla, he had an Achilles' heel, that Achilles' heel was his excessive daring, his complete contempt for danger.

And this is where we can hardly agree with him, since we consider that his life, his experience, his capacity as a seasoned leader, his prestige and everything his life signified were more valuable, incomparably more valuable, than he himself perhaps believed.

His conduct may have been profoundly influenced by the idea that men have a relative value in history, the idea that causes are not defeated when men fall, that the powerful march of history cannot and will not be halted when leaders fall.

And that is true, there is no doubt about it. It shows his faith in men, his faith in ideas, his faith in examples. However, as I said a few days ago, with all our heart we would have liked to see him as a forger of victories, to see victories forged under his leadership, since men of his experience, men of his caliber, of his really unique capacity, are not common.

We have a full understanding of the value of his example. We are absolutely convinced that many men will strive to live up to his example, that men like him will emerge from the heart of the peoples.

It is not easy to find a person with all the virtues that were combined in him. It is not easy for a person, spontaneously, to develop a personality like his. I would say that he is one of those men who are difficult to match and virtually impossible to surpass. But I would also say that the example of men like him contributes to the appearance of men of the same ilk.

In Che, we not only admire the fighter, the man capable of performing great feats. And what he did, what he was doing, the very fact of his rising with a handful of men against the army of the ruling class, trained by Yankee advisers sent in by Yankee imperialism and backed by the oligarchies of all neighboring countries, in itself constitutes an extraordinary feat.

And if we search the pages of history it is likely that we will find no other case in which a leader with such a limited number of men has set about a task of such import, a case in which a leader with such a limited number of men has set out to fight against such large forces. Such proof of confidence in himself, such proof of confidence in the peoples, such proof of faith in men's capacity to fight, can be looked for in the pages of history, but the like of it will never be found.

And he fell.

The enemy believes it has defeated his ideas, his guerrilla concepts, his points of view on revolutionary armed struggle. And what they accomplished by a stroke of luck, was to eliminate him physically; what they accomplished was to gain an accidental advantage that an enemy may gain in war. And we do not know to what degree that stroke of luck, that stroke of fortune, was helped along in a battle like many others, by that characteristic of which we spoke before—his excessive aggressiveness, his absolute disdain for danger.

This also happened in our War of Independence. In a battle at Dos Rios they killed the Apostle of our Independence. In a battle at Punta Brava they killed Antonio Maceo, a veteran of hundreds of battles. Countless leaders, countless patriots of our War of Independence, were killed in similar battles. And that did not spell defeat for the Cuban cause.

The death of Che, as we said a few days ago, is a hard blow for the revolutionary movement, in that it deprives it, without a doubt, of its most experienced and able leader.

But those who are boasting of victory are mistaken. They are mistaken when they think that his death is the end of his ideas, the end of his tactics, the end of his guerrilla concepts, the end of his theses. For the man who fell, as a mortal man, as a man who faced bullets time and again, as a soldier, as a leader, is a thousand times more able than those who killed him by a stroke of luck.

However, how must revolutionaries face this serious setback? How must we face this loss? If Che had to express an opinion on this point, what would it be? He gave his opinion. He expressed that opinion quite clearly when he wrote in his Message to the Latin American Conference of Solidarity that if death surprised him anywhere, it would be welcome as long as his battle cry had reached a receptive ear and another hand stretched out to take up his rifle.

And his battle cry will reach not just one receptive ear, but millions of receptive ears! And not one hand, but millions of hands will stretch out to take up arms!

New leaders will emerge. And the men, of the receptive ears and the outstretched hands, will need leaders who emerge from the ranks of the people, just as leaders have emerged in all revolutions. Those hands will not have available a leader of Che's extraordinary experience and enormous ability. Those leaders will be formed in the process of struggle; those leaders will emerge from among the millions of receptive ears, from the millions of hands that will sooner or later stretch out to take up arms.

It isn't that we feel that his death will necessarily have immediate repercussions in the practical sphere of revolutionary struggle, that his death will necessarily have immediate repercussions in the practical sphere of development of the struggle. The fact is that when Che took up arms again he was not thinking of an immediate victory; he was not thinking of a speedy victory against the forces of the oligarchies and of imperialism. As an experienced fighter, he was prepared for a prolonged struggle of five, ten, fifteen, or twenty years if necessary. He was ready to fight for five, ten, fifteen, twenty years, or all his life if need be!

And within this time perspective his death, or rather his example, will have tremendous repercussions. The force of that example will be invincible.

Those who cling to the idea of luck try in vain to deny his experience and his capacity as a leader. Che was an extraordinarily able military leader. But when we remember Che, when we think of Che, we do not think fundamentally of his military virtues. No! Warfare is a means and not an end; warfare is a tool of revolutionaries. The important thing is the revolution, the revolutionary cause, revolutionary ideas, revolutionary objectives, revolutionary sentiments, revolutionary virtues!

And it is in that field, in the field of ideas, in the field of sentiments, in the field of revolutionary virtues, in the field of intelligence, that—apart from his military virtues—we feel the tremendous loss that his death means to the revolutionary movement.

Because Che's extraordinary personality was made up of virtues which are rarely found together. He stood out as an unsurpassed man of action, but Che was not only an unsurpassed man of action, he was a man of visionary intelligence and broad culture, a profound thinker. That is, in his person the man of ideas and the man of action were combined.

But it is not only that Che possessed the double characteristic of the man of ideas, of profound ideas, and the man of action, but that Che as a revolutionary united in himself the virtues which can be defined as the fullest expression of the virtues of a revolutionary; a man of complete integrity; a man of a supreme sense of honor, of absolute sincerity; a man of Stoic and Spartan living habits; a man in whose conduct not one stain can be found. He constituted, through his virtues, what can be called a truly model revolutionary.

When men die it is usual to make speeches, to emphasize their virtues, but rarely can one say of a man, with greater justice, with greater accuracy, what we say of Che: that he was a pure example of revolutionary virtues!

But he possessed another quality, not a quality of the intellect nor of the will, not a quality derived from experience, from struggle, but a quality of the heart: He was an extraordinarily human man, a man of extraordinary sensitivity!

That is why we say, when we think of his life, that he constituted the singular case of a most extraordinary man, able to unite in his personality not only the characteristics of the man of action, but also the man of thought, the man of immaculate revolutionary virtues, and of extraordinary human sensibility, joined with an iron character, a will of steel, indomitable tenacity.

And because of this he has left future generations not only his experience, his knowledge as an outstanding soldier but also, at the same time, the fruits of his intelligence. He wrote with the virtuosity of a master of our language. His narratives of the war are incomparable. The depth of his thinking is impressive. He never wrote about anything with less than extraordinary profundity; and we have no doubt that some of his writings will pass on to posterity as classic documents of revolutionary thought.

And thus, as fruits of that vigorous and profound intelligence, he left us an infinity of memories, an infinity of narratives that, without his work, without his efforts, might have been lost forever.

An indefatigable worker, during the years that he served our country, he did not know a single day of rest. Many were the responsibilities assigned to him: as president of the National Bank, as director of the National Planning Board, as Minister of Industries, as commander of military regions, as the head of political or economic or fraternal delegations.

His versatile intelligence was able to undertake with maximum assurance any task of any kind. And thus he brilliantly represented our country in numerous international conferences, just as he brilliantly led soldiers in combat, just as he was a model worker in charge of any of the organizations to which he was assigned, and for him there were no days of rest, for him there were no hours of rest! And if we looked through the windows of his offices, we would see he had the lights on until all hours of the night, studying, or rather working or studying. For he was a student of all problems, he was a tireless reader. His thirst for learning was practically insatiable, and the hours he stole from sleep he devoted to study.

He devoted his scheduled days off to voluntary work. He was the inspiration and provided the greatest incentive for that work which is today carried out by hundreds of thousands of persons throughout the country; he stimulated that activity in which our people are making greater and greater efforts.

And as a revolutionary, as a communist revolutionary, a true Communist, he had a boundless faith in moral values, he had a boundless faith in the conscience of men. And we should say that he saw, with absolute clarity, moral resources as the fundamental lever in the construction of communism in human society.

He thought, worked out, and wrote many things. And it is fitting to bring out, on a day like today, that Che's writings, Che's political and revolutionary thinking, will be of permanent value in the Cuban revolutionary process and in the Latin American revolutionary process. And we do not doubt that his ideas, as a man of action, as a man of thought, as a man of untarnished moral virtues, as a man of unexcelled human sensitivity, as a man of spotless conduct, have and will continue to have universal value.

The imperialists boast of their triumph at having killed this guerrilla fighter in action; the imperialists boast of a triumphant stroke of luck that led to the elimination of such a splendid man of action. But perhaps the imperialists do not know, or pretend not to know, that the man of action was only one of the many facets of the personality of that combatant. And if we speak of sorrow, we are saddened not only at having lost a man of action; we are saddened at having lost a morally superior man; we are saddened at having lost a man of exquisite human sensitivity; we are saddened at having lost such a mind. We are saddened to think that he was only thirty-nine years old at the time of his death. We are saddened at missing the additional fruits that we would have received from that intelligence and that ever richer experience.

We have an idea of the dimension of the loss for the revolutionary movement. But nevertheless, here is the weak side of the imperialist enemy; they think that by eliminating a man physically they have eliminated his thinking; that by eliminating him physically, they have eliminated his ideas, eliminated his virtues, eliminated his example. And so shameless are they in this belief that they have no hesitation in publishing, as the most natural thing in the world, by the now almost universally accepted circumstances in which they murdered him after he had been seriously wounded in action. They do not even seem to be aware of the repulsiveness of the procedure, they do not even seem to be aware of the shamelessness of the admission. They have published it as if thugs, oligarchs, and mercenaries had the right to shoot a seriously wounded revolutionary prisoner. And even worse, they explain why they did it. They assert that Che's trial would have been quite an earthshaker, that it would have been impossible to place this revolutionary on the dock.

And not only that, but neither have they hesitated to spirit away his remains. And be it true or false, they certainly announced they had cremated his body, thus beginning to show their fear, beginning to show that they are not so sure that by physically eliminating the combatant they can liquidate his ideas, liquidate his example.

Che fell defending the interests, defending the cause of the exploited and the oppressed peoples of this continent; Che fell defending the cause of the poor and disenfranchized of this earth. And the exemplary manner and the selflessness with which he defended that cause cannot be disputed by even his most bitter enemies. And before history, men who act as he did, men who do all and give all for the cause of the oppressed, grow in stature with each passing day and find a deeper place in the heart of the people with each passing day.

The imperialistic enemies are beginning to see this, and it will not be long before it will be proved that his death will, in the long run, be like a germ which will give rise to many men determined to imitate him, many men determined to follow his example.

And we are absolutely convinced that the revolutionary cause on this continent will recover from the blow, that the revolutionary movement on this continent will not be crushed by this blow.

From the revolutionary point of view of our people, how must we view Che's example?

Do we feel we have lost him? It is true that we will not see new writings of his, true that we will never again hear his voice. But Che has left a heritage to the world, a great heritage, and we who knew him so well can become in a great degree his beneficiaries.

He left us his revolutionary thinking, his revolutionary virtues; he left us his character, his will, his tenacity, his spirit of work. In a word, he left us his example! And Che's example will be a model for our people; Che's example will be the ideal model for our people!

If we wish to express what we expect our revolutionary combatants, our militants, our men to be, we must say, without hesitation: "Let them be like Che!" If we wish to express what we want the men of future generations to be, we must say: "Let them be like Che!" If we wish to say how we want our children to be educated, we must say without hesitation: "We want them to be educated in Che's spirit!" If we want the model of a man who does not belong to our time, the model of a man who belongs to the future, I say from the depths of my heart that such a model, without a single stain on his conduct, without a single stain on his actions, is Che! If we wish to express what we want our children to be, we must say from our very hearts as ardent revolutionaries: "We want them to be like Che!"

Che has become a model of what men should be, not only for our people but also for people everywhere in Latin America. Che carried to its highest expression revolutionary stoicism, the revolutionary spirit of sacrifice, revolutionary combativeness, the revolutionary's spirit of work. Che brought the ideas of Marxism-Leninism to their freshest, purest, most revolutionary expression. No other man of our time has carried the spirit of proletarian internationalism to its highest possible level, as Che did.

And in the future, when an example of a proletarian internationalist is spoken of, when an example of a proletarian internationalist is sought, that example, high above any other, will be Che's example! National flags, prejudices, chauvinism, and egoism had disappeared from his mind and heart. And he was ready to shed his generous blood spontaneously and immediately, in behalf of any people, for the cause of any people!

And thus, his blood fell on our soil when he was wounded in several battles; and his blood was shed in Bolivia, for the redemption of the exploited and the oppressed. That blood was shed for the sake of all the exploited and all the oppressed; that blood was shed for all the peoples of America and for the people in Vietnam, because while fighting there in

Bolivia, fighting against the oligarchies and imperialism, he knew that he was offering Vietnam the highest possible expression of his solidarity!

It is for this reason, comrades of the Revolution, that we must face the future with optimism. And in Che's example we will always find inspiration, inspiration in struggle, inspiration in tenacity, inspiration in intransigence toward the enemy, inspiration in internationalist sentiment!

Therefore, after tonight's impressive ceremony, after this incredible demonstration of multitudinous recognition, incredible for its magnitude, discipline, and spirit of devotion; which demonstrates that our people are a sensitive, grateful people, who know how to honor the memory of the brave who die in combat, and our people recognize those who serve them; which demonstrates the people's solidarity with the revolutionary struggle and how this people will raise aloft and maintain ever higher aloft their revolutionary banners and revolutionary principles—in these moments of remembrance let us lift our spirits with optimism in the future, with absolute optimism in the final victory of the peoples, and say to Che and to the heroes who fought and died with him; Ever onward to Victory!

Patria o muerte!

Venceremos!

92
Guevara